The Contemporary Russian Economy

Marek Dabrowski
Editor

The Contemporary Russian Economy

A Comprehensive Analysis

Editor
Marek Dabrowski
Bruegel
Brussels, Belgium

Higher School of Economics
Moscow, Russia

CASE—Center for Social and Economic Research
Warsaw, Poland

ISBN 978-3-031-17381-3   ISBN 978-3-031-17382-0 (eBook)
https://doi.org/10.1007/978-3-031-17382-0

© The Editor(s) (if applicable) and The Author(s), under exclusive license to Springer Nature Switzerland AG 2023
This work is subject to copyright. All rights are solely and exclusively licensed by the Publisher, whether the whole or part of the material is concerned, specifically the rights of translation, reprinting, reuse of illustrations, recitation, broadcasting, reproduction on microfilms or in any other physical way, and transmission or information storage and retrieval, electronic adaptation, computer software, or by similar or dissimilar methodology now known or hereafter developed.
The use of general descriptive names, registered names, trademarks, service marks, etc. in this publication does not imply, even in the absence of a specific statement, that such names are exempt from the relevant protective laws and regulations and therefore free for general use.
The publisher, the authors, and the editors are safe to assume that the advice and information in this book are believed to be true and accurate at the date of publication. Neither the publisher nor the authors or the editors give a warranty, expressed or implied, with respect to the material contained herein or for any errors or omissions that may have been made. The publisher remains neutral with regard to jurisdictional claims in published maps and institutional affiliations.

This Palgrave Macmillan imprint is published by the registered company Springer Nature Switzerland AG
The registered company address is: Gewerbestrasse 11, 6330 Cham, Switzerland

Preface

We offer an international textbook on the contemporary Russian economy for undergraduate and graduate students of various universities and faculties that teach Russian studies, the Russian economy, Russian politics, the economics of transition and emerging markets, international relations, and other relevant topics. Some chapters may also be helpful for post-graduate courses, academics, analysts, and practitioners in their daily work.

The textbook contains broad characteristics of the economic geography of Russia, its natural and human resources, the contemporary Russian economic history, institutions and governance, major sectors, a regional dimension, Russia's role in the global economy, and economic and social policy challenges. It consists of 19 chapters grouped into seven thematic parts.

Part I analyses the geographic conditions and natural and human resources that determine Russia's economic and social development. It consists of two chapters. Chapter 1, authored by Leonid Limonov and Denis Kadochnikov, contains the major geographic characteristics of Russia, its climate, natural resources, and transport infrastructure. Chapter 2, written by Irina Denisova and Marina Kartseva, deals with demographic trends, health, and education.

Part II is about the historical roots of the contemporary Russian economy. It also contains two chapters, both authored by Carol Scott Leonard. Chapter 3 presents the period of capitalist industrialisation and modernisation until WWI. Chapter 4 describes the period of communist industrialisation between the October Revolution in 1917 and the collapse of the Soviet Union in 1991.

Part III provides an overview of the institutional settings which determine the functioning of the Russian economy since the beginning of the 1990s. It contains three chapters. Chapter 5, written by Christopher Hartwell, discusses the constitutional foundations of the economic system and the role of government in economic activity. Chapter 6 of Marek Dabrowski analyses the factors that determine Russia's business and investment climate and governance system. Chapter 7, authored by Alexander Radygin and Alexander Abramov, presents the evolution of the ownership structure of the Russian economy, corporate governance, and stock market.

Part IV is about the Russian economy's key sectors and Russia's regional diversity. It is composed of four chapters. Chapter 8, written by Svetlana Avdasheva, provides an overview of the structural changes in the Russian economy since 1992. Chapter 9 of Przemyslaw Kowalski is devoted to the energy sector, its evolution, and future challenges. Chapter 10 of Evgeniya Serova presents changes in the agriculture sector since 1992. Chapter 11, authored by Leonid Limonov, Olga Rusetskaya, and Nikolai Zhunda, deals with regional diversity.

Part V is devoted to Russia's role in the global economy, trade and investment relations with leading partners, and membership in international and regional economic and financial organisations. It also presents the negative impact of geopolitical choices and sanctions since 2014. It consists of three chapters. In Chapter 12, Arne Melchior analyses changes in trade flows and trade systems. Chapter 13 of Kalman Kalotay discusses foreign direct and portfolio investment, both incoming and outgoing. In Chapter 14, Marek Dabrowski and Svetlana Avdasheva analyse the subsequent sanctions against Russia since 2014, including an unprecedented package of sanctions that followed Russia's invasion of Ukraine in February 2022 and Russia's policy responses to these sanctions.

Part VI analyses the economic and social policy challenges faced by the Russian economy, such as the declining growth rate, sources of macroeconomic and financial vulnerability, inflation and monetary policy, fiscal policy and the tax system, labour market conditions, poverty and income inequality, the role of social policy and the public pension system, and others. It consists of four chapters. Chapter 15 of Ilya Voskoboynikov analyses the factors of economic growth in post-Soviet Russia. In Chapter 16, Marek Dabrowski discusses sources of macroeconomic vulnerability and the evolution of monetary and fiscal policies, including the tax system. Chapter 17 of Vladimir Gimpelson deals with the specific features of the labour market in Russia. In Chapter 18, Irina Denisova and Marina Kartseva analyse trends in living standards, poverty, and inequality in Russia and a broad spectrum of social policy measures and institutions, including a public pension system.

Finally, Part VII (Chapter 19), prepared by Marek Dabrowski and having a summary character for the entire volume, provides an overview of the changes in economic policy and the economic and governance system since the early 1990s. It also signals some development challenges the Russian economy may face in the forthcoming years.

One of the motivations for undertaking this project was to offer students worldwide and a broader academic and analytical community an updated picture of a contemporary Russian economy in the situation when similar publications were produced at least a decade earlier. When we started working on this project in 2020, we could not predict the dramatic and unexpected developments that shocked the entire world in February 2022, the war in

Ukraine. Instead, we were preoccupied with the potential impact of the COVID-19 pandemic.

Most chapters were written between September 2021 and January 2022, before the invasion of Ukraine and accompanying sanctions and counter-sanctions. Chapters 14 and 19 that deal extensively with this issue were written later—in May and June 2022. Some other chapters include last-minute updates that try at least signal potential consequences of the war and sanctions for the Russian economy. However, given the conflict's far-going political and economic implications, the high degree of uncertainty and unpredictability concerning future developments, and lack of data, we know that the picture presented in some chapters may change substantially in the coming months and years. Nevertheless, we believe we provide a professional, honest, and correct analysis of how the Russian economy and Russian economic system looked and worked in the early 2020s.

An international team of 18 authors has prepared the textbook (see the 'Contributors' section for their bio notes), representing the highest expertise in the respective topics and having long experience analysing the Russian economy.

This textbook idea was born in the Higher School of Economics (HSE) in Moscow and its Faculty of Economic Sciences. Professors Evgenii Yasin and Yaroslav Kuzminov, Academic Supervisors of the HSE, were among those who inspired me to undertake this difficult task. The final thematic plan benefited from the comments of anonymous referees invited by the publisher.

At the stage of project implementation, Kristen Hartwell provided extensive assistance in language editing and editorial harmonisation of all chapters. My granddaughter Joanna Dabrowska, a fresh graduate of the University of Strathclyde in Glasgow, helped with their technical formatting.

This work also would not have been possible without the generous contribution of the Atlas Foundation, who provided a grant (number G-0486-22Q2-1) under their illiberalism programme, to allow for the English language editing of the final volume. Thanks are also due to the ZHAW School of Management and Law's International Management Institute, based in Winterthur, Switzerland, which oversaw the administration of this grant on behalf of the Editor and the contributors.

The views and opinions presented in this volume are those of the respective authors only. They do not necessarily reflect the position of the institutions with which they have been associated and other contributors to this publication. Authors take sole responsibility for the content and scientific quality of the respective chapters. As the scientific coordinator and editor of this volume, I am responsible for its conceptualisation, thematic composition, choice of the authors, and overall editorial coherence.

Brussels, Belgium Marek Dabrowski
June 2022

Contents

Part I   Natural and Human Resources

1   **Natural Resources, Geography, and Climate**   3
    Leonid Limonov and Denis Kadochnikov
    1.1   Geography   4
    1.2   Climate and Environment   5
    1.3   Natural Resources   5
          1.3.1   Aquatic Resources   5
          1.3.2   Land   8
          1.3.3   Mineral Resources   8
    1.4   An Overview of Key Mineral Resources   10
          1.4.1   Oil   10
          1.4.2   Natural Gas   10
          1.4.3   Coal   11
          1.4.4   Uranium   11
          1.4.5   Iron   12
          1.4.6   Copper   12
          1.4.7   Nickel   12
          1.4.8   Gold   13
          1.4.9   Silver   13
          1.4.10 Diamonds   13
          1.4.11 Phosphates and Potassium Salts   14
    1.5   Natural Resources and Environmental Factors
          of Human Settlement Patterns   14
    1.6   Infrastructural Aspects   16
    References   19

2	**Human Resources**		21
	Irina Denisova and Marina Kartseva		
	2.1	Human Capital in Russia from an International Perspective	22
		2.1.1 Population Size and Growth Rate	22
		2.1.2 Human Development Index	22
	2.2	Population Structure and Main Demographic Trends	24
		2.2.1 Trends in Fertility and Mortality	24
		2.2.2 Regional Variation	25
		2.2.3 Mortality from an International Perspective: Russia's Mortality Crisis	26
		2.2.4 Fertility in Russia from an International Perspective	27
		2.2.5 Age and Gender Structure of the Population	30
		2.2.6 Aging (Dependency Ratios)	31
	2.3	Health	33
		2.3.1 Causes of Death	33
		2.3.2 Socially Significant Diseases: Tuberculosis and Diabetes	34
		2.3.3 Health Detrimental Behaviour: Alcohol Consumption and Smoking	35
	2.4	Education	36
		2.4.1 Enrolment Rates and Education Structure	36
		2.4.2 Quality of Education	38
	2.5	Conclusions	39
	References		40

Part II Historical Roots

3	**Capitalist Industrialisation and Modernisation: From Alexander's Reforms Until World War I (the 1860s–1917)**		45
	Carol Scott Leonard		
	3.1	Introduction	46
	3.2	Reforms Between 1861 and 1905	46
		3.2.1 Overview	46
		3.2.2 Emancipation of the Serfs	47
		3.2.3 Education Reform	48
		3.2.4 Judicial Reform	49
		3.2.5 Administrative Reform	49
		3.2.6 Modernisation of the Army and Navy	50
		3.2.7 Laws Improving the Conditions of Factory Labour	50
		3.2.8 Summary	51
	3.3	The 1905 Revolution and Institutional Transformation	51
		3.3.1 Political Changes	51

		3.3.2	The Stolypin Land Reform	52
	3.4	Sectoral Transformation: The 1880s–1913		53
		3.4.1	Agriculture and Trade	53
		3.4.2	Financing Industrial Development	54
	3.5	Society		56
		3.5.1	Standard of Living, 1880s–1913	56
	3.6	The Intelligentsia and the Emergence of Radical Activism		57
	3.7	World War I and Revolution		59
	References			60
4	**The Soviet Economy (1918–1991)**			**61**
	Carol Scott Leonard			
	4.1	Introduction		62
	4.2	Civil War and 'War Communism' (1918–1921)		62
	4.3	The 'New Economic Policy' (1921–1928)		64
		4.3.1	Retreat	64
		4.3.2	Command Institutions	64
		4.3.3	Leadership Struggle Over Rapid Industrialisation	65
		4.3.4	Rapid Post-WWI Economic Recovery.	66
		4.3.5	Comparative Performance Estimates, 1913 and 1928	67
	4.4	Constructing Soviet Economic Institutions		67
		4.4.1	The First Wave of the Forced Stalinist Industrialisation (1929–1940)	67
		4.4.2	The Period of World War II (1941–1945)	69
		4.4.3	The Performance of the Economy After Stalinist Industrialisation	70
	4.5	Reforming the Soviet Economy (1945–1991)		71
		4.5.1	The Period of the Post-War Stalinist Reconstruction (1945–1953)	71
		4.5.2	Partial Changes in the Political System and Economic Policy in the Post-Stalin Era (1953–1985)	72
		4.5.3	The Performance of the Late Soviet Economy	73
		4.5.4	The Period of Gorbachev's Perestroika (1986–1991)	74
	References			76

Part III Institutions and Their Transformation

5	**Constitutional Foundations of the Post-communist Russian Economy and the Role of the State**		**81**
	Christopher A. Hartwell		
	5.1	Introduction	82

5.2	The Move Towards Legalising the Market Economy: Promises and Problems	83
	5.2.1 **The Constitution and the Civil Code**	83
	5.2.2 The Problem of Delay	86
5.3	When Politics and Economics Clash: The Period After 2000	87
	5.3.1 **The Russian Economy Under Putin**	91
5.4	The Future of the State in the Russian Economy	93
References		96

6 Business and Investment Climate, Governance System — 99
Marek Dabrowski

6.1	Introduction	100
6.2	Definitions and Measurement Methodology	100
6.3	International Perception of the Business and Investment Climate in Russia	102
6.4	International Perception of Governance and Political System in Russia	106
6.5	Flawed Governance as the Factor Responsible for Poor Business and Investment Climate	108
6.6	Economic Consequences of a Poor Business and Investment Climate and Flawed Governance	111
References		112

7 Evolution of Ownership Structure and Corporate Governance — 115
Alexander Radygin and Alexander Abramov

7.1	Introduction: Private Versus Public Sector	116
7.2	Privatisation from the Origins: Discussions, Models, and Results	117
7.3	Public Sector: Quantitative Dynamics and Comparative Effectiveness	121
7.4	Corporate Governance: Panacea or Imitation?	124
7.5	Stock Market: Historical and Future Challenges	130
7.6	Conclusions	137
References		139

Part IV Major Sectors and Regional Diversity

8 Structural Changes in the Russian Economy Since 1992 — 145
Svetlana Avdasheva

8.1	Introduction	146
8.2	Structure of the Russian Economy: International Comparisons	148
8.3	Liberalisation Shock and Further Restructuring of Russian Industries	149

		8.4	Industrial Policies in Russia	155
	References			159
9	**Energy Sector**			161
	Przemyslaw Kowalski			
	9.1	Introduction		162
	9.2	Energy Consumption and CO2 Emissions		162
	9.3	Overview of Russia's Policy Framework Relevant to the Energy Sector		165
	9.4	Russia's Energy Mix		168
		9.4.1	Natural Gas	168
		9.4.2	LNG	171
		9.4.3	Gas Pricing	172
		9.4.4	Oil	174
		9.4.5	Oil Pricing	175
		9.4.6	Coal	176
		9.4.7	Coal Pricing	177
		9.4.8	Renewables	177
		9.4.9	Electricity	177
		9.4.10	Electricity Pricing	179
	9.5	Russia's Approach to the Challenges of Climate Change		179
		9.5.1	A Green Economy Transition	180
		9.5.2	Russia's Energy Strategy and Its Challenges and Opportunities Associated with a Green Transition	181
	9.6	Consequences of Russia's Military Aggression on Ukraine		183
	9.7	Conclusion		184
	References			185
10	**Agriculture**			187
	Eugenia Serova			
	10.1	Introduction		188
	10.2	Soviet Agriculture: Major Challenges and Transformation Objectives		188
	10.3	The Original Shape of Agrarian Transformation in the Early 1990s		189
	10.4	Transformation-Related Output Decline in Agriculture		191
	10.5	Contemporary Agri-Food Sector in Russia		193
	10.6	Future Challenges		197
		10.6.1	Sustainability in the Agri-Food Sector	198
		10.6.2	Innovativeness of the Agri-Food Sector	199
		10.6.3	Rural Development	200
	References			202

11 Regional Diversity — 203
Leonid Limonov, Olga Rusetskaya, and Nikolay Zhunda

- 11.1 Demographic and Social Diversity of the Russian Regions — 204
- 11.2 Economic Diversity — 207
  - 11.2.1 Differences in Gross Regional Product — 207
  - 11.2.2 GRP Per Capita — 212
  - 11.2.3 Capital Investment Dynamics and Variation Across Regions — 213
- 11.3 Challenges of Spatial Development and Regional Policy of Russia — 217
  - 11.3.1 Intergovernmental Transfers — 219
  - 11.3.2 Federal Budget Expenditures in the Regions — 220
  - 11.3.3 Federal Tax Incentives in Selected Territories — 220
- 11.4 Summary — 222
- References — 223

Part V Russia in the Global Economy

12 Russia in World Trade — 227
Arne Melchior

- 12.1 Introduction — 228
- 12.2 Russia's Trade Growth During Transition — 229
- 12.3 Russia's WTO Membership — 232
- 12.4 Russia's Bilateral and Regional Trade Agreements — 236
- 12.5 The Geography of Russia's Foreign Trade — 237
- 12.6 Trade Policy Challenges in the Early 2020s: From Security Tensions to the Green Transition — 240
- References — 244

13 Foreign Investment — 247
Kalman Kalotay

- 13.1 Introduction and Context — 248
- 13.2 Trends and Patterns of Foreign Investment — 249
  - 13.2.1 Dynamics of Foreign Investment — 249
  - 13.2.2 The Role of Stocks and Flows in Measuring Foreign Investment — 251
  - 13.2.3 Modes of Entry of FDI — 251
  - 13.2.4 Selected Sectoral and Geographical Patterns of Foreign Investment — 253
  - 13.2.5 Measurement Problems ('Through a Glass Darkly') — 256
- 13.3 The FDI and FPI Intensity of Russia in International Comparison — 258
  - 13.3.1 How the Foreign Investment Indices are Constructed — 258
  - 13.3.2 Why are the Indices of Russia Low? — 259

| | | 13.4 | Key Issues in Foreign Investment and Development in Russia in an International Context | 262 |

      13.4 Key Issues in Foreign Investment and Development in Russia in an International Context   262
           13.4.1 The Flow of Financial Resources in Foreign Investment   262
           13.4.2 The Package of Resources in FDI   263
           13.4.3 Dealing with the Flipsides of the FDI Impact   264
      13.5 The Role of MNEs   265
           13.5.1 The Universe of the Largest Russian MNEs   265
           13.5.2 The Role of the State   267
      13.6 Looking Forward   267
      References   269

14 Sanctions and Forces Driving to Autarky   271
Marek Dabrowski and Svetlana Avdasheva
      14.1 Introduction   272
      14.2 The 2014 and 2018 Rounds of Western Sanctions   273
      14.3 Russia's Policy Response in 2014 and the Following Years   274
      14.4 Economic Impact of the First Two Rounds of Sanctions and Countersanctions   276
      14.5 The 2022 Round of Western Sanctions   278
           14.5.1 Individual Sanctions   278
           14.5.2 Financial Sanctions   279
           14.5.3 Energy Sanctions   279
           14.5.4 Trade Sanctions   279
           14.5.5 Transportation Sanctions   280
           14.5.6 Media Sanctions   280
           14.5.7 Diplomatic Sanctions   280
           14.5.8 Withdrawal from Russia and Spontaneous Boycott   280
      14.6 Russia's Response Measures to the 2022 Sanctions   281
           14.6.1 Short-Term Stabilisation Measures   281
           14.6.2 Support for Aggregate Demand and Supply   282
           14.6.3 Retaliation (Countersanction) Measures   283
           14.6.4 Sectoral Measures to Compensate for the Withdrawal of Imports and FDI   284
      14.7 Impact of Sanctions and Geopolitical Confrontation on Russia's Economic Development   285
      References   286

Part VI Economic and Social Policy Challenges

15 Economic Growth   291
Ilya Voskoboynikov
      15.1 Introduction   292

		15.2	The Global Economy and Russia During 1990–2019: An Overview	293
		15.3	Structural Change, Labour Reallocation, and Productivity Growth	296
		15.4	Transformational Recession (1990–1998)	299
			15.4.1 The Post-Transition Recovery (1999–2008)	304
		15.5	The Decade of Stagnation (2009–2019)	306
		15.6	Conclusions	308
		Appendix 15.1: Country Grouping		310
		References		311
16	Macroeconomic Vulnerability, Monetary, and Fiscal Policies			313
	Marek Dabrowski			
		16.1	Introduction	314
		16.2	Episodes of Macroeconomic and Financial Instability	314
			16.2.1 Collapse of the Soviet Rouble and Failure of Macroeconomic Stabilisation After the Collapse of the Soviet Union (1989–1995)	315
			16.2.2 The Crisis of 1998–1999	318
			16.2.3 Fallout from the Global Financial Crisis (2008–2009)	319
			16.2.4 The 2014–2016 Crisis	320
			16.2.5 The COVID-19 Crisis (2020–2021)	320
			16.2.6 Macroeconomic Consequences of the War with Ukraine (2022)	321
		16.3	Sources of Balance-of-Payments and Currency Fragility	322
		16.4	Inflation, Monetary Policy, Central Bank Independence	324
		16.5	Evolution of Fiscal Policy	327
		16.6	Tax System	330
		16.7	Conclusions	332
		References		333
17	Labour Market, Employment, and Migration			335
	Vladimir Gimpelson			
		17.1	Introduction	336
		17.2	A Concise Story of Labour Market Adjustment	336
			17.2.1 The First Decade—From Plan to Turmoil	337
			17.2.2 Unexpected Boom and Surprising Recovery	338
			17.2.3 The New Crisis and Endless Stagnation	338
		17.3	A Miracle of Low Unemployment?	339
		17.4	Puzzles of Adjustment: How Does It Work?	341
		17.5	The Role of Labour Market Institutions	342
			17.5.1 Employment Regulations	342
			17.5.2 Wage Setting and a Two-Tier Wage Structure	344
			17.5.3 Trade Unions and Wage Agreements	345

17.6	Structural Change and Informality	345
17.7	Wages, Low Pay, and Inequality	348
	17.7.1 Dynamics and Levels	348
	17.7.2 Low Pay	349
	17.7.3 Inequality	350
17.8	Human Capital, Educational Boom, and High Returns	352
17.9	Conclusions	356
	References	357

18 Standard of Living and Social Policy — 359
Irina Denisova and Marina Kartseva

18.1	Introduction	360
18.2	Living Standard, Income, and Wealth Inequality in Russia from an International Perspective	360
18.3	Income and Wealth Inequality: Measurement, Dynamics, and Determinants	362
	18.3.1 Income Inequality	362
	18.3.2 Regional Income Inequality	363
	18.3.3 Determinants of Inequality: Inequality of Opportunities	364
	18.3.4 Wealth Inequality	365
18.4	Poverty: Dynamics, Determinants, and Measurement Issues	366
	18.4.1 Poverty Measures and Dynamics	366
	18.4.2 International Perspective	368
	18.4.3 Determinants of Poverty, Poverty Profiles, and Poverty Risk Factors	369
	18.4.4 Regional Dimension of Poverty	370
18.5	Social Security and Social Policy Instruments	371
	18.5.1 Configuration of the Social Security System in Russia	371
	18.5.2 Social Protection Components	372
	18.5.3 The Impact of Social Transfers on Poverty	373
	18.5.4 Social Policy Instruments: Maternity and Child Benefits	374
	18.5.5 Social Policy Instruments: Labour Pension	374
18.6	Conclusions	377
	References	379

Part VII Summary

19 Russia's Two Transitions (1992–2003 and 2003–2022) — 383
Marek Dabrowski

19.1	Introduction	384
19.2	From Plan to Market: The Heroic Decade of the 1990s	385

19.3	The Turning Point of the Russian Transition (the Early 2000s)	389
19.4	The Autocratic and Dirigiste Drift (2003–2014)	391
19.5	Towards the War Economy (2014–2022)	394
19.6	The Russian Economy in the Early 2020s	396
References		397

Index 399

Notes on Contributors

Abramov Alexander is the Head of the Laboratory for the Analysis of Institutions and Financial Markets at the Institute of Applied Economic Research at the Russian Academy of National Economy and Public Administration (RANEPA) in Moscow. Since the 1990s, he has held various advisory positions in Russian institutions dealing with economic and financial policy, privatisation, and the securities market. He is the author and co-author of more than 200 publications on these issues and a member of the Board of Directors of the National Association of Securities Market Participants (NAUFOR).

Avdasheva Svetlana is a Professor of Applied Economics at the Faculty of Economic Sciences, Higher School of Economics in Moscow, and Head of its Department of Applied Economics. She specialises in industrial organisation and competition economics as well as institutional economics. Her main field of interest is the comparative analysis of institutional aspects of competition enforcement. She is the author of several publications on corporate and value chain governance in the Russian economy under transition.

Dabrowski Marek is a Non-Resident Fellow at Bruegel, Brussels, Professor at the Higher School of Economics in Moscow, and Co-founder and Fellow at CASE—Center for Social and Economic Research in Warsaw. He was the First Deputy Minister of Finance of Poland (1989–1990) and a Member of the Monetary Policy Council of the National Bank of Poland (1998–2004). He has also been involved in policy advising and research in several countries of Central and Eastern Europe, the former Soviet Union, the Middle East, and Africa. He was a Fellow under the 2014–2015 Fellowship Initiative of the European Commission—DG ECFIN. He is a member of the Academia Europaea and the author of more than 300 international publications analysing, among others, the transition in Russia and other emerging market economies.

Denisova Irina is an Associate Professor at the Moscow State University and Senior Lecturer at the New Economic School in Moscow. She holds a Ph.D. in Economics from the University of Manchester (UK). In the 2000s, she was an expert in several OECD and World Bank projects as well as the author and co-author of numerous academic publications on the political economy of transition, social policy, demography, health, the labour market, and income distribution.

Gimpelson Vladimir is a Professor and Director of the Centre for Labour Market Studies at the Higher School of Economics in Moscow. He is also a Fellow at the Institute of Labour Economics (IZA) in Bonn. He is the leading expert on the Russian labour market. He has participated as an expert and consultant in many OECD, World Bank, ILO, and EU projects. During 1998–1999, he was a Professor in the Economic Department at the University of Tokyo. He is the author and co-author of over 150 academic publications on the labour market and employment policies in transition countries.

Hartwell Christopher A. is a Professor of International Business Policy and Head of the International Management Institute at ZHAW School of Management and Law, Zurich. Previously, he was a Professor at Bournemouth University, UK (2018–2021), President of CASE—Center for Social and Economic Research in Warsaw (2014–2018), and Head of Global Markets and Institutional Research, Institute for Emerging Market Studies (IEMS) at Moscow School of Management—SKOLKOVO, Moscow (2012–2014). He has participated in several USAID and EU projects in countries of the former Soviet Union, Central and Eastern Europe, and other emerging market economies. He is the author of numerous publications on political economy, institutional economics, and the economics of transition. He holds a Ph.D. from the Warsaw School of Economics, an MPP from Harvard University, and a B.A. in Political Science and Economics from the University of Pennsylvania.

Kadochnikov Denis is a Senior Research Fellow at the International Centre for Social and Economic Research—Leontief Centre in St. Petersburg and an Associate Professor at Saint Petersburg State University. He is the author of several academic publications on public finance and fiscal federalism issues in Russia and China, the economics of language, and international economics and finance.

Kalotay Kalman is an External Research Fellow at the Institute of World Economics, Centre for Economic and Regional Studies in Budapest, Hungary (since 2022) and an Honorary Professor of the Corvinus University of Budapest, Hungary (since 2013). In 2021, he retired from the Division on Investment and Enterprise of the United Nations Conference on Trade and Development (UNCTAD) in Geneva and from the World Investment Report team. He has broad experience in transition, emerging market, and developing economies, including Russia. He has experience in teaching investment policy issues to different audiences (close to 30 courses taught) and a publication record of more than 30 academic articles and more than 20 book chapters, primarily on inward and outward FDI in transition economies. He holds a Ph.D. from Corvinus University.

Kartseva Marina is a Senior Fellow at the Institute for Social Analysis and Forecasting, Russian Presidential Academy of National Economy and Public Administration (RANEPA) in Moscow. She was previously a Senior Fellow at the Center for Economic and Financial Research in Moscow. She is the author of several academic publications on social policy, income distribution, demography, the labour market, and economic sociology related to Russia and other transition economies.

Kowalski Przemyslaw is a Senior Economist at the Organisation for Economic Co-operation and Development (OECD) specialising in international trade and macroeconomics. His previous roles include President of CASE—Center for Social and Economic Research in Warsaw; teaching and research positions in economics at the Institut d'Etudes Politiques de Paris, Sciences Po in Paris and the University of Sussex, UK; and various consultancy roles in international macroeconomics and finance, development economics, and international trade. He graduated with a Ph.D. in Economics from the University of Sussex, UK and holds an M.A. and M.Sc. in Economics from the University of Sussex and the University of Warsaw, respectively. He has contributed to several articles and books on economics and economic policy.

Limonov Leonid is the leading Russian expert on regional economic development. He is the Research Director of the International Centre for Social and Economic Research—Leontief Centre in St. Petersburg and a Professor at the St. Petersburg campus of the Higher School of Economics. He is (from May 2021) an Honorary Professor of Cardiff University, UK (School of Geography and Planning). He has also held visiting posts at the University of Liverpool, the Ecole Polytechnique (France), and the University of Maryland (USA). From 2012 to 2018, he was a Research Professor at the IWH (Institute of Economic Research in Halle-am-Saale, Germany). He has published over 100 academic books and papers on social and economic transformation, subnational territorial strategic planning, and spatial development in Russia and other countries of the former Soviet Union. He is the Editor of *Area Development and Policy*, an international journal published by Francis and Taylor Group (Routledge).

Melchior Arne is a Senior Research Fellow at the Norwegian Institute of International Affairs (NUPI) in Oslo and an Associate Professor at the Arctic University of Norway, Tromsø. He has a Ph.D. in Economics from the University of Oslo. His areas of expertise include international trade and global development, trade policy and international economic institutions, international inequality, geographical economics, and regional development. He has written numerous publications on, among others, trade and economic development in Europe, Russia, India, China, and the global economy, often using numerical models as a tool. An example is the book *Free Trade Agreements and Globalisation—In the Shadow of Brexit and Trump* (Palgrave Macmillan, 2018), analysing the world economy, China's growth and the role of commodity trade, and Russia split into regions. Before starting his research career, he gained experience from international trade negotiations as a government official, including via multilateral and bilateral negotiations with several Asian countries.

Radygin Alexander is the Head of the Department for Institutional Development, Ownership, and Corporate Governance at the Gaidar Institute for Economic Policy in Moscow and Director of the Institute of Applied Economic Research and Professor at the Russian Academy of National Economy and Public Administration (RANEPA) in Moscow. Since the 1990s, he has held various advisory and consultancy positions in Russian and international institutions dealing with economic policy, privatisation, corporate governance, the stock market, and structural and industrial policy, among others. He is the author and co-author of more than 400 publications on these issues and a member of the editorial boards of *Economic Policy* and the *Russian Journal of Economics*.

Rusetskaya Olga is the Head of the Investment Planning Department of the International Centre for Social and Economic Research—Leontief Centre in St. Petersburg and docent at the Saint Petersburg State University of Economics and the St. Petersburg campus of the Higher School of Economics. Since 1994, she has served as a coordinator and expert in numerous research and consulting projects in municipal and regional development. Between 2004 and 2007, as a Consultant at the World Bank Institute, she provided training for representatives of federal, regional, and municipal authorities, instructors, and consultants in the World Bank Institute's distance learning course Municipal Governance. She is the author and co-author of several publications on the socio-economic development of cities and regions in Russia.

Scott Leonard Carol is an Emeritus Fellow at St. Antony's College, University of Oxford, Lead Researcher at the Institute of Regional Studies and Urban Planning at the Higher School of Economics, and Professor and former Director of the Center for Russian Studies at the Russian Presidential Academy of National Economy and Public Administration (RANEPA) in Moscow. Previously, she was a University Lecturer in Regional Studies of the Post-Communist States at the University of Oxford and has been a Fellow at St. Anthony's College since 1997. She has also held positions at Lafayette College in Pennsylvania, the State University of New York, and Harvard University's Russian Research Center. She is the author of several books on the Russian economy, including *Agrarian Reform in Russia: The Road from Serfdom* (2010). In the 1990s, she was a Consultant on economic reforms to the Government of the Russian Federation.

Serova Eugenia is the leading Russian expert on the agriculture sector and agrarian and land reforms in post-Soviet Russia. She is a Professor and Director of the Institute of Agrarian Studies at the Higher School of Economics in Moscow. Between 2007 and 2018, she worked in various positions at the United Nations Food and Agriculture Organization (FAO). Previously, she participated in multiple projects for the World Bank, OECD, and the International Food Policy Research Institute (IFPRI). She also has teaching experience at several US and UK universities. She is the author and co-author of several publications on agriculture, agri-food business, rural development, and land reform. She is also a member of the editorial boards of several academic journals.

Voskoboynikov Ilya is a Leading Research Fellow and Director of the Centre for Productivity Studies and Assistant Professor at the Faculty of Economic Sciences at the Higher School of Economics in Moscow. He is Head of the Russia KLEMS Group, part of the global World KLEMS initiative, which has been set up to promote and facilitate the analysis of growth and productivity patterns worldwide based on a growth accounting framework. He is the author of several publications on the factors of economic growth and productivity in Russia from an international comparative perspective.

Zhunda Nikolay is a Senior Researcher at the International Centre for Social and Economic Research—Leontief Centre in St. Petersburg and Associate Professor at the Saint Petersburg State University of Economics. He was awarded a Ph.D. in Economics from the Institute for Regional Economic Studies of the Russian Academy of Sciences in 2002. Since 1998, he has held various consultancy positions within research projects and technical assistance programmes run by international organisations, including the World Bank and the UNDP, among others. Between 2011 and 2017, he held various academic positions at the St. Petersburg campus of the Higher School of Economics. He is the author and co-author of several publications on urban and regional economics and finance, and development issues.

Abbreviations

AIDS	Acquired Immunodeficiency Syndrome
AO	*Avtonomnyi Okrug* (Autonomous District)
AZLK	*Avtomobil'nyi zavod Leninskogo Komsomola* (Lenin Komsomol Automobile Factory)
BMIE	Balance of Monetary Incomes and Expenditures
BRIC	Brazil, Russia, India, and China
BTI	Bertelsmann Stiftung's Transformation Index
CAATSA	Countering America's Adversaries Through Sanctions Act
CBAM	Carbon Border Adjustment Mechanism
CBRF	Central Bank of the Russian Federation
CEO	Chief Executive Officer
CET	Carbon Emission Trading
CIS	Commonwealth of Independent States
CIT	Corporate Income Tax
CMEA/COMECON	Council for Mutual Economic Assistance
CO2	Carbon Dioxide
COP26	(UN) Climate Change Conference
COVID-19	Coronavirus Disease 2019
CPRF	Communist Party of the Russian Federation
CPSU	Communist Party of the Soviet Union
CSO	Civil Society Organisation
EAEU	Eurasian Economic Union
EBRD	European Bank for Reconstruction and Development
EIUDI	Economist Intelligence Unit Democracy Index
EU	European Union
EUR	Euro
FAO	Food and Agriculture Organization
FAS	Federal Antimonopoly Service
FCL	Federal Constitutional Law
FCTC	Framework Convention on Tobacco Control
FDI	Foreign Direct Investment
FEHL	Far-Eastern Hectare Law

FFMMI	Federal Fund for Mandatory Medical Insurance
FGC	Federal Grid Company
FHFIW	Freedom House's Freedom in the World
FHNIT	Freedom House's Nations in Transit
FLW	Food Loss and Waste
FPI	Foreign Portfolio Investment
FSB	*Federal'naya sluzhba bezopasnosti* (Federal Security Service)
FSU	Former Soviet Union
FTA	Free Trade Agreement
G20	Group of Twenty
G7	Group of Seven
G8	Group of Eight
GATS	General Agreement on Trade in Services
GATT	General Agreement on Tariffs and Trade
GDP	Gross Domestic Product
GFC	Global Financial Crisis
GFSI	Global Food Security Index
GG	General Government
GNI	Gross National Income
GNP	Gross National Product
GOSPLAN	*Gosudarstvennyi planovyi komitet* (State Planning Committee)
GRP	Gross Regional Product
HBS	Household Budget Survey
HDI	Human Development Index
HFIEF	Heritage Foundation Index of Economic Freedom
HIV	Human Immunodeficiency Virus
HQ	Headquarter
ICLS	International Conference of Labour Statisticians
ICRG	International Country Risk Guide
ICT	Information and Telecommunication Technologies
IEA	International Energy Agency
IFS	International Financial Statistics
ILO	International Labour Organization
IMF	International Monetary Fund
IPO	Initial Public Offering
IPR	Intellectual Property Rights
ISCO	International Standard Classification of Occupations
IT	Information Technologies
KBC	Knowledge-Based Capital
LNG	Liquified Natural Gas
M&A	Mergers and Acquisitions
MET	Mineral Extraction Tax
MFN	Most Favoured Nation
MICEX	Moscow Interbank Currency Exchange
MNE	Multi-National Enterprise
NATO	North Atlantic Treaty Organization
NEP	New Economic Policy
NGO	Non-Governmental Organisation
NLMK	New Lipetsk Metallurgy Company

NWF	National Wealth Fund
OECD	Organisation for Economic Co-operation and Development
OJSC	Open Joint Stock Company
P/BV	Price-To-Book Value
PCA	Partnership and Cooperation Agreement (with the EU)
PISA	Programme for International Student Assessment
PIT	Personal Income Tax
pp	Percentage Point
PPP	Purchasing Power Parity
PSE	Producer Support Estimate
PSEDA	Priority Social and Economic Development Area
R&D	Research and Development
RAO EES/UES	Russian Joint-Stock Company 'United Energy Systems'
RCA	Revealed Comparative Advantage
RF	Russian Federation
RLMS-HSE	Russia Longitudinal Monitoring Survey of the Higher School of Economics
ROE	Return on Equity
Rosstat	Federal State Statistics Service
ROW	Rest of the World
RSFSR	Russian Soviet Federative Socialist Republic
RTS	Russian Trading System
RUB	Rouble
SAR	Special Administrative Region
SDGs	Sustainable Development Goals
SEZ	Special Economic Zone
SMEs	Small- and Medium-Sized Enterprises
SNA	System of National Accounts
SOE	State-Owned Enterprise
SPIMEX	Saint-Petersburg International Mercantile Exchange
SSIPSP	Statistical Survey of Income and Participation in Social Programmes
STRI	Services Trade Restrictiveness Index (of OECD)
SUE	State Unitary Enterprise
SWIFT	Society for Worldwide Interbank Financial Telecommunication
TFP	Total Factor Productivity
TFR	Total Fertility Rate
TICPI	Transparency International Corruption Perception Index
TNK-BP	*Tyumenskaya neftyanaya kompaniya* (Tyumen Oil Company)—British Petroleum
TRIPS	Trade-Related Intellectual Property Rights
UGSS	Unified Gas Supply System
UK	United Kingdom (of Great Britain and Northern Ireland)
UMMC	Ural Mining Metallurgical Company
UN	United Nations
UNCTAD	United Nations Conference on Trade and Development
UNDP	United Nations Development Programme
US	United States

USD	United States dollar
USE	United State Examination
USSR	Union of the Soviet Socialist Republics
VAT	Value Added Tax
VEB	*Vnesheconombank* (Foreign Economic Affair Bank)
WBDB	World Bank Doing Business
WBWDI	World Bank's World Development Indicators
WBWGI	World Bank's World Governance Indicators
WEFGCR	World Economic Forum's Global Competitiveness Report
WEO	World Economic Outlook
WHO	World Health Organization
WTO	World Trade Organization
WWI	World War I
WWII	World War II

List of Figures

Fig. 2.1	Crude death, crude birth, and natural population growth rates in Russia, per 1000 people, 1980–2019 (*Source* World Bank, World development indicators, https://datatopics.worldbank.org/world-development-indicators/)	24
Fig. 2.2	Life expectancy at birth, men (Panel A) and women (Panel B) (*Source* World Bank, World development indicators [https://datatopics.worldbank.org/world-development-indicators/])	27
Fig. 2.3	Total Fertility Rate in Russia, Poland, France, and the United States, 1970–2018 (*Source* Human Fertility Database, http://www.humanfertility.org)	28
Fig. 2.4	Mean age of mother at birth by parity (Panel A), 1970–2018 and Unadjusted and Bongaarts-Feeney (BF) Adjusted Period TFR, 1970–2018 (Panel B) (*Source* Human Fertility Database, http://www.humanfertility.org)	29
Fig. 2.5	Number of people by age and sex in Russia in 2019 (*Source* Federal State Statistic Service [Rosstat], https://rosstat.gov.ru/)	30
Fig. 2.6	Age dependency ratio, %, 1970–2050, Old-age (Panel A) and Total (Panel B) (*Source* OECD statistics http://www.oecd.org/std)	32
Fig. 2.7	Performance in reading, mathematics, and science (mean scores), OECD members and candidate countries and Russia, 2018 (*Note* Results for Spain based on 2015 data. *Source* OECD. https://pisadataexplorer.oecd.org/ide/idepisa/dataset.aspx)	38
Fig. 5.1	Federal Government expenditures as % of GDP and annual growth, in %, 1991–2020 (*Source* World Bank World Development Indicators)	93

xxx   LIST OF FIGURES

Fig. 5.2	GDP per capita and executive constraints in Russia, 1992–2020 (*Note* Constraints are measured on a scale of 1–7, with lower values indicating lower levels of executive constraints. *Source* World Bank's World Development Indicators database [GDP per capita], the Polity V database ['executive constraints'] [Center for Systemic Peace, 2021, available at https://www.systemicpeace.org/polityproject.html])	95
Fig. 6.1	Russia: HFIEF overall scores, 1995–2022 (*Source* https://www.heritage.org/index/visualize?cnts=russia&type=8)	105
Fig. 6.2	Russia: WBWGI indicators, 1996–2020 (*Source* https://databank.worldbank.org/reports.aspx?source=worldwide-governance-indicators#)	106
Fig. 6.3	Russia: FHFIW scores (a simple average of political rights and civil liberties scores), 1992–2021 (*Source* https://freedomhouse.org/sites/default/files/2022-03/Country_and_Territory_Ratings_and_Statuses_FIW_1973-2022%20.xlsx)	108
Fig. 6.4	Russia: EIUDI scores, 2006–2021 (*Source* EIU [2022], Table 3, p. 33)	109
Fig. 7.1	Nominal trend: a decrease in the number of economic entities with state participation, 1999–2020 (*Note* SOEs—state-owned enterprises; FSUEs—federal state unitary enterprises; FSIs—federal state institutions. *Source* Federal Agency for State Property Management)	120
Fig. 7.2	Shares of SOEs, SUEs, and GGS in GDP in 2000–2020, in % (*Source* Authors' calculations)	123
Fig. 7.3	Average financial ratios and performance indicators of private companies and SOEs in Russia over the period 2006–2020 (*Notes* ROE—net income available for common shareholders/average total common equity, in %; P/BV—price-to-book value ratio; operating margin—operating income/total sales, in %; total debt to total assets, in %. *Source* authors' calculations)	125
Fig. 7.4	Indicators of the capitalisation value and volume of stock trading in shares of Russian companies in GDP (%) and similar indicators in the world (%) (*Source* authors' calculations based on the World Bank's World Development Indicators, data of the World Federation of Exchanges https://statistics.world-exchanges.org/Account/Login, the IMF International Financial Statistics (IFS) database, and data of the Russian stock exchanges https://www.moex.com/)	131
Fig. 8.1	Physical output index of selected Russian industries, 1993–2016: 1992 = 1 (*Source* Federal State Statistics Service [Rosstat])	154

LIST OF FIGURES   xxxi

Fig. 9.1	Primary energy consumption per unit of GDP and per capita, world economy and Russia, 1980–2020 (*Source* Author's calculations based on IMF's World Economic Outlook, October 2021 for world GDP in purchasing power parity international dollars and BP [2021] for world's primary energy consumption)	163
Fig. 9.2	CO2 emissions, per USD 1000 of GDP, world economy and Russia, 1985–2020 (*Source* Author's calculations based on IMF's World Economic Outlook, October 2021 for world GDP in purchasing power parity international dollars and BP [2021] for CO2 emissions)	164
Fig. 9.3	The energy and related sectors and the Russian economy—selected indicators (*Sources* ∧Federal State Statistics Service [Rosstat [2020]; *WITS [2021]; #NRGI [2021])	165
Fig. 9.4	Primary energy consumption and production by fuel: Russia and the world economy (*Note* shares calculated on the basis of calorific values. *Source* BP [2021]; author's calculations)	169
Fig. 9.5	IEA's Net Zero CO2 emissions by 2050 scenario: total global energy supply by source (*Source* IEA [2021] and author's calculations)	181
Fig. 10.1	Russia: structure of gross agricultural output by farm type (% of total in current prices), 1990–2018 (*Note* AgEnt—agricultural enterprises; HH—household plots; PF—peasant farms *Source* Yanbykh et al. [2020])	190
Fig. 10.2	Russia: support to the agri-food sector (PSE*), in %, 1986–2020 (*Note* PSE—producer support estimate, the conventional measure of level of price and budget transfer to agricultural producers. Conventional measure of support to agriculture, developed by the OECD *Source* OECD)	191
Fig. 10.3	Russia: annual growth rate of gross agricultural output (previous year = 100), 1990–2020 (*Source* The Federal State Statistics Service [Rosstat])	192
Fig. 10.4	Russia: dynamic of production of major crops, million tonnes (*Source* The Federal State Statistics Service [Rosstat])	194
Fig. 10.5	Russia: agri-food trade, USD million (*Source* The Federal State Statistics Service [Rosstat]; for 2019 and 2020—Customs data)	196
Fig. 10.6	The Global Food Security Index, top 10 countries and Russia from 113 monitored, 2021. Note: 100 is the highest level of food security (*Source* https://impact.economist.com/sustainability/project/food-security-index/)	196
Fig. 11.1	Growth of real monetary incomes of the population in 2020 against 1999, % (bars) (*Note* The ratio of the population's average nominal monetary income to the subsistence level in 2020, % (line). *Note* AO—autonomous okrug (district). *Source* authors' calculations based on the Federal State Statistics Service [Rosstat] data)	206

Fig. 11.2	Ratio of investment in fixed capital to GRP, in %, 2000–2018 (*Source* Authors' calculations based on the Federal State Statistics Service [Rosstat] data)	216
Fig. 12.1	Russia's foreign trade in % of GDP, 1996–2020 (*Source* World Bank's World Development Indicators)	229
Fig. 12.2	Russia's share of the world total, 2018 (*Source* ITC trade map, World Bank's World Development Indicators)	230
Fig. 12.3	Russia's trade versus commodity prices, 1996–2020 (*Sources* COMTRADE and IMF Commodity Price Index)	231
Fig. 12.4	Russia's applied tariffs, 1993–2020 (*Source* WITS/COMTRADE)	233
Fig. 12.5	The changing geography of Russia's foreign trade, 1996–2020, % of Russia's trade with all countries for each trade flow (*Source* WITS/COMTRADE)	238
Fig. 13.1	Foreign direct investment flows of Russia, 1992–2020, USD billions (*Source* Author's calculations based on UNCTAD data)	250
Fig. 13.2	Foreign portfolio investment flows of Russia, 1994–2020, USD billions (*Source* Author's calculations based on IMF data)	250
Fig. 13.3	Value of announced greenfield FDI projects in Russia and by Russian investors abroad, 2003–2020, USD billions (*Source* Author's calculations based on UNCTAD data)	252
Fig. 13.4	Value of net cross-border M&As in Russia and by Russian investors abroad, 1992–2020, USD billions (*Source* Author's calculations based on UNCTAD data)	253
Fig. 13.5	Main industries of the cumulative FDI inflows to Russia, 2010–2020, % of total (*Source* Author's calculations based on UNCTAD data)	254
Fig. 13.6	Main sources of the inward FDI stock in Russia by country and country group, 2009 and 2020, % of total stock (*Source* Author's calculations based on UNCTAD data)	255
Fig. 13.7	Main destinations of the outward FDI stock in Russia by country and country group, 2009 and 2020, % of total stock (*Source* Author's calculations based on UNCTAD data)	255
Fig. 13.8	Main destinations of the outward FPI stock in Russia by country and country group, 2009 and 2020, % of total stock (*Source* Author's calculations based on Central Bank of the Russian Federation [CBRF] data)	256
Fig. 13.9	Inward FDI index of Russia and selected countries of comparison, 2008 and 2020, World average = 1 (*Source* Author's calculations based on UNCTAD and IMF data)	259
Fig. 13.10	Outward FDI index of Russia and selected countries of comparison, 2008 and 2020, World average = 1 (*Source* Author's calculations based on UNCTAD and IMF data)	260
Fig. 13.11	Inward FPI index of Russia and selected countries of comparison, 2008 and 2020, World average = 1 (*Source* Author's calculations based on UNCTAD and IMF data)	260

Fig. 13.12	Outward FPI index of Russia and selected countries of comparison, 2008 and 2020, World average = 1 (*Source* Author's calculations based on UNCTAD and IMF data)	261
Fig. 15.1	Changes in real GDP in Russia in a comparative perspective, 1990 = 100, 1990–2021 (*Notes* The figure is represented in logarithmic or ratio scale. See more about ratio scale in [Weil, 2013, p. 31, Fig. 1.3]. For the country grouping—see Appendix 15.1. *Source* The Conference Board Total Economy Database™, August, 2021)	295
Fig. 15.2	Conceptual framework for understanding sources of economic growth (*Source* Rodrik, 2003, p. 5, and author's analysis)	295
Fig. 15.3	Capital growth rates and oil prices in 1990–2021 (*Sources* The Conference Board Total Economy Database™, August [2021], Thomson Reuters, U.S. Energy Information Administration—for oil prices)	305
Fig. 16.1	Commodity price indices, 1992–2020, 2016 = 100 (*Source* IMF Primary Commodity Price System, http://www.imf.org/external/np/res/commod/External_Data.xls)	318
Fig. 16.2	Russia's international reserves in USD billion, 1998–2022 (*Source* http://www.cbr.ru/hd_base/mrrf/mrrf_7d/?UniDbQuery.Posted=True&UniDbQuery.From=05.1998&UniDbQuery.To=04.2022)	319
Fig. 16.3	Russia: savings, investment, current account balance, and natural resource rent, % of GDP, 1994–2020 (*Source* IMF World Economic Outlook database, October 2021; World Bank's World Development Indicators, last update 28 October 2021)	322
Fig. 16.4	Russia: net private capital flows, USD billion, 1994–2020 (*Note* Sign (−) means net capital inflows, sign (+)—net capital outflow. *Source* http://www.cbr.ru/statistics/credit_statistics/bop/outflow.xlsx)	323
Fig. 16.5	Russia: Inflation, end of the period, annual % change, 1993–2021, logarithmic scale (*Source* IMF World Economic Outlook database, April 2022)	325
Fig. 16.6	Russia: fiscal indicators, in % of GDP, 1998–2021 (*Source* IMF World Economic Outlook database, April 2022)	328
Fig. 16.7	Russia: General government gross debt, in % of GDP, 1998–2021 (*Source* IMF World Economic Outlook database, April 2022)	329
Fig. 17.1	GDP, employment, and real wage, 1991 = 100% (*Source* The Federal State Statistics Service [Rosstat])	337
Fig. 17.2	Unemployment rates, %, 1992–2020 (*Source* Federal State Statistics Service [Rosstat])	340
Fig. 17.3	Differentiation of earnings: Gini and decile ratios, p90/p50 and p50/p10 (*Source* Author's RLMS-HSE-based estimates)	351
Fig. 17.4	Composition of employment by occupation, 2000 and 2020 (*Source* Rosstat, author's estimates)	354

Fig. 17.5	Number of foreign workers,* 2010–2019, in thousands (*Note* * the number of foreigners registered for the first time at a place of temporary residence in Russia with the declared purpose 'work'. *Source* Brunarska & Denisenko, 2021, Table A6)	356
Fig. 18.1	Gross household disposable income, including social transfers in kind, PPP USD per capita, 2011–2019 (or nearest) (*Note* For Costa Rica [CRI], Japan [JPN], New Zealand [NZL], and Turkey [TUR]—2017 instead of 2019; for CRI—2012 instead of 2011. *Source* OECD statistics)	361
Fig. 18.2	Gini index and S90/S10 decile share, incomes, OECD member countries, candidate countries, and Russia, 2019 (or nearest) (*Source* World Bank's World Development Indicators)	362
Fig. 18.3	Gini index and S90/S10 decile share, Russia, 2000–2019 (*Source* The Federal State Statistics Service [Rosstat])	363
Fig. 18.4	Population distribution by average monthly household per capita monetary income (in USD) in Russia, 2018 (*Note* Annual average exchange rate in 2018 used for conversion into USD 2019. *Source* authors' calculations based on the Statistical Survey of Income and Participation in Social Programmes, Rosstat)	364
Fig. 18.5	Distribution of income and average per capita income in Russia in 2018, by decile (*Source* The Federal State Statistics Service [Rosstat])	365
Fig. 18.6	Poverty headcount ratio, various poverty lines, Russia, 2000–2019 (*Sources* Federal State Statistics Service [Rosstat] https://www.fedstat.ru/indicator/33460; World Bank)	367
Fig. 18.7	Poverty headcount ratio at half of the median income, OECD member countries, candidate countries, and Russia, 2019 (or the nearest) (*Source* OECD statistics https://data.oecd.org/inequality/poverty-rate.htm)	368

List of Tables

Table 2.1	Age-standardised death rates by leading causes of death, Russia and OECD average, 2000 and 2019, males and females	34
Table 3.1	GDP in the Russian Empire estimated by the author, 1860–1913	55
Table 6.1	Russia: WBDB 2020 rankings and scores (Data for 2019)	103
Table 6.2	Russia: 2022 HFIEF scores	104
Table 7.1	Main stages of privatisation in Russia	118
Table 7.2	Compliance with corporate governance practices in Russian public companies in 2015–2019, monitoring by the Bank of Russia	130
Table 7.3	Average annual indicators of the Russian stock market at various stages of its development on the time horizon, 1993–2020	132
Table 7.4	Average annual share of Russia in the world by individual indicators of the stock market at various stages of its development, 1993–2020	136
Table 8.1	Indicators of the structure of the Russian economy: international comparisons, 2019 and 2020	148
Table 8.2	Revealed comparative advantages of Russian industries across product groups: 1996 and 2019	151
Table 11.1	Interregional differences in the ratio of the average per capita cash income to the subsistence level, %, 2003–2020	207
Table 11.2	Dynamics of interregional disparities in socio-demographic indicators	208
Table 11.3	GRP by federal district in 2000 prices, RUB billions, 2018–2000	210
Table 11.4	Regions with the highest and lowest cumulative GRP growth rates, 2000–2018	211
Table 11.5	The largest regions by contribution to national GRP, %	212
Table 11.6	Regions with the highest and lowest levels of GRP per capita, 2000 and 2018	214

Table 11.7	Regions with the highest and lowest levels of investment per capita (average for the period 2000–2018)	217
Table 11.8	Regions with the largest and smallest stock of investments for the period 2000–2018	218
Table 12.1	The composition of Russia's non-fuel exports, 1996–2020	239
Table 13.1	Direct investment income and reinvested earnings in Russia, 2013–2020 (USD billions and %)	263
Table 13.2	The 20 largest Russian MNEs, ranked by foreign assets in 2019	266
Table 15.1	GDP yearly average growth rates in Russia and in the World 1990–2019, in comparable prices, %	294
Table 15.2	Structural changes in the Russian economy in 1995–2015	298
Table 15.3	Growth accounting of the Russian economy in 1990–2019	303
Table 16.1	Russia: structure of general government expenditure (functional classification), % of GDP, 2000–2020	330
Table 16.2	Russia: Structure of general government revenue (selected items), % of GDP, 2000–2020	331
Table 17.1	Educational composition of employment, of all employed, %	352

List of Boxes

Box 2.1	The Human Development Index (HDI)	23
Box 2.2	Maternity (Family) Capital	29
Box 2.3	Pension Age Reform	32
Box 7.1	Mass Privatisation Schemes	120
Box 9.1	Definition of Primary Energy	164
Box 10.1	Contemporary Russian agriculture—basic facts (2020)	197
Box 16.1	Typology of financial crises	315
Box 18.1	Measuring household income in Russia	366
Box 18.2	Official definition of the poverty rate in Russia	370
Box 18.3	Evolution of the social protection system	376
Box 18.4	Poverty reduction as a national policy priority: families with children	377

PART I

Natural and Human Resources

CHAPTER 1

Natural Resources, Geography, and Climate

Leonid Limonov and Denis Kadochnikov

Highlights

- The size of Russia's territory exceeds 17 million square kilometres, or one-eighth of the Earth's surface. It stretches for about ten thousand kilometres from east to west and for more than four thousand kilometres from north to south. The maritime area under the country's jurisdiction extends for more than eight million square kilometres.
- Russia, being the largest country in the world, possesses vast and diverse natural resources, from land and aquatic resources to mineral resources

---

L. Limonov (✉) · D. Kadochnikov
International Centre for Social and Economic
Research 'Leontief Centre', St. Petersburg, Russia
e-mail: limonov@leontief.ru

D. Kadochnikov
e-mail: denis@leontief.ru

L. Limonov
The Higher School of Economics, St. Petersburg, Russia

D. Kadochnikov
St. Petersburg State University, St. Petersburg, Russia

© The Author(s), under exclusive license to Springer Nature
Switzerland AG 2023
M. Dabrowski (ed.), *The Contemporary Russian Economy*,
https://doi.org/10.1007/978-3-031-17382-0_1

(most notably, oil, natural gas, coal, gold, silver, iron, copper, nickel, uranium, diamonds, phosphates, and potassium salts).
- Natural resources provide the foundation for the country's processing industries and bring in a substantial share of export revenues.
- Historically, access to natural resources and climatic and environmental conditions have always been important in determining not only Russia's economic specificity but also its human settlement patterns and infrastructural needs and challenges.
- Today, the changing climate along with the need to develop new reserves creates new challenges as well as opportunities for the Russian economy.

1.1 Geography

Russia is the world's largest country in terms of area, occupying more than 17 million square kilometres, or one-eighth of the Earth's surface. It stretches for about ten thousand kilometres from east to west and for more than four thousand kilometres from north to south. About one-third of Russia's territory is located in Europe and two-thirds in Asia. Most of the country's territory is a continuous landmass; however, it also includes the exclave of Kaliningrad Oblast (on the coast the Baltic Sea), as well as numerous islands.

The maritime area under Russian jurisdiction extends for 8.6 million square kilometres, including 3.9 million square kilometres of the continental shelf and 4.7 million square kilometres of deep-water areas. Russia's coastlines are washed by 12 seas from 3 oceans (the White, Barents, Kara, Laptev, East Siberian, and Chukchi Seas of the Arctic Ocean; the Baltic, Black, and Azov Seas of the Atlantic Ocean; and the Bering and Okhotsk Seas and the Sea of Japan of the Pacific Ocean) and one landlocked body of water (the Caspian Sea). Most of Russia's rivers flow into the Arctic Ocean, the trade and transportation importance of which has been limited for centuries but is now growing due to global warming as well as the development of Russia's fleet of icebreakers. Russia's major seaports have long been those on the coasts of the Baltic and Black Seas; however, the role of its Pacific seaports is also growing.

Although there are different approaches to identifying the physiographic divisions of Russia, one widely used approach recognises 12 regions: the Arctic Islands; Fennoscandia, the Russian (or East European) Plain, and the Caucasus in the European part of Russia; the Ural Mountains—separating Europe and Asia; and the West Siberian Plain, Middle Siberia, Northeast Siberia, Koryakia-Kamchatka-Kurils, the Altai-Sayan Mountains, the Baikal Mountains, and Amur-Sakhalin in Asia (Vampilova & Manakov, 2012). Each of these physiographic divisions is characterised by distinctive landscapes and natural features, and there is further significant variety of natural conditions within each division. About one-fifth of the Russian territory lies within the North Polar Circle and approximately 60% of Russia's surface is underlain by permafrost, mostly in Siberia.

1.2 Climate and Environment

The four major climate zones found in Russia are arctic, sub-arctic, temperate, and subtropical. In Russia as a whole, climatic conditions change not so much from south to north, but rather from south-west to north-east, which is why areas located at certain latitudes in the west (in Europe) are warmer than areas at the same latitude in the east (in Siberia). However, the variety of climatic and microclimatic conditions between and within the country's physiographic divisions is substantial and determined by a complex set of factors including, but not limited to, latitude, longitude, elevation, proximity to oceans (in particular to the Atlantic Ocean and its warm Gulf Stream), type of landscape, soil, and water resources. Thus, while there is no denying that, relative to the rest of the world, Russia is a generally cold country, its size and natural variety should be remembered to avoid overgeneralisation. Throughout most of Russia, winters tend to be snowy and cold while summers are relatively warm; air temperature fluctuations during the year and the difference between winter temperature lows and summer highs can be quite significant.

As the global climate changes, climatic conditions in Russia are also changing. The consequences of global warming for the country are likely to include increases in the occurrence of extreme weather conditions and natural disasters, similar to the rest of the world. There is however an aspect of global warming which is of special importance for Russia and other northern countries: the future of the permafrost. The possible thawing of the soil may have disastrous effects for the infrastructure, nature, and people in the affected areas. As permafrost is a natural carbon sink, its destruction will release large amounts of greenhouse gases into the atmosphere thus additionally stimulating the process of warming (Streletskiy et al., 2019). Global climate change creates serious risks and challenges for Russia, although in some respects it also creates new opportunities (e.g., the development of the Northern Sea Route, described later in this chapter).

1.3 Natural Resources

Russia is richly endowed with natural resources of various types. These include aquatic, land, and mineral resources.

1.3.1 Aquatic Resources

The water or aquatic resources of Russia include rivers, lakes, swamps, glaciers, underground water, and ice, as well as water flora and fauna. For centuries, rivers and lakes have been important waterways and sources of a variety of biological resources and freshwater. In Russia, there are 221 rivers with lengths exceeding 500 kms, 3316 rivers with lengths between 101 and 500 kms, and 137,302 shorter rivers (Federal State Statistics Service of the Russian Federation, 2020, p. 70). Russia's longest river is the Lena (4.4 thousand kilometres long), which flows through Siberia to the Arctic Ocean. However, the river that played a key role in the historical development of the Russian state and economy is the Volga (3.5 thousand kilometres long; it is also Europe's longest river), which flows to the Caspian Sea. A system of human-built canals augments the natural system of rivers. Most of these canals can be found in European Russia, ensuring connections between the rivers flowing into the Baltic Sea, the Black Sea, and the White Sea, thus connecting these seas. Canals also serve to bring water to water-scarce agricultural areas in the south.

The size of Russia's freshwater reserves is estimated at around 89 thousand cubic kilometres (Ministry of Natural Resources and Ecology of the Russian Federation, 2019, p. 10)—almost one-fifth of the world's total. Of this amount, 23 thousand cubic kilometres of freshwater is contained in Lake Baikal alone. The geographical distribution of water resources (including freshwater) is uneven; thus, along with the water abundant regions, there are regions experiencing a shortage of water resources.

Swamps are primarily found in the north-western regions of European Russia as well as in western Siberia. They play an important role in the bio-ecological system due to, among other things, the ability of swamp plants to effectively bind carbon thus decreasing its concentration in the atmosphere. At the same time and for the same reason, peat (accumulated remnants of swamp plants and organic matter) is a valuable natural fuel and fertiliser, although its use inevitably releases substantial amounts of carbon. Russia (along with Canada) possesses a substantial share of the world's peat reserves.

Russia's aquatic biological resources include the fish, shellfish, other aquatic animals, algae, and water plants which are naturally living in the country's lakes, rivers, swamps, man-made water reservoirs, internal seas, and in the 200-mile maritime exclusive economic zone (on the country's continental shelf). The volume of harvested aquatic biological resources in Russia grew substantially during the twentieth century due to advances in catching and storage technologies, as well as due to the growing Soviet fishing fleet, which by the 1980s became the largest in the world. In the 1980s, the amount of catch in Russia reached its maximum of more than eight million tonnes (the Soviet Union's total was 14 million tonnes). Following the breakup of the Soviet Union, the Russian fishing industry and fishing fleet experienced a period of decay, accompanied by the growth of poaching and shadow trade schemes; the amount of catch by 2004 decreased to less than three million tonnes, a historical low since the 1960s. Reforms in the fishing industry and anti-poaching measures, however, allowed for a reversal of this trend, bringing Russia back among the world's top five capture producers by 2016 (Food and Agriculture Organization, 2020) and the top 10 exporters of fish products. As of 2019, the harvesting of aquatic biological resources by Russian companies amounted to almost five million tonnes, 97% of which were harvested from maritime fisheries and 3% from inland lakes, river, and other water reservoirs (Federal Agency for Fishery—Rosrybolovstvo, 2020). Furthermore, almost 70% of these aquatic biological resources were harvested in the Pacific Ocean. Russia is a net exporter of fish and crustaceans, molluscs, and other aquatic invertebrates. Aquaculture (i.e., growing aquatic products rather than capturing them) is also developing in Russia, but currently plays minor role in production.

An important facet of a country's aquatic resources is the potential for hydropower. Hydropower is a renewable energy source (see Chapter 9), although not without a controversial impact on the environment. The construction of hydropower stations often requires flooding large areas, which can affect animals and plants and may change the microclimate in adjacent areas. However, building hydropower stations prevents burning fuel, which emits carbon dioxide into the atmosphere, expands the water supply, and can help to prevent seasonal floods. The earliest (small) hydropower stations were built in Russia at the end of the nineteenth century. Russia's first large-scale station was constructed in the 1920s and most of its existing hydropower stations were built during the 1930s–1980s. There are currently more than 100 hydropower stations in Russia (each with a capacity of over 10 megawatts), which brings the total capacity to 51.8 gigawatts (Federal State Statistics Service of the Russian Federation, 2020, p. 395). Of these, 15 hydropower stations have a capacity of over 1000 megawatts, seven of which are located in the Volga River Basin (European Russia), five in the Yenisei River Basin (Siberia), two on the Amur River (Far East), and one on the Sulak River (Dagestan). Several large-scale hydropower station construction projects were suspended or cancelled in the 1990s due to the economic crisis and related decrease in electricity consumption. The construction of new large-scale stations has only resumed in the twenty-first century.

According to some estimates (Soloviev, 2020, pp. 26–35), Russia's theoretical gross hydropower generation capacity (including small rivers) equals approximately 2800 terawatt-hours per year, making it the second in the world in this respect, after China but ahead of the United States, Brazil, and Canada; the attainable potential without small rivers is 1670 terawatt-hours per year. Most of Russia's hydropower potential is concentrated in Siberia. The actual total annual electric power production (using all sources) in Russia in 2019 amounted to 1121 billion kilowatt-hours, and the hydroelectric power production—to 196 billion kilowatt-hours (Federal State Statistics Service of the Russian Federation, 2020, p. 394). This means that only a fraction of the existing hydropower potential is realised; in particular, the extent to which the existing potential is realised in the Russian Far East is especially low. In certain regions of Russia, such as the northern part of the Caucasus, the construction of hydropower stations is possible without the significant flooding of adjacent areas.

1.3.2 Land

Russia is the largest country in the world according to its total land mass; therefore, it is not surprising that one of its largest natural resources is land. As of 2019, 66% of Russia's total land mass was covered by forests and 22% was used for agricultural purposes (Federal Service for State Registration, Cadastre and Cartography—Rosreestr, 2019). Russia's remaining land is used for settlements, industry, infrastructure and transportation, military and other special purposes, protected and recreational areas, and reserved lands. During the Soviet period, all land was owned by the state; however, along with the market reforms beginning in the 1990s, private ownership of land was permitted and the process of privatisation began (see Chapters 7 and 10). In 2019, the share of lands of all kinds in private ownership was around 7%, the share of private agricultural lands was 33%, and the share of private lands under settlements was 25% (Federal Service for State Registration, Cadastre and Cartography—Rosreestr, 2019).

Agricultural lands include lands used for crop cultivation, cattle farming, and aquaculture, among others. The relative share of agricultural lands in Russia is not high compared to the world's average, in particular, due to its climatic conditions, but the absolute area of lands suitable for agricultural use is substantial. As of 2019, in terms of the total area of agricultural lands, Russia ranked fifth in the world after China, the United States, Australia, and Brazil (it ranked close to the latter, despite obvious differences in climate) (see Food and Agriculture Organization of the United Nations, 2021). While the climate, even in the southern parts of Russia, is generally not as beneficial for crop production as in countries located closer to the Earth's equator, the large area and quality of its soil partially compensate for this (see Chapter 10 for more information on agriculture production).

Russian forest lands account for one-fifth of the world's total, commensurate in their area to the combined forest lands of Brazil and Canada; Russia is one of the world's top producers and exporters of roundwood and sawn wood (Food and Agriculture Organization of the United Nations, 2021). Russian forests play an increasingly important ecological role globally: according to some estimates, over the last three decades, despite deforestation and natural disasters (such as fires), the productivity of the vegetation, tree cover, and total biomass of Russian forests have increased substantially, thus balancing the net forest stock losses in tropical countries (Schepaschenko et al., 2021).

1.3.3 Mineral Resources

Russia's mineral resources are vast and diverse, making it one of the world leaders in terms of both discovered reserves and the production and export of natural gas, oil, coal, iron ore, copper, nickel, zinc, gold, palladium, and diamonds, among others. Its discovered mineral deposits are found throughout Russia's territory and continental shelf. They are often located in remote areas with limited transportation access and/or harsh natural conditions. In many cases, there are high relative and absolute costs associated with the extraction and transportation of certain minerals, which leads to lower economic efficiency and profitability as compared to some other international examples. Nevertheless, the mineral resources of Russia are strategically important for the development of its processing industries, agriculture, and exports, as well as to ensure the country's security and sustainability.

In 2018, the Federal Government adopted the strategy for the development of the mineral resource base until 2035 (Ministry of Natural Resources and Ecology of the Russian Federation, 2018). This document is intended to guide Russia's executive bodies in formulating and carrying out policies aimed at the effective exploration, exploitation, and renewal of the nation's mineral resources. The strategic goal in this sphere is to ensure sustainable access to the mineral resources needed for the country's economic development and to maintain the economic and energy security of Russia. To achieve this goal, the strategy envisages various measures of state support for geological exploration, the introduction of new mining and processing technologies, and the recovery of the existing resource base, among others.

The strategy identifies three groups of minerals based on reserve size, production volume, and prospects.

The first group includes minerals with reserves sufficient for the needs of the national economy up to the year 2035 and beyond under all development scenarios: natural gas, copper, nickel, tin, tungsten, molybdenum, tantalum, niobium, cobalt, scandium, germanium, platinoids, apatite ores, iron ores, potassium salts, coal, and the mineral components of cement (carbonates and clay minerals). It is noted that while the economy-wide needs for these minerals are—and for the foreseeable future will be—largely met by domestic production, the accessibility of these minerals for some regions of Russia is currently limited (due to infrastructural and other reasons). This results in higher costs and/or unstable supplies and calls for the development of new infrastructure and the exploration of new reserves.

The second group includes minerals where the existing levels of production cannot be maintained in the long term without the development of new mines or fields: oil, lead, antimony, gold, silver, diamonds, zinc, and pure quartz. It is also reasonable and possibly even necessary to find and use non-traditional sources of these minerals.

The third group includes the scarce minerals which Russia must import in significant amounts due to either a lack of natural reserves or their low quality: uranium, manganese, chromium, titanium, bauxite, zirconium, beryllium, lithium, rhenium, yttrium, fluorspar, bentonites for foundry production, feldspar raw materials, kaolin, large-leaf muscovite, iodine, bromine, and optical raw materials. While substantial reserves of chromium and certain rare earth metals can be found in Russia, they remain underdeveloped. One way envisioned in the Strategy to ensure an increase in the domestic production of these minerals—and to reduce Russia's dependence on imports—is to stimulate investments into exploration and production facilities and infrastructure. Another solution, also mentioned in the Strategy, is for Russian companies to participate in joint international exploration and development projects.

1.4 An Overview of Key Mineral Resources

An overview of the country's key mineral resources is presented below.

1.4.1 Oil

As of 2019, Russia possessed 8% (18.7 billion tonnes) of the discovered world reserves of liquid hydrocarbons (including oil), ranking among the top six countries, and has extracted about 12% (558.5 million tonnes) of the global annual production volume, being one of the top three major producers and exporters of oil (Ministry of Natural Resources and Ecology of the Russian Federation, 2020, p. 15). More than half of Russian oil is extracted in the Ural Federal District (i.e., the Khanty-Mansi Autonomous District, the Yamal-Nenets Autonomous District, and the Tyumen Oblast). Another oil-rich territory, producing about one-fifth of the total, is the Volga Federal District (i.e., the Republic of Tatarstan, the Orenburg Oblast, the Samara Oblast, Perm Krai, the Republic of Bashkortostan, and the Udmurt Republic). The remaining oil is extracted predominantly in Siberian regions. The significance of Russia's continental shelf in oil extraction is expected to increase in the future.

As the productivity of existing oil fields is decreasing with time, Russian corporations are undertaking projects to discover new oilfields; some of these newly discovered oilfields are expected to start production in the 2020s, which is important for maintaining and increasing the overall production volume. Untraditional oil sources, such as shale oil fields, have only recently begun to be exploited, although there is growing interest in them among Russian oil producers, as the country's estimated shale oil reserves are among the largest (and possibly—the largest) globally.

Around half of Russia's extracted oil and processed oil products are exported (see Chapter 9). Oil pipelines deliver Russian oil directly to Germany, Eastern Europe, and China; there are also oil pipelines leading to Russia from Azerbaijan and Kazakhstan. Some oil pipelines end at Russian seaports, where oil and oil products are transported in oil tankers.

1.4.2 Natural Gas

Russia's proved natural gas reserves are the largest in the world (49 trillion cubic metres), representing a quarter of the global amount. In 2019, Russia was the world's leading exporter of natural gas and the second major producer after the United States (Ministry of Natural Resources and Ecology of the Russian Federation, 2020, p. 42). The production and export volumes of natural gas from Russia have been growing over the last decade (see Chapter 9), although the dynamics have lagged behind that of the United States, where untraditional sources of natural gas (shale) were being actively exploited, while Russia relied solely on traditional sources.

As of 2021, the network of gas pipelines used to transport gas to Russian and foreign consumers had a total length of 177 thousand kilometres. In recent years, many new gas pipelines are under construction, which is key to ensuring that the increased demand from international consumers is met. Recently completed major gas pipelines include the Nord Stream and Nord Stream 2 (which has not become operational due to sanctions—see Chapter 14), delivering gas from Russia to Germany and Central Europe; the Power of Siberia, delivering gas to Russia's Pacific coast with a second pipeline to China; and the Turkish Stream, delivering gas from Russia to Turkey.

While gas pipelines have traditionally been the most important means of gas delivery, liquefied natural gas (LNG) trade is growing rapidly. The demand for LNG increased dramatically in the 2010s and is primarily shipped in tankers to consumers without sufficient access to gas pipelines—mostly to consumers in Asia. In 2019, Russia was among the major exporters of LNG, ranked third after Qatar and Australia (Ministry of Natural Resources and Ecology of the Russian Federation, 2020, p. 51).

As of 2019, 86% of Russia's natural gas production was concentrated in the Ural Federal District (primarily in Yamal-Nenets Autonomous District). Major ongoing projects to develop new natural gas fields are also being implemented on the Yamal Peninsula, as well as on the Island of Sakhalin and on Russia's continental shelf.

1.4.3 Coal

Russian proved reserves of coal (of all types) account for 11% (113 billion tonnes) of the world's total, ranking it fourth in this respect (after the United States, China, and Australia). During 2010–2019, coal production in Russia expanded, reaching more than 400 million tonnes (Ministry of Natural Resources and Ecology of the Russian Federation, 2020, p. 64). More than half of all production is concentrated in the Kuznetsk Basin (Kuzbass) in the Kemerovo Oblast (south-western Siberia), which possesses one of the world's largest coal deposits; the rest is also produced mostly in Siberia (see Chapter 9). More than 100 companies are involved in coal mining.

1.4.4 Uranium

Russia possesses 8% of the proved world uranium reserves, sharing third place with Canada after Kazakhstan and Australia and ranking seventh in terms of uranium production—producing 2997 tonnes in 2019 (Ministry of Natural Resources and Ecology of the Russian Federation, 2020, p. 82). Most of

Russia's uranium is extracted in Siberia—in Zabaikalskiy Krai, the Republic of Buryatia, the Kurgan Oblast, and the Republic of Yakutia. Uranium extraction and processing are controlled by the state-owned holding Rosatom (comprised of several hundred companies operating in the atomic industry), which is also engaged in the construction and operation of nuclear power stations in Russia and internationally. Russia exports almost no crude uranium; however, it imports it (mostly from Kazakhstan) for processing. Rosatom is one of the world's leading producers and exporters of fuel for nuclear power stations.

1.4.5   Iron

Russia's proved reserves of iron ore represent about 15% of the global reserves, ranking it second in the world after Brazil (Ministry of Natural Resources and Ecology of the Russian Federation, 2020, p. 94). Almost half of all iron ore is extracted on the territory of the Kursk Magnetic Anomaly (Kursk and Belgorod oblasts) in the European part of Russia, about one-fifth—in the Urals, and the rest—mostly in Siberia and in the north-west. Iron ore production and processing is primarily carried out by several corporate groups, including Metalloinvest, which controls two-thirds of the national production. The country's iron ore reserves are sufficient for current and projected domestic needs and most (around 80%) of the produced ore is supplied to Russian metallurgical plants; the rest is exported, with China and Ukraine being the major buyers. However, production sites/mines and processing sites/metallurgical plants are rather remote from each other, leading to high transportation costs. Some metallurgical plants located close to Kazakhstan import iron ore from them to save on transportation costs.

1.4.6   Copper

Russia's proved reserves of copper represent 8% of the global figure (Ministry of Natural Resources and Ecology of the Russian Federation, 2020, p. 150). Its production volume is largely sufficient for domestic needs and for exports of processed copper; however, some copper concentrates are imported for processing. Most of Russia's copper extraction is carried out in the Urals and Krasnoyarsk Krai, the rest—in the north of European Russia and in Siberia. Copper production and processing is conducted primarily by three major vertically integrated companies—Nornickel, the Russian Copper Company, and UMMC.

1.4.7   Nickel

Nickel is one of Russia's strategic minerals, the reserves and production of which cover Russia's own needs and allow for exports. As of 2019, Russia is the world's third major holder and producer of nickel (Ministry of Natural Resources and Ecology of the Russian Federation, 2020, p. 170). Almost all nickel extraction is conducted in the Norilsk area in the north of Krasnoyarsk Krai, with small amounts also produced in the Murmansk Oblast and Kamchatka. Nickel extraction and processing is carried out predominantly by the vertically integrated holding Nornickel. Most of the nickel produced in Russia is exported.

1.4.8 Gold

Russia's proved gold reserves are the largest in the world (13% of the global amount), with Canada being close second as of 2019. In terms of the global share of gold production, Russia ranks third (9%) after China (12%) and Australia (10%) (Ministry of Natural Resources and Ecology of the Russian Federation, 2020, p. 312). Over the last decade, gold ore extraction in Russia has grown substantially, and the extent of domestic gold ore processing has also increased. Most gold production is concentrated in Siberia (Krasnoyarskiy Krai and the Republic of Yakutia, among others) and the Russian Far East (particularly in the Magadan Oblast). Two-thirds of Russia's gold production is carried out by 10 companies, of which the largest producer (controlling almost one-third of Russia's reserves and production) is the Polus holding company. The share of gold exports to production varied during 2010–2019, depending on the policy of the Central Bank of the Russian Federation (CBRF), which is usually the largest purchaser of Russian gold. The discovered reserves of gold and ongoing investments to Russia's capacity to extract gold may increase Russian gold production by about half of its current volume until 2030.

1.4.9 Silver

In terms of proved silver reserves and production volume, Russia currently ranks fifth in the world (Ministry of Natural Resources and Ecology of the Russian Federation, 2020, p. 334). Most silver reserves are located in the Urals, Siberia, and the Far East of Russia. However, it is expected that the existing mines may be nearly exhausted by 2040, thus requiring the development of new mines located in areas currently insufficiently equipped with transportation and/or processing infrastructure.

1.4.10 Diamonds

Diamonds are found primarily in two Russian regions—the Republic of Yakutia (Siberia) and in the Archangelsk Oblast (north of European Russia). The country's diamond reserves are the largest in the world—nearly half of the global discovered reserves (Ministry of Natural Resources and Ecology of the Russian Federation, 2020, p. 372), making it the top producer and exporter of diamonds, providing about one-third of the global supply. Russia's leading producer of diamonds (with a market share of almost 90%) is the

Alrosa Group. If current production levels are maintained, Russia's currently exploited diamond mines will be largely exhausted within a couple decades. To maintain Russia's diamond production, it is crucial to develop new mines (the process of which is currently under way). Nearly all diamonds mined in Russia are exported (primarily to Belgium, as well as to India and the United Arab Emirates).

1.4.11 *Phosphates and Potassium Salts*

Russia possesses sufficient reserves of phosphates and potassium salts to produce all major types of mineral fertilisers, meeting both domestic and international demands. Although Russia's natural reserves of phosphates (two-thirds of which are apatite) are relatively small, their quality is high—even unique—making Russia one of the world's top suppliers of phosphates and phosphate fertilisers (Ministry of Natural Resources and Ecology of the Russian Federation, 2020, p. 400). Almost all production of apatite is concentrated in the Murmansk Oblast (north of the European part of Russia) and is carried out predominantly by three companies—PhosAgro, EuroChim, and Akron, as well as by some smaller ones. There are also minor phosphate mines in the Republic of Buryatia (Siberia) and the Tula Oblast (European Russia), as well as other regions of Russia. Most of Russia's extracted apatite concentrate is processed within the country, primarily into fertilisers; some phosphate concentrates and phosphate fertilisers are exported.

Russia is also one of the top producers of potassium salts (Ministry of Natural Resources and Ecology of the Russian Federation, 2020, p. 414), together with Canada, Belarus, and China providing three-quarters of the global supply. Potassium production is concentrated in Perm Krai (Urals), Irkutsk Oblast (Siberia), Volgograd Oblast, and the Komi Republic (European part of Russia). The production of potassium salts and potassium fertilisers is dominated by Uralkali, which is also one of the top global exporters, as well as by several smaller companies. Most of the potassium salts and fertilisers produced are exported.

1.5 Natural Resources and Environmental Factors of Human Settlement Patterns

Since the ancient times, climate, environmental conditions, the presence of natural resources, and proximity to natural (rivers and seas) and man-made transportation routes (along with political and security considerations) were among the most important factors determining the settlement of people. These factors are also influencing human migration and settlement patterns in modern-day Russia. In the traditional (largely subsistence-oriented) agricultural economy and society of the past, it was fertile land and a relatively favourable climate as well as an abundance of rivers that made the Russian (East European) Plain sought after and fought for. Natural waterways provided connections between settlements on the Plain, also connecting them with the seas in the north and south.

The oldest cities in Russia developed centuries ago in the vicinity of the Black, Caspian, Baltic, and White Seas and on the fertile lands along the rivers serving as trade routes connecting northern Europe with Byzantium and the Arab Caliphate. The growth of cities and the development of trade drove the people of ancient Russia farther to the north and east in search of furs, metals, and other natural resources. This quest was championed by the Great Novgorod Republic and the principality of Vladimir-Suzdal as early as the twelfth and thirteenth centuries; their exploratory expeditions reached the Ural Mountains, thousands of kilometres afar. Since the beginnings of Russia's unification in the fifteenth and sixteenth centuries, military and security considerations made the state push its frontier as far as possible from the Russian heartland. A combination of trade and military considerations made it crucial for the growing Russian state during the seventeenth to nineteenth centuries to regain access to the Baltic and Black Seas as well as the White Sea in the north (which were lost centuries earlier), establishing new seaports and cities on their coasts, and later to explore the shores of the Pacific Ocean, establishing Russian settlements as far as the modern-day US state of California (Fort Ross in Sonoma). Generally avoiding extremely cold regions, lands unsuitable for farming, and areas distant from trade routes, people (beyond the Russian plain) tended to settle in the southern areas of Siberia and the Russian Far East, establishing new towns close to exploitable natural resources—fertile land, water rich with fish, forests with fur-bearing animals, and, later on, mineral deposits.

The core of the urban system of modern-day Russia—its network of its major urban centres—was largely formed in the twentieth century (see Pivovarov, 2001). It should be remembered, however, that prior to the late twentieth century, the country's urban system evolved as an integral part of the urban system of the Russian Empire, and later of the Soviet Union. This explains the rather vivid gap in the size of the population between Russia's two major cities (Moscow and St. Petersburg) on the one side and the next largest Russian cities on the other. The Soviet urban system also included several cities (such as Kiev, Minsk, and Tashkent) outside Russia that used to fill that gap.

The role of natural resources, especially that of coal, oil, and gas—that is, sources of energy, as well as of metal ores, grew substantially after the start of Russia's industrialisation. In the centrally planned economy of the Soviet Union, the process of industrialisation was advanced by the state and accompanied by rapid urbanisation as new large-scale industrial enterprises needed more labour. This industrialisation also required the increased production of resources and energy, both for the industry itself and for a source of export revenue, which was needed to finance the purchase of machines and equipment as well as new large-scale construction projects. This called for the development of new facilities to extract mineral deposits in remote, usually scarcely populated areas.

A vast number of new towns and cities were planned and built (especially during the 1930s–1970s) close to resource-rich areas and to new energy power stations, as well as along the new transportation routes (see Lappo, 2012). Some of these settlements eventually evolved into relatively large cities, but most of them remained small, single-industry towns. Some of them grew close to prisons and labour camps and were populated by former prisoners or forced labourers. Many people, especially post-World War II (WWII) when many cities in the western part of the Soviet Union had been damaged or destroyed, came willingly, being attracted to these places by employment opportunities and the numerous benefits (e.g., higher salaries, earlier retirement, and longer annual vacations, among others) guaranteed by the government to those working in harsh climates. However, even before the economic challenges of the 1980s, most of these single-industry towns experienced an outflow of people, the expectations and ambitions of whom had changed.

The collapse of the central planning system, followed by economic decline in the 1990s, left the government unable to finance most of its earlier guarantees to the residents of the extreme north and similar territories. At the same time, enterprises previously engaged in the extraction of natural resources were privatised, while others were forced to cut labour or went bankrupt. Outmigration from single-industry towns increased further due to the easing of restrictions on choosing a place of residence and due to the development of the housing market nationwide. While some of these settlements continue to prosper under new conditions, many—being a legacy of a different socio-economic and political system—are depressive places with high unemployment, representing a serious challenge for local authorities and federal policymakers (see Fattakhov et al., 2019).

The process of the concentration of the population in large Russian cities (with Moscow, St. Petersburg, and the Black Sea coast being the top attractors), which began in the 1990s, negatively affected not only remote single-industry towns but even the older cities of European Russia. This may be regarded as an indication of the gradual and inevitable erosion of the Soviet legacy of spatial planning. As for the exploitation of remotely located new mineral resource deposits and other natural resources, the current approach is different from the Soviet one: instead of establishing permanent settlements for employees, work is organised in seasonal shifts.

1.6   INFRASTRUCTURAL ASPECTS

To make effective use of its natural resources, to develop new mineral deposits, to expand the processing of natural resources on its own territory (thus reducing exports of raw materials), and to deepen its integration into international trade, it is essential for Russia to expand and modernise its transport infrastructure.

Russia's infrastructure currently includes all types of transport linkages, the capacity of which is generally sufficient to meet the needs of the national economy in the short run. Nevertheless, in the medium and long run, its transport infrastructure requires further expansion and modernisation for several reasons.

First, ensuring the conditions for increased human mobility is important from the perspective of effectively engaging the nation's human capital in the social and economic development of the country and thus lowering its reliance on the exploitation of natural resources.

Second, the expansion of old and the development of new transportation routes and linkages within the country is needed to connect remotely located resource-rich areas with domestic industrial enterprises and domestic markets, which will allow the greater development of domestic processing industries.

Third, as global trade and the global economy are transforming and new markets grow fast in the east and south (see Chapter 11), it is important for Russia to integrate its own transport infrastructure into the evolving Eurasian and global trade routes to gain access to new markets for its exports as well as to engage in transit trade and to participate in global value chains.

Fourth, it is important to increase the safety and reliability of all types of transport connections.

Fifth, efficient transportation infrastructure is crucial for the needs of national defence and security.

Sixth, more attention must be paid to the environmental impact of the transport sector as well as to the challenges and opportunities created by the climate change.

In 2008, the Russian government adopted a strategy on transport through 2030 (Ministry of Transport of the Russian Federation, 2008). To achieve the strategic goal of having the transportation system serving the innovative and socially oriented economy, several specific goals are identified:

- Creation of a unified national transport space, combining transportation routes and hubs as well as logistical infrastructure, ensuring direct linkages between major economic centres and the availability of alternative routes.
- Ensuring the accessibility and quality of transport-logistical services through the development of a competitive business environment in this sector.
- Guaranteeing the accessibility and quality of transport services to the population based on social standards.
- Integration into the global transport space and using the country's transit potential.
- Ensuring the safety of the transport system.
- Decreasing the negative impact of the transport system on the environment, particularly by switching to cleaner types of fuel and to more ecological types of transportation.

There are multiple indicators defined for each of these goals, and financing is provided from the federal budget along with other sources. The implementation of the transport strategy is monitored based on a system of 78 statistical indicators. As of 2020, substantial progress has been made towards achieving the first, second, and fifth goals, while progress towards the other goals has been moderate (Ministry of Transport of the Russian Federation, 2021).

During the 2010s, Russia actively constructed new motorways and developed its seaports and airports; however, the needed upgrades of its existing motorways and the development of additional railways have been slower than planned. The achieved level of reliability of passenger and cargo transportation services is generally high; for example, much of Russia's railway rolling stock and airplanes were upgraded in the 2010s, but its fleet of water vehicles is still in need of renovation. The shift to new environmentally friendly types of fuels and vehicles remains an important task, the progress towards which has so far been limited.

A key infrastructure project, seen as a strategic priority and involving a number of major Russian corporations, is the development of the Northern Sea Route—a water passage connecting the Atlantic, Arctic, and Pacific oceans, mostly through Russia's territorial waters and exclusive economic zone along its northern coast. This route between Northern Europe and Southeast Asia is shorter than the traditional routes through the Suez and Panama Canals or the Northwest Passage via the Canadian Arctic Archipelago.

Historically, the earliest attempts to discover and use water routes in the Russian Arctic were undertaken centuries ago but were limited in their extent due to the ocean's extensive ice cover. Only at the turn of the twentieth century, with the advent of steam-powered seagoing icebreakers, long-distance navigation in the Arctic waters became possible. Following several research-oriented sea voyages, transport navigation along the Northern Sea Route began in 1935, when two vessels carrying timber sailed from Leningrad (now St. Petersburg) to Vladivostok. The active development of transport navigation along fragments of the Northern Sea Route started in the 1960s in connection with the intensification of mineral resource extraction in the areas close to the Arctic coast and were supported by the novel Soviet fleet of nuclear icebreakers.

In the twenty-first century, due to both reduced ice cover in the Arctic and the development of Russia's state and corporate fleets of icebreakers, the transport potential of the Northern Sea Route is increasing. In the circumpolar territories of Russia, particularly on the Yamal Peninsula, new oil and gas fields are being developed and large-scale gas liquefication facilities have been constructed and will be expanded further, along with the new seaport of Sabetta on the Yamal Peninsula designed primarily for LNG tankers. As the global demand for LNG is expected to grow, especially in Asia, the importance of Russian gas and oil shipments via the Northern Sea Route cannot be overestimated. In addition to servicing export shipments, the Northern Sea Route is useful for organising the delivery of various cargos to the northern regions of Russia, otherwise poorly accessible in certain seasons. The Northern Sea Route may also play an important role in integrating Russia into international trade routes, allowing it to export transit transport services (see also Stepanov, 2019; Zvorykina & Teteryatnikov, 2019).

Questions for Students

1. What types of climates are found in Russia?
2. What are the most important risks and opportunities created by climate change for Russia?
3. What types of natural resources are the most important for the country's economy?
4. What factors hinder the exploitation of the country's discovered natural resources?
5. How are the country's human settlement patterns related to the climate and natural resources?
6. What are the main reasons for expanding and modernising the transportation system of Russia in the medium and long run? What goals are to be achieved and what major projects could you mention in this regard?

References

Fattakhov, R. V., Nizamutdinov, M. M., & Oreshnikov, V. V. (2019). Analysing and modelling of trends in the development of the territorial: Settlement system in Russia. *Ekonomika Regiona [Economy of Region]*, *15*(2), 436–450 (in Russian).

Federal Agency for Fishery—Rosrybolovstvo. (2020). *Data on the fish catch and harvesting of other aquatic biological resources for January-December 2019* (in Russian). https://fish.gov.ru/wp-content/uploads/documents/otraslevaya_dey atelnost/ekonomika_otrasli/statistika_analitika/2020/f407-01-12_2019.pdf

Federal Service for State Registration, Cadastre and Cartography—Rosreestr. (2019). *Data on the state and structure of lands in the Russian Federation on 01.01.2019* (in Russian). https://rosreestr.gov.ru/site/activity/gosudarstvennoe-upravlenie-v-sfere-ispolzovaniya-i-okhrany-zemel/gosudarstvennyy-monitoring-zemel/sostoy anie-zemel-rossii/gosudarstvennyy-natsionalnyy-doklad-o-sostoyanii-i-ispolzovanii-zemel-v-rossiyskoy-federatsii

Federal State Statistics Service of the Russian Federation (2020). *Russian statistical yearbook 2020*. Moscow.

Food and Agriculture Organization of the United Nations. (2020). The state of world fisheries and aquaculture 2020: Sustainability in action. *Rome.* https://doi.org/10.4060/ca9229en

Food and Agriculture Organization of the United Nations. (2021). *Food and agriculture data*. http://www.fao.org/faostat/en/#data/RL

Lappo, G. M. (2012). *Goroda Rossii. Vzgljad geografa (Cities of Russia. Geographer's view)*. Novyj hronograf (in Russian).

Ministry of Natural Resources and Ecology of the Russian Federation. (2018). The strategy for the development of the mineral resource base of the Russian

Federation until 2035 (Adopted by the Resolution of the Government of the Russian Federation No 2914-r on 22.12.2018) (in Russian). http://www.mnr.gov.ru/docs/strategiya_razvitiya_mineralno_syrevoy_bazy_rossiyskoy_federatsii_do_2035_goda/strategiya_razvitiya_mineralno_syrevoy_bazy_rossiyskoy_federatsii_do_2035_goda/

Ministry of Natural Resources and Ecology of the Russian Federation. (2019). *On the state and the utilization of water resources of the Russian Federation in 2018: The state report*. Moscow (in Russian).

Ministry of Natural Resources and Ecology of the Russian Federation. (2020). *On the state and the utilization of mineral resources of the Russian Federation in 2019: State report*. Moscow (in Russian).

Ministry of Transport of the Russian Federation. (2008). *The transport strategy of the Russian Federation for the period of up to 2030* (Adopted by the Resolution of the Government of the Russian Federation No 1734-r on 22.11.2008) (in Russian). https://mintrans.gov.ru/documents/3/1009

Ministry of Transport of the Russian Federation. (2021). *The report on the implementation of the Transport Strategy of the Russian Federation for the period of up to 2030. The reporting year 2020* (in Russian). https://mintrans.gov.ru/documents/11/11430

Pivovarov, Y. (2001). Urbanization in Russia in the XX century: Ideas and reality. *Social Sciences and Contemporary World, 6*, 101–113 (in Russian).

Schepaschenko, D., Moltchanova, E., Fedorov, S., et al. (2021). Russian forest sequesters substantially more carbon than previously reported. *SciRep, 11*, 12825. https://doi.org/10.1038/s41598-021-92152-9

Soloviev, D. A. (2020). Russia's hydropower complex: New opportunities and prospects for development. *Energy Policy, 1*(143), 26–35 (in Russian).

Stepanov, N. (2019). Arctic and the development of the Northern Sea route in the institutional modernization of Russian economy. *Federalism, 1*, 5–23 (in Russian).

Streletskiy DA, Suter LJ, Shiklomanov NI, Porfiriev, B. N., & Eliseev, D. O. (2019). Assessment of climate change impacts on buildings, structures and infrastructure in the Russian regions on permafrost. *Environmental Research Letters, 14*(2), 025003. https://doi.org/10.1088/1748-9326/aaf5e6

Vampilova, L. B., & Manakov, A. G. (2012). Natural and cultural indications of historical-geographical zoning of Russia. Izvestiya RAN (Akad. Nauk SSSR). *Seriya Geograficheskaya, 6*, 7–16 (in Russian).

Zvorykina, Y. V., & Teteryatnikov, K. S. (2019). The Northern Sea Route as a tool of Arctic development. *Russian Economic Journal, 4*, 21–44 (in Russian). https://doi.org/10.33983/0130-9757-2019-4-21-44

CHAPTER 2

Human Resources

Irina Denisova and Marina Kartseva

Highlights

- The multi-ethnic and multicultural population of Russia has been subject to substantial demographic changes since the last decade of the twentieth century, including negative population growth, a shrinking working-age population, and population aging. These changes pose challenges to the country's economic growth potential and public finances.
- The health status of the population—and in particular males—improves slowly. The missed cardiovascular revolution is responsible for continued high mortality rates in Russia.
- Russia's population is well educated compared to other middle-income countries, which is in part a positive legacy of the Soviet era. In the post-Soviet period, however, quality of education is a growing concern,

---

I. Denisova (✉)
New Economic School, Moscow, Russia
e-mail: idenisova@nes.ru

Moscow State University, Moscow, Russia

M. Kartseva
Russian Academy of National Economy and Public Administration, Moscow, Russia
e-mail: kartseva-ma@ranepa.ru

© The Author(s), under exclusive license to Springer Nature Switzerland AG 2023
M. Dabrowski (ed.), *The Contemporary Russian Economy*,
https://doi.org/10.1007/978-3-031-17382-0_2

especially given the increased pace of technological change. Equal opportunities in access to high-quality education is a central issue in social policy.

2.1 Human Capital in Russia from an International Perspective

2.1.1 Population Size and Growth Rate

Russia is a large country not only in terms of its territory but also in terms of the size of its population. In 2020, Russia ranked ninth among the most populated countries of the world, with a population of approximately 146 million people (United Nations, 2019), with Bangladesh ranked eighth and Mexico ranked tenth.

At the same time, Russia has been experiencing depopulation (negative population growth) for several decades. Russia had negative annual population growth both in 2000 (−0.42%) and in 2019 (−0.05%), though for the latter, the magnitude was much less.[1] In other words, Russia lost 4.2 people for every 1000 people living in the country in 2000 and 0.5 person for every 1000 people in 2019. In comparison, among members of the Organisation for Economic Co-operation and Development (OECD), only Italy, Latvia, Lithuania, Japan, Greece, Hungary, and Poland had negative population growth rates in 2019.

Persistent negative population growth can limit extensive economic growth. Intensive economic growth via the more productive use of resources—in particular, human resources—is the alternative. In this situation, it is then especially important that people possess a high level of human capital (productive capacity).

We first discuss an aggregate measure of human capital development in Russia as reflected by the Human Development Index (HDI) and examine Russia from an international perspective. Sections 2.3 and 2.4 discuss the health and educational components of human capital in Russia.

2.1.2 Human Development Index

Russia, with an HDI value of 0.824 in 2019, belongs to the group of countries with very high human development (with an HDI of 0.800 and above); it ranked 52nd out of 189 countries. Moreover, Russia has made significant progress since 2000, when its HDI value amounted to 0.722. However, Russia is not a leader in this respect: India, China, Turkey, and Latvia have shown even more progress, improving their HDI values by 0.15 (India), 0.17 (China), 0.16 (Turkey), and 0.13 (Latvia) between 2000 and 2019.[2]

---

[1] https://datatopics.worldbank.org/world-development-indicators/.

[2] http://hdr.undp.org/en/content/human-development-index-hdi.

Progress in human development in Russia during the analysed period was driven by a sharp increase in the standard of living component—gross national income (GNI) per capita—and a significant increase in the life expectancy component (see Box 2.1 for HDI components). Russia's GNI component of the HDI almost doubled during 2000–2019, from USD 14.19 thousand (in purchasing power parity [PPP] terms) in 2000 to USD 26.2 thousand in 2019. Life expectancy at birth increased by 7.5 years during this period, from 65.1 in 2000 to 72.6 in 2019.[3] The educational component also improved during the same period. Mean years of education of adults increased modestly from 11.3 in 2000 to 12.2 in 2019 (a more sizeable increase by 2.4 years occurred from 1990 to 2000) and expected years of schooling of children—from 12.5 in 2000 to 15 in 2019 (an increase of 2.5 years).

Despite improvements, there is still a long way to go for Russia to reach the level of the leading countries. The maximum values of the HDI components are currently set at 15 years for mean schooling of adults, 18 years for expected years of schooling of children, 85 years for life expectancy, and USD 75 thousand per capita GNI (constant prices of 2017 PPP adjusted). Russia ranked 110th of 189 countries in 2019 based on life expectancy at birth. At the same time, Russia ranked 32nd of 189 countries based on the mean schooling years of adults, 54th of 189 countries based on GNI per capita, and 55th of 189 countries based on expected years of schooling of children. This multidimensional gap reflects the losses in human development Russia currently has as compared with its potential. The underlying trends and policy measures to improve health, education, and living standards are discussed in Sects. 2.3 and 2.4 (health and education) and in Chapter 18 (standard of living).

Box 2.1 The Human Development Index (HDI)

The HDI is a way to characterise the level of human capital in a country. It is a composite index of a country's advancement in each of three dimensions: health (measured by life expectancy at birth), education (measured by mean years of schooling for adults aged 25+ and expected years of schooling for children of school entering age), and standard of living (as captured by GNI per capita) (UNDP, 2020). Each component of the HDI is scaled to a value between zero and one, with a higher value being better. The composite HDI value is the geometric mean of the three components and is also transformed into the zero–one scale.[4]

---

[3] See https://ourworldindata.org/human-development-index#health.

[4] For technical details see https://hdr.undp.org/sites/default/files/data/2020/hdr 2020_technical_notes.pdf.

2.2 Population Structure and Main Demographic Trends

2.2.1 Trends in Fertility and Mortality

One of the key trends underlying recent economic and social development in Russia is its shrinking population. Indeed, as is clear from Fig. 2.1, what looked like a decline in the natural population growth rate in the mid-1980s resulted in a prolonged negative trend until the mid-2000s, with a growth rate of −0.46% in 2002 and 2003. It is only in 2009 that births equated deaths and the natural population growth rate became positive. The natural population growth rate continued to increase until 2014 when the trend reversed; growth rates again became negative in 2018.

The trends in crude death rate (number of deaths per 1000 population) and crude birth rate (number of live births per 1000 population) in Fig. 2.1 clearly demonstrate the cause of Russia's negative population growth. Increasing mortality rates and decreasing fertility rates in 1985–2000 formed 'the Russian Cross'—an unusual situation for a non-war period. The decreasing tendency in fertility reversed in 2001, while for mortality, the reversal of the trend took longer, occurring only in 2006. A second decline in the natural population growth rate occurred when the trend for the crude birth rate again reversed; the mortality rate continued to decrease.

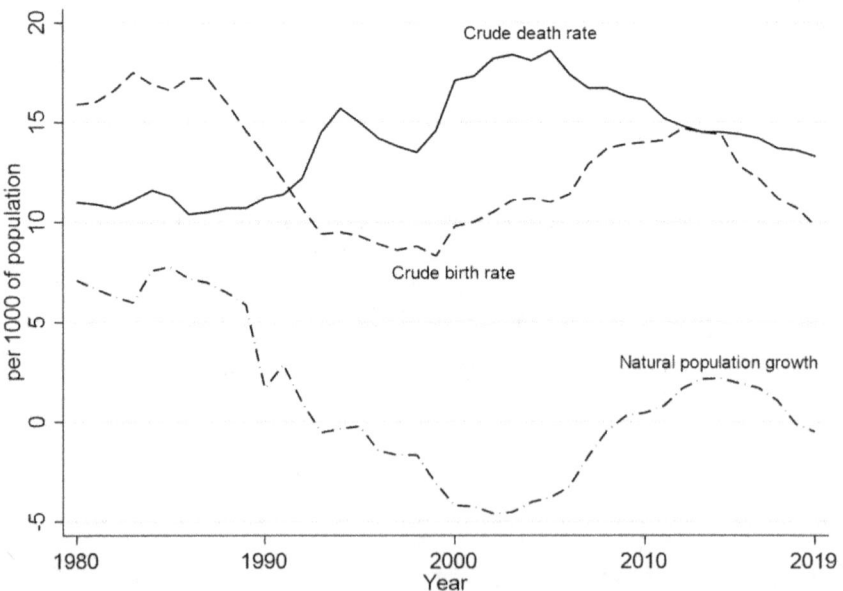

Fig. 2.1 Crude death, crude birth, and natural population growth rates in Russia, per 1000 people, 1980–2019 (*Source* World Bank, World development indicators, https://datatopics.worldbank.org/world-development-indicators/)

An active migration policy, the promotion of birth, and population saving programmes aim to either reverse or compensate for the negative natural population growth rate. Despite some success along these three dimensions, Russia's population decreased during 2018–2020 and is also expected to decrease in 2021. In particular, net migration to Russia in 2019 amounted to 285.1 thousand people, which was not enough to compensate for the natural population decrease of 316.2 thousand.

Excessive mortality in 2020 and 2021 due to COVID-19 added to the natural population decrease in Russia. Migration flows were also negatively affected by the circumstances of the pandemic.

2.2.2 Regional Variation

Russia is a very geographically, ethnically, economically, and socially diverse country (see Chapter 11). According to the 2010 Census, almost 190 ethnic groups speaking about 100 languages inhabit its territory. Russians comprise 77% of the population (111 million people). The Tatars are the next largest group, amounting to 4% (5 million people), followed by Ukrainians (1.35%, 2 million people), Bashkirs (1.1%, 1.5 million people), Chuvash (1%, 1.4 million people), Chechens (1%, 1.4 million people), and Armenians (0.86%, 1.2 million people).

Diversity in Russia as measured by the ethnic, language, and religion fractionalization indices is 0.25, 0.25, and 0.44, respectively (each index is scaled on a zero–one interval, with a higher index value meaning a higher degree of fractionalization) (Alesina et al., 2003). This is higher than in Poland (with indices of 0.12, 0.04, and 0.17), lower than in the United States for two out of the three indices (0.49, 0.25, and 0.82), and much lower than in Southern Africa (0.75, 0.86, and 0.86).

The average birth and death rates for Russia presented in Fig. 2.1 conceal very sizeable variations—in particular, in the regional population growth rates. In 2019, the mode regional birth rate was about nine births per 1000 of the population; however, there were regions with 7 or 20 births per 1000 of the population. The regions with the highest birth rates were Chechnya (20.3), Tyva (18.6), Ingushetia (16.4), and Dagestan (14.8). At the same time, the crude birth rate was below 8 per 1000 of the population in the following regions: Leningrad, Smolensk, Tula, Tambov, Ivanovo, and Penza oblasts as well as in Republic of Mordovia.

The same is true for crude mortality rates. In 2019, the mode regional death rate was about 14 per 1000 of the population; however, there were regions with higher mortality rates (i.e., above 16 in Pskov, Novgorod, and Tver oblasts). There were also a significant number of regions with lower mortality rates (9.5 in Moscow, 11 in St. Petersburg and Tatarstan, and less than 5 per 1000 in Dagestan, Ingushetia, and Chechnya).

As a result, there was considerable variation in regional natural population growth rates—from a negative rate of between -0.7 and -0.8% in Pskov, Tula,

Ivanovo, Tver, Novgorod, and Smolensk oblasts to positive growth rates of 1% in Tyva and Dagestan, 1.3% in Ingushetia, and 1.6% in Chechnya.

2.2.3 Mortality from an International Perspective: Russia's Mortality Crisis

Russia's persistent high mortality in the 1990s and 2000s, at the level of the least developed countries in the world, attracted a lot of attention. Such high rates of mortality among working-age adults are rarely observed in non-war periods; this period in its history was referred to as 'Russia's mortality crisis'. In 2005, Russia ranked 162nd out of 219 countries according to male life expectancy at birth[5] and 116th out of 219 according to female life expectancy at birth. In 2005, a newborn boy in Russia had a mean life expectancy which was 7 years shorter than a boy in Brazil; 10 years shorter than a newborn boy in China; and 15 years shorter than a newborn boy in Germany, the United Kingdom, or the United States. The gap in mean life expectancy between a newborn girl in Russia and the United Kingdom or the United States was 6 years in 2005.

This unfortunate male mortality pattern in Russia captured by the life expectancy indicator was driven by the extremely high mortality rates of working-age adults, with cardiovascular diseases and external causes being the leading causes of deaths (Shkolnikov et al., 1998). The problem originated not in the 1990s, but much earlier.

Figure 2.2 depicts life expectancy at birth for males (Panel A) and females (Panel B) for 1970–2019 for Russia, Poland, the United States, and France. As seen in Fig. 2.2, in the beginning of the 1970s, male and female life expectancy rates were similar among the analysed countries.

In the 1970s, France and the United States began to deviate from the group, showing a pronounced upward trend and improved life expectancies, while Russia and Poland stagnated, showing no improvement. The reason for the stagnation of mortality rates in Russia and Poland was the missed cardiovascular revolution—a sustainable and non-reversible decrease in mortality rates from cardiovascular diseases caused by improvements in medical technologies and lifestyles (Mesle & Vallin, 2011). Poland managed to join the positive trend in the beginning of the 1990s, while it took Russia 15 years longer to begin the same process. In 2019, Russia ranked 105th in male life expectancy and 72nd in female life expectancy, which was an improvement. The gaps in male life expectancy in 2019 decreased to 12 years in comparison with the United States, 8 years with China, and 5 years with Brazil. Thus, progress has been achieved but there still is a long way to go.

---

[5] Life expectancy at birth is the average number of years a newborn child would live if the current age-specific mortality rates stood the same through his or her life.

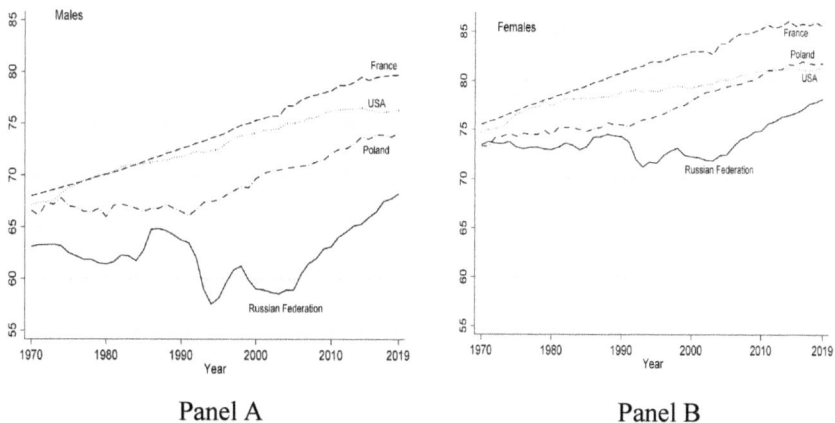

Fig. 2.2 Life expectancy at birth, men (Panel A) and women (Panel B) (*Source* World Bank, World development indicators [https://datatopics.worldbank.org/world-development-indicators/])

2.2.4 Fertility in Russia from an International Perspective

The decline in fertility rates in the second half of the twentieth century was one of the most important global trends, reflecting the modernisation of life in general. Russia, lagging behind other countries with its mortality decline, was rather early with its fertility decline. Indeed, in 1972, the total fertility rate (TFR), which is the average number of children per woman,[6] in Russia was similar to that in the United States (about 2 children per woman) and below that in Poland (2.2) and France (2.4) (Fig. 2.3, Panel A). In the 1970s, there was a gradual decline in the TFR in Russia and a rapid decline in the United States and France. By 1980, Russia and the United States again had similar TFRs of 1.8. Over the next 40 years, the TFR in the United States was relatively stable, with some mild fluctuations in the range of 1.8–2.1. France also entered a period of stabilisation of the TFR, with a level of 1.8 children per woman until the mid-2000s and then almost 2 children per woman in the 2010s. In contrast, the TFR in Russia showed an increase to 2.23 in 1987 followed by a sharp decrease to 1.16 in 1999. The trend in the TFR reversed again in the 2000s, peaking at 1.78 in 2015 and then followed by a decline to 1.6 in 2018. Interestingly, the TFR in Poland also decreased from 2.2–2.3 during the 1970–1980s to 1.2 in 2004, before increasing slightly to 1.3; however, these changes were not as rapid as in Russia.

---

[6] The TFR is the average number of children that would be born to a woman over her lifetime if the current age-specific fertility rates would stay the same through her reproductive years, and the woman would survive until the end of her reproductive life (15–49).

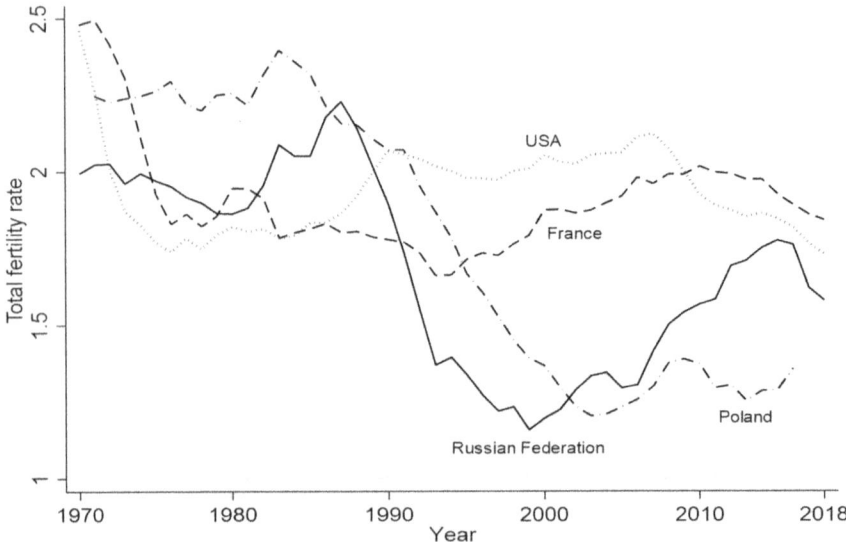

Fig. 2.3 Total Fertility Rate in Russia, Poland, France, and the United States, 1970–2018 (*Source* Human Fertility Database, http://www.humanfertility.org)

The shift to a lower TFR in Russia seems to be disturbed by sizeable interventions to stimulate birth rates. Indeed, the rise of the TFR in the early 1980s is attributed to measures promoting motherhood, such as extensive parental leaves and child benefits (Zakharov, 2008). The reversal of this trend in 2006 is related to the maternal capital programme (Box 2.2).

These interventions are likely to be responsible not only for the rise in the TFR soon after their introduction but also for its subsequent fall—at least partially. The fall in the TFR in the 1990s was associated not only with the economic and social hardships of Russia's transition period, but also with the pro-natalist policies of the 1980s (Denisova & Shapiro, 2013). These interventions affected the birth calendar of families, incentivising them to have children earlier than planned. As a result, the rise in the TFR in the 1980s was mirrored by a fall in the TFR in the 1990s (Avdeev & Monnier, 1994).

The nature of the TFR as a measure of fertility assumes stability in age-specific fertility rates, which in turn assumes stability in preferences in reproductive age across cohorts. At the same time, many nations seem to have transitioned from early childbearing to later motherhood. This transition is captured by the mean age of the mother at the birth of the first, second, third, and higher parity child (Panel A in Fig. 2.4).

As shown in Fig. 2.4, the mean age of mothers at the birth of a child in Russia has been rising steadily for all parities (birth orders) beginning from the mid-1990s. The largest increase was observed for the mean age of childbearing of the first child: it increased from age 22 in 1990 to almost age 27 in 2018.

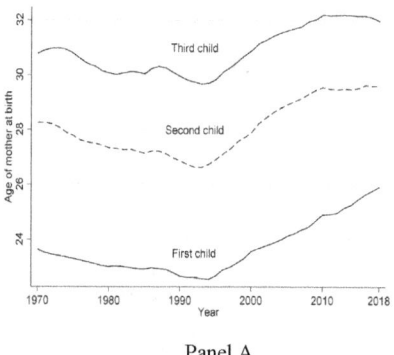 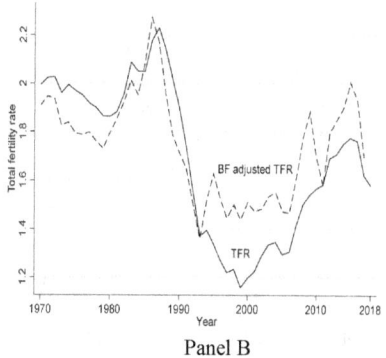

Panel A   Panel B

Fig. 2.4 Mean age of mother at birth by parity (Panel A), 1970–2018 and Unadjusted and Bongaarts-Feeney (BF) Adjusted Period TFR, 1970–2018 (Panel B) (*Source* Human Fertility Database, http://www.humanfertility.org)

The mean age of childbearing for the second and the third+ child increased by 3 and 2 years, respectively, over the period and were 30 and 32 in 2018.

This is a clear manifestation of the ongoing changes in the preferences of families over the timing of childbearing. To correct the TFR measure for changes in the mean age of the mother at the birth of a child, an adjusted measure of the TFR was suggested by Bongaarts and Feeney (1998). Adjusted and unadjusted TFRs for Russia are shown in Panel B of Fig. 2.4. Adjusting the shift in preferences for later motherhood makes the TFR of 1999 not that dramatic—1.44 children per woman instead of 1.16.

Box 2.2 Maternity (Family) Capital

Maternity capital was introduced in 2007 as a measure to support families with a second or higher order parity child born or adopted since 2007. The idea was to stimulate second and further births, while the first birth was assumed to be a cultural norm. The amount of support was RUB 250 thousand in 2007 (equivalent to USD 10 thousand at 2007 exchange rates or 18 monthly average wages in Russia) and is indexed annually for inflation. From 2012, regional governments added additional support for newborn children. The capital could be used when the child reached 3 years old. The initial instructions of use were limited to purchasing housing, paying for education, or investing in a future pension. They were later relaxed to allow more ways to improve the material welfare of families with children.

In 2020, the programme was reformed to motivate families for the birth of the first child. The change seems intuitive given the rapid recent increase in the mean age of mothers at the birth of the first child. Since 1 January 2020, families having a first child are also entitled to maternity capital. The payments to families who give birth to second and higher order parity children remain a part of the programme.

The maternity capital programme has had short-term and long-term effects on fertility, including an increase in completed fertility for a large cohort of Russian women (Sorvachev & Yakovlev, 2020).

2.2.5 Age and Gender Structure of the Population

A population pyramid best describes the age and gender structure of the Russian population. The pyramid for 2019 is depicted in Fig. 2.5. Each horizontal bar is scaled to reflect the age and gender structure of the population (in thousands of people). The mortality and fertility trends discussed previously provide an explanation of the specifics of the age and gender structure of the Russian population. In particular, low fertility rates result in a rather narrow base of the pyramid: the share of children, age group 0–14, is only 17.7%. The low life expectancy due to the high mortality rates of Russian adults explains the sharp decline in the number of males 65+ and females 70+, which is in contrast to population pyramids in developed countries and is more like that of a developing country. The share of those aged 65+ in Russia is only 15% and the share of those of a working age (15–64) is 67.3%.

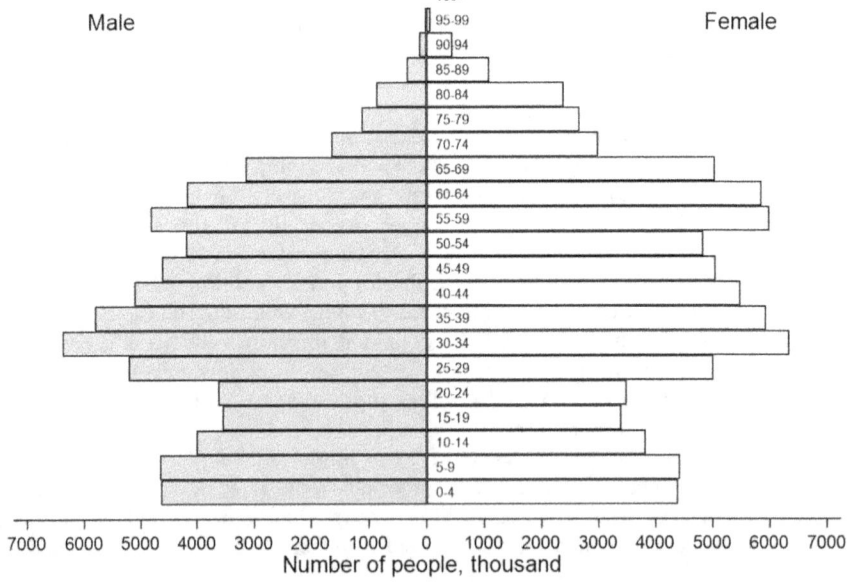

Fig. 2.5 Number of people by age and sex in Russia in 2019 (*Source* Federal State Statistic Service [Rosstat], https://rosstat.gov.ru/)

There are clear signs of demographic waves in Russia, where some age groups are less populated than the preceding and following age cohorts. This is clear for the 45–54 age cohorts as well as for the 10–14 and especially the 15–24 age cohorts. The former is an echo of World War II—fewer children were born during the period of the war and thus there were fewer potential parents for the 45–54 age cohort. The latter is a combination of the less populated age group 45–54 and the sharp decline in fertility in the 1990s after its increase in the mid-1980s. The maternity capital programme (Box 2.2) appears to have been successful at least in stimulating births during the period of 2010–2019 as the 0–9 age cohort is larger. Notice that the increased fertility rates were also able to compensate for the relatively smaller group of potential parents in the 20–29 age cohorts.

In addition, gender parity in younger age cohorts disappears after age 45 and becomes more pronounced in senior age cohorts, reflecting the much higher mortality rates of Russian males. As a result, almost two-thirds of Russians in the age group 70–74 are females, and three-fourths in age group 80+.

2.2.6 Aging (Dependency Ratios)

The demographic transition from high fertility and mortality rates to moderate or even low rates has caused population aging in many countries. The growth in the share of the elderly population in Russia began in the late 1960s. By 2019, the share of those aged 65+ reached 15%, with 11% among men and 19% among women (Fig. 2.5). Aging in Russia will continue in the near future, as it has done in many countries. At the same time, the problem of population aging in Russia is not as acute as in some developed countries. For instance, the share of the population aged 65+ is 28% in Japan, 23% in Italy, and 21% in Germany. Moreover, aging is occurring rather gradually in Russia, allowing Russia time to adapt to the challenge. The increase of the share of those aged 65+ from 7 to 14% stretched over 50 years in Russia, while in China this growth took place over 25 years, in Brazil over 20 years, and in Vietnam over 15 years (Mirkin & Weinberger, 2000). The slow aging in Russia is explained by its stagnation in life expectancy: fewer children are born in Russia, but Russians still live relatively short lives.

Nevertheless, the demographic burden placed on the working-age population by the elderly is increasing. One of the measures of the demographic burden adopted in international comparisons is the ratio of the population aged 65+ to the population of those of a working age: 15–64. Panel A of Fig. 2.6 depicts the ratio for Russia, France, Poland, and the United States for 1970–2050 (forecast for 2021–2050). All four countries experience an increase in the old-age dependency ratio over the period, along with an acceleration of this increase starting from the 2010s. The old-age dependency ratio in Russia is very similar to that of the United States after the 2000s. France

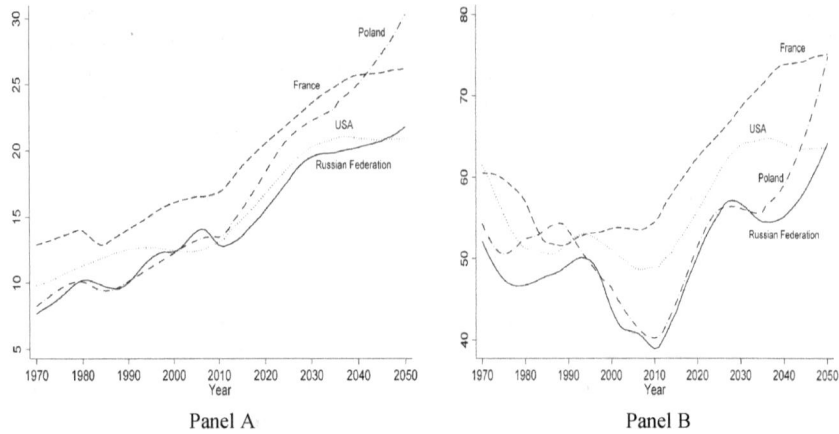

Fig. 2.6 Age dependency ratio, %, 1970–2050, Old-age (Panel A) and Total (Panel B) (*Source* OECD statistics http://www.oecd.org/std)

has and will have a much higher old-age dependency ratio, and Poland is converging rapidly to France's level.

This comparison confirms that the old-age dependency ratio is an important issue for Russia to consider in its policymaking, though both the level and the expected rate of increase in the near future are not remarkable when compared internationally. Moreover, the total dependency ratio, that is, the ratio of the sum of the 0–14 and 65+ population to working-age population, is and will remain much smaller in Russia than in France or the United States, though will be rising in the near future (Panel B of Fig. 2.6).

Overall, the growing demographic pressure on the pension and health systems needs to be addressed through economic policy; the pension age reform of 2018 is an example of one of Russia's policy responses (Box 2.3). The contraction of the labour supply due to the decline in the size of the working-age population is another demographic challenge for Russia. A mixture of an active migration policy and increasing labour productivity through technological modernisation seems to be a remedy.

Box 2.3 Pension Age Reform
The retirement age for eligibility for old-age pensions was first established in the Soviet Union in 1928; it was set at age 55 for women and age 60 for men. Eligibility rules initially defined for textile workers only were expanded in 1932 to other industries except agriculture. In 1964, agricultural workers became eligible for old-age pensions albeit with a 5-year higher retirement age. In 1968, a uniform retirement age was adopted for all workers: 55 for women and 60 for men. Since then, the eligibility age for old-age pensions has remained

unchanged. In October 2018, a new retirement age was set, which will gradually reach 60 for women and 65 for men by 2028. These changes will occur incrementally over 10 years.

2.3 Health

It is not an easy task to measure the health of a population. Mortality rates as summarised by life expectancy at birth are informative about the prevalence of severe life-threatening health conditions. The relatively short lives of Russians, especially of males, manifest as the bad health of the population (Sect. 2.2). In this section, we examine the primary causes of death in Russia to get a better sense of the main health problems. In addition, we study morbidity rates for some socially significant diseases and provide evidence on the health hazardous habits of the Russian population.

2.3.1 Causes of Death

Cardiovascular diseases are the leading cause of mortality in Russia. In 2019, it accounted for 49% of deaths among men and 56% of deaths among women. The age-standardised death rate from cardiovascular diseases was 549 per 100,000 for men in 2019 (934 in 2000) and 351 per 100,000 for women (579 in 2000) (Table 2.1). For comparison, the OECD average in 2019 was 164 per 100,000 for men and 112 per 100,000 for women. The fourfold higher death rate for males and threefold higher death rate for females from cardiovascular diseases are indications of the still non-exhausted potential of the cardiovascular revolution for Russia. The death rates from this cause decreased almost twofold in the first two decades of the twenty-first century, but there is still a long way to go.

Neoplasms (tumours) as a cause of death explained 18% of the deaths of males and 17% of the deaths of females in 2019. Russia's death toll from this cause is at the OECD average level if compared via age-standardised death rates: 180 per 100,000 for males and 100 per 100,000 for females, as compared to 168 and 100 per 100,000 males and females in the OECD, respectively.

Self-harm and interpersonal violence, unintentional injuries, and substance use disorders together explain 13.2% deaths of males and 8.5% deaths of females in Russia in 2019 (as compared to 20.5 and 14%, respectively, in 2000). Russia's age-standardised death rates for males from each of the three are almost threefold higher than the OECD average: 61 versus 23 per 100,000 for self-harm; 50 versus 18 per 100,000 for unintentional injuries; and 31 versus 12 per 100,000 for substance use disorders. Note the enormous progress Russia has accomplished since 2000 in reducing the death rates from

Table 2.1 Age-standardised death rates by leading causes of death, Russia and OECD average, 2000 and 2019, males and females

Cause	Russia		OECD countries	
	2000	2019	2000	2019
Males				
Cardiovascular diseases	934.4	549.2	257.5	164.4
Neoplasms	238.6	179.8	207.2	168.3
Self-harm and interpersonal violence	138.1	61.5	25.6	23.5
Digestive diseases	55.0	57.5	36.9	29.8
Unintentional injuries	110.0	50.0	22.5	17.9
Respiratory infections and tuberculosis	67.0	33.5	34.1	22.8
Chronic respiratory diseases	65.6	31.7	42.6	33.6
Substance use disorders	56.6	31.0	7.8	12.3
Neurological disorders	29.4	28.5	31.2	32.1
Transport injuries	42.6	23.3	21.9	13.2
HIV/AIDS and sexually transmitted infections	9.3	16.5	3.6	1.7
Diabetes and kidney diseases	13.4	13.1	32.1	32.9
Females				
Cardiovascular diseases	579.6	351.2	174.5	111.6
Neoplasms	114.5	99.3	122.8	106.1
Digestive diseases	25.2	30.4	21.2	17.9
Neurological disorders	26.7	26.6	30.3	30.9
Unintentional injuries	26.8	13.2	11.0	9.1
Diabetes and kidney diseases	11.5	13.1	25.0	24.0
Self-harm and interpersonal violence	29.7	13.1	7.4	6.6
Respiratory infections and tuberculosis	18.1	11.3	20.4	13.2
Chronic respiratory diseases	15.9	9.1	20.8	19.3
Other non-communicable diseases	14.2	8.9	13.4	11.5
Transport injuries	12.9	7.2	7.6	4.4
Substance use disorders	13.7	6.9	2.0	4.4
HIV/AIDS and sexually transmitted infections	2.3	6.6	1.2	0.7

Source Global Health Data Exchange http://ghdx.healthdata.org/gbd-results-tool

these causes. It is this reduction, together with progress made improving death rates from cardiovascular diseases, which explain the bulk of the reduction in mortality rates and the increase in life expectancy during this period.

2.3.2 Socially Significant Diseases: Tuberculosis and Diabetes

In 2004, the Russian government defined a list of socially significant diseases, aiming at taking control over their incidence and prevalence. The list comprises eight groups: sexually transmitted infections, tuberculosis, viral hepatitis B and C, malignant neoplasms, HIV, diabetes, diseases characterised by elevated blood pressure, and behavioural and mental disorders.

One needs to be careful interpreting the data on incidence of a disease as it reflects not only the arrival of new cases but also the ability to diagnose them. However, this is less an issue with tuberculosis, which is a severe and persistent problem in Russia. The incidence rate amounted to 144 per 100,000 of the population in 2004–2005, a very high level for an upper-middle-income country. Measures to fight tuberculosis resulted in a twofold decline in the incidence rate, which was 72 per 100,000 in 2019. However, this was still a very high rate by international comparison: 6 times higher than in Poland, 11 times higher than in France, and 32 times higher than in the United States.

The cross-country comparison is less obvious for diabetes as its latent forms are more widespread. The incidence rate for diabetes in Russia steadily increased between 1990 and 2019 from 109 to 152 per 100,000 of the population. This was very close to the incidence rate in France throughout the period and less than in Poland (290) or the United States (380) during the same years.[7]

2.3.3 Health Detrimental Behaviour: Alcohol Consumption and Smoking

The Russian mortality crisis is related to the excessive consumption of strong alcohol and smoking (Denisova, 2010; Shkolnikov et al., 1998). The total estimated consumption of alcohol in Russia in 2000 reached almost 19 liters of pure alcohol per capita (adults 15+), which was 30% higher than in the top drinking countries of Ireland (14.2) and France (13.9). Moreover, the consumption of strong alcoholic beverages (vodka mainly) in Russia far exceeded the consumption of beer and wine both in terms of the aggregate volume of pure alcohol and the prevalence among the population. In addition, the 'northern' type of consumption, with large doses within a short time, was characteristic for Russia (Nemtsov, 2002).

The situation improved in the 2010s. Total pure alcohol consumption decreased almost twofold and amounted to 10.8 liters per capita in 2019. Russia was no longer the international leader in this respect. These changes were driven mainly by a shift from the consumption of vodka to the consumption of beer in younger cohorts. There was also a trend for better educated and wealthier people to switch to the consumption of wine rather than strong spirits (Yakovlev, 2018). This improvement contributed to an increase of the life expectancy in Russia via a decrease of cardiovascular causes of death (see above).

Smoking causes significant health losses which are translated into economic losses. Russia traditionally had a high smoking prevalence, and this further increased in the 1990s–2000s. The prevalence of tobacco smoking among males rose from less than 50% in the mid-1980s to 65% in the 2000s (World Health Organization, 2009). The 2000s demonstrated a rise in female smoking, which increased from less than 10% in the 1980s (Cooper, 1982)

---

[7] http://ghdx.healthdata.org/gbd-results-tool.

to 22% in 2010 (WHO GHO, 2014). Russia was among the most smoking countries in the world, with 35% of adults (15+) being daily smokers in 2000.

The situation changed significantly in the 2010s. The number of daily adult smokers decreased to 25.8% by 2019. The tendency of decreased smoking is observed worldwide. Between 2000 and 2019, the number of daily smokers dropped from 31 to 16% in South Korea, from 33 to 22% in Spain, and from 44 to 28% in Turkey. This positive change is associated with the World Health Organization (WHO) Framework Convention on Tobacco Control (FCTC) which came into force in 2005 and was ratified by 168 countries (Husain et al., 2021).

The WHO FCTC outlined effective practices to reduce the demand for tobacco. Six types of interventions were stressed in the MPOWER Policy Package to Reverse the Tobacco Epidemic of the WHO: (i) monitoring tobacco use; (ii) protecting people from tobacco smoke; (iii) offering help to quit tobacco use; (iv) warning about the dangers of tobacco; (v) enforcing bans on tobacco advertising, promotion, and sponsorship; and (vi) raising taxes on tobacco products. Russia adopted the package in 2013. The policies contributed to the decrease in smoking prevalence in Russia. However, there is a long way yet to go to reach the level of the least smoking countries.

Overall, poor health resulting in low life expectancy remains the major challenge for Russia, which is still lagging behind the leaders of the cardiovascular revolution. The new tasks of fighting the increasing risks of neoplasms and neurodegenerative diseases complicate the agenda for health policy reforms. On top of this is the challenge to ensure vertical and horizontal equity in geographically, ethnically, and socially diverse Russia (see Chapter 11).

2.4 EDUCATION

2.4.1 *Enrolment Rates and Education Structure*

Russia ranks high based on indicators of educational attainments: 32nd of 189 countries based on mean schooling years of adults and 55th of 189 countries based on expected years of schooling of children (both in 2019). These high rankings reflect the affordability of education in the country, both at secondary school and tertiary levels. The gross secondary school enrolment ratio, i.e., the ratio of total secondary school enrolment, regardless of age, to the population of the age group that officially corresponds to the level of education, was as high as 103.6% in 2019, which was slightly below the OECD average of 105.8%.[8,9]

According to another measure of access to education, the out-of-school rate, Russia is similar to other leading countries and performing better than

---

[8] The gross enrolment ratio can exceed 100% due to the inclusion of over-aged and under-aged students because of early or late school entrance and grade repetition.

[9] https://data.worldbank.org/indicator/SE.SEC.ENRR.

the OECD average: only 0.2% of children in the official age range are not in primary or lower secondary school and 3% are not in upper secondary school (OECD, 2020). The high secondary school enrolment ratio and very low out-of-school rates lay the grounds for lifelong learning and human development in Russia.

The success of Russia—geographically a very large and heterogeneous country—in access to education is confirmed by the highest educational attainment of those aged 25–64. In 2018, Russia recorded the next to the leader (Japan) result of only 4.8% of people in the 25–64 age group with a below-upper-secondary education level. This is two times lower than in the United States (9%), four times lower than the OECD average of 21.4%, ten times lower than in Brazil (47%), and fifteen times lower than in China (as of 2010, 75%).

In 2019, Russia was among the top three countries with the highest share of adults (aged 25–64) with tertiary education (57%), just behind Canada and Ireland (both 59%). This was 50% higher than the OECD average (38%), three times higher than the level of Brazil (18.4%), and almost six times higher than the level of China (9.7% as of 2010).

Tertiary education is a wide group encompassing short-cycle, bachelor, master, and doctoral programmes. Based on the information on adults in the 25–34 age group, one-third of tertiary education (22% of adults) in Russia represents short-cycle programmes and the remaining two-thirds (40% of adults)—other programmes: bachelor (7% of adults), master (32% of adults), and doctoral programmes (1% of adults) (OECD, 2020).

Russia's structure of tertiary education is comparable to Canada's except for the fact that bachelor programmes are more popular in Canada while master programmes are more in demand in Russia. The structure of tertiary education in Russia is biased towards short-term programmes in comparison with the European Union (EU)'s average structure, which has only 13% of tertiary education from short-term programmes and the remaining 87% from bachelor, master, and doctoral programmes. Another difference with the EU's average structure is the almost 50:50 division between bachelor and master programmes in the EU, while the proportion of bachelor and master's degrees is 20:80 in Russia.

The expansion of university education in Russia responded to increased demand and the liberalisation of regulation in this sector in the 1990s–2000s. It came with the increased number and diversity of higher education institutions, improved institutional autonomy, and academic self-governance. In 2003, Russia joined the Bologna process and the two-tier system of bachelor and master's degrees was gradually introduced together with the redesign of educational programmes and qualifications. As a result, the share of adults aged 15 + with a university degree increased from 11% in 1989 to 16% in 2002, 23% in 2010, and 26% (30.2% in 25–64 group) in 2015 (Gokhberg et al., 2020).

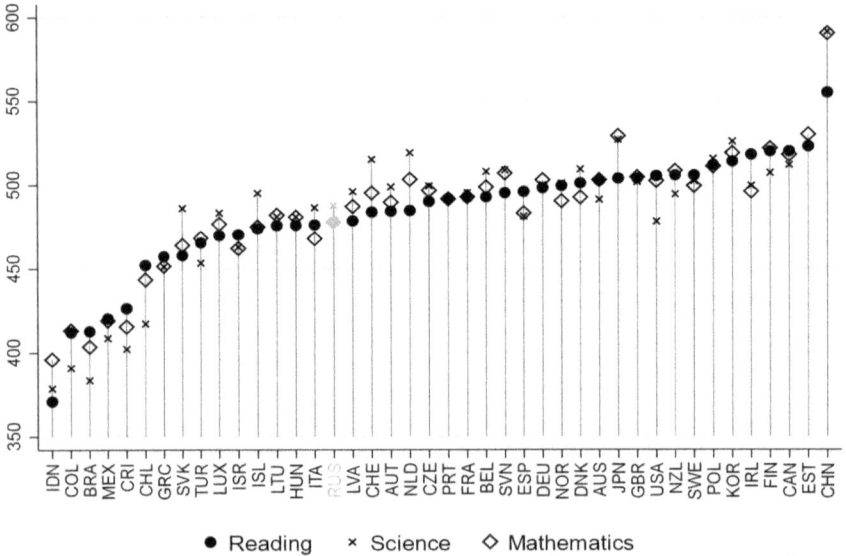

Fig. 2.7 Performance in reading, mathematics, and science (mean scores), OECD members and candidate countries and Russia, 2018 (*Note* Results for Spain based on 2015 data. *Source* OECD. https://pisadataexplorer.oecd.org/ide/idepisa/dataset.aspx)

2.4.2 Quality of Education

Quality of education is an important concern and is especially challenging in a rapidly changing socio-economic environment. The Programme for International Student Assessment (PISA) was launched by the OECD in 1997 to evaluate 15-year-old school pupils' performance in mathematics, science, and reading. The results for the 2018 PISA round are presented in Fig. 2.7 (mean scores for each country, the maximum score is 600). Russia performs at the level of the OECD average in math (488 in Russia versus 489 for the OECD average) and slightly lower in reading (479 versus 487) and science (478 versus 489). At the same time, there is considerable room for improvement. The difference in the mean scores in math with the top performers is substantial: China[10] is the outperformer with a score of 591, followed by Japan (527), South Korea (526), and Estonia (523). The gap is equally large in reading (China 555, Estonia 523, and Finland and Canada 520) and in science (China 590, Estonia 530, Japan 529, and Finland 522).

---

[10] The results for China should be treated with caution, as they are not nationally representative.

The variation in the Unified State Examination (USE)—the mandatory test for all high school graduates in Russia since 2009—is a proxy for the variation in the quality of education within Russia.[11] The average USE score of school graduates in 2015 in the Russian language varied from 44 to 72 (out of 100) depending on the region. Similarly, the USE score in mathematics (as a profiling test) varied from 38 to 54 (Lazareva & Zakharov, 2020).

The large variation in USE results across regions, and inside regions across rural and urban areas and across good and not so good schools, suggests issues with the equality of opportunities to access higher education. The introduction of the USE in 2009 was a step towards diminishing the gap in the opportunities between university cities and peripheral areas. Indeed, as shown by Francesconi et al. (2019), the reform resulted in the increased geographical mobility of high school graduates from small cities and towns to start college. At the same time, there is no sign of changes in the educational mobility of high school graduates from rural areas.

Overall, equality of opportunities and quality of education are the major concerns. In addition, a lack of vision regarding vocational education within the tertiary system, little integration of the tertiary system nationally and internationally, limited collaboration between institutions, and the limited role of the sector in research and development and innovation are the most important challenges to tertiary education in Russia (OECD, 1999).

2.5 Conclusions

Russia is one of the largest countries in the world in terms of population size. Moreover, Russia's population is well educated, making the country rich in terms of human resources. The major challenges for the future development of the human potential in Russia are threefold.

First, the mortality rates of the working-age population, especially males, are still extremely high and are unobserved nowadays in a developed country. Attempts to 'catch-up' with the cardiovascular revolution bring initial results. More efforts, however, are needed in fighting premature and preventable deaths.

Second, demographic modernisation in terms of low fertility rates and later motherhood is the reality. Active pro-natalist policies soften the decline in birth rates at least in the short run. At the same time, these policies seem to be responsible for creating demographic waves. A balance is still to be found to stabilise fertility rates at a level sufficient for non-negative natural population growth.

Third, quality of education is an increasing concern, especially given the increased pace of technological change. The modernisation of secondary and tertiary education is at the top of the economic policy agenda. The provision

---

[11] More precisely, the variation in the USE is a result of the interaction of the quality of education and the efforts and talents of pupils.

of equal opportunities in access to high-quality education is the central issue in social policy. Success or failure here would shape the social development of the country for many years.

Population aging is an issue for Russia, though the rate and the pace is not high in international comparison. The declining working-age population in Russia is both a challenge and an opportunity. Decreased fertility rates, setting limits to extensive economic development, however, provide strong incentives for the technological modernisation of the country.

Questions for Students

1. The HDI is a way to measure human development in a country (Box 2.1). What is Russia's position internationally as measured by the index? Are there possibilities to improve the index? What are the key challenges for human development in Russia?
2. Demographic development in Russia in the mid-1980s through the end of the 1990s is described as 'the Russian Cross'. Explain the origin of this name, paying special attention to the underlying demographic processes.
3. Russia has a sizable gender gap in life expectancy. Suggest explanations based on the age-standardised death rates in Table 2.1.
4. Provide a rationale for pension age reform in Russia (hint: look at the age pyramid).
5. Describing education in Russia, people talk about educational attainment, accessibility, and quality of education. Describe the situation with education in Russia according to these three criteria.

References

Alesina, A., Devleeschauwer, A., Easterly, W., Kurlat, S., & Wacziarg, R. (2003). Fractionalization. *Journal of Economic Growth, 8*(2), 155–194.

Avdeev, A., & Monnier, A. (1994). A survey of modern Russian fertility. *Population, 49*(4–5), 859–901.

Bongaarts, J., & Feeney, G. (1998). On the quantum and tempo of fertility. *Population and Development Review, 24*(2), 271–329.

Cooper, R. (1982). Smoking in the Soviet Union. *British Medical Journal (clinical Research Edition), 285*(6341), 549–551.

Denisova, I. (2010). Adult mortality in Russia: A microanalysis. *Economics of Transition, 18*(2), 333–363.

Denisova, I., & Shapiro, J. (2013). Recent demographic developments in the Russian Federation. In M. Alexeev & S. Weber (Eds.), *The Oxford handbook of the Russian economy* (pp. 800–826). Oxford University Press.

Francesconi, M., Slonimczyk, F., & Yurko, A. (2019). Democratizing access to higher education in Russia: The consequences of the unified state exam reform. *European Economic Review, 117*(4), 56–82.

Gokhberg, L. M., Ozerova, O. K., Sautina, E. V., & Shugal, N. B. (2020). *Obrazovanie v Tzifrakh (Education in Figures)*. Higher School of Economics

Husain, M. J., Datta, B. K., Nargis, N., et al. (2021). Revisiting the association between worldwide implementation of the MPOWER package and smoking prevalence, 2008–2017. *Tobacco Control, 30*, 630–637.

Lazareva, O., & Zakharov, A. (2020). Teacher wages and educational outcomes: Evidence from the Russian school system. *Education Economics, 28*(4), 418–436.

Mesle, F., & Vallin, J. (2011). Historical trends in mortality. In R. G. Rogers & E. M. Crimmins (Eds.), *International handbook of adult mortality* (pp. 9–47). Springer.

Mirkin, B., & Weinberger, M. (2000). *The demography of population aging. Paper presented at the technical meeting on population ageing and living arrangement of older persons: critical issues and policy responses population division*. United Nations.

Nemtsov, A. (2002). Alcohol-related harm losses in Russia in the 1980s and 1990s. *Addiction, 97*, 1413–1425.

OECD. (1999). *Reviews of national policies for education: Tertiary education and research in the Russian Federation*. OECD Publishing.

OECD. (2020). *Education at a Glance 2020: OECD indicators*. OECD Publishing.

Shkolnikov, V. M., Cornia, G. A., Leon, D. A., & Mesle, F. (1998). Causes of the Russian mortality crisis: Evidence and interpretations. *World Development, 26*(11), 1995–2011.

Sorvachev, I., & Yakovlev, E. (2020). *Short- and long-run effects of a sizable child subsidy: evidence from Russia* (IZA Discussion Papers 13019). Institute of Labour Economics.

UNDP (United Nations Development Programme). (2020). *Human Development report*. UNDP.

United Nations, Department of Economic and Social Affairs, Population Division. (2019). *World population prospects 2019*. UN.

WHO (World Health Organization). (2012). *Global report: mortality attributable to tobacco*. WHO.

WHO GHO (World Health Organization Global Health Observatory). (2014). *WHO GHO observatory database*. http://apps.who.int/gho/data/node.main.Tobacco?lang=en

World Health Organization, Regional Office for Europe. (2009). *Global adult tobacco survey*. Country Report.

Yakovlev, E. (2018). Demand for alcohol consumption in Russia and its implication for mortality. *American Economic Journal: Applied Economics, 10*(1), 106–149.

Zakharov, S. V. (2008). Russian Federation: From the first to the second demographic transition. *Demographic Research, 24*(19), 907–972.

PART II

Historical Roots

CHAPTER 3

Capitalist Industrialisation and Modernisation: From Alexander's Reforms Until World War I (the 1860s–1917)

Carol Scott Leonard

Highlights

- Reforms under Alexander II (1855–1881) started catching-up industrialisation of a relatively backward servile economy chiefly by railroad construction in a revolutionary transformation, which helped make Russia the world's largest exporter of grain by 1913.
- The 'Great Reforms' of Alexander II began with a fundamental institutional transformation, the emancipation of the serfs in 1861, but in the sphere of justice, there was also a thorough and radical break with the past.
- The powerful finance minister of the 1890s, Sergei Witte (1892–1903), later serving as Prime Minister (1905–1906), put Russia on the gold standard in 1896 and brought about favourable conditions for industry. Currency reform helped the government attract significant foreign investment and borrow foreign technology to accelerate railroad building.

C. Scott Leonard (✉)
St. Antony's College, University of Oxford, Oxford, United Kingdom
e-mail: carol.scott.leonard@gmail.com

The Russian Presidential Academy of National Economy and Public Administration (RANEPA), Moscow, Russia

Higher School of Economics, Moscow, Russia

© The Author(s), under exclusive license to Springer Nature Switzerland AG 2023
M. Dabrowski (ed.), *The Contemporary Russian Economy*,
https://doi.org/10.1007/978-3-031-17382-0_3

- The February Revolution of 1917 began spontaneously over food lines in the capital, where protestors called for an end to autocracy.

3.1 Introduction

The emancipation reform of Emperor Alexander II of 1861 freed more than 23 million serfs, opening the doors to capitalist industrialisation and the modernisation of the previously servile agrarian economy. This fundamental systemic change was supplemented by several other reforms carried out between the 1860s and 1880s—financial reform, judicial reform, education reform, administrative reform, modernisation of the army and navy, and laws designed to improve the conditions of factory labour. These reforms allowed catching-up industrialisation led by railroad construction, a revolutionary transformation, which helped make Russia the world's largest exporter of grain by 1913. Despite a high rate of growth after 1885 and increased prosperity, rural Russia only shrank from 90.5% to 84.7% of the total population between 1867 and 1914. On fertile soils, archaic cultivation methods, including three-field rotations and wooden ploughs, held back productivity growth and rural emigration, and in regions of less fertile agriculture, subsistence agriculture continued to dominate. Persistent rural poverty and the rise of strikes by factory labour, encouraged by the radical early-twentieth century Marxist intelligentsia's labour activism, led to revolutionary action in 1905 that resulted in the creation of a limited constitutional regime. After 1907, the new parliament enacted major reforms introducing universal education, freedom of the press, and peasant landholding rights, and this period witnessed rapid economic growth and far-going social changes. Russia's entry into World War I (WWI), however, the most devastating war in Russian history, led to the collapse of the Russian monarchy by revolution in February 1917. This chapter will provide an overview of the reforms undertaken in this period as well as the socio-economic performance of Russia.

3.2 Reforms Between 1861 and 1905

3.2.1 Overview

Governing one of the poorest countries on the periphery of Europe in the 1850s, the Russian tsar Nicholas I (1824–1856) thought of economic policy as preserving the country's resources rather than expanding them. The aim was to preserve Russia's political and social order, where peasants were attached to the land where they lived and worked, while the land and its output were owned by the nobility and the state. Serfdom was the source of weak state capacity; it held back industry and agriculture and made the country uncompetitive among rapidly modernising European states in the early nineteenth century.

A disastrous defeat in the lengthy Crimean War (1853–1856), which ended in the humiliating Peace of Paris, exposed Russia's relative backwardness along with the failures of the rigid social and political system and the elite interests that upheld it. Under social pressure and financial stress with sharply elevated levels of debt, the next tsar, Alexander II (1856–1881), began major reforms. He ended private ownership of lands with villages, freeing peasants of the landlords' power over their personal lives. He overhauled the weak military and financial institutions, transformed the justice system, introduced local self-government, and in 1874, introduced universal conscription. He also lifted censorship and eased restrictions on travel. The laws, he declared, were to be *'equally just for all and equally protective of all'*. However, Alexander II's reforms were not coordinated over time.

His more conservative successors, Alexander III (1881–1894) and Nicholas II (1894–1917), reversed some reforms but maintained stability in state finance. With the help of foreign investment, from the late 1880s, they accelerated railroad construction, the basis of the extensive industrialisation through 1913. Alexander III's powerful finance minister of the 1890s, Sergei Witte (1892–1903), retained by Nicholas II and later serving as Prime Minister (1905–1906), put Russia on the gold standard in 1896. After years of tight fiscal policy to accomplish this, he had nevertheless brought about favourable conditions for industry, with legislation in place to improve working conditions. Currency reform helped the government attract significant foreign investment and borrow foreign technology to accelerate railroad building. Foreign investment remained strong despite the partial nationalisation of the railroads and a protective tariff to encourage domestic production.

In 1905, following months of civil unrest and outbreaks of violence after Russia's defeat in the Russo-Japanese war (1903–1905), Russia's 'First Revolution', Nicholas II ceded significant political reforms. As Prime Minister after 1905, Witte designed Russia's first constitution. By the outbreak of WWI, Russia was a constitutional monarchy with new liberal institutions that included a multi-party system and a parliament (Duma).

3.2.2 Emancipation of the Serfs

The emancipation reform freed more than 23 million serfs, opening the doors to capitalist industrialisation and modernisation of the largely agrarian economy. It improved possibilities for the export of grain by stimulating agricultural productivity. It encouraged former serfs to labour off the land, gradually contributing to industrial development. Railroad construction accelerated, after a sluggish start in the 1850s, and as trade grew from the south, bringing iron and coal as well as grain to the capital cities and ports, Russia's markets grew along dense new rail networks. By 1900, Russia's GDP significantly increased from 1850 (by about 17%).

By the 1861 reform, peasants could use the land, but nobles retained ownership until agreement to transfer was reached with the commune at a price determined by negotiation or through a government arbitrator. Peasant land holdings grew with some delay, as a consequence, and in many cases, peasants paid inflated prices for land acquisitions. According to the 1877 census, the noble class owned nearly 80% of privately held arable land, with the peasants' share about 5%. By 1900, nobles owned less than 54% and the peasants' share rose to roughly 28%, with the remaining land belonging to urban residents and traders (Goodwin & Grennes, 1998, p. 407).

The results of this reform were powerful but slow. The delayed response was due to its transfer of ownership rights over land (and the authority to negotiate their transfer) to the peasant commune rather than to households. Households received only their garden plots in perpetuity, as a traditional right. Allotment land belonged, also by tradition, to communes, which could redistribute parcels, whose size could be adjusted to the work capacity of households. The ongoing constraints on landed assets and peasant mobility were removed only after 1905 during the era of the Russian Duma (see below), when Prime Minister Petr Stolypin imposed a reform to end the authority of the commune.

During the revolutionary year, 1917, the spontaneous seizure of nobles' lands by the peasants showed continued frustrations lasting from the time of the Great Reforms due essentially to weak individual property rights in land. In brief, despite its failures, the serf emancipation was of profound economic significance: without it, serfdom would have imposed a binding constraint on the rate of economic growth. Its implementation, creating a thriving land market, was boosted after the founding of a Peasants' Land Bank in 1883. To be sure, some weaknesses in this reform contributed to continued rural unrest through the early twentieth century. From 1905 through 1907 and after the outbreak of WWI, with encouragement by socialist revolutionary activists, land ownership became an explosive issue.

3.2.3 Education Reform

New policies in education were given shape by regulatory codes in 1863, which restored autonomy to universities by allowing self-governing councils. A reform in 1864 introduced two kinds of specialised gymnasia, one preparing pupils for universities and others for training at higher technical institutions. The Elementary Schools Code of 1864 allowed *zemstvo* (see Sect. 3.2.5) and town councils to provide and maintain schools supervised at the district level. The reign of Alexander II witnessed an extraordinary expansion of women's medical education. The post-Crimean War regime saw the establishment of the first Russian medical courses that trained female physicians. From 1850s, when censorship was lifted from the popular press, this question, women's medical education, had become a significant domestic issue. By the end of the century, Russia's total number of women doctors was far greater than in any contemporary European state.

3.2.4 Judicial Reform

New judicial statutes declared equality of all before the law (although peasants were to be judged in separate courts) and created public trial by jury, incorporating the right of the defence to produce witnesses, and the election of officials for district courts. Previously divided by estate into nobles, clergy, urban, and rural dwellers, judicial reform helped unify subjects of the monarchy. Reform brought public hearings along with jury trials and professional advocates. There were provisions for judicial settlements, civil proceedings, criminal proceedings, and new regulations for punishment guiding justices of the peace, with one exception, extrajudicial punishment, which was commonly used in the latter decades of the century. Only political cases and certain offences committed by government officials were exempted from trial by jury. The judicial system was separated from state and local administration, and educated jurists gained appointment as judges, who were paid and not subject to arbitrary removal. Lower courts, presided over by justices of the peace elected by the provincial assemblies and town councils, could adopt a simplified set of procedures. These reforms in the sphere of justice marked a thorough and radical break with the past.

3.2.5 Administrative Reform

The ordinary administrative system, controlled by the central government, continued to exist unchanged in the era of the 'Great Reforms', and many matters that in Western European countries are considered as part of the work of local authorities were left under the control of the central government officials. Representative administrative organs (*zemstva*) were created in provinces and districts to oversee economic activity and support education, medicine, and welfare. Property qualifications for office underscored the continuity of noble privilege in the councils and executive office, however, by excluding peasants from this governance reform. Estates also retained traditional corporative institutions in bodies of the local nobility and merchant guilds. However, local planning for road infrastructure, famine relief, schools, hospitals, and charitable institutions formed only a small part of the work *zemstva* eventually took up as civic activities, for which they were allowed to levy supportive taxes.

Municipal government reform in 1870 also invested in an elected assembly to make laws, although property qualifications for holding office again ensured the maintenance of traditional authority, with, in the town council, the wealthiest holding a position in the council similar to that held by nobles in rural areas. Municipal authorities, however, were hobbled. They faced the difficulty of raising funds, with shortfalls for development projects. They could change public laws regarding health and sanitary conditions, but they had no independent powers of enforcement, which was carried out by police who were controlled by the central government. As a consequence, municipal government was less transformed after the serf emancipation than other public spheres. In general, governance remained centralised. But reform was significant in that it brought educated estates into the public service, which generated broad responsiveness of the professional classes to issues of social progress. The peasantry was excluded from these reforms, but they were active as before in the traditional peasant institution of self-government, the commune, and after the reforms in municipal courts.

3.2.6 Modernisation of the Army and Navy

In 1874, universal conscription from the age of 20 replaced recruitment. This radical change was to provide the country with a professional army after Russia's defeat in Crimea. Reforms focused on communications and transport, modernised military equipment, and training to improve the competence of the military leadership. Active military service was reduced to 6 or 7 years, and corporal punishment in the military was eliminated. New military schools were a significant social reform in spreading literacy among the male populace. A code of military offences and court-martial procedures ended harsh punishment and made soldiers subject to the civil law reforms of 1864. Youths attaining the age of 20 were automatically called up for six years, followed by 9 in the reserve and service in the militia up to the age of 40. Total exemption, or a considerable reduction of the 6 years' period, was granted to men who could bring proof of exceptional domestic obligations, and those who had completed the course of elementary or secondary school or university received privileges corresponding to the standard of education they had attained. The army was placed on a territorial basis, and the annual quota of recruits required from each military district was chosen by lot. The efficiency of the army was further increased by the provision for education.

3.2.7 Laws Improving the Conditions of Factory Labour

Some decades after Europe and Britain, the Russian government acted to ease working conditions at factories. A new law in 1886 ordered the terms and procedures by which factory owners could hire labour, directed that wages be paid at least once a month, prohibited payment in kind and the charging of interest on advances made to workers, and created new supervisory agencies in major industrial centres. Regulations further eased terms of employment by controlling the arbitrariness of factory owners through fines and by shortening the length of the working day to 11.5 h. For some cities, stricter safety measures and better sanitary conditions were required, and as in most of industrialised Europe, Russia barred labour under the age of 12. Workers' demands for association from the 1890s were met only after 1906, when trade unions were legalised, encouraging organised activity among workers in some industries on behalf of tangible material improvements by means of collective bargaining.

3.2.8 Summary

To summarise the key components of the 'Great Reforms', the freeing of serfs from landlords' control and decentralised governance unified the country under a new social order, even as it failed to shift political authority to the larger governing group or place limitations on the personal powers of the autocrat. These reforms did encourage civic activism at the provincial level, where social welfare programmes developed. They also introduced secure property rights for landowners, although these rights did not extend to all individual producers or households and, for peasants, were conditional on negotiations and then, the payment of redemption fees.

3.3 THE 1905 REVOLUTION AND INSTITUTIONAL TRANSFORMATION

In 1905, the monarchy faced massive political and economic strikes, which were set off by the shooting by the government into a crowd of protesting factory workers in St. Petersburg. Concentrated in cities with industrial workers and encouraged by revolutionaries and trade unionists who mobilised some 800,000 workers by the end of the year, unrest spread into the countryside and built into a general strike led by railroad workers, after which the monarchy ceded to demands for civil and political liberties and an elected legislature in the 'October manifesto'.

3.3.1 Political Changes

The imperial state Duma, the elected legislative assembly, was created in 1906, but its first deputies were considered too radical by the government. It convened four times between 1906 and the collapse of the Empire in February 1917. The First and Second Dumas, with all classes and nationalities electing deputies, were dissolved. The Third Duma, after a new electoral law was put in place, was more inclined to support the government. It was dominated by gentry, landowners, and businessmen, whose party was called the 'Octobrists'; it lasted for its full session.

The priority of all parties was land reform, in view of the sweeping peasant unrest during and after the 1905 Revolution. Immediate interest in legislation was stimulated especially among peasants. In May 1905, an All-Russian Peasant Union was formed with radical organisers, whose demands included the redistribution of noble landholdings. Most parties in the Third Duma sought less radical reforms and united behind Stolypin's market-oriented agrarian programme (see below). The Third Duma also voted spending bills for an expansion of education that was to introduce compulsory primary schooling. Although it could not create or bring down governments, the Duma could exert real pressure on ministers, especially during the budget debates in which ministers, even of foreign and military departments, came under the deputies' scrutiny. These debates were extensively reported in the newspapers, where they could not be censored, and raised public awareness of political issues. As a result of liberalising reforms, this period saw growth in the publication of newspapers, periodicals, and books, both in the capital cities and in the provinces. The Fourth Duma had far more limited political influence than the Third, however, and it was prorogued in 1915.

3.3.2 *The Stolypin Land Reform*

Imposed initially by decree but implemented in stages as a flexible experiment, the land reform of 1906 designed by Prime Minister Petr Stolypin (1906–1911) was a major institutional transformation in support of capitalist market development. Stolypin's decree abolished control over the distribution of land by the Russian land commune (*obshchina*) and replaced it with individual property rights, highlighting private ownership and consolidating allotment shares into modern farmsteads. The government provided technical assistance and made available for purchase new lands previously belonging to the crown and state in central Russia and Siberia. The political objective was to reduce peasants' revolutionary aspirations by supporting farm ownership. The commune was prohibited from stopping individuals who wished to leave, and communes that resisted were dissolved. Peasants were also given financial incentives to move to remote areas of Siberia in an attempt to encourage settlement.

After 1906, land purchase by peasants spread far faster and wider than immediately after abolition, and between 1908 and 1913, demand for agricultural machines increased so significantly that the domestic production of agricultural machines approximately doubled. Land sales no doubt mostly benefited wealthier peasants rather than the poorest; the land that was sold to them was then rented out to local peasants. The fact that outsiders or newcomers bought extensive land holdings in consolidated lots to be rented out led to peasant dissatisfaction and land seizures when the revolution was underway in 1917.

Stolypin embraced a broader reform than only the introduction of land markets in agricultural regions. He also sponsored bills to address key issues in the judicial system. He worked with Duma legislation to protect those who had been arrested during preliminary investigations and introduced the suspended sentence, by which punishment could be deferred or an early release could be justified by post-jail monitoring. The government proposed that there be civil and criminal liability for officials who violated the subjects' legal rights and liberties. In brief, his larger aim was to strengthen the professional citizenry as a foundation for a civil society, although the main body of a middle class not yet created would have to be peasants, which in 1897, was some 70% of the population (Goodwin & Grennes, 1998, p. 407). Therefore, the urgency of reform lay in accustoming peasants to the ownership of landed property.

Reform, however, added substantially to state expenditures during years of weak state capacity, which applied pressure for the increase in extraordinary revenues. Proposals in the Duma for a personal income tax were rejected, and Russia continued to rely on indirect taxes of basic consumption items, including kerosene, matches, tobacco, and spirits.

3.4 Sectoral Transformation: The 1880s–1913

3.4.1 Agriculture and Trade

The agricultural sector grew more rapidly than the population with visible gains in consumption from the mid-1880s. The demand for land rose as nobles sold their holdings to the peasants, which showed the peasants' rising purchasing power. In the 1880s and 1890s, a time of relative macroeconomic stability, the impact of reform along with railroad building helped Russian agriculture advance at rates close to those observed in that era in Europe and the United States. Historical writing focuses on Russia's rural poor, but the empirical evidence does not support the familiar notion of a deep and widespread agrarian crisis, drawn mainly from revolutionaries' writings. Peasant living standards and real wages were rising, and exports of wheat led to Russia's world dominance, despite major expansions in wheat exports by the United States, Canada, Argentina, Australia, and India. Odessa became a major exporting port.

Russian wheat exports grew rapidly as a consequence of the re-regionalisation of wheat production from northern core industrial regions to the south, especially in areas around port cities. The location of production changed to represent the new pattern of comparative advantage. During the tsarist period and into the 1920s, as railroad construction accelerated within Russia and regional price differences narrowed, wheat production was encouraged far into the new agricultural areas of western Siberia. The government allowed railroads to become credit-granting agents, which significantly stimulated production and export. Wheat production was also stimulated by demand, which shifted from rye to wheat as consumption expanded, following a pattern similar to that in other countries. Yields of wheat in the late tsarist period averaged 5–10 bushels less per acre than in the United States, but this difference shrank by the late 1930s (Goodwin & Grennes, 1998, p. 410).

Russia's fiscal weakness imposed limitations on the structure of reform and thus affected the transformation of agriculture. Once landlords' authority over villages was removed, the state could not collect its own taxes. Therefore, reform allowed communal forms of landholding, along with tax liability, to persist in most European provinces of Russia, so that the state could collect redemption fees by which peasants paid off the land they were given. It is clear from recent research that labour flows into cities in the early decades after serf emancipation were mainly from those peasant properties where the state not the nobility had previously been the landowner (Markevich & Zhuravskaya, 2018). One anticipated benefit of agrarian reform was the release of labour to industry. But the transactions that might release labour were inhibited by the state's lack of capacity to assist the negotiation process or contribute to technological improvement on former serf estates. Meanwhile, for nobles, too, the impact of reform was hobbled by the inability to adequately compensate nobles for the loss of their settled land. The nobility received interest-bearing bonds and redemption certificates which could be used only to pay off state obligations in the amount of up to 80% of a sum capitalised at 6% of the value of previous dues minus the landlord's debt to the credit institutions. Neither the peasants nor the nobles were significantly better off after reform in regard to their agricultural assets. However, the poll tax on peasants was abolished, contributing to their mobility, and a high protective tariff to be paid in gold encouraged domestic industry. The Russian government decades later learned that state encouragement and support of industry should go further in assuring military power and fiscal stability.

3.4.2 Financing Industrial Development

The Russian state's industrialisation policy, often called the Witte system after Sergei Witte, the minister of finance from 1892 to 1903, played a prominent role in determining the course of Russian industrialisation and its opening to the West. Heavy industry increased considerably. The production of iron and steel rose by 50% and by the outbreak of WWI, Russia was the fourth largest producer of steel, coal, and iron. The boom began in the 1890s associated with a burst of railroad building in the late 1880s and gains from a long stable macroeconomic regime maintained by Russia's successive ministers of finance. Russia joined the international gold standard in 1897. But as Russia became a heavily indebted nation, some critics have talked about the costs of the fiscal conservatism and protectionism required to adopt the gold standard. The role of industry in the economy can be seen in Table 3.1.

Tariffs on imported pig iron and steel raised revenues from French investment but the Russian metallurgical industry stagnated before the 1880s without direct connections between coal and iron sources until the first railroad linked the Urals with the Donets Basin. After the 1880s, consolidation of the railroads mainly under state control had the enormous benefit in attracting foreign capital to Russian industry in part because the network of rail lines was now, after the 1880s, connected with the industrial regions of the south. After the turn of the century, economic crisis again slowed the course of industrialisation. Then, the war with Japan ending in Russia's defeat in 1905, along with the revolutionary disturbances of 1904–1905, revealed a low point in industrial outcomes, signifying to the government that Russian policy was still held back by inferior industry and technology, which required a larger kind of political as well as economic base of resources. As a result of dislocations in

Table 3.1 GDP in the Russian Empire estimated by the author, 1860–1913

	Agriculture	Industry	Construction	T&C	Trade	Services	GDP
At 1913 prices: RUB million							
1860	4332.1	530.5	100.6	113.6	328.7	537.4	5942.8
1885	4818.1	1188.7	251.3	283.6	587.6	862.6	7991.9
1913	10629.40	4561.6	1142	1288.7	1639.7	1884.6	21146.00
Index (1913 GDP = 100)							
1860	20.5	2.5	0.5	0.5	1.6	2.5	28.1
1885	22.8	5.6	1.2	1.3	2.8	4.1	37.8
1913	50.3	21.6	5.4	6.1	7.8	8.9	100
Average real annual growth rate, in %							
1860–1913	1.7	4.1	4.7	4.7	3.1	2.4	2.5
1860–1885	0.4	3.3	3.7	3.7	2.4	1.9	1.2
1885–1913	2.9	4.9	5.6	5.6	3.7	2.8	3.5

Source Appendix Table 11.1.1. in Kuboniwa et al. (2019)
Note T&C: Transportation and communications

the country's industry, agriculture, commerce, and transportation due to military mobilisation in 1905, the strike movement, and the loss of authority by government agencies, normal revenue totals in 1904 and 1905 were actually below that of 1903.

In these years, the treasury could not cover extraordinary expenditures. Between 1890–1900 and 1900–1913, the ordinary and extraordinary expenditures of the budget doubled. Meanwhile, payment on the state debt rose between 1861 and 1901 and further by 1913. Military expenditures, which had fallen to 30% of the budget by 1900, rose briefly during the Russo-Japanese war to some RUB 6.5 billion, over twice the size of the annual budget. They had to be funded by extraordinary resources. Sergei Witte eventually obtained a loan from the French stock exchange for nearly RUB 1 billion which allowed Russia to stay on the gold standard but added to an already massive state debt, entailing larger interest payments and the complete liquidation of short-term loans.

With Russia increasing state support for railroads and spending on the military, state finance was stretched by an ambitious military budget, which was aimed also to boost industry, but dominated state expenditures up to Russia's entry into WWI in 1914, with almost a doubling of annual military expenditures between 1900 and 1913. Added to this priority were the costs of the great reforms, the new administration of justice, higher and secondary education institutions, and infrastructure expenditures by local *zemstva*.

The loss of revenues from the poll tax after serf emancipation reduced the tax burden on the peasantry but weakened revenues and led to the increase in indirect taxes: alcohol became a lucrative government monopoly, the tobacco tax doubled from 1880 to 1895, the sugar tax grew by a multiple of 10, oil and matches were taxed, stamp duties increased, and tariff duties increased on imported goods during the 1880s. Tariffs on imports aimed to stimulate domestic production. The foreign sector, as a whole (exports, imports, tariff revenues, capital flows, and capital investment), played a large role in converting domestic resources into investment in the modernisation of the economy (Dohan, 1991, p. 213).

There were serious consequences of the dependence on indirect taxes as Russia entered WWI. One consequence was the burden on peasant consumption, even though the overall tax burden on the peasantry was reduced, indirect taxation increased by some 10%. To be sure, peasants could avoid the excise duty on alcohol by home-distilled spirits, and they could avoid the consumption of other taxed goods. Urban residents paid more in taxation during this period.

Russia joined the gold standard in 1897, gaining prestige and enhanced standing in the world financial community. The Russian state also hoped to attract significant foreign capital as a consequence of gold standard membership. By the end of the tsarist period, Russia had become a large international debtor, with substantial investments from France, Germany, and England as well as liabilities. This point alone demonstrates the success of the strategy, although tight financial controls had slowed what might have been additional decades of industrial growth before the turn of the century. The rebound in foreign confidence after 1905–1907, when foreign investment dipped, might not have taken place without the assurance of the gold standard. The fact that the Russian economy attracted so much capital after 1897 despite the tumultuous events of 1904 suggests the payoff to Russia's strategy.

Russia's relative strength was in agriculture, where output per capita grew significantly. In industry, the most impressive per capita change was in textiles rather than in heavy industry. Russia was indeed one of the world's major economic powers, however. In 1913, Russia's aggregate output was exceeded only by that of the United States, the United Kingdom, and Germany.

3.5 Society

3.5.1 *Standard of Living, 1880s–1913*

Although backward by comparison with the states of Europe, the standard of living in Russia was improving rapidly before the revolution, and cities were growing in the last decades of the imperial era. In 1869, 9.5% of Russians were residents in urban areas of at least 10,000 in population. By 1914, quite a few previously ordinary towns grew to impressive urban centres, and the urban population increased to 15.3% of the total population. With a weaker definition of urbanisation, including settlements of 2000 or more, then the percent urban in Russia reached over 30. The Russian population rose in large part due to a sharp decrease in mortality rates. It grew by 1.5% per annum between 1867 and 1913.

Even though urban living conditions were overcrowded and unsanitary, they did not slow city growth and the differential in mortality, larger in rural than in urban populations, remained throughout the century. In St. Petersburg, workers tended to live in barracks, and the number of people living in each room or cellar was two times that in Berlin, Vienna, or Paris. Russian infant mortality and death rates in 1861 were not much different from those of Germany, Italy, and Austria-Hungary a decade earlier. Forty years later, Russian infant mortality was virtually unchanged, whereas in the other countries it had declined significantly. The advances in public health services experienced in Europe were shared in Russian cities but not in Russian villages. Thus, the 'urban penalty' disappeared during the late nineteenth century in Russia and the overall mortality in cities dropped due in large part to improvements in health care and health knowledge. Russia was obviously backward relative to its major European competitors both at the beginning of its 'modern period' (1861) and at the end of the tsarist era. This conclusion emerges unambiguously from the per capita figures and from social indicators.

However, in summary, in Russia, as elsewhere, living conditions improved, even though there were rural and urban differences. Literacy rates were rising as the rural education system expanded.

3.6 The Intelligentsia and the Emergence of Radical Activism

Beginning in the late eighteenth and early nineteenth century, in this society divided by social estate into rigid exclusive categories, there emerged a well-educated and thoughtful element that came to be called 'the intelligentsia'. To belong to this group, it was not sufficient to be a professional, an urban dweller, or a member of one of the many noble salons in the capital cities of Moscow and St. Petersburg. One of the first members was Alexander Radishchev, an author and social critic, who was arrested and exiled during the relatively enlightened rule of Catherine II for having published in 1790 *Journey from St. Petersburg to Moscow*, a fictionalised journey in which he recounted scenes of social injustice, poverty, and brutality—essentially, an indictment of serfdom, autocracy, and censorship. Other circles of social critics formed around universities and the thick journals that became popular in the 1830s and 1840s. Later in the century, the term intelligentsia became associated both with the nihilist movement of the 1860s and then, as it affected society more broadly by the turn of the century, any educated or self-educated person who possessed a critical mind, a secular code of ethics, a commitment to social justice, and cultural refinement. Self-identifying as in the intelligentsia implied a critical approach to conditions and the government of Russia.

The narrow social context in which such an identifiable group of critics could emerge was to a great extent reflected in the specific environment of censorship following the French Revolution, when Catherine II attempted to suppress radicalism in publications by French and American political writing.

In general, the political context, however, was also important in that the tsars rejected discussion or depiction of the Empire as a personalised autocracy with rigidly subordinated officialdom and suppressed corps, corporations, or legal entities. The idea of constitutional order and limitations of sovereign authority were rejected by the autocracy and subjected to censorship through the mid-nineteenth century, but such ideas flourished nevertheless, and there were broad layers of society, consisting of nobles and townspeople of diverse rank who created in Russia a lively non-revolutionary civic life in capital cities and provincial urban centres. Joseph Bradley (2002, p. 1105) summarises the current understanding about the environment that gave birth to the Russian intelligentsia and its broadening to include new layers of society in the 1860s and 1870s:

> Economic growth, mobility, urbanization, and advances in education, coupled with the Great Reforms of the 1860s, fostered the development of organized structures that mediated between the individual and the state. New professional, entrepreneurial, and artistic elites aspired to create new public identities. Bureaucratic service to the state or visionary service "to the people" no longer defined the concept of public duty.

Despite the modernisation of society and the economy beginning most visibly in the era of Alexander II, waves of revolutionary activity spread across the country organised first by populists and later by Marxists. In Russia, by contrast with Germany and other countries in Europe, the target of the intelligentsia's criticism was not the bourgeoisie but the autocracy itself. Moreover, the driving force of radicalism, by contrast, again, with elsewhere at the time, was not the labour movement, insignificant in a country with a rudimentary industry, but the intelligentsia. These two factors: the necessity of concentrating the struggle against the monarchy (at the time of its most conservative phase) instead of the bourgeoisie, and of having to wage the struggle with the help of an intelligentsia instead of a labour movement, had a profound effect on the nature and history of Russian Marxism.

Marxism became important in Russia from the 1880s, when industrialisation helped create workers' movements and an urban elite that welcomed the Marxist social and political doctrines. Marxist leaders, such as Georgy Plekhanov and Vladimir Lenin, helped shift the focus in revolutionary circles in Russia and abroad from the populist orientation to the conditions of the peasantry to the radicalisation of workers in towns. In brief, Russian Marxist revolutionaries were heavily influenced by radical populists (e.g., People's Will) and populists were influenced by Marxism (Pipes, 1960).

3.7 World War I and Revolution

Witte's negotiation of a large French loan helped solidify the Franco-Russian alliance, which would be one factor drawing Russia into WWI. Other interests dominated in the opening years of war. Russia was mainly interested in Balkan affairs, where the weakening of the Ottoman Empire and the Hapsburg monarchy was leading to aspirations by different powers for greater influence among Slavic peoples, who aspired to be free of colonial powers. Russia came to an understanding with Austria that broke down when Austria-Hungary occupied Bosnia and Herzegovina in 1908. After the assassination of Archduke Franz Ferdinand in 1914, Austria-Hungary issued an ultimatum to Serbia, in whose defence Russia mobilised forces on the border with Austria-Hungary, leading to German intervention and escalation into world war.

The Russian government was supported domestically by civil action to provide support for economic priorities and coordinate medical relief, supplies, and transport. By 1915, with the Russian army lacking adequate munitions, Germany and Austria-Hungary advanced into the Western territories of the Russian empire. As Nicholas II took personal charge of the army and went to the front, the government fell apart at home, largely due to personal intrigues of the Empress' favourite, Grigoriy Rasputin. Nicholas began, from his headquarters in Belarus, acceding to some of Rasputin's requests by dismissing members of the government perceived as a threat. In December 1916, Rasputin was murdered, even as the fortunes of Russia's military were improving with the reorganisation of military production. But the call-up of peasants and the inflation, resulting from the strain of financing the war without adequate state revenues, led to the outbreak of strikes, which tended more and more to be political.

The February Revolution of 1917 began spontaneously over food lines in the capital, where protestors called for an end to autocracy. With the collapse of military support for the tsar, the workers and soldiers revived the *soviets* (councils) they had created in 1905 to represent their interests, and a provisional government, as agreed by the Petrograd *soviet* and the Duma, led by Prince Georgy Lvov of the *zemstvo* and consisting mainly of representative of liberal parties, took control in Petrograd and secured the tsar's abdication. The countrywide revolution, brought to fruition by strikers and by other urban and rural massive support against the government, reflected the economic and social conditions generated after the draining years of war. The gulf that emerged between the monarchy and educated society and between the tsar and subjects from all social classes left the tsar isolated, with palace intrigues seemingly representing all that was left of his powers.

In February 1917, a Provisional Government was formed with the intent of a future convening of a Constituent Assembly in 1918. But as unrest grew in major cities, the temporary liberal parliamentary government's weakness relative to powerful workers' *soviets* in cities and the Socialist Revolutionary party, which dominated the countryside, was apparent. The Provisional Government continued prosecution of the unpopular war, in which Russian forces were weakened by the mass desertion of soldiers returning to Russia, and it witnessed radical socialists winning in local elections. A failed coup in August by the right-wing General Kornilov only increased the popularity of the Bolsheviks, who seized power from the government on 25 October 1917 (according to the old-style Julian calendar).

Questions for Students

1. Many historians have viewed the serf emancipation in 1861 as a failed reform: do you agree?
2. How important was Russia's entry into World War I among the reasons for the outbreak of the revolution in February 1917?
3. How important was 'state capacity' in imperial Russia to the pace of modernisation in the late nineteenth century?

References

Bradley, J. (2002). Subjects into citizens: Societies, civil society, and autocracy in tsarist Russia. *The American Historical Review, 107*(4), 1094–1123.

Dohan, M. R. (1991). Foreign trade. In R. W. Davies (Ed.), *From tsarism to the new economic policy: Continuity and change in the economy of the USSR* (pp. 212–236). Springer.

Goodwin, B. K., & Grennes, T. J. (1998). Tsarist Russia and the world wheat market. *Explorations in Economic History, 35*(4), 405–430.

Kuboniwa, M., Shida, Y., & Tabata, S. (2019). Gross domestic products. In M. Kuboniwa et al. (Eds.), *Russian economic development over three centuries*. Palgrave Macmillan. https://doi.org/10.1007/978-981-13-8429-5_11, https://rdcu.be/cKLJ9

Markevich, A., & Zhuravskaya, E. (2018). The economic effects of the abolition of serfdom: Evidence from the Russian Empire. *The American Historical Review, 108*(4–5), 1074–1117.

Pipes, R. (1960). Russian marxism and its populist background: The late nineteenth century. *The Russian Revolution, 19*(4), 316–337.

CHAPTER 4

The Soviet Economy (1918–1991)

Carol Scott Leonard

Highlights
- The Bolsheviks had aimed when they took power for a state capitalist system to keep skilled capitalist managers in place while slowly moving towards socialism; they rapidly laid the foundations of a socialist economy under the coercive policies of 'War Communism' (1918–1921).
- After introducing the New Economic Policy (NEP) in 1921, within a few years, small and medium-scale industries thrived, and the price of industrial goods was affordable to the urban and rural populace.
- The rapid restoration of markets during the NEP was resisted among some Bolshevik theorists who argued that rural markets might hold back the financing of the needs and supply of workers for rapid industrialisation. Stalin closed the debate on this issue in deciding on the rapid industrialisation launched by the first 5-year plan in 1929.

C. S. Leonard (✉)
St. Antony's College,
University of Oxford, Oxford, United Kingdom
e-mail: carol.scott.leonard@gmail.com

The Russian Presidential Academy of National Economy and Public Administration (RANEPA), Moscow, Russia

Higher School of Economic, Moscow, Russia

© The Author(s), under exclusive license to Springer Nature Switzerland AG 2023
M. Dabrowski (ed.), *The Contemporary Russian Economy*,
https://doi.org/10.1007/978-3-031-17382-0_4

- Stalin's industrialisation policy was characterised by the total elimination of private entrepreneurship, the redistribution of investment in favour of heavy and military industry, the collectivisation of agriculture, the reallocation of large groups of the population, the system of forced labour, and mass political terror.
- After World War II, the Soviet Union became a modern, urban, non-agricultural economy, with its strength demonstrated in mobilising resources to rebuild after the war. However, the workforce still lacked crucial incentives for innovation and productivity improvement, and without property rights, production required imports of advanced technology, including for the extraction of resources upon which the economy heavily depended.
- The continued inefficiency of the command economic system showed by the mid-1980s that past achievements of military and industrial objectives by means of mobilising new resources, as in collectivisation, was no longer an adequate model for growth.
- In 1987, President Gorbachev introduced a 'new economic mechanism' giving considerable scope in decision-making to enterprises and allowing independent worker-owned cooperatives to operate alongside state cooperatives to encourage the private sector.
- Growth stalled in 1987–1988.
- The collapse of the Soviet Union in 1991 occurred when its sovereignty over Soviet republics ended as a consequence of political liberalisation.
- On 25 December 1991, President Gorbachev resigned, and this date marks the end of the Soviet Union.

4.1 Introduction

World War I (WWI) caused heavy human losses and suffering and material damage and the collapse of the Russian monarchy. Two revolutions in 1917 eventually led to the grab of political power by the Bolshevik party, which proclaimed the goal of building a socialist/communist state and society and a non-market economy based on central planning and state ownership of the means of production. The subsequent 74 years of the communist regime changed the Russian economy and society radically.

This chapter offers a general overview of the centrally planned economy (how it functioned) and analyses its development (institutional and policy characteristics as well as economic and social performance).

4.2 Civil War and 'War Communism' (1918–1921)

The period of civil war and 'War Communism' (1918–1921) magnified the human and material losses of WWI (see Chapter 3).

Roughly half a million Russian soldiers, deserters from the front during WWI, were detained on trains attempting to return to their villages. After the Bolsheviks seized power in October 1917, Lenin used the massive desertion along with the economic effects of war to justify a swift if punishing conclusion of peace at Brest Litovsk (1918). By this peace, Russia was left with Moscow, Petrograd, and the industrial heartland, and was separated from Ukraine, the Polish and Baltic territories, and Finland. Ukraine was recovered in 1919, and Georgia, Armenia, and Azerbaijan by 1921. The Bolsheviks had abrogated the Constituent Assembly in 1918, before the war was over, thus preventing opposition to the peace, consolidating power, and ending participation in the governing coalition by the more moderate Socialist Revolutionaries, the party of the peasantry.

Opposition grew, and civil war broke out. 'The Reds' faced a formidable enemy, in addition to the peasantry, a joint front of the Whites, or anti-communists, monarchists, and anarchists, who were supplied with materials by foreign countries, including Britain, Italy, France, the United States, Japan, and others. To feed cities and defeat peasant resistance, the Bolsheviks established a 'food dictatorship'—or War Communism—modelled initially on the German regulatory system. Forced requisitions from the peasants, however, led to further resistance and extensive loss of life along with deeper economic collapse. The Bolsheviks gained the upper hand with the advantage of a remarkably well-trained and capable cadre of former tsarist officers, restored to their military positions by Leon Trotsky. Bolshevik victory against a remarkable coalition led to the memorialisation of the rhetoric of campaigns, political fronts, and economic struggles, and this was later turned against Russia's own citizens. The VChK (*Cheka*), or the first in a series of Soviet secret police organisations, was formed in December 1917 as the government arm of domestic protection from internal foes.

The Bolsheviks had aimed initially for a state capitalist system to keep skilled capitalist managers in place while slowly moving towards socialism, but within months, the struggle against those opposed to their government led them to more rapidly lay the foundations of a socialist economy. They nationalised the banking system and foreign trade as part of their coercive policies under War Communism. They established a Supreme Council of the National Economy (*Vesenkha*) to control the supply of coal and iron and from June 1918 seized 'the commanding heights' of large-scale industry and transport. Initially, agriculture had remained in private hands, while farmers were obligated to deliver their food produce above a subsistence norm for government distribution to others. With a government monopoly over trade, important commodities were purchased at fixed prices. However, the resulting scarcity, a condition in which the black market flourished and inflation accelerated, was failing to produce sufficient revenues or improve the competence and reduce corruption among officials. Coercive means ignored property rights and civil rights and allowed extreme penalties for resistance, turning policy rhetoric into campaigns against 'enemies of the people' who were working with the foreign enemy to 'strangle the revolution'. Violence and corruption deprived the War Communist state of legitimacy, while it drained state revenues, and it ended with a tactical retreat. Peasant revolt, especially the Tambov Revolt in 1920, contributed along with economic collapse to a rethinking of economic strategy and the end of War Communism in 1921.

4.3 The 'New Economic Policy' (1921–1928)

The 'New Economic Policy' (NEP) between 1921 and 1928 brought economic liberalisation and partially rehabilitated private entrepreneurship in agriculture, trade, services, and small and medium-size industry.

4.3.1 Retreat

Building the NEP (1921–1928), the state retained the organisational structures from War Communism and continued to control key sectors of the economy—heavy industry, communications, and transport—while temporarily reviving markets in light and consumer goods industries. A monetary reform in 1923 introduced a money tax ending the food dictatorship. This 'breathing space' helped restore village markets and allowed peasants to retain the surplus after the payment of a graduated levy in proportion to the harvest. Because of continued control over large-scale industry, transport, and banking, the government succeeded in boosting productivity by demanding managers produce more while not raising wages to match output. The price of manufactured goods fell for farmers and pushed down industrial costs making manufacturing more profitable. In summary, by the mid-1920s, small and medium-scale industry thrived, and the price of industrial goods was affordable to the urban and rural populace.

Agriculture too, despite harvest failures and widespread famine in 1921, recovered under the NEP and justified by the mid-1920s the partial restoration of markets. Since the food supply was ample, distribution was no longer a policy issue and peasant households experienced relief. This meant, however, that peasants were no longer pressed to leave the land for jobs in rural and urban factories. For the future, the government would have to have a far larger supply of workers through rural emigration as demand increased among the critical industries at the 'commanding heights'; discussions focused on how to mobilise the labour essential to the industrialisation drive. One means was to return to a more coercive policy squeezing labour and extracting food resources from the agricultural sector. The NEP was proving itself capable of meeting some of this demand although at too slow a pace.

4.3.2 Command Institutions

The NEP reforms improved state capacity with recruitment and training to develop competence and managerial discipline for control over wages and investment in profit-making enterprises. The foundations of state planning institutions were laid: a planning commission (Gosplan) from before the NEP continued to coordinate goals for output targets and for the supply of intermediate goods to meet those targets. Gosplan used a 'material balances' approach to balance estimates of supply and demand. During the NEP, centralised price controls resulted in the rationing of some capital goods, but there was a significant economic recovery by the mid-1920s.

The Soviet government maintained as its priority the industrial economy, while the development of agriculture was reduced to a secondary concern. The particular focus was labour policy, to increase the size of the working class and improve discipline and productivity at factories. Party membership was used to spread socialist norms in the state administration and required under Iosif Stalin, general party secretary from 1922, for important positions in the government and the economy. Personnel files identified competences, records of achievement and failings, and the promotions of party members from who was demanded loyalty and the implementation of party policies. Security also meant country-wide control from Moscow from 1918 when the party made Moscow the capital city, and Russian interests became dominant in the central party apparatus over those of the other nationalities. The party in Moscow was a power base for Stalin, and he used it in the power struggle after Lenin's death in 1924 to determine the fate of governance as well as the path to socialism. The key question in government circles was the need for rapid industrialisation; this became a succession struggle for control of overall policy affecting society and the economy.

4.3.3   Leadership Struggle Over Rapid Industrialisation

The NEP restored the marketing of grain by ending the forced requisitions, the main feature of War Communism. But the rapid restoration of markets, as noted above, was resisted among Bolshevik theorists who argued that rural markets might hold back the financing of the needs and supply of workers for rapid industrialisation. They broadly agreed on the need for rapid growth and industrialisation but disagreed on the specific measures needed to increase the volume of output, change the composition of output and employment, and determine the interrelations of agriculture and industry. The disagreement seemed increasingly urgent to resolve from the mid-1920s because of the threat of war. Harrison (2017, p. 24) writes:

> 'Bolsheviks hardly had to be reminded of the threat of foreign enemies, but real or not, war scares in the late 1920s gave external tensions an urgency and a priority in the likelihood of military mobilization.'

Bolsheviks on the Left, inspired by Leon Trotsky and defended by the theoretician Evgenii Preobrazhenskii, a prominent party member and economist, argued that the state should proceed faster towards industrialisation by increasing its capital accumulation, letting the terms of trade move firmly against the peasants, with the small producer to face heavy taxation. They argued that a massive shift of resources from agriculture to industry would enable industry to achieve a higher technological level. The Right, led by Nikolai Bukharin, using the already clear achievements of the NEP as support for the argument, insisted that only if agriculture was rapidly growing could industry continually advance; what was needed was agricultural exports and investment in the branches that served the export sector, such as grain elevators, to provide resources for progress to a higher technological level in industry. Stalin successively took policy positions that defeated his rivals, first, by attacking the Left as 'super-industrialist', and then, using their arguments after he defeated them, by attacking the Right and prioritising the needs of heavy industry. Closing the debate, Stalin formulated a course of policy, 'Socialism in One Country', essentially autarky. All out, for the 5-year plan in 1929, he commanded investment in heavy industry in particular and industry as a whole.

4.3.4   Rapid Post-WWI Economic Recovery.

By 1927/28, domestic production probably reached 1913 levels of the tsarist economy, although the data are difficult to verify. Post-war recovery was substantial, although the Soviet economy still lagged far behind the great industrial powers. The gap in industrial capacity is demonstrated in the high proportion in Russia of textile and food industries combined with the weak development of machine building and electrical engineering, a relatively small percentage of iron and steel, the almost complete absence of the chemical industry, and a low level of the production of consumer goods (Gatrell & Davies, 1990, p. 134). The Soviet budget benefitted from the decline of military expenditure, a major strain in the war years, and, helping to finance industrial capacity, the budget also experienced relief in the balance of payments and, in particular, by abrogation of the tsarist debt. The NEP advanced industry, directing imports towards its investment needs, for example, improving the product mix in engineering, which showed gains in sophistication. The hourly productivity of labour went up as incentives were designed to improve competence; the output in large-scale industry by 1927 can verifiably be said to have surpassed the pre-war level.

In agriculture, the NEP encouraged a more intensive, high-yielding non-grain production mix and more investment of sales in the village. Households created networks to market products and purchase equipment and start independent farms by leasing land and implements from other peasants. Migrant labour also increased. Peasants participated widely in industrial development: 3.8%, or 5.7 million, engaged in migrant labour, of which more than one-half were engaged in non-agricultural labour (Harrison, 1990, p. 122). Within certain limits during the NEP, *kulaks*, or wealthy peasants, thrived, although they were subject to taxation and exclusion from the privileges of citizenship.

The foreign sector, by contrast, changed and grew smaller. The Soviet government abandoned the market export mechanism of prices and profitability in favour of administrative decisions on exports, with grain exports falling to a minimal level. The priority was to continue the tsarist model of import substitution, importing foreign technicians and technology raw material and machinery and exporting timber and oil. Shortages of imports, however, limited the growth of industrial output. And while the rouble itself was inconvertible, a new currency was created, *chervontsy*, to be directly exchangeable for gold, although actual exchange was delayed, indeed, and never made a reality. Gosbank (the State Bank; a central bank of the USSR) purchased *chervontsy* for gold and foreign currency only as a mechanism for supporting the exchange rate at a certain level. A Special Foreign Currency Commission was formed in 1923 to concentrate demand for foreign currency in a few large all-Russian centres and to preserve currency resources inside the country by means of export control. There was no direct transfer of actual currency from seller to purchaser but through a Gosbank account, transforming economic institutions.

4.3.5 *Comparative Performance Estimates, 1913 and 1928*

The comparison of national income at the end of the NEP, 1928, and 1913, as noted above, is controversial in view of the fragility of the data as well as overstatement in the officially reworked Soviet estimates of the achievement of the NEP. Statistics published by the Soviet government, using a low implicit deflator, are not supported by contemporary price indices; they had recovery to the pre-revolutionary peak completed by 1926 and national income at 19% and per capita at 9% above 1913 levels (Gregory, 1990, p. 247). A close review by Paul Gregory (1990) based on western and alternate Russian economists' estimates, by contrast, finds output in 1928 about equal to that in 1913, with a substantial per capita gap still remaining.

4.4 Constructing Soviet Economic Institutions

4.4.1 *The First Wave of the Forced Stalinist Industrialisation (1929–1940)*

The first wave of the forced Stalinist industrialisation (1929–1940) was characterised by the total elimination of private entrepreneurship, the redistribution of investment in favour of heavy and military industry, the collectivisation of agriculture, the reallocation of large groups of the population, the system of forced labour, and mass political terror.

The end of the NEP signified a move to the command economy, ending the leadership struggle and reviving the forced requisition of food from the peasants, while reimposing the state monopoly of the grain trade. Peasants who resisted were put on trial for sabotage and collaboration with enemies of the country, the first steps of a campaign to be a model for the rest of the country.

Formally, the first 5-year plan (1929) introduced centralised planning of industry, collectivisation of agriculture, isolation of the economy from foreign trade and rearmament, and forced labour. Stalin aimed in 5 years to double the national income and treble the output of investment goods, while lifting consumption per head by two-thirds. Hundreds of large-scale industrial and infrastructure projects set optimistic goals for harvests. The plan was intended to produce things not services, to outproduce all other countries in coal, steel, and cement, numbers of lathes, and megawatts of electrical power so that Russia would be as modern and as powerful as its rivals. It was a system initially without incentives for individual self-improvement, with weak ones introduced later by reform, acknowledging the problem but using chiefly administrative means to improve lagging productivity.

According to the plan, the economy's stocks of fixed capital were to expand rapidly, and the size of the labour force in industry, drawn mainly from agricultural households, was to increase dramatically. Industrial output did indeed grow by 50% over 5 years and 80% over 6 years. Transport activity rose so quickly above plan levels—reaching 227% of 1928 by 1932—that there were backlogs of unshipped freight clogging the railroads for several years, and passenger travel conditions were chaotic.

Agriculture, however, did not respond as anticipated to plans for its modernisation. There were demands for the expansion of fields and quick results, which meant that available animal draft power was inadequate and tractor production had to increase substantially. Processing in villages fell, as food, cotton, flax, and leather supplies dropped, creating a demand for emergency imports. Shortages of food and other consumer goods forced the introduction of rationing. Coercion led to resistance by the rural population and the failure of the agriculture sector driven into collective farms, from which the wealthiest NEP households were now driven for ideological reasons, as the 'liquidation of the kulaks as a class'.

Collectives were a new form of land use under a general regime of nationalised land. Numerous collective farms and a smaller number of powerful state farms were created by force and with speed for the production of field crops. The first 5-year plan aimed to bring up to one in five peasant households into the collective farm sector in order for the state to invest in a substantial agriculture sector. It aimed to control the uses of new machinery, which the state would supply, and to produce bigger surpluses from larger farms with that machinery. After initial efforts, the aim expanded to force producers of all kinds into collective farms—in early 1930, they covered half of all family farms and by 1936, 90%. Among enormous immediate costs was the collapse of the horse population after poor weather in 1932, when food became scarce and costly. Famine causing the death of around six million people led to the consumption of feed by humans. Forced collectivisation drove the campaign to 'liquidate' the wealthy peasants, or kulaks, as a 'class', which resettled or imprisoned two million peasants. Some private farming was allowed for supplementary production of vegetables, but this was on a very small scale, the average of which was about 0.25 hectares from a permitted 0.50 hectares of garden and field and a number of livestock. Rural households that sold produce formed a private collective farm market, which allowed them an outlet for the sale of vegetables and animal products, outside procurement, which brought them low prices for their goods. The household economy realised some commercial profit, and it was endorsed in Soviet law, part of the long historical norm; in fact, the private sector provided an essential economic contribution at roughly one-quarter of gross agricultural output (GAO) and a remarkable 31% share of animal production.

4.4.2 The Period of World War II (1941–1945)

In 1941–1945, the USSR emerged as a world power after defeating the Axis powers on the Eastern Front of World War II (WWII), called the Great Patriotic War, in battles unprecedented in ferocity and brutality, destruction, deportations, and large loss of life in combat and due to starvation, exposure, disease, and massacres. Of the estimated 70–80 million deaths in WWII, 30 million occurred on the Eastern Front, and over 20 million were lost in the Soviet Union. Before war broke out, the Soviet Union had agreed to a non-aggression pact with Nazi Germany (the Molotov-Ribbentrop Pact, 1939), which included a secret protocol dividing the territories of Romania, Poland, Lithuania, Latvia, Estonia, and Finland into German and Soviet spheres of influence. After Germany invaded Poland on 1 September 1939, Russia also invaded Poland, and in November engaged in the 'winter war' to gain part of Finland and then taking Estonia, Latvia, Lithuania, and parts of Romania. Then on 22 June 1941, Hitler invaded the Soviet Union, but the result of this conflict, opening the Eastern Front in WWII, was the decisive Soviet victory that determined the defeat of Nazi Germany and the allied Axis powers in the European theatre of war.

These victories reflect the considerable strength of the Soviet Union, which had by 1940 narrowed the gap in output per capita with Europe and the United States. From 1928 through 1937, the rapid Soviet advance in gross domestic product (GDP) per capita boosted its wartime economic performance. This was despite enormous population losses with a staggering demographic cost. By contrast with the limits of its food procurement during WWI, in WWII, Russia had a well-developed procurement system. Despite a disastrous fall in food output per head of the collective farm population, military-style procurement campaigns increased the confiscation of food, and collective farm peasants accepted the sacrifice to feed the army in war time.

4.4.3 The Performance of the Economy After Stalinist Industrialisation

The Soviet command economy from the late 1920s was built with the construction of a war economy in mind. With the aim of protecting against infiltration by internal and external enemies acting together, as they had in the civil war, policy suppressed market forces and strengthened the role of the state with the application of a military level of secrecy. The interest of military security was behind Stalin's decisions to accelerate industrialisation, to collectivise peasant farming, and to squeeze consumption for the sake of accumulation and defence. Some of the permanent effects of this policy on governance were the priority of state over private ownership and the resort to the political mobilisation of resources, including the use of forced labour.

The Soviet economic system is best described as one of centralised planning, implemented administratively through the issuing of direct commands and extensive, detailed coordinating instructions (a summary of traditional Soviet economic institutions and procedures can be found in Bornstein, 2019). Subordinates provided information and suggestions, but they had little autonomy in determining what to do, or even how to do it. All authority resided with the central authorities, though the fine detail of implementation was delegated to operational units. Central direction and control determined the nature and defined the logic of the Soviet economic system. The state owned all natural resources (land and minerals) and almost all of the reproducible capital (buildings, machinery, equipment, and inventories) and conducted virtually all activity in industry, mining, construction, transportation, and wholesale trade.

This traditional Soviet economic system was very good at mobilising scarce resources and concentrating on a few clear, well-defined objectives that can be expressed in measurable, quantitative, and communicable terms and that yielded large observable changes as outcomes. The Soviet 5-year plans were a programme of action based on simple objectives, the building of major heavy industrial capacities (1930s–1950s), the collectivisation of agriculture (1930s), the post-war reconstruction of industry, and an unprecedented military-industrial complex (1960s–1970s).

Overall success in these objectives did not lead to any particular well-functioning sector, as, for example, agriculture, whose failure was evident in the scarcity of food products and the long lines in major cities for essential items. However, the command system achieved the goals of industrialising and collectivising the economy rapidly, to be sure, with huge waste and human loss. Both reconstruction after the mass destruction of war and development through extensive growth were facilitated by the existence of detailed knowledge of the final state to be achieved.

By rapid industrialisation, the Soviet Union acquired a powerful defence industry, a multi-million-person army, thousands of aircraft and tanks, and nuclear weapons. The collective farms ensured that the defence industry and the army would be fed first when the country was under attack. The economy's centralised institutions for oversight and enforcement guaranteed his authority. Here was the command economy's comparative advantage: the production of economic and military power. The industrialisation policies put into place from 1928 made Russia by 1970 one of the world's most successful economies in regard to industrial output. The political repression and the famine mortality following the collectivisation of agriculture weigh heavily against calling this achievement a success, as do constraints on consumption and a standard of living that did not compare at the time to Western standards.

4.5 Reforming the Soviet Economy (1945–1991)

4.5.1 The Period of the Post-War Stalinist Reconstruction (1945–1953)

By 1950, the economy was recovering economically from the effects of WWII. Reconstruction was bringing fixed capital and employment to a level higher than before WWII, and housing increased, although the need was still substantial. The railway network in use in 1945 was actually longer than in 1940. There was a steady climb of GDP per capita after the war years.

During the war, Russia experienced a net decline of 7 million in population, by no means the total loss; this was easily made up with a rapid population growth of 2% per annum by 1950. For much of the period, investment in agriculture was significant. The stock of trucks and tractors grew at up to 10% per annum. Agricultural inputs included petroleum products, hardware and spare parts, fertilisers, wood, and electric power, but their consumption increased more rapidly than their production; investment was not matched by output in the agricultural sector.

After the war, through 1953, when Stalin died, reconstruction dominated economic activity, continuing the war time emphasis on the sinews of national power. Economic policy, organisation, and ideas were frozen in their focus on heavy industry and rail transport. In post-war years, Soviet development did not produce rapid growth in productivity, but there was tremendous expansion in output—metallurgical output quickly reached its pre-war level, the great Dnieper dam was rebuilt within 2 years and producing electricity, and the revival of consumer goods from exceedingly low levels in 1945 was rapid. The Soviet Union became a modern, urban, non-agricultural economy and increased the supply of inputs to production and outputs in cities networked territorially across the country. The enormous contribution of this period showed the strength of the Soviet system, mobilising resources to rebuild after the war. New groups were drawn into the Soviet workforce—women and rural dwellers—and the stock of capital, including human capital, expanded. However, the workforce still lacked crucial incentives for innovation and productivity improvement, and without property rights, production required imports of advanced technology, including for the extraction of resources upon which the economy heavily depended.

The following were the salient characteristics for understanding the nature and performance of the Soviet economic system: the hierarchical structure of authority, which has sole vertical accountability for outcomes; the rigid, highly centralised planning of production and distribution; the commitment to maximal resource utilisation, which gave tautness and pressure in planning; administrative allocation in mostly physical terms of produced goods and services; price control; the lack of liquidity or flexible response capability and the lack of a true money; superiors' control of norms, indices, and parameters of plan targets and rewards; and incentives that are oriented to meeting targets rather than to consequences. Any economic reforms, as follows in the Sects. 4.5.2–4.5.2, can change the administrative regime, but production routines only very slowly (Ericson, 1991, p. 29).

4.5.2 Partial Changes in the Political System and Economic Policy in the Post-Stalin Era (1953–1985)

After Stalin's death in 1953, a leadership struggle elevated Nikita Khrushchev as General Secretary of the Communist Party of the Soviet Union (CPSU). A reformer, responsible for détente in foreign affairs, brought about 'the thaw' in domestic affairs, resulting in considerable freedom of cultural expression after the stifling of artistic creativity under Stalin. He also freed political prisoners and closed the gulag, or forced labour camp system. Announced by a secret speech at the 20th Party Congress in 1956, a denunciation of Stalin leaked abroad, and the new policies led to 'de-Stalinization' across the Eastern and Central European states occupied by Soviet troops during WWII and then incorporated into an Eastern Bloc (which excluded Yugoslavia and Albania). De-Stalinization loosened ties with the Soviet Union for some of these states. In Hungary (1956), a resistance movement was suppressed, and in Czechoslovakia in 1968, resistance was put down by East bloc troops.

In economic policy, there were reforms leading to organisational improvements without departing from the principle of centralised planning and allocation. There was some effort to slow the dissipation of power from Moscow to the provinces by the centralisation of industrial structures by ministry. Reforms addressed the concerns for improving consumption. Khrushchev moved policy away from collective housing arrangements, and his government began the massive construction of modern apartment blocks, known as *'khrushchevkas'*. He freed peasants to travel and relocate—they received passports, enabling them to move out of poor villages to big cities. Slow growth in productivity in agriculture was addressed by a new programme, his Virgin Lands project to cultivate 13 million hectares of previously unfarmed land east of the Volga, in western Siberia, Kazakhstan, and the Northern Caucasus, where the land was broken by hundreds of thousands of volunteers. The project had no effect on productivity; years of good yields were followed by years of droughts, and the new technologies applied to the dry soils caused severe erosion. Growth dropped dramatically in the 1970s, as soil erosion caused a decline in land under cultivation, and declining growth in capital stock and declining employment led to weak per capita progress.

The next period of reform began in 1965 under the post-Khrushchev Prime Minister, Alexei Kosygin, when Leonid Brezhnev was selected as the new General Secretary of the CPSU. Essentially, there were two kinds of reform measures, those aimed at improving central planning and control and those aimed at decentralising the implementation of central objectives by expanding the autonomy of operational units. Both involved attempts to rationalise the economic environment in which subordinates had to operate and give state-owned firms more autonomy. The 'Kosygin' reforms introduced profit incentives, or 'economic levers'. There were new price indicators in the plan, profitability (*rentabel'nost'*), defined as the ratio between profits and capital, and sales (*realizatsiya*). By making profits, firms were to accumulate incentive funds, which could generate cash bonuses for workers, social and cultural housing projects, and general development, and firm managers were given some discretion in the use of these funds. A second innovation was the replacement of 'administrative methods' by contracts to gain workers' compliance. Finally, land rent was introduced to contribute to what was called the economic optimisation of resource use, and the government embraced 'cybernetics', the application of mathematical methods and computational economics, in the planning process.

Major reforms in 1966–1967 did not produce immediate success, and some were withdrawn, including the autonomy of enterprises in making decisions about labour and investment. Some ministries gained decision-making power to self-finance, but others did not. Punishment for the failure of these reforms to deliver was the return of mandatory targets. However, the organisational approach to reform remained in effect for the entire Soviet era and was codified in a major decree of 1979.[1] Another round of Kosygin reforms in 1973 further attempted to weaken the powers and functions of the central ministries by establishing associations at the republic and local level of government so that enterprises cooperate with each other in regard to technology, innovation, and education. Most treatments emphasise inefficiencies within the Soviet planned economy, which persist despite reform, as leading to the fall in Soviet GDP. Prolonged recession, along with other political factors eventually caused the break-up of the Soviet Union.

4.5.3 *The Performance of the Late Soviet Economy*

The Soviet centralised economy throughout this period experienced a slowing rate of growth, a falling rate of return on investment, dragging improvement of the technological level of the capital stock, and poor quality of design, which affected consumption and exports. The total factor productivity (land, labour, and capital inputs) slipped from an annual growth of 1.7% between 1928 and

---

[1] Schroeder (1979) refers to government activity in this period as a 'treadmill of reforms'.

1940 to 0.0% from 1970 to 1975 and -0.5% from 1980 to 1985 (Allen, 2001, p. 862).

The Soviet government had achieved recognition as a world superpower under Brezhnev in the mid-1970s, attaining nuclear parity with the United States. But economic performance continued to deteriorate, while reforms increased rather than decreased bureaucracy, which interfered with decision-making and cost savings. There was no evidence of a relationship between plan indicators and incentive funds or between effort and reward. External concerns from 1971 to 1979 applied further pressure for reforms: windfall gains as the rise in oil and gold prices allowed the importation with those funds of a significant amount of goods and services. However, by the 1980s, the prices of oil and gas were falling, and the economy experienced windfall losses, which made imports of goods and services, as the dollar strengthened, more costly. The terms of trade with the Eastern bloc countries were affected as those states became deeply indebted. They were paying the costs of the rising Soviet energy prices in 1975 as energy importers, and they had borrowed extensively in hard currency to secure technology imports. While rising prices led to pressures for economic change in Eastern bloc countries, the Soviet invasion of Afghanistan in December 1979 postponed reform considerations in the Soviet Union.

4.5.4 *The Period of Gorbachev's Perestroika (1986–1991)*

The continued inefficiency of the command economic system showed that past achievements of military and industrial objectives by means of mobilising new resources, as in collectivisation, was no longer an adequate model for growth. The system could not deliver advances in computer technology, modernise consumer goods industries, or improve the productivity of agriculture to the level found in advanced market economies. The administrative reforms from 1965 and in the 1970s had not succeeded. There was an increase in dysfunctional behaviour at the firm level, obvious waste in low-quality output, declining economic growth and productivity, and too frequent failures to achieve planned goals. A surge of interest in reform brought to power a key reformer, Mikhail Gorbachev, a lawyer, originally from a poor peasant family in Stavropol Krai and an admirer of Khrushchev's de-Stalinization. Widely considered one of the most significant figures of the second half of the twentieth century for his role in foreign affairs in bringing the Cold War to an end, for which he received the Nobel Peace Prize, his domestic reforms were sweeping. He introduced '*glasnost*' (openness)—increased openness and transparency in government institutions and activities, allowing Soviet citizens to discuss publicly the problems of their system and potential solutions. He spoke on open radio, for example, about the Chernobyl disaster in 1986, its causes and consequences. He called for the creation of a modern industrial base equal to any in the West, the elevation of living standards, and the provision of strong defence during a period of rapid technological change.

Gorbachev called his economic reforms *'perestroika'* (reconstruction), a term that showed their base in the human factor, to tighten political discipline, in the technological modernisation of industry, and in the acceleration of growth. A steady and rapid rate of growth was anticipated by the year 2000: net material product (NMP) growth (utilised) would be about 3.2% per year during 1981–1985, 3.5–4.1% during 1986–1989, and then 5.0–5.3% in the 1990s (Hewett, 1991, p. 8). For human factor development, he focused on campaigns against corruption, drunkenness, and illegal economic activity. For example, he led an anti-alcohol campaign in 1986, which reduced alcohol production by about 40%, raised the legal drinking age from 18 to 21, and prohibited its sale before 2 pm. The costs to the economy were enormous, leading to the cessation of this campaign in 1988; however, crime rates fell and life expectancy rose slightly from 1986 to 1987, and there was some per capita productivity increase. In 1987, he introduced a 'new economic mechanism' and a law on State Enterprise giving considerable scope in decision-making to enterprises. The law embraced enterprise self-financing, wholesale trade, a change in the banking and credit system, wage reforms, and ministerial reorganisation. Gosplan's place was reduced to long-term goal setting; everyday operations would be handled at the enterprise level. Another major reform in the new economic mechanism was the 1988 law allowing independent worker-owned cooperatives to operate alongside state cooperatives to encourage the private sector. This law resulted in the start of significant agrarian reform, allowing the exodus of small farmers from the collectives.

The results were not promising. Some improvement in the economy was shown in 1986, but growth stalled in 1987–1988 with declines in farm output and in the construction and transportation sectors. *'Perestroika'* did not succeed in overcoming institutional inertia in high technology machine-building sector. Moreover, having abandoned the former administrative controls, autonomy in spending led the macroeconomic imbalances to deepen in a soaring state budget deficit, and the volume of inter-enterprise credit and the growth of money flowing to the population in their incomes after 1988 brought about inflationary pressures (see Chapter 16). In 1989, incomes in the population rose by almost 13% as goods and services rose far more slowly. Shortages were pervasive. Noren (1991, p. 376) summarises the results of 5 years of Gorbachev's economic leadership:

> 'bad luck, bad policies, half measures, the emergence of ethnic turmoil on an unimaged scale, an erosion in popular morale [...] developments in Eastern Europe, and tenacious opposition within the lower reaches of the bureaucracy.'

The collapse of the Soviet Union in 1991 occurred as a consequence of the disintegration of its sovereignty over Soviet republics, as the government moved towards partially free elections and the establishment of a new assembly in December 1988, the first Congress of People's Deputies of the Soviet Union. The Soviet republics held parliamentary elections in March

1990, and the CPSU party lost in six of them. Estonia, Latvia, and Lithuania were the first to leave the Soviet Union in August 1991; most of the others, including the Russian Federation, declared their sovereignty during 1990–1991. To stop this movement from ending the regime in Moscow, there was a coup attempt in August 1991, when communist hardliners and military elites tried to overthrow Gorbachev, but it was defeated by massive protests in Moscow and across the country and ended after 3 days. The CPSU was delegalized and pro-independence movements in the Soviet republics gained momentum. On 25 December 1991, President Gorbachev resigned; this date marks the end of the Soviet Union. Boris Yeltsin, the first president of the Russian Federation, launched market-oriented reforms (with the Deputy Prime Minister Yegor Gaidar as their main architect) as of November 1991.

In summary, the period of Gorbachev's *'perestroika'* brought about the gradual demise of the command system of central planning and, eventually, the collapse of the Soviet Union in 1991.

Questions for Students
1. Why did the considerable accomplishments of the NEP not meet the objectives of many in the Communist Party in the late 1920s?
2. Why did the long-term slowdown of economic growth lead to the collapse of the central planning system?
3. Did Gorbachev's *perestroika* go well beyond the Kosygin reforms?

References

Allen, R. C. (2001). The rise and decline of the Soviet economy. *Canadian Journal of Economics, 34,* 859–881.
Bornstein, M. (2019). *The Soviet economy: Continuity and change.* Routledge.
Ericson, R. E. (1991). The classical Soviet-type economy: Nature of the system and implications for reform. *Journal of Economic Perspectives, 5*(4), 11–27.
Gatrell, P., & Davies, R. W. (1990). The Industrial Economy. In R. W. Davies (Ed.), *From tsarism to the new economic policy: Continuity and change in the economy of the USSR* (pp. 127–159). Springer.
Gregory, P. (1990). National Income. In R. W. Davies (Ed.), *From tsarism to the new economic policy: Continuity and change in the economy of the USSR* (pp. 237–337). Springer.
Harrison, M. (1990). The Peasantry and Industrialization. In R. W. Davies (Ed.), *From tsarism to the new economic policy: Continuity and change in the economy of the USSR* (pp. 104–124). Springer.
Harrison, M. (2017). Foundations of the Soviet command economy, 1917 to 1941. In S. Pons and S. Smith (Eds.), *The Cambridge history of communism* (Vol. 1, pp. 327–347). Cambridge University Press.
Hewett, E. (1991). Gorbachev's Economic strategy: A preliminary assessment. In E. A. Hewett & V. H. Winston (Eds.), *Milestones in Glasnost and Perestroyka: The economy* (pp. 5–22). Brookings Institution.

Maddison, A, (1995). *Monitoring the world economy, 1820–1992*, OECD.
Maddison A (2001). *The world economy: A millennial perspective*. OECD.
Noren, J. H. (1991). The economic crisis: Another Perspective. In E. A. Hewett & V. H. Winston (Eds.), *Milestones in Glasnost and Perestroyka: The economy* (pp. 360–407). Brookings Institution.
Ofer, G. (1987). Soviet economic growth: 1928–1985. *Journal of Economic Literature, 25*(4), 1767–1833.
Schroeder, G. E. (1979). The Soviet economy on a treadmill of reforms. In *Soviet economy in a time of change: A compendium of papers* (Vol. 1, pp. 312–340). Gov. Printing Off.

PART III

Institutions and Their Transformation

CHAPTER 5

Constitutional Foundations of the Post-communist Russian Economy and the Role of the State

Christopher A. Hartwell

Highlights

- The legal basis of the market economy in Russia is the 1993 Constitution and the 1995 Civil Code.
- Both documents have been amended since being originally introduced to reflect political changes in the country.
- In most instances, the original strong legal protections have been watered down to make room for political decisions.
- The changes in Russia's legal regime regarding the market economy have, thus, allowed for much more room for state intervention than were desired by reformers in the early 1990s.

C. A. Hartwell (✉)
ZHAW School of Management and Law, Winterthur, Switzerland
e-mail: christopher.hartwell@zhaw.ch

Kozminski University, Warsaw, Poland

© The Author(s), under exclusive license to Springer Nature Switzerland AG 2023
M. Dabrowski (ed.), *The Contemporary Russian Economy*,
https://doi.org/10.1007/978-3-031-17382-0_5

5.1 Introduction

The transition from communism to capitalism with the fall of the Soviet Union at the end of 1991 was accomplished via a multi-faceted approach involving the change of legal norms, institutional orderings and functions (Hartwell, 2013), and, of course, personalities in power. Of these, the most basic and fundamental was the reorientation in the authorising framework for the newly independent Russian Federation, away from one guarding communist tenets and towards one which facilitated a market economy. In particular, the shift in the Russian Constitution and in the institutions charged with enforcing its provisions (including the executive, legislative, and judicial branches) created a sea change in economic relations within Russia, legalising natural rights which, for decades, had been officially illegal under the Soviet legal framework.

However, the Constitution also had a goal to set the rules of the federal system, defining the rights and responsibilities of republics, territories, and regions (federal entities) against the prerogatives of the federal government. This construction of a new series of political institutions, with new relationships among each other, created a parallel structure for the development of the market economy, one which was meant to support such an evolution but one also with the potential to intrude and/or retard this development. Indeed, while the Constitution outlined a broad set of principles related to the market economy and what was 'allowed' within the borders of the Russian Federation, in many ways it offered an idealised version of economic outcomes. As in every other country, the Constitution represented a starting point for discussion in defining the actual parameters of the role of the state in the economy, a point which would then be hashed out in the political arena and could shift over time due to changing political currents. In the case of Russia, and for most of its post-communist experience, this struggle between the economic foundation of the Constitution and the political apparatus it spawned has resulted in a move away from these economic ideals and towards a subordination under political realities.

This chapter will examine this tension in the Russian post-communist experience, analysing the main provisions of the Constitution and other important legislation related to the market economy (such as the Civil Code) that determine the shape of the economic system in Russia and how it affects its implementation in practice. Specifically, we will focus on the role of the state as envisioned in the legal framework of Russia and how this has evolved since the Russian Federation became independent at the end of 1991. Which is a more accurate representation of the extent of state involvement in the Russian economy: is it the Constitution? Is it the supporting legislation and the institutional structure that the Constitution laid out? Or has it been the political imperatives of the Russian government and the personalities which have been in charge?

5.2 The Move Towards Legalising the Market Economy: Promises and Problems

5.2.1 The Constitution and the Civil Code

The Russian legal framework writ large consists of several authorising pieces of legislation, including, most prominently, the Constitution of 1993 (*Konstitutsiya Rossiyskoy Federatsii, Prinyata vsenarodnym golosovaniyem 12 Dekabrya 1993*). The Constitution is the supreme law throughout the territory of Russia, supplemented by Federal Constitutional Laws (FCL) adopted on constitutional issues, decrees of the President, and decisions of state authorities. As noted above, the Constitution also sets out the structure of the Russian government, dividing authority across the executive, legislative, and judicial branches, with Chapter 5 outlining the legislative bodies of the Russian Federation; similar to democracies elsewhere around the world, the legislative framework which was created under the Constitution's aegis is primarily determined by the legislative branch (the State Duma), although (especially under President Vladimir Putin) this has not precluded close coordination between the legislative and executive branches (and, to some extent, the judiciary as well). As can be expected from a document that is primarily political, the overall purpose of the Constitution is to elucidate basic principles but more concisely to lay out the functions and structure of the Russian state.

It is crucial to note, however, that the 1993 Constitution was conceived during a protracted political struggle in Russia, specifically between President Boris Yeltsin and the legislative branch, centred on one of the most important issues about the structure of the Russian state: the distribution of power across the various branches. The legal reality of the validity of the Constitution of the Russian Soviet Federative Socialist Republic (RSFSR) after 1991—and the ambiguities attached to the lack of an immediate replacement—inhibited necessary measures to move forward, in both the political and economic sphere. In particular, despite the reality of the Soviet Union having highly centralised power (and in particular in the executive), the Constitution from 1977 on paper at least had a much more balanced delegation of authority between the legislative and the executive branch (Osakwe, 1979). This constraint on the democratically elected administration of Boris Yeltsin (and the uncertainty regarding what could be done) was found to be intolerable from the point of view of the executive, and many times in 1992, the Yeltsin administration simply set aside the Soviet Constitution and acted in unilateral ways (Kubicek, 1994). The infighting between Yeltsin and the Congress of Peoples' Deputies and Supreme Council came to a head with Yeltsin's 'presidential coup' in 1993, culminating in the shelling of the White House and a victory in the constitutional referendum of 12 December 1993 (Roeder, 1994). The result of these events was the enhancement of the power of the Presidency and the executive in the Russian political system, a reality that was enshrined in the 1993 Constitution and (as we will see) would have ramifications for the future of the market economy.

But from the vantage point of 1993, and specifically focused on the economy and its regulation, the Constitution of 1993 was a massive positive change from the previous foundational document from the Soviet Union, the 1977 Constitution of the Union of Soviet Socialist Republics (USSR) and RSFSR. Itself a third revision of the Soviet Constitution (previous versions were approved in 1924 and 1936), the 1977 Constitution of the USSR and RSFSR continued to define economic relations as a function of the collective, recognising 'social property' (but not private property) as the basis of the socialist system. By contrast, the Constitution of 1993, as the aggregation of fundamental principles of the Russian Federation, acknowledges the principles (on paper at least) of what is necessary for a successful open market economy, repudiating the *'supremacy of the fundamental principles of the socialist state order [democratic centralism, socialist legality, absence of protection of private property...]'* of the Soviet order (Kalinichenko & Kochenov, 2021, p. 342).

Instead, the Constitution of 1993 focused on the basic principles required for a functioning market economy, laid out most clearly in Articles 8 and 9: Article 8 explicitly provides for the free flow of goods, services, and capital within the territory of the Russian Federation, as well as outlining 'support for competition' within the framework of economic relations. Perhaps more importantly, Article 9(2) establishes the right of private property ownership, a right further enhanced by Article 35 (which also prohibits takings of private property without a court decision and guarantees the right of inheritance), but with provisions that ownership of land and other natural resources by state and municipal authorities is still allowed. Finally, Article 34 of the Constitution explicitly carves out a space for the private sector, upholding the right of Russian citizens to engage in entrepreneurial activity as long as they are not engaged in activities aimed at monopolisation.

Enforcing the Constitution of 1993 was entrusted to the Constitutional Court of the Russian Federation, a judicial body that actually was founded before the Soviet Union fell (in July 1991) and, thus, for two and a half years of its existence was meant to oversee the implementation of the 1977 Constitution. Given its reliance on an antiquated document—and a major part in the power struggle between the executive and the legislative branches after the fall of the Soviet Union—Russian President Boris Yeltsin suspended the Constitutional Court in late 1993, before the new Constitution came into being. Legal experts were intimately involved in making sure that the Court was part of the Constitutional process, in order to avoid legislative changes after the fact, and the Court received impressive powers to issue legally binding interpretations of the Constitution (Trochev, 2008). However, being included in the protracted process of the Constitution meant that it was not until 1994 that a new Act authorising the organisational creation of the Court was passed, and the Court itself began operations again only in 1995 (and a further law in 1996 allowed for the creation of courts at the local level).

Following the Constitution in 1995 was a more detail-oriented and legalistic document, the Civil Code of the Russian Federation, replacing the antiquated 1964 Civil Code of the Soviet Union. The new Civil Code laid out the legal basis for protecting the principles that the Constitution affirmed and could be thought of as (in the words of Boris Yeltsin) the 'economic constitution' of the country, displaying a shift towards building a distinct legal culture regarding economic activities and enshrining in legal practice and norms the foundations of the market economy. In this regard, the Civil Code went even further than the Constitution in affirming the rights of entrepreneurs, with much of the document '*carv[ing] out major areas of economic activity to be decided by the private parties to a transaction, free from state interference*' (Blumenfeld, 1996, p. 479). An example of this is Article 209, which explicitly referred to the right of land ownership ('*The owner possesses the rights to hold, to use, and to dispose of his property*'), whereas elsewhere in the document as enacted in 1995, there are stipulations regarding private contracts and prohibitions against state interference stronger than even in some Western countries at the time (Lametti, 2005); most importantly, perhaps (and with an eye on the political struggle between the Duma and the President), was the supremacy clause of the Code, which stipulated that legislation or executive decrees could not be used to alter the Code, but instead the actual text of the Code itself needed to be amended. Any legislation that was thus in conflict with the code was null and void unless the Code was changed to allow for it (Blumenfeld, 1996).

In many ways, the key attribute of both the Constitution of 1993 and the Civil Code of 1995 was to signify a historic break with the past of modern Russia and lay the foundation for a new market economy. By starting with the basic documents of a legal framework, Russian reformers hoped to break the personal and transactional approach to the law which had dominated under the Soviet Union, where the rule of law did not exist, and laws were applied according to the whims of the Communist Party (Hendley, 1997). This 'top-down' approach found favour with international advisors who were eager to build the institutions necessary for Russia's market transition (Boycko & Shleifer, 1995) and was also welcomed by Russian policymakers, who saw such enshrinement of principles as a relatively quick way to build acceptance of the market economy. Although many of the basic policies for transition had already been underway by the time the Constitution was approved (see below), it was hoped that the creation of a coherent legal commitment to the market economy would allow for its rapid development. Moreover, by rolling into the legislative changes the institutional foundations for the legal profession and the judiciary in an independent Russian Federation, it was also hoped that the judiciary would become another guarantor of rule of law.

5.2.2 The Problem of Delay

The specific Articles in the Constitution dealing with private property and entrepreneurship came about as part of the general debates on the Constitution's protections but were also affected by the prevailing economic climate at the time. As noted, the economic transformation of Russia on the basis of private property had begun already in earnest in 1992, even without the foundational laws present. While macroeconomic stabilisation was a prerequisite for transition, the long road to stabilisation was accompanied by a broader programme of privatisation to undercut the power of state-owned enterprises (SOEs) and build up a nascent private sector.

The efficacy of Russia's privatisation programme has been debated vigorously in the economics literature and will be discussed more in-depth in Chapter 7. Observing the privatisation debate in terms of the overall enabling environment for property rights, and especially with regard to legal protection of property rights, for many firms, ownership had been transferred but many of the issues related to the operation and position of these industrial behemoths had not been resolved. More importantly, the legal framework regarding property was still absent and, without a coherent set of legal protections, competition could not flourish to erode the power of these large firms. Political scientist Michael McFaul (1995, p. 210) noted that '*by the summer of 1993, insiders had acquired majority shares in two-thirds of Russia's privatized and privatizing firms...little if any restructuring (bankruptcies, downsizing, unbundling) had taken place within enterprises, and few market institutions had been created.*' But even though these firms had been moved to private hands, subsidies continued to be a major part of the Russian budget (still at 10.74% of gross domestic product [GDP] by the end of 1993, according to the World Bank—see Freinkman & Haney, 1997). More importantly, the lack of explicitly delineated formal property rights meant that informal property rights generated during the late Soviet period at the worker and industrial level made restructuring difficult (Sachs, 1992); charges of asset stripping and looting of public investments for private gains were made in firms which were not privatised (Shleifer & Treisman, 2005).

The Russian government's inability to generate the legal protections for property rights in the interim between the fall of the Soviet Union and 1993, combined with the misplaced focus on garnering more powers for the executive (while de-prioritising the need to replace the 1977 Constitution), made such sweeping provisions for protecting the market economy in the 1993 Constitution both necessary and somewhat unrealistic. At the time that the Constitution was under formation, interests opposed to reform had already become entrenched and powerful in their opposition to the President, meaning that much of the protections offered were already being eroded in reality (Trochev, 2008). Entrenched interests within SOEs supported keeping firms state-owned, while the existence of opposition in the Duma related to discredited ideologies (above all, the Communists) impeded swift legalisation of fundamental economic institutions from 1992 to 1993. The Communists also found unlikely but willing allies from the oligarchs, the new titans of industry who had started to acquire assets before the Soviet Union fell and who had consolidated their positions afterwards. In an influential paper in 2003, Konstantin Sonin argued that the Russian transition had created a class of the economy (the oligarchs), which actively opposed broad-based property rights. The reasoning was that the oligarchs had achieved a sufficient level of rights to protect their own property (whether through wealth acquisition, rent-seeking, or political activity) and had no need for functioning economic institutions which may threaten their own rent streams (Sonin, 2003).

This reality meant that the guiding legislation under these broader principles (the Civil Code) was also incredibly delayed, not being proposed until 1994 and enacted only in 1995; this long delay meant that the small window of reform available to remove many Soviet-era institutions had closed and, instead, the political compromises and obstruction which had occurred in the interim were actually codified.[1] This could be seen most clearly in the lack of progress on broad-based property rights, as the protections offered by the Constitution and Civil Code required a new Land Code to become effective. However, the existing Land Code at the time of the passing of the Constitution *'allowed regions to decide questions of land ownership, and at least 10 regions had land laws that did not recognize private ownership of land as late as 1995'* (Wegren, 2012, p. 195). It was not until 2001—and a new Presidential regime—that a land code was actually passed (see below), and it too was a reflection of this delay.

5.3 When Politics and Economics Clash: The Period After 2000

The delay between the end of the Soviet Union and the creation of a new set of legislation to govern the transformation was problematic but not fatal for Russia's transition; however, married with the emphasis on increasing executive power, it was to create a myriad of difficulties for the development of economic institutions in the country. The ramifications of this early neglect are still felt today, especially when one considers the relative weight that politics and economics have in the Russian system under President Vladimir Putin.

As Semyakin (2021, p. 16) noted regarding the body of Russian law, *'property relations are regulated by various laws that are quite contradictory.'* Indeed, there were contradictions within the Constitution (noted above) on private property but, more problematic was a myriad of caveats included in the Civil Code, which could then be utilised to infringe on economic rights. For example, in Article 1 of the Civil Code, there is a stipulation that *'civil rights*

---

[1] Polish economist and former Finance Minister Leszek Balcerowicz called this time after a crisis or during a transition, 'extraordinary politics' (Balcerowicz, 1995) where there is only a small window to get transformative reforms passed.

may be restricted on the basis of the Federal Law and only to the extent to which it shall be necessary for the purposes of protecting the foundations of the constitutional system, morality, the health, the rights and the lawful interests of other persons, of providing for the defence of the country and for the state security.' This broad exception for matters of state security (which is not defined) may then allow for all forms of transgressions by the state, including especially confiscation of property due to legal infractions (Article 243 of the Civil Code). Additional stipulations on expropriation for public needs in the Code and follow-on legislation (including the Land Code of 2001, see below) have also created an expansive allowance for state interference (Kosareva et al., 2018).

Indeed, these caveats and hedges created a hole to allow the state back into the Russian economy, and this has been the case in Russia since 1999, when an ailing President Yeltsin appointed Vladimir Putin as his Prime Minister and then stepped aside at the end of the year, making Putin the President. Although Yeltsin had been associated with liberal economic reforms, he was also forever linked to the financial crisis of 1998 (see Chapter 16). The political atmosphere after the crisis was not favourable for future market-based reforms, and the nomination of Yevgeny Primakov as Prime Minister led to a number of restrictive measures (including on foreign currency) and selected bank bailouts (Vavilov, 2010).

Following Yeltsin's resignation, Putin appeared to push forward on some salutary economic reforms, reclaiming the liberal mantle from its post-1998 nadir. During Putin's first term from 2000 to 2004, the government instituted a proportional personal income tax of 13% and pushed through some of the long-delayed legislation needed in the country, including the Land Code in 2001 and a joint stock company law (Desai, 2005). Early moves from Putin in the economy also took on the power of the oligarchs (highly unpopular because of 1998), but as a way to remove potential political rivals rather than to demonstrate an explicitly pro-market orientation: the case of businessmen such as Mikhail Khodorkovsky marked a move in Putin's reign away from the rule of law, breaking the economic power of the oligarchs (a popular move in theory) by using questionable means (Goldman, 2004).

These initial economic policies by Putin were soon shelved by Putin's second term in favour of a rapid change on the legal front, with three separate series of comprehensive amendments to the Constitution occurring at the end of Putin's second term and during his third and fourth terms. The Constitution had been amended several times before Putin came to power and even during his first two terms, with changes in 1996, 2001, 2003, 2004, 2005, 2006, and 2007; however, these changes were focused exclusively on Article 65 of the Constitution, i.e., the Article that regulates the structure of the Federation, and most of these changes were just name changes as sub-national territories were changed (Petersen & Levin, 2016).

By contrast, the set of Constitutional changes in 2008 was focused on removing constraints to the executive, extending the term of the President to 6 years (and the Duma's terms to 5 years) and amending Articles 81 and 96 of the Constitution concerned with these terms. The changes were instituted mainly with an eye on Vladimir Putin's return to power but also signalled an important shift away from the legislative oversight of the Duma, bringing all legislative power within the executive (an argument has been made that the continued legalism of Russia during this period was merely a case of intra-executive rivalries rather than actual legislation, see Noble, 2020). In short, the amendments of 2008 were in line with the many earlier changes to the Constitution but signalled a move towards moving beyond merely Article 65 and changing other sections of the Constitution if they stood in the way of greater executive power.

This effect could be seen in the second sweeping set of Constitutional amendments that occurred in 2014, building on the 2008 changes and allowing for massive changes outside of the political system. While the 2014 amendments allowed for the President to appoint 10% of the membership of the Federation Council (the upper house of the Russian parliament, now known as the Senate) directly, the changes in the overall judicial system were more consequential. In particular, the Supreme Arbitrage Court was abolished, removing the institutional mechanism which was utilised exclusively for commercial disputes; this change made the Supreme Court of the Russian Federation the final venue for commercial cases (as well, as of August 2014, the final court for criminal, administrative, and military cases), a substantial institutional reorientation which placed considerable power in the Supreme Court's hands. Unlike previous amendments, these far-reaching changes meant substantive alterations throughout the Constitution, including Articles 71, 83, 102, 104, and 125 through 129 (Petersen & Levin, 2016). Finally, in line with earlier amendments to the Constitution, Article 65 was also altered to include the 'Republic of Crimea' and the 'city of federal importance Sevastopol' into the Russian Federation after their annexation.

The final set of changes, in 2020, has perhaps been the most controversial, as it allowed President Putin to claim a clean slate on his term limits and allowed him to serve for two additional terms (removing the stipulation that a President could not serve more than two terms in a row). The shift in the Federation Council begun in 2014 also continued in 2020, with the creation of up to 30 senate positions appointed by the President and the addition of 'former Presidents' to the Senate. In tandem with this further expansion of Presidential power into the legislature, the Constitutional amendments of 2020 also included economic points explicitly for the first time. Unlike other countries, which keep their constitutions limited to broader economic and political principles, Russia's Constitution now includes a mandate to index pensions to inflation and outlines the floor of the country's minimum wage (i.e., not lower than the subsistence minimum as defined by the Russian State Statistics Service [Rosstat]). These moves were widely seen as a way to secure popular support for the whole package of amendments.

Perhaps much more consequential than merely enshrining a particular person in power or raising the minimum wage, the amendments of 2020 also expanded the power of the Federation Council (and, in reality, the President) over the judiciary. A key provision in the amendments was to allow for the Council to propose to the President that specific judges may be removed, while further powers allowed for the Council to remove judges from the highest bodies (i.e., the Supreme and Constitutional Courts) on the recommendation of the President. This violation of the tenets of judicial independence thus meant that judges across the judiciary served at the leisure of the President, and any missteps (as perceived by the Kremlin) could end in removal. This power was indeed used by the Kremlin in the wake of the Constitutional amendments becoming law in July 2020, as by November 2020, two out of seven deputy chairs of the Supreme Court were replaced, the Prosecutor General was replaced, and all three major investigation chiefs in the government (in the Federal Security Service [FSB], the Ministry of Internal Affairs, and the Investigative Committee of the Russian Federation) were also summarily replaced (Noble & Petrov, 2021).

Similarly, changes have been made to the Civil Code and other supporting legislation regarding economic relations within the Russian Federation. For example, the Land Code was passed in 2001 and was (in theory) meant to further define the relations of property rights and their protection, as noted in both the Constitution and the Civil Code. However, given the continued opposition to expansive private property rights evidenced by the Duma, the compromise Land Code that was actually enacted only applied to approximately 2% of all of the land within the Russian Federation (Kratzke, 2003). As in other countries in the former Soviet Union (FSU), principally Ukraine and Kazakhstan, the Land Code prohibited foreigners from owning agricultural land, as well as owning land 'near state borders'. Further amendments to the Land Code, including an approved change in 2013 and a package introduced in 2014, waded further into the legal definitions of 'land plots' but, more importantly, established procedures for expropriation of private land by governmental agencies. With reference to the 2013 amendment, a procedure was introduced for remission of property rights if there was found to be 'improper utilisation of the land', a broad category that also covered agricultural land and that detailed more about how property rights could be lost than how they would be protected. This 'land use restriction' was also the basis of the 'Far-Eastern Hectare Law (FEHL)', passed by the Russian government in 2016 to encourage settlement in the Far Eastern regions of the country. Under the FEHL, any Russian citizen could apply for and receive for free one hectare of federal or republican land in these regions, similar to the Homestead Act of 1862 in the United States. However (and despite protests against the giving away of land in the Sakha Republic, the largest republic in terms of territory), the law made it clear that the land rights would be revoked if significant improvements to the land had not been undertaken within 5 years (Belolyubskaya, 2021). In tandem with the political issues presented by the law (including the ability of regions to define their own property rights regimes), the FEHL once again underlined how vast swathes of Russian territory are seen as the property of the state, to give and take away as needed.

5.3.1 The Russian Economy Under Putin

Much as with the early years of the Constitution, the changes in the legal framework in Russia starting in 2008 merely followed the reality that had developed in the country, where the state had already begun its re-assertion of power over the economy. Richard Sakwa saw this happening already after the first two terms of Putin:

> Russia today is characterized by two competing political orders. The first is the constitutional state, regulated by law and enshrining the normative values of the democratic movement of the late Soviet period and contemporary liberal democracies, populated by political parties, parliament, and representative movements and regulated by electoral and associated laws. The second is the administrative regime, which has emerged as a tutelary order standing outside the normative state although not repudiating its principles. (Sakwa, 2010, p. 185)

Similarly, as Oversloot (2007) presciently noted in a legal article, Putin had used the Russian government from his first and second administration to help re-order Russian society, undercutting the Constitution via other means and expanding the prerogatives of the state *vis a vis* other actors in the country. Given this state of affairs, the Constitutional changes noted above were done to codify the facts on the ground rather than to enable a shift in the balance of power between state and society. In reality, formal changes were only created to make Russia's path to 'superpresidentialism' irrevocable (Fish, 2000).

It is important to recognise at this point that, like during the Constitutional crisis of 1993, the changes done under Putin's third and fourth terms as President did not specifically concern the economy and/or the relationship of the state to the economy. Putin has actually appeared to not be overly concerned with state intervention in the economy as a principle or ideological tenet; however, the emphasis on expanding the power of the executive to become *primus inter pares* has resulted in powers aggregated to the President which can be utilised within the economy as well as within civil society. For example, the move towards direct appointments of regional governors in 2004 was a way to centralise power over regional initiatives within the Kremlin, but it also allowed for a move towards homogeneous policies rather than allowing Russian regions the freedom to experiment. At the same time, given that businesses had expanded into the regions and were able to make inroads in building a viable private sector outside of Moscow in the 1990s, re-centralisation also took away the leverage business had to restrain the powers of the governors (Orttung, 2004).

This is precisely what has happened since the interregnum of Dimitry Medvedev as President (with Prime Minister Vladimir Putin) from 2008 to 2012, as the return of Putin to the Presidency in 2012 heralded additional involvement of the state in the economy. Whereas the Constitution and the Civil Code spoke of principles regarding the rights of individuals to engage in entrepreneurship, the Russian government since the global financial crisis (2008–2009) has been more involved in the ways in which the government itself can propel the economy. 'Mega-projects' such as the Sochi Olympics in 2014 allowed for private participation but had goals set exclusively by the government, not only encouraging economic development but built around a narrative of 'Russian greatness' (Mueller, 2011). In this manner, the state utilised the levers given to it by successive waves of expansion of executive power to harness the economy (and, by extension, to direct it) in a way which comported with overall political and geopolitical goals.

The results of this approach can be seen in the aggregate economic statistics on the state's role in the economy and also, particularly, in the structure of the economy. Since 2012, and especially since the imposition of sanctions by the West for Russia's annexation of Crimea in 2014 and continued direct involvement in Ukraine's Donbas region (see Chapter 14), the Russian economy has become far less diversified and far more controlled by the state. First, the economic downturn in the mid-2010s caused by the decline of the world price of oil and given further impetus by Western sanctions after 2014 did little to spur on diversification of the Russian economy, leaving it heavily dependent upon the energy sector (see Chapters 8, 9, 15, and 16) and, in particular, the energy giants (closely overseen by the political authorities).

In line with these trends has been an increase in the federal government's expenditures in the economy, although this has also been tied to revenues and the world price of oil. As Fig. 5.1 shows, federal government expenditures shrank after the imposition of sanctions in 2014, but have been on an upward trajectory ever since, remaining within the 18% of GDP range in the post-2014 era. These broad macroeconomic aggregates obscure just how much of a hand the state has in the microeconomics of firms, however, by not including state-run companies and their expenditures. A paper by Abramov et al. (2017) notes that, over 2006–2014, the state became involved either directly or indirectly with 52.5% of the Russian economy (with only 47.5% of the economy fully privately owned), while Radygin and Abramov (Chapter 7) show that, as of 2020, the state still comprised 51.1% of GDP in Russia. The International Monetary Fund (IMF) also concurred with these assessments, noting that employment in Russian state organs has grown to 50% of all employment, with a formal footprint of the Russian state of approximately 40% of the economy; more problematic was the fact that both state-owned enterprises were less efficient than their private counterparts *and* the pervasiveness of the government skewed incentives even in sectors where they were not directly involved, leading to high levels of concentration in the private sector as well

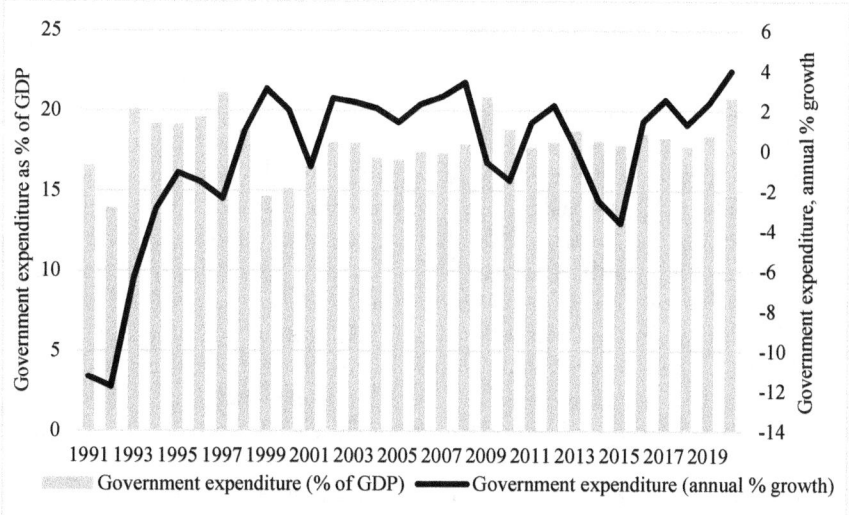

Fig. 5.1 Federal Government expenditures as % of GDP and annual growth, in %, 1991–2020 (*Source* World Bank World Development Indicators)

(Di Bella et al., 2019). With the legal protections provided for state intervention into the economy, the state has enthusiastically utilised these precisely to intervene.

5.4 The Future of the State in the Russian Economy

The reform of the legal regime in post-Soviet Russia was originally predicated on making a break with the recent Soviet past, enshrining the tenets of the new market economy in the foundational documents of the country. However, as this chapter has shown, the development of the market economy could never be divorced from the process of political wrangling after the USSR, and indeed much of the economic development of the Russian Federation has been subsumed under this very wrangling. From early attempts to define the role of the executive in the economy to more recent moves to expand the powers of the President, define national champions, and bring the 'commanding heights' of the economy under closer state supervision, there has been a consistent struggle of politics against economics and a clear victory of politics in this struggle.

The growth of executive power has continued unabated due to an issue that has been observed in Russia and elsewhere: legal institutions do not have enough gravitas or heft to be able to protect the market economy or even the rule of law on their own (Hartwell & Urban, 2021). Unlike the lawyers and legal experts who believed that the formal recognition of the Constitutional

Court in the Constitution of 1993 would guarantee its independence from political turbulence (Trochev, 2008), the reality has been that the executive has been able to shape the legal landscape, first by decree, second by erosion of institutional norms, and finally by changing the foundational documents related to the legal sector. In many ways, the gradual changing of norms has forced the judiciary to acquiesce in the expansion of the power of the state and made it unable to push back. Concerning themselves with narrow interpretations of the law and increasingly side-lined as a force for judicial review, the 2020 amendments to the Constitution '*officially politiciz[ed] and instrumentaliz[ed] the Court for the president's benefit, marking a significant departure from the previous institutional development*' (Grigoriev, 2021, p. 21).

What this reality bodes for the future of the state in the Russian economy is not optimistic. There is a wealth of economic evidence on the relationship between executive constraints and economic development, with unconstrained executives correlated highly negatively with growth trajectories (Besley & Mueller, 2018). The changes in the legal framework in Russia over the past 30 years have shifted the balance decisively towards fewer executive constraints, and this has already resulted in subpar economic performance for the country; Russia was facing an economic downturn even before the Western sanctions following the annexation of Crimea in 2014 (see Chapter 14), and the rigidity of the state-interventionist model has kept its growth paths low as executive constraints have been lowered (Fig. 5.2).

An additional two points must be noted here with regard to the role of the state in the economy. Political scientists often speak of the issue of 'state capacity', i.e., the ability of a government and/or bureaucracy to be able to implement its preferred policies. The Russian government has consistently shown low state capacity, with overall bureaucratic quality within the Russian government unable to cope with the executive's desires to play a more prominent role in the economy. According to the International Country Risk Guide (ICRG),[2] a private agency undertakes risk analysis in many countries globally, the 'bureaucratic quality' of Russia has been rated at 1 (the lowest score possible) on a scale from 1 to 4 since August 1997 (prior to 1997, Russian bureaucracy scored a 2 on the same scale). Part of this problem may be the reality of a power imbalance within the Russian government when it comes to political versus economic development. Key ministries such as the Federal Security Service (the Russian language abbreviation FSB), the Ministry of Defence, the Ministry of Justice, and the Ministry of Extraordinary Situations have been steadily growing in power since the return of Vladimir Putin as President in 2012 (Veselova, 2019) and, subsequently, have been increasing their ability to intervene in the economy; for example, expenditures classified as 'national defence' in the Russian government budget rose from RUB 681.8

---

[2] The ICRG is put out by the PRS Group in its International Country Risk Guide Annual Publication. All variable definitions are available at: https://epub.prsgroup.com/list-of-all-variable-definitions.

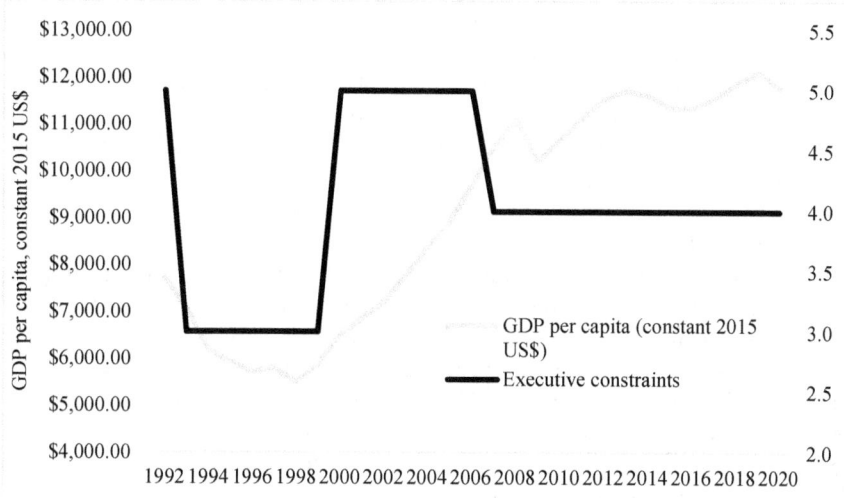

Fig. 5.2 GDP per capita and executive constraints in Russia, 1992–2020 (*Note* Constraints are measured on a scale of 1–7, with lower values indicating lower levels of executive constraints. *Source* World Bank's World Development Indicators database [GDP per capita], the Polity V database ['executive constraints'] [Center for Systemic Peace, 2021, available at https://www.systemicpeace.org/polityproject.html])

billion in 2006 to a peak of RUB 3.775 trillion in 2016 (settling at approximately RUB 3 trillion each year afterwards), a growth of 453%.[3] This move towards militarising the economy and its management (Huskey, 2010) has meant that the traditional economic policymaking organs of the government (including the Ministry of Finance, the Ministry of Economic Development, and the Central Bank of the Russian Federation) have been treated more as technocratic bodies, charged with ensuring macroeconomic stability, rather than gatekeepers of the private sector.

The second point, somewhat related to state capacity, is the issue of corruption (see Chapter 6). The expansion of the powers of the state has also resulted in a shift away from the informal corruption and crime of the 1990s towards more oppressive formal requirements from the state. Indeed, corruption has manifested itself in several political institutions within the Russian government, including public procurement, where political connections are required to help access funding from the government (Belokrylov, 2017; Yakovlev & Demidova, 2012). More importantly, the inability of the judicial system to constrain the executive has led to a widespread perception of corruption and derogation of the rule of law, including the pervasiveness of 'telephone law', where calls

---

[3] Based on numbers from the Ministry of Finance of the Russian Federation (https://minfin.gov.ru/en/statistics/fedbud/?id_65=119255-annual_report_on_exe cution_of_the_federal_budget_starting_from_january_1_2006).

from powerful officials can change the results in a criminal or commercial trial. The weakness of the judiciary and the access to it via corruption have been cited in numerous studies as a hindrance to the economic development of the country (Arslanova, 2012). And with the judiciary removed as a barrier to executive power, it appears that businesses need to treat official corruption as yet another cost for them to operate in Russia.

In sum, the Constitutional order in post-Soviet Russia has shifted from a much more laissez-faire demonstration of principles allied with the market economy towards, as the political winds have shifted, a much more interventionist mentality. At every step of the way, the shift in the legal foundations has trailed the executive's whims, codifying reality rather than setting the framework for a range of outcomes. What happens in a Russia without Vladimir Putin will show if the judiciary and other interested actors—such as businesses and civil society—can claw back the legal foundations of a Russian free market economy, or if the Constitutional basis for the Russian economy will remain dependent on the power of the executive.

Questions for Students

1. Describe, in your own words, the main reason for the new Constitution in 1993.
2. What were the main aspects regarding private property in the 1993 Constitution?
3. What obstacles were there to the Civil Code being passed in an expedient manner?
4. What changes were made to the Constitution in 2008 and 2014?
5. What are the 'two competing orders' in the Russian legal system today?

References

Abramov, A., Radygin, A., & Chernova, M. (2017). State-owned enterprises in the Russian market: Ownership structure and their role in the economy. *Russian Journal of Economics, 3*(1), 1–23.

Arslanova, H. D. (2012). Corruption as a restraining factor of economic development of the region. *Regional problems of economic transformation 4.* https://cyberleninka.ru/article/n/korruptsiya-kak-sderzhivayuschiy-faktor-razvitiya-ekonomiki-regiona

Balcerowicz, L. (1995). *Socialism, Capitalism, Transformation.* Central European University Press.

Belolyubskaya, G. (2021). The Far-Eastern Hectare Law and land in the Sakha Republic (Russia). *Polar Science*, 100683.

Belokrylov, K. A. (2017). Public procurement reform in Russia: Ways to reduce the risk of corruption. *International Journal of Applied Business and Economic Research, 15*(8), 127–139. http://serialsjournals.com/serialjournalmanager/pdf/1495269236.pdf

Besley, T., & Mueller, H. (2018). Institutions, volatility, and investment. *Journal of the European Economic Association, 16*(3), 604–649.

Blumenfeld, L. H. (1996). Russia's new civil code: The legal foundation for Russia's emerging market economy. *International Lawyer, 30*(3), 477–519.

Boycko, M., & Shleifer, A. (1995). Next steps in privatization: Six major challenges. In I. W. Lieberman & J. Nellis (Eds.), *Russia: Creating Private Enterprises and Efficient Markets*. The World Bank.

Center for Systemic Peace. (2021). *Polity V Project*. https://www.systemicpeace.org/polityproject.html

Desai, P. (2005). Russian retrospectives on reforms from Yeltsin to Putin. *Journal of Economic Perspectives, 19*(1), 87–106.

Di Bella, G., Dynnikova, O., & Slavov, S. (2019). The Russian state's size and its footprint: Have they increased? IMF Working Paper, WP19/53. https://www.imf.org/~/media/Files/Publications/WP/2019/WPIEA2019053.ashx

Fish, M. S. (2000). *The executive deception: Superpresidentialism and the degradation of Russian politics*. Routledge.

Freinkman, L., Haney, M. (1997, July 11). What affects the propensity to subsidize: Determinants of budget subsidies and transfers financed by the Russian regional governments in 1992–1995. World Bank Policy Study. https://papers.ssrn.com/sol3/papers.cfm?abstract_id=82048

Goldman, M. I. (2004). Putin and the oligarchs. *Foreign Affairs, 83*(6), 33–44.

Grigoriev, I. S. (2021). What changes for the constitutional court with the new Russian constitution? *Russian Politics, 6*(1) 27–49. https://doi.org/10.30965/24518921-00601003

Hartwell, C. (2013). *Institutional barriers in the transition to market: Examining performance and divergence in transition economies*. Palgrave Macmillan.

Hartwell, C. A., & Urban, M. (2021). Burning the Rechtsstaat: Legal institutions and protection of the rule of law. *Journal of Institutional Economics, 17*(1), 105–131.

Hendley, K. (1997). Legal development in post-Soviet Russia. *Post-Soviet Affairs, 13*(3), 228–251.

Huskey, E. (2010). Elite recruitment and state-society relations in technocratic authoritarian regimes: The Russian case. *Communist and Post-Communist Studies, 43*(4), 363–372.

Kalinichenko, P., & Kochenov, D. (2021). Amendments to the 1993 constitution of the Russian Federation concerning international law. *International Legal Materials, 60*(2), 341–346. https://doi.org/10.1017/ilm.2021.10

Kosareva, N. B., Baykova, T. K., & Polidi, T. D. (2018). Real estate expropriation in Russia: Statutory regulation and enforcement. In F. Plimmer & W. McCluskey (Eds.), *Routledge Handbook of Contemporary Issues in Expropriation* (pp. 298–320). Routledge.

Kratzke, W. P. (2003). Russia's New Land Code: A Two Percent Solution. *Minnesota Journal of International Law, 12*(1), 109–197.

Kubicek, P. (1994). Delegative democracy in Russia and Ukraine. *Communist and Post-Communist Studies, 27*(4), 423–441.

Lametti, D. (2005). Rights of private property in the civil code of the Russian Federation and in the civil code of Quebec. *Review of Central and East European Law, 30*(1), 29–48.

McFaul, M. (1995). State power, institutional change, and the politics of privatization in Russia. *World Politics, 47*(2), 210–243.

Mueller, M. (2011). State dirigisme in megaprojects: Governing the 2014 winter Olympics in Sochi. *Environment and Planning A, 43*(9), 2091–2108.

Noble, B. (2020). Authoritarian amendments: Legislative institutions as intraexecutive constraints in post-Soviet Russia. *Comparative Political Studies, 53*(9), 1417–1454.

Noble, B., & Petrov, N. (2021). From constitution to law: Implementing the 2020 Russian constitutional changes. *Russian Politics, 6*(1), 130–152.

Orttung, R. W. (2004). Business and politics in the Russian regions. *Problems of Post-Communism, 51*(2), 48–60.

Osakwe, C. (1979). The theories and realities of modern Soviet constitutional law: An analysis of the 1977 USSR constitution. *University of Pennsylvania Law Review, 127*(5), 1350–1437.

Oversloot, H. (2007). Reordering the state (without changing the constitution): Russia under Putin's rule, 2000–2008. *Review of Central and East European Law, 32*(1), 41–64.

Petersen, F., Levin, I. (2016). The Russian Federation. In A. Fruhstorfer & M. Hein (Eds.), *Constitutional Politics in Central and Eastern Europe: From Post-Socialist Transition to the Reform of Political Systems* (pp. 519–545). Springer Fachmedien Wiesbaden. https://doi.org/10.1007/978-3-658-13762-5_21

Roeder, P. G. (1994). Varieties of post-Soviet authoritarian regimes. *Post-Soviet Affairs, 10*(1), 61–101.

Sachs, J. D. (1992). Privatization in Russia: Some lessons from Eastern Europe. *The American Economic Review, 82*(2), 43–48.

Sakwa, R. (2010). The dual state in Russia. *Post-Soviet Affairs, 26*(3), 185–206.

Semyakin, M. (2021). The revival of property rights in post-Soviet Russia and the problems of their further development. *Russian Juridical Journal Electronic Supplement, 2*, 16–26.

Shleifer, A., & Treisman, D. (2005). A normal country: Russia after communism. *Journal of Economic Perspectives, 19*(1), 151–174.

Sonin, K. (2003). Why the rich may favor poor protection of property rights. *Journal of Comparative Economics, 31*(4), 715–731.

Trochev, A. (2008). *Judging Russia: The role of the constitutional court in Russian politics 1990–2006*. Cambridge University Press.

Vavilov, A. (2010). *The Russian public debt and financial meltdowns*. Palgrave Macmillan.

Veselova, E. S. (2019). The Leftovers of the Arctic Pie. *Problems of Economic Transition, 61*(7–9), 571–582.

Wegren, S. K. (2012). Institutional impact and agricultural change in Russia. *Journal of Eurasian Studies, 3*(2), 193–202.

Yakovlev, A., & Demidova, O. (2012). Access of firms to public procurement in Russia in the 2000s: Before and after radical reform of regulation. *International Journal of Economic Policy in Emerging Economies, 5*(2), 140–157.

CHAPTER 6

Business and Investment Climate, Governance System

Marek Dabrowski

Highlights

- Russia's rankings in the most prominent global surveys, dealing with various aspects of business and investment climate and economic and political governance, have systematically deteriorated since the 1990s.
- Failure of democratisation in the 1990s and the autocratic drift since the early 2000s can be considered the leading cause of the poor governance and business and investment climate.
- The deficit of the rule of law and insecure property rights underpinned by the politically dependent judiciary and the dismantling of other systemic checks and balances are the key obstacles to business activity and the leading risk factor in making investment decisions in Russia.
- Excessive centralisation and bureaucratisation, instability of the regulatory environment, infrastructure underdevelopment, and financial sector fragility are other obstacles to business activity. These obstacles increase

---

M. Dabrowski (✉)
Bruegel, Brussels, Belgium
e-mail: marek.dabrowski@bruegel.org

Higher School of Economics, Moscow, Russia

CASE—Center for Social and Economic Research, Warsaw, Poland

© The Author(s), under exclusive license to Springer Nature Switzerland AG 2023
M. Dabrowski (ed.), *The Contemporary Russian Economy*,
https://doi.org/10.1007/978-3-031-17382-0_6

transaction costs and investment risk premia and lead to such pathologies as corruption, state capture, and business harassment by administrative and law enforcement agencies.
- A prudent macroeconomic policy, periodic attempts at administrative deregulation, and Russia's comparative advantages such as its large internal market, high-quality human capital, and abundant natural resources cannot fully compensate for these systemic shortcomings.
- The poor business and investment climate hurt growth dynamics, the innovativeness of the economy, structural diversification, and macroeconomic stability (due to capital outflows).

6.1 Introduction

Like many emerging market economies, as demonstrated by various international surveys, Russia faces business and investment climate problems. The insufficient protection of property rights is the biggest challenge. Other negative factors include excessive regulation, the unstable regulatory environment, the outsized role of law enforcement and security agencies, the underdeveloped technical infrastructure and financial sector, and periodic episodes of macroeconomic and financial instability (see Chapter 16).

Problems with business and investment climate seem to have a persistent character despite domestic and external economic liberalisation and mass privatisation in the early 1990s and several attempts at business deregulation and easing administrative procedures in the subsequent decades.

This chapter begins by defining business and investment climate, regulatory environment, and governance and discusses the methodology for measuring them (Sect. 6.2). Section 6.3 contains an overview of Russia's scores in the most prominent global business and investment climate surveys. Section 6.4 presents an overview of Russia's governance and political system. Section 6.5 analyses the impact of governance and the characteristics of the political system on the business and investment climate. Section 6.6 summarises the microeconomic, structural, and macroeconomic consequences of a poor business and investment climate.

6.2 Definitions and Measurement Methodology

The terms *business climate*, *investment climate*, *regulatory environment*, and *governance* are widely used but rarely defined precisely. As a result, there are several explicit and, quite often, implicit definitions of these concepts in the literature and policy debate (see Uzunidis, 2013 regarding *business climate*).

Let us start with business climate. According to Dabson et al. (1996), it '…refers to the perceived hospitality of a state or locality to the needs and desires of businesses located in, or considering a move to, that jurisdiction.' The same authors underline that '…government has a major impact on business climate, for it is that combination of public services, taxation and regulation that creates the context within which companies operate.'

There are also other meanings of business climate, such as measuring business opinions on short-term macroeconomic conditions and prospects such as sales, profits, employment, and investment, among others (Sauer & Wohlrabe, 2018; Uzunidis, 2013), that is, typical business cycle analyses. This is not an interpretation that will be used in this chapter.

The *investment climate* is defined similarly to business climate, and often these two terms are used as synonyms. We also use them interchangeably in this chapter. We assume that investment decisions are an integral part of business activity.

According to Hayes (2021), '*...investment climate refers to the economic, financial, and socio-political conditions in a country or region that impact whether individuals, banks, and institutions are willing to lend and acquire a stake (i.e., invest) in the businesses operating there.*' It is affected by factors such as '*...poverty level, crime rate, infrastructure, workforce participation, national security considerations, political (in)stability, regime uncertainty, taxes, liquidity and stability of financial markets, rule of law, property rights, regulatory environment, government transparency, and government accountability.*'

A similar approach is proposed by the European Bank of Reconstruction and Development (EBRD), according to which the investment climate is defined '*...by a wide range of factors that determine whether domestic and foreign investment happens: by the soundness of macroeconomic policies, the strength of economic and political institutions, the functioning of the legal and regulatory framework, the quality of infrastructure and other services, amongst others.*'[1]

The *regulatory environment* is a narrower concept, and it is defined as '*...the set of taxes, rules, and laws or regulations that businesses must adhere to.*'[2] The regulatory environment can be seen as a component of the business and investment climate.

Finally, *governance* can be defined as '*...the traditions and institutions by which authority in a country is exercised*' (Kaufmann et al., 2009). The World Bank uses this broad definition in its annual survey on the World Governance Indicators (WGI)[3] (see Sect. 6.4). A more detailed specification of this concept includes '*...the process by which governments are selected, monitored and replaced; the capacity of the government to effectively formulate and implement sound policies; and the respect of citizens and the state for the institutions that govern economic and social interactions among them.*'

According to the United Nations Development Programme (UNDP, 2007), '*governance* is the system of values, policies and institutions by which a

---

[1] https://www.ebrd.com/what-we-do/sectors-and-topics/investment-climate-govern ance.html.

[2] https://study.com/academy/answer/define-regulatory-environment.html.

[3] See https://datacatalog.worldbank.org/search/dataset/0038026.

society manages its economic, political and social affairs through interactions within and among the state, civil society and private sector.'

The EBRD distinguishes between '...*political governance (the type of political system, constitutional set-up, relations between state and society), economic governance (state institutions that regulate the economy, competition, property and contract rights) and corporate governance (national and company laws and practices that determine corporate conduct, shareholder rights, disclosure and transparency, accounting standards).*' Corporate governance will not be discussed in this chapter because it is the subject of Chapter 7.

The most frequent way of measuring the various dimensions of business and investment climate, regulatory environment, and governance and comparing them between countries is by using composite numeric indices produced by global development institutions and non-governmental organisations (NGOs). They allow for cross-country comparison and a dynamic analysis of changes in individual countries. In Sects. 6.3 and 6.4, we review the results of selected surveys for Russia.

However, one must be aware of the methodological difficulties in constructing and interpreting such indices. First, they try to quantify phenomena that have a qualitative character. Therefore, they must rely on some selected proxy indicators. Second, most surveys rely on the opinions of either experts or business practitioners. That is, they have, by definition, a subjective character. There is also the question of the representativeness of these opinions. Third, the construction of composite indices can also be disputable in terms of their composition (selection of detailed measures) and the weights attached to the individual components. Fourth, there are frequent correlations between these components (multicollinearity), which may distort the final results.

With all the above-mentioned methodological questions involved (which suggest caution in interpreting survey results), using a global business/investment climate and governance survey seems the best available way of empirical analysis.

6.3 International Perception of the Business and Investment Climate in Russia

Global surveys dealing with various business and investment climate aspects provide a contradictory picture of the Russian economy. Below we analyse[4] four of them: the World Bank Doing Business (WBDB) survey, the Heritage Foundation Index of Economic Freedom (HFIEF), the Transparency International Corruption Perception Index (TICPI), and the Global Competitiveness Report of the World Economic Forum (WEFGCR).

---

[4] Sections 6.3–6.5 draw partly from Dabrowski (2019).

Table 6.1 Russia: WBDB 2020 rankings and scores (Data for 2019)

Category	Rank	Score
Starting a business	40	93.1
Dealing with construction permits	26	78.9
Getting electricity	7	97.5
Registering property	12	88.6
Getting credit	25	80.0
Protecting minority investors	72	60.0
Paying taxes	58	80.5
Trading across borders	99	71.8
Enforcing contracts	21	72.2
Resolving insolvency	57	59.1
Overall	28	78.2

Source https://www.doingbusiness.org/en/data/exploreeconomies/russia#

The WBDB survey was published annually between 2003 and 2019 but was discontinued in September 2021 due to data irregularities.[5] In the 2020 survey, the last one published (containing data for 190 countries in 2019), Russia obtained a high 28th place in the country ranking and a score of 78.2 on a scale from 0 to 100. Furthermore, Russia's scores and rankings have systematically improved since 2013. However, the methodology of the WBDB survey changed several times, limiting the comparability of WBDB scores and rankings from different years.

The disaggregated scores (Table 6.1) inform us that in the 2020 survey, Russia performed best in getting electricity (94.00), starting a business (93.04), and registering property (88.74), while scoring worst on protecting minority investors (61.67) and resolving insolvency (58.61).

Three other global surveys—the HFIEF, TICPI, and WEFGCR—offer less optimistic pictures.

In the 2022 HFIEF (data for 2021),[6] Russia was ranked 113th out of 177 countries and 43rd out of 45 European countries. Its score amounted to 56.1 (on a scale from 0 to 100). It found itself in the group of 'mostly unfree' countries. The HFIEF scored Russia best on fiscal health (99.3), tax burden (93.1), trade freedom (69.0), and monetary freedom (68.0), and worst on government integrity (29.7), investment freedom (30.0), financial freedom (30.0), judicial effectiveness (34.7), and property rights (36.8) (Table 6.2).

---

[5] https://www.worldbank.org/en/news/statement/2021/09/16/world-bank-group-to-discontinue-doing-business-report.

[6] For methodology see https://www.heritage.org/index/pdf/2022/book/02_2022_IndexOfEconomicFreedom_METHODOLOGY.pdf.

Table 6.2 Russia: 2022 HFIEF scores

Categories	12 Economic freedoms	Score
The rule of law	Property rights	36.8
	Judicial effectiveness	34.7
	Government integrity	29.7
Government size	Tax burden	93.1
	Government spending	62.6
	Fiscal health	99.3
Regulatory efficiency	Business freedom	62.5
	Labour freedom	57.3
	Monetary freedom	68.0
Open markets	Trade freedom	69.0
	Investment freedom	30.0
	Financial freedom	30.0
Overall score		56.1
Ranking		113

Source https://www.heritage.org/index/country/russia

Between 1995 and 2016, Russia was at the bottom of the 'mostly unfree' group (scores between 50 and 60) or sometimes fell below 50 (the 'repressed' group). Since the 2017 ranking, the scores substantially improved, and in the 2020–2021 rankings, Russia was upgraded into the 'moderately free' group (Fig. 6.1). One of the factors that could help in upgrading the ranking was the addition of new indices to the aggregate index, including 'fiscal health,' in which Russia scored very well. However, the 2022 ranking brought a visible reversal, and one may expect that the war in Ukraine and associated sanctions and countersanctions (see Chapter 14) will cause further deterioration.

In the TICPI 2021 survey, Russia was ranked 136 out of 180 countries, with a score of 29, the same as Angola, Liberia, and Mali. The ranking scores countries from 0 (most corrupt) to 100 (free from corruption). Since 2012, Russia's score has changed little, oscillating between 27 (2014) and 30 (2020).[7]

The WEFGCR is another composite index built from 103 detailed indicators, which are grouped into 12 pillars: institutions, infrastructure, adoption of information and communication technologies (ICT), macroeconomic stability, health, skills, product market, labour market, financial system, market size, business dynamism, and innovation capacity. The 2019 WEFGCR ranked Russia 43rd out of 141 countries assessed. It received a score of 66.7 (on a scale of 0–100, with higher scores meaning a more competitive economy), an improvement of 1.1 points compared to the 2018 WEFGCR (Schwab et al., 2019, pp. 482–485).

---

[7] https://www.transparency.org/en/cpi/2021/index/rus. See also https://images.transparencycdn.org/images/CPI-2021-Methodology.zip for methodological explanations.

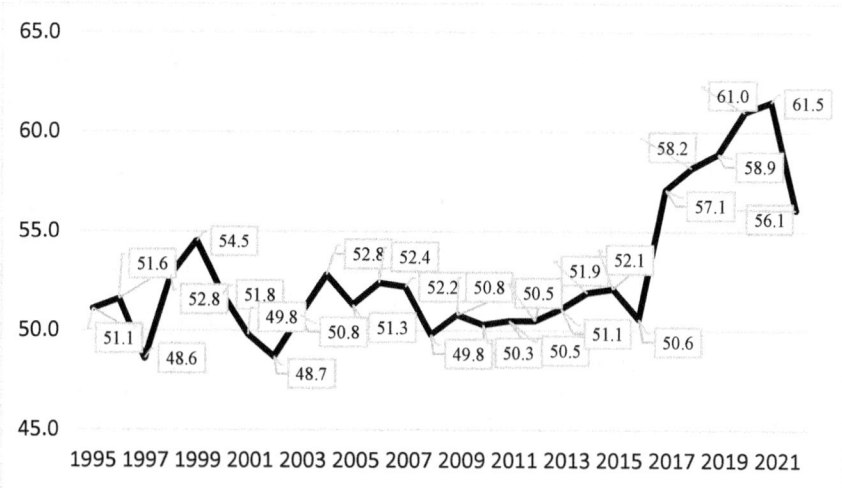

Fig. 6.1 Russia: HFIEF overall scores, 1995–2022 (*Source* https://www.heritage.org/index/visualize?cnts=russia&type=8)

The disaggregation of the overall score by pillars shows the high notes on macroeconomic stability (score of 90.0 but rank of only 43), market size (score of 84.2 and rank of 6), ICT adoption (score of 77.0 and rank of 22), and infrastructure (score of 73.8 but rank of only 50). Looking at individual indices, Russia ranked well in research institution prominence (score of 94.7, 9th rank), scientific publications (92.2, 22nd rank), costs of starting a business (99.4, 27th rank), flexibility of wage determination (78.2, 17th rank), competition in services (74.5, 17th rank), mobile telephone subscription (100, 9th rank), electricity access (100, 2nd rank), quality of land administration (86.7, 15th rank), e-participation (92.1, 23rd rank), and budget transparency (72.0, 15th rank).

On the negative side, the worst pillar scores and rankings concerned product market (52.9, 87th rank), institutions (52.6, 74th rank), financial system (55.7, 95th rank), and health (69.2, 97th rank). In the detailed indices, the worst notes were attributed to freedom of the press (49.7, 122nd rank), incidence of corruption (28.0, 116th rank), property rights (44.7, 113th rank), social capital (45.3, 104th rank), complexity of trade tariffs (44.4, 109th rank), prevalence of non-tariff barriers (51.9, 103rd rank), internal labour mobility (52.7, 103rd rank), labour tax rate (60.6, 134th rank), financing of small and medium-sized enterprises (SMEs) (38.1, 118th rank), and soundness of banks (48.5, 115th rank).

6.4 International Perception of Governance and Political System in Russia

The World Bank's World Governance Indicators (WBWGI) is a composite index that summarises various dimensions of a governance system. In line with the World Bank's definition of governance presented in Sect. 6.2, it summarises scores in six categories (control of corruption, government effectiveness, political stability and absence of violence/terrorism, regulatory quality, rule of law, voice and accountability) on a scale from +2.5 (good governance) to –2.5 (poor governance) in each category.

Figure 6.2 shows that since the beginning of the WBWGI rating in 1996, Russia recorded negative scores (below zero) in each category, with one exception—'government effectiveness' in 2018–2020 (amounting to zero or slightly above zero). The 'voice and accountability' variable (the proxy of democratisation) deteriorated systematically over the surveyed period. 'Rule of law' and 'control of corruption' stayed firmly in 'negative' territory (between –0.700 and –1.100). 'Political stability and absence of violence/terrorism' fluctuated between –0.700 and –1.500 until 2015, with some improvement in the second half of the 2010s. The two more 'technocratic' variables—'regulatory quality' and 'government effectiveness' looked slightly better, however, with the former deteriorating since the mid-2000s and the latter improving in the 2010s.

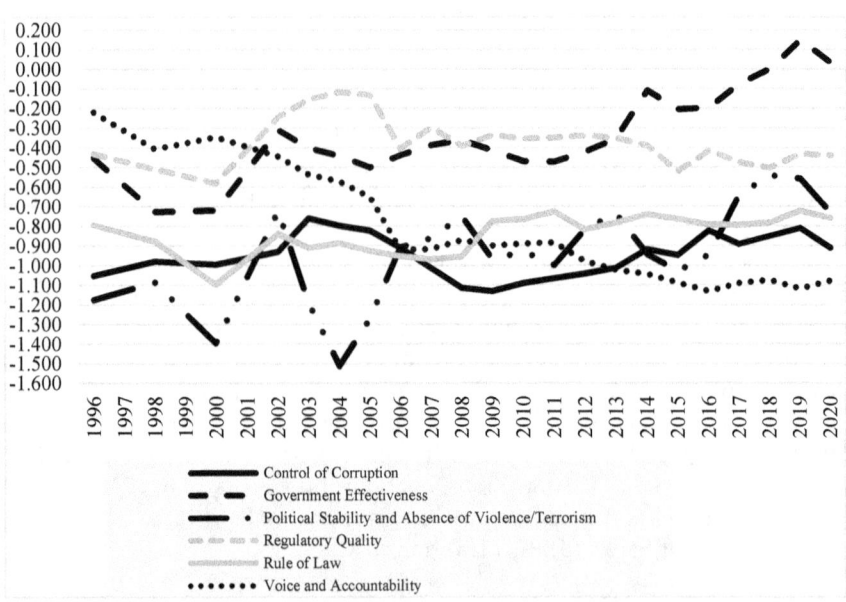

Fig. 6.2 Russia: WBWGI indicators, 1996–2020 (*Source* https://databank.worldbank.org/reports.aspx?source=worldwide-governance-indicators#)

Another worldwide governance survey—the Bertelsmann Stiftung's Transformation Index (BTI)—assesses various dimensions of political and economic governance in 137 post-communist, emerging market, and developing countries (advanced economies with stable democracies are excluded) (Bertelsmann Stiftung, 2022a). It produces three subindices, which characterise political transformation, economic transformation, and governance. The first one (political transformation) summarises the indices of stateness, political participation, rule of law, stability of democratic institutions, and political and social integration. The second one (economic transformation) considers socioeconomic level, market organisation, monetary and fiscal stability, private property, welfare regime, economic performance, and sustainability. Finally, the governance index assesses level of difficulty, steering capacity, resource efficiency, consensus building, and international cooperation. All indices are scaled between 1 (the lowest note) and 10 (the highest).

The BTI 2022 awarded Russia an overall (status) index of 5.27 and a ranking of 66 (Bertelsmann Stiftung, 2022b). The economic transformation index amounted to 6.14 (39th rank), the political transformation index—4.40 (84th rank; moderate autocracy), and the governance index—3.48 (111th rank). In all these indices and most of their components, Russia's scores have deteriorated since 2006, when the BTI was first published.

Other international surveys concentrate on the political dimension of a governance system. The Freedom House's Freedom in the World (FHFIW) rating measures seven categories and 25 detailed indicators of political rights and civil liberties in 195 countries and 15 dependent or unrecognised territories since 1972. These are electoral process, political pluralism and participation, the functioning of the government, freedom of expression and belief, associational and organisational rights, the rule of law, and personal autonomy and individual rights (Repucci & Slipowitz, 2022). The scores are awarded on a scale from 1 (the freest) to 7 (the least free).

Figure 6.3 shows a systematic deterioration of Russia's scores that resulted in its downgrading from the partly free to the non-free category (in 2004). A more detailed picture is provided by another Freedom House survey—Nations in Transit (FHNIT), which monitors changes in political systems in the post-communist countries of Central and Eastern Europe (CEE) and the former Soviet Union (FSU). The overall FHNIT democracy score is the average of seven categories: national democratic governance, electoral process, civil society, independent media, local democratic governance, judicial framework and independence, and corruption.

The 2022 FHNIT report (Smeltzer & Buyon, 2022) assessed the political system in Russia as a 'consolidated authoritarian regime' with an overall democracy score of 1.32 on a scale from 1 to 7, with one representing the lowest level of democratic progress and seven—the highest. The democratic percentage amounted to 5.36% on a scale running from 0 (the least democratic regime) to 100 (the most democratic). In all seven categories, Russia's scores were below 2, with the highest score (1.75) in 'civil society'. It is also worth

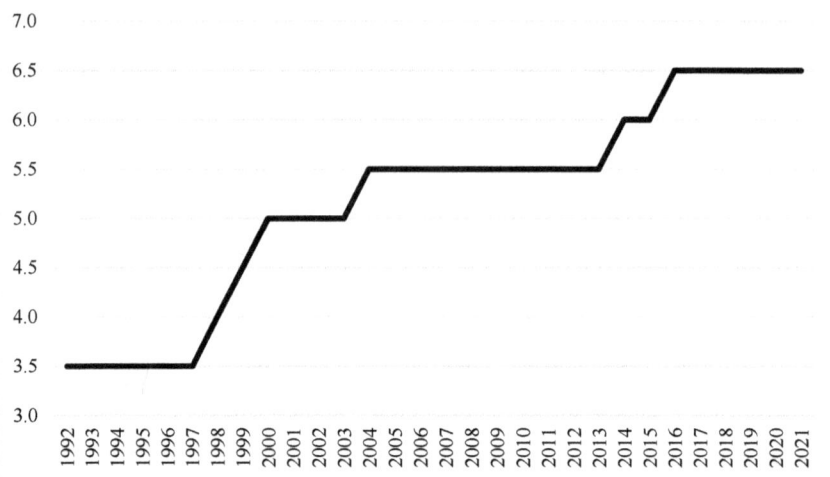

Fig. 6.3 Russia: FHFIW scores (a simple average of political rights and civil liberties scores), 1992–2021 (*Source* https://freedomhouse.org/sites/default/files/2022-03/Country_and_Territory_Ratings_and_Statuses_FIW_1973-2022%20.xlsx)

noticing that Russia's score in the FHNIT survey systematically deteriorated in the 2000s and 2010s.

Finally, the Economist Intelligence Unit Democracy Index (EIUDI) includes five components: electoral process and pluralism, functioning of the government, political participation, political culture, and civil liberties. It applies a scale from 0 (no democracy) to 10 (full democracy). The EIUDI 2021 (EIU, 2022) ranked 165 independent states and two territories. Russia received a score of 3.24 and a ranking of 124 in the group of authoritarian countries. Its best component scores related to political participation (4.44) and civil liberties (4.12), and the worst—electoral process and pluralism (1.75). As in the case of other surveys, Russia's scores represent a downward trend over time, with the lowest value recorded in 2018 (Fig. 6.4).

6.5 Flawed Governance as the Factor Responsible for Poor Business and Investment Climate

The overview of international governance surveys in Sect. 6.4 provides a picture of an oversized and overcentralised (given the federal character of Russia) government (the power vertical as frequently phrased by Russian politicians and analysts). Such a government interferes in the business activity and private life of citizens. However, it cannot provide essential public goods such as public security, property rights, and civil rights protections and sufficient technical and social infrastructure.

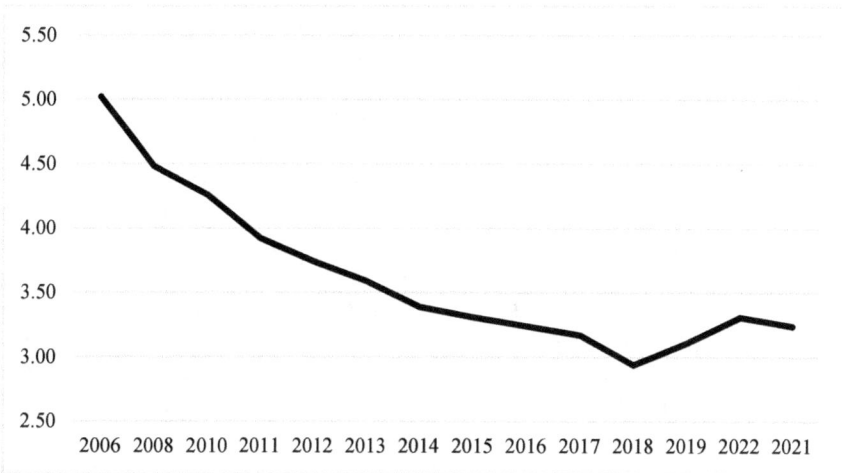

Fig. 6.4 Russia: EIUDI scores, 2006–2021 (*Source* EIU [2022], Table 3, p. 33)

Overregulation, the oppressive Criminal Code, and the ambiguous content of many other pieces of legislation allow the public administration and law enforcement agencies to interpret and enforce them arbitrarily. This leads to frequent power abuse for private benefit, administrative harassment, and extorting money and assets from private businesses. The Russian business community often calls it state 'racketeering'. In practical terms, such practices involve a specific kind of privatisation of public authority and public goods to benefit those who perform political and administrative power. Some authors (e.g., Lanskoy & Myles-Primakoff, 2018 and Aslund, 2019) call this phenomenon a kleptocratic state.

'Privatisation' of the Russian state was possible thanks to an authoritarian drift in the political system that started at the end of the 1990s. Some flaws of the constitutional system (see Chapter 5), for example, the dominance of the executive branch of government over the legislative and judicial ones and the extensive prerogatives of the president, allowed for such a drift. It led to the gradual dismantling of constitutional checks and balances: political dependence of judiciary, reduction in regional autonomy, and political control over media and civil society organisations (CSOs), for example, by using the infamous Foreign Agent Law adopted in 2012 and its subsequent tightening.

Limiting the independence of the legislative and judicial branches of government and media and CSOs reduced their monitoring capacities over the executive branch. It resulted in the lack of transparency and accountability of the latter and created a fertile ground for groups of special interests, rent-seeking, state and business capture by oligarchic groups, and various forms of corruption.

Several comparative cross-country analyses confirm a positive correlation between changes in political and economic systems (Bertelsmann Stiftung,

2022a; Dabrowski, 2021). This should not be surprising if one analyses the impact of democratic mechanisms and institutions on the functioning of a market economy (De Haan & Sturm, 2003). Beyond the already mentioned arguments (the role of political checks and balances in limiting the concentration and abuse of political power and the monitoring role of the media and CSOs), the democratic rotation of political elites and their accountability to the electorate may also reduce the incidence of power abuses, corruption, and state capture. Furthermore, civil liberties support and supplement economic freedom. It is hard to imagine the effective functioning and development of a contemporary post-industrial (service-based) economy without the freedom of movement, expression, speech, and assembly and the right to private property, privacy, and equal treatment under the law, among others, and their adequate judicial protection. Autocratic regimes are also less open to the external world (Gable, 2005), hurting economic and social development.

In the light of the above findings and arguments, no one should be surprised by the negative impact of the autocratic drift and the resulting deterioration in governance quality on the business and investment climate. Regulations, procedures, and institutions that have a more technocratic character and often use digital tools and platforms (for example, business and property registration and issuing construction permits, among others) are more immune to the flaws in the governance system, corruption, and power abuse. However, frequently repeated campaigns of business deregulation (for example, reducing the number and frequency of inspections) serve as indirect evidence that progress in this sphere is not necessarily sustainable and requires periodic reinforcement.

The business and investment climate in Russia also benefits, in comparison with other emerging market economies, from the country's level of socioeconomic development (an upper-middle-income status) and some elements of its social and technical infrastructure such as its relatively good education system, research capacities, human resources, access to cheap energy, communications, and digital networks, among others. Russia's large domestic market and rich natural resources are other incentives for business involvement. Since the beginning of the twenty-first century, its relatively prudent monetary and fiscal policies (although unable to prevent periodic episodes of macroeconomic and financial crises—see Chapter 16) has partly mitigated other shortcomings of the governance system and improved the business climate.

However, the practices of state 'racketeering', corruption, the politically motivated expropriation of business assets,[8] selective enforcement of repressive legislation, and more generally, 'selective' justice (adopting criminal penalties based on doubtful evidence against selected business people), the instability of

---

[8] The best-known cases of politically motivated expropriation relate to the dismantling of the YUKOS oil company in 2003–2005, taking over a majority stake in the Sakhalin-2 project by Gazprom in 2006, and the nationalisation of Bashneft oil company in 2014—see Chapter 7.

legislation, and ignoring the rulings of international arbitrage bodies, among others, undermine the stability of property rights and create business uncertainty. These are the most damaging factors behind Russia's poor business and investment climate, which are not always fully captured by international surveys (see Sect. 6.3), particularly the WBDB.

The renationalisation of the Russian economy after 2003 has given state-owned enterprises (SOEs) a privileged status (see Chapter 7). The same applied to private business groups close to political power. As a result, other market participants have suffered from an uneven playing field. This is another factor discouraging genuine private investment and distorting competition.

6.6 Economic Consequences of a Poor Business and Investment Climate and Flawed Governance

As discussed earlier in this chapter, the unfavourable business and investment climate has roots in Russia's failure of political and institutional reforms. Democratisation and building a rule-of-law governance system were not completed in the 1990s and were then reversed in the 2000s and 2010s. The invasion of Ukraine in February 2022 and associated Western sanctions along with Russia's retaliatory measures (see Chapter 14) can further worsen the business and investment climate, especially for non-residents and in all activities dependent on foreign trade and investment as well as international finance. It will also additionally consolidate the autocratic character of Russia's governance system.

So far, insecure property rights, the lack of an independent and impartial judiciary, 'selective' justice and law enforcement, an uneven playing field, and the abuse of political and administrative power for private benefits (especially in the case of law enforcement agencies) proved the most critical obstacles to business activity in Russia.

These fundamental shortcomings in the governance system and business and investment climate cannot be compensated for by prudent macroeconomic policies, low and relatively simple taxation (see Chapter 16), and repeated measures aimed at the administrative simplification of business registration, property registration, tax payments, court procedures, and the inspection regime, among others. They also diminish the potential investment attractiveness of the Russian economy stemming from its large territory and population, abundant natural resources (see Chapter 1), human capital (see Chapter 2), vast domestic market, elements of modern infrastructure (for example, in the ICT sphere), and upper-middle-income status.

There are multi-dimensional consequences of these shortcomings. In a microeconomic sphere, they increase the cost of doing business and risk premia of the potential investment projects (see Chapter 8). By limiting market entry and granting privileged market access for SOEs and private owners closely associated with political power (oligarchs), they distort market competition at the cost of consumers and the economy's innovativeness. They also discriminate against SMEs because their transaction costs and investment risks are too high. As a result, the weight and role of SMEs are smaller in Russia than in many other advanced and emerging market economies. This limits the development of a middle class, the natural political base of a liberal democratic order (Lu, 2005; Moyo, 2018).

Structurally, a poor business and investment climate helps to consolidate the dominant position of resource (upstream) industries, particularly the energy sector, and halts the economy's diversification in favour of high value-added manufacturing and services. Where the service sector develops (the example of business and financial services and the ICT sector), it is inward rather than outward-oriented, i.e., it focuses on serving the domestic market.

Macroeconomically, precarious property rights and business uncertainty are causes of the continuous net private capital outflows, particularly during periods of macroeconomic turbulence and financial crises (see Chapter 16).

Questions for Students

1. What are the most frequently used definitions of business and investment climate, regulatory environment, and governance, and the differences between these concepts?
2. Which methodological problems are involved in measuring business and investment climate and governance changes?
3. Please present the examples of the most prominent global surveys of various aspects of business and investment climate and governance.
4. How has the international assessment of Russia's business and investment climate and governance evolved since the 1990s?
5. How does political governance influence Russia's economic governance and business and investment climate?
6. Please characterise the main factors determining insecure property rights in Russia.
7. How does a poor business and investment climate contribute to macroeconomic fragility despite prudent monetary and fiscal policies?

References

Aslund, A. (2019). *Russia's crony capitalism: The path from market economy to kleptocracy*. Yale University Press.

Bertelsmann Stiftung. (2022a). *Transformation index BTI 2022: Governance in international comparison*. Verlag Bertelsmann Stiftung.

Bertelsmann Stiftung. (2022b). BTI 2022b Country Report—Russia. Bertelsmann Stiftung, Guetersloh. https://bti-project.org/fileadmin/api/content/en/downloads/reports/country_report_2022_RUS.pdf

Dabrowski, M. (2019). Factors determining Russia's long-term growth rate. *Russian Journal of Economics, 5*(4), 328–353. https://rujec.org/article/49417/download/pdf/366392

Dabrowski, M. (2021). The antidemocratic drift in the early 21st century: Some thoughts on its roots, dynamics and prospects. *Central European Business Review, 10*(2), 63–83. https://cebr.vse.cz/pdfs/cbr/2021/02/04.pdf

Dabson, B., Rist, C., & Schweke, W. (1996, June 1). Business climate and the role of development incentives. *Federal Reserve Bank of Minneapolis.* https://www.minneapolisfed.org/article/1996/business-climate-and-the-role-of-development-incentives

De Haan, J., & Sturm, J.-E. (2003). Does more democracy lead to greater economic freedom? New evidence for developing countries. *European Journal of Political Economy, 19*(3), 547–563. https://doi.org/10.1016/S0176-2680(03)00013-2

EIU. (2022). Democracy index 2021. *The China Challenge. The Economist Economic Intelligence Unit.* www.eiu.com

Gable, S. (2005). The effect of democracy on different categories of economic freedom. *European Journal of Political Economy, 21*(4), 967–980. https://doi.org/10.1016/j.ejpoleco.2004.11.005

Hayes, A. (2021, September 1). Investment climate. *Investopedia.* https://www.investopedia.com/terms/i/investmentclimate.asp

Kaufmann, D., Kraay, A., & Mastruzzi, M. (2009, June 29). Governance matters 2009: Learning from over a decade of the worldwide governance indicators. *Brookings.* https://www.brookings.edu/opinions/governance-matters-2009-learning-from-over-a-decade-of-the-worldwide-governance-indicators/

Lanskoy, M., & Myles-Primakoff, D. (2018). The rise of Kleptocracy: Power and Plunder in Putin's Russia. *Journal of Democracy, 29*(1), 76–85.

Lu, C. (2005). Middle class and democracy: Structural linkage. *International Review of Modern Sociology, 31*(2), 157–178.

Moyo, D. (2018, April 20). Why the survival of democracy depends on a strong middle-class. *The Globe and Mail.* https://www.theglobeandmail.com/opinion/article-why-the-survival-of-democracy-depends-on-a-strong-middle-class/

Repucci, S., Slipowitz, A. (2022). Freedom in the World 2022: the global expansion of the authoritarian rule. *Freedom House.* https://freedomhouse.org/sites/default/files/2022-02/FIW_2022_PDF_Booklet_Digital_Final_Web.pdf

Sauer, S., & Wohlrabe, K. (2018). The new IFO business climate index for Germany. *CESIFO Forum, 19*(2), 59–64. http://test1.cesifo.org/en/publikationen/2018/article-journal/new-ifo-business-climate-index-germany

Schwab, K. et al. (2019). The global competitiveness report 2019. World economic forum. http://www3.weforum.org/docs/WEF_TheGlobalCompetitivenessReport2019.pdf

Smeltzer, M., & Buyon, N. (2022). Nations in transit 2022: From democratic decline to authoritarian aggression. Freedom House. https://freedomhouse.org/sites/default/files/2022-04/NIT_2022_final_digital.pdf

UNDP. (2007). *Governance Indicators: A Users' Guide.* Second Edition. United Nations Development Programme, Oslo Governance Centre. https://www.un.org/ruleoflaw/files/Governance%20Indicators_A%20Users%20Guide.pdf

Uzunidis, D. (2013) Business Climate a/nd Entrepreneurialism. In: Carayannis EG (eds) Encyclopedia of Creativity, Invention, Innovation and Entrepreneurship. Springer. https://doi.org/10.1007/978-1-4614-3858-8_194

CHAPTER 7

Evolution of Ownership Structure and Corporate Governance

Alexander Radygin and Alexander Abramov

Highlights

- While theoretical conclusions about the advantages of different ownership forms are rather controversial, most empirical studies show that private companies outperform state-owned ones in numerous financial indicators.
- In Russia, the search for sources of economic growth and social stability led to a significant transformative development of ownership structures and corporate governance models. The reforms of the 1990s reduced state involvement in the economy; however, since the early 2000s, the public sector once again began to expand as measured by the share of GDP. The question of whether the economic growth model and scope of state involvement in the early 2020s are optimal has remained open.

A. Radygin (✉)
Gaidar Institute for Economic Policy, Moscow, Russia
e-mail: arad@ranepa.ru

A. Radygin · A. Abramov
Russian Academy of National Economy and Public Administration (RANEPA), Moscow, Russia
e-mail: abramov-ae@ranepa.ru

© The Author(s), under exclusive license to Springer Nature Switzerland AG 2023
M. Dabrowski (ed.), *The Contemporary Russian Economy*,
https://doi.org/10.1007/978-3-031-17382-0_7

- Although a modern corporate governance model was implemented in Russia, its further development is hindered by a high degree of ownership concentration, a lack of transparency in business operations, and an orientation to own resources and debt as major sources of financing.
- During the years of reform, a liquid and open exchange market for shares and bonds emerged and effective stock market infrastructure was created. The key remaining issues are the development of the internal savings system, the implementation of new technologies, and the improvement of financial regulation.

7.1 Introduction: Private Versus Public Sector

The global trend towards a reduction in state ownership (state participation in commercial enterprises) has been characteristic of the late twentieth and early twenty-first centuries, although this trend can sometimes slow down or be temporarily reversed, especially during financial and economic crises.

The effect of privatisation on transformation and efficiency at the micro level is largely beneficial, although such changes can occur faster and easier where economic and government institutions are stronger and the quality of the legal and regulatory framework of economic activity is higher. On the other hand, partial privatisation can produce positive effects where institutions are weaker (Marcelin & Mathur, 2015). At the same time, when the government retains the controlling interest after partial privatisation, it can weaken the company's performance (Boubakri et al., 2005).

In practice, the privatisation process follows a cyclical pattern, reflecting the specific interests and preferences of the ruling elites and serving various goals—from systemic post-communist transformation to the achievement of certain ideological, structural, or budgetary (fiscal) objectives. It cannot be said that all the privatisation programmes implemented around the world since the 1980s have actually been successful. However, privatisation is not a goal in itself, but an economic policy instrument designed to introduce market rules for economic agents.

Russia, similar to other transition economies, has gone through the difficult process of institutional reform—from the choice of a primary privatisation model to modern standards of the public sector and corporate governance.[1] This chapter analyses the key trends in privatisation and corporate governance since the late 1980s.

---

[1] See, for example, Radygin (1995), Boyko et al. (1996), Blasi et al. (1997), Gaidar et al. (2003), Tambovtsev et al. (2009), Alexeev and Weber (2013), Grigoriev and Kurdin (2016), Radygin et al. (2019), Gurevich et al. (2020).

7.2 Privatisation from the Origins: Discussions, Models, and Results

In Russia, as in other post-communist countries, privatisation started in the late 1980s. The period 1985–1989 was characterised by minor changes in the Soviet system when any alternative forms of ownership were considered only in the context of a 'multi-structured socialist economy' with a dominant public sector (see Chapter 4). The years 1990–1991 saw more systematically implemented reforms or—to be more precise—the emergence of more systematic concepts of a pro-market transformation. There was a noticeable shift in the ideological approaches to ownership issues, which was reflected in the legislation adopted during that period (concerning ownership and joint stock companies, among others). Meanwhile, against the ongoing discussions about the alternative forms of ownership and the methods of privatisation, there was a surge in the spontaneous process of asset withdrawal from the public sector in the interests of the Soviet nomenclature and directors of state-owned enterprises (SOEs) (Radygin, 1992).

Although Russia, during privatisation, avoided facing problems like the restitution of property rights from the pre-communist period or a noticeable regional separatism, the scale of the Soviet economy, its high level of sectoral concentration, and the extremely politicised nature of the privatisation process predetermined the choice of a privatisation model that was focused on maximising social compromise. Table 7.1 presents the main stages of privatisation.

The most important systemic transformation period was the mass privatisation of 1992–1994 because it formed the primary ownership structure of Russian enterprises. The emergence of a significant stratum of private owners of various types was perceived as a necessary precondition for preventing a communist restoration. The process of the post-privatisation redistribution of property lasted for about a decade, and its main characteristic was the concentration of ownership in the hands of private majority shareholders.

Numerous studies (Aukutsionek et al., 2007; Dolgopiatova, 2002, 2007; Radygin, 2000; Radygin & Entov, 1999) present the main trends in the ownership structure of Russian companies: a reduction in employee ownership; stabilisation or growth in management ownership; a significant increase in the ownership share of large external investors; stabilisation or a reduction in the share of small external investors (individuals); and a consistent contraction in state ownership. Overall, ownership by internal shareholders declined (due to a decrease in ownership by ordinary employees), while that of external and pseudo-external shareholders increased. During this period, the key feature of the ownership structure of the biggest Russian joint stock companies was the ownership of stock by large state and private financial-industrial groups (holding companies) as well as low employee stock ownership with relatively high non-resident stock ownership.

Table 7.1 Main stages of privatisation in Russia

Period	Stage characteristics	Priority goals
1987–1991	Spontaneous privatisation process	Lack of specialised legislation, no formalised goals at the macro level
1992–1994	Mass privatisation (see Box 7.1)	Dominance of political goals and the search for social compromise, launch of reforms based on privatisation legislation, intensive build-up of 'critical mass' of relevant institutional changes
1995–1998	First monetary stage, including loan-for-share auctions in 1995	Combination of political and fiscal goals resulting in an unsuccessful transition to monetary model
1999–2009	Second monetary stage	Combination of fiscal goals and the consolidation of state-owned assets, the quantitative growth of the public sector
2010–present	Emphasis on public sector management, declarations of new large-scale privatisations in non-resource sectors	Combination of fiscal (mainly renewable sources—dividends, rent, among others) and optimisation tasks, continued policy of public sector consolidation

Source Authors' analysis

The impact of privatisation and the post-privatisation ownership changes on the performance of enterprises remains debatable, but empirical analyses revealed some positive trends. According to Megginson (2017), most studies show significant improvements in the financial and operational performance indicators of the former SOEs after privatisation. In addition, privatisation boosts the potential and efficiency of national capital markets. Claessens and Djankov (2002), using the example of Eastern European enterprises, demonstrated the positive effect of privatisation on revenues and labour productivity coupled with job losses. The economic and statistical significance of the post-privatisation positive effect increased over time. Estrin et al. (2009) assessed the impact of privatisation on the performance of companies in transition economies and in most cases found a positive effect. In countries of the former Soviet Union (FSU), such positive effects were observed only when control had been transferred to foreign investors. The degree of concentration of ownership can affect the efficiency of companies.

Most of the studies that covered Russia also found similar conclusions. The best performance was demonstrated by those enterprises where ownership was concentrated either in the hands of managers (in small- and medium-sized enterprises) or certain types of outsiders (in large enterprises), although there is also some opposing evidence (Aukutsionek et al., 1998). Radygin and Entov (2001) note that a shrinking share of state ownership translated into an increased return on fixed assets. At the same time, alongside an increasing concentration of joint stock ownership, indicators like revenue per employee, return on fixed assets, and profit margin generally improved. Brown et al. (2006) showed that privatisation in most cases led to labour productivity growth, but in Russia, it produced an opposite effect. The obvious positive effect of privatisation by domestic investors could be seen in the short term in Hungary, Romania, and Ukraine, and in later years, it continued to grow; however, in Russia, the positive effects were only revealed five years after privatisation. The results of privatisation vary dramatically across different countries depending on the degree of involvement of foreign investors.

Abramov et al. (2017) show that the size of the state-owned stake negatively influences a company's performance, and its increase is associated with a rising debt burden. Radygin et al. (2019), by comparing the economic and financial performance indicators of the largest SOEs, prove that they usually underperform private Russian companies and their foreign competitors.

In the early 2000s, the pace of privatisation in Russia slowed down. Monetary privatisation in the second half of the 1990s, which had been aiming at generating higher budget revenues and enterprise restructuring, did not bring satisfactory results. The bulk of property remaining in state ownership was represented either by low-liquid assets or, on the contrary, by very attractive ones (for example, state-owned stakes in monopolies of national importance), the sale of which at an adequate market price could be possible only upon meeting certain prerequisites. After the financial crisis of 1997–1998 (see Chapter 16) followed by the stock market collapse, the prospects for any serious growth in budget proceeds through privatisation sales dimmed even more.

In 2000–2005, government policy was aimed, for the most part, at optimising the state's participation in the economy. In subsequent years, it became more prominent due to the expansion of SOEs and their participation in mergers and acquisitions (M&As).

After 2005, the processes of consolidating scattered state-owned assets and pooling them into vertically integrated structures under state control (pseudo-privatisation), increasing the state's stakes in the biggest public companies, among others, sharply intensified. In some instances, these integrated structures covered entire industries (e.g., aviation, nuclear industry, and shipbuilding).

Furthermore, the years 2007–2008 saw the creation of state corporations and development institutions. Similar to other countries, the global financial crisis (GFC) of 2008–2009 led to an increase in indirect state ownership. However, Russia, unlike other countries, did not re-privatise these assets in 2010–2012. The expansion of indirect state ownership went on throughout the period 2014–2021, affecting a variety of sectors (i.e., oil, banking and finance, and trade, among others).

In summary, one may say that the privatisation trends in the 2000s and 2010s appear ambiguous. The number of economic entities with state participation (the indicator applied in official Russian statistics, government documents, and statements to illustrate the role of state versus private ownership) declined, which suggests a consistent denationalisation trend (Fig. 7.1). At the same time, the role of the state has been gaining in strength by inertia, according to the growing share of the public sector in GDP and other macro indicators (see Sect. 7.3).

In the political and economic sense, the situation can be described in terms of a 'reluctant' or 'delayed' privatisation (Bortolotti & Faccio, 2004). Evidently, the choice was made in favour of the model of state capitalism, which essentially implies government control over key national assets, promotion of the development of 'national champions' in globally competitive industries, and investment through state-controlled institutions (Megginson, 2017, p. 1).

> **Box 7.1 Mass Privatisation Schemes**
> The total number of enterprises at the beginning of mass privatisation (1992) was about 240,000, which thus meant that standardised procedures were required. A significant component of the model was the privatisation voucher, which was designed to build up political support and effective demand. The State Programme of Privatisation of State and Municipal Enterprises in the

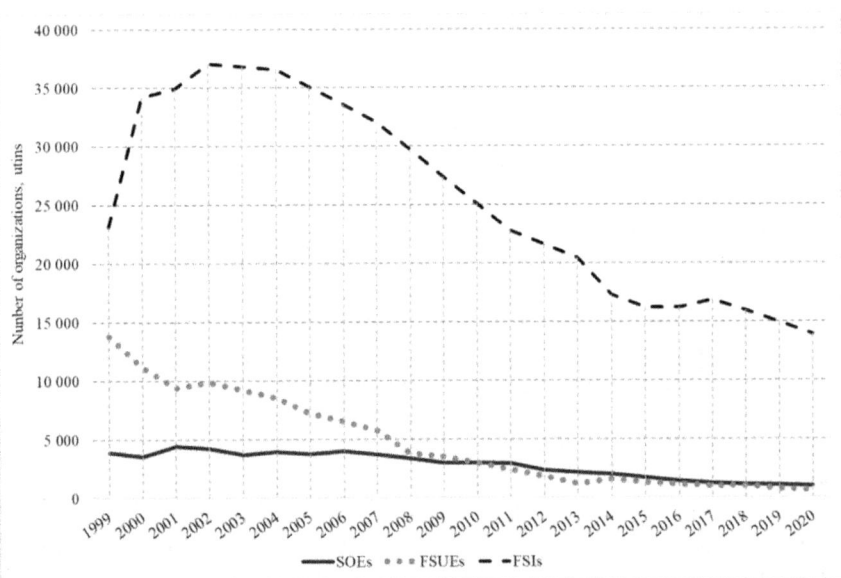

Fig. 7.1 Nominal trend: a decrease in the number of economic entities with state participation, 1999–2020 (*Note* SOEs—state-owned enterprises; FSUEs—federal state unitary enterprises; FSIs—federal state institutions. *Source* Federal Agency for State Property Management)

Russian Federation for 1992, which became fundamental for the mass privatisation of 1992–1994, was approved by the Supreme Council of the Russian Federation on 11 June 1992. For the purposes of privatisation, all enterprises in Russia were divided into three groups: small enterprises (with fewer than 200 employees and with a book value of fixed assets below RUB 1 million), which were privatised through auctions and tenders; large enterprises (with more than 1000 employees and with a book value of fixed assets above RUB 50 million), which were reorganised into open joint stock companies (corporatised) with a mandatory stock market offering; and all other (medium-sized) enterprises, which could use any method of privatisation, including voluntary corporatisation. If employees decided to privatise the company through a market offering of stocks in an open joint stock company (OJSC), one of the following three privatisation methods would be applied: option 1, which included the transfer of registered non-voting shares worth 25% of the authorised capital at par value to all employees, the sale to the employees of ordinary (voting) shares worth up to 10% of the authorised capital at a discount of 30% of the par value, and the sale to the managers of ordinary shares worth 5% of the authorised capital at par value; option 2, which granted all employees the right to buy ordinary shares worth up to 51% of the authorised capital at par value multiplied by a factor of 1.7; and option 3, which granted a group of employees the right to purchase at par value ordinary shares in their enterprise worth up to 20% of its authorised capital if they fulfilled certain conditions as well as the sale of ordinary shares worth up to 20% of the authorised capital to all employees at a 30% discount. Evidence shows that the second option was the most attractive for employees of privatised enterprises—it was chosen by 70–80% of companies.

7.3 Public Sector: Quantitative Dynamics and Comparative Effectiveness

The size of the public sector and its share in the business ownership structure have a significant impact on the performance of companies and the economy as a whole. However, there are no unified methods for measuring the size of the public sector, and no single definition of SOEs. In this chapter, we define SOEs as organisations with the state acting as their sole owner or holding the direct or indirect majority stake or a substantial minority stake (shares in the authorised capital) of at least 10%.

To estimate the share of the public sector in GDP, we rely on our own methods using the calculated added value of three sectors of the Russian economy: SOEs,[2] state unitary enterprises (SUEs), and general government (GG).[3]

The share of the public sector in GDP, according to our estimates, jumped from 31.2% in 2000 to 51.1% in 2020, which was caused primarily by the increasing share of the largest SOEs in the fuel and energy, finance, and transport industries; the creation of large development institutions; the nationalisation of several major companies (TNK-BP, Bashneft, Magnit, Otkrytie Bank, Binbank, and Promsvyazbank); and an expanding share of the GG in GDP.

These estimates can be compared with data on the share of the public sector in GDP in 1992–2010 released by the European Bank for Reconstruction and Development (EBRD) in its annual Transition Reports. According to these data, in the 1990s, the share of the public sector in GDP shrank from 75% in 1992 to 30% in 1997 and then remained at that level until 2004. In 2005, it increased to 35%, remaining the same until 2010.

According to IMF (2019) estimates, the size of the public sector in the Russian economy was 32% of GDP in 2012 and 33% of GDP in 2016.[4]

According to the estimates of the Federal Antimonopoly Service (FAS) cited in its annual reports on competition in Russia, the share of the public sector in the Russian economy increased from 25% in 1998 to 70% in 2019. Incidentally, the FAS does not disclose its calculation methodology.

As noted earlier, the public sector in Russia expanded in quantitative and qualitative terms from the 2000s onwards. The quantitative expansion trend in the public sector prevailed in 2000–2008, and then in the 2010s, the situation changed when the inputs of SOEs in the key economic indicators stabilised or slightly increased, mainly due to cyclical changes in certain sectors characterised by different levels of state presence. Meanwhile, the strengthening position of the state in the economy acquired a qualitative character. This was

---

[2] Value added was estimated for a sample of the 144 largest SOEs. In the absence of data on the components of value added for a number of companies, their share in GDP was calculated based on their revenues and the ratio of value added in revenues for the rest of the SOEs.

[3] General government (GG) includes two types of organisations: public authorities and administrations at all levels—ministries, departments, services, agencies, and state extra-budgetary funds, among others, as well as non-market non-profit organisations funded and controlled by the state (schools, hospitals, and cultural organisations, among others). The share of GG in GDP is calculated based on the value added of the GG, reflected in the System of National Accounts (SNA). For indicators of the share of the public sector in GDP, see https://ipei.ranepa.ru/kgu.

[4] In the IMF (2019) methodology, the share of SOEs in the value added of industries was determined separately for each sector. Depending on the data availability, these shares were calculated using revenue or number of employees, and in the banking system—by the value of the banks' assets. Such a method may result in an underestimation of the final data because the share of the largest SOEs in value added is significantly higher than their shares in revenue and employment in the economy as a whole. In addition, the use of non-consolidated data for large Russian holding companies and their subsidiaries is a serious limitation of these calculations.

achieved primarily by increasing the role of state institutions in the distribution of financial resources and the control of economic agents, expanding the spheres (control zones) subject to state regulation, boosting the activity of state corporations and development institutions, transferring to their authorised capital the property of state-owned companies that were not publicly traded, and involving private companies in non-market mechanisms for coordinating certain management decisions. The ambivalence and inconsistency of the position of the state as a legislator, regulator, and direct owner of large companies give rise to a conflict of interests, which in practice manifests itself in the policy of double standards towards Russian businesses.

As shown in Fig. 7.2, the share of SOEs in GDP increased from 20.0% in 2000 to 34.4% in 2020. Over the same period, the share of SUEs dropped from 4.1% of GDP to 1.9% as a result of government policy aimed at the gradual elimination of this generally inefficient organisational and legal form. The share of the GG increased from 7.1% to 14.6% (close to the average of 27 European Union [EU] Member States, which stood at 14.0%).

In the 2000s and 2010s, the increasing presence of the state in the economy was observed alongside a significantly strengthening role of SOEs as issuers of securities in the stock and corporate bond markets. The share of SOEs in the capitalisation of the Russian stock market increased from 47.4% in 2000 to 49.9% in 2020. Their share in the value of outstanding corporate bonds increased from 11.2% in 2003 to 71.0% in 2020. The share of SOEs in the dividends paid likewise increased significantly, from 9.7% in 2006 to 56.0% in 2020. This is an indication of the domestic market's stronger orientation

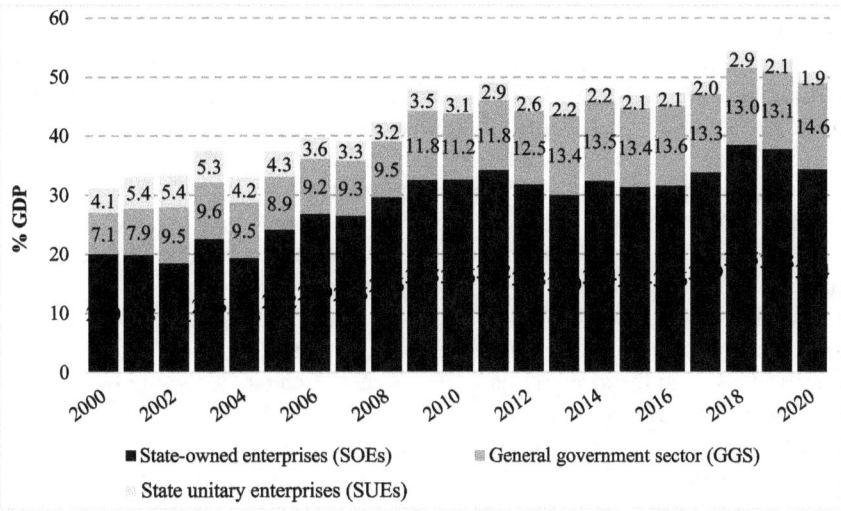

Fig. 7.2 Shares of SOEs, SUEs, and GGS in GDP in 2000–2020, in % (*Source* Authors' calculations)

to issuers operating in the industries where SOEs dominate (i.e., fuel and energy, finance, transport), to the detriment of new private issuers, and to the expansion of the already existing privately owned companies.

The mandatory requirement that the largest SOEs should earmark at least 50% of their net profit for dividends helped increase budget revenue and boost the market value of shares in those companies.

A comparison of the samples of 144 SOEs and the 169 largest (by their proceeds level) private companies operating in Russia over the period 2006–2020 reveals the fact that private companies consistently outperformed SOEs in terms of return on equity (ROE) and the price-to-book value (P/BV) ratio (Fig. 7.3). At the same time, SOEs outperformed private companies in terms of operating margin (the ratio of operating profit to revenue), which, as a rule, indicates that these companies more frequently resorted to the policy of price increases to improve their financial performance indicators. Besides, from 2013, SOEs demonstrated a lower debt burden on assets. This means that private companies are forced to borrow more actively in order to finance their projects. In terms of the growth rate of their sales (proceeds), both groups performed similarly.

7.4 Corporate Governance: Panacea or Imitation?

Globalisation and competition, changes in the structure of shareholders, the emergence of new industries, the development of financial markets, and digital technologies are the driving forces of corporate governance reform in many countries around the world. Corporate governance issues have gone beyond national borders and become the subject of international regulations, for example, the OECD Principles of Corporate Governance (OECD, 2015).

In Russia, the regulations and practices of corporate governance have evolved over time. In the 1990s, despite the adoption of the basic norms of corporate law,[5] the standards of good corporate governance practices were not complied with, which can be explained by the primary post-privatisation redistribution of property in the corporate sector.

The second period (approximately 2000–2003) was characterised by obvious progress when corporate governance issues began to interest the largest companies (corporate groups). This happened alongside an ongoing concentration of equity capital, enterprise M&As, the reorganisation of established business groups (holding companies), intra- and inter-industry expansion, and a search for foreign financial sources. The first Corporate Governance Code was adopted in 2002.

It was intended to fill the existing gaps in the Russian legislation on joint stock companies. In the early 2000s, some large Russian companies disclosed

---

[5] Federal Law No. 208-FZ dated 26 December1995 'On Joint Stock Companies', with amendments to Federal Law No. 120-FZ dated 07 August 2001 'On Joint Stock Companies'.

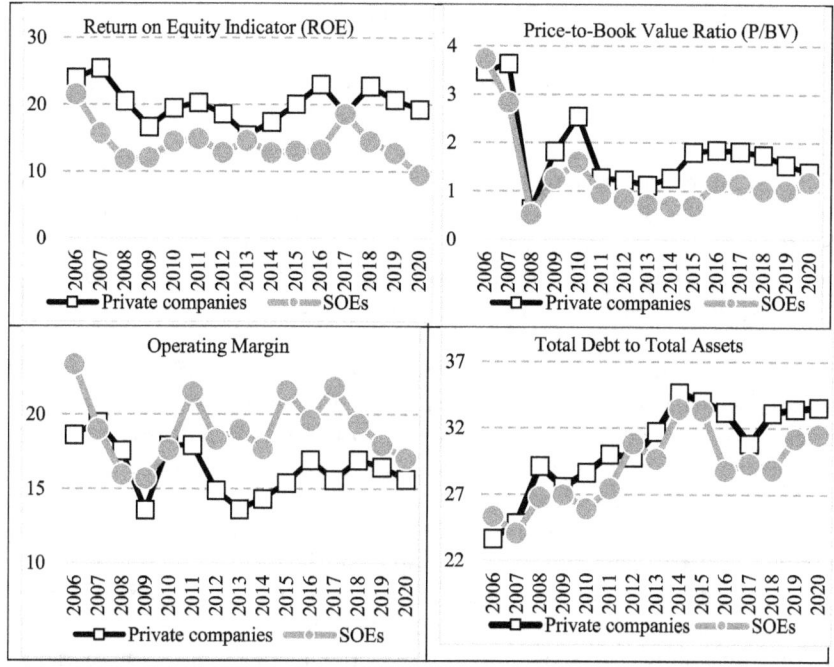

Fig. 7.3 Average financial ratios and performance indicators of private companies and SOEs in Russia over the period 2006–2020 (*Notes* ROE—net income available for common shareholders/average total common equity, in %; P/BV—price-to-book value ratio; operating margin—operating income/total sales, in %; total debt to total assets, in %. *Source* authors' calculations)

information on their beneficial owners, the remuneration of the members of their boards of directors, and the number of their independent directors, including foreign ones, among others. An increasing percentage of Russian companies began to pay dividends to their shareholders and disclosed the rules of transactions in their own shares conducted by their senior managers and members of boards of directors.

However, these positive practices were demonstrated only by the largest private companies. The assessment of the level of corporate governance in 140 Russian companies undertaken in 2004 by the Russian Institute of Directors and the Expert RA agency showed that only one company corresponded to the highest level ('A'). A 2003 study of 307 open joint stock companies revealed no broad commitment to the implementation of good practices. Furthermore, 50% of companies believed it to be important and one of their three priority goals, 17% of companies considered the development of corporate governance standards to be their priority goal, and, for about one-third of companies, it was insignificant (compared with their other goals). According to the corporate governance index calculated on the basis of 18 indicators, only 11% of companies were rated to have 'good practices'.[6]

The third period (2004–2008) was characterised by the deep freeze put on *high-quality* corporate initiatives and the increasing role of the state and SOEs in the corporate control market. The new trends translated primarily into increased opportunities for developing ownership structure transparency, beneficial owners, and financial openness, among others. There was growth in the number of initial public offerings (IPOs)—which peaked in 2006–2007—and cross-border M&As, which were often viewed as a tool for protecting businesses by attracting large foreign investors.

In the early 2000s, the arrival of external shareholders with a stake of 3–4% in some of the largest companies, usually of foreign origin, made it possible to speak of the emergence of a new type of outsider in Russia's corporate governance system. This was a partial transition from 'oligarchic' to 'public' corporate governance principles.

Meanwhile, the formation of a transparent corporate governance infrastructure in large companies was completed. It included corporate codes, internal regulations, quotas for independent directors, committees for working with shareholders, and corporate secretaries, among others. Nevertheless, the demand for innovation came primarily from the 'second-tier' companies which were preparing to enter the financial market.

Among the leaders were newly founded companies and a narrow group of companies that publicly raised funds on the international financial market and were listed in the United States (Shvyrkov, 2008). On the other hand, the least transparent aspects of corporate activities were ownership structure, the remuneration of top management and boards of directors, related party transactions, and relations with minority shareholders (see, e.g., Alexeev & Weber, 2013; Guriev et al., 2004; Chapter 9). Seemingly, there also exists a certain relationship between a company's achieved equity concentration level and ownership structure transparency.

The GFC of 2008–2009 provided a new impetus for corporate governance reform on a global scale and in Russia. First of all, there were some noticeable alterations in corporate legislation. In 2009, the Concept of the Development of Civil Legislation was approved, and on 1 September 2014, a new version of 'The Legal Entities' chapter of the Civil Code of the Russian Federation came into force.[7] In June 2015, significant changes were also made to the Federal Law 'On Joint Stock Companies'. The scale of amendments to the

---

[6] The project 'National rating of corporate governance' of the consortium 'RID-Expert RA' (www.rid.ru, www.raexpert.ru); Corporate governance practice in the regions of Russia. IRG research and commissioned by the International Finance Corporation (IFC), 2003.

[7] Federal Law No. 99-FZ dated 5 May 2014 'On Amendments to Chapter 4 of Part 1 of the Civil Code of the Russian Federation and on Invalidation of Certain Provisions of Legislative Acts of the Russian Federation'.

Civil Code was comparable with 1995 when Part I of the Civil Code replaced Soviet legislation (see Chapter 5).

The next few years (2015–2021) can be described as a period of adjusting the regulatory infrastructure of the largest public and private companies to international standards and the formal requirements issued by the national mega-regulator (i.e., the Bank of Russia[8]).

Russia's new Corporate Governance Code[9] adopted in 2014, this time at the initiative of the Bank of Russia, was more consistent with the OECD Framework Principles of Corporate Governance.[10] In this connection, the companies listed on the Russian stock exchange demonstrate the highest degree of compliance with best corporate governance practices, formally meeting nearly all requirements stipulated in the Code.

The Russian Corporate Governance Code is a form of soft law, and together with hard law (legislation), it makes up a system of hybrid regulation. In such a model, laws regulate the organisation of the board of directors, the rights of shareholders, the presence of an audit committee, and mandatory external audit. The Code addresses the issues of the independence of board members, internal control and risk management, and the remuneration and appointment of committees. Compliance with the Russian Corporate Governance Code is voluntary, but the companies whose securities are traded at organised auctions are required to follow its principles on a 'comply-or-explain' basis.

The comply-or-explain approach is believed to be more effective, as it allows companies to adapt the corporate governance rules more flexibly to their own specific features and gives them relative freedom in adopting the most appropriate management structures to improve their performance. Nevertheless, it is more costly to implement, especially in less developed economies.

The formal expert assessment of the new regulations rated them very high. As early as 2016–2017, the EBRD (2017) ranked Russia as a country with a moderately strong code (on a scale of 1 to 5): '4'—most of the code meets its purpose, but further reforms are needed in some of its aspects.[11] It is significant that the countries practicing the comply-or-explain approach received the highest scores (besides Russia, these were Estonia ['4–5']; Poland, Slovenia,

---

[8] The alternative name of the Central Bank of the Russian Federation.

[9] See: Letter of the Bank of Russia dated 10 April 2014 No. 06-52/2463 'On the Corporate Governance Code' // Bulletin of the Bank of Russia, No. 40, 18 April 2014; Information Letter of the Bank of Russia dated 26 April 2019 No. IN-06-28/41 'On recommendations for organising and conducting self-assessment of the Effectiveness of the Board of Directors (Supervisory Board) in public Joint Stock Companies' // Bulletin of the Bank of Russia, No. 29, 30 April 2019.

[10] The new OECD/G20 Corporate Governance Principles adopted in 2015 retained the main features and content of the 2004 principles but included more detailed recommendations. By no means being revolutionary, they nevertheless sought to raise standards in a number of areas, better reflect differences in the global corporate governance system, and recognise the limits of global convergence of corporate governance practices.

[11] See http://www.ebrd.com/what-we-do/sectors/legal-reform/corporate-governance/sector-assessment.html.

and Croatia ['4']; and Latvia and Lithuania ['3–4']). However, despite the upgrade of Russia from a good ('3') to a moderately strong ('4') ranking in December 2017 (OECD, 2017), it was noted that only 5 of the top 10 listed companies disclosed information on their compliance with the code. Incidentally, most of the explanations provided were too formal and lacked important references to the companies' current corporate governance practices. In addition, the EBRD pointed out the absence of references to the Code as a source of rights and obligations of companies in judicial practice.

Since 2015, the Bank of Russia has been reviewing reports on compliance with the 2014 Corporate Governance Code submitted by public joint stock companies included in the Levels 1 and 2 quotation lists of the Moscow Exchange. The results of this analysis (Table 7.2) show an increase in the number of principles that these companies were complying with fully. In the 12 state-controlled joint stock companies, the average compliance index was 90%. The provisions set forth in 'Board of Directors' chapter were complied with the least. The largest SOEs explain their non-compliance, in particular, by the specificity of their capital structure.

However, in their monitoring, both the Bank of Russia and other institutions primarily applied the open information released by the companies (quarterly and annual reports, reports on compliance with the principles of the Code, lists of affiliated persons, and reports on material facts, among others) and did not verify its reliability.

The institutions that conducted the analyses noted the highly formal nature and incompleteness of information in the reports provided by companies, especially their explanations for non-compliance with the corporate governance rules. According to the Deloitte CIS Corporate Governance Centre, the level of compliance of Russian companies with the best corporate governance practices is not increasing because of the waning interest of foreign investors in their assets as a result of Western sanctions (see Chapter 14). Among the existing constraints, the highly concentrated ownership structure in Russian companies is also noted, with an average controlling stake amounting to 57.6%, whereas usually it is minority shareholders who desire to appoint independent directors. Meanwhile, in 2014–2015, the practice of placing high-ranking civil servants on the boards of directors of SOEs was resumed, and the comply-or-explain principle was not yet fully realised (Petrova et al., 2016).

The National Corporate Governance Index 2020[12] showed, after 2017–2018, a more limited disclosure of information on compliance with the Code by the top 100 companies by market capitalisation monitored by the Bank of Russia. In 2020, the positive trends included the presence of independent directors in almost all companies (against 20% in 2015); the inclusion in

---

[12] National Corporate Governance Index 2020. TopCompetence. https://corpshark.ru/p/natsionalnyj-indeks-korporativnogo-upravleniya-2020-rucgi/.

their board meeting agendas issues like sustainable development, social responsibility, and digital business transformation; and regard for environmental, social, and governance factors when making investment decisions. Nevertheless, only 25% of companies made significant efforts to improve their corporate governance quality and increase transparency.

A joint study by Ernst and Young and the Skolkovo Club of Independent Directors (2020) gave a generally positive assessment of the response of boards of directors to the COVID-19 pandemic, but also noted several drawbacks: insufficient attention to risk management, crisis scenarios, and strategy; unsatisfactory quality of information provided to boards of directors; and lack of trust between the board and management.

Russia has adopted the one-tier (Anglo-Saxon) structure of the board of directors (sometimes called a supervisory board). Therefore, the board of directors (supervisory board) is the central element in the corporate governance system of a public joint stock company in Russia. However, contrary to world practices, the board of directors (supervisory board) in Russia is quite often the body that simultaneously performs the functions of strategic management, control, and supervision, and, in some cases, the current management of the corporation. The inclusion of a certain number of independent directors into a board of directors operating in such a format cannot eliminate the conflict (of interests).

The law 'On Joint Stock Companies' of 1995, with all the amendments introduced there up to 2002, attempted to copy the Anglo-Saxon model of protecting the rights of minority shareholders. However, the concept of corporate legislation development until 2008 (Ministry of Economic Development of the Russian Federation), which was updated in 2018, in a sense became a manifesto of the pro-majority model designed to protect the rights of the largest shareholders. Indeed, this was more in line with the real processes in the field of corporate control that were typical of a vast majority of Russian companies (Continental European model). At the same time, a radical change in the regulatory strategy should not give rise to new imbalances that would be detrimental to one or another group of subjects of corporate relations.

The development of a national model of corporate governance is influenced by numerous factors—for example, the situation in Russia's stock market and corporate control market; competition in commodity, financial, and labour markets; a balanced bankruptcy procedure; the general institutional environment; property rights protection; contract enforcement mechanisms; and incentives for external and internal investments, among others.

Internal corporate initiatives and corporate culture are no less important. While corporate culture is the product of a long historical development, specific initiatives at the company level can be adopted only after appropriate objective conditions have been created. At the same time, real improvements across all aspects of corporate governance practices can also be considered generally to be an indicator of the institutional environment quality.

Table 7.2 Compliance with corporate governance practices in Russian public companies in 2015–2019, monitoring by the Bank of Russia

Chapter of Corporate Governance Code 2014	Number of Principles	All public joint stock companies, %*				
		2015	2016	2017	2018	2019
Shareholder Rights	13	5	6	7	21	23
Board of Directors	36	0	0	0	0	2
Corporate Secretary	2	45	77	85	86	87
Remuneration System	10	6	5	11	13	15
System of Internal Control and Management of Risks	6	42	55	60	65	69
Information Disclosure	7	15	17	25	33	48
Significant Corporate Actions	5	7	9	7	10	11

Notes Number of joint stock companies: 2015—99, 2016—84, 2017—75, 2018—65, 2019—64. Since 2018, monitoring also includes companies whose shares are included in the Level 3 quotation list (155 in 2018 and 154 in 2019)
Source https://www.cbr.ru/issuers_corporate/analitics; https://www.cbr.ru/Collection/Collection/File/31741/Review_corp_14122020.pdf

7.5 Stock Market: Historical and Future Challenges

The first legal acts regulating the Russian stock market were adopted in 1990–1991. The creation of a liquid stock market was primarily the result of mass privatisation, which was launched in 1992 with the corporatisation of large SOEs and the issuance of privatisation vouchers.

As shown in Fig. 7.4, the development of the Russian stock market during 1993–2020 was uneven. Over 28 years, it experienced four major financial crises: in 1997–1998, 2008–2009, 2014, and 2020. As a result of the rapid stock market growth in the late 1990s-early 2000s, the capitalisation and liquidity indices peaked in 2007. Then, in 2014, the capitalisation and exchange trading volume plunged to 24.9% and 7.8% of GDP, respectively, and after 2015, they once again rose to 48.1% and 18.6% in 2020. Nevertheless, the capitalisation and trading volume of the Russian stock market in 2020 stood approximately at the level of 2003. The share of capitalisation of Russian companies in the global capitalisation index hit its record high of 2.5% in 2007 and 2010, and the share of stock trading volumes amounted to 1.4% in 2007. In 2020, the global share of the Russian stock market by capitalisation and stock trading volume was only 0.8% and 0.3%, respectively.

Given the insufficient level of development of domestic institutional investors, the capitalisation and liquidity of the Russian stock market largely depend on commodity prices in global markets and the behaviour of foreign

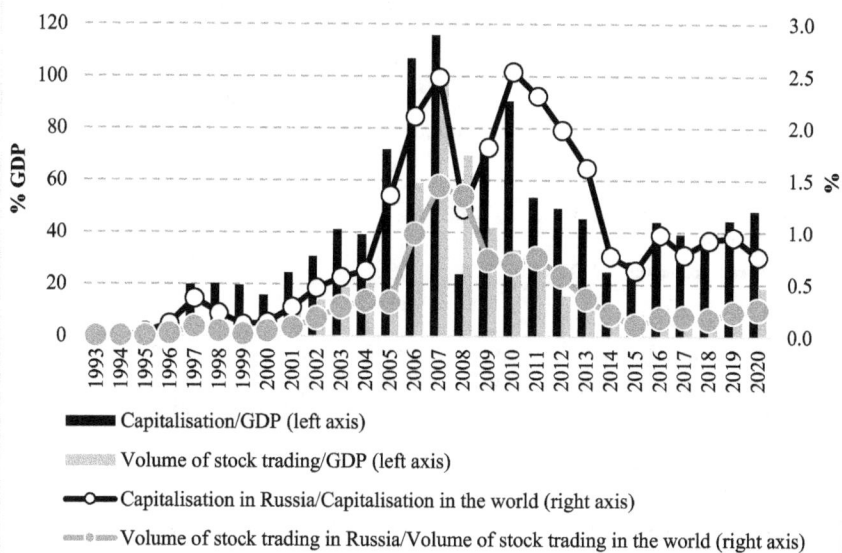

Fig. 7.4 Indicators of the capitalisation value and volume of stock trading in shares of Russian companies in GDP (%) and similar indicators in the world (%) (*Source* authors' calculations based on the World Bank's World Development Indicators, data of the World Federation of Exchanges https://statistics.world-exchanges.org/Account/Login, the IMF International Financial Statistics (IFS) database, and data of the Russian stock exchanges https://www.moex.com/)

portfolio investors.[13] It was only in the late 2010s that domestic retail investors began to play a more active role in stock market transactions. Their share in these transactions, according to the Moscow Exchange, increased from 35% in 2017 to 44% in 2020.

To understand the peculiarities of stock market evolution since the early 1990s, four equal time periods—seven years each—can be distinguished (Table 7.3). During the first period (1993–1999), the domestic stock market and its infrastructure were created in the course of mass privatisation. The second (2000–2006) was a period of steady stock market growth sustained by climbing raw material commodity prices, foreign investment inflow, and structural reforms in the economy. This was followed in 2007–2013 by the GFC of 2008–2009 and the subsequent recovery, with the increased volatility of oil prices and stock indices. And finally, 2014–2020 was a period of volatile commodity prices, weak investment activity, rising geopolitical risks, and the strengthening role of the government in the economy.

---

[13] According to the estimates of the Bank of Russia in 2019, the share of non-residents in the Free Float of shares of Russian companies was 52% (Bank of Russia, 2020).

Table 7.3 Average annual indicators of the Russian stock market at various stages of its development on the time horizon, 1993–2020

Indicator	Years			
	1993–1999	2000–2006	2007–2013	2014–2020
Growth rate of real GDP, %	−3.8	7.0	2.9	0.4
Growth rate of investments in fixed assets in USD, %	−19.3	33.8	20.0	−4.0
Price of Brent crude oil, USD per barrel	17.6	37.9	91.7	61.0
Inflation, %	191.4	13.9	8.8	6.3
USD to RUB exchange rate	9.7	29.3	30.9	64.7
Capitalisation, share in GDP, %	9.6	47.0	64.0	39.1
Stock exchange transactions, share in GDP, %	1.9	21.2	42.2	10.7
Number of listed companies per 1 million population	0.3	1.1	2.2	1.6
RTS Total Return Index, in USD, % per annum	88.0*	45.9	11.6	4.3
Corporate bonds, share in GDP, %	0.4**	1.5	5.7	11.5
Share of SOEs in capitalisation, %	N/A	40.9	49.4	49.4
Share of SOEs in outstanding corporate bonds, %	N/A	17.7***	33.5	61.1
Pension reserves and savings, share in GDP, %	0.2****	1.1	3.6	5.7
Net assets of mutual funds, share in GDP, %	0.04****	0.2	0.2	0.3

Notes * for the period 1996–1999; ** for the period 1998–1999; *** for the period 2003–2006; **** for the period 1997–1999

Source: authors' calculations based on the data of the World Bank's World Development Indicators, World Federation of Exchanges, the IMF International Financial Statistics (IFS), Bloomberg https://www.bloomberg.com/professional/solution/bloomberg-terminal/, Cbonds https://cbonds.ru/ and SPARK https://spark-interfax.ru/about, and companies' annual reports for different years.

In 1993–1999, the stock market was born in the unfavourable conditions of negative economic growth, a decline in investment in fixed assets in US dollar (USD) terms, and average annual inflation exceeding 190% per annum. In this situation, the goal of creating an organised stock market was part of market reforms aimed at building private ownership, boosting competition, and attracting foreign investment into the Russian economy.

In accordance with the Executive Order of the President of the Russian Federation No. 721 dated 1 July 1992, the State Property Committee and its regional agencies, over the period from July 1992 through June 1994, reorganised more than 22,000 state enterprises into joint stock companies

(Boyko et al., 1996), of which between December 1992 and June 1994, 15,100 companies were privatised with an average stake of 20% of the authorised capital (Blasi et al., 1997). Voucher privatisation involved millions of individuals in the stock market. More than 98% of Russian citizens received privatisation vouchers. In the course of voucher privatisation, 25% of privatisation vouchers were invested in voucher investment funds, 25% were sold to intermediaries, and the remaining 50% were invested in shares purchased either by employees in their own companies through closed auctions or at open voucher auctions (Chubais et al., 1999).

Privatisation gave rise to new financial intermediaries involved in transactions with vouchers. Some of them evolved into large investment companies operating according to Western standards. The stock market was organised on liberal principles, and from the very beginning, it became attractive to major foreign investment banks and funds. The risks of the Russian stock market during that period were very high, but the high rate of return for the most part offset those risks. Our calculations show the average annual return of the Russian Trading System (RTS) Index in 1996–1999 to be 88% per annum.

In November–December 1995, during the next wave of privatisation, the 'loans-for-shares' auctions were held, during which the shares in 12 major joint stock companies (Norilsk Nickel, Lukoil, YUKOS, Sibneft, Surgutneftegaz, Mechel, NLMK, and others) to the total value of USD 780 million were taken over by private entities controlled by financial oligarchs or former top managers of the privatised companies. To this day, these transactions raise criticism in society, because they are viewed as collusion between the executive power and oligarchs. Nevertheless, Treisman (2010) notes also some of their positive aspects, in particular, the fact that the consolidation of control over privatised companies by the oligarchs has significantly improved their performance measured against comparable SOEs.

In the second half of the 1990s, due to active privatisation, a liquid stock market emerged, and this was what the other FSU countries failed to achieve at that time. The most important steps in this direction included the following:

- Creation of a reliable system for registering title to shares in privatised companies with independent registrars;
- Introduction of the institution of a nominee holder of shares (1993);
- Creation of PAUFOR (hereinafter—NAUFOR), a self-regulating organisation of brokers (1994);
- Development of a regulatory framework for mutual funds as an alternative to the numerous financial pyramids of the 1990s (1995);
- Creation of an organised stock market based on the RTS (1995);
- Adoption of Federal Law No. 39-FZ dated 22 April 1996 'On the Securities Market'; and
- Creation of the Federal Securities and Stock Market Commission as a separate and independent executive authority.

As a result, by the end of the 1990s, Russia had developed a dynamically growing domestic stock market based on competition and private initiative, which, unlike the banking system, successfully survived the crisis of 1997–1998.

The period 2000–2006 was the most dynamic one for Russia in terms of economic and stock market growth. The average annual growth rates of GDP and investment reached 7.0% and 33.8%, respectively, and the average inflation rate plunged to 13.9%. The share of capitalisation in GDP increased to 47.0% and the volume of stock exchange transactions, to 21.2%, compared with the corresponding average indices of 9.6% and 1.9% over the previous seven years. The average annual return of the RTS Index was 45.9% per annum.

The growth of the economy and the stock market during that period was based on rising global commodity prices and an inflow of foreign portfolio investors. However, according to Kudrin and Gurvich (2014), economic development was also influenced by the ongoing market reforms. These included new budget, tax, labour, and land codes; an improving business climate; a programme of 'de-bureaucratisation' of the economy; and a reduction of the tax burden on the raw materials sector. In the early 2000s, foreign exchange legislation was liberalised, and Russia received investment-grade credit ratings from the rating agencies Moody's, Standard & Poor's, and Fitch, which contributed to an increased foreign portfolio investment inflow.

The stock market growth was facilitated by privatisation deals, the liberalisation of the market for shares in Gazprom, and the onset of the restructuring of RAO United Energy System (UES) Russia.

The biggest privatisation deals of the first half of the 2000s were the sales of a 49% stake in Rosgosstrakh in 2001, of 74.95% of shares in Slavneft to a consortium of Sibneft and TNK-BP in 2002, and of a stake in Lukoil (oil company) to ConocoPhillips in 2004. In 2006, an IPO of 15% of shares in Rosneft was completed, which were sold for USD 10.4 billion, and the following year saw IPOs by Sberbank and VTB Bank.

In 2005, the market for shares in Gazprom was liberalised: the 20% limit on ownership of its shares for non-residents was lifted, and so Gazprom shares could now be listed on Russia's major exchanges, the RTS and the MICEX.

In 2006–2008, in order to create a competitive electricity market and attract investments in the electric power industry, the state-owned holding company RAO UES Russia was reorganised by being divided into 23 independent private companies and only two state-owned ones—the Federal Grid Company (FGC) and IDGC Holding Company (Chubais, 2018; Urinson et al., 2020).

A serious test for the market was the conflict between the Russian government and Yukos Oil Company, whose CEOs in 2003–2004 were accused of tax evasion and other offenses. As a result of that conflict, the company's main asset, Yuganskneftegaz, was eventually taken over by Rosneft and Yukos itself was liquidated in 2007.

The GFC of 2008–2009 put an end to the long-standing trend of rising oil prices, their volatility increased, the growth of domestic investment slowed down, and foreign investment began to outflow. In 2007–2013, the average annual GDP growth rate plunged to 2.9% from 7.0% in 2000–2006, that is, by 2.4 times. Alongside an economic slowdown, the average rate of return of the RTS Index dropped from 45.9% to 11.6% per annum. The economic indicators point to the strengthening role of the state in the stock and bond markets. The economic policy choice was made in favour of increasing state participation in the economy and the allocation of financial resources. In 2007, state corporations and development institutions began to be rapidly set up (STLC, Rosatom, RVC, Rostec, Rusnano, and SME Corporation, among others). In 2014–2020, the average annual GDP growth rate plummeted from 2.9% in 2007–2013 to 0.4%, or by 7.2 times. From July 2014, sectorial sanctions were imposed against Russian businesses (see Chapter 14). However, an economic and investment slowdown had been triggered by internal factors even earlier, in the second half of 2012, when oil prices were relatively high and there were no sanctions (see Chapter 15).

In an effort to support the banking system's activity, from late 2012, the Bank of Russia began to increase its refinancing of banks (primarily state-owned ones) channelled through repo transactions, the volume of corresponding outstanding debt increasing as a result from RUB 3.0 trillion in December 2012 to RUB 9.5 trillion in December 2014. From 2014, the Bank of Russia took over the role of a mega-regulator of the financial market. This increased financial sector stability, while the financial market stagnated. Also from 2014, a moratorium was imposed on new contributions to the second pillar fully funded pension system (see Chapter 18).

This period was also marked by large transactions, during which shares of private entities passed into direct state ownership or to SOEs. In 2012, the state-owned company Rosneft bought 100% of shares in TNK-BP from its private shareholders. In 2016, by decision of the Arbitration Court of Moscow in response to the claim of the Prosecutor General's Office of the Russian Federation, 71% of shares in Bashneft, an oil company privatised in the early 2000s, were transferred into federal ownership, and later on, 50.075% of these shares were sold to Rosneft. In 2017, in the course of bankruptcy preventing measures, the Bank of Russia became the owner of shares in Otkrytie Bank, as well as in Binbank, the latter being merged with Otkrytie on 1 January 2019. Meanwhile, Promsvyazbank was also rehabilitated, and its shares transferred to the Federal Agency for State Property Management. In 2018, 29% of shares in the Magnit retail chain were transferred to VTB Bank.

Thus, the domestic stock market and the economy at large are currently faced with the task of finding new growth drivers. As shown in Table 7.4, Russia's share in the world by its key indicators of the depth of the stock market (share of capitalisation and stock trading in GDP, number of listed companies) is significantly below Russia's input in global GDP and share in world population. At the same time, the financial market development index calculated by the IMF was steadily on the decline.

The future prospects of the Russian stock market are for the most part associated with its reliance on domestic investors. The years 2020–2021 saw a massive inflow of private investors into the market. According to data released by the Moscow Exchange, the number of individual accounts with brokers increased from 3.9 million in 2019 to 16.8 million in 2021, or by 4.3 times. The number of investors in market mutual funds jumped from 0.5 million to 4.7 million over the same period, or by 9.4 times. The share of retail investors in stock trading increased from 35% in 2018 to 40% in 2021.

At the same time, the domestic stock market remains constrained by the underdeveloped domestic institutional investors, uncertainty about the prospects of mandatory pension savings and corporate pension plans, the low level of competition between financial structures, outdated standards for retail sales of financial products, the high collective investment costs for private investors, a limited inflow of new Russian companies listed on the domestic exchanges, and the volatility of foreign portfolio investment flows in the stock and bond markets (Radygin et al., 2021).

As the history of the Russian stock market demonstrates, its development could be facilitated by the privatisation of stakes in large SOEs. However, the question as to its future evolution remains open.

Table 7.4 Average annual share of Russia in the world by individual indicators of the stock market at various stages of its development, 1993–2020

Indicator	Years			
	1993–1999	2000–2006	2007–2013	2014–2020
GDP in USD at purchasing power parity, %	2.2	2.4	3.4	3.2
Investment in fixed assets, %	1.1	1.1	2.4	1.7
Population, %	2.6	2.3	2.1	1.9
Capitalisation, %	0.1	0.8	2.0	0.8
Stock trading volume, %	0.03	0.3	0.8	0.2
Number of listed companies, %	0.12	0.38	0.71	0.53
Average annual Financial Market Development Index for Russia, IMF coefficient	0.51	0.61	0.56	0.37

Source Own calculations based on the World Development Indicators (WDI) databases of the World Bank, the statistics portal of the World Federation of Exchanges, and the Financial Development Index Database of the International Monetary Fund https://data.imf.org/?sk=F8032E80-B36C-43B1-AC26-493C5B1CD33B

7.6 Conclusions

Despite the mass privatisation of the 1990s and the continuously declining number of registered SOEs, Russia in the 2010s had one of the largest public sectors in the world in terms of its share in GDP, capitalisation, and share in employment, among others. The public sector increased in the 2000s mainly in its SOE segment.

Unlike the situation in the early 1990s, political arguments in favour of privatisation have disappeared. Fiscal considerations are still important, but they are not as strong as in the 2000s. Accordingly, the main argument in favour of further denationalisation is the need for optimisation across the public sector as a whole and economic efficiency. This policy requires a pragmatic balance between retaining government influence in some sectors and its complete withdrawal from others, and replacement of state ownership with sectoral regulation and other forms of control over strategic companies.

Overall, the corporate governance model in Russia, both in its hard (the Civil Code and the Federal Law 'On Joint Stock Companies') and soft (the Corporate Governance Code) components, is no worse and no better than other national models, including in the OECD and EU countries. It covers all significant areas of corporate governance. The Russian Corporate Governance Code is a high-quality well-structured document, and its content is consistent with the international standards of corporate governance, including the OECD Principles of Corporate Governance. It is by no means inferior to, and sometimes surpasses, the codes of other countries.

The central question is what steps should be taken next to improve the quality of corporate governance? The easiest way would be to follow the path of formal improvement, in particular, a revision of legislation on joint stock companies and efforts to properly implement the Corporate Governance Code (e.g., the monitoring of private enterprises and SOEs and administrative pressure to improve their indicators, among others).

However, this is not enough. The main constraints are rooted in the period of the 1990s and 2000s: a relatively high level of joint stock ownership concentration, the 'closed' nature of most companies (while they formally remain public), the organisation of businesses in the form of groups of companies, the combination of management and ownership functions, the prevalence of own resources and debt as sources of financing, and over-compliant boards of directors, among others.

This majority-dominated model of joint stock ownership and corporate governance, in spite of the adequate quality of legislation, actually lacks a well-functioning classical system of checks and balances capable of protecting the interests of all parties. For obvious reasons, this is even more typical of SOEs, where the strategic and fiscal interests of the government can radically diverge from those of private minority shareholders.

The improvement of corporate governance quality in SOEs should not be reduced just to modifying its rules. It is necessary to stimulate the transformation of SOEs into public companies with IPOs and secondary public offerings of their stocks. Reducing the scale of direct state involvement in the economy also means increasing the scale of privatisation of large companies and synchronising federal and regional denationalisation policies.

The introduction of Western sanctions since 2014, which will probably be long term, inevitably brings to the forefront the issue of domestic competition, thus implying the increasing role of a market mechanism, including the continuation of privatisation programmes.

The large-scale privatisation carried out in the 1990s contributed to the formation of a liquid domestic stock market, which demonstrated rapid growth in the early 2000s, thanks to an inflow of forex earnings generated by exports and foreign portfolio investment. As these growth factors were exhausted, after the 2008–2009 GFC the investment mechanism was reoriented towards state development institutions and SOEs, and the role of financial regulation strengthened to maintain financial stability. The competition level in the stock market became lower. Alongside the increased volatility in global financial markets and rising geopolitical risks, all this brought down the pace of stock market recovery. The prospects for its further evolution will depend on the growth potential of domestic savings and the use of modern digital technologies. A new wave of privatisation could also give an additional impetus to its development.

Questions for Students

1. What were the main stages of privatisation in Russia, what were their major characteristics, and which of the stages was of the greatest importance for the systemic transformation of the Russian economy?
2. What was the dynamic of the public sector in Russia's GDP in 1992–2020 and its major characteristics?
3. Characterise the long-term changes in the ownership structure of Russian companies caused by privatisation. How have they affected their effectiveness?
4. What are the main features of the corporate governance model in Russian joint stock companies?
5. How has mass privatisation affected the Russian stock market and its features in comparison with other countries?

References

Abramov, A., Radygin, A., Entov, R., & Chernova, M. (2017). State ownership and efficiency characteristics. *Russian Journal of Economics, 3*(2), 129–157. https://doi.org/10.1016/j.ruje.2017.06.002

Alexeev, M., & Weber, S. (Eds.). (2013). *The Oxford handbook of the Russian economy.* Oxford University Press.

Aukutsionek, S., Kapeliushnikov, R., & Zhukov, V. (1998). Dominant shareholders and performance of industrial enterprises. *The Russian Economic Barometer, 1*, 8–41. https://www.imemo.ru/files/File/magazines/REB_kvartal_EN/1998/1998_01_reb_kvartal_eng.pdf

Aukutsionek, S., Dyomina, N., & Kapelyushnikov, R. (2007). Ownership structure of the Russian industrial enterprises in 2007. *The Russian Economic Barometer, 3*, 3–11. https://www.imemo.ru/en/publications/periodical/reb-quarterly-eng/archive/2007/1-4

Bank of Russia. https://www.cbr.ru/issuers_corporate/analitics

Bank of Russia. (2020). *Obzor rossiiskogo finansovogo sektora i finansovykh instrumentov. 2019 god. Analiticheskii material* [Overview of the Russian financial sector and financial instruments, 2019. Analytical material]. Bank of Russia. http://www.cbr.ru/Collection/Collection/File/32167/overview_2019.pdf

Blasi, J., Kroumova, M., & Kruse, D. (1997). *Kremlin capitalism: The privatisation of the Russian economy.* Cornell University Press.

Bloomberg Information Resources. https://www.bloomberg.com/professional/solution/bloomberg-terminal/

Bortolotti, B., & Faccio, M. (2004). *Reluctant privatisation* (EGGI Working Paper 4). https://EconPapers.repec.org/RePEc:hit:hitcei:2006-5

Boubakri, N., Cosset, J., & Guedhami, O. (2005). Postprivatisation corporate governance: The role of ownership structure and investor protection. *Journal of Financial Economics, 76*(2), 369–399. https://doi.org/10.1016/j.jfineco.2004.05.003

Boyko, M., Shleifer, A., & Vishny, R. (1996). *Privatising Russia.* The MIT Press.

Brown, J. D., Earle, J. S., & Telegdy, A. (2006). The productivity effects of privatisation: Longitudinal estimates from Hungary, Romania, Russia, and Ukraine. *Journal of Political Economy, 114*(1), 61–99. https://doi.org/10.1086/499547

Cbonds statistics. https://cbonds.ru/

Chubais, A. B. (Ed.). (1999). *Privatizatsiia po-rossiiski* [Privatisation Russian-style]. Vagrius Publishing House.

Chubais, A. B. (2018). Reforma rossiiskoi elektroenergetiki: desiat' let spustiya [Russian Electric Power Industry Reform: 10 Years Later]. *Voprosy Ekonomiki, 8*, 39–56. https://dlib.eastview.com/browse/doc/51592930

Claessens, S., & Djankov, S. (2002). Privatisation benefits in Eastern Europe. *Journal of Public Economics, 83*(3), 307–324. https://doi.org/10.1016/S0047-2727(00)00169-9

Dolgopiatova, T. (2002). Corporate control in the Russian industry: Actors and mechanisms, east-west. *Journal of Economics and Business, 5*(2), 197–215. https://www.u-picardie.fr/eastwest/fichiers/art20.pdf

Dolgopiatova, T. (2007). Ownership concentration and Russian company development: Empirical evidence. *Problems of Economic Transition, 50*(5), 7–23. https://doi.org/10.2753/PET1061-1991500501

EBRD. (2017). *Corporate Governance in transition economies: Russian country report.* European Bank for Reconstruction and Development. http://www.ebrd.com/documents/ogc/russia.pdf

Ernst & Young Corporate Governance Services Group and SKOLKOVO Independent Directors Club. (2020). *The impact of the COVID-19 pandemic on the activities of the Board of Directors.* https://roscongress.org/en/materials/vliyanie-pandemii-covid-19-na-deyatelnost-soveta-direktorov/

Estrin, S., Hanousek, J., Kocenda, E., & Svejnar, J. (2009). The effects of privatisation and ownership in transition economies. *Journal of Economic Literature, 47*(3), 699–728. https://doi.org/10.1257/jel.47.3.699

Gaidar, Y. (Ed.). (2003). *The economics of Russian transition.* The MIT Press.

Grigoriev, L. M., & Kurdin, A. A. (2016). Nereshennyi vopros legitimnosti chastnoi sobstvennosti v Rossii [The unsolved question of the legitimacy of private property in Russia]. *Voprosy Ekonomiki, 1,* 36–62. https://dlib.eastview.com/browse/doc/46029120

Gurevich, V. S. (Ed.). (2020). *Ekonomicheskaia politika Rossii. Turbulentnoe desiatiletie 2008–2018* [Russia's economic policy. The turbulent decade 2008–2018]. Delo Publishing House.

Guriev, S., Lazareva, A., Rachinsky, S., & Tsukhilo, S. (2004). Corporate governance in Russian industry. *Problems of Economic Transition, 47,* 6–83. https://doi.org/10.1080/10611991.2004.11049910

IMF. (2019). *Reassessing the role of state-owned enterprises in Central, Eastern, and Southeastern Europe* (European Departmental Paper Series No. 19). European Department. https://www.imf.org/en/Publications/Departmental-Papers-Policy-Papers/Issues/2019/06/17/Reassessing-the-Role-of-State-Owned-Enterprises-in-Central-Eastern-and-Southeastern-Europe-46859

International Financial Statistics (IFS) databases of the International Monetary Fund: https://data.imf.org/?sk=4c514d48-b6ba-49ed-8ab9-52b0c1a0179b

Kudrin, A., & Gurvich, E. (2014). Novaia model' rosta dlya rossiiskoi ekonomiki [A new growth model for the Russian economy]. *Voprosy Ekonomiki, 12,* 4–36. https://doi.org/10.32609/0042-8736-2014-12-4-36

Marcelin, I., & Mathur, I. (2015). Privatisation, financial development, property rights and growth. *Journal of Banking & Finance, 50,* 528–546. https://doi.org/10.1016/j.jbankfin.2014.03.034

Megginson, W. L. (2017). Privatisation, state capitalism, and state ownership of business in the 21st century. *Foundations and Trends in Finance 11*(1–2), 1–153. https://doi.org/10.1561/0500000053

National Corporate Governance Index 2020 RUCGI: https://corpshark.ru/p/natsionalnyj-indeks-korporativnogo-upravleniya-2020-rucgi/

OECD. (2015). *Guidelines on corporate governance of state-owned enterprises.* OECD Publishing. https://www.oecd.org/corporate/guidelines-corporate-governance-soes.htm

OECD. (2017). *The size and sectoral distribution of state-owned enterprises.* OECD Publishing. https://www.oecd.org/publications/the-size-and-sectoral-distribution-of-state-owned-enterprises-9789264280663-en.htm

Petrova, S., Podtcerob, U., & Romanova, S. (2016). Korporativnoe upravlenie v Rossii ne uluchshaetsia s 2012 goda [Corporate governance in Russia has not improved since 2012]. *Vedomosti,* 5 April. https://www.vedomosti.ru/management/articles/2016/04/06/636572-korporativnoe-upravlenie

Radygin, A. (1992). Spontaneous privatisation: Motivations, forms and stages. *Studies on Soviet Economic Development, 3*(5), 341–347.

Radygin, A. (1995). *Privatisation in Russia: Hard choice, first results, new targets*. CRCE-The Jarvis Print Group.

Radygin, A. D., & Entov, R. M. (1999). *Institutsional'nye problemy razvitiia korporativnogo sektora: sobstvennost', kontrol', rynok tsennykh bumag* [Institutional problems of corporate sector development: ownership, control, securities market] (Vol. 12P). IEPP. https://www.iep.ru/ru/publikatcii/publication/452.html

Radygin, A. (2000). The redistribution of property rights in post-privatisation Russia. *Problems of Economic Transition, 42*(11), 6–34. https://doi.org/10.2753/PET1061-199142116

Radygin, A. D., & Entov, R. M. (2001). *Korporativnoe upravlenie i zashchita prav sobstvennosti: empiricheskii analiz i aktual'nye napravleniia reform* [Corporate governance and the protection of property rights: An empirical analysis of current trends and reforms]. (Working Papers 36P). Institute for the Economy in Transition. https://www.iep.ru/files/text/usaid/corporation.pdf

Radygin, A., Abramov, A., Entov, R., Chernova, M., & Malginov, G. (2019). *Privatisation in Russia: 30 years after. The size and effectiveness of the state sector*. Delo Publishing House. https://EconPapers.repec.org/RePEc:rnp:ppaper:021904

Radygin, A. D., Abramov, A. E., & Chernova, M. I. (2021). Rossiiskii fondovyi rynok: tendencii, vyzovy I orientiry rapvitiya [The Russian stock market: trends, challenges, development guidelines]. *Voprosy Ekonomiki, 11*, 5–32. https://dlib.eastview.com/browse/doc/71309667

Shvyrkov, O. (2008). *Opyt otsenki korporativnogo upravleniia v rossiiskikh kompaniiakh. Materialy rossiiskogo 'kruglogo stola' po voprosam koporativnogo upravleniia* [Experience in assessing corporate governance in Russian companies. Materials of the Russian 'round table' on corporate governance]. OECD and Ministry of Economic Development. http://docplayer.com/storage/80/80674740/1654949667/dtAYkVXbB6HMZhxniHe30Q/80674740.pdf

SPARK: https://spark-interfax.ru/about and annual reports of companies for different years.

State property indices IPEI RANEPA: https://ipei.ranepa.ru/en/soe/indices

Tambovtsev, V. L. (Ed.). (2009). *Prava sobstvennosti, privatizatsiia i natsionalizatsiia v Rossii [Property rights, privatisation and nationalisation in Russia]*. Liberal Mission Foundation.

Treisman D (2010) *'Loans for shares' Revisited* (NBER Working Paper 15819). NBER. http://www.nber.org/papers/w15819

Urinson, Y. M., Kozhukhovskii, I. S., & Sorokin, I. S. (2020). Reformirovanie rossiiskoi elektroenergetiki: rezul'taty i nereshennye voprosy [Reforming the Russian electric power industry: results and unresolved issues]. *HSE Economic Journal, 3*, 323–339. https://doi.org/10.17323/1813-8691-2020-24-3-323-339

World Development Indicators (WDI) databases: https://databank.worldbank.org/source/world-development-indicators

World Federation of Exchanges: https://statistics.world-exchanges.org/Account/Login

PART IV

Major Sectors and Regional Diversity

CHAPTER 8

Structural Changes in the Russian Economy Since 1992

Svetlana Avdasheva

Highlights

- The overall structure of the Russian economy does not differ much from most industrialised countries: market and non-market services account for the largest part of employment.
- This structure is a result of the considerable decline of industry—and especially manufacturing—during the 30 years after liberalisation reforms.
- International competition has been the most important driver of structural changes in Russia since 1992.
- Thirty years of structural transformation after liberalisation contain two processes: the adaptation of old capacities to sustain competition in the market economy (the restructuring of brownfields) and the emergence of new businesses and sectors (the growth of greenfields).
- Restructured brownfield industries are still more competitive internationally than greenfield ones.
- Vertical industrial policy measures, with a high ratio of public versus private financing, prevail over horizontal industrial policy measures.

S. Avdasheva (✉)
Higher School of Economics, Moscow, Russia
e-mail: avdash@hse.ru

8.1 Introduction

There is a widespread view of Russia as the 'world's gas station'—a country highly skewed towards the extraction and primary refining of natural resources. This view strengthened in 2022 after the waves of international sanctions and retaliatory measures, which substantially limit exports from and imports to Russia. The projected impact of sanctions and countersanctions on the global trade is driven by the fact that the Russian share in the global trade of essential commodities is incredibly large: 10–14% for crude oil; 15% for coal briquettes; 13–23% for fertilizers; 18–21% for wheat; 14% for sunflower oil; 25% for palladium; 14% for nickel; and 13% for platinum (Ruta, 2022). All the products in the list are categorised as either fuels, metals, or agricultural raw materials.

The most well-known large Russian corporations come from these sectors. Among the 10 largest oil and gas companies by number of employees, one-half are Russian companies (Gazprom, Rosneft, Transneft, Lukoil, and Surgutneftegas).[1] In the global energy market, Russia is the third largest primary energy producer, the second largest producer of oil and gas, and the largest supplier of pipeline gas (see Chapter 9).

Today, the Russian economy and especially Russian fiscal and monetary policy highly depend on energy exports (see Chapter 16). Almost every economic indicator in Russia—budget deficit or surplus, rouble exchange rate, birth of new companies, and bankruptcy rate—depends on the oil price. This may seem strange when we recall that the Soviet economy—for which Russia is a legal heir—was not deeply integrated into global markets or the international division of labour. With no free flow of goods, capital, or labour and almost 300 million inhabitants, the Soviet economy should have had a complex structure.

This chapter explains why the Russian economy participates in global markets with predominantly primary products, how the structure of the economy changed during the transition period, the challenges that the Russian economic structure created for governments, and how the Russian government has faced these challenges.

In this chapter, we consider economic structure as a composition of the national economy (measured by value added and gross domestic product as the sum of value added, or by employment) in terms of sectors and industries. Any classification of economic sectors or industries contains several levels. A common classification into industry, agriculture, and services uses the attribute of technologies used. Industry then might be divided into mining and manufacturing, and services—into market (provided for money) and non-market (provided for individuals or communities free of charge) services. Another way to classify sectors and industries uses groups of goods sold in the country. All the goods produced are divided into traded and non-traded goods and

---

[1] https://www.statista.com/statistics/717302/largest-oil-and-gas-companies-worldwide-by-employment/.

traded and non-traded sectors, respectively. Traded goods can be imported or exported, and therefore, companies from different countries compete with each other in the markets for these goods. The Revealed Comparative Advantage[2] (RCA) index shows how successful the competition between companies from different countries is. The supply of non-traded goods is localised within the country (for instance, heating or construction). For analytical purposes, all goods could be divided along a simplified chain of value creation, as capital goods (buildings, machinery, and equipment used in the production of finished goods), raw materials and intermediate goods (materials or substances used in primary production as well as semi-finished materials), and consumer goods. Further classification is also possible. The structure of the economy might be described under different levels of detail or generalisation. In this chapter, we attempt to analyse specific industries and the production of certain goods to explain the content of the competition Russian companies face in global and domestic markets; however, we are limited to the statistics available.

Important conceptual frameworks for this chapter are *economic system* and *transition*. After 1992, Russia went through a transition from an *administrative command economy*, where the government determines the allocation of resources and the distribution of the value added, to a *market economy*, where these decisions are made independently by economic actors, using pricing information that the market provides. The comparative advantage of a market economy is that the decentralised system of market allocation accumulates and provides incentives to economic decisions, which, at the end (with reservations well-known from the theory of market failures), result in an efficient outcome. Therefore, the transition from an administrative command economy to the market one in an ideal world should increase the efficiency of resource allocation. In this chapter, we are going to explain why the transition was so difficult for Russian producers individually and in large sectors, keeping in mind that this issue is still debatable, and why many industries did not reach efficiency gains.

First, we present the structure of the Russian economy in comparison with other countries (Sect. 8.2). Next, we analyse the main features of the structural changes in the Russian economy (Sect. 8.3). Finally, we provide a brief overview of the policies that the government applies in order to improve the composition of industry in the Russian economy as well as the patterns of their development (Sect. 8.4).

---

[2] The Revealed Comparative Advantage (RCA) index is ratio, where the numerator is the share of a particular country's exports of the commodity of interest in the total exports of the country, and the denominator is the share of the exports of the same commodity in total global exports. An RCA exceeding 1 is interpreted as a comparative advantage of a country in the international division of labour.

8.2 Structure of the Russian Economy: International Comparisons

At first glance, the structure of the Russian economy does not differ much from those of other industrialised countries (Table 8.1). The share of industry in employment exceeds the respective indicator for the world and is only slightly smaller than in China or Germany. Industry as a sum of mining and manufacturing contributes more than 41% of the total value added, that is, it is slightly less than in Germany and substantially less than in China. However, the share of manufacturing in the Russian gross domestic product (GDP) is only 14.9%, which is substantially less than in Germany or China (20.0 and 26.2%, respectively). In 1991, the last year before transition, the share of industry in employment was 40%, and the share of manufacturing in value added was 24%. Over the next 30 years, the Russian economy deindustrialised. This structural change requires an explanation.

Deindustrialisation is not a unique phenomenon in the modern world (see Rodrik, 2016). The traditional explanation of deindustrialisation in developed countries involves the international division of labour and the industrialisation of developing countries. As industrialisation takes place in developing countries, industrial capacities, especially those that are environmentally hazardous, move there from high-income countries. In high-income countries, the economy grows using their comparative advantages in technology

Table 8.1 Indicators of the structure of the Russian economy: international comparisons, 2019 and 2020

Indicator	Sector	Russia	World	European Union	Germany	China**
Share of employment (2019), %	Industry	26.8	22.7	25	27.2	27.4
	Agriculture	5.8	26.7	4.4	1.2	25.3
	Services	67.4	50.6	70.7	71.6	47.3
Share of GDP (2020), %	Agriculture	4.1			0.8	8.0
	Mining	26.6			23.4	30.8
	Manufacturing	14.9			20.0	26.2
	Construction	6.9			5.8	7.2
	Wholesale, retail trade, restaurants, and hotels	17.2			11.4	11.0
	Transport	7.7			9.3	7.8
	Others	37.5			49.2	35.2

Note For share of GDP—China mainland
Source For structure of employment: World Development Indicators, International Labour Organization projection; for share of the value added by economic activities: UNCTAD data. Sum of shares in GDP exceeds 100% because of the methodology used.

and knowledge creation. In turn, increasing productivity in high-income countries allows value added in manufacturing to increase together with the decrease in employment. This explains the U-inverted dependence between GDP per capita and the share of manufacturing in employment and value added. However, deindustrialisation in Russia can hardly be explained in this way. First, in the analysed period (1992–2019), Russia was an upper-middle-income country, not a high-income country. Second, deindustrialisation took place together with a decline in GDP per capita. In constant USD (that is, in comparable values), Russian GDP per capita from 1989 (the last year before the radical collapse of the Soviet economy) to 2019 increased by only about 23%. Moreover, the market-oriented development of Russia started with a 45% decrease in GDP per capita between 1989 and 1998.

An alternative explanation of deindustrialisation (Rodrik, 2016) is applicable for small developing countries, in the process of trade liberalisation as a transition from a closed to an open economy. Under conditions of free trade, countries specialise in the products in which they are relatively more productive. If the national industry is unable to produce goods at sufficiently low costs, it loses to foreign competitors and imports replace domestic production. This is often the case if the country is a late industrialiser. When a new industry has insufficient time to reach high productivity, under conditions of free international trade, it shrinks.

There is evidence that supports this explanation for Russian deindustrialisation. First, liberalisation reforms began with the radical opening of the Russian economy to free trade. In 1992, both the ratios of exports and imports to GDP exceeded 100%.[3] Second, as many late industrialisers, Russia exhibits comparative advantages in primary products, first of all, oil and natural gas. While fuel and energy products account for only 15–20% of Russian GDP,[4] they represent about 50% of the country's exports. At the same time, one can doubt that Rodrik's explanation is completely right for Russia. We know that Russia is hardly a 'late industrialiser'. Russia was an industrial country long before liberalisation. Should we further analyse or reject Rodrik's explanation for Russia?

8.3 Liberalisation Shock and Further Restructuring of Russian Industries

The transition from a planned to a market economy in Russia in the 1990s changed the environment of decision-making for domestic businesses. First,

---

[3] To some extent, this is a matter of statistics. In 1992, Russia experienced a very high inflation rate with substantial adjustments to the rouble exchange rate. At the same time, prices for some groups of goods remained frozen. In this context, statistics both for GDP and export and import flows are imperfect. However, the roughness of the estimates does not call into question the fact that Russia jumped from a closed to an open economy very quickly.

[4] The volatility of oil prices explains the large variation.

after privatisation, new owners had to make decisions based on the criteria of their private benefits (profit maximisation). Even if we are far from considering the state as a 'welfare-maximising social planner', there is no doubt that under the centrally planned economy, decisions were motivated by a more complex set of objectives. The conventional advantage of a market over planned economy is that private owners have more incentives to allocate resources efficiently. This means that private owners choose other quantities, other product mixes, and other buyers as well as set different prices (unless the individual is a price-taker). Second, liberalisation implies free prices. In the Soviet planned economy, prices were not only distorted in comparison to market prices, but they were also entirely artificial. The rapid opening of Russia to international trade also meant rapid price adjustments.

The adaptation process for owners of privatised capacities (inherited from the Soviet period)—let's call them brownfield—is known as restructuring. Developed as 'enterprises' within Soviet planned system, the capacities should become 'firms'. This was a fairly difficult process for many reasons, with specific challenges for different sectors. First, investment priorities during the socialist period induced several distortions that became important factors of the development after transition. The fact that the Russian economy was skewed towards investment-intensive industries at the expense of the production of consumer goods was commonly recognised. In turn, in knowledge-intensive industries, due to their lengthy isolation from global commodity markets, domestic technological decisions were largely incompatible with those of the rest of the world. Consequently, most industries producing capital goods were unable to compete on the open global markets. This was not always because of a low technological level. Incompatibility with technological decisions applied outside the Soviet bloc made innovations and inventions too fragile. Second, underinvestment in the production of consumer goods (fully acknowledged by the government) accompanied by the isolation of consumer goods industries from global competition explains the inability of most companies in this sector to survive after the entry of international rivals.

Disorganisation (Blanchard & Kremer, 1997) became an important obstacle to the restructuring of brownfield capacities. In a market economy, firms govern their vertical contracts, choosing buyers and suppliers as well as the type of contract—for example, buying commodities with the use of one-off contracts, long-term contracts, or vertical integration, among others. In the planned economy, vertical contracts and vertical structures did not matter. The State Planning Committee (GOSPLAN) was responsible for establishing and enforcing contracts between enterprises. Even in the late years of the Soviet Union, when the power of the government and GOSPLAN had eroded, enterprises were unable to organise and enforce contracts in a manner similar to that of a market economy.

In competing for buyers, brownfield companies in different stages of production—upstream and downstream—found themselves in very different positions. In the upstream industries which produced commodities (such as oil and ferrous and non-ferrous metals), many Russian suppliers found themselves highly price competitive. For them, export orientation became the dominant restructuring strategy. Russian suppliers of natural gas, oil, oil products, and metals provide examples of this type of transformation. Industries with significant exports before the 1990s, e.g., oil and natural gas, increased the quantities supplied and found new customers. Industries oriented largely towards domestic markets, e.g., metals, found new buyers abroad.

Price competitiveness was rarely the case for the companies supplying downstream. At the same time, they faced sharply decreasing demand, fierce competition from new entrants, inflationary depreciation of working capitals, the inability to finance operations due to underdeveloped financial markets, and macroeconomic vulnerability. The insolvency of downstream producers further deteriorated due to their lack of competitiveness against rapidly growing imports. They became unable to compete for the exported raw materials. In turn, the producers of primary products became competitive in international markets just after the opening of the economy (see Table 8.2, compare the RCA index in 1996 for intermediate goods and raw materials with capital and consumer goods across industries and agricultural raw materials, fuel, and ore and metals with food, manufacturers, textiles, and machinery and transport equipment).

Owners of the brownfield capacities rarely succeeded in re-establishing traditional vertical contracts along the value chain. Russian ferrous metallurgy was an important exception. Shortly after privatisation, the owners of the metal processing capacities acquired their suppliers of iron ore and coal. However, most other brownfield downstream industries lost their suppliers, becoming

Table 8.2 Revealed comparative advantages of Russian industries across product groups: 1996 and 2019

Indicator	Product Groups	1996	2019
Stages of Processing Classification	Capital Goods	0.11	0.10
	Consumer Goods	0.65	0.88
	Intermediate Goods	1.51	1.14
	Raw Materials	2.43	3.11
Standard International Trade Classification SITC Rev. 2	Agricultural Raw Materials	1.80	1.80
	Chemicals	0.85	0.51
	Food	0.55	0.73
	Fuel	4.81	4.67
	Manufacturers	0.39	0.29
	Ore and Metals	4.26	1.81
	Textiles	0.20	0.07
	Machinery and Transport Equipment	0.14	0.10

Source World Integrated Trade Solution https://wits.worldbank.org

uncompetitive against foreign importers of Russian raw materials. The *disorganisation* hypothesis predicted the negative dependence of the speed and success of restructuring on the complexity of the technology applied. Simpler technologies and the production of less complex products are restructured faster. This is true not only for industry; in the agricultural sector, the fastest growth after 2000 was recorded for the production of grain. Wheat, barley, and corn became important Russian exports (see Chapter 10).

In addition to contractual inefficiencies, many downstream capacities faced technological inefficiencies because of their size. There were privatised companies that were too small (for instance, in the food industry) or too large to be price competitive. Many brownfield capacities kept suboptimal sizes in the 2010s (Golikova & Kuznetsov, 2017). Again, primary products and fuels, where large capacities induce cost competitiveness due to economies of scale, demonstrated advantages in this respect.

The competitiveness of brownfield capacities and the process of their restructuring predicted the performance of the Russian economy before 1998 almost entirely (Dolgopyatova et al., 2009). Greenfield investments were rare for various reasons. First, investments in Russia during the 30 years after the collapse of the Soviet system faced high risks (see Chapter 6) and, therefore, required high returns. The period of the 1990s was similar to 2022 in this respect. In addition, under conditions of high macroeconomic vulnerability, the emergence of new financial businesses and instruments provided greenfield businesses with opportunities which did not require substantial investments. Greenfield businesses focused on financial operations and the redistribution of ownership.

Macroeconomic policy before 1998 also disincentivised investments in domestic production *vis a vis* import operations. From 1995 up to the August 1998 crisis, Russia maintained its policy of the pegged exchange rate. The rouble was overvalued, which stimulated substantial amounts of imports. Furthermore, the overvalued rouble contributed to the sharp decline of textile manufacturing and food and agricultural production during this period.

After the rouble's sharp devaluation in 1998 (see Chapter 16) and the increase of global oil prices, which resulted in the rapid increase of GDP and domestic demand up to 2008, structural changes intensified, both for brownfield and greenfield companies. Decreasing import profitability motivated global companies to increase their foreign direct investment (FDI) in Russia. During 1999–2008, food production increased faster than the industry average and was comparable with fuels, mining, and extraction. The revival of the domestic auto industry (see Sect. 8.4) also took place during this period.

From the beginning of the twenty-first century, Russia experienced digitalisation and Internet penetration. In the early 2020s, the ratio of penetration of the Internet (including mobile Internet) corresponded to the level of high-income countries. Russia has a relatively strong domestic digital sector. The Russian company '*Yandex*' developed a search platform that shares the Russian market with *Google Search*. Since 2000, there are Russian social networks and web browsers that compete with those offered by international companies, and they have been protected by the Russian government since 2020. This sector is among the few where greenfield companies do not face competition from brownfield ones.

The fallout of the global financial crisis (GFC) in 2008–2009 interrupted the growth of Russian GDP. Flows of FDI declined, respectively, with a partial restoration during 2011–2018. However, the sanctions regime adopted against Russia in 2014 and in subsequent years (see Chapter 14) discourages both domestic and foreign investment. This was especially true for investments in physical assets. The last year that recorded a substantial increase in investments was 2007. Since 2013, investments in physical assets declined in absolute terms.

Overall, changes in the economic structure of the Russian economy have been driven by the macroeconomic environment and geopolitical risks (Fig. 8.1). Fuels, mining, and extraction was the only industry during 1992–1998 that exhibited a lower decline than the industry average. The decline of the textiles, machinery and equipment, and transport and transportation equipment production industries exceeded the averages. These sectors were never restored to the outputs that were achieved in pre-reform period. Since 1999, there has been an acceleration in the production of food and metallurgy and metal products. The food industry received substantial inflows of FDI. Concerning metallurgy and metal products, brownfield companies increased their competitiveness after acquiring suppliers of raw materials.

Since 2008, the structure of the Russian economy has changed largely by inertia. Fuels, metals, and food increased their shares in industrial output, while most other industries decreased in relative terms. By comparing the RCA index by product group and industry in 2019 and 1996, we observe that the position of Russia in the global division of labour did not change substantially.

Over a quarter of a century, the competitiveness of consumer goods slightly increased; the same was true for food. However, their RCA index values of less than 1 indicate that while food products and other consumer goods are competitive in domestic markets, they are not competitive in global markets. The international competitiveness of raw materials increased. Capital goods, manufacturers, and machinery and transport equipment have retained a low global competitiveness.

After 1992, the Russian economy experienced deep structural changes. The most substantial market-driven changes took place between 1992 and 1998, during a transition-related output decline. The changes had origins in geography and the endowments of natural resources, the history of economic development before 1992, the transition from a planned to a market economy, and the circumstances in which market liberalisation took place. While having a positive impact on efficient resource allocation, liberalisation did create challenges. The most important was the break-up of Soviet era economic ties, both inside and outside Russia.

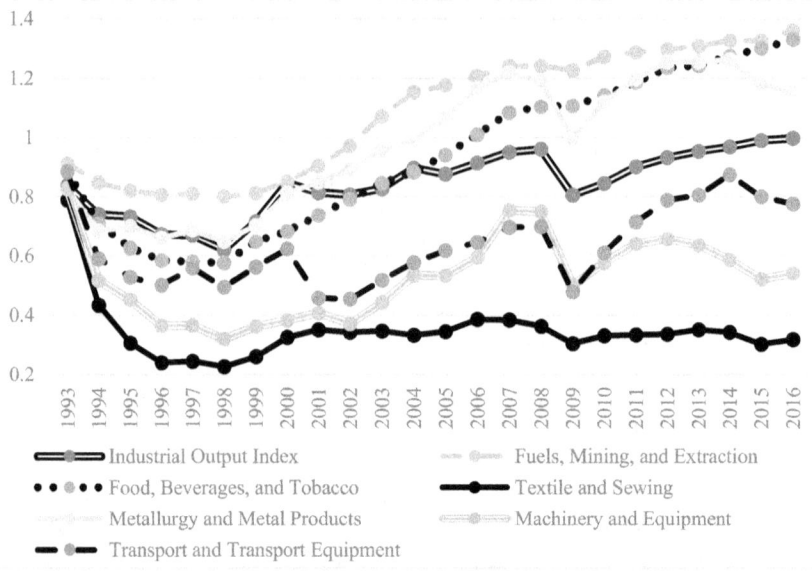

Fig. 8.1 Physical output index of selected Russian industries, 1993–2016: 1992 = 1 (*Source* Federal State Statistics Service [Rosstat])

Geography and natural resource endowments explain the comparative advantages inherited by post-Soviet Russia from the Soviet Union—and some of them, from the Russian Empire. Using the advantages of natural resource endowments, and also due to investments in mining during the Soviet period, post-Soviet Russia strengthened its position among the largest producers and exporters of oil and natural gas. Contrary to any expectations in the early 1990s, 30 years later, Russia restored its historical competitive advantages as a producer and exporter of wheat, sunflowers, and other crops that it had obtained in the nineteenth century.

From the Soviet period, Russia inherited investments in large-scale capacities in the primary products sectors as well as those closely related with them—mining, oil refining, and metallurgy. Brownfield capacities in these industries survived restructuring, developing their competitive advantages in export markets. Greenfield capacities established after 1992, in turn, are rarely competitive in international markets. Agricultural raw materials are the exception. The food industry, being the most attractive target for private investments, both domestic and FDI, obtained competitiveness mainly in domestic markets.

The economic structure, skewed towards primary products—and among primary products, oil and natural gas—challenged economic growth and macroeconomic stability in Russia. Energy products account for more than 50% of export revenue and about 50% of tax revenue. Oil price volatility affects most macroeconomic indicators—the fiscal balance, the rouble exchange rate, GDP, poverty, and the birth and death of new firms, among others.

During 30 years of a market economy, Russian economic policy has attempted to develop domestic industries with higher value added. In the first years of transition, efforts were made to support brownfield capacities outside the primary products sector. Most of these efforts were revealed to be unfruitful. Later, the Russian government concentrated on providing direct and indirect support to greenfield investments, both private and public.

8.4 Industrial Policies in Russia

The structure of the Russian economy is not only an outcome of the functioning of free markets and the international division of labour driven by comparative advantages, but also of economic policy. Economy-wide policies aimed at improving the business and investment climate may stimulate the use of those resources (i.e., the development of those industries) that would be under-utilised (underdeveloped) otherwise. Among specific measures, one can mention industrial policies and protectionist measures.

Industrial policies, in short, aim at the reallocation of resources towards sectors with higher productivity. These policies may be divided into horizontal or vertical measures (Simachev et al., 2014, with examples for Russia). Conventionally, horizontal industrial policy supports productivity-enhancing activities, such as research and development and innovation, without selecting between industries and economic sectors. Vertical industrial policy supports specific sectors. Horizontal industrial policy is closely interconnected with innovation policy. In turn, sector-specific vertical industrial policy often uses protectionist measures aimed at discriminating against foreign producers as compared to domestic ones in order to support the latter.

Overall, protectionist measures decrease economic efficiency by distorting resource allocation. In the real world, many sectors which were developed using protectionist measures, at the end, were revealed to be non-competitive. The overall explanation is that under protectionism, inefficient projects are not separated out, inefficient firms do not go bankrupt, and the management of these firms does not face strong incentives to make efficient decisions.

Conventional wisdom is that horizontal industrial policy is preferable to vertical industrial policy. In addition, under vertical industrial policy, there is a risk of rent-seeking because the government supports selected industries and companies, and interest groups can influence this process of selection. Corruption is an inevitable result. In spite of these limitations and drawbacks, many countries apply vertical industrial policies as well as horizontal ones (to different extents, however).

One can expect that the Russian economy, with its high share of state ownership and its autocratic political regime, will apply large-scale industrial policy projects aimed at improving the competitiveness of particular industries and sectors. The questions of interest are what are the targets of these projects and what are the outcomes of these interventions?

The strategic objectives of Russian industrial policy result from weaknesses in its economic structure. Shortly after the beginning of its liberalisation, it became clear that Russian downstream sectors had lost competitiveness.

Since 2000, several economic policy programmes, including 'Diversification of the Economy', 'Improvement of Business and Investment Climate', and 'New Highly Productive Jobs', were developed in order to improve the competitiveness of domestic downstream products. Overall, these policies brought limited effects. During the course of 30 years, investments in new capacities remained too low to ensure effective diversification and a rapid increase in the number of highly productive jobs.

The primary explanation is the low investment attractiveness of Russia due to the government's overbearing interference in business activity and the discretionary actions it takes (see Chapter 6) as well as an unfavourable and rapidly changing political environment.

To make an investment in Russia, an investor expects substantially higher returns than in other countries, and this requirement thus excludes many investment projects that would otherwise be efficient. In 2021, the market rate of return in Russia was 13.8% (including a risk-free rate of 5.7% and a market premium of 8.1%), while in most European countries, this rate falls between 6 and 8% (for instance, in Germany—6.4%) (Fernandes et al., 2021). In an environment of a high required rate of return, which leads to low investment activity, economic structure cannot substantially change. Industrial policies are largely ineffective unless there is substantial public financing for investment projects.

During these 30 years, the re-establishment of high value-added domestic industries was the primary target of domestic industrial policy. In addition to horizontal policy measures, which did not differentiate between sectors and markets (scientific grants; improving information and communication infrastructure, education, and public services; support of cooperation between universities and companies; and tax incentives for spending on research and development), several industry-specific projects of a vertical nature were implemented. The projects varied in terms of the proportion of private versus public financing.

The most successful example of a vertical industrial policy project that relied primarily on private financing was the investment of global car producers in Russia. At the beginning of the 2000s, sales of used imported passenger cars in Russia accounted for about one-third of the market. In order to attract international car producers, the Russian government first imposed high import duties on passenger cars (for used cars—prohibitive import duties) and, second, provided specific support measures for auto producers concerning the industrial assembling of passenger cars in Russia. Contracts implied the positive dependence of support measures on the level of localisation (share of components and parts that companies procured in Russia).

Starting in 2002, the programme proved to be very successful. During 2000–2001, domestic car producers Avtovaz and AZLK sold less than 1 million new cars. In 2001, AZLK shut down its activity. After only seven years, in 2008, the overall capacity of car producers in Russia accounted for 3 million new cars, and more than half of them were developed by international companies. Kia, Hyundai, Renault, Skoda, Volkswagen, Toyota, and BMW successfully competed with the Russian automobile maker Avtovaz. The GFC of 2008–2009 and the sanctions and countersanctions in 2014 (see Chapter 14) hurt the development of automobile manufacturing in Russia considerably. General Motors and Ford left Russia. But still, in 2021, out of the 1.3 million passenger cars sold in Russia, about 75% were those assembled by international automobile manufacturers.

There were several dimensions in which this project was successful. First, in full compliance with the strategic objectives of Russian industrial policy, it contributed to the diversification of downstream industry and the creation of new jobs with high value added. Second, there were positive spillovers (externalities) from the project. There was additional demand for domestic producers of materials and components stemming from the improving quality standards. The increasing competences of Russian subcontractors and suppliers of global car producers supported their competitiveness. The share of value added domestically to the cars assembled by global producers gradually increased. In competition with internationally recognised brands, Russian Avtovaz substantially increased the quality of its cars. In this respect, greenfield automobile manufacturing in Russia did not suppress but instead supported the modernisation and restructuring of brownfield capacities. Last but not least, industrial assembling projects were complemented by a number of joint ventures with Russian car producers, in the passenger, light commercial vehicle, and truck segments. The combination of protectionist (i.e., increasing import duties) and industrial policy (i.e., conditional import preferences and support of infrastructure, among others) was revealed to be effective.

Another vertical industrial policy project was the development of the domestic production of large-diameter pipeline tubes. Historically, despite gas and oil pipeline construction and developed steelmakers, Russia had no domestic production of large-diameter steel tubes for pipelines. During the construction of the first natural gas pipeline to Europe (Urengoy-Pomary-Uzhhorod) in 1982–1983, German companies supplied the tubes. During the next quarter century, the construction, renovation, and repair of the Russian oil and gas pipelines relied on tubes produced in Germany and Japan. At the same time, Russian steelmakers were revealed to be globally competitive in markets for products with low value added (for instance, iron), but less competitive in markets with higher value added (including products from steel and special types of steel, among others).

Natural gas pipeline extension projects by Gazprom at the beginning of the twenty-first century provided the momentum to support investment in new capacities for large-diameter pipeline tube production. Together with announcements of future pipeline construction, the government increased import duties on pipeline tubes and granted preferences to domestic producers in the procurement of pipelines by state-owned enterprises Gazprom and Transneft to stimulate investment in the new capacities. The four largest Russian steelmakers quickly developed their capacities of tubes. The government succeeded in stimulating private investment, but at the cost of a substantial increase in the prices of the tube and, therefore, the cost of constructing the pipelines.

There were investigations of collusion and corruption during project implementation. To control price increases, Gazprom revised the rules of procurement several times. On the positive side, Russia's large-diameter tubes appeared to be internationally competitive, with increasing exports to countries of the former Soviet Union (FSU) and East Asia. Similar to the auto assembling project, investments in the production of large-diameter steel tubes contributed to a change in Russia's economic structure towards higher value-added sectors. Comparing these two projects, we may see the risks of vertical industrial policy. If a project is implemented in the absence of effective competition, it likely brings losses due to rent-seeking.

After 2014, in the context of the increasing country risk premium, the private financing of investment projects has become rare. Public sources have replaced private investments in financing innovation projects. In 2007, special development institutions in the form of 'state corporations' were created to concentrate the financing, coordination, and implementation of investments in knowledge-intensive projects and sectors. The largest state corporations are Vnesheconombank (VEB), Rostec (State Corporation for Assistance to Development, Production, and Export of Advanced Technology Industrial Product), Rosatom (State Nuclear Agency Corporation), and Roscosmos (State Space Corporation).

VEB is an institute focused on public venture financing for innovation projects. Rostec governs several hundred scientific institutes and firms in three main sectors: aviation, arms, and electronics. Rosatom manages several hundred organisations and firms in the nuclear energy sector, from mining to transportation. Roscosmos conducts research and development as well as economic activity in the space industry. State corporations are clear examples of vertical industrial policy projects based wholly on public financing.

Questions for Students

1. Deindustrialisation is a global economic trend (see, for instance, Rodrik, 2016). Can you discuss the similarities and differences between deindustrialisation globally and the decreasing share of manufacturing in the Russian economy from 1992 onward?
2. Please list the key differences between an 'enterprise' under a command planned economy and a 'firm' in a market economy (see, for instance, Dolgopyatova et al., 2009).

3. How did the transition from 'enterprise' to 'firm' affect the structure of Russian companies during the transition period? How did this transition affect the proportions of large and small companies as well as the vertical integration of companies?
4. What was the difference between 'brownfield' (restructured ex-Soviet enterprises) and 'greenfield' (new establishments founded after 1992) during the period of transition? Is it similar to the difference between an 'incumbent' and 'new entrant' in a market?
5. What is the difference between vertical and horizontal industrial policy?
6. In Russia, can you expect horizontal or vertical industrial policy measures? Why? How do industrial policy goals internationally (see, for instance, Aiginger & Rodrik, 2020) differ from the objectives of Russian industrial policy?

References

Aiginger, K., & Rodrik, D. (2020). Rebirth of industrial policy and an agenda for the twenty-first century. *Journal of Industry, Competition and Trade, 20*(2), 189–207.

Blanchard, O., & Kremer, M. (1997). Disorganization. *The Quarterly Journal of Economics, 112*(4), 1091–1126.

Dolgopyatova, T. G., Iwasaki, I., & Yakovlev, A. A. (2009). The Emergence of Russian Corporations: From the Soviet Enterprise to a Market Firm. In T. Dolgopyatova, I. Iwasaki, & A. A. Yakovlev (Eds.), *Organization and Development of Russian Business* (pp. 12–35). Palgrave Macmillan.

Fernandez, P., Bañuls, S., & Fernandez, Acin P. (2021, June 6). Survey: market risk premium and risk-free rate used for 88 countries in 2021. IESE Business School Working Paper. https://ssrn.com/abstract=3861152 or https://doi.org/10.2139/ssrn.3861152

Golikova, V., & Kuznetsov, B. (2017), Suboptimal size: Factors preventing the growth of Russian small and medium-sized enterprises. *Foresight 11*(3) (Eng), 83–93.

Rodrik, D. (2016). Premature deindustrialization. *Journal of Economic Growth, 21*(1), 1–33.

Ruta, M. (2022). The impact of war in Ukraine on global trade and investments. *World Bank.* https://openknowledge.worldbank.org/handle/10986/37359

Simachev, Y., Kuzyk, M., Kuznetsov, B., & Pogrebnyak, E. (2014). Russia on the path towards a new technology industrial policy: Exciting prospects and fatal traps. *Foresight, 8*(4) (Eng), 6–23.

CHAPTER 9

Energy Sector

Przemyslaw Kowalski

Highlights
- The energy sector contributes significantly to Russia's economy, supports its competitiveness, and shapes the country's internal political economy and foreign relations.
- Russia's high energy and emission intensities reflect the country's advantage as owner of vast fossil fuel endowments and high energy consumption needs as well as its legacy of Soviet-forced industrialisation and post-Soviet economic policies, which tend to support energy production and keep domestic energy prices at relatively low levels.
- Management of the energy sector is still dominated by the government, particularly in the natural gas sector, although the country has introduced reforms aimed at increasing efficiency and the role of market-based principles.

The chapter is based on the work completed during the author's sabbatical from the OECD. The views expressed in this chapter are solely those of the author and do not implicate the OECD or its Member States.

P. Kowalski (✉)
Organisation for Economic Co-operation and Development (OECD), Paris, France
e-mail: przemyslaw.kowalski@oecd.org

© The Author(s), under exclusive license to Springer Nature Switzerland AG 2023
M. Dabrowski (ed.), *The Contemporary Russian Economy*,
https://doi.org/10.1007/978-3-031-17382-0_9

- In the period leading up to Russia's invasion of Ukraine in February 2022, the implications of an imminent global energy transition for Russia could arguably be seen as both a cause of concern and an opportunity.
- Following the invasion, it is hard to see how Russia will be able to maintain its position as a key energy exporter, let alone become a key shaper of the global debate on combating climate change.

9.1 Introduction

This chapter starts with analysing the trends in energy consumption and CO_2 emissions in Russia (Sect. 9.2). Next, it sketches the contours of Russia's policies in the energy sector (Sect. 9.3) before presenting the trends in Russia's production, consumption, and external trade of different fuels and outlining the key economic and institutional features of Russia's principal energy subsectors (natural gas, oil, coal, and electricity generation) (Sect. 9.4). Section 9.5 discusses the implications of a global transition to a low emissions economy for the Russian energy sector and, in this context, discusses Russia's opportunities and challenges as well as its strategic approach to tackling climate change, and Sect. 9.6 consequences of Russia's aggression onUkraine. Section 9.7 presents conclusions.

9.2 Energy Consumption and CO_2 Emissions

In 2019, the generation of USD 1000 worth of global gross domestic product (GDP) was on average associated with the consumption of about 1 billion calories of primary energy (equivalent to 0.7 barrels of oil) (see Box 9.1) and with about 255 kilogrammes of CO_2 emissions.[1] This was approximately four to five times less than four decades earlier, illustrating significant reductions in energy and emission intensity of output (Fig. 9.1).

In the same period, global per capita energy consumption has actually increased (Fig. 9.2). The corresponding figures for Russia show even steeper reductions—albeit from much higher initial levels—but also that the country's energy and emission intensities are currently still 64% and 48% higher, respectively, than the world averages. Per capita consumption of primary energy in Russia is almost triple the world average.[2]

---

[1] This calculation is based on BP (2021), which shows the world economy consumes daily 380,779 trillion calories of primary energy, which is equivalent to some 260 million of barrels of crude oil, and that it emits 94 million tonnes of CO_2. The world GDP data used for the calculation is in international dollars at purchasing power parities.

[2] Note that the category 'consumption' is not restricted to final consumption by individuals but also includes demand from downstream sectors such as industry, residential, services, transport, and agriculture.

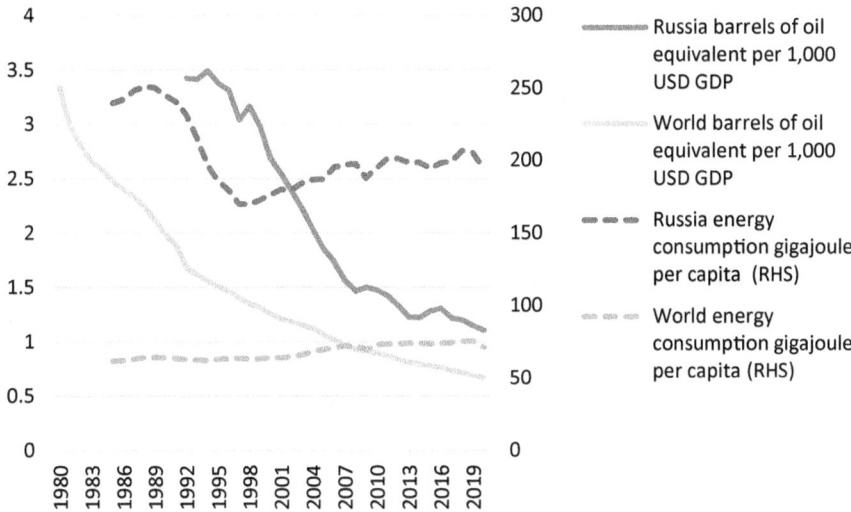

Fig. 9.1 Primary energy consumption per unit of GDP and per capita, world economy and Russia, 1980–2020 (*Source* Author's calculations based on IMF's World Economic Outlook, October 2021 for world GDP in purchasing power parity international dollars and BP [2021] for world's primary energy consumption)

In Russia, the relatively high energy and emission intensity reflect several unique factors, such as Russia's advantage as owner of vast fossil fuel endowments, its high energy consumption needs due to its large territory and harsh climatic conditions, its legacy of Soviet-forced industrialisation (see Chapter 4), and the post-Soviet economic policies which tended to support energy production and kept domestic energy prices at relatively low levels. The production, distribution, domestic use, and export of energy resources have indeed played an important role in the Russian economy and society for a long time, and energy still contributes significantly to the country's GDP, budget revenues, and export receipts (Fig. 9.3).

Note that the contribution of the energy sector to GDP, employment, and other economic aggregates depends on how the sector is defined. For example, while the estimate of the GDP contribution of the energy sector (mining, quarrying, electricity and gas, steam, and air conditioning supply systems) from the Federal State Statistics Service (Rosstat) was 14% in 2019, some estimates posit contributions of around 20–23% (Mitrova & Yermakov, 2019).

Access to relatively inexpensive energy is supporting the competitiveness of Russia's non-energy sectors, such as, for example, metallurgy or chemicals (European Commission, 2020). Proceeds from energy extraction and their concentrated distribution play an instrumental role in Russia's internal political economy (Kolesnikov & Volkov, 2021). The country's leading position

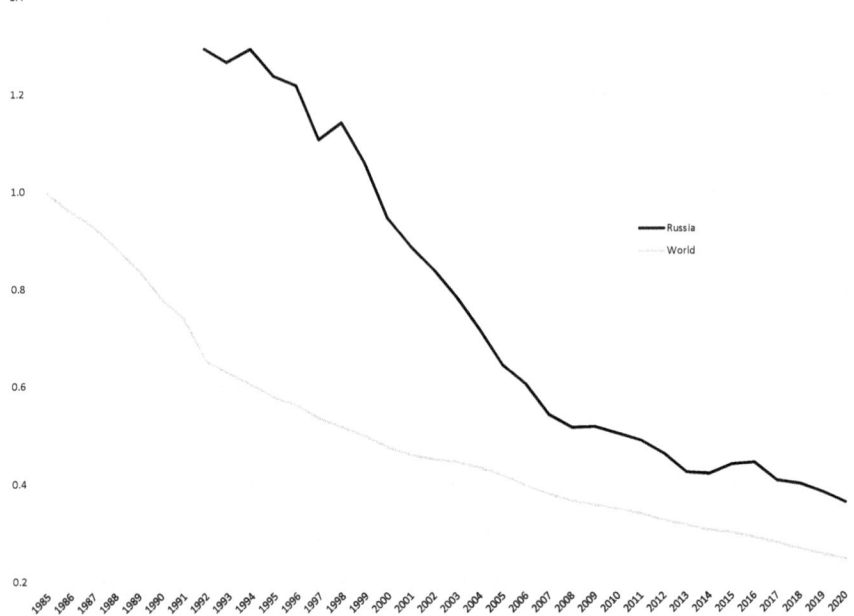

Fig. 9.2 CO2 emissions, per USD 1000 of GDP, world economy and Russia, 1985–2020 (*Source* Author's calculations based on IMF's World Economic Outlook, October 2021 for world GDP in purchasing power parity international dollars and BP [2021] for CO2 emissions)

as a top energy exporter, particularly to Europe and the former Soviet Union (FSU), has also been often used as a leverage in its foreign relations.

These realities might continue for some time but there are two major factors that are likely to cause reductions in demand for Russian fossil fuels, perhaps even in the most immediate future. These are the international policy responses to climate change (Sect. 9.5) and Russia's large-scale military aggression of Ukraine in February 2022 (Sect. 9.6).

> **Box 9.1 Definition of Primary Energy**
> Primary energy is defined in this chapter after BP (2021) as energy comprising commercially traded fuels, including modern renewables used to generate electricity. It includes oil, natural gas, coal, nuclear energy, and hydroelectric energy as well as renewables used to generate electricity such as solar and wind power. More generally, primary energy is defined as the energy which is extracted or captured and separated from other materials (e.g., coal from rocks), but not further processed. To avoid double counting, it is distinguished from secondary

energy which comprises all sources of energy that result from the transformation of primary and secondary sources (e.g., electricity generated from natural gas).

9.3 Overview of Russia's Policy Framework Relevant to the Energy Sector

Economic efficiency is an important consideration in energy policies across the world because, under conducive conditions, market-based interactions between suppliers and consumers of energy help determine its true economic and social value and thus the socially optimal levels of its production and use. However, energy is also a strategic resource, and energy markets are subject to market failures. The extent of state intervention in energy markets across the world is considerable, including through state ownership or control of key energy companies, subsidies, and regulations, which affect the costs and prices of different fuels across local and international energy markets.

Three decades after the breakup of the Soviet Union, Russia still presents a state-dominated approach to the management of its energy sectors, although it has also introduced several reforms aimed at increasing efficiency and the

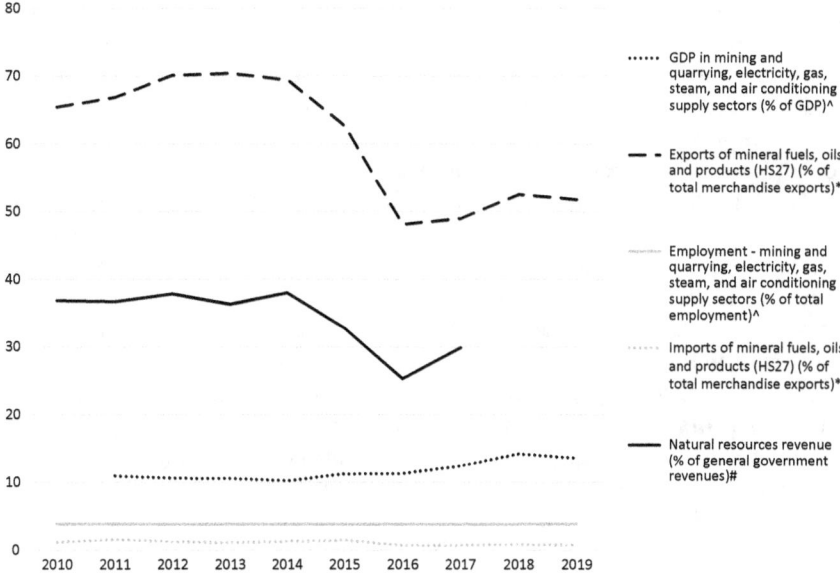

Fig. 9.3 The energy and related sectors and the Russian economy—selected indicators (*Sources* ^Federal State Statistics Service [Rosstat [2020]]; *WITS [2021]; #NRGI [2021])

role of market-based principles. Market-oriented initiatives emerged in the 1990s and intensified in the 2010s, with gradual deregulation and the expansion of the share of producers independent from the state in the total volume of domestic sales of natural gas as well as reforms of the taxation of extraction and exports of energy products. However, a host of monopoly rights, the taxation of exports, and regulated prices, particularly in the natural gas sector, remain an important mechanism influencing the production and consumption of energy and continue to exercise a downward pressure on domestic energy prices. This likely leads to its suboptimal use by households and industry and introduces distortions in downstream economic sectors.

Similar to other countries, the range of policies used in Russia to shape the economic performance and social contribution of its energy sectors is wide and includes the statutory rights (and obligations) of natural monopolies, competition regulations, the tax regime, and government support.

Systemic aspects of the energy sector, such as the transmission of oil and gas products via trunk pipelines as well as natural gas transportation using pipelines, services on the transmission of electric power and heat energy, and natural monopolies are strictly regulated and many key players in this sector are state-owned or otherwise state-influenced. At the time of writing of this chapter, the following companies fall into the category of natural monopolies[3]: Transneft (transportation of oil through pipelines), Transnefteprodukt (transportation of oil products through pipelines), Gazprom (production and transportation through pipelines of natural gas), and Inter RAO (electricity). Natural monopolisation is most prominent in the gas subsector due to Gazprom's leading position in the production and export of natural gas and its statutory ownership and control of the Unified Gas Supply System (UGSS)—the world's largest gas transmission system (see also Sect. 9.5.1).

The implementation of laws related to natural monopolies, the regulation of prices for certain energy goods and services (e.g., gas and electricity tariffs), and foreign investments in business entities deemed strategically important in terms of national defence and state security are entrusted with the Federal Antimonopoly Service (FAS). The FAS ensures compliance with antimonopoly regulations at all levels of economic activity, including in the energy sector, and it also plays an active role in the process of developing policies in which it promotes competitive behaviour in the sector. Past cases investigated by the FAS concerning the energy sector include, for instance, incidents in which Gazprom was found to have violated competition law through its stock exchange activities, through its indexing of tariffs on gas transportation for independent producers, or by creating a competition-restricting environment (European Commission, 2020).

---

[3] Federal Law of 19 July 1995 'On Natural Monopolies', as amended, available at: http://pravo.gov.ru/proxy/ips/?docbody=&nd=102037075&intelsearch=%CE+%E5% F1%F2%E5%F1%F2%E2%E5%ED%ED%FB%F5+%EC%EE%ED%EE%EF%EE%EB%E8% FF%F5, accessed on 16 March 2020.

Accounting for about one-third of the federal budget revenue, energy taxation is an important source of public revenues, but it is also an instrument used to shape the sector's development and the domestic prices faced by consumers. Taxes applying to the energy sector include royalties (such as the mineral extraction tax [MET], with different tax rates applicable to different resources and a complex range of coefficients and parameters), an additional income tax on hydrocarbon extraction (introduced to support the exploitation of low-margin areas yielding oil, gas, and liquefied natural gas [LNG]), corporate profit tax, value added tax (VAT), excise duties, and export taxes.

Being a large net exporter of energy and a country which has relied on energy for its economic and social development, it is not surprising that the taxation of energy in Russia has traditionally focused on exports. The reforms proposed in the late 2010s[4] and known informally as the 'tax manoeuvre' with a view of improving Russia's budgetary situation have however aimed to gradually equalise the tax treatment of domestically consumed and export-oriented oil products by decreasing export taxes and increasing the MET (Khrennikova, 2018). Before the COVID-19 pandemic, major elements of this reform were still to be implemented and the current policies related to the taxation of energy exports seemed to continue to exercise a downward pressure on domestic energy prices across the different energy sectors (European Commission, 2020). The pandemic, which caused a temporary collapse of world oil prices and led to a significant budget deficit in Russia, triggered the largest tax reform in the oil and gas industry since the early 2000s, which resulted in abolishing a number of MET benefits and a more rapid transition to a sales-revenue-based system.

The energy sector is also receiving state support promoting the development of the sector, in particular, in the form of budgetary grants and allocations specified in the national Energy Development Programme. In the most recent version of this programme, which covers the period 2013–2024, budgetary allocations amounted to the equivalent of USD 2.2 billion and included project funding in areas such as energy savings and increasing energy efficiency, the development and modernisation of the energy sector, the development of the hydrocarbon sector, the restructuring and development of the Russian coal sector, and the development of renewable energy.

Adding together the direct budgetary support measures and tax benefits, the OECD (2021) estimated that the amount of annual Russian fossil fuel subsidies increased from USD 4.6 billion in 2015 to USD 17.3 billion in 2017, before decreasing to USD 9.3 billion in 2020. The bulk of these subsidies was in the form of reduced extraction taxes for oil depending on

---

[4] The reforms were part of a revival plan accepted by the State Duma in May 2018 which defined broad economic development goals up to the year 2024 inclusive (see: http://en.kremlin.ru/events/president/news/57425). The original announcement is available at: https://minenergo.gov.ru/view-pdf/11246/84473, accessed on 2 September 2019.

the specific properties of the subsoil deposit exploited or on the production properties, benefitting mainly large oil producers.

Defining state support more broadly as the amounts that energy producers benefit from being able to sell energy products at too high prices (producers' support) and the amounts consumers receive buying at too low prices (consumers' support), the IMF estimated the amount of the subsidies to fossil fuels in Russia at USD 551 billion in 2015, which made it the world's third largest subsidiser (after China with USD 1432 billion and the United States with USD 649 billion) and the world number one when it came to subsidies per capita (USD 3832 per capita) followed by Saudi Arabia (USD 3709) and the United Arab Emirates (USD 2452) (Coady et al., 2019).

9.4 Russia's Energy Mix

In 2019, Russia was the world's third largest primary energy producer, accounting for 11% of global energy production, after China (19%) and the United States (16%) (BP, 2021).

It was the second largest producer of both natural gas and oil (17.1% and 12.8% of global production, respectively, in both cases after the United States), the fifth largest coal producer (after China, Australia, India, and the United States) accounting for 5.5% of global production, the fourth largest producer of nuclear energy (after China, the United States, and France), and the fifth largest producer of hydroelectricity (after China, Brazil, Canada, and the United States). However, Russia was only the 61st largest producer of energy from renewable sources.

Russia's energy consumption and production mixes diverged in important ways from world averages (Fig. 9.4). Differences in production structures between Russia and the world, while still affected by consumer preferences and policies, are good indicators of differences in natural endowments (and thus of Russia's comparative advantages), while differences in consumption structures also reflect geographical conditions and policies that shape the domestic relative prices (and thus the use) of different fuels within the country. They reveal Russia's strong advantage and support policies in natural gas and oil, a steadily expanding advantage in coal, and negligible involvement in renewables other than nuclear and hydropower.[5]

9.4.1 Natural Gas

Russia harbours the world's largest proven reserves of natural gas (estimated at 37.4 trillion cubic metres in 2020, i.e., 20% of the global stock), which are located in West Siberia, mainly in the Yamal-Nenets Autonomous Okrug

---

[5] Whether nuclear energy and hydropower are renewable energy sources is a subject to debate.

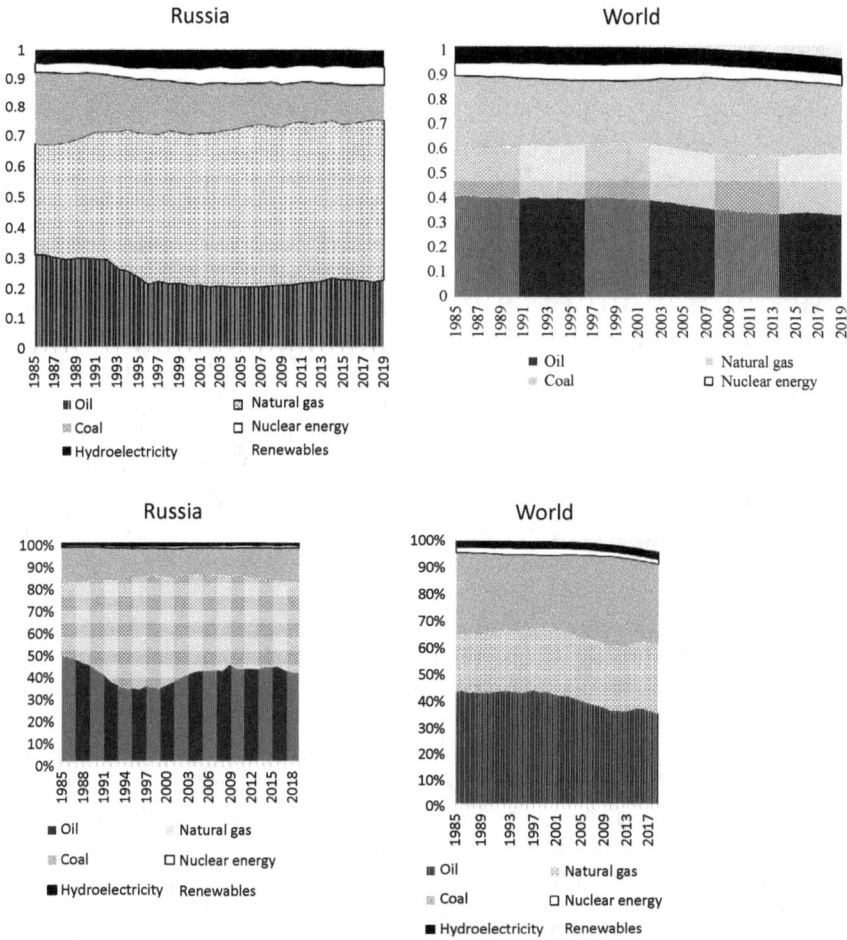

Fig. 9.4 Primary energy consumption and production by fuel: Russia and the world economy (*Note* shares calculated on the basis of calorific values. *Source* BP [2021]; author's calculations)

(District). The country's reserve-to-production ratio[6] of 58.6 years is above the world average (48.8 years). This suggests a relatively long time to the potential exhaustion of Russian gas reserves at the current rate of extraction.

In 2019, natural gas accounted for 53% of the energy consumed in Russia, which was more than twice the world average (24%). The growth in reliance on natural gas for consumption has also been more rapid than on average across the world, and it is one of the most prominent characteristics of the transformation of Russia's energy sector since the mid-1980s. The production

---

[6] The reserves-to-production ratio is the outcome of dividing the end-of-year reserves by the production achieved that year.

share of natural gas, at 41% in 2019, was also much higher than the world average (26%).

In 2019, Russia was the world's largest exporter of pipeline gas (44% of global exports) and the fourth largest exporter of LNG, accounting for 8.1% of the world's total. Exports of natural gas started picking up after a period of stagnation between the early 1990s and the mid-2010s, mainly due to institutional reforms in the Russian gas sector and the growing role of independent producers and LNG technology (see below).

At the beginning of the 2020s, there were more than 250 gas and associated petroleum gas mining companies registered in Russia; however, gas production has long been dominated by the majority state-owned Gazprom Group (Gazprom thereafter), which has the status of a natural monopolist in the natural gas sector. Despite a gradual deregulation and the opening of the gas market to independent companies, Gazprom accounted still for close to three-quarters of the national natural gas production. Another state-owned—but considered independent—company, Rosneft,[7] accounted for some 10% of Russia's gas production, while Novatek and Lukoil, which are both fully privately owned companies, accounted for a further 10% and 4%, respectively, of production.

Gazprom is an undisputed leader in the domestic gas market. It has been estimated that it directly satisfies almost one-half of domestic consumption while a further 30% is satisfied by other producers through the Gas Transmission System—the transportation part of Russia's UGSS—over which Gazprom maintains statutory ownership and control granted to it by the government.

The UGSS is the main part of Russia's Federal Gas Supply system. It is the world's largest gas transmission system comprising some 158,200 kms of gas trunklines and branches and 218 compressor stations, covering the European part of Russia, but excluding eastern Siberia and the Far East where gas is supplied via the regional gas supply systems.

As the statutory owner of the UGSS, Gazprom is obliged to provide access to UGSS' gas pipelines to independent gas suppliers. The latter, unlike Gazprom, which has to follow government-determined gas tariffs (see below), can supply gas to consumers at unregulated prices but are still subject to regulated gas transportation tariffs, in the setting of which Gazprom takes part[8] and which also depend on the transport routes allocated to these companies by Gazprom. In allocating routes, Gazprom is supposed to take into account the parameters and balance of the whole system and is not legally obliged to offer transport by the shortest routes to independent companies. This allegedly gives Gazprom information advantages and ultimately the ability to obstruct independent gas producers' access to the transmission and distribution facilities and influence their prices to their own advantage (Yafimava, 2015). Thus,

---

[7] Rosneft is referred to as 'independent', because it is not a part of the Gazprom Group.

[8] These tariffs are themselves set by the government on the basis of unique information possessed and reported by Gazprom.

in practice, Russia's gas prices and supplies are determined by Gazprom and its dominant owner—the government.

Gazprom is also by far the largest gas producer internationally, outdistancing by a factor of four or more such international players as the Royal Dutch Shell, Petro China, Exxon Mobil, or British Petroleum (BP). This leading position is clearly linked to Russia's natural gas endowments combined with Gazprom's statutory monopoly over exports of Russian gas via pipelines.

In 2020, Russia exported some 35% of its natural gas production. Europe, including Turkey and Ukraine, was a chief destination accounting for 85% of Russia's pipeline gas exports. The bulk of exports to Europe was destined for Germany (28% of Russia's total exports) and Italy (10%). Other FSU countries accounted for 13% of Russian exports, with Belarus alone accounting for 9%. Russian gas constituted 38% of total pipelined gas imports by Europe and 66% of imports by the FSU region.

9.4.2 LNG

The production and international trade of LNG are not regulated as heavily by the government as pipeline gas. Independent companies play more important roles in LNG production and exports since the 2013 amendment of Russia's Law on Gas Exports, when Gazprom no longer had a monopoly over exporting LNG and other companies fulfilling specific criteria could also do so. This has been estimated to have benefitted Novatek and Rosneft with their respective LNG projects in Sakhalin and in the Arctic but, at least for some time since the liberalisation, entry to the export market was still not possible for other market participants as they did not meet the export criteria (European Commission, 2020; Mitrova, 2013). Gazprom's share of LNG exports, estimated by the European Commission (2020) at above 20% in 2018, was already much smaller than the share in pipelined gas exports and has been gradually falling.

At least partially as a result of these reforms, Russia's LNG market developed rapidly in the 2010s. In 2020, exporting 40.4 billion cubic metres of LNG, Russia accounted for 8.3% of global LNG exports, almost triple the share in 2009 (2.7%). LNG exports accounted for 6.3% of Russia's total natural gas production—43% of Russia's LNG exports were destined for Europe; Japan and China accounted for 21% and 17%, respectively; and the Asia Pacific region as a whole accounted for 56%.

Russia's LNG exports were therefore more regionally diversified than its exports via pipelines and encompassed new dynamic centres of economic growth in Asia Pacific. The dependencies of the LNG importing countries on imports from Russia were also weaker than in the case of pipelined gas. These figures reflect both Russia's more liberal approach to the LNG segment and stronger international competition in LNG markets as compared to pipeline gas.

9.4.3 Gas Pricing

The production, domestic consumption, and export of Russian natural gas are strongly shaped by the government through its regulation of gas prices. Price regulation reflects the role natural gas has played in Russia's economic and social development, including its impact on inflation.

Since the beginning of the 1990s, the regulation of gas prices has been a tool used by the government to limit increases in the prices paid by domestic non-industrial consumers and to shape the competitiveness of Russian downstream industries. Accounting for large shares of pipeline gas imports in Europe and the FSU, Russia also has considerable market power in these markets, and it has been using it to its advantage. Since the early 1990s—albeit to different degrees in different periods—the regulated prices paid for gas by residential consumers (household prices) have tended to be lower than those paid by industrial users (wholesale prices), and the latter have tended to be lower than export prices (e.g., European Commission, 2020; Henderson, 2011).

Russia's approach to gas price regulation has evolved significantly over the last three decades. In the 1990s, gas prices were indexed to inflation and, with the galloping inflation at the time, reached very high levels, contributing to non-payment problems.[9] The early 2000s saw a departure from the inflation-indexation and a move—at least officially—towards the conditioning of wholesale gas pricing on the costs of production and a regulated mark-up.[10] In reality, however, it is difficult to gauge whether and how economic costs were taken into account because the data and methodology used for these calculations were not public and several analyses argue that the cost-plus principle was generally not followed and that prices were set discretionally at the top political level (see, e.g., European Commission, 2020; Idrisov & Gordeev, 2017).

The late 2000s saw a further shift towards the market-based pricing principle based on the 'European netback parity', where the domestic wholesale price is calculated on the basis of the prices of exports to Europe with some discounts,[11] which were supposed to diminish over time so as to achieve equal pricing of domestic supplies and exports. The deadlines for achieving such

---

[9] Non-payments peaked in 1997 when Gazprom reported being paid for only 29% of its domestic sales (Henderson, 2011).

[10] Government Decree No. 1021 of 29 December 2000 on State Regulation of Gas Prices, Tariffs for Transportation Services and Fees for Technological Connection of Gas-using Equipment to Gas Distribution Networks in the Russian Federation ('Decree on State Regulation of Gas Prices').

[11] Government Resolution No. 333 of 28 May 2007 on Improvement of State regulation of Gas Prices.

parity were first set for 2011 and then for 2014 and 2017; however, these deadlines were not met and it has been estimated that, throughout the period 2010–2018, Russian export prices were over three times higher than their domestic counterparts (European Commission, 2020).

In the early 2020s, wholesale gas prices are still set according to the regulations and formula from the mid-2010s[12] based on the netback parity approach. The domestic wholesale gas price is thus calculated by first deducting the customs duties from the export price at the Russian border, the value of the costs of the transportation and storage of the gas when it is sold outside the FSU, and the difference between the average cost of transport from production sites to the border of Russia and the average cost of transporting gas from production sites to consumers within Russia. This price is scaled down further using a 'reduction coefficient'—also called a netback discount coefficient—which is supposed to ensure the downward correspondence of gas price changes with past consumer gas price changes and a price zone differentiation coefficient. This further lowers prices in individual regions, taking into account a range of factors such as different levels of socioeconomic development and distance from gas production sites as well as the routing of gas flows, the costs and degree of use of alternative fuels, and the presence of independent gas suppliers (European Commission, 2020).

Since 2008, the Saint-Petersburg International Mercantile Exchange (SPIMEX) has provided additional opportunities for the organised trade of, among others, crude oil and oil products and of gas that is not covered by the government regulation of wholesale gas prices. However, the ability of this exchange to compete with the regulated market and significantly influence Russia's domestic gas prices is limited by relatively shallow competition, rigid price-setting mechanisms, the low liquidity and depth of the market, and the inadequacy of the trading infrastructure (European Commission, 2020). For example, it has been estimated that, in the late 2010s, Gazprom itself played a major role in trading gas on SPIMEX. Access of gas traded on SPIMEX to the pipeline network must be agreed upon with Gazprom at its discretion in advance of any trade being completed, thus raising questions about conflict of interests. Overall, in the late 2010s, transactions on SPIMEX constituted less than 10% of the entire domestic natural gas trade, and the prices of gas traded there usually remained some 3–5% below the administratively regulated level (European Commission, 2020).

Overall, market forces play a much larger role in gas pricing in the early 2020s than in the 1990s, but price formation is still very much influenced by the government. The wholesale gas pricing formula, which links the domestic price to the export price rather than to the actual cost of production in Russia, does not clearly factor in domestic market conditions or the commercial considerations of gas suppliers. Instead, by its construction, it creates a wedge between domestic and export prices. Importantly, the key parameters of

---

[12] FTS Order No. 1142-e of 9 July 2014 (as amended on 24 March 2015).

this pricing formula are determined by state-owned entities such as Gazprom based on criteria and information which do not appear transparent. Furthermore, price regulation seems conducive to non-transparent cross-subsidisation and price distortions across regions and industrial sectors and between the domestic and export sales. This is concerning both from the point of view of domestic environmental and welfare effects and the efficiency of the allocation of productive resources within Russia as well as in the context of international gas and product market distortions.

The pricing of gas used by other industries has indeed been identified as an issue when Russia was acceding to the WTO as well as in a number of trade remedy cases (Furculita, 2017).

9.4.4 Oil

Russia's 108 billion barrels of proven crude oil reserves accounted for 6.2% of the world's total reserves in 2020, making Russia the world's sixth largest oil reserve holder. Russia's production of oil in that year accounted for 13% of global production, which was the second largest share after the United States (17%) (BP, 2021).

Oil was also the second most important fuel consumed and produced in Russia, and its shares in overall energy consumption and production have been growing steadily in the last two decades. At 22%, the share of oil in Russia's energy consumption was however significantly lower than the world average (33%), while its production share was higher (41%, with 34% for the world average), revealing the export orientation of the sector.

Russia's net exports of oil have seen a significant expansion since the 1990s. The value of Russian hydrocarbon exports, and thus the overall value of merchandise exports, are strongly influenced by the international price of oil and so thus is the exchange rate of the national currency (see Chapters 12 and 16). Russia is not a member of the Organization of the Petroleum Exporting Countries (OPEC), but it has co-ordinated its oil output strategy with the organisation in order to influence international prices of oil on some—but not all—occasions. Since 2019 it has been part of the larger 'OPEC+' group and central to its many vital decisions.

In 2020, 53% of Russian oil exports were destined for Europe, 32% for China, an additional 7% for other countries in Asia Pacific, and 6% for FSU countries. As far as dependence on imports of Russian oil is concerned, shipments from Russia accounted for 98% of oil imports of the FSU, 29% of imports of Europe, and 15% of imports of China.

At the beginning of the 2020s, there were close to 300 entities licensed to produce oil and gas condensate (oil liquids) from subsoil resources, although about 83% of Russia's production was delivered by 100 entities included in the structure of 11 vertically integrated companies.[13] In 2018, the largest shares were contributed by Rosneft (35%), Lukoil (15%), Surgutneftegas (11%), Gazprom Neft (7%), Tatneft (5%), Bashneft (3%), Slavneft (2%), Novatek (2%), and Russneft (1%). The largest oil companies that accounted for more than one-half of production were state-owned. There was also a fair amount of cross-ownership between the different state companies (European Commission, 2020).

At the beginning of the 2020s, Rosneft's major shareholder was Rosneftegaz, fully owned by the government. Gazprom Neft is a subsidiary of the majority state-owned Gazprom. Tatneft is partially owned by the Republic of Tatarstan, while Bashneft is majority-owned by Rosneft. Slavneft is a formerly state-owned company of the government of Belarus and it is currently jointly controlled by two Russian state-owned companies: Rosneft and Gazprom. Lukoil is a former state-owned enterprise which was privatised in 1993 and is currently the largest private Russian oil-producing company. Surgutneftegas, created in 1993 by merging previously state-owned companies, is a fully privately owned company. Russneft and Novatek are also privately owned (European Commission, 2020).

9.4.5 Oil Pricing

The domestic prices of oil and oil products are generally subject to supply and demand forces, although discretionary government interventions have happened fairly often. These included instances of price fixing agreements with market players, for example, in November 2018, to tame the growth of retail prices for petroleum products (European Commission, 2020).

As discussed in Sect. 9.3, and similar to other energy and mineral products, the prices of oil and oil products are also shaped by the taxes applied on the extraction or sales of these resources. They influence the competitiveness of different segments of the oil and oil products industry, for example, by setting higher tax rates on exports of crude oil than on exports of processed products. In addition, the government has the right to deploy specific fiscal instruments if the prevailing market conditions push the Urals Crude oil prices in directions that endanger the financial security of the national economy.[14] Informally, the so-called tax manoeuvre aimed to push companies to invest in refineries and reduce the amount of low-value heavy fuel oil exports while expanding high-quality diesel production to target the European market.

---

[13] Ministry of Energy of the Russian Federation (2018), *Extraction of crude oil*, available at: https://minenergo.gov.ru/node/1209, accessed on 1 September 2019.

[14] Urals Crude oil prices are the official benchmark for the pricing of the Russian crude oil earmarked for international markets and are used in planning budgetary expenditures and other macroeconomic indicators.

SPIMEX maintains indices for regional producers' prices for the most significant oil sites (i.e., Timan-Pechora, Volga-Ural, and West Siberia) and provides information on the prices of some oil derivatives.

9.4.6 Coal

As of 2020, Russia held the world's second largest proved coal[15] reserves, after the United States (15% of the world's total), and its reserve-to-production ratio of 407 years was almost three times higher than the world average (139).

The share of coal in Russia's domestic primary energy consumption has decreased from 24% in the mid-1980s to 11% at the beginning of the 2020s, while the world average has been hovering around 25–30%. The share of coal in Russia's total energy production has been increasing since the mid-2000s, which coincided with world trends and followed an increase in crude oil prices. Growing external demand for coal was a primary driver, as testified by a significant expansion in net exports.

In 2020, Russia was the world's third largest exporter of coal (18% of global exports), after Australia (29%) and Indonesia (27%). Asia and Asia Pacific accounted for 56% of Russia's coal exports, with China itself accounting for 18%, South Korea for 13%, and Japan for 10%. European destinations accounted together for 35% of Russian coal exports while the FSU accounted for 2%.

Several countries and regions depend strongly on coal imports from Russia. In 2020, Russia accounted for 50% of coal imports by Europe, 47% of imports by all African countries, 30% of imports by the Middle East, 22% of imports by South Korea, and 15% and 13% of imports by China and Japan, respectively (BP, 2021).

At the beginning of 2021, close to 180 coal mines were active in Russia.[16] Accounting for close to 60% of total production, the largest centre is the Kuznetsk Coal Basin (Kuzbass). Other significant coal-producing regions include Kansk-Achinsk (9% of production), South Yakutia (4%), and Pechora (2%). The industry has been almost completely privatised, with state and municipal enterprises accounting for less than 0.5% of production (Rosstat, 2018). The market is however relatively concentrated, with the largest three coal producers accounting for over 40% of total production. These are SUEK (26% market share), the Ural Mining Metallurgical Company, incorporating Kuzbassrazrezugol (11%), and SDS Ugol (6%) (Central Dispatch Management of Fuel & Energy Complex, 2018). According to estimates of the Analytical

---

[15] The BP (2019, p. 40) definition used in this chapter includes commercial solid fuels, i.e., bituminous coal and anthracite (hard coal), lignite and brown (sub-bituminous) coal, and other commercial solid fuels. It also includes coal produced for coal-to-liquids and coal-to-gas transformations.

[16] Ministry of Energy of the Russian Federation (2018), *Gas: About the industry*, available at: https://minenergo.gov.ru/node/433.

Center for the Government of the Russian Federation (2017), about 39% of the coal consumed in Russia was destined for coking plants and 35% for large industrial sectors such as metallurgy, cement production, and railways.

9.4.7 Coal Pricing

Similar to oil, the domestic prices of coal and derivative products, while influenced by applicable taxes, are shaped to a large extent by market forces. One additional channel of potential governmental influence is through the regulation of railway transportation tariffs. The main coal mining regions are located long distances from the nearest seaports and railways serve as the most important means of the delivery. For example, delivering coal to one of the Pacific coast ports from the Kuznetsk Coal Basin requires transportation by some 4000 kms. On average, coal and coke have average hauls of around 1500 kms, a distance on which railways are an economically preferred mode of transport (Pittman, 2011).

Railway tariffs are set by Russian authorities and coal belongs to a privileged class of commodities which enjoy relatively low transport tariffs, deemed in the literature as priced below cost and being cross-subsidised by higher tariffs for the transport of other goods (European Commission, 2020).

9.4.8 Renewables

The share of energy generated from renewable sources (nuclear, hydroelectric, wind, and solar) in consumption has increased from 8% in the mid-1980s to 12% at the beginning of the 2020s, which was quicker than across the world on average. Nevertheless, at the beginning of the 2020s, the share was still lower than the world average of 16%, indicating the potential for further expansion. Nuclear and hydroelectric energy were the principal sources of Russia's renewable energy, while wind and solar power have not increased markedly and accounted for less than 0.1% of Russia's energy consumption in 2019.

The production shares of renewable energy are even smaller. While Russia is a relatively significant producer of both hydroelectric and nuclear energy, it is actually still a net importer. The relatively low production of wind and solar energy suggests unrealised potential, especially given that Russia occupies 11% of the world's land mass (see Chapter 1 and Sect. 9.5).

9.4.9 Electricity

In 2020, Russia was the world's fourth largest producer of electricity, after China, the United States, and India, accounting for 4% of global production. The share of electricity in Russia's total energy consumption has been increasing since the 1980s, following world trends. However, it flattened in the 2010s and remains below the world average. In 2019, it accounted for 13% in Russia, as compared to 17% globally.

Russia's electric power generation sector has undergone extensive reforms since the late 1990s when the United Energy System of Russia (RAO UES; the Russian language abbreviation RAO EES), the incumbent state-controlled monopoly dominating at that time, with over two-thirds of generation capacity and almost the entire transmission and distribution network, was gradually unbundled. It was separated into regulated entities, including an independent system operator, trading and transmission systems administrators at the federal level, several distribution companies at the regional level, and market-based competitors in the generation and retail segments. The aim of the reforms was the creation of competitive wholesale and retail markets for both electricity and capacity governed by a set of market rules and procedures.

The unified national electric grid is owned by the state-owned Federal Grid Company (FGC). However, the FGC and its affiliates are prohibited from selling and purchasing electric energy, which makes them different from Gazprom, who is the main producer and trader of gas while also being the manager of the UGSS and the main implementing body of regulated gas price policies (see Sects. 9.4.1 and 9.4.2).

In the generation segment, the unbundling of RAO UES resulted in the separation and privatisation of several wholesale and territorial power-generating companies, with several of the privatised companies being purchased by foreign energy firms. These reforms are deemed to have resulted in the significant deregulation of certain market segments and in new capacity investments. However, in 2018, over 80% of power generation was concentrated among the top 10 players, several of whom were majority state-owned. These were RusHydro, in which more than 60% of shares belong to the state, Inter RAO (where the state-owned Rosneftegaz Group owns approximately 28% of shares and FGC—an additional 9%), Gazpromenergoholding (owned by Gazprom), and the state-owned Rosenergoatom, an electric power division of Rosatom (Khokhlov, 2018).

State control over the retail segment is considered less significant than in the generation segment but market concentration, due to the strong positions held by legacy companies in their historic territories, is still deemed high (Khokhlov, 2018).

In 2020, 46% of electricity was generated in Russia from natural gas (compared to 23% across the world on average), and only 16% from coal (36% across the world) and 1% from oil (3%). Nuclear energy and hydro-electric power also had relatively high shares in electricity generation, but the contribution of other renewables was minimal.

The dominance of gas as the principal fuel in the electricity sector makes Russian electricity greener than it would be if it was generated in oil or coal-fuelled power plants. At the same time, companies that generate electricity from gas and which pay relatively low regulated prices for it de facto compete for gas with more lucrative export markets. This provides an incentive to Russian policymakers and the electric power-generating companies themselves to gradually diversify away from gas towards other, preferably renewable, energy sources.

9.4.10 Electricity Pricing

Russia has a two-tier electricity market—wholesale and retail. In the wholesale market, electricity generating companies or electricity importers supply electric power on the day-ahead market or under unregulated bilateral agreements within the same geographic zone. The wholesale power and capacity market is divided into three independent geographic zones: (1) the first price zone (Russia's European area and the Urals); (2) the second price zone (Siberia); and (3) the non-price zone (remote regions isolated from the unified energy system of Russia).

In price zones, the day-ahead wholesale market price is derived through the clearing of price bids submitted by suppliers and buyers, and thus it reflects the interaction of demand and supply as well as the structure of the given market. There are also additional regulated components which are added to the equilibrium price of the wholesale market, such as, for example, allowances for capacity or renewable energy generation. In the non-price zone, electricity is supplied at prices regulated by the FAS.

Thus, the wholesale market prices are a combination of both regulated tariffs and market forces, with market forces playing a larger role in the price zones and regulated tariffs dominating in non-price zones. In the retail market, power is supplied to industrial consumers and households at tariffs regulated by the FAS, which partially reflect the costs of system services and market conditions in the wholesale markets, but which are also differentiated by the categories of end users (European Commission, 2020).

9.5 Russia's Approach to the Challenges of Climate Change

Russia's specialisation in natural gas is a structural characteristic which, on the one hand, poses a challenge and, on the other, could turn into an opportunity. Natural gas, and particularly pipeline gas, while not as 'green' as renewables, has the lowest emissions per unit of energy obtained among the conventional fossil fuels (U.S. Environmental Protection Agency, 2021). It is envisaged as a non-negligible share of energy consumed even in scenarios with low or zero emissions. In addition, subsoil cavities, which remain after gas extraction, can be used as 'natural sinks' for the storage of captured carbon. The relatively low reliance on oil and coal sources for domestic energy consumption can also be conducive to such a transition because the direct impact on Russian consumers would be relatively small. However, the significant export orientation of these industries—and their contribution to the value of the country's overall merchandise exports—makes Russia vulnerable to climate change and other policies adopted by major importers of its oil and coal. The relatively low levels of production of renewable energy other than nuclear and hydropower (see Sect. 9.4.8) are a definite challenge.

9.5.1 A Green Economy Transition

The global challenge of reducing CO_2 and other greenhouse gas emissions is a formidable one not just for Russia. The energy sector—the source of an estimated three-quarters of global greenhouse gas emissions—is at its centre. The International Energy Agency (IEA, 2021) sets out a trajectory for the global energy sector to achieve net zero CO_2 emissions by 2050 to allow limiting the long-term increase in the average global temperature to 1.5 °C.

The implications of the IEA's scenario in terms of the level and structure of the global primary energy supply in the lead-up to 2050 are shown in Fig. 9.5. The global economy transforms from one dominated by fossil fuels to one progressively led by known renewable energy technologies. In 2050, wind and solar account together for 37% of energy supplies while fossil fuels account for only slightly more than one-fifth. Some fossil fuels such as natural gas and oil, which either cannot be substituted for renewable energy sources or are not combusted when used in production, are still used at the end of this timeline. Notably, natural gas, which has relatively low emissions relative to its calorific content and has versatile applications, will account for 11% of the total energy supply in that year, while oil for 8%.

Electrification and the substitution of the direct combustion of fossil fuels for indirect use via electricity generation are two additional important elements of a green transition. Electricity generation and electrification allow reducing greenhouse gas emissions not only when electricity comes from renewable sources but also when it is generated from fossil fuels, because the transformation of fossil fuels into electric energy in specialised power plants allows for a better control of emissions.

While this is not the only trajectory to reach a low emission economy—and certainly it is very ambitious—it is in the view of the IEA the most technically feasible, cost-effective, and socially acceptable one, and it also allows continued economic growth, further improvements to energy efficiency,[17] and maintaining the security of energy supplies. In terms of technology requirements, the scenario assumes the increased use of existing renewable and emission capture technologies as well as improvements in their cost-effectiveness and the investments in infrastructure these will need. It also assumes considerable investments in further innovation focusing on the commercialisation of

---

[17] According to this scenario, in 2050 the world economy is more than twice as big but uses 8% less energy than in 2021.

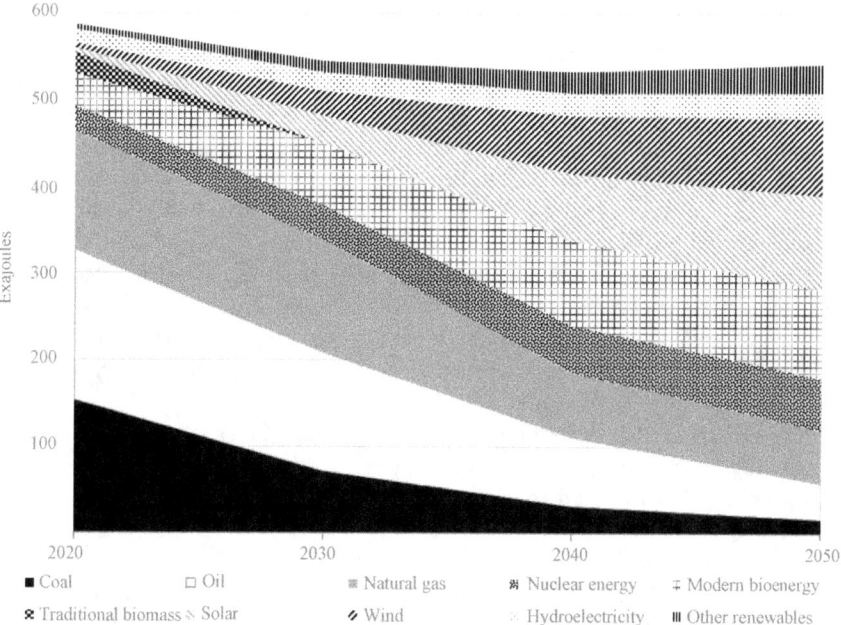

Fig. 9.5 IEA's Net Zero CO_2 emissions by 2050 scenario: total global energy supply by source (*Source* IEA [2021] and author's calculations)

technologies which are not yet on the market,[18] such as advanced batteries, hydrogen electrolysers, and direct air capture and storage (IEA, 2021).

9.5.2 Russia's Energy Strategy and Its Challenges and Opportunities Associated with a Green Transition

As communicated in a number of presidential and governmental decrees issued during 2019–2021, Russia's official energy strategy and its position on climate change and the green transition seem to have recently undergone a radical change.

The Energy Security Doctrine decreed by the President in 2019[19] is a strategic planning document which focused on ensuring Russia's energy security and set out the key directions of the country's energy strategy for the period up to 2030. It was followed by the government's executive orders, which adopted concrete implementation measures.[20] Energy security was

---

[18] In this scenario, half of the cumulative emission cuts in 2050 come from technologies that are at the demonstration or prototype phase.

[19] Decree of the President of the Russian Federation of 13 May 2019 N 216 'On Approval of the Energy Security Doctrine of the Russian Federation'.

[20] These are the Decree of the Government of the Russian Federation of 06 September 2021 No. 1523-r 'On approval of the Energy Strategy of the Russian Federation for the

defined in these documents not only in terms of the ability to supply energy to citizens and national businesses but also as the ability of doing so based on domestic energy production.

Climate change and the transition to a green economy were referred to explicitly in the challenges section of the Doctrine, as belonging to a '*set of conditions and factors that create new incentives for the development of world energy [...] but also can lead to a threat to energy security*'. While supporting '*...international efforts aimed at combating climate change*' and declaring readiness '*...to cooperate in this area with all states*', the Doctrine considered the idea of the green transition an unacceptable infringement of '*the interests of energy producing states and deliberately ignoring such aspects of sustainable development as ensuring universal access to energy and developing clean hydrocarbon energy technologies*'.

The Doctrine also described a number of other external threats and challenges to Russian energy security, which made it clear that the country sees itself as discriminated in global energy markets and energy development projects.

A more progressive view—albeit also revealing Russia's strategic interests—was expressed in Russia's 2021 'Strategy for the Socioeconomic Development of the Russian Federation with Low Greenhouse Gas Emissions Until 2050'.[21] Prepared just before the United Nations (UN) Climate Change Conference (COP26) in Glasgow in November 2021—and announced unexpectedly on the first day of COP26 talks—the strategy explicitly acknowledged negative anthropogenic impacts on climate and the associated dangers for Russia, and it reiterated Russia's international commitments[22] to fighting climate change. To illustrate the need to overhaul the Russian energy sector and Russia's economy as a whole in this context, the document portrayed two alternative socio-economic development scenarios.

The 'inertial' scenario, in which Russia's energy mix and energy efficiency would not change significantly, would be a threat to its socio-economic development which would materialise as a reduction in its medium-term rate of GDP growth to 1%, mainly due to negative growth in Russia's raw energy exports caused by the global transition towards greener energy sources. In

period up to 2035', and the Decree of the Government of the Russian Federation of 06 January 2021 No. 1447-r (as amended on 14 September 2021) 'On approval of the Action Plan for the implementation of the Energy Strategy of the Russian Federation for the period up to 2035'.

[21] See the Presidential Decree No. 666 from 4 November 2020 'On the reduction of greenhouse gas emissions' and the associated Governmental Decree N 3052-r from 29 October 2021 'On Approval of the Strategy for the Socioeconomic Development of the Russian Federation with Low Greenhouse Gas Emissions Until 2050'.

[22] Russia is a party to the Framework Convention, the Kyoto Protocol, and the Paris Agreement.

contrast, in the preferred 'target (intensive) scenario', Russia would cut its greenhouse gas emissions by up to 70% by 2030, as compared to the 1990 level, and become completely carbon neutral by 2060. Among others, the intensive scenario featured the development and application of low and zero carbon technologies, the increased use of secondary energy sources, changes in tax and customs policies, new financing for green initiatives, more than doubling the greenhouse gas absorption capacities of Russia's forests and other ecosystems, and the promotion of carbon capture, storage, and utilisation. In addition, hydrogen was seen in this context as a way for Russia to use its extensive pipeline export network into Europe amidst its worries that European Carbon Border Adjustment Mechanism would eventually apply to its fossil fuel exports. In the intensive scenario, Russia would gradually diversify away from raw energy production and exports towards more modern economic activities which are less energy intensive and which rely on greener energy sources. This scenario was portrayed as allowing the economy to achieve a medium-term growth rate of 3%.

At face value, these policy statements may have been be interpreted as showing the Russian authorities' increasing appreciation of the stakes involved in a transition to a greener global economy for a country like Russia. These statements were also likely part of a strategy to lay the groundwork for defending Russia's strategic interests in this debate (as illustrated by an emphasis on increasing the greenhouse gas absorption capacities of forests rather than on cutting emissions, technology neutrality in order to accept nuclear energy as a source of green energy, and developing international standards and mechanisms for accounting for carbon emissions in different countries (Likhacheva, 2021; Sharushkina, 2021; Trenin, 2021).

9.6 Consequences of Russia's Military Aggression on Ukraine

The illegal large-scale military aggression of Russia on Ukraine, which commenced on 24 February 2022, shocked the world. Many countries, including some of the main importers of Russian oil, gas, and coal, demanded an immediate cessation of the aggression and, in its absence, imposed on Russia a suite of economic sanctions (see Chapter 14). Russia responded with threats of energy supply cuts and imposed new payment conditions, which were in breach of current contracts.

These events have become a major incentive for consumers of Russian energy (represented by both governments and private firms) to diversify away as quickly as possible towards other sources. By the end of March 2022, some countries have already announced bans on imports of Russian oil and coal or have presented emergency plans for gradually introducing such bans on all Russian fuels, and others may follow in the near future. It has also been reported that major oil importing firms have already reduced purchases of Russian oil, not wanting to be seen as financing the aggression. Shifting to other suppliers is costly and takes time but, if enough actors decide to pursue this path—or if Russia itself decides to cut supplies with a view of inflicting economic costs on its political adversaries—this could well mean the end of dominance of the Russian energy sector and the Russian economy the way we have known it in the last three decades.

9.7 Conclusion

In the period leading up to Russia's invasion of Ukraine in 2022, the implications of a global energy transition for Russia could be arguably seen as both a cause of concern and an opportunity. More than in countries which do not produce as much energy from fossil fuels, in Russia, the transition to an economy based primarily on renewable energy would require not only very significant economic changes, but social and political ones as well (Kolesnikov & Volkov, 2021). This explains why, for a long time, Russian political elites viewed the policy responses to climate change deliberated by the international community mainly as a threat.

At the same time, a global transition to a low emission economy would have to build on existing sectoral expertise and would require large investments in innovation, technology deployment, and infrastructure development. It could thus, in principle, also arguably be an opportunity for Russia, and this seems to have been reflected in its strategy on tackling climate change prepared in Autumn 2021 in the context of the COP26. Participating in international discussions and having the ability to shape the global debate on climate change and energy transition would make good sense from Russia's point of view. Furthermore, having Russia on board would also be in the interest of the international community.

Unfortunately, following Russia's invasion of Ukraine and the threats of energy supply cuts subsequently made by Russia to some of its main energy trading partners, it is hard to see how Russia will be able to maintain its position as a key energy exporter, let alone become a key shaper of the global debate on combating climate change.

Questions for Students
1. Why does energy play such an important role in Russia's economy and economic policies?
2. What roles do government and market forces play in the management of Russia's energy sector?
3. What are the main implications of international climate change policies for Russia's energy sector?

REFERENCES

Analytical Center for the Government of the Russian Federation. (2017). Statistical collection: Fuel and energy complex of Russia, June 2017 Issue. http://ac.gov.ru/files/publication/a/13691.pdf. Accessed 29 March 2022.

BP. (2021). Statistical review of world energy, 70th edition. British Petroleum. https://www.bp.com/content/dam/bp/business-sites/en/global/corporate/pdfs/energy-economics/statistical-review/bp-stats-review-2021-full-report.pdf. Accessed 29 March 2022.

Central Dispatch Management of Fuel and Energy Complex. (2018). Coal in Russia and the World: Production, consumption, export, import. http://www.cdu.ru/tek_russia/articles/5/499/. Accessed 29 March 2022.

Coady, D. et al. (2019). *Global fossil fuel subsidies remain large: An update based on country-level estimates* (International Monetary Fund Working Paper 19/89). https://www.imf.org/en/Publications/WP/Issues/2019/05/02/Global-Fossil-Fuel-Subsidies-Remain-Large-An-Update-Based-on-Country-Level-Estimates-46509. Accessed 29 March 2022.

Commission, E. (2020). *Commission Staff Working Document on significant distortions in the economy of the Russian Federation for the purposes of trade defence investigations*. European Commission.

Furculita, C. (2017). *russian gas dual pricing consistency with WTO law: A question that might have been answered*. https://doi.org/10.2139/ssrn.3169167.Accessed29March2022

Henderson, J. (2011). *Domestic gas prices in Russia – Towards export netback?* Oxford Institute for Energy Studies. NG 57, November. https://www.oxfordenergy.org/wpcms/wp-content/uploads/2011/11/NG_57.pdf

Idrisov, G., & Gordeev, D. (2017). *Theoretical and practical aspects of natural gas pricing in domestic and foreign markets: The case of Russia* (Working Papers). Gaidar Institute for Economic Policy. https://EconPapers.repec.org/RePEc:gai:wpaper:wpaper-2017-274

IEA. (2021). *Net zero by 2050: A roadmap for the global energy sector*. International Energy Agency.

Khokhlov, A. A. (2018). *Market liberalization and decarbonization of the Russian electricity industry: Perpetuum pendulum*. OIES Oxford Energy Comment. https://www.oxfordenergy.org/publications/market-liberalization-decarbonization-russian-electricity-industry/. Accessed 29 March 2022.

Khrennikova, D. (2018). *Russian oil getting ready for biggest tax overhaul in 20 years*. https://www.bloomberg.com/news/articles/2018-07-25/russian-oil-getting-ready-for-biggest-tax-overhaul-in-20-years. Accessed 29 March 2022.

Kolesnikov, A., & Volkov, D. (2021). *The coming deluge: Russia's looming lost decade of unpaid bills and economic stagnation*. Carnegie Moscow Center. https://carnegiemoscow.org/2021/11/24/coming-deluge-russia-s-looming-lost-decade-of-unpaid-bills-and-economic-stagnation-pub-85852. Accessed 29 March 2022.

Likhacheva, A. (2021). *A greener Russia? Moscow's Agenda at the COP26 Climate Summit*. Carnegie Moscow Center. https://carnegiemoscow.org/commentary/85737. Accessed 29 March 2022.

Mitrova, T. (2013). *Russian LNG: The long road to export*. IFRI Russia/NIS Center. https://www.ifri.org/sites/default/files/atoms/files/defifrimitrovalngengdecember2013.pdf. Accessed 29 March 2022.

Mitrova, T., & Yermakov, V. (2019). *Russia's energy strategy-2035: Struggling to remain relevant*. IFRI. https://www.ifri.org/en/publications/etudes-de-lifri/russieneireports/russias-energy-strategy-2035-struggling-remain. Accessed 29 March 2022.

NRGI. (2021). *Natural resource revenue dataset*. Natural Resource Governance Institute. https://www.resourcedata.org/dataset/natural-resource-revenue-dataset. Accessed 29 March 2022.

OECD. (2021). OECD companion to the inventory of support measures for fossil fuels. *OECD Publishing, Paris*. https://doi.org/10.1787/e670c620-en.Accessed29March2022

Pittman, R. (2011). *Blame the switchman? Russia railways restructuring after ten years* (Economic Analysis Group Discussion Papers). U.S. Department of Justice. https://www.justice.gov/sites/default/files/atr/legacy/2011/03/08/267882a.pdf. Accessed 29 March 2022.

Rosstat. (2018). *Russian statistical yearbook, table 16.4: 'Volume of shipped own produced goods, works performed and services rendered by ownership type in 2017'*. The Federal State Statistics Service (Rosstat). https://www.gks.ru/free_doc/doc_2018/year/year18.pdf. Accessed 29 March 2022.

Rosstat. (2020). *Statistical yearbook 2020*. The Federal State Statistics Service (Rosstat).

Sharushkina, N. (2021). *COP26: Russia unveils new low-carbon strategy*. Energy Intelligence Group.

Trenin, D. (2021). *After COP26: Russia's path to the global green future*. Moscow Carnegie Center.

U.S. Environmental Protection Agency. (2021). *Carbon factors provided by the U.S. Environmental Protection Agency, Inventory of U.S. Greenhouse Gas Emissions and Sinks 1999–2019*. https://www.epa.gov/ghgemissions/inventory-us-greenhouse-gas-emissions-and-sinks-1990-2019. Accessed 29 March 2022.

WITS. (2021). *World integrated trade solution*. https://wits.worldbank.org/. Accessed 29 March 2022.

Yafimava, K. (2015). *Evolution of gas pipeline regulation in Russia: Third party access, capacity allocation and transportation tariff* (Oxford, Institute of Energy Studies Paper No. 95). https://www.oxfordenergy.org/publications/evolution-o. Accessed 29 March 2022.

CHAPTER 10

Agriculture

Eugenia Serova

Highlights

- Since the 1990s, the agriculture sector in Russia has undergone a deep systemic transformation in terms of land ownership, market-based production and investment, market pricing, external openness, and technical modernisation.
- As a result of its systemic transformation, three types of agricultural farms emerged: (i) large private enterprises, including agri-holdings (which play a dominant role in grain production); (ii) family farms; and (iii) household plots.
- Russia, forced to import large quantities of grain and other food products during the Soviet era, has now become a major exporter of wheat and other crops as well as agricultural products.
- The future development of Russia's agricultural sector faces three main challenges: environmental sustainability (including CO2 emissions and the impact of climate change on agriculture), innovation, and rural development.

E. Serova (✉)
Higher School of Economics, Moscow, Russia
e-mail: evserova@hse.ru

© The Author(s), under exclusive license to Springer Nature Switzerland AG 2023
M. Dabrowski (ed.), *The Contemporary Russian Economy*,
https://doi.org/10.1007/978-3-031-17382-0_10

10.1 Introduction

During 30 years of transition (1992–2021), Russian agriculture experienced an extraordinary change: a traditionally backwards sector has become a leading sector of the national economy. Food security, an uncertainty that Russia faced in the last century, is no longer an acute issue on the national agenda. Russia, previously a major agri-food importer, has now become a key supplier for global agri-food markets. In this chapter, we analyse the major achievements of Russia's transition as well as the development challenges of agriculture in post-Soviet Russia.

10.2 Soviet Agriculture: Major Challenges and Transformation Objectives

State agriculture under central planning was characterised not only by a high level of state regulation, but also by the direct management of agricultural production by the state. Investment and working capital (to a considerable extent) for agricultural producers were centrally allocated by the government; the government also set production tasks which, in turn, determined the branch and regional structure of agricultural production. The input and output prices (both levels and ratios), interest rates, and wages were centrally administered. Moreover, each climatic zone had its own price levels adjusted to the zonal cost of production. Therefore, profitability (as reflected in the books) was not an indicator of performance, and the regional specialisation of production was set artificially by zonal prices. Russia's economy was closed: producers could not reach global markets and the government regulated consumer access to foreign commodities. *Kolkhozes* and *sovkhozes* (collective and state farms) were a form of agricultural enterprise appropriate to this economic system. The state was the only owner of lands, and the farms acquired the lands for 'eternal and free use'.

Six decades of development (since collectivisation in the 1930s) demonstrated, on the one hand, the stability of its internal structure. However, on the other hand, it revealed two fundamental problems, the resolution of which was impossible without making changes to the foundations of this system.

The first problem was the lack of endogenous economic incentives in the functioning of these enterprises. Prices as a source of market information had no effect on production decisions: in 1988–1991, the correlation between procurement price changes and changes in planted areas under the respective crops was −0.91, between procurement price changes and changes in the respective animal populations −0.37 (Serova, 1999).

The sector was also not responsive to investments. For example, the use of electricity in agriculture from 1980 to 1990 increased by 61%, the use of mineral fertilisers—by 22%, and capital investments—by about 40%; however, during the same period, labour productivity in agricultural production increased by only 28% and gross output—by only 12%.

The second problem of the state agricultural system was caused by the low motivation of farm workers. The performance of large collective and state farms was not directly correlated with the contributions of individual workers. At the same time, and unlike in the industrial sectors, it was difficult to monitor each individual operation in agriculture, for example, the quality of ploughing or milking, among others. Therefore, in Soviet agriculture, one could observe extreme opportunistic behaviour among farm workers, such as overreporting, poor performance, and the pilfering of farm resources.

Thus, in the Soviet economy, neither farms nor farm workers were interested in enhancing productivity and efficiency. The poor motivation of enterprises and workers resulted in Soviet agriculture falling far behind the rest of the world, and despite its ongoing reforms, it gradually fell into stagnation. In the 1980s, the average annual growth of its gross agricultural output was close to 0 and its productivity level lagged behind developed countries (Serova, 1999).

By the beginning of the 1990s, the state agriculture system had reached the limits of its development. It had become an obstacle to technological progress and thus required fundamental reform. By the end of the 1980s, there was also an evident deficit of agri-food products in the Soviet Union. Agriculture stagnated and did not respond to investment, price signals, or partial reforms.

In addition, total subsidies to the agri-food sector comprised up to one-third of sales and were a heavy burden for the national budget, especially at a time when its revenue fell substantially as a result of a decline in world oil prices. Thus, by the beginning of the 1990s, there was an acute need for radical reform in the agri-food sector.

10.3 The Original Shape of Agrarian Transformation in the Early 1990s

The agrarian transformation in Russia began after the break-up of the Soviet Union in 1991; its first steps included land reform and farm restructuring.

There are a number of different mechanisms for land privatisation and de-collectivisation. Russia opted to issue conditional land shares. The workers of the *kolkhozes* and *sovkhozes* as well as pensioners and social service officers received equal conditional shares in the land of their farms. The conditional shares were not marked on the ground and could be considered as a type of option: they granted the holder the right to withdraw with a physical plot at any time, without the permission of the other land shareholders—the only consideration was that the location of the plot had to be agreed. Additionally, these land shares were transferable in all types of legal transactions. During 1992–1994, around 12 million such shares were allotted to rural dwellers (the rest of the lands were held in various forms of state and municipal ownership). By 1997, 53% of farmlands belonged to land shareholders and an additional 10% were fully privately owned. These land shares were the major tool used by modern agricultural companies in Russia in the accumulation of land banks.

The former collective and state farms had to be transformed into one of the legal company forms envisaged by the Civil Code.

In only a few years, the structure of agriculture had changed remarkably: three major segments appeared—private agricultural enterprises (heirs of collective and state farms), private family farms, and household plots (Fig. 10.1). Unlike in other FSU countries, almost all types of land transactions were legalised.

After 1998, a new form of agribusiness started to emerge in Russia: *agroholdings*. These are large farm operations—much larger than the traditional Soviet farm enterprises or their current heirs—established with outside capital. This capital can originate from a downstream sector, for example, when a processor invests in farms supplying raw materials, or it can originate from an upstream sector, for example, when a supplier controls the purchase of inputs. However, very often, the capital originates from entirely outside the sector, for example, from the energy, finance, or metallurgy sectors. In some cases, many farms are held by one holding company; however, in others, there could be a single large farm enterprise. Sometimes, such companies are organised under the control and with the participation of regional and/or local administrations; however, in the majority of cases, they are purely private initiatives. Management structures differ tremendously from company to company. Land

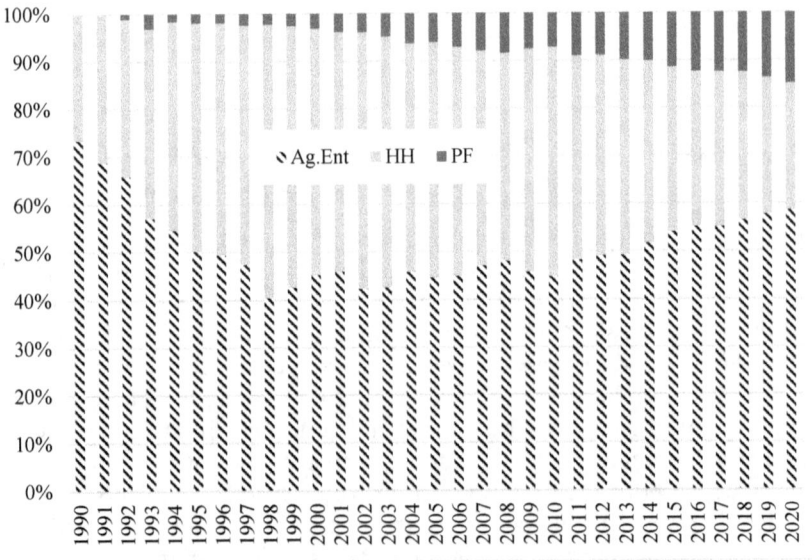

Fig. 10.1 Russia: structure of gross agricultural output by farm type (% of total in current prices), 1990–2018 (*Note* AgEnt—agricultural enterprises; HH—household plots; PF—peasant farms *Source* Yanbykh et al. [2020])

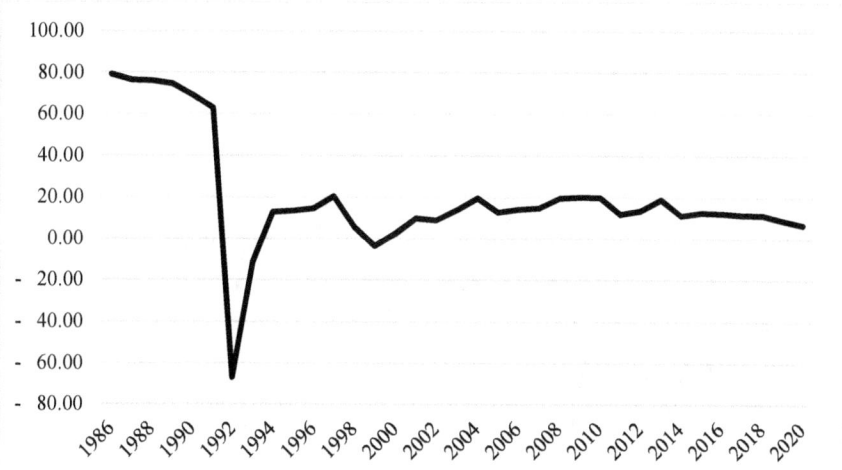

Fig. 10.2 Russia: support to the agri-food sector (PSE*), in %, 1986–2020 (*Note* PSE—producer support estimate, the conventional measure of level of price and budget transfer to agricultural producers. Conventional measure of support to agriculture, developed by the OECD *Source* OECD)

tenures may also be arranged differently: vast areas of land may be owned by a company, but most often, these are rented land shares (Serova, 2007).

At the same time as the food industry and the major segments of the middleman sector were privatised, output and input markets were also liberalised. Hence, the new infrastructure for market-oriented agriculture began to take shape.

New elements of agrarian policy were introduced: state procurements were sharply reduced, a new system of subsidies for producers was put in place, trade was significantly liberalised, and price controls were lifted, among others. The level of state support to agriculture fell dramatically (Fig. 10.2).

10.4 Transformation-Related Output Decline in Agriculture

As in all post-communist industrial countries, the agrarian transformation in Russia was coupled with a severe decline in agricultural production, which lasted approximately nine years (Fig. 10.3). This decline was explained by three factors: (i) trade liberalisation; (ii) a decline in the purchasing power of the population; and (iii) a restructuring of the sector associated with the collapse of the old institutions and the disorientation of managers and governing officers on all levels (see Chapters 8 and 15).

Trade liberalisation and the resulting massive inflow of imported food commodities partly pushed out the domestic producers. Domestic producers

Fig. 10.3 Russia: annual growth rate of gross agricultural output (previous year = 100), 1990–2020 (*Source* The Federal State Statistics Service [Rosstat])

could not compete with international suppliers: in many cases, their production was more expansive. Furthermore, the logistics of the planned economy were not conducive to private marketing, which increased transaction costs, and managers were not sufficiently skilled to operate in the new economic and social environment. In addition, consumers were more interested in the imported foodstuffs to which they had no access in the Soviet era. During the Soviet period, many non-food goods were rationed due to physical shortages (see Chapter 4), which led to a shift in consumer spending towards food items. After trade liberalisation, Russian consumers gained access to many foreign non-food goods and services and this diverted part of these consumer incomes from agri-food items.

During the last 30 years of the Soviet system, retail food prices (in the state retail system) were frozen, while nominal wages and other incomes of the population grew progressively. It created a kind of hidden (suppressed) inflation (Howard, 1976), where prices remained nominally stable, but goods were in deficit, thus increasing forced savings. When prices were liberalised in 1992, this hidden inflation was unfrozen. The real incomes of the population fell dramatically and thus the demand for food contracted, especially for commodities with a high-income elasticity, such as meat or dairy products. The contraction of demand also led to the contraction of production.

The market infrastructure designed for the centrally planned economy was not appropriate for the market system. There were no marketing institutions, such as middlemen, wholesale markets, cooperatives, or market information systems. Soviet food safety and veterinary systems could not work in this new environment. Emerging small producers could not purchase small-scale equipment and machinery which was not produced in the Soviet Union. Market institutes could not be built overnight, and their absence became an obstacle between producers and consumers: actual food demand could not be satisfied while producers suffered from overproduction and inventories.

The transition to a market economy took about five or six years, after which the agri-food sector could begin its recovery.

The recovery of production in the agri-food sector started with the financial crisis of 1998, when the four-fold devaluation of the national currency (see Chapter 16) led to the creation of protection from import pressure and provided a window of opportunity for domestic producers. Imports thus became more expensive and could not compete with domestic producers. Some producers used this opportunity to gain competitiveness by modernising their production facilities and building efficient food chains. The effects of the global financial crisis (GFC) of 2008–2009 (another devaluation of the rouble) provided similar support for the agri-food sector.

The market-oriented agricultural sector was also characterised by significant changes in its production structure. Russia, a large grain importer in the late Soviet era, emerged as a large meat importer (although later it gained a high level of self-sufficiency in meat production as well). Sugar and sunflower seed production recorded the highest levels in Russian history, and intensive cattle breeding emerged as a completely new subsector. The regional distribution of agricultural production also changed notably. Under the Soviet system of differentiated prices adjusted to local production costs, it was equally profitable to produce all commodities throughout the country. Hence, regional specialisation was not strong. After Russia's market transformation, specialised areas of production for individual products emerged.

The structure of food also changed. The consumption of mostly subsidised food items in the Soviet economy (meat and dairy products) reduced sharply, while that of potatoes and bread products increased. Poultry and pork began to dominate meat consumption, as compared to beef which was more popular during the Soviet period (thanks to subsidies).

10.5 Contemporary Agri-Food Sector in Russia

As a result of its market transition, Russia has managed to solve its long-standing problem of food shortages. The agri-food sector has been one of the most steadily developing sectors of the national economy. According to the Federal State Statistics Service (Rosstat), between 2013 and 2020, GDP grew by 4.2%, while the agriculture value added—by 31%. The production of selected crops has reached historical records (e.g., sunflower seeds and sugar beet). On the other hand, Russia's pre-reform level of livestock production has not been achieved due to limited consumer demand (after eliminating the

Soviet era subsidies—see Sect. 10.4). For instance, in 1992, 47 million tonnes of milk were produced, in 2020—just about one-half of that.

Russia, which was once a stable importer of staple foods, has become a significant supplier to the world market. Russia is now a world champion in exports of wheat and buckwheat. In 2020, Russia was the world's largest wheat exporter and the second largest for sunflower oil and barley.

The livestock sector contracted by about one-half during the 1990s, and as a result, Russia became a big meat importer. However, since 2000, this sector has rebounded and meat imports (especially chicken and pork) have fallen considerably (Fig. 10.4).

Russia has never in its history had an intensive cattle breeding programme. This sector was first established in the 2000s and now the country even exports beef. The quantities exported are still 15–20 times smaller than the quantities of the world leaders such as Poland, the Netherlands, and France; however, in the 2010s, beef exports grew to almost 4000 tonnes. In 2021, Russian agri-food exports comprised almost USD 37 billion, having grown in the 2010s by almost five times (Fig. 10.5). According to customs data, most agri-food exports are cereals, fish and seafood, and oils and oil seeds.

The country continues to be a net-importer of agri-food products; however, its trade deficit was largely reduced.

Conventional indicators of food security show that Russia is consistently in the top 20% of the world's countries (Fig. 10.6). This means that the

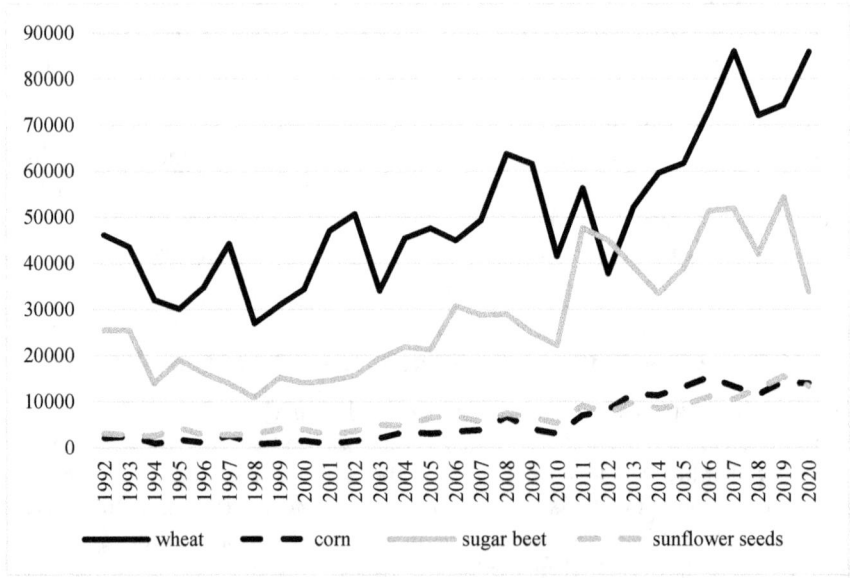

Fig. 10.4 Russia: dynamic of production of major crops, million tonnes (*Source* The Federal State Statistics Service [Rosstat])

historically permanent threat of famine no longer hangs over the country. The relatively low level of food availability in Russia in the Global Food Security Index (GFSI), despite sufficient production, is primarily explained by unstable policy and corruption.[1]

Both partial sector performance indicators (such as yields per hectare, yields per head, and labour productivity) and total factor productivity (TFP) are growing. According to Federal State Statistics Service (Rosstat), between 1990 and 2020, grain yield per hectare increased from 1.94 to 3.1 tonnes, corn—from 3.14 to 5.32, sugar beet—from 2.4 to 3.7 (or 4.8 in 2019), and potatoes—from 9.1 to 27.1. The annual yield per cow in the same period increased from 2.8 tonnes to 6.7 tonnes of milk per year, and so on. In the 2010s, labour productivity in agriculture grew faster than in the entire Russian economy. Productivity growth was achieved primarily due to new technologies. Also, possibilities for high levels of profitability in the major agriculture subsectors brought in large private investment and good management.

Agribusiness in Russia and some academic studies (Shick, 2020) believe that budget support had a positive impact on the growth in agricultural production. State support for agriculture in Russia is consistently between the levels of the European Union (EU) and the United States (US), although a number of support programmes are not always effective in achieving their goals.

Between 2010 and 2019, the main policy goal was to increase the volume of production for import substitution. Figure 10.5 confirms that this goal was largely achieved. Russia is self-sufficient in most staple agri-food commodities.

The structure of state support has been relatively stable since 2006, with 15–30% of the funds allocated to investment support through mid- and long-term credit support programmes. Other subsidies to producers, especially input subsidies (feed, seeds, fertilisers, and diesel fuel) were always among the main policy instruments.

In 2019, the goal of national agricultural policy changed: export expansion became the central goal. It should reach USD 45 billion of agri-food exports by 2024. By 2021, 80% of this goal has already been achieved.[2]

In 2014, due to the political conflict around Crimea and responding to the Western sanctions (see Chapter 14), Russia imposed import restrictions for agri-food commodities from the EU, the US, Canada, Australia, and Norway (later—from some other countries). There is an opinion that these restrictions supported Russia's producers although Fig. 10.3 does not support this claim (Fig. 10.6).

---

[1] The Global Food Security Index (GFSI) considers the issues of food affordability, availability, quality and safety, and natural resources and resilience (last one since 2020) across a set of 113 countries. The index is a dynamic quantitative and qualitative benchmarking model constructed from 58 unique indicators that measure the drivers of food security across both developing and developed countries—see https://impact.economist.com/sustainability/project/food-security-index/Country/Details#Russia.

[2] In 2021, in order to fight food product inflation, Russia's government introduced limitations on agri-food exports, which led to its decline.

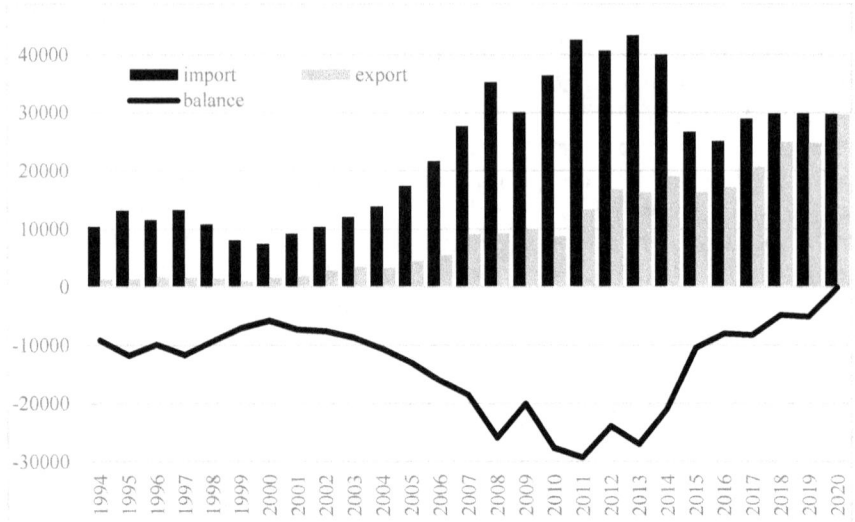

Fig. 10.5 Russia: agri-food trade, USD million (*Source* The Federal State Statistics Service [Rosstat]; for 2019 and 2020—Customs data)

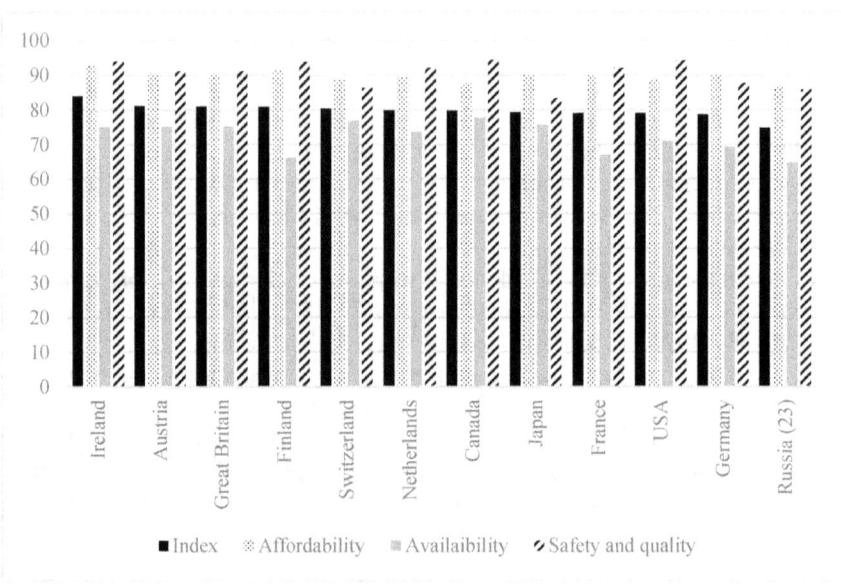

Fig. 10.6 The Global Food Security Index, top 10 countries and Russia from 113 monitored, 2021. Note: 100 is the highest level of food security (*Source* https://impact.economist.com/sustainability/project/food-security-index/)

The agriculture structure in contemporary Russia has a dual character: there are very large agricultural holdings operating on hundreds of thousands of hectares, and small producers who still provide a significant part of the gross agricultural output, especially for certain products such as potatoes and open field vegetables (Fig. 10.1). At the same time, the share of market production of household plots is insignificant and declined between two agricultural censuses—from 12.5% in 2006 to 11.2% in 2016.[3] This means that household plots are mostly subsistence and produce for family consumption.

The total land bank of the 10 biggest agricultural companies in Russia amounts to almost 6 million hectares, that is, about 7% of total arable lands. However, the size of these companies in terms of revenues is not very impressive in comparison with the leading international agricultural companies. In 2020, the annual revenue of the largest Russian agroholding *(Agrocomplex Tkacheva)* amounted to USD 1.23 billion, the second largest *(Prodimex)*— USD 0.9 billion (Lyalikova, 2021), while the annual revenues of global agricultural companies such as Olam International totalled more than USD 21 billion, the Dairy Farmers of America—almost USD 16 billion, and Fonterra—more than USD 13 billion (Laughman, 2020).

Box 10.1 Contemporary Russian agriculture—basic facts (2020)
Russia has 222 million hectares of agricultural land, which is about 5% of global agricultural lands. Agricultural lands comprise 13% of Russia's overall territory—7% of these lands contain the highly fertile black soil *chernozem*. The largest *chernozem* fields can be found on Russia's territory. Much of Russia's territory (47%) is covered by forests. Russia has abundant freshwater resources (see Chapter 1); however, most of these resources are located in the Eastern part of the country where only 20% of the population lives. Agriculture uses 14% of annual water withdrawals. Agricultural value added (including fishery and forestry) comprises 4.5% of Russia's GDP. The share of agriculture in the total labour force of Russia is around 6%. Approximately 25% of Russians live in rural areas.
  Source: Data of the Federal State Statistics Service (Rosstat) and FAOSTAT.

10.6 Future Challenges

During 30 years of transition, Russia's agricultural sector made notable progress. This progress was achieved through better management and large public and private investments. Both of these factors are about to be exhausted. The future development of the sector faces three major challenges: environmental sustainability, innovation, and rural development.

---

[3] Data from Agricultural Census—https://rosstat.gov.ru/519 and https://rosstat.gov.ru/folder/520.

10.6.1 Sustainability in the Agri-Food Sector

The main challenge to global development nowadays is the requirement for sustainable development in all spheres of human activity, including agriculture. In order to feed a growing and—what is even more important—increasingly rich population, more resources are required if conventional agricultural technologies continue ('business as usual' scenario). More lands, more fresh water, and more energy will be needed to meet global food (and fibre) demand. However, world resources are already limited (more land for agriculture is possible mainly at the expense of forests, which is highly undesirable from an environmental point of view), and the availability of these resources is further restricted by intense use, urbanisation, and climate change. This is why the concept of sustainable agriculture was brought to the global agenda. Among the 17 Sustainable Development Goals (SDGs) adopted by the United Nations (UN) in 2015, the second states the goal of ending all forms of hunger and malnutrition by 2030 and promoting sustainable agriculture.[4]

The main obstacle to the sustainable development of agriculture in Russia is the 'resource curse': the availability of vast land and water resources and its relatively high level of biodiversity do not yet pose an urgent need for the country to protect them. Russia is still the planet's environmental donor. Therefore, the challenges to sustainable development are not always felt the same way as in other parts of the world. Sometimes, it seems to producers and policymakers that the problem is somewhere in the developing world and that it does not concern Russia. The issue of sustainable agriculture only entered into the national policy agenda in 2020.

First, Russia will be significantly affected by global warming, although it is not clear yet how it will influence Russian agriculture (FAO, 2021). One view is that global warming will enable agricultural production in the large territory of Siberia, which could not be used for this purpose thus far. To a certain extent, this is already happening, for example, in the Tyumen oblast in western Siberia. On the other hand, in Russia's traditional agricultural regions—the Volga area and south of European Russia—the instances of extreme weather events (floods and droughts) have become more frequent due to climate change. And these are the areas where the infrastructure and labour force for agriculture are located. The relocation of production more to the north-east of the country may require additional large investments.

Second, agriculture is rather far from being carbon neutral. According to FAO statistics, each unit of agricultural production in Russia causes 23 times greater greenhouse gas emissions than in the EU.

Russia, as with other countries in the world, is faced with a severe problem of soil degradation. It is asserted that the total area of eroded and deflated lands and lands potentially prone to wind and water erosion is over 50%

---

[4] See https://sdgs.un.org/goals/goal2.

of its agricultural lands (Tsymbarovich et al., 2020). This can challenge the sustainability of agricultural production in the country.

Water stress measures such as the irrigated agriculture water use efficiency (in USD/m^3) in Russia are 10 times lower than the world average.[5] This shows that agricultural water is not used in a sustainable way.

In several regions, the limits of the ecological burden associated with agricultural production have already been reached. In some regions, livestock production (poultry, pork) generates large farm waste, which in an extreme situation can enter the underground aquifer and cause an ecological catastrophe. In a number of southern regions, the maximum allowable share of sunflower crops in crop rotations has been exceeded, which leads to the extreme exhausting of soil fertility. There is also data on overfishing. The rapid development of aquaculture in Russia has not been accompanied by adequate measures of environmental sustainability, which can lead to the collapse of the industry (as has happened in several other countries).

Food loss and waste (FLW) is a serious threat to sustainable agricultural development nowadays. FLW expresses the extreme level of inefficiency of using resources, but it is also a source of massive greenhouse gas emissions.[6] As there is essentially no official monitoring system for FLW in Russia, we have to rely on the expert opinions of market participants. For the main branches of the agri-food sector, losses reach up to 40% of the output, which means that all types of resources are used in an unproductive manner. Unlike the majority of other countries, Russia does not have any national strategy to reduce FLW.

Last but not the least, Russian agri-food exports can be restricted by importing countries looking at the sustainability of the production techniques of the imported goods.

On the other hand, there are also positive trends. For example, the reduction in the area used for agricultural production due to increases in productivity per hectare has led to some improvements in the conservation of biodiversity in the country.

10.6.2 Innovativeness of the Agri-Food Sector

Food production today is one of the world's most knowledge-intensive industries. In order to maintain and strengthen its position in both domestic and foreign markets, Russia urgently needs to switch to an innovative method of developing its agri-food sector.

Russian agriculture output is very volatile. For example, the volatility of yields of main crops exceeds many times the same indicator in Canada, which has similar agri-climatic conditions and a similar size of agricultural

---

[5] Irrigated agriculture water use efficiency (USD/m3) is defined as the value added in irrigated agriculture divided by the volume of water used. See https://sdg.tracking-progress.org/indicator/6-4-1-water-use-efficiency-usd-per-cubic-meter/.

[6] See https://www.fao.org/platform-food-loss-waste/flw-data/en/.

production. This is a sign of a technological gap. Other evidence of such a technological gap can be found in the very high dependence of Russia's agriculture on the imports of breeding materials.

What are the main constraints to the innovative development of Russia's agriculture? First, there is a huge generation gap in agricultural sciences dating back to the 1930s and 1940s when restrictions were imposed in many academic fields (for example, agricultural economics, agricultural statistics, and genetics), and existing scientific schools were destroyed. Further, in the 1990s, the influx of young people into agricultural sciences declined sharply. This was also due to a very large financing gap in Russia's agricultural sciences in comparison with its main trade competitors. This generational gap cannot be eliminated merely by monetary measures.

Second, it is necessary to take into account that the private sector is the main investor in applied agricultural science (for comparison, in the US, 76% of research and development [R&D] investments in agriculture are made by private corporations). The investment cycle in applied agricultural research is 12–20 years on average worldwide. This means that R&D investments are only possible in a stable business environment. In Russia, even the largest agribusiness companies have an average planning horizon of four to five years. In these conditions, investments in R&D and personnel become high risk.

To encourage agribusinesses to invest in R&D, the Federal Programme of Scientific and Technological Progress in the Agri-food Sector was launched in 2019, the main tool of which is the governmental co-financing of R&D.

Third, innovative development and new technologies require a different approach to agricultural education. The modern system of agricultural education in Russia, on the one hand, is detached from fundamental research; on the other hand, it trains specialists in isolation from the practical needs of business.

10.6.3 Rural Development

With increasing productivity in the agricultural sector, large segments of rural areas in Russia have been marginalised. This has led to the degradation of rural areas in these territories, the migration of the rural population to the cities, and the disappearance of a large number of settlements. Moreover, large-scale agribusiness in search of skilled labour has switched in some cases to shift methods of organising work.

The underdevelopment of rural areas also becomes an obstacle to the development of agriculture. The marginalised social environment creates risks for production, and businesses cannot attract qualified employees on a permanent basis. Agribusiness is often forced by regional authorities to invest in the technical infrastructure and social development of the territories of its production, which increases costs of production and reduces competitiveness. Thus, rural development today is not only a social challenge for the country's development, but also a condition for further development of the agricultural sector.

Since 2009, the decline in the rural population in Russia has averaged 100 thousand annually, and since the beginning of the twenty-first century, the rural population of Russia due to depopulation and migration to cities decreased by 1.6 million people.

Rural areas in Russia have always lagged behind urban territories in their development. Despite the fact that, since the beginning of the twenty-first century, the government has taken steps to increase the standard of living in the countryside, the problem of rural underdevelopment remains urgent. In rural areas of Russia, the income level of the population is noticeably lower—every fifth rural resident belongs to the group of the population with incomes below the subsistence level. The unemployment rate is twice as high as in urban territories.

In the 2010s, some progress has been achieved in equalising the standard of living of the population in rural and urban areas in Russia. The State Programme on Rural Development adopted in 2019 involves, for the first time, a local community-driven approach. It also tends to attract private businesses to its implementation. Furthermore, it targets innovative solutions in the development of physical and social infrastructure, such as alternative sources of energy supply, remote education, and telemedicine.

Return migration is a new trend in rural development. Some residents of the biggest cities choose rural areas as the place of second residence. The development of rural infrastructure should support this new tendency.

Questions for Students

1. What were the major problems of centrally planned agriculture?
2. Describe land shares as a mechanism of land privatisation in Russia and other post-Soviet countries.
3. What were the major reasons for the transformation-related output decline in agriculture in the 1990s?
4. What are the factors underlying the agricultural structure of modern Russia?
5. What are the major results of Russia's agricultural transformation since the 1990s?
6. Where is Russia's place in global agri-food production?
7. What are the major challenges for further agricultural development in Russia?

References

FAO. (2021). *The state of the world's land and water resources for food and agriculture*. Food and Agriculture Organization. https://www.fao.org/3/cb7654en/cb7654en.pdf

Howard, D. H. (1976). A note on hidden inflation in the Soviet Union. *Soviet Studies*, 28(4), 599–608. https://www.jstor.org/stable/150363?seq=1#metadata_info_tab_contents

Laughman, C. (2020, August 21). The 2020 top 100 food and beverage companies. *Food Engineering*. https://www.foodengineeringmag.com/articles/99063-the-2020-top-100-food-and-beverage-companies

Lyalikova, A. (2021, March 3). 20 krupneishikh zemlevladel'cev Rossii. Reiting Forbes (20 largest landowners of Russia. Rating Forbes). *Forbes*. https://www.forbes.ru/biznes-photogallery/422283-20-samyh-dorogih-chastnyh-zemlevladeniy-rossii-2021-reyting-forbes

Serova, E. (1999). *Agrarnaya ekonomika [Agricultural Economics]*. Publishing House of the Higher School of Economics.

Serova, E. (2007). Agro-holdings: Vertical integration in agri-food supply chains in Russia. In J. Swinnen (Ed.), *Global supply chains, standards and the poor: How the globalization of food systems and standards affects rural development and poverty* (pp. 188–206). CABI.

Shick, O. (2020). Public expenditure for agricultural sector in Russia: Does it promote growth? *Russian Journal of Economics*, 6(1), 42–55. https://rujec.org/article/49756/

Tsymbarovich, P., Kust, G., Kumani, M., Golosov, V., & Andreeva, O. (2020). Soil erosion: An important indicator for the assessment of land degradation neutrality in Russia. *International Soil and Water Conservation Research*, 8(4), 418–429. https://www.sciencedirect.com/science/article/pii/S209563392030040X/pdfft?md5=635eadb7bb658a43fd2325df6992c47c&pid=1-s2.0-S209563392030040X-main.pdf

Yanbykh, R., Saraikin, V., & Lerman, Z. (2020). Changes in Russia's agrarian structure: What can we learn from agricultural census? *Russian Journal of Economics*, 6(1), 26–41. https://doi.org/10.32609/j.ruje.6.49746

CHAPTER 11

Regional Diversity

Leonid Limonov, Olga Rusetskaya, and Nikolay Zhunda

Highlights

- The population of Russia is extremely unevenly distributed over its territory. The average population density as of 1 January 2021 was 8.54 people per square kilometre. The majority of the population (68.53%) lives in the European part of Russia, which constitutes one-fifth (20.82%) of Russia's territory and has the most favourable climatic conditions.
- The foremost modern spatial development trend in Russia is the steady migration of the factors of production—from the east and north to the west, south, and centre of the country. This has led to the spatial concentration of economic development in a small number of federal

L. Limonov (✉) · O. Rusetskaya · N. Zhunda
International
Centre for Social and Economic Research 'Leontief Centre', St. Petersburg, Russia
e-mail: limonov@leontief.ru

O. Rusetskaya
e-mail: olga@leontief.ru

N. Zhunda
e-mail: nzhunda@leontief.ru

Higher School of Economics, St. Petersburg, Russia

© The Author(s), under exclusive license to Springer Nature Switzerland AG 2023
M. Dabrowski (ed.), *The Contemporary Russian Economy*,
https://doi.org/10.1007/978-3-031-17382-0_11

entities and, consequently, to a high level of interregional socio-economic disparities.
- In the 2010s, there has been a reduction in interregional socio-economic disparities as a result of the state's policy of regional development. However, a high level of interregional socio-economic inequality remains.

11.1 Demographic and Social Diversity of the Russian Regions

The population of Russia is extremely unevenly distributed over its territory. The average population density as of 1 January 2022 was 8.49 people per square kilometre (km^2).[1] The majority of the population (68.53%) lives in the European part of Russia, which constitutes one-fifth (20.82%) of Russia's territory and has the most favourable climatic conditions. The remaining population is largely dispersed across southern Siberia and the Far East—in particular, along the Trans-Siberian Railway.[2]

The lowest population density (0.07 persons/km^2) among federal entities of the Russian Federation is in the Chukotka Autonomous Okrug (AO), which is located in the Russian Far East in the Far North. The highest population density is found in the two federal capital cities of Moscow (4933 people/km^2) and St. Petersburg (3832 people/km^2).

The influence of natural resources and environmental factors on the settlement of people in contemporary Russia is discussed in detail in Sect. 1.4 of Chapter 1.

Foreign and internal migration began to play an important role in the Russian demographic situation in the 1990s. The main inflow of immigrants came from the former Soviet Union (FSU) and the Baltic countries. Foreign migration made it possible to compensate partly for the natural loss of population and to replenish approximately three million people during this decade (Vishnevskiy, 2000). At the same time, intra-Russia population migration, which was centripetal in nature—from the north and east to the west, centre, and south of the country—increased significantly. In addition to the traditional form of migration associated with a change of permanent residence, temporary labour migration also developed (Karachurina, 2007).

Since 2000, Russian regions have experienced different situations in terms of population dynamics (Leontief Centre, 2020). Only 23 regions out of 83 experienced stable population growth. Population growth, mainly due to internal and external migration, occurred in economically developed territories as well as in those with good natural and climactic conditions: Moscow

---

[1] Calculated using Federal State Statistics Service (Rosstat) data.

[2] The Trans-Siberian Railway is a railroad between Chelyabinsk and Vladivostok built during 1891–1916, connecting the European part of Russia with the largest East Siberian and Far Eastern industrial cities.

and St. Petersburg's urban agglomerations, Krasnodar Krai, Belgorod Oblast, the Ural part of Tyumen Oblast, and the Karachay-Cherkess Republic. Natural population growth (see Chapter 2) occurred mainly in the national republics and autonomous *okrugs* (districts, AOs)—for example, in northern European Russia (Nenets AO), the North Caucasus (Chechnya, Ingushetia, and Dagestan), and Siberia and the Far East (Tyva, Altai, Yamalo-Nenets, Khanty-Mansi, and Sakha [Yakutia]).

Fifty-three regions recorded population decreases, usually due to negative population growth combined with migratory outflows. These regions are predominantly territories with unfavourable climatic conditions as well as deindustrialised or old industrialised regions with limited economic restructuring. The leaders in terms of migration outflows are the northern regions of European Russia (Komi Republic, Murmansk Oblast, and Arkhangelsk Oblast), the regions of the Far East (Magadan Oblast, Chukotka AO, Kamchatka Krai, and the Jewish Autonomous Oblast), the Republic of Kalmykia near the Caspian Sea, and the Kurgan Oblast in the West Siberian Plain. In the remaining seven regions, there was no clear trend of population change.

Despite a population decline, the process of urbanisation continues. The population is growing in the cities located in the south of European Russia and in large urban agglomerations. At the same time, there is a steady decline in the population of cities with less than 100 thousand people and in rural areas. Gradual changes in the urban system are determined by both market and nonmarket factors: the size and structure of the potential market, the level of specialisation, infrastructure, the administrative status of the city, and its geographical location (Kolomak, 2021).

Demographic changes result in growing disparities in territorial dispersion and the economic development of territories. These trends, combined with the general European trends of declining birth rates and population ageing, entail a growing demographic burden on the working-age population (see Chapter 2) and imbalances in regional labour markets (see Chapter 17).

Greater heterogeneity in the ethno-demographic structure of the populations of individual regions is positively associated with their productivity and innovation (Limonov & Nesena, 2016).

The highest values of this indicator are in the rich oil and gas-producing northern Yamal-Nenets AO, as well as in the capital cities of Moscow and St. Petersburg, where it is more than four times higher. In another 15 economically developed regions, it exceeds the subsistence level more than three times. On the opposite end of the spectrum (the right-hand side of Fig. 11.1), there are regions where it barely doubled: the Republic of Ingushetia, the Karachay-Cherkess Republic, the Kabardino-Balkarian Republic, the Republic of Tyva, and the Jewish Autonomous Oblast.

As a result of a government policy to support poor regions, the gap between the rich and poor regions more than halved between 2003 and 2020—from 7.5 times in 2003 to 3.3 times in 2020, and the coefficient of variation

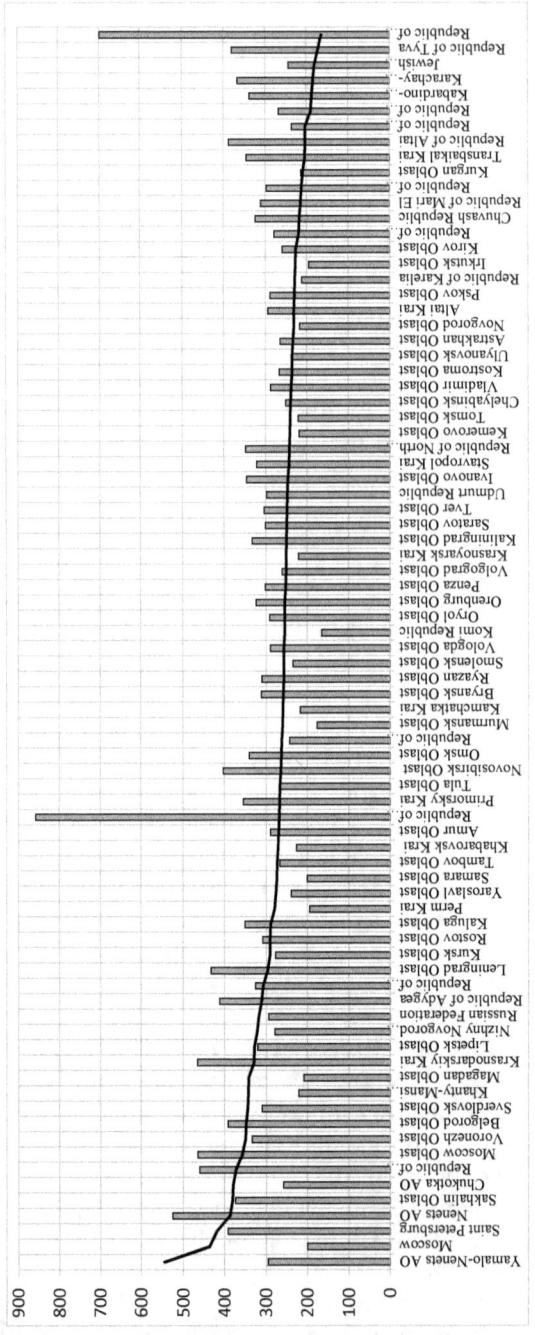

Fig. 11.1 Growth of real monetary incomes of the population in 2020 against 1999, % (bars) (*Note* The ratio of the population's average nominal monetary income to the subsistence level in 2020, % (line). *Note* AO—autonomous okrug (district). *Source* authors' calculations based on the Federal State Statistics Service [Rosstat] data)

Table 11.1 Interregional differences in the ratio of the average per capita cash income to the subsistence level, %, 2003–2020

Indicator	2003	2007	2013	2018	2019	2020
Average value of the index in the Russian Federation	243.8	324.6	351.7	323.3	324.9	318.2
Minimum value of the index	71.1	135.7	169.3	157.4	158.3	164.1
Maximum value of the index	531.0	598.4	530.3	500.6	510.5	545.0
Ratio of the maximum value of the index to the minimum value	7.5	4.4	3.1	3.2	3.2	3.3
Coefficient of variation, %	36.1	31.0	22.3	22	22.9	23.3

Source Authors' calculations based on the Federal State Statistics Service (Rosstat) data

decreased by more than 1.5 times (from 36.1% to 23.3%)—that is, interregional disparities decreased (Table 11.1). However, the coefficient of variation, despite its decline, continues to be significant.

Between 2003 and 2020, life expectancy at birth in Russia grew by more than six years on average (Table 11.2). Despite reducing the differences, the gap between the best and worst performing regions in regard to life expectancy at birth in 2020 was still more than 15 years. The infant mortality rate decreased by more than three times on average (from 15.3 to 4.5). However, interregional differences have grown and are significant. Differences in housing and healthcare infrastructure (number of hospital beds, outpatient clinics, and doctors) have diminished.

11.2 Economic Diversity

In this section, we analyse interregional economic differences since 2000. The early and mid-2000s was a period of fairly intensive growth, which was facilitated by a slowdown in inflation, strengthening monetary policy, and the situation of the world commodity markets (see Chapter 15). The key economic indicators illustrating regional economic performance are gross regional product (GRP)[3] and investment in fixed capital.

11.2.1 Differences in Gross Regional Product

Between 2000 and 2018, GRP growth in comparable (2000) prices amounted to almost 200% in Russia (Table 11.3). However, this growth rate gradually slowed down and was largely dependent on external shocks, such as the global financial crisis (GFC), changes in commodity prices, and geopolitical conflicts. In particular, growth was interrupted in 2009 and during 2015–2016.

---

[3] Gross Regional Product (GRP) is defined as the sum of value added contributed by economic agents residing in a given region.

Table 11.2 Dynamics of interregional disparities in socio-demographic indicators

Indicator	2000	2007	2013	2018	2019	2020
Life expectancy at birth, total population (number of years)						
Average value for Russia	65.34	67.61	70.76	72.91	73.34	71.54
Minimum value of the index	55.16	58.83	61.79	63.58	67.57	65.82
Maximum value of the index	71.98	75.19	78.84	82.41	83.40	81.48
Ratio of the maximum value of the index to the minimum value, times	1.3	1.3	1.3	1.3	1.2	1.2
Infant mortality rate (number of deaths per 1,000 live births)						
Average value of the index in the Russian Federation	15.3	9.4	8.2	5.1	4.9	4.5
Minimum value of the index	9.4	4.3	4.4	1.6	1.4	2.1
Maximum value of the index	33.0	21.4	23.9	12.7	10.9	14.7
Ratio of the maximum value of the index to the minimum value, times	3.5	5	5.4	7.9	7.8	7
Number of hospital beds, per 10,000 population (at the end of the year; beds)						
Average value of the index in the Russian Federation	115.0	106.6	90.6	79.9	80	81.3
Minimum value of the index	43	50.6	46.1	44.4	44.1	48.7
Maximum value of the index	241.4	230	148.9	131.3	126.9	128.8
Ratio of the maximum value of the index to the minimum value, times	5.6	4.5	3.2	3.0	2.9	2.6
Capacity of outpatient and polyclinic organisations, per 10,000 population (at the end of the year; visits per shift)						
Average value of the index in the Russian Federation	243.2	257.4	264.5	272.4	277.5	283.7
Minimum value of the index	79	111.4	113.1	124.1	119.6	181.2
Maximum value of the index	481.1	562.8	483.6	471.6	476.5	487.6
Ratio of the maximum value of the index to the minimum value, times	6.1	5.1	4.3	3.8	4.0	2.7

Indicator	2000	2007	2013	2018	2019	2020
Number of doctors of all specialties, per 10,000 people (people)						
Average value of the index in the Russian Federation	46.5	49.6	48.9	47.9	48.7	50.4
Minimum value of the index	20.5	22.8	27.0	29.3	29.3	28.9
Maximum value of the index	74.5	79.1	81.2	81.2	84.9	89.3
Ratio of the maximum value of the index to the minimum value, times	3.6	3.5	3.0	2.8	2.9	3.1
Total area of residential premises per inhabitant on average (at the end of the year; square metres)						
Average value of the index in the Russian Federation	19.2	21.4	23.4	25.8	26.3	26.9
Minimum value of the index	6.9	5.0	12.9	14.1	14.2	14.3
Maximum value of the index	28.9	28.0	29.0	32.7	33.5	34.2
Ratio of the maximum value of the index to the minimum value, times	4.2	5.6	2.2	2.3	2.4	2.4

Source authors' calculations based on Federal State Statistics Service (Rosstat) data

Table 11.3 GRP by federal district in 2000 prices, RUB billions, 2018–2000

Federal district	2000	2018	Rate of growth 2018 to 2000, %
Russian Federation, total	5753.7	11,264.5	196
Central Federal District	1841.5	3651.4	198
North-Western Federal District	578.5	1170.2	202
Southern Federal District	329.7	703.0	213
North Caucasus Federal District	105.2	278.6	265
Volga Federal District	1036.8	1923.5	186
Ural Federal District	866.1	1666.5	192
Siberian Federal District	635.5	1210.7	191
Far Eastern Federal District	360.4	651.7	181

Source Authors' calculations based on the Federal State Statistics Service (Rosstat) data

Analysing the dynamics of GRP, we can distinguish regions with high and low growth rates. In the first group, GRP growth between 2000 and 2018 amounted to 250% or more. This group included.

- Regions that are part of the largest agglomerations, excluding the city of Moscow: St. Petersburg (255%), Leningrad Oblast (282%), and Moscow Oblast (250%). The city of Moscow ranked 40th with a growth rate of 189%, which is slightly below the national average.
- Regions with a developed manufacturing industry and a diversified economic structure: Kaluga (250%), Kaliningrad (252%), and Belgorod (287%) oblasts; in Belgorod, along with industry, mineral resources (more than 40% of the country's proven iron ore reserves) play a significant role in GRP growth.
- Selected republics in the North Caucasus and southern regions: the Republic of Dagestan (429% by 2000), the Republic of Adygea (260%), and Rostov Oblast (268%). It should be noted that the North Caucasus and Southern Federal Districts as a whole show GRP growth that exceeded the Russian average (Table 11.3)—265% and 213%, respectively. Such high growth was due to a number of factors, including the development of agriculture and the growth of domestic demand in the southern regions and, in the North Caucasus, the effects of federal fiscal support and a low initial base (i.e., Dagestan).
- Two Far Eastern regions—Sakhalin Oblast (322%) and the Chukotka AO (265%)—thanks to the development of natural resource deposits (gold and hydrocarbons) (Tables 11.4 and 11.5).

The regions lagging behind the national average belong to two categories: (i) deindustrialised peripheral regions such as the Republic of Buryatia, the Republic of Kalmykia, the Republic of Komi, and Kamchatka Krai; and (ii)

Table 11.4 Regions with the highest and lowest cumulative GRP growth rates, 2000–2018

Regions	GRP in RUB billion		Change in %
	2000	2018	2018/2000
Regions with the highest GRP growth (250% or more)			
Republic of Dagestan	20.9	89.8	429
Sakhalin Oblast	34.8	112.1	322
Belgorod Oblast	42.1	120.8	287
Leningrad Oblast	56.0	157.8	282
Rostov Oblast	89.0	238.0	268
Chukotka AO	3.9	10.4	265
Republic of Adygea	5.5	14.4	260
St. Petersburg	188.2	480.8	255
Kaliningrad Oblast	23.3	58.7	252
Kaluga Oblast	23.9	59.7	250
Moscow Oblast	176.7	441.2	250
Regions with the lowest GRP growth (less than 150%)			
Republic of Buryatia	21.6	32.2	149
Kurgan Oblast	18.7	27.9	149
Kostroma Oblast	16.7	24.1	145
Kamchatka Krai	18.1	25.9	143
Vologda Oblast	69.2	97.9	142
Pskov Oblast	16.2	22.8	141
Kemerovo Oblast	88.7	123.4	139
Magadan Oblast	13.0	17.7	136
Republic of Karelia	28.2	37.1	131
Kirov Oblast	35.8	46.7	131
Ivanovo Oblast	16.9	21.3	126
Republic of Komi	59.5	72.5	122
Murmansk Oblast	55.1	59.9	109
Republic of Kalmykia	6.2	5.6	90

Source Authors' calculations based on the Federal State Statistics Service (Rosstat) data

old industrial regions in the centre and the north of the European part of Russia: Kirov, Murmansk, Vologda, Kostroma, and Ivanovo oblasts.

Between 2000 and 2018, changes in the group of regions with the highest absolute values of GRP were insignificant. In 2000, the cities of Moscow and St. Petersburg; the Tyumen, Moscow, Sverdlovsk, and Samara oblasts; the Republics of Tatarstan and Bashkortostan; and Krasnoyarsk and Krasnodar krais were the top 10 regions by GRP value. In 2018, only one region, the Samara Oblast, dropped out of this list. At the same time, the contributions of the city of Moscow, the Tyumen Oblast, and Krasnoyarsk Krai to the national GRP slightly decreased. The remaining regions, on the contrary, strengthened their positions. The shares of St. Petersburg (+1 percentage point [pp]), the

Table 11.5 The largest regions by contribution to national GRP, %

Region	Rank		Share in GRP		Change between 2018 and 2000, in pp, %
	2000	2018	2000	2018	
Moscow	1	1	20.14	19.42	−0.72
Tyumen Oblast	2	2	9.92	9.70	−0.23
Krasnoyarsk Krai	3	5	3.73	3.63	−0.10
St. Petersburg	4	3	3.27	4.27	1.00
Republic of Tatarstan	5	6	3.24	3.61	0.37
Moscow Oblast	6	4	3.07	3.92	0.85
Sverdlovsk Oblast	7	7	2.71	3.09	0.38
Republic of Bashkortostan	8	8	2.52	2.86	0.34
Samara Oblast	9	–	2.44	–	−0.55
Krasnodar Krai	10	9	2.38	2.52	0.14
Rostov Oblast	–	10	–	2.11	0.57
Total			53.43	55.13	1.7

Note A dash denotes the absence of the region in the top 10 in a given year
Source Authors' calculations based on the Federal State Statistics Service (Rosstat) data

Moscow Oblast (+0.85% pp), and the Rostov Oblast (+0.57 pp) increased most significantly, which allowed the latter to join the group of the top 10 regions.

As of 2009, the differences in GRP between regions have been decreasing. This is largely due to smaller contributions from two federal entities (the city of Moscow and the Tyumen Oblast, including its AOs) as a result of the GFC and the decline in hydrocarbon prices during 2014–2015. Between 2008–2018, their share in the national GRP decreased by 3 pp, but still remains high at 29.1%.

If one excludes these two federal entities from the calculation, the differences in the remaining group of regions continued to increase, although at a lower rate. In the analysed period, the top 10 regions accounted for 53% to 56% of the national GRP.

11.2.2 GRP Per Capita

GRP per capita is used to compare differences between regions in the level of economic development. However, the dynamic of national GRP per capita does not differ substantially from that of GRP due to insignificant changes in the size of the population. As a result, during 2000–2018, the national GRP per capita in comparable prices also nearly doubled. Differences in GRP per capita between regions increased during 2000–2003, which was then followed by a long-term downward trend; exceptions occurred post-financial crisis in 2009 and in 2018.

We can identify a number of regions where the average level of GRP per capita exceeds 1.5 or more. In addition to the capital city (Moscow), these are the main resource-producing territories: the Tyumen Oblast, the Republic of Sakha, Krasnoyarsk Krai, the Magadan Oblast, and the Sakhalin Oblast.

These regions maintained their positions throughout the period under consideration. In 2000, the Murmansk and Vologda oblasts as well as the Republic of Komi were among the top 10 regions by this indicator; however, this later changed (Table 11.6). The Arkhangelsk and Irkutsk oblasts as well as the Republic of Tatarstan were able to increase their GRP per capita significantly.

The regions with the lowest GRP per capita are found in the deindustrialised areas of the south and east of the country as well as in the Volga region. In the Republic of Ingushetia, in 2018, the GRP per capita was only 12% of the national average, 5 pp worse than in 2000.

Only two regions were able to graduate from the list of the 10 regions with the lowest GRP per capita during the analysed period—the Republic of Mari El and the Kabardino-Balkarian Republic. In 2018, their per capita GRP increased by 231% and 224%, respectively, relative to 2000. Their places on the list were taken by the Chuvash Republic and the Republic of Kalmykia, where in 2018 their GRP per capita amounted to 174% and 102%, respectively, relative to 2000. Dagestan, despite a rapid increase of almost 3.5 times, remained on the list of the 10 regions with the lowest GRP per capita.

A comparison of GRP per capita across Russia's regions with the level of GDP of other countries in terms of purchasing power parity (PPP) can serve as an illustration of the scale of regional differences in the level of economic development. Before the devaluation of the rouble in 2014, the GRP per capita of the Tyumen and Sakhalin oblasts (in PPP terms) reached more than USD 70 thousand, which roughly corresponded to the GDP per capita of Norway, while the GRP per capita of Ingushetia was only USD 5.3 thousand, similar to India, Uzbekistan, and Vietnam. Meanwhile, Moscow's GRP per capita was USD 51 thousand per capita, on par with the United States.

11.2.3 Capital Investment Dynamics and Variation Across Regions

Between 2000 and 2018, investment in fixed assets in comparable prices increased 2.8 times. However, this growth trend was interrupted twice: in 2009 and 2015. In the first period, between 2000 and 2008, investment increased 2.7 times. In 2009, as a result of the GFC, the volume of investments fell by 13.5% from the previous year. Growth resumed in 2010 and continued until 2012, after which there was a period of stagnation. In 2015, a fall of 10% from the 2014 level was recorded, after which growth resumed again only in 2017.

The highest ratio of investment to GRP (32%) was reached in 2012 (Fig. 11.2). The ratio then decreased until 2016, after which it then began to

Table 11.6 Regions with the highest and lowest levels of GRP per capita, 2000 and 2018

Regions	Rank		GRP per capita, RUB thousands, in 2000 prices		In % to the national average, %		Growth 2000–2018, %
	2000	2018	2000	2018	2000	2018	
Regions with the highest level of GRP per capita							
Tyumen Oblast	1	1	176.9	294.5	448	384	166
Moscow	2	4	115.6	174.2	292	227	151
Republic of Sakha (Yakutia)	3	5	85.4	150.4	216	196	176
Krasnoyarsk Krai	4	6	71.3	142.3	180	185	200
Chukotka AO	5	3	66.0	210.2	167	274	319
Magadan Oblast	6	7	65.7	124.3	166	162	189
Sakhalin Oblast	7	2	61.6	228.9	156	298	372
Murmansk Oblast	8	(18)	59.2	79.7	150	104	135
Komi Republic	9	(12)	56.6	86.7	143	113	153
Vologda Oblast	10	(14)	53.4	83.5	135	109	156
Arkhangelsk Oblast	(13)	8	44.8	115.7	113	151	258
Republic of Tatarstan	(11)	9	49.1	104.4	124	136	212
Irkutsk Oblast	(18)	10	39.1	97.3	99	127	249
Regions with the lowest level of GRP per capita							
Republic of Ingushetia	1	1	6.7	9.5	17	12	143
Republic of Dagestan	2	8	8.5	29.2	21	38	344
Republic of Tyva	3	2	11.7	18.8	30	24	160
Republic of North Ossetia-Alania	4	5	12.0	21.7	30	28	181

Regions	Rank		GRP per capita, RUB thousands, in 2000 prices		In % to the national average, %		Growth 2000–2018, %
	2000	2018	2000	2018	2000	2018	
Republic of Adygea	5	10	12.3	31.7	31	41	257
Karachay-Cherkess Republic	6	6	12.4	22.9	31	30	184
Republic of Altay	7	7	13.5	24.3	34	32	180
Ivanovo Oblast	8	4	14.2	21.1	36	28	148
Republic of Mari El	9	(13)	15.1	34.8	38	45	231
Kabardino-Balkarian Republic	10	(14)	15.9	35.8	40	47	224
Chuvash Republic	(12)	9	17.3	30.1	44	39	174
Republic of Kalmykia	(21)	3	20.2	20.5	51	27	102

Note Data for regions that were not included in a given category in an analysed year are shown in parentheses
Source Authors' calculations based on the Federal State Statistics Service (Rosstat) data

grow. In 2018, it amounted to 29% of GRP—an increase of 9 pp as compared to 2000.

The list of the top 10 regions in terms of per capita investment includes those with extractive industries and major agglomerations, with the exception of the Moscow Oblast, which ranked only 32nd in terms of average per capita investment (Table 11.7).

The lowest levels of fixed capital investment per capita are recorded in the republics of the North Caucasus, the old industrialised and deindustrialised regions of Siberia, the Volga region, and in the north of the country.

During 2000–2018, the 10 regions with the largest investment stock accounted for slightly more than half of the total volume of national investment (50.6%). The leaders were the largest Russian agglomerations as well as the industrially developed and export-oriented extractive regions. Low levels of accumulated investment were recorded in the economically weak regions, particularly in the republics of the North Caucasus and the remote deindustrialised regions.

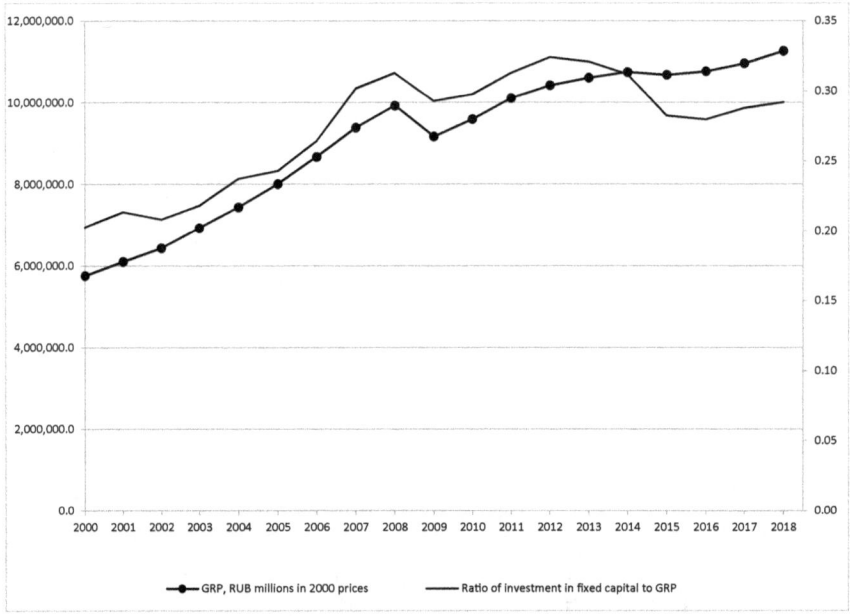

Fig. 11.2 Ratio of investment in fixed capital to GRP, in %, 2000–2018 (*Source* Authors' calculations based on the Federal State Statistics Service [Rosstat] data)

Table 11.7 Regions with the highest and lowest levels of investment per capita (average for the period 2000–2018)

Region	Investment in fixed capital, average per capita, 2000–2018		Investment in fixed capital, total for 2000–2018		
	Rank	RUB in 2000 prices	Rank	RUB millions in 2000 prices	share in national total, %
Regions with the highest level of investment per capita					
Tyumen Oblast	1	116.8	1	7157.0	14.7
Sakhalin Oblast	2	103.6	9	1111.6	2.3
Chukotka AO	3	54.2	74	61.4	0.1
Republic of Sakha (Yakutia)	4	52.5	12	956.9	2.0
Republic of Komi	5	34.7	20	692.9	1.4
Leningrad Oblast	6	32.9	10	1052.7	2.2
Magadan Oblast	7	31.1	66	117.1	0.2
Krasnoyarsk Krai	8	27.0	7	1547.5	3.2
Moscow	9	25.2	2	4799.7	9.9
St. Petersburg	10	24.1	3	2169.7	4.5
Regions with the lowest level of investment per capita					
Ivanovo Oblast	1	4.9	67	109.7	0.2
Karachay-Cherkess Republic	2	5.5	77	45.9	0.1
Republic of Ingushetia	3	5.5	79	41.0	0.1
Kabardino-Balkarian Republic	4	5.6	70	94.2	0.2
Kurgan Oblast	5	6.0	65	120.9	0.2
Altai Krai	6	6.1	42	308.2	0.6
Pskov Oblast	7	6.1	71	91.8	0.2
Kostroma Oblast	8	6.9	68	99.9	0.2
Republic of Dagestan	9	7.1	39	331.5	0.7
Bryansk Oblast	10	7.2	58	194.2	0.4

Source Authors' calculations based on the Federal State Statistics Service (Rosstat) data

11.3 Challenges of Spatial Development and Regional Policy of Russia

The centralised management of the Soviet period caused a shift of productive forces to the east and north as well as a decrease in the spatial concentration of economic activity. The market reforms of the 1990s, in the absence of a targeted spatial policy, initiated a move in the opposite direction. The major trend of Russia's modern spatial development is the steady migration of the factors and results of production from the east and north to the west,

Table 11.8 Regions with the largest and smallest stock of investments for the period 2000–2018

Region	Investment in fixed capital, total for 2000–2018			Investment in fixed capital, average per capita for 2000–2018	
	Rank	RUB millions in 2000 prices	Share in national total, %	Rank	RUB in 2000 prices
Regions with the highest values of accumulated investment					
Tyumen Oblast	1	7157.0	14.7	1	116.8
Moscow	2	4799.7	9.9	9	25.2
St. Petersburg	3	2169.7	4.5	10	24.1
Krasnodar Oblast	4	1943.0	4.0	18	19.9
Moscow Oblast	5	1776.0	3.7	32	14.1
Republic of Tatarstan	6	1683.2	3.5	12	23.4
Krasnoyarsk Krai	7	1547.5	3.2	8	27.0
Sverdlovsk Oblast	8	1294.9	2.7	29	14.9
Sakhalin Oblast	9	1111.6	2.3	2	103.6
Leningrad Oblast	10	1052.7	2.2	6	32.9
Regions with the lowest values of accumulated investment					
Republic of Altai	1	35.4	0.1	56	9.2
Republic of Ingushetia	2	41.0	0.1	78	5.5
Republic of Tyva	3	44.2	0.1	68	7.6
Karachay-Cherkess Republic	4	45.9	0.1	79	5.5
Republic of Kalmykia	5	52.8	0.1	58	9.0
Jewish Autonomous Oblast	6	59.7	0.1	23	16.2
Chukotka AO	7	61.4	0.1	3	54.2
Republic of Adygea	8	71.7	0.1	63	8.4
Republic of Khakassia	9	85.8	0.2	66	8.1
Pskov Oblast	10	91.8	0.2	74	6.1

Source Authors' calculations based on the Federal State Statistics Service (Rosstat) data

south, and centre of the country, which has led to the spatial concentration of economic development in a small number of federal entities and consequently to a high level of interregional socio-economic inequality (Kryukov & Kolomak, 2021).

Government policy in the sphere of spatial and regional development is defined by a diverse set of legal acts, the most important of which is the Strategy of spatial development of the Russian Federation for the period up to 2025.[4] According to this document, spatial development is understood as improving the settlement system and territorial organisation of the economy, including through an effective government policy of regional development. The goal is to ensure the sustainable and balanced spatial development of the country, aimed at reducing interregional differences in the level and quality of life of the population, and accelerating the pace of economic growth and technological development. Another document guiding regional policy in Russia is the Main provisions of the state policy of regional development of the Russian Federation for the period up to 2025.[5]

Federal support for Russia's regions is regulated by a number of normative legal acts, which outline the three main forms of federal support: intergovernmental transfers, federal budget expenditures earmarked for regional development, and federal tax benefits for select territories (Klimanov et al., 2017).

11.3.1 Intergovernmental Transfers

The purpose of intergovernmental transfers is to either ensure the fiscal equalisation of territories or stimulate their economic development. This type of transfer is used in a country with a federal form of government. However, federal states differ significantly based on the degree of centralisation of their budget revenues and expenditures and by the principles and mechanisms of the distribution of transfers (Hueglin & Fenna, 2006; Wallack & Spinivasan, 2006). The need to reduce interregional differences is the primary justification for the high centralisation of public finances and large-scale intergovernmental redistributions.

One of the foremost reasons for vertical transfers is the budget inequality of the federal entities and the need to finance the public goods and services guaranteed by the state, the provision of which should not differ greatly among territorial units. Regions have comparable expenditure commitments; however, as a rule, they have different economic opportunities to finance these expenditures from their own revenues. Such gaps in available revenues and necessary expenditures are partially compensated by transfers from the central government.

The main revenue items of regional budgets are tax revenues, non-tax revenues, and transfers, largely from the federal budget. The level of independence of regional budgets can be characterised by the share of tax and non-tax revenue in their total revenue.

---

[4] Strategy for the Spatial Development of the Russian Federation for the period up to 2025. Approved by the Decree of the Government of the Russian Federation of February 13, 2019. N 207-r.

[5] Main provisions of the state policy of regional development of the Russian Federation for the period up to 2025. Approved by the Decree of the President of the Russian Federation of January 16, 2017. N 13.

The dependence of Russian regions on non-repayable transfers from the federal government varies greatly. In 2018, the share of federal transfers ranged from 10 to 40% for most regions (56 out of 85) (Kolomak & Sumskaya, 2020). Between 2012 and 2018, the number of regions whose budgets saw a reduction in the share of transfers increased. However, in 2018, the share of federal transfers in the budget revenues of 12 regions was over 50%. The concentration of financial resources at the federal level and active transfer activity indicates the excessive centralisation of budget resources in Russia, which does not correspond to the principle of fiscal federalism. The revenues of a large number of regions are unstable and dependent on federal transfers. This makes it difficult for regional authorities to work out long-term development programmes, since the budgetary resources available for their implementation are uncertain. The budgetary policy pursued in the pre-pandemic period did not solve the problem of Russia's significant interregional inequality.

During the 2020 crisis caused by the coronavirus pandemic, a number of researchers (Klimanov et al., 2020; Zubarevich, 2021) pointed out that federal transfers became the leading factor of regional budget stability. At the same time, the share of own tax and non-tax revenues decreased, which indicates an increasing level of fiscal centralisation in Russia. Thus, fiscal decentralisation faces significant limitations in Russia. In the future, fiscal decentralisation will be determined by how long crisis phenomena last and the course of economic and political transformations (Klimanov & Mikhailova, 2021).

11.3.2 Federal Budget Expenditures in the Regions

Direct federal budget expenditures in the regions are implemented in accordance with the programme-targeted method of management via the development and implementation of government programmes, including those focused on the socio-economic development of individual macro-regions and federal entities, for example in the Far East and Baikal region, the North Caucasian Federal District, the Kaliningrad Oblast, and the Arctic zone. The main activities under these programmes are the construction of engineering, transport, and social infrastructure. Most programmes are sectoral, but they also include measures aimed at regional development. For example, as part of the government's 'Economic development and innovation economy' programme, 26 clusters in 21 regions were approved to be subsidised. Additionally, the 'Development of industry and increasing its competitiveness' programme included support for individual industrial parks (Klimanov et al., 2017).

11.3.3 Federal Tax Incentives in Selected Territories

Federal transfers to less developed regions, while ensuring high growth rates, were insufficient to overcome the development gap. Meanwhile, the growth of the Russian economy as a whole slowed down considerably in the second half of the 2010s (see Chapter 15). The period of high prices for hydrocarbons, which was one of the main drivers of growth, ended and the emerging restrictions in international relations became a significant obstacle to the inflow of investment and technological innovation. Under these conditions, improving regional policy with an emphasis on the use of stimulating instruments has become particularly urgent.

Stimulating instruments include, among others, special economic zones (SEZs), special administrative regions (SARs), and priority social and economic development areas (PSEDAs). These territories enjoy special economic regimes which are intended to support the development of the individual territories. In particular, they aim to stimulate investment inflow, industry creation, infrastructure development (transport, energy, and social), job creation, and structural diversification as well as solve the further socio-economic problems of a given territory.

Special economic zones (SEZs) began operating in 2005. SEZs aim to attract direct investment in priority economic activities. As of October 2021, a total of 39 SEZs were operating in Russia in four areas: industrial production (20 SEZs), technology and innovation (7), tourism and recreational (10), and port-area (2).

Investors in SEZs receive infrastructure support at the expense of budgetary funds as well as special tax and customs treatment. There are also a number of benefits for SEZ residents related to social insurance contributions, personal income tax, and exemption from property and land tax for five years or more. The size of benefits may vary depending on the type of zone. Additional preferences may be associated with the special customs regime, for example: (i) exemption from customs duties and VAT for the placement and use of imported goods and (ii) exemption from adhering to selected prohibitions and restrictions in force in Russia.

Between 2005 and 2020, more than 778 resident companies registered in SEZs—this includes more than 144 companies with foreign capital from 41 different countries. The total volume of investments in SEZs amounted to more than RUB 440 billion. Furthermore, over 38 thousand jobs were created and approximately RUB 100 billion were paid in taxes, customs payments, and deductions to non-budgetary funds.

Special administrative regions (SARs) are areas which offer flexible tax and foreign exchange regulations for companies which have decided to relocate to Russia from a foreign jurisdiction.

Priority social and economic development areas (PSEDAs) are another federally initiated mechanism for regional development. The first PSEDAs were created in 2015 in the Far Eastern regions. Subsequently, these areas spread to single-industry towns with complex social and economic conditions. As a result, by 2020, two-thirds of the federal entities took advantage of the opportunity to create PSEDAs; the total number of such areas exceeded 110.

About one-half of all existing PSEDAs are concentrated in 15 regions. The Republic of Tatarstan, Bashkortostan, and the Chelyabinsk Oblast have the most PSEDAs—five each. In the beginning of 2020, there were 639 registered companies in PSEDAs, which created more than 27 thousand jobs and attracted more than RUB 69 billion in investment; the revenue of their residents amounted to more than RUB 149 billion.[6]

However, many of these PSEDAs are not yet able to assume the role of the driver of economic growth and attract sustainable investment. Furthermore, in a number of regions where PSEDAs have been established, there has been a decline in investment for several years in a row. Investment activity in existing PSEDAs is heterogeneous, with investors primarily looking towards large industrial cities. As a result, the top 10 largest PSEDAs (excluding the Far East) are home to more than half of the registered companies, with the leading PSEDAs operating in Togliatti, Naberezhnye Chelny, and Novokuznetsk (Zubova, 2019).

If we consider the experience of the creation and functioning of territories with special status, their main shortcomings are the following:

- Operational management is excessively centralised and conducted by government bodies against the foreign practice of involving commercial management companies;
- A high degree of centralisation constrains local initiatives and limits opportunities for representatives of the business community to participate;
- Territories with special status are often located in relatively prosperous and investment-attractive regions, which leads to the increased concentration of economic activity;
- Privileges enjoyed by territories with special status boost intraregional competition, but do not always have a positive influence on economic development;
- Diversity among the types of territories with special status and the lack of a unified system of evaluation criteria make it difficult to fully assess them.

At the same time, examples of successful sites testify to the sustainability of such tools of territorial development.

11.4 Summary

To summarise, several conclusions arise. The level of economic inequality among regions is largely predetermined by the heterogeneity of space. The rate of economic growth is largely influenced by the capacity of the consumer

---

[6] Ministry of Economic Development. https://www.economy.gov.ru/material/directions/regionalnoe_razvitie/instrumenty_razvitiya_territoriy/tor/.

market, the diversification and development of the production base, the degree of its export orientation, and, of course, the presence of natural resources that are in demand on international commodity markets.

In the first two decades of the twenty-first century, one saw the formation of fairly stable groups of both highly developed regions, with above-average national growth rates of GRP per capita and investment, and lagging regions. At the same time, the gap between the most economically developed and the lagging regions remains substantial. Export-oriented resource-producing regions, major agglomerations, and regions with a developed manufacturing industry and diversified economic structure can be counted as the most economically successful. The lagging regions are the deindustrialised and old industrial regions and cities located in the north and east of the country as well as in the North Caucasus region. At the same time, many lagging regions have strategic importance. These are primarily the regions located on the periphery of the country and, in particular, in the Far East.

Questions for Students

1. What are the differences between Russian regions in terms of population density?
2. What was the situation in Russian regions during the first 20 years of the twenty-first century in terms of population dynamics?
3. How do Russian regions differ in terms of income level and basic socio-demographic indicators?
4. What are the main forms of federal support for Russian regions?

References

Hueglin, T., & Fenna, A. (2006). *Comparative federalism: A systematic inquiry.* Broadview Press.

Karachurina, L. (2007). Regional'nye osobennosti rossijskoj demograficheskoj situacii [Regional peculiarities of the Russian demographic situation]. *Demoscope Weekly*, pp. 273–274. http://www.demoscope.ru/weekly/2007/0273/analit05.php

Klimanov, V. V., Ivas'ko, E. V., & Nedopivtseva, D. A. (2017). Inventarizaciya aktual'nyh form federal'noj podderzhki regionov [Inventory of current forms of federal support for regions]. *Gosudarstvennyi autit. Pravo. Ekonomika (State Audit. Law. Economy)*, 2, 47–51.

Klimanov, V., Kazakova, S., Mikhaylova, A., & Safina, A. (2020). Fiscal resilience of Russia's regions in the face of COVID-19. *Journal of Public Budgeting, Accounting & Financial Management*, 33(1), 87–94. https://doi.org/10.1108/JPBAFM-07-2020-0123

Klimanov, V. V., & Mikhailova, A. A. (2021). Budgetary decentralization in pandemic and post-pandemic conditions. *Journal of the New Economic Association*, 3(51), 218–226.

Kolomak, E. A., & Sumskaya, T. V. (2020). Assessing federal transfers' role in the subnational budget system of the Russian Federation. *Economic and Social Changes: Facts, Trends, Forecast, 13*(2), 89–105. https://doi.org/10.15838/esc.2020.2.68.6

Kolomak, E. (2021). The urban system of Russia from 1991–2020: Gradual development instead of radical transformation. *Area Development and Policy*. https://doi.org/10.1080/23792949.2021.2002168

Kryukov, V. A., & Kolomak, E. A. (2021). Prostranstvennoe razvitie Rossii: Osnovnye problemy i podkhody k ikh preodoleniyu [Spatial development of Russia: Main problems and approaches to overcoming them]. *Nauchnye Trudy Vol'nogo Ekonomicheskogo Obshchestva Rossii [scientific Proceedings of the Free Economic Society of Russia], 227*(1), 92–114.

Leontief Centre. (2020). *Report on the research work "Features of Spatial Development of Russia in the XXI Century: Growth Drivers, Challenges for Territories and State Regional Policy"*. International Centre for Social and Economic Research.

Limonov, L., & Nesena, M. (2016). Regional cultural diversity in Russia: Does it matter for regional economic performance? *Area Development and Policy, 1*(1), 63–93. https://doi.org/10.1080/23792949.2016.1164016

Vishnevskiy, A. (Ed.). (2000) *Naselenie Rossii 1999. Sed'moj ezhegodnyj demograficheskij doklad* [Population of Russia 1999: Seventh annual demographic report]. http://www.demoscope.ru/weekly/knigi/ns_r99/sod_r.html Accessed 15 March 2022

Wallack, J., & Spinivasan, T. N. (2006). *Federalism and economic reform: International perspectives*. Cambridge University Press.

Zubarevich, N. V. (2021) Vozmozhnosti decentralizacii v god pandemii: chto pokazyvaet byudzhetnyj analiz? [Possibility of decentralization during the year of pandemic: What does the analysis of public budgets reveal?] *Regional Studies, 1*, 46–57. DOI: https://doi.org/10.5922/1994-5280-2021-1-4

Zubova, Y. (2019). *Territorii operezhayushchego razvitiya buksuyut* [Territories of advanced development are stalled]. Akademiya gorodskikh tekhnologiii SREDA [Academy of urban technologies SREDA]. https://sreda-academy.ru/showcase/territorii-operezhayushchego-razvitiya-buksuyut/

PART V

Russia in the Global Economy

CHAPTER 12

Russia in World Trade

Arne Melchior

Highlights

- Transition has increased Russia's openness and trade, but Russia is still a medium-sized trader and not a giant in the field. However, Russia is a very large commodity exporter.
- Russia's foreign trade grew exponentially from 1991 to 2012, and then slowed down. Fuel exports with rising commodity prices were a strong driver and led to fluctuations over time.
- During the first stage of transition, Russia turned to Western Europe, and later China entered the field, both at the expense of trade with the former Soviet Union (FSU). Russia has benefited from China's growth and could likely benefit from further trade integration with Western Europe as well as China.
- Russia's WTO accession took 19 years and led to liberalisation for trade in goods and important institutional reforms. But Russia's regime for services trade and foreign direct investment (FDI) is more restrictive.

A. Melchior (✉)
Norwegian Institute of International Affairs (NUPI), Oslo, Norway
e-mail: AM@nupi.no

Arctic University of Norway, Tromsø, Norway

- The Eurasian Economic Union (EAEU) is an important achievement, but trade with the FSU area had slow growth, and Western Europe and China are Russia's most important trade partners.
- In the early 2020s, geopolitical tensions and security issues, including the Russia-Ukraine conflict, are limiting Russia's trade policy development. The green transition may also be a future key issue for Russian trade, with carbon border taxes and the phasing out of fossil fuels on the global agenda.

12.1 Introduction

During the Soviet period, foreign trade was heavily regulated and limited. The rouble was not convertible, so trade was not possible without special permission to use foreign currency. In 1989, the foreign trade of the Soviet Union amounted to 15% of the gross national product (GNP), and more than half of its foreign trade in goods was with members of COMECON or Council for Mutual Economic Assistance (CMEA).[1,2] At this time, trade within the FSU area was domestic and not counted as international trade.

After the fall of the Iron Curtain in 1989, COMECON and the Soviet Union were dissolved in 1991. The collapse of the central planning system led to the external opening and increased trade with the whole world, and particularly Western Europe. A major event was Russia's membership in the World Trade Organization (WTO) from 2012, following a 19-year period of preparation and arduous negotiations starting from 1993.

At the same time, Russia pursued the aim of continued economic integration in the FSU area, with several steps from the Commonwealth of Independent States (CIS) in 1991, various free trade agreements (FTAs), and eventually the Eurasian Economic Union (EAEU) from 2015.

Third, the growth of China and Asia changed the world including Russia's trade, again with growing trade and another geographical turn of trade flows, this time towards China. From the turn of the century, the share of China in Russian imports increased dramatically, mainly at the expense of the CIS.

Fourth, Asia's growth contributed to commodity price hikes: from the turn of the century, commodity prices rose sharply for a whole decade, followed by a decade of strong fluctuations.[3] For Russia, being one of the world's largest

---

[1] The figure is for trade in goods (export plus imports), based on data from the Slavic-Eurasian Research Center, Hokkaido University, Japan; see https://src-h.slav.hokudai.ac.jp/database/SESS.html#USSR-S1.

[2] COMECON was formed in 1949 as a response to the Marshall plan and the emerging Western European Integration. COMECON included the USSR, six European countries that are now part of the European Union (Poland, Czechoslovakia, East Germany, Hungary, Bulgaria, and Romania), and four other countries (Albania, Cuba, Mongolia, and Vietnam).

[3] See https://www.imf.org/en/Research/commodity-prices.

commodity exporters, the changing terms of trade had a strong influence on the volume and patterns of trade.

In this chapter, we examine Russia's trade and trade policy in the light of these changing tides, leading up to the pre-war situation of early 2022, where increased geopolitical tensions, including the Russia-Ukraine conflict, and the green transition have been added to the trade agenda.

12.2 Russia's Trade Growth During Transition

After the collapse of the Soviet Union and the COMECON in 1991, the foreign trade of Russia exploded. Figure 12.1 shows the trade openness of Russia (exports plus imports as a share of GDP) during 1996–2020.

In 2021, Russia was a much more open economy than it was in 1989. After the initial rapid transition in the 1990s, the trade/GDP share has stabilised just below 50%. Hence, Russia is more open than large nations such as the United States (26% in 2019) or China (36%), but more closed than the majority of Western European countries (for example, Germany 88%, and France, Italy, and the United Kingdom in the 60–64% range).

While transition created a more open Russia, the country is still a relatively small trader in global comparison. The trade of Russia is much smaller than that of the United States and China, and smaller than the trade of medium-sized European nations such as Germany, France, the United Kingdom, and Italy. For example, the trade of Germany in 2018 was more than four times

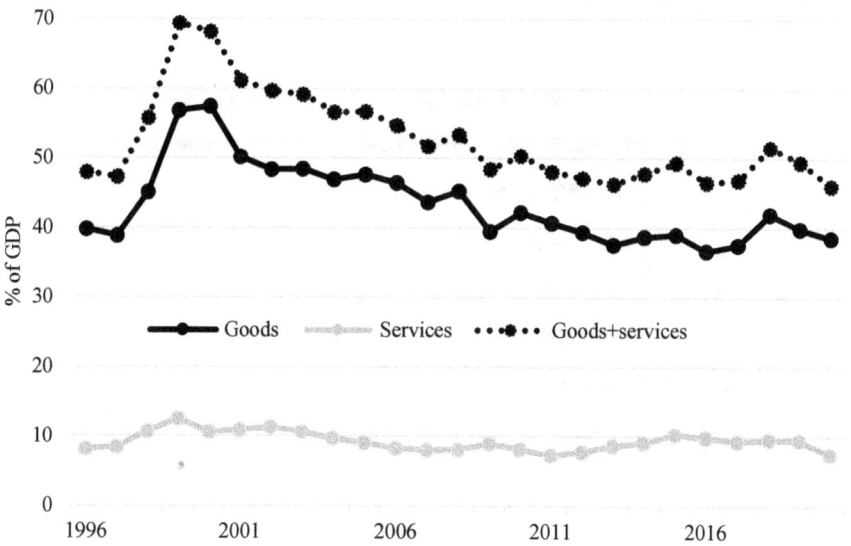

Fig. 12.1 Russia's foreign trade in % of GDP, 1996–2020 (*Source* World Bank's World Development Indicators)

that of Russia. For trade, therefore, Russia is not a superpower, but a medium-sized nation at par with Western European countries. This is revealed in Fig. 12.2, showing Russia's share of the world total for selected variables.

For trade in goods, Russia's trade is at par with its share in world nominal GDP, however with exports larger than imports, rendering a significant trade surplus. For trade in services, Russia is relatively larger, but this time with more imports than exports and a corresponding trade deficit.

Corresponding to Russia's massive land area, Russia has a very large share of total natural resource rents in the world economy (Fig. 12.2). This share has grown in the 2000s, illustrating Russia's role as a major commodity exporter in the world economy. This is a key feature of Russia's foreign trade and the reason for the sizeable trade surplus for goods in recent years.

Price fluctuations are generally stronger for commodity trade than for manufacturing, so we expect that Russia's fuel exports vary over time. But changing oil and gas prices do not only affect fuel trade, they also affect Russia's imports and non-fuel exports. This correlation between commodity trade fluctuations and other trade flows is quite strong for Russia. As an illustration, Fig. 12.3 shows nominal Russian exports and imports, with exports split into fuel and non-fuel, together with the commodity price index of the International Monetary Fund (IMF) during 1996–2020.

The influence of commodity price fluctuations is remarkable, with two of the trade curves following commodity prices like shadows. The correlation between fuel exports and the commodity price index is 0.99, so most of the variation in fuel exports is due to price changes. But Russia's imports were also strongly correlated with commodity prices, with a correlation of 0.94. For

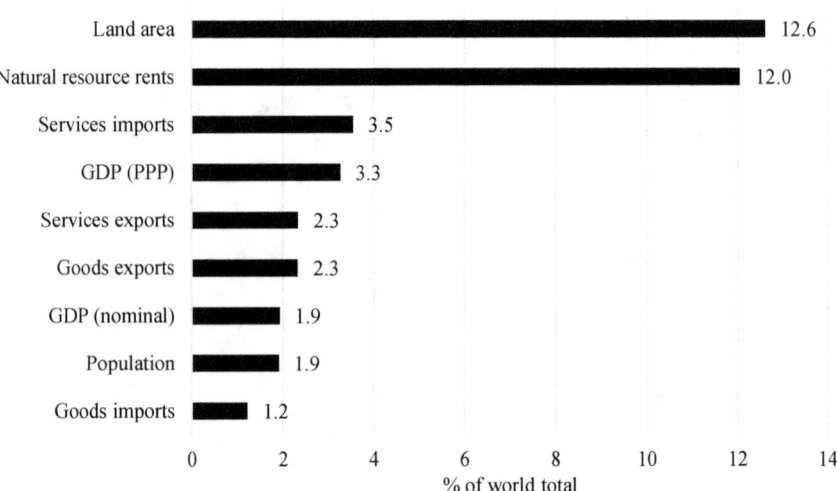

Fig. 12.2 Russia's share of the world total, 2018 (*Source* ITC trade map, World Bank's World Development Indicators)

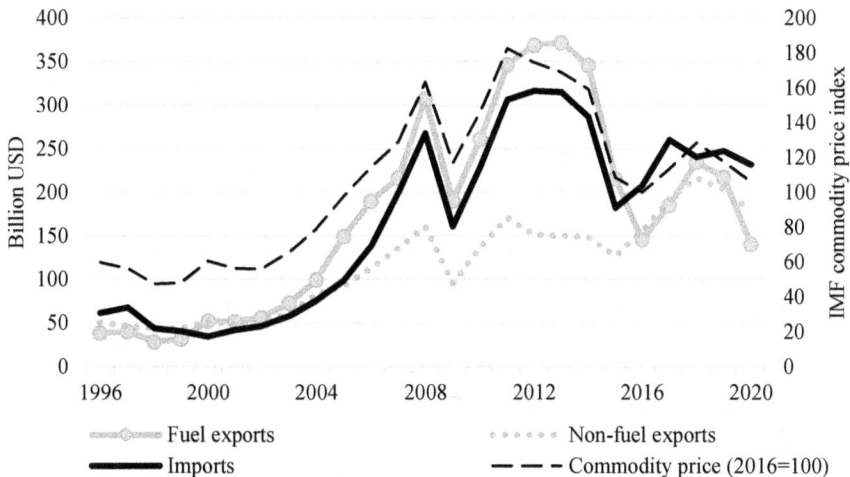

Fig. 12.3 Russia's trade versus commodity prices, 1996–2020 (*Sources* COMTRADE and IMF Commodity Price Index)

non-fuel exports, the development was less volatile, but still with a correlation of 0.76.

This co-variation may occur for different reasons: it may be due to a macroeconomic effect (commodity revenues allow more imports); value chain effects (upstream impact of changed commodity prices); or a 'spurious' correlation whereby commodity trade and other trade are affected by the same underlying shock. While an in-depth causal analysis is beyond the scope of this chapter, the persistence of the co-variation over time suggests that the macroeconomic mechanism may have been at work: commodity trade revenues were largely spent on importing. But the other causal mechanisms were of importance as well, for example, the global financial crisis (GFC) in 2007–2009 affected all trade flows. The exchange rate also played a role; the rouble rate dropped considerably from 2014, making imports more expensive and declining in dollar terms.

Figure 12.3 also reveals that during the 25-year period, Russia's trade experienced strong growth. This was partly driven by commodity prices and peaked around 2012. During the 2000s, Russian trade grew exponentially, with five-year moving growth annual averages of about 30% over several years. During this period, Russia's share of world trade increased (Melchior, 2018, 2019). This was followed by shrinking trade in the five-year periods ending from 2015 to 2018.

With rising oil prices, the share of fuels in Russia's exports of goods soared from 43% in 1996 to a peak level of 71% in 2012–2013. Even if this share dropped again to 44% in 2020, a continuous post-Soviet worry in Russia has been about diversification: Has Russia become over-reliant on fuels and commodity exports, and how is this affected by trade policy? Will liberalisation lead to further deindustrialisation? These questions (see, e.g., EBRD, 2012 for a broad discussion) are important in Russia's trade policy debates.

12.3 Russia's WTO Membership

With memories of the centrally planned economy of the Soviet Union, the pro-communist opposition to President Yeltsin resisted liberalisation after 1991. The agricultural lobby and some oligarchs also supported the idea of building new industries sheltered from import competition (Aslund, 2010). Proponents of liberalisation and Russia's WTO membership, on the other hand, maintained that the WTO would guarantee market access abroad for non-oil exports, and thereby contribute to industrial diversification. According to this view, Russian exports of metals and other industrial goods might be subject to protectionist measures from other countries, unless protected by WTO rules. A study for the World Bank, however, suggested that less than one-tenth of Russia's gains from WTO membership would be due to better market access abroad: the largest gains would be due to domestic reforms, replacing former bureaucracies by new and modern institutions and regulations (Tarr, 2007). According to this analysis, such reforms would be particularly important for the services sectors.

Russian trade reform started in the 1980s in the perestroika period: some foreign trade operations were decentralised from 1988, and the Soviet Union applied for observer status in the General Agreement on Tariffs and Trade (GATT), normally a step towards membership. Observer status was approved by the GATT in 1990 (GATT, 1990). Russia became a member of the IMF (and the World Bank) in 1992, establishing a trade-friendly currency regime (current account convertibility). In 1993, Russia also applied for GATT membership, which widened to the WTO when it was established in 1995.[4] While GATT accession procedures had been relatively easy in the past, the WTO established a more demanding process, where incumbent members made more stringent demands and negotiations were difficult. The process was especially demanding for Russia and China, due to their importance and non-market legacy. During this process, Russia had to negotiate bilaterally with about 60 of the WTO's members until membership was finally approved in 2012. This was a frustrating process for Russia, also re-fuelling domestic debates about the virtues of membership. But President Putin made WTO membership a top priority in 2000 (Aslund, 2010), and President Medvedev supported the final steps in 2012. Russia's WTO accession thereby took 19 years. In the WTO Trade Policy review of Russia (WTO, 2021, p. 32),

---

[4] WTO included not only GATT but also General Agreement on Trade in Services (GATS), Trade-Related Intellectual Property Rights (TRIPS), and common institutional arrangements (on dispute settlement and notification requirements, among others).

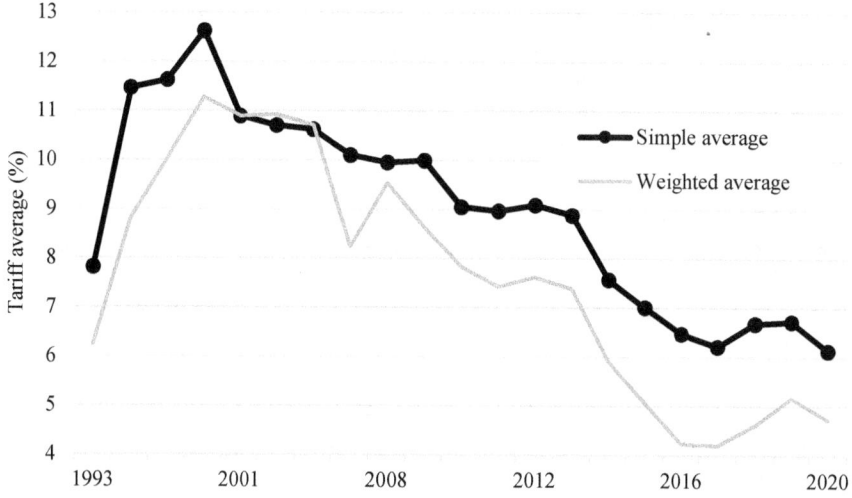

Fig. 12.4 Russia's applied tariffs, 1993–2020 (*Source* WITS/COMTRADE)

Russia's continuous unambiguous support for the global trading system is emphasised, in spite of some domestic reservations.

Figure 12.3 suggests that Russia's trade stagnated just after its WTO entry in 2012. But we have seen that commodity price fluctuations played a key role in this development. Disentangling the impact of WTO membership from other determinants of trade is not an easy task, in the presence of transition, Chinese growth, and more on top of commodity prices. Transition implied that liberalisation also took place independently from the WTO. Figure 12.4 shows that Russia's average tariffs[5] also declined before Russia joined the WTO.

For WTO accession, Russia agreed to reduce average tariffs from 10 to 7.8%, immediately for some goods and with transition periods up to seven years for sensitive sectors (agriculture, automotive, and civil aircraft) (Tochit-skaya, 2012). These tariff cuts were completed in 2020 and are reflected in Fig. 12.4.

Beyond tariffs, Russia committed to several reforms as part of the WTO package. In many institutional areas, Russian reforms took place during the 19-year WTO accession process, and it is not always easy to say what was due to WTO negotiations and what would have happened anyway. Some reforms also took a very long time—for example, the transition of Russia's veterinary control from the former 'prescriptive' regulations to a more modern

---

[5] The figure shows the 'MFN', i.e., Most Favoured Nation, tariffs that apply to countries without any trade preferences. A technical issue is how to include so-called specific tariffs, i.e., tariffs of the form 'x roubles per kilogram' and the like; see Tarr (2007) for a discussion. In Fig. 12.4, we have used the 'UNCTAD method' available in the World Integrated Trade Solution (WITS) software.

risk-based approach as advocated by the Food and Agriculture Organization (FAO) (Black & Kireeva, 2015). This process started with WTO membership but continues 10 years after accession.

For trade in goods, the WTO agreement had several implications beyond tariffs. This e.g. included the following:

- Administration of tariffs was simplified;
- Product regulations such as veterinary standards would be subject to WTO rules;
- Russia was subjected to WTO rules for safeguard measures and duties against dumping or illegal subsidies.

Has Russia implemented these reforms as appropriate? A useful source in this respect is the trade policy reviews of the WTO, with the latest edition in 2021 (WTO, 2021).[6]

On tariff administration, Russia has improved its regime, now jointly with partners in the EAEU—see Sect. 12.5. Over time, there have been some WTO disputes on customs valuation. Recently, some concerns have been raised about digital product tracing systems established in 2019, potentially raising costs for traders (USTR, 2021).

Anti-dumping duties against imports at too low prices are frequently used by WTO members, particularly for 'homogeneous' goods where prices may easily be compared. Russia is a major exporter of such goods, for example, metals or fertilisers, and therefore subject to anti-dumping duties. Being subject to WTO rules was an advantage for Russia, not being treated as a 'non-market' economy any longer. Since 1995, Russia has been subject to anti-dumping measures by other countries 126 times, 37 of these in 2012 or later. At the same time, Russia imposed anti-dumping measures on other exporters 48 times, of which 30 were imposed in 2012 or later. For Russia, WTO membership improved the legal regime on anti-dumping and increased its own use of this trade remedy tool.

For veterinary standards and other product regulations, Russia has introduced important reforms, but there are still concerns among other WTO members. However, if one counts the number of complaints, Russia does not stand out as exceptional. If one counts the number of 'specific trade concerns' in the WTO Technical Barriers to Trade Information Management System, Russia received 24 complaints during 2012–2021, at the same level as the United States but much lower than China, India, and the EU.[7] These complaints are often about domestic product regulations with an impact on

---

[6] Other sources are the bi-annual reports on Russia by the US Trade Representative (the latest is USTR 2021) and the WTO trade monitoring reports on the G20 (see www.wto.org). Furthermore, the European Commission (2020) presents a comprehensive analysis of potentially trade-distorting practices in Russia.

[7] See http://tbtims.wto.org/en/SpecificTradeConcerns/Search.

trade. In general, the impression is that for trade in goods, there are things to complain about in Russia, but Russia does not stand out as a particularly 'bad' case.

There are other areas, however, where the reach of Russia's WTO membership is limited.

- Russia is not yet a member of the WTO's agreement on public procurement, and recent reports indicate increased 'buy Russian' policies using national preferences in various forms. This applies to trade in goods as well as services.
- Based on measures of the Organisation for Economic Co-operation and Development (OECD) for trade in services, Russia has a relatively restrictive trade policy in this field. The OECD's Services Trade Restrictiveness Index (STRI) estimates by sector indicate that Russia's trade restrictiveness is above the average for most services sectors, compared to the 35 countries for which the STRI is calculated. The Russian regime has also become somewhat more restrictive in the second half of the 2010s.[8] Three sectors stand out as particularly restrictive: rail freight transport, cargo-handling and storage, and storage/warehouse. Restrictions on foreign entry, barriers to competition, and the lack of regulatory transparency are key drivers behind the high STRI scores for these sectors. Services are often delivered through foreign affiliates, and restrictions on FDI therefore limit services trade. In recent years, Russia has generally tightened its FDI regime, limiting foreign access, including new 'investment screening' from 2017 (USTR, 2021; WTO, 2021).

On this basis, one may conclude that WTO membership led to important Russian reforms and liberalisation in some areas. But some trade barriers remain for goods, and the regime for FDI and services is more restrictive.

As noted earlier, the analysis of Tarr (2007) suggested that institutional changes in Russia would provide the most important benefits for Russia. The model-based analysis of Melchior (2018, 2019) suggests that multilateral trade integration of the WTO type leads to a welfare gain for Russia, mainly due to lower import prices. Interestingly, there is no deindustrialisation effect, and the benefits are rather evenly shared across Russian regions. Here, Rutherford and Tarr (2006) obtain different results, with the highest benefits in northwest Russia, St. Petersburg, and the Russian Far East. This is perhaps because they use a different type of model and account for the WTO impact on FDI in services. Hence, it is important to take into account FDI and domestic reforms, in addition to cross-border trade barriers.

---

[8] See https://www.oecd.org/trade/topics/services-trade/documents/oecd-stri-country-note-rus.pdf. These STRI country notes are renewed every year and we refer to the version of January 2021.

12.4 Russia's Bilateral and Regional Trade Agreements

At the same time as Russia embraced globalisation and the WTO, it aimed to maintain strong ties with the FSU countries. The formation of the CIS in 1991 was the new platform, followed by a later 'spaghetti bowl' of various agreements with varying trade ambitions and mixed successes with respect to implementation. While the three Baltic states dropped off this wagon from the start, the other FSU countries joined, at least during the early stages.

The most successful track of integration in the FSU area has been the various steps leading to the formation of the EAEU in 2015; with no less than seven preceding agreements—the first dating from 1995 and the customs union implemented in 2010.[9] The EAEU is a deep trade agreement, starting with Russia, Belarus, and Kazakhstan, and later joined by Armenia and Kyrgyzstan. The EAEU has a common external trade policy; it is currently the EAEU and not Russia alone that initiates new FTAs with third countries. The EAEU also has common trade legislation in an increasing number of fields, however with a tentative flavour in the sense that exceptions are allowed. For example, Kazakhstan had lower external tariffs than the common external tariff of the EAEU, and this is accepted, although temporarily, for more than one thousand tariff lines (WTO, 2018). The EAEU also develops common product regulations, for example, in the veterinary field, but many regulations are still national, and partners are allowed to introduce temporary national measures in some circumstances. Hence, the EAEU has not yet developed a binding common trade machinery like the EU, but it is on its way as the most successful trade agreement in the FSU and is an advanced trade agreement by global standards. While the ambition is broad, the focus so far is mainly on trade in goods, but the migration regime is also advanced by global standards (Vinokurov, 2017). The EAEU aims for a comprehensive internal market for goods, services, and investment, and allows labour migration between members. In terms of power relationships, the EAEU is probably more inequitable than the EU, where smaller countries have more influence, and no single nation can dominate. Armenia, Kazakhstan, and Kyrgyzstan had to accept almost doubling their external tariffs, since the common external tariff was set close to Russia's tariffs.[10] Another exception to the united external policy is that the EAEU states have not agreed about Ukraine sanctions.

Russia hopes that more CIS countries and perhaps others may join the EAEU. Recently, observer status has been offered as an intermediate step, granted to Moldova (2018), Cuba, and Uzbekistan (2020).

Beyond the EAEU, in 2021 Russia had other FTAs in the FSU:

---

[9] For a detailed overview, see WTO (2018).

[10] According to Tarr (2016), the countries lose from this but could potentially gain from migration and the reduction of non-tariff barriers in the EAEU.

- An FTA with Georgia from 2001;
- The CIS FTA from 2013, including the EAEU countries plus Moldova, Tajikistan, and Ukraine[11];
- FTAs with Azerbaijan, Turkmenistan, and Uzbekistan from 2012–2013;
- Bilateral agreements with Belarus and Kazakhstan also remain in force.

Beyond the CIS, Russia concluded an FTA with Serbia in 2012. More recently, the EAEU has initiated joint FTAs with third countries, starting with Vietnam (2016) and followed by Iran (2019), Singapore, and Serbia (concluded in 2019, but not yet in force by late 2021). At the end of 2021, negotiations were ongoing with Egypt, India, and Israel.

On the whole, Russia's bilateral trade policies have had some achievements, but mainly in the FSU, with only a few FTAs beyond, and few major markets involved so far. Melchior (2018, Chapter 3) compares the coverage of FTAs between the 41 largest trading countries in the world (with the EU as one), and Russia comes out close to the bottom of this list.

12.5 The Geography of Russia's Foreign Trade

Regarding the geographical composition of trade, Russia's point of departure in 1989 was that 61% of trade beyond the Soviet Union was with 'socialist countries', mainly COMECON, and about one-fourth with 'developed capitalist countries'. This changed rapidly with transition. We can distinguish two phases:

- Early transition, 1990s: Strong reallocation of trade from COMECON towards Western Europe and the rest of the world (ROW);
- From 2000: Strong reallocation towards China, particularly for imports and mainly at the expense of the FSU area.

Figure 12.5 shows the change during 1996–2020 (data for the early 1990s are not included in the COMTRADE database, perhaps because they are less reliable). Exports are split into fuel and non-fuel.

The main patterns are

- The FSU remains an important market for Russian non-fuel exports, but the FSU share of fuel exports declined in the 1990s and the share of the CIS in Russia's imports declined dramatically, especially during the 2000s and 2010s;
- After a decrease in the 1990s, the EU-28 has a continuously high share of Russia's foreign trade, especially fuel exports. A closer look reveals

---

[11] Russia revoked the FTA with Ukraine from 1 January 2016.

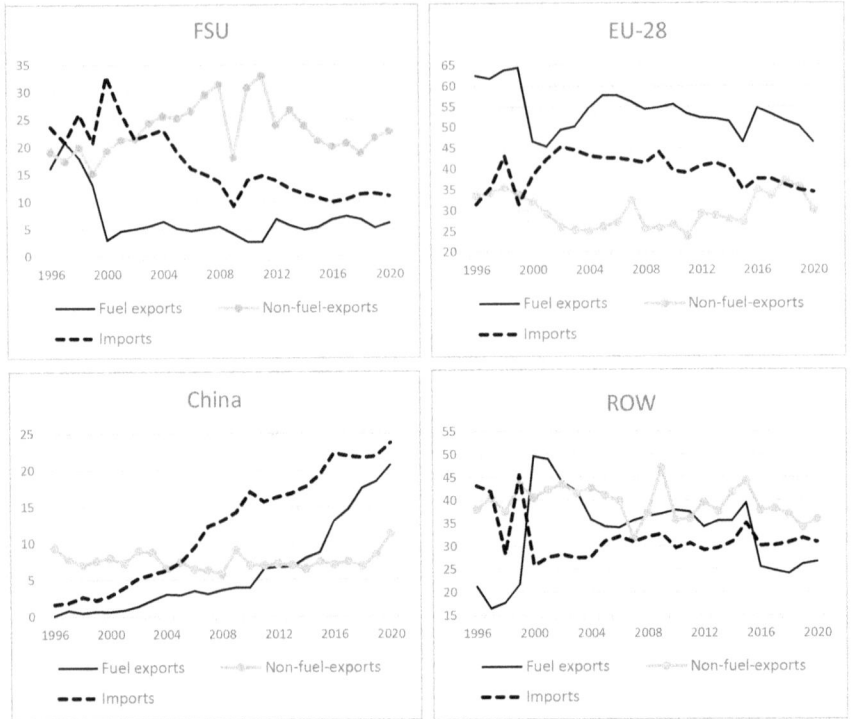

Fig. 12.5 The changing geography of Russia's foreign trade, 1996–2020, % of Russia's trade with all countries for each trade flow (*Source* WITS/COMTRADE)

that the drop in the 1990s was particularly for the forthcoming new EU Member States (including Central Europe);
- There was spectacular growth in imports from China and fuel exports to China. China's share of Russia's imports grew from 1.6% in 1996 to 24% in 2020. The share of China in non-fuel exports was relatively stable, and much lower than for the FSU and EU-28;
- The ROW had a significant share of about one-third of Russia's trade, with some fluctuations. The United States and North America represent only a modest part of this, so Russia has extensive trade with many countries all over the world. Commodity trade tends to be more globally oriented than manufacturing trade (Melchior, 2018), and the extensive global trade of Russia is in line with this.

The analysis shows that the EU became Russia's largest trade partner after 1991, but trade with China accelerated strongly from the 2000s and partly replaced Russia's imports from the FSU area. This reallocation has continued also after the formation of the EAEU and other FTAs in the FSU area. While

China's growth is the main reason for this development, it is also evident that Russia's FTAs in the FSU area have not been able to reverse this trend.

We have already seen that fuel exports in the 2010s accounted for up to 71% of Russia's exports of goods (in 2012–2013). In Russia's trade with the EU-28 and increasingly with China, the exchange of fuel exports for manufacturing imports is the main component. Is Russia about to become deindustrialised, and a pure commodity exporter? Has trade policy failed to promote Russian manufacturing production?

A qualification to the questions above is that the non-fuel exports of Russia have not always declined in absolute terms; there was a significant decline during 1996–2002 but then very strong growth until the financial crisis. Later recovery followed, but there was again a strong setback in 2015, and then eventually some growth towards 2020.

Table 12.1 shows the composition of Russia's non-fuel exports during 1996–2020, split into main categories.

While ores and metals had a stable share and arms exports are more volatile, agricultural/food exports have recently increased considerably. Other non-fuel exports (various manufacturing sectors) were more hit by the GFC in 2007–2009 and COVID-19 in 2020; otherwise, the trend is not so clear.

On the whole, we are not able to conclude that there has been a massive deindustrialisation of Russia, even if the manufacturing trade balance has deteriorated over time, especially due to growing imports from China. For Russia, the EU and the FSU remain important markets also for non-fuel exports. A reason to worry, however, is the steep decline in FSU market shares in Russian imports. So perhaps other FSU countries have more reasons to worry.

For Russia in 2022, Western Europe and China are the major trading partners, not the FSU. The FSU is nevertheless still important to Russia, since a prospering neighbourhood is vital also for Russia's growth, and a prospering Russia is crucial for other FSU economies. Likewise, for the FSU countries, trade with Western Europe and China will be of key importance, with proportions depending on whether they are located more to the west (such as Belarus

Table 12.1 The composition of Russia's non-fuel exports, 1996–2020

Year	Share (%) of Russia's non-fuel exports					Non-fuel % of total exports
	Food	Ores and metals	Arms	Other	Sum non-fuel	
1996	3.1	17.7	30.9	48.3	100	56.9
2000	2.5	18.8	28.8	49.9	100	49.4
2005	4.2	17.4	27.3	51.1	100	38.2
2010	5.5	16.2	34.9	43.4	100	34.4
2015	12.6	16.4	13.3	57.7	100	37.0
2020	15.7	16.2	25.3	42.9	100	56.0

Source WITS/COMTRADE

and Ukraine) or to the east (Central Asia). The same geography applies inside Russia; Western Europe is top of the list for St. Petersburg, while Russia's Far East trades mainly with China. From a trade and growth perspective, neither Russia, Russian regions, nor FSU countries should be forced to choose between east and west, both doors should be open. In this light, it makes sense that the EAEU in their strategic plan have this dual approach: integration with China as well as with the EU (EAEU, 2020, p. 8). According to Melchior (2018, 2019), Russia has nothing to fear, in the sense that such integration will not only provide welfare benefits but also stimulate industrial diversification.

In this context, it should be recalled that while the growth of China has led to deindustrialisation in some countries, it has also been the main driver behind the commodity price increase of the 25-year period studied here. The model-based analysis of Melchior (2018, Chapter 7) suggests that commodity-producing countries and regions obtained among the highest welfare gains from China's growth, due to the terms of trade gain: getting cheaper industrial goods in return for more expensive commodity exports. On the other hand, this also caused manufacturing contraction and falling nominal wages in the same countries. Trade integration with China, on the other hand, is different from Chinese growth and may potentially lead to a welfare gain combined with higher nominal wages and re-industrialisation (Melchior, 2018). And preferential trade integration via FTAs with China and the EU will be better for industrialisation than multilateral free trade, according to this analysis (ibid.).

12.6 Trade Policy Challenges in the Early 2020s: From Security Tensions to the Green Transition

The election of President Donald Trump in the United States in 2016 marked the end of a 30-year period of globalisation and liberalism in trade. Under President Trump, the United States introduced new protectionist measures, started a trade war with China, and partly blocked the dispute settlement system of the WTO.[12] At the time of writing (January 2022), the world trade system has not yet settled after this earthquake, the acceleration of FTAs across the globe has generally been put on hold, and the prospects of new WTO reforms are highly uncertain. A new feature of US trade policy under President Trump was its 'securitisation'—i.e., protectionist measures motivated by geopolitical and security reasons. For example, new steel and aluminium safeguard measures were introduced in 2018 for alleged security reasons, the trade war with China was geopolitically motivated, and investment screening and export controls were tightened for security reasons.

While Russia has been a rather innocent victim of some of President Trump's measures (notably the new barriers for steel and aluminium), it has a

---

[12] For extensive documentation of US trade policies under President Trump, see www.piie.com.

long history of geopolitics in trade, dating from the COMECON era and with Iran recently on the top of the FTA priority list. At the time of writing (January 2022), the Russia-Ukraine conflict is a major obstacle to Russia's trade integration with Western Europe. In addition to the sanctions and countersanctions (see Chapter 14), conflicts in the FSU are harmful to economic growth in the region, affecting Russia as well as the countries concerned.

A challenge for commodity-trading countries is the potential conflict between export industries and domestic consumers: Russian consumers would like to have cheap electricity, energy, and grains; but the exporters benefit from selling abroad at the highest possible prices. With cables, pipelines, and international trade, prices may be bid up to the benefit of exporters but to the detriment of consumers. An illustration is the growing integration of European energy markets, leading to electricity and natural gas prices far above normal levels towards the end of 2021.

Russia has several times used export restrictions as a method to separate export markets from domestic consumer markets, for example, for not only grains but also other commodities (WTO, 2021, p. 56ff). Russia is not alone; another example was provided in 2020, when several countries introduced export restrictions for medical equipment, including the EAEU. This also illustrates that supply shortages can also be a motive for export restrictions, not only a means to maintain lower domestic prices. Such measures are generally harmful to consumers abroad; they limit supply and bid up prices. For exporters, they can have ambiguous effects; quantity limitations may bid up export prices and generate rents, but outright export bans will force exporters to sell domestically at lower prices. Russia abolished several export restrictions as part of WTO accession, and export taxes for oil and gas have recently been reduced (see Chapter 9). The WTO generally aims to limit the use of export restrictions even if they are allowed in special circumstances, especially in the presence of critical shortages of food or other essential goods (GATT Article XI).

In the future, export restrictions may be an increasingly controversial issue, for the following reasons:

- The green transition may increase global electricity demand and bid up electricity prices, which are linked to energy markets in general. An illustration is the European debate in 2022 about the delayed opening of the Nord Stream 2 natural gas pipeline from Russia to the EU, and to what extent variations in the Russian supply of natural gas contributed to the EU's electricity price hikes;
- Supply shortages for rare commodities may become more common in the future;
- Climate change may affect agriculture unevenly and create food shortages in some regions.

Such developments may create incentives for the increased use of export restrictions and conflicts in the future.

There are also growing tensions about security-based restrictions (for exports or imports), where the line between legitimate security concerns and economic motives such as protectionism has been blurred under President Trump. In the previous era of liberal world markets, this did not generate many serious conflicts. However, there is the potential for more conflict in the future if GATT's security clause (GATT Article XXI) is used as a blanket waiver for protective measures. An interesting case was the WTO dispute between Russia and Ukraine, where Russia used this clause to stop transit trade from Ukraine through Russia, and Ukraine filed a WTO complaint. The WTO panel ruling in 2019 mainly supported Russia. Ukraine accepted the ruling and said it would not appeal.[13] The case illustrates the important role of the WTO in trade conflict resolution.[14]

The infamous 2018 steel and aluminium tariffs of President Trump were also introduced for security reasons, and Russia plus a dozen other countries complained in the WTO at the end of 2021. Some (including Russia), but not all, introduced countersanctions.[15] The common front by China, Russia, Western Europe, Canada, and Mexico in this case illustrates that the United States was the odd man out in that context.

While security-related sanctions are not examined in this chapter, President Trump's policies also illustrate that sanctions may also be used for protectionist purposes. A grey area is also when security concerns are legitimate, but their implementation is influenced by trade policy concerns. A case in question is Russia's import ban for agricultural goods from the United States, the EU, and other countries, which fits into Russia's import substitution policies that were introduced from 2014 (see Chapters 14 and 19).[16] While subsidies are more important than import restrictions in this context, these policies also create a possible motivation for non-liberal trade policies at the sector level, including non-tariff barriers and resistance to liberalisation.

An emerging trade policy challenge is coming from policies aimed to prevent climate change. The green transition will raise costs for industries worldwide, and the EU has presented a proposal for the Carbon Border

---

[13] See https://www.wto.org/english/news_e/news19_e/dsb_26apr19_e.htm.

[14] In spite of this, Russia has—at the time of writing—not yet joined the initiative to create a parallel dispute settlement body while the United States is still blocking the appointment of new judges in the WTO system. This Multi-Party Interim Appeal Arbitration Arrangement was set up in 2020, and by early 2022, the EU and 24 other WTO members including China were members. But not yet Russia.

[15] The countries that complained were Canada, China, the EU, India, Japan, South Korea, Mexico, New Zealand, Norway, Russia, Sweden, Chinese Taipei, and Turkey. Some complained about steel only, others for steel and aluminium. See www.wto.org for information.

[16] See also European Commission (2020, Chapter 6) for information on import substitution policies.

Adjustment Mechanism (CBAM) (European Commission, 2021). The EU has, along with many other countries, introduced a carbon emissions trading (CET) system, whereby EU industries must acquire quotas to cover their CO_2 emissions. While CET quotas were initially allocated for free, they could be traded in the CET market, and allocation will become increasingly restrictive and lead to higher quota prices. This will raise the costs of EU producers, which risk losing out in competition with third-country producers that do not have to pay for their CO_2 emissions. CBAM intends to re-establish a 'level playing field' in the EU market by taxing imports with rates linked to the CET price, also taking into account CET systems in the exporting country. In early 2022, it is not yet clear when and how CBAM will eventually be implemented, and there are vivid debates about the issue in the EU itself and with its trade partners, including about its WTO compatibility. In the initial proposal, the sectors covered were electricity, iron and steel, aluminium, cement, and fertilisers. These represent a small share of EU imports but a large share of CO_2 emissions. CBAM is particularly important to Russia because of its exports to the EU of metals and fertilisers.

Another key issue for Russia with respect to the green transition is the role of oil and natural gas. Cutting consumption of oil and natural gas would be a heavy blow to Russia, the Middle East, Norway, and other fuel exporters, and a core issue in debates about energy transition and climate change. While the world as a whole is not ready for such a step in 2022, CO_2 pricing will also affect demand in the near future. Given that the EU is the main customer for Russian fuel exports, EU policies in the field will be important. An important sub-issue is whether natural gas will be considered as a legitimate component of the green transition in the EU: for example, by replacing energy from coal. At the time of writing, the EU Commission has presented new proposals related to the so-called 'taxonomy' on which sectors are considered 'environmentally sustainable'. The draft proposal added nuclear energy and natural gas to the list, subject to certain conditions.[17] However, this is controversial in some corners, and the political outcome on the issue will be important for Russia's trade in the future.

Questions for Students

1. What were the main changes in Russia's foreign trade regime from 1985 to 1995?
2. In what way is it true that commodity price changes have been a major driver for Russia's foreign trade during 1995–2020?
3. What were the main consequences of Russia's WTO membership (list some of these)?

---

[17] See European Commission press release 1.1.2022: EU Taxonomy: Commission begins expert consultations on Complementary Delegated Act covering certain nuclear and gas activities. https://ec.europa.eu/commission/presscorner/detail/en/ip_22_2.

4. What does it mean that the EAEU is a customs union with common external trade policies?
5. Is competition from China a threat to Russian manufacturing production and diversification?

References

Aslund, A. (2010). Why doesn't Russia join the WTO? *The Washington Quarterly*, *33*(2), 49–63. https://doi.org/10.1080/01636601003661670

Black, R., & Kireeva, I. (2015). Sanitary and phytosanitary issues for the customs union of Russian Federation, Belarus and Kazakhstan in relation to trade with other CIS countries and the EU, with special reference to food of non-animal origin and phytosanitary control. *Journal of World Trade, 49*(5), 805–835.

EAEU. (2020). *Strategic directions for developing the Eurasian economic integration until 2025*. Approved by Decision No. 11 of the Supreme Eurasian Economic Council dated December 11, 2020. https://eec.eaeunion.org/upload/medialibrary/820/Strategy_2025.pdf. Accessed 5 January 2022.

EBRD. (2012). *Diversifying Russia. Harnessing regional diversity*. https://www.ebrd.com/news/publications/special-reports/diversifying-russia.html. Accessed 5 January 2022.

European Commission. (2020). *Commission Staff Working Document on significant distortions in the economy of the Russian Federation for the purposes of trade defence investigations*. Brussels, 22.10.2020. Document SWD (2020) 242 final. https://trade.ec.europa.eu/doclib/docs/2020/october/tradoc_158997.pdf

European Commission. (2021). *Proposal for a regulation of the European Parliament and of the Council establishing a carbon border adjustment mechanism*. Brussels, 14.7.2021 document COM(2021) 564 final. https://bit.ly/3zGSiBt

GATT. (1990). GATT grants observer status to the Soviet Union. GATT Newsletter No. 71 – May-June 1990.

Melchior, A. (2018). *Free trade agreements and globalisation*. Palgrave Macmillan.

Melchior, A. (2019). Russia in world trade: Between globalism and regionalism. *Russian Journal of Economics, 5*, 354–384. https://doi.org/10.32609/j.ruje.5.49345

Rutherford, T., & Tarr, D. (2006). *Regional impacts of Russia's accession to the WTO* (World Bank Policy Research Working Paper No. 4015). https://bit.ly/3sYfwlc. Accessed 5 January 2022.

Tarr, D. (2007). *Russian WTO accession: What has been accomplished, what can be expected?* (World Bank Policy Research Working Paper No. 4428, December 2007). https://openknowledge.worldbank.org/handle/10986/7612. Accessed 5 January 2022.

Tarr, D. G. (2016). The Eurasian Economic Union of Russia, Belarus, Kazakhstan, Armenia, and the Kyrgyz Republic: Can it succeed where its predecessor failed? *Eastern European Economics, 54*(1), 1–22.

Tochitskaya, I. (2012). *Russia's accession to the WTO: Impacts and challenges*. CASE Network E-briefs 01/2012. https://www.case-research.eu/files/?id_plik=2818

USTR (United States Trade Representative). (2021). *2021 Report on the Implementation and Enforcement of Russia's WTO Commitments*. https://bit.ly/3JZ9G90

Vinokurov, E. (2017). Eurasian Economic Union: Current state and preliminary results. *Russian Journal of Economics, 3*, 54–70.

WTO. (2018). *Factual presentation. Treaty on the Eurasian Economic Union (goods and services)*. Report by the Secretariat, document WT/REG358/1. https://bit.ly/3GdvUlm. Accessed 5 January 2022.

WTO. (2021). *Russian Federation. Trade policy review*. Report by the Secretariat. Document WT/TPR/S/416, 22 September 2021. https://www.wto.org/english/tratop_e/tpr_e/tp516_e.htm

CHAPTER 13

Foreign Investment

Kalman Kalotay

Highlights

- Investment flows into and out of Russia have been rather limited compared with the flows of other major economies of the world.
- Foreign investment to and from Russia has been sensitive to the international political environment, which improved at the beginning of transition but deteriorated significantly in the aftermath of the Crimean crisis in 2014, and especially after the 2022 Russia–Ukraine conflict.
- The two main modes of entry of foreign direct investment—greenfield investment and cross-border mergers and acquisitions (M&As)—have fluctuated largely over the past three decades.
- Natural resource-based activities have played a major role in the foreign investment flows of Russia.
- Foreign investment data reflect real economic activities imperfectly, 'through a glass darkly'.
- The three main forms of 'indirect FDI'—round-tripping, transhipping, and corporate inversion—all play a major role in Russia, usually transiting through offshore centres such as Cyprus.

K. Kalotay (✉)
Institute of World Economics, Budapest, Hungary
e-mail: kalotayk@gmail.com

- The largest Russian multi-national enterprises are based in natural resources and have close links with the Russian government; some of them are state-owned, others state-influenced.
- The COVID-19 pandemic has sped up major transformations in global investment flows due to the acceleration of digitalisation, adjustment to environmental issues, and climate change, and to increasing economic nationalism, affecting the flows of Russia deeply.

13.1 Introduction and Context

In the contemporary world economy, *foreign investment*, alongside trade, is one of the main channels of international economic relations between countries. In Russia, the history of such investment started by and large with the end of the Soviet system and the transition from a centrally planned to a market economy. Before 1991, the investment links of the Union of Soviet Socialist Republics (USSR) with the outside world used to be extremely limited. With the end of the USSR, not only foreign economic relations were liberalised, but also new international relations were created with the newly independent successor states.

This chapter explores the main characteristics of foreign investment coming to and leaving Russia, going back to the 1990s. Most of the statistics used the internationally accepted standard definition of foreign investment. However, not all data are available for all details of foreign investment flows and stocks.

The investment flows into and out of Russia have been rather limited compared with those of other major economies of the world. They have also been volatile, affected by the fluctuations of the national and the world economy, and provoked by a series of crisis situations emerging since the end of the Soviet Union (see Chapter 16). Foreign investment is also sensitive to the international political environment, which improved at the beginning of transition but deteriorated significantly in the aftermath of the Crimean crisis in 2014 and especially after the 2022 Russia–Ukraine conflict.

Foreign investment consists of the transfer of financial assets from one country to another, with all its economic, social, and political consequences. In each country, it consists of inward and outward investment. In the case of Russia, inward foreign investment denotes the transfer of funds by legal or physical persons residing in foreign countries to Russia as a host country, and outward foreign investment denotes the transfer of funds abroad by legal or physical persons residing in Russia as a home country. Statistics record foreign investment as inflows or outflows in the financial account of the balance of payments of the country in a given period of time. They are registered on a net basis, i.e., divestment is deducted from gross inflows. This way, flows in a given period may be positive or negative. As for foreign investment stocks, they refer to the value of cumulative flows from the beginning of recording transactions until a given point of time, usually the end of a given year, adjusted to exchange rate fluctuations and changes in the valuation of assets. They are recorded in the international investment position of the country—inward stocks as liabilities and outward stocks as assets.

Foreign investment is divided into *direct*, *portfolio*, and *other* investments. From a substantial point of view, direct investment is different from portfolio and other investments because it contains an element of control by the investor in the invested company and because it is a package of resources going beyond finances (usually in terms of job creation, skills development, transfer of technology, access to production systems and international markets, and other resources, among others—see Sect. 13.4). Statisticians measure this control by differentiating between foreign investors who own or acquire at least 10% of the shares of the invested companies (treated as direct investors) and investors whose participation remains below 10% (treated as portfolio or other investors).

Income derived from foreign investment (called foreign investment income) is recorded separately in the current account of the balance of payments of countries (see Sect. 13.4). This income, if it is not reinvested in the original project, forms the basis for the repatriation of profits.

To ensure the international comparability of foreign investment statistics, all countries of the world, including Russia, follow in their official reports the same global standards set in the Balance of Payments and International Investment Position Manual established by the International Monetary Fund (IMF) in cooperation with other international organisations.

13.2 Trends and Patterns of Foreign Investment

13.2.1 Dynamics of Foreign Investment

To allow the measurement of longer term dynamics, data series have been available for foreign direct investment (FDI) since 1992 and foreign portfolio investment (FPI) since 1994. They are shown in Figs. 13.1 (FDI) and 13.2 (FPI). While both kinds of flows have exhibited large fluctuations following the developments of the Russian and the world economy—sometimes with a lag—FDI has been consistently more stable and larger than FPI. Moreover, only FPI flows reached negative values in certain years, especially in 2008 and 2014.

In FDI inflows, an upward and accelerating trend could be observed until 2008, with a record level (USD 76 billion) registered at the end of that period. The global financial crisis (GFC) hit inflows severely, and only a partial recovery took place up to 2013. However, the level in 2013 (USD 53 billion) was still well below the previous record. Moreover, in 2014, the upward trend was broken in the aftermath of the Crimean crisis. Post-2014 flows remained volatile, and they were hit again by the COVID-19 pandemic in 2020.

With very few exceptions, FDI outflows moved in parallel with inflows, with a high of USD 57 billion recorded in 2008. However, the post-2009 recovery

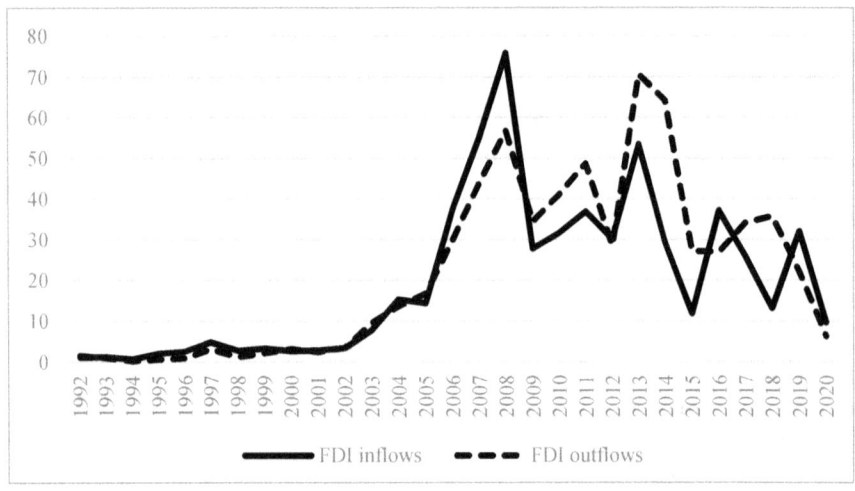

Fig. 13.1 Foreign direct investment flows of Russia, 1992–2020, USD billions (*Source* Author's calculations based on UNCTAD data)

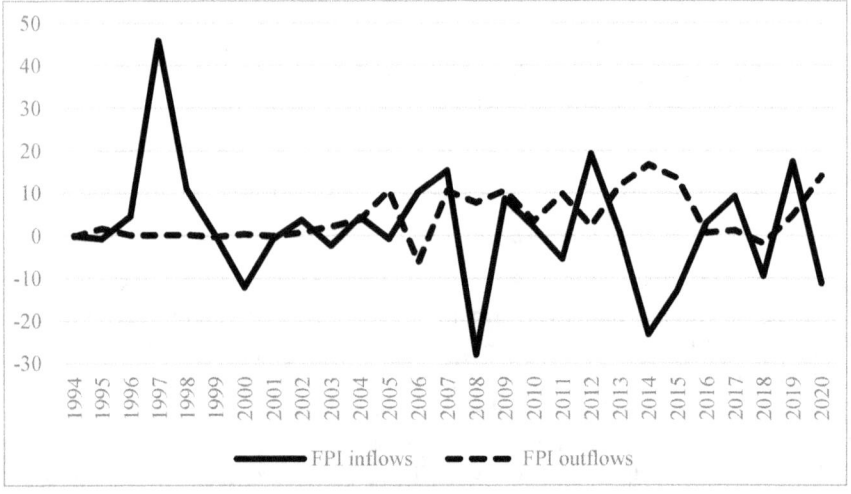

Fig. 13.2 Foreign portfolio investment flows of Russia, 1994–2020, USD billions (*Source* Author's calculations based on IMF data)

was stronger in outflows than in inflows, and the former reached an all-time record of USD 71 billion in 2013. After the 2014 crisis, the decline was sharp in outflows, exceeding the one registered in inflows.

In FPI, an exceptionally large one-time inflow was recorded in 1997 (USD 46 billion), just before the Russian financial crisis in 1998 (see Chapter 16). Afterwards, FPI inflows fluctuated and never exceeded USD 20 billion per year. FPI outflows remained more stable. Investment in assets abroad played the role of a safe haven, therefore it declined less in crisis years. It even increased in the COVID year of 2020.

13.2.2 The Role of Stocks and Flows in Measuring Foreign Investment

In Russia and other countries, there has been an ongoing debate if flows or stocks are more reliable in measuring foreign investment patterns (see, e.g., Antaloczy & Sass, 2015; Kalotay, 2012; Kuznetsov, 2018). This debate usually concludes that flows are more useful when measuring the dynamics of investment, but stocks are better when looking at the structural features of investment. This is so because of the lumpiness of investment, especially in its direct investment form. Large projects/transactions tend to exaggerate flows in a given year and show a big decline in the subsequent year when the transaction has been completed and not replaced by another similarly large one.

13.2.3 Modes of Entry of FDI

There are two main modes of entry of FDI: *greenfield* investment (meaning the creation of new assets) and cross-border *M&As* affecting existing assets (UNCTAD, 2000). This differentiation does not exist in FPI because the latter rarely contains a 'greenfield' element. There are also intermediate modes of entry in the case of joint ventures and the expansion of projects. And there are '*brownfield*' projects which combine the two modes of entry. They take place, for example, in the privatisation of state-owned assets (see Chapter 7), when the transformation of firms starts with an acquisition, but it is followed by investment in new assets. In the data sets measuring the different modes of entry, the intermediate forms are usually assimilated into one of the two main forms, depending on with which they show more similarities.

Differentiation between the main modes of entry is important from the point of view of gauging the development impact of FDI. In general, greenfield investment adds more to productive capacities than M&As, but acquired firms usually have more inherited links with local partners (UNCTAD, 2000). However, in the long term, the difference between the two modes of entry tends to diminish. To be noted also is that the acquisition of existing assets can raise more political concerns than greenfield investment, depending on the nationality and main features of the investor. Acquisitions by a state-owned entity from a country deemed to be 'hostile' usually face strong merger control hurdles in the host country.

As for the size of the individual modes of entry, their statistics do not follow the Balance of Payments standards and are thus not directly comparable with overall FDI flows. Instead of measuring the financial flows, greenfield and M&A data reflect more the value of announced projects. For that reason, especially, greenfield data are more the indicator of investor intentions than actual flows.

With those reservations in mind, the following observations can be made on the two main modes of entry into Russia (Figs. 13.3 and 13.4):

- In greenfield projects, data availability starts only in 2003. There is a clear indication of a downward trend in the value of new projects targeting Russia after the onset of the GFC in 2008. Paradoxically, there was no full recovery to pre-crisis levels at the end of the decade and the beginning of the new one, but a slight increase of the value of projects after 2014, very probably related to the opportunities offered by the Russian policy of stimulating local production. Trends in projects initiated by Russian firms abroad are less clear. There was a one-time peak of USD 37 billion in 2017. Both inward and outward project announcements declined sharply during the COVID-19 crisis.
- In net M&A inflows and outflows (net of divestments), the lumpiness of large transactions is very apparent, especially in the sales of Russian assets to foreigners, with a large divestment in 2013 and a large new project in 2011. In general, the values of both ways of transactions (M&As targeting Russian firms and M&As carried out by Russian firms abroad) are very small in a global market, which moves hundreds of billions of dollars per year. It is to be added that during the COVID-19 crisis in 2020, M&As were relatively little Affected, related to the paradoxical buoyancy of stock markets in the same year.

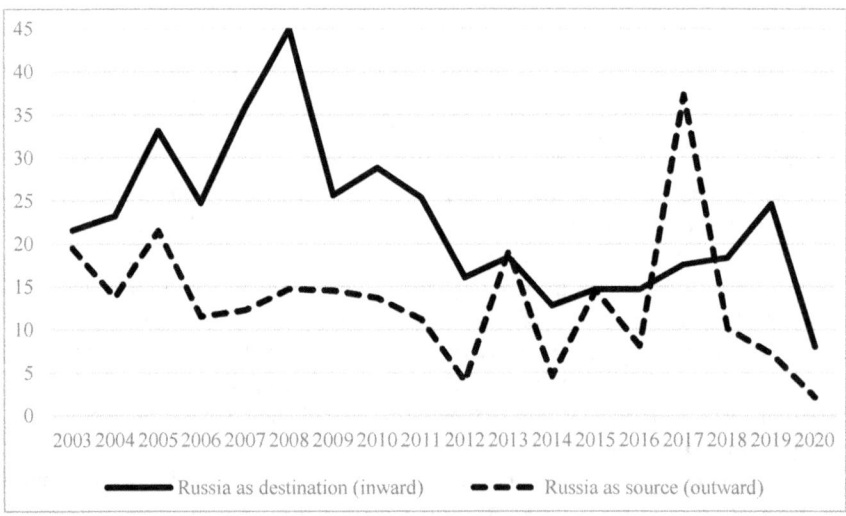

Fig. 13.3 Value of announced greenfield FDI projects in Russia and by Russian investors abroad, 2003–2020, USD billions (*Source* Author's calculations based on UNCTAD data)

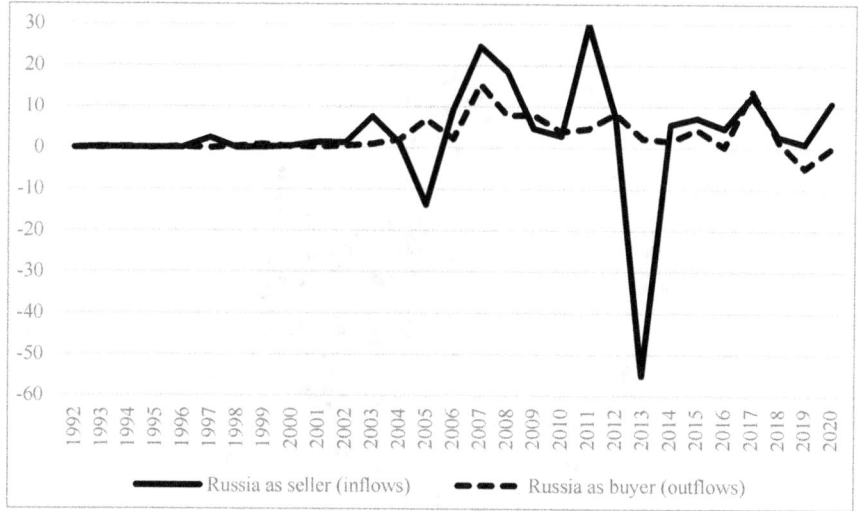

Fig. 13.4 Value of net cross-border M&As in Russia and by Russian investors abroad, 1992–2020, USD billions (*Source* Author's calculations based on UNCTAD data)

13.2.4 Selected Sectoral and Geographical Patterns of Foreign Investment

The industry and sectoral composition is available for inward FDI only. In the data series for FDI flows between 2010 and 2020 (Fig. 13.5), natural resource-based activities played a major role, with mining (including oil) and refining together accounting for more than one-third and metallurgy another 5%. In non-resource-based activities, finance and trade each accounted for around one-fifth. The share of all other economic activities combined reached 22% only.

Data are not available on the overall industrial and sectoral composition of outward FDI. However, the list of the largest multi-national enterprises (MNEs) of the country presented in Subsect. 13.5.1 suggests that oil and gas, metallurgy, transport, and telecommunications play a major role in Russian outward FDI.

As for the geography of inward FDI, FDI stocks indicate very small structural changes between 2009 and 2020. A caveat is to be added here: data register the nationality of the immediate investor and not of the final beneficial owner. For that reason, in a data set where transactions transiting offshore locations play an important role (see Subsect. 13.2.5), some of the information may be misleading about the real nationality of final investors. Keeping in mind these reservations, the 'raw' numbers show that the share of developed economies remains around four-fifths and that of Europe over two-thirds (Fig. 13.6). However, that share includes Cyprus and the Netherlands, which together account for over two-fifths of the total number. In principle, the

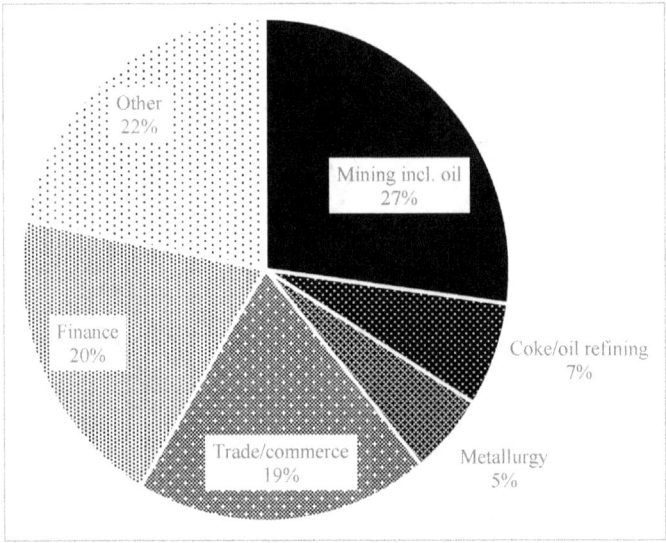

Fig. 13.5 Main industries of the cumulative FDI inflows to Russia, 2010–2020, % of total (*Source* Author's calculations based on UNCTAD data)

share of developing and transition economies remained quite low. However, if one considers that a large part of transactions flowing via Cyprus and the Netherlands originates in these countries, their real share is to be supposed to be much higher.

Similarly, the share of developed economies and Europe remained high in the outward FDI stock of Russia, with practically no change in it between 2009 and 2020 (Fig. 13.7). The importance of Cyprus even increased, despite the financial crisis plaguing that economy in 2012–2013. There are also some individual country differences with inflows. In outflows, Austria and Singapore, two trading nations, occupy a much higher share.

In the FPI outward stock of Russia, economies and country groups with large and sophisticated capital markets dominate even more than in the country's outward FDI stock (Fig. 13.8). The share of developed economies came to close to 90% in both 2009 and 2020. The largest recipients are Ireland, Luxembourg, the United Kingdom, and the United States. The share of Cyprus and the Netherlands, though not negligible, remained more modest.

These data sets do not give a definitive answer to the question if diversification towards new foreign investment partners outside the group of developed countries takes place. However, it indicates that even if we set aside offshore or transit partners, developed countries still play an important role in foreign investment relations with the world.

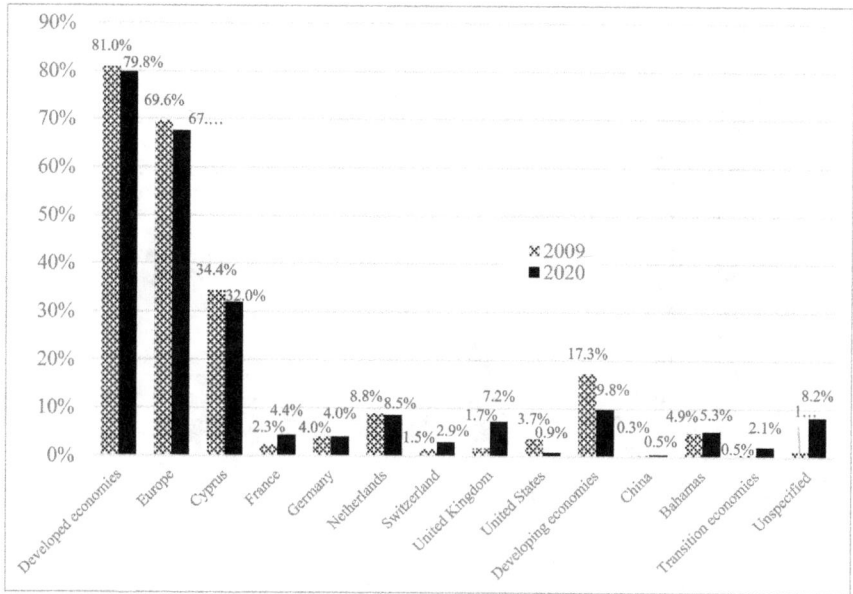

Fig. 13.6 Main sources of the inward FDI stock in Russia by country and country group, 2009 and 2020, % of total stock (*Source* Author's calculations based on UNCTAD data)

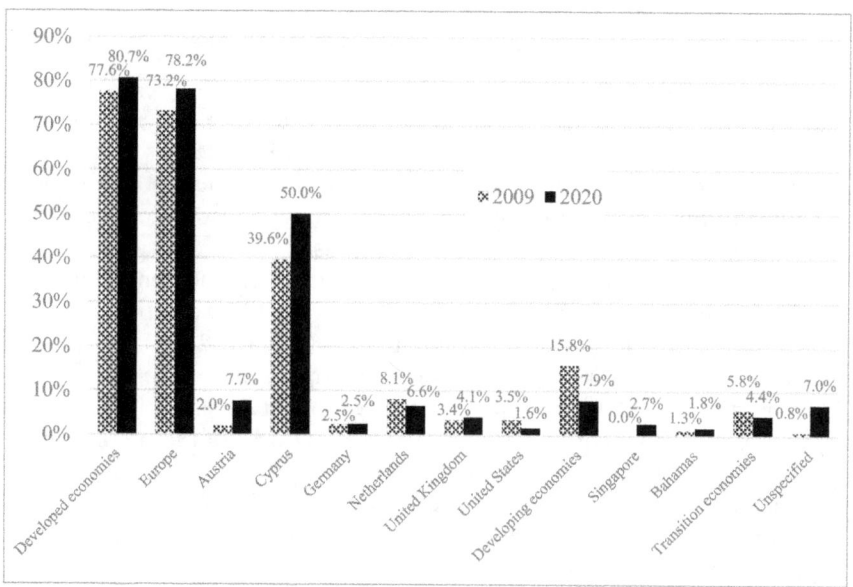

Fig. 13.7 Main destinations of the outward FDI stock in Russia by country and country group, 2009 and 2020, % of total stock (*Source* Author's calculations based on UNCTAD data)

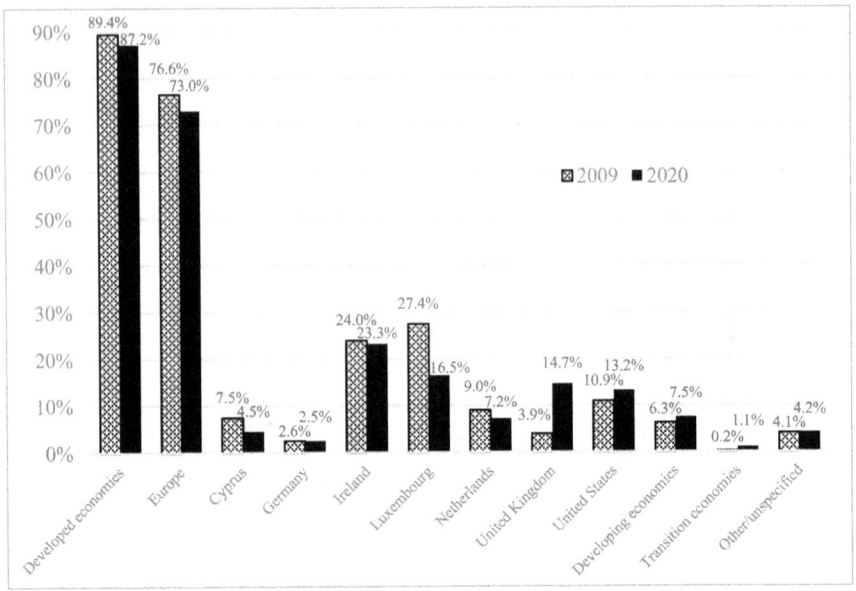

Fig. 13.8 Main destinations of the outward FPI stock in Russia by country and country group, 2009 and 2020, % of total stock (*Source* Author's calculations based on Central Bank of the Russian Federation [CBRF] data)

13.2.5 Measurement Problems ('Through a Glass Darkly')

Subsection 13.2.4 already has provided insights into the complexity and limitations of foreign investment data. They reflect trends in an imperfect manner, 'through a glass darkly' (see Antaloczy & Sass, 2015). The fact that in many cases the immediate investor is not the same as the final beneficial owner means that some of the transactions registered in the statistics lead to an overestimation compared with trends in the real economy as the same transaction flowing through various countries is counted more than once. The generic name of this type of transaction is 'indirect' FDI (Kalotay, 2012). Sometimes, but less frequently, the literature calls it 'conduit' FDI (Casella, 2019), referring to the use of transit countries. In other cases, it is referred to as 'phantom' FDI (Damgaard et al., 2019) as in the transit locations it does not lead to direct creation of new productive capacities. However, it does not mean non-existent transactions and for that reason, the adjective phantom may be misleading. This chapter therefore uses the most usual term of indirect FDI.

Indirect FDI has three main forms: round-tripping, transhipping, and corporate inversion. To visualise it in the Russian context, we present them as follows:

Round-tripping: Russia → transit country (e.g., Cyprus) → Russia

Transshipping: Russia → transit country (e.g., Cyprus) → final destination country
  Country of origin → transit country (e.g., Cyprus) → Russia
Corporate inversion:
Original headquarter (HQ) country becoming affiliate location (Russia) ↔
Old affiliate location becoming HQ (e.g., in the Netherlands)

The prevalence of indirect FDI (with a key role played by offshore centres such as Cyprus) is one of the reasons why trends in inward and outward FDI move together. It is particularly evident in the case of round-tripping, when the same funds leave and enter the country, and are registered in both inward and outward FDI. Other forms of indirect FDI are related to the phenomenon called liability of foreignness. In some cases, Russian firms have the interest to enter host countries under different nationalities, especially in a world where the regulation of FDI is closely related to international politics such as sanctions and countersanctions (see Chapter 14). These forms are also important for firms from the perspective of managing their corporate network optimally. Investing via geographically and culturally close affiliates instead of a faraway parent company can facilitate the setting up and management of operations. In addition, in all forms of indirect FDI, tax considerations play an important role.

Policymakers and civil society representatives around the world increasingly emphasise the importance of knowing the ultimate beneficiary owners and ultimate targets of FDI. This information may better guide their decision-making process (UNCTAD, 2016). Part of the effort is in an increasingly sophisticated collection of FDI data, in which both the immediate investors and the ultimate beneficial owner are identified. Some countries already publish such differentiated reports on their inward FDI (but not on outward FDI yet). It is also increasing practice to report FDI on the so-called directional basis, allowing the elimination of part of the indirect FDI practices from the FDI data.

FDI data do not only overestimate some transactions in the real economy, but they also underestimate others. The best-known case is in the so-called *non-equity modes* of activities by MNEs (UNCTAD, 2011). This is so because MNEs do control and manage important parts of their value chains without formally owning the assets of the companies working within the given value chain and getting instructions about the quantity and quality to be produced and the timing of the production process. In other words, the differentiation between internalisation (in-house activities) and externalisation (transactions with business partners) is increasingly blurred. This phenomenon also affects activities in Russia and the transactions of Russian firms abroad. The most common forms are licensing, franchising, business process outsourcing, and contract manufacturing. In all these forms, the business partners enjoy formal independence from the MNE. The advantage for MNEs is that these business links are less costly than FDI (there is no need to carry on formal investment with sunk costs) and in case of crisis, these links are easier to liquidate than FDI (in the latter, the company needs to divest with all the adjacent costs linked to that). Non-equity modes are also a preferred way in activities in which there are fewer material movements (such as digital services). These activities lend themselves to non-equity modes easily.

To be noted also is that some emerging countries such as China have also moved their transactions into projects in which outward FDI is intricately interlinked with other transactions, for example state-to-state loans, trade transactions, and barters, among others, especially in the framework of the Belt and Road Initiative. In some cases, it is impossible to disentangle the FDI element or classify elements correctly. In the case of the foreign activities of the Russian state and Russian firms, such packages are less frequent and less developed, though in the case of declarations signed at the Russia–Africa Summits, there have been efforts to emulate the Chinese example.

The rise of non-equity modes provokes questions about control and responsibility. In various parts of the world, especially in the developed world, civil society and courts increasingly make MNEs responsible for all activities carried out in their value chains, independently of the ownership of the assets. In some cases, like in the production of consumer goods, social pressure has an immediate impact on business. So far, Russian firms may have been less affected by these moves because they produce less consumer goods. However, cases about the environmental and social impact of their activities may be brought up in the future in any court of the world as the principle of universal competence is gaining ground. In other words, a court in a developed country may declare itself competent in a complaint against the activities of a Russian MNE in a faraway developing country, and it could be either via FDI or any other form.

13.3 THE FDI AND FPI INTENSITY OF RUSSIA IN INTERNATIONAL COMPARISON

13.3.1 How the Foreign Investment Indices are Constructed

To assess the role of foreign investment (both inward and outward) in the development strategy of Russia in international comparison, we use a modified and further developed version of UNCTAD's Performance Index in its *World Investment Report 2002* (UNCTAD, 2002), which measures the FDI intensity of individual economies or groups. Its formula to be applied to all types of foreign investment is the following:

$$\text{FI Performance Index}_i = \frac{\text{FI}_i / \text{FI}_v}{\text{GDP}_i / \text{GDP}_v} \tag{13.1}$$

where

- FI Performance Index$_i$ is the index value for country i
- FI$_i$ is the FI flow or stock of country i in the given period

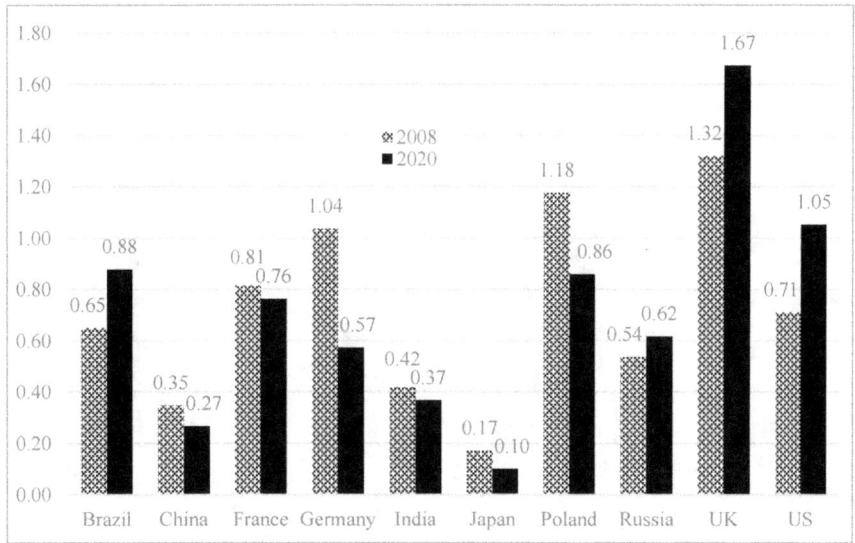

Fig. 13.9 Inward FDI index of Russia and selected countries of comparison, 2008 and 2020, World average = 1 (*Source* Author's calculations based on UNCTAD and IMF data)

- FI_p is world FI flow or stock in the given period
- GDP_i is the GDP for country i in the given period
- GDP_p is world GDP in the given period.

In this chapter, we measure separately the indices for the FDI and FPI inward and outward stocks of Russia and nine comparison countries: Brazil, China, France, Germany, India, Japan, Poland, the United Kingdom, and the United States. These countries have been selected because either they are among the largest economies of the world (the United States, China, Japan, Germany, United Kingdom, India, and France), because they are of similar size to Russia (Brazil), or because they are the largest transition economy that joined the European Union (EU) (Poland).

The results of the comparison are presented in Figs. 13.9–13.12.

13.3.2 Why are the Indices of Russia Low?

Overall, all the intensity indices of Russia remain below 1. In other words, in all cases, the country's reliance on the given segment of foreign investment is lower than what one would expect on the basis of the size of Russian gross domestic product (GDP). They are particularly low in inward and outward FPI. However, all four indices increased between 2008 and 2020, reflecting a slowly growing reliance on foreign investment.

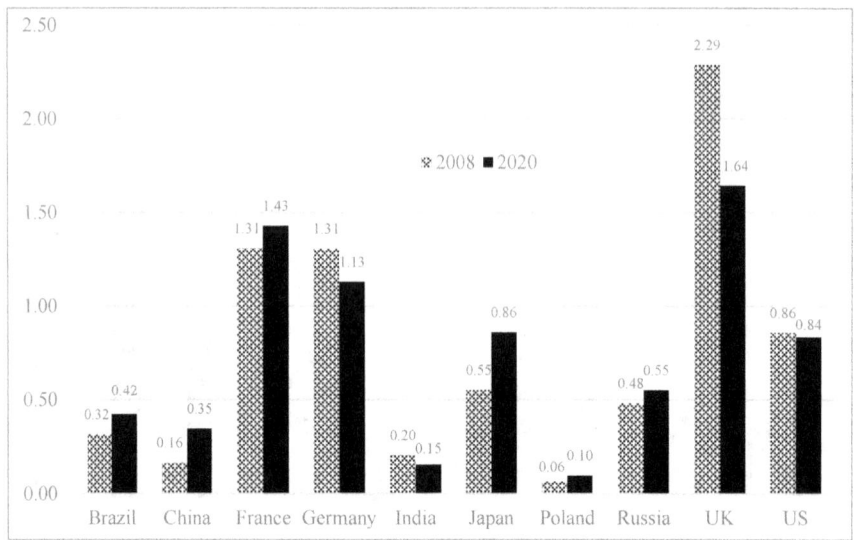

Fig. 13.10 Outward FDI index of Russia and selected countries of comparison, 2008 and 2020, World average = 1 (*Source* Author's calculations based on UNCTAD and IMF data)

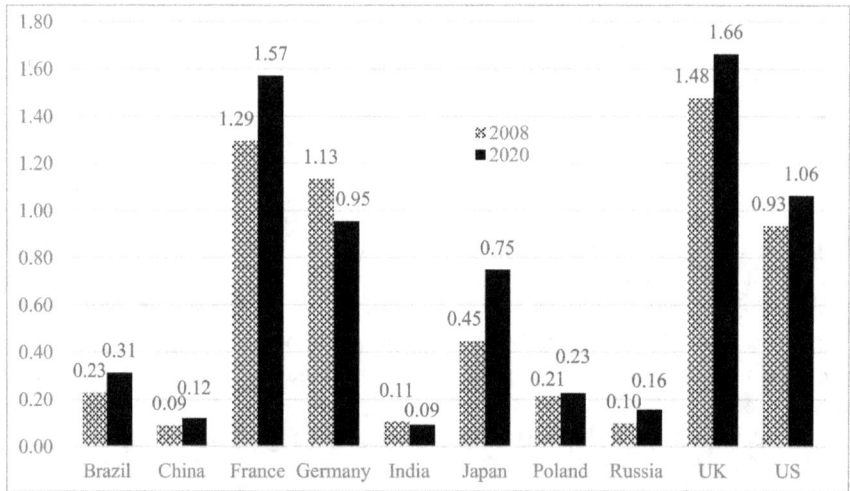

Fig. 13.11 Inward FPI index of Russia and selected countries of comparison, 2008 and 2020, World average = 1 (*Source* Author's calculations based on UNCTAD and IMF data)

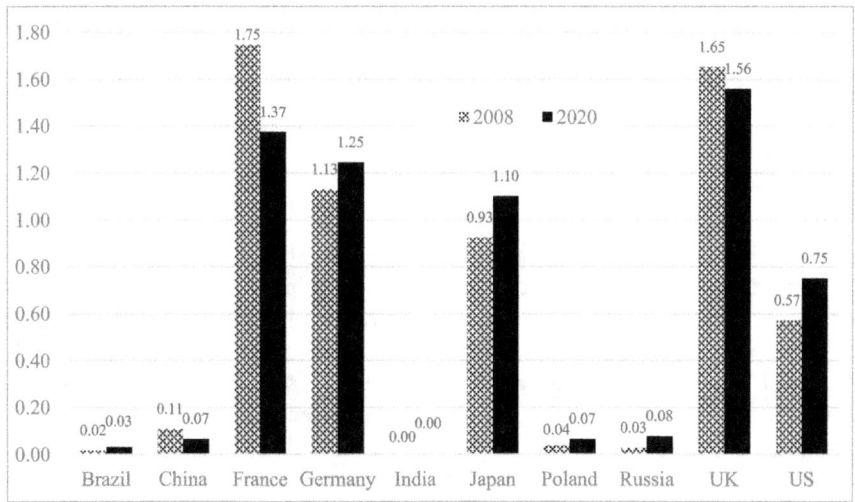

Fig. 13.12 Outward FPI index of Russia and selected countries of comparison, 2008 and 2020, World average = 1 (*Source* Author's calculations based on UNCTAD and IMF data)

It is also important to compare the indices of the Russian economy with the selected nine benchmark economies. Please note that among them some, too, show lower than 1 value in some indicators. For example, in terms of the inward FDI index, Russia exhibited a higher value than Germany, India, China, and Japan. Naturally, a lower reliance does not necessarily mean a failure in the development path of a country but can be a choice of development strategy (like in the case of Japan). No wonder three of the four have in turn higher outward FDI index values than Russia. The only surprise comes from China, which, in comparison with its GDP, relies less, and not more, on inward and outward FDI than Russia (though with the rapid expansion of the Chinese multinationals abroad, the country's outward FDI index is rising very fast).

The comparison group can be divided into two, especially in the outward FPI index. On the one hand, the BRIC[1] countries including Russia show very low values, reflecting the relative novelty and shallowness of their capital markets, while the developed countries with mature markets have much higher values.

In sum, the relatively low foreign investment intensity of the Russian economy is in part the result of its historical development, with a transition to a market economy starting only in 1991, but also of policy choices that resulted in the selected and partial promotion of inward and outward FDI. Finally, the indices of the Russian economy also reflect the international policy

---

[1] The BRIC acronym stands for Brazil, Russia, India, and China.

environment, which is limiting the possibilities of both inward and outward foreign investment.

13.4 Key Issues in Foreign Investment and Development in Russia in an International Context

The Russian government—or any government for that matter—does not allow or sometimes promote inward and outward foreign investment just for the sake of maximising its volume but for deriving development benefits from it. All types of foreign investments include an element of financial flows. In inward FDI, they represent additional financial resources for the country, which can be helpful in realising economic projects or counterbalancing an eventual deficit (for example, a trade deficit) in the current account of the balance of payments of the country. However, from these flows are to be deducted profit repatriation (which is registered as part of the investment income in the current account; see Sect. 13.1). The aim of policymakers in this context is to reduce the potential of profit repatriation by convincing investors to reinvest their net gains in the country, instead of sending them abroad.

13.4.1 The Flow of Financial Resources in Foreign Investment

Outward foreign investment is an outflow of financial resources from the country, which is then counterbalanced by profits repatriated to Russia. In this case, the government allows outward foreign investment because it expects other development benefits from it, described below. The outflow of financial resources can be motivated by pull factors (i.e., business opportunities in foreign markets), and in this case we talk about reasons for expansion, or by push factors (i.e., difficulties in the national business environment), and here, we talk about reasons of exodus. In the economic history of Russia, both in the early stages of transition and in the crisis episodes, reasons for exodus prevailed, and foreign investment outflows were partly mixed with a phenomenon called 'capital flight' (capital flight has no firmly set definition; the term is used when assets or money rapidly flow out of a country due to an event of economic consequence). However, in the growth episodes of the post-1999 Russian economy, the bulk of outward foreign investment was motivated by considerations of expansion.

The breakdown of direct investment income into repatriated profits and reinvested earnings in Russia in recent years is shown in Table 13.1. It indicates that income on inward FDI largely exceeded income on outward FDI, due to the higher profitability of the former. It also suggests that Russian MNEs had more propensity to reinvest their earnings abroad than the propensity of foreign investors to reinvest their profits in Russia. Still, the net balance of reinvested earnings was positive, though the difference was shrinking.

Table 13.1 Direct investment income and reinvested earnings in Russia, 2013–2020 (USD billions and %)

Indicator	2013	2014	2015	2016	2017	2018	2019	2020
Direct investment income, net	−48.9	−43.9	−23.7	−26.5	−29.8	−24.5	−35.8	−25.1
Direct investment income on inward FDI, payable	69.4	68.6	41.0	48.1	57.1	59.6	71.0	53.7
Of which reinvested earnings	21.7	21.7	11.2	17.2	16.7	16.6	19.5	5.4
Share of reinvested earnings (% of total)	31.3	31.6	27.3	35.8	29.3	27.8	27.5	10.1
Direct investment income on outward FDI, receivable	20.5	24.7	17.3	21.7	27.3	35.2	35.2	28.6
Of which reinvested earnings	11.4	14.5	5.9	10.8	11.7	13.9	14.2	2.9
Share of reinvested earnings (% of total)	55.7	58.6	34.2	50.0	42.7	39.6	40.4	10.3

Source Author's calculations based on CBRF data

13.4.2 The Package of Resources in FDI

While FPI consists mainly of financial flows, FDI is a package of resources which contains, to varying degrees, the following elements:

- **Contribution to structural change in the home and host economies**: in the case of Russia, both inward and outward FDI are concentrated in natural resources, therefore this impact is modest.
- **Access to international markets and foreign business partners**: both inward and outward FDI play an important role in this. In the case of inward FDI, it allows entities located in Russia to join international value chains; in the case of outward FDI, these are the Russian firms that extend the scope and reach of their own value chains.
- **Jobs**: job creation takes place both in inward FDI (at the affiliates of foreign firms located in Russia) and in outward FDI (at the corporate HQs of Russian MNEs). Usually, the number of jobs at the HQs is smaller but the qualifications higher. Job creation also depends on the capital versus labour intensity of the activities. In most resource-based activities, the number of jobs created is limited.
- **Transfer of labour skills**: MNEs have a vested interest in training their employees. The latter, even if they have good general education, do not have exactly the skills required for the job. The advantage of such training is that even if employees leave the MNE at a later stage (or the MNE separates from those employees), they retain the skills learned and can use them in a new context in the local economy.

- **Transfer of management skills**: MNEs usually bring new management techniques with them to the host country, skills that local business partners can learn and emulate. The reverse transfer also happens when an MNE from an emerging market economy acquires a firm in a developed economy and adopts some of the management practices found there.
- **Transfer of technology**: this flows in the majority of cases from corporate HQs to host (recipient) countries of FDI. However, in the case of the so-called 'strategic asset seeking' when emerging market MNEs target assets in developed countries (see below), a reverse transfer of technology, from affiliates to HQs, is also common.

The development impact also depends on the main motivation of investors. We can identify four main types of *motivations*: (natural) resource, market, efficiency, and strategic asset seeking FDI. In the case of FDI inflows to Russia, the first three motivations are present, reflecting its diverse competitive advantages. However, the industry structure indicates that most investors target the country's natural resources and/or the large market and are less motivated by efficiency seeking considerations (in this case, there would be more export-oriented manufacturing or services located in the country). In the case of the outward FDI, the fourth motivation, accessing strategic assets (for example, technology, know-how, or unique skills) abroad also plays a significant role. Natural resource-seeking motives still exist when Russian MNEs access the resources of developing countries to integrate them into their own value chains.

13.4.3 *Dealing with the Flipsides of the FDI Impact*

The development impact of foreign investment is not always positive. Sudden changes in financial flows can destabilise the local markets. Some of the foreign investment flows are pro-cyclical, which can particularly be a problem in a downturn, when authorities wish to counter the negative effects.

As for FDI, as it entails the control of assets in the host country, it raises the question of *dependency* on foreign capital, which can become a political issue, too, especially if there is a sensitivity about the nationality of the investor. No country has thus a fully liberalised regime in which investors are allowed to enter into any activity without limitations and without screening. Indeed, many countries, including Russia, have their lists of *strategic sectors* in which foreign investment is not allowed or is restricted. The Strategic Investment Law of the Russian Federation, adopted in 2008 and modified subsequently several times, the last time in 2021, lists the prohibited and restricted sectors (close to 50 in total). Prohibition applies, for example, to operating mass media, owning agricultural land, diamond mining, regional gas supply and gas distribution systems, insurance, air transportation, armaments, and security services. Russian law is quite restrictive but has the advantage of certain clarity.

The competitiveness of foreign investors also has double-edged consequences. It can lift the competitiveness of the host economy but can also lead to the *crowding out* of local firms unable to compete with foreign firms having better technology or more financial resources. In such cases, intervention from the competition authority can be required. One should not forget that the entry of foreign investment by default provokes changes in society, in culture, and in consumption patterns which the authorities may wish to monitor.

Policy intervention in this area is a difficult balancing act. It must find a middle-way compromise between local firms that expect protection and foreign investors who expect non-arbitrary rules, based on the principle of *national treatment* (meaning that local and foreign firms are to be treated on equal footing). At the end of 2021, UNCTAD's Investment Dispute Settlement Navigator registered 740 concluded and 354 pending cases of *Investor-State dispute settlement*, under which disagreement about the treatment of investors has been brought by these firms to international arbitration fora. Of these, 26 have been initiated against Russia. At the end of 2021, 9 cases were pending, 11 had been decided in favour of the investors, 4 had been decided in favour of the Russian State, 1 had been settled by the parties outside the arbitration forum, and 1 had been discontinued by the parties.

13.5 The Role of MNEs

This section briefly presents the main characteristics of Russian MNEs, which are the main agents of outward FDI. In principle, natural persons can also undertake inward and outward FDI. However, the transactions of the latter are usually very small, except for some diaspora and suitcase investors in economies from which large parts of the population have moved to work abroad (the example of transition economies, such as Kyrgyzstan, Tajikistan, and Moldova). However, in the case of Russia, though such phenomena exist, their value is very small compared with the overall FDI.

13.5.1 The Universe of the Largest Russian MNEs

The bulk of outward FDI transactions of Russia is carried out by a handful of large MNEs. The total foreign assets of the 20 largest MNEs amounted to USD 108 billion in 2019 (Table 13.2) out of a total outward FDI stocks of USD 407 billion in the same year.

The industry composition of the top 20 is concentrated, and dominated by natural resource-based firms, with oil and gas companies occupying the top three posts. Their strategies are related to the control of their value chains, typically upstream in developing counties and downstream in developed countries. Some of these firms are actively involved in indirect FDI, too. Two of them, VEON and NMK, have undertaken corporate inversion, and have now their official HQs registered abroad while Russian individuals remain the

Table 13.2 The 20 largest Russian MNEs, ranked by foreign assets in 2019

Rank	Company	Industry	Long-term foreign assets, USD billions		Total foreign assets, USD billions		Share of foreign assets in total assets, %	
			2018	2019	2018	2019	2018	2019
1	Lukoil	Oil and gas	18.37	21.29	24.76	28.82	30	30
2	Gazprom	Oil and gas	14.75	15.61	18.49	18.92	6	5
3	Rosneft	Oil and gas	8.31	11.11	10.79	13.63	6	7
4	VEON	Telecom	6.20	6.76	7.95	8.01	56	50
5	RUSAL	Metallurgy	3.68	4.19	5.42	6.46	34	36
6	Sovcomflot	Transport	5.55	5.51	6.00	6.09	84	83
7	Atomenergoprom	Nuclear energy	3.77	4.07	5.71	5.46	12	10
8	Russian Railways	Transport	1.68	1.98	3.07	3.32	4	4
9	Evraz	Steel	2.13	1.88	3.71	3.17	40	32
10	NLMK	Metallurgy	1.35	1.34	2.92	2.53	29	24
11	EuroChem	Fertilizers	1.36	1.43	1.72	1.78	18	15
12	NordGold	Metallurgy	1.32	1.32	1.63	1.68	64	61
13	Russneft	Oil and gas	1.20	1.59	1.36	1.65	37	36
14	VSMPO-Avisma	Metallurgy	0.10	0.22	1.20	1.38	25	25
15	Zarubezhneft	Oil and gas	0.48	0.56	1.01	1.15	37	35
16	MegaFon	Telecom	0.20	0.52	0.24	1.02	3	9
17	TMK	Steel	0.90	0.28	1.93	0.83	38	15
18	Norilsk Nickel	Metallurgy	0.48	0.44	0.68	0.67	4	3
19	MMK	Metallurgy	0.33	0.32	0.53	0.50	7	6
20	AFK Sistema	Conglomerate	0.91	0.27	1.63	0.48	8	2
Total of the top 20			73.07	80.69	100.75	107.55		

Source Data courtesy of Alexander Kuznetsov, edited by the author. Please also refer to Kuznetsov (2021)

main shareholders. With the exception of state-owned entities (see below), they have rich individuals (commonly known as 'oligarchs') among their key shareholders.

13.5.2   *The Role of the State*

The list of the largest Russian MNEs includes four fully state-owned firms (Sovcomflot, Atomenergoprom, Russian Railways, and Zarubezhneft), as well as three companies in which the state holds significant shares (Gazprom, Rosneft, and VSMPO-Avisma). Together, these firms account for almost half of the assets of the top 20 group. However, the impact of the Russian government does not stop there. The bulk of the rest of the companies can be considered as state-influenced companies, in whose major strategic decisions the government has an informal say (Panibratov 2013). Historically, this was not always the case. In the 1990s, it was mostly the large firms that captured the state, influencing its policies. After 1999, the state gradually recovered the upper hand (see Chapter 7). It took back some of the assets (most notably from the company Yukos by state-owned Rosneft in 2004). In the case of the rest, the government changed its relationship with private owners, with the state gaining independence from and influence on those companies.

State ownership has advantages and disadvantages. The main advantage is that the state is expected to help out its firms if they find themselves in a difficult financial situation. In other words, the budget constraint of state-owned firms is supposed to be softer than that of privately owned firms, though in crisis conditions, the state may also help the latter. One disadvantage of state ownership is that the firm is supposed to have less management autonomy and may need to follow more closely government priorities in its business decisions. State ownership also has an ambiguous impact on the operations of firms abroad. In host countries with friendly relations with the country of origin, state backing may be an advantage, but in countries with less friendly relations, the attitude of host government countries may be more restrictive. They may treat state-influenced firms in the same way as state-owned firms.

13.6   Looking Forward

The COVID-19 crisis is not just another crisis. If it were the case, one could easily conclude that the foreign investment links of Russia are going to survive it as they did in the former crises. They were mostly of a financial nature. The current one affects the organisation of society and the economy globally.

The pandemic has accelerated three pre-existing trends, which would be very challenging for the Russian economy as a whole and its foreign investment links of the world (UNCTAD, 2020).

One of them is *digitalisation*. In the future, many activities will need fewer physical transactions and thus less FDI than before. The Russian economy has some bright spots but overall is a physical transaction-based economy with its dependence on natural resources.

The second is the adjustment to *environmental issues* and *climate change*. What remains of FDI will increasingly move towards producing 'sustainable' goods and services. That may be a major challenge not only for the large Russian MNEs based on fossil fuels, but also for inflows, although full transition to a carbon-neutral world will not happen overnight and so far, the appetite of emerging economies, especially China, for fossil fuels seems to be insatiable.

The third trend is towards increasing *economic nationalism* at the expense of multilateralism (see Chapter 12), which also affects policies towards foreign investment in all countries of the world. In this area, COVID-19 has exacerbated the recourse to national solutions, despite the calls of international organisations to do it differently and some rhetoric here and there. The Russian government has to navigate in the future in a rather fragmented world when trying to ensure the development benefits of foreign investment for the country. It is a large country but not with endless resources (see Chapters 1 and 2). Political relations with 7 of the top 10 economies of the world are quite tense, which do not augur well for foreign investment promotion. The Russian government needs to find a solution to leverage its development policies in the international arena in promoting not just investment but also its senior twin sister, trade (see Chapter 12).

In sum, it is not easy, though not fully impossible, to transform the current strengths of the Russian economy into levers for future competitiveness. Structural transformation from dependence on energy and raw materials is underway though data suggest rather slow progress so far (see Chapter 8). The country also has some technological strengths, but these have not yet transformed any part of the country into a global hub. As a recent example of missed opportunities in technological development, Russia could have transformed itself into a global centre of production for anti-COVID vaccines. However, its vaccine, though developed as the first in the world, did not receive the licence from the WHO for a long time because of murky administrative and documentation errors, and the country failed to scale up its productive capacity. The country would also need better institutions to deal with issues related to business (see Chapter 6). It also needs to negotiate a new place in the global political order, at least with the countries with which it has had its traditional foreign investment links. This is a very ambitious agenda but can be done. The future of foreign investment coming in and going out of Russia also hinges on the country's place in global political cooperation. The 2022 armed conflict in Ukraine does not bode well with that requirement. Indeed, that war may be a major blow to both types of investment.

Questions for Students
1. What are the main reasons for the low level of investment flows into and out of Russia compared with other major economies of the world?

2. Why are investment flows to and from Russia sensitive to developments in international politics?
3. What are the main differences between direct and portfolio investments from the point of view of development impact?
4. What are the main problems of foreign direct investment statistics in Russia?
5. Is the involvement of the Russian government beneficial for outward foreign direct investment?
6. How has the COVID-19 pandemic changed the prospects for foreign investment in the world and Russia?

References

Antaloczy, K., & Sass, M. (2015). Through a glass darkly: The content of statistical data on foreign direct investment. *Studies in International Economics: Special Issue of Kulgazdasag, 1*(1), 34–61. Accessed 7 January 2022. http://real.mtak.hu/29247/1/Antaloczy_Sass_Through_a_glass...Kulgazdasag_u.pdf

Casella, B. (2019). Looking through conduit FDI in search of ultimate investors—a probabilistic approach. *Transnational Corporations, 26*(1), 109–146. https://doi.org/10.18356/8a8b094c-en

Damgaard, J., Elkjaer, T., & Johannesen, N. (2019). The rise of phantom investments. *Finance & Development, 56*(3), 11–13. Accessed 7 January 2022. https://www.imf.org/external/pubs/ft/fandd/2019/09/pdf/the-rise-of-phantom-FDI-in-tax-havens-damgaard.pdf

Kalotay, K. (2012). Indirect FDI. *The Journal of World Investment & Trade, 13*(4), 542–555. https://doi.org/10.1163/221190012X649841

Kuznetsov, A. (2018). Metody otsenki pryamykh rossiyskikh investitsii za rubezhom (Assessment methods of direct Russian investment abroad). *Ekonomicheskaya nauka sovremennoy Rossii (Economic Science of Contemporary Russia), 4*(2018), 37–50. Accessed 7 January 2022. https://www.ecr-journal.ru/jour/article/view/333

Kuznetsov, A. (2021). Direct investment from Russia abroad: Changes since 2018. *Herald of the Russian Academy of Sciences, 91*, 700–707. https://doi.org/10.1134/S1019331621060162

Panibratov, A. (2013). *The Influence of the State on Expanding Russian MNEs: Advantage or Handicap?* Russie.Nei.Visions № 73, IFRI Russia/NIS Center, Paris. Accessed 7 January 2022. https://www.ifri.org/sites/default/files/atoms/files/ifriandreypanibratovrussiancompagniesengdecember2013.pdf

UNCTAD. (2000). *World investment report 2000: Cross-border mergers and acquisitions and development.* United Nations, New York—Geneva.

UNCTAD. (2002). *World Investment Report 2002: Transnational Corporations and Export Competitiveness.* United Nations, New York—Geneva.

UNCTAD. (2011). *World Investment Report 2011: Non-Equity Modes of International Production and Development.* United Nations, New York—Geneva.

UNCTAD. (2016). *World Investment Report 2016. Investor Nationality: Policy Challenges.* United Nations, New York—Geneva.

UNCTAD. (2020). *World Investment Report 2020: International Production Beyond the Pandemic*. United Nations, New York—Geneva.

CHAPTER 14

Sanctions and Forces Driving to Autarky

Marek Dabrowski and Svetlana Avdasheva

Highlights

- Economic sanctions introduced in 2014 by the United States (US), the European Union (EU), and other advanced economies, in response to the annexation of Crimea and the conflict in Donbas, together with Russia's domestic and international countermeasures, started the process of decoupling the Russian economy from global markets, reversing the earlier trend of global integration.
- Additional and much stronger sanctions came in response to Russia's invasion of Ukraine in February 2022. Similar to 2014, these sanctions were followed by retaliatory measures from Russia against 'unfriendly' countries, which also deepened the sanctions' negative effects on the Russian economy.

M. Dabrowski (✉)
Bruegel, Brussels, Belgium
e-mail: marek.dabrowski@bruegel.org

M. Dabrowski · S. Avdasheva
Higher School of Economics, Moscow, Russia
e-mail: avdash@hse.ru

M. Dabrowski
CASE—Center for Social and Economic Research, Warsaw, Poland

© The Author(s), under exclusive license to Springer Nature Switzerland AG 2023
M. Dabrowski (ed.), *The Contemporary Russian Economy*,
https://doi.org/10.1007/978-3-031-17382-0_14

- As a result of the sanctions and countersanctions, the Russian economy has become partly closed to the external world, less competitive, less innovative, and more autarkic. Quality of life will suffer and the costs of production will increase. Even if the Russian economy overcomes the sanction-related recession, its long-term growth trend will be slower as compared to a non-sanction scenario.
- Other effects of the sanctions and countersanctions will include the increasing role of the government in economic management, more state ownership, further deterioration of the business and investment climate, and more macroeconomic fragility.

14.1 Introduction

Since the second half of the 2000s, political relations between Russia and its Western[1] partners, in the first instance, the United States and the EU, have gradually deteriorated. Both caused by the Russian authorities' military and foreign policy decisions, two turning points dramatically accelerated this deterioration. First, in March 2014, Russia annexed Crimea, a part of the Ukrainian territory. It shortly after began to actively support the separatist movement in Donbas, which led to Ukrainian authorities losing control over approximately half of this region as well as the formation of two unrecognised territorial entities—the Donetsk and Luhansk People's Republics. Despite an international effort to end the conflict in eastern Ukraine (the two Minsk agreements signed on 5 September 2014 and 11 February 2015), it was never resolved. Second, on 24 February 2022, Russia started a military invasion of the Ukrainian territory (called in official Russian terminology a 'special military operation') that led to a full-scale war, which continues at the time of writing this chapter (May 2022).

The analysis of the geopolitical causes and dynamics of the conflict between Russia and its Western partners is beyond the thematic remit of this chapter. However, we will analyse its negative impact on economic relations between Russia and its major trade and investment partners, the functioning of the Russian economy, and, consequently, Russia's economic performance in the short, medium, and long run. Below, we present and analyse the first (2014) and second (2018) rounds of Western sanctions against Russia (Sect. 14.2), Russia's countersanctions and other policy response measures (Sect. 14.3), and estimates of their negative impact on the Russian economy (Sect. 14.4).[2] Then we move to the new, much more comprehensive and robust packages of sanctions following the invasion of Ukraine in February 2022 (Sect. 14.5) and Russia's response measures to these sanctions (Sect. 14.6). Finally, Sect. 14.7

---

[1] In this chapter, we use the adjective 'Western' in a broad geopolitical (membership in US- and EU-initiated alliances) rather than precise geographical sense (for example, Japan, Australia, and South Korea are not located west of Russia).

[2] The content of Sects. 15.2 and 15.4 partly draws from Dabrowski (2019).

attempts to assess the potential economic impact of the war and sanction/countersanction regime on the Russian economy from a short-, medium- and long-term perspective.

14.2 The 2014 and 2018 Rounds of Western Sanctions

The annexation of Crimea and Russia's engagement in the conflict in the Donbas region of Ukraine in 2014 triggered a series of international sanctions against Russia initiated by the US and the EU. To various degrees, Canada, Australia, Norway, Iceland, Switzerland, Japan, some EU candidate countries, and international organisations such as the European Bank for Reconstruction and Development (EBRD) joined the anti-Russian measures. Sanctions were put in place in 2014 and are still in force, subject to regular renewal (in the case of the EU) and updates (concerning the list of sanctioned individuals and companies).

The 2014 US and EU sanctions had a multipronged character,[3] involving four groups of measures (Russell, 2016): political/diplomatic (Tier 1), sanctions against individuals and entities (Tier 2), economic sanctions (Tier 3), and those related to Crimea.

The Tier 1 sanctions excluded Russia from the Group of Eight (G8). They suspended negotiations on Russia's accession to the Organisation for Economic Co-operation and Development and the International Energy Agency, a new EU-Russia treaty (which could include a free trade agreement), and EU-Russia visa liberalisation. They also stopped the semi-annual EU-Russia summits, the NATO-Russia cooperation, and the voting rights of the Russian delegation to the Parliamentary Assembly of the Council of Europe (this sanction was terminated in 2019).

The Tier 2 sanctions have been targeted against named individuals and companies, for example, those engaged in doing business in Crimea. Measures include visa bans and asset freezes. Russian public money has supported some affected companies to compensate for sanction-related losses.

In the economic sphere (Tier 3), sanctions have concentrated on three areas:

- A ban on medium- and long-term financing for the largest state-owned banks and companies;
- A ban on trade in military and dual-use equipment and some oil exploration and production equipment and services;

---

[3] See https://www.state.gov/ukraine-and-russia-sanctions/ for the list and content of US sanctions and https://www.consilium.europa.eu/en/policies/sanctions/restrictive-measures-against-russia-over-ukraine/history-restrictive-measures-against-russia-over-ukraine/ for the list and content of EU sanctions.

- A ban on trade, including tourism, travel, and communication services, with the annexed Crimea, and prohibition on the use of Crimean ports and involvement in investment activity in this territory.

In April 2018, the US adopted the Countering America's Adversaries Through Sanctions Act (CAATSA), which partly codified the existing sanctions and introduced new ones against selected Russian businesspeople and companies in response to Russia's alleged interference in the US 2016 presidential election. Another wave of US sanctions followed in August 2018 in response to the attempted assassination in the United Kingdom (UK) of a former Russian intelligence officer.

14.3 Russia's Policy Response in 2014 and the Following Years

In August 2014, the Government of the Russian Federation responded to the Western sanctions (see Sect. 14.2) with a ban on imports of most food products from countries that adopted sanctions against Russia. Imports of meat, milk products (especially cheese), fruits, and vegetables became the most affected. Geographically, food imports from European and especially Eastern European and Baltic states declined dramatically. Domestic consumers became the main losers (see Sect. 14.4), while domestic agricultural and food producers were the leading gainers. The food imports embargo meant the implementation of much earlier proposals of an agriculture lobby for more robust protection against imports, justified on the grounds of the country's food security (Korhonen et al., 2018).

Since 2014, Russia has also started to introduce a series of economic sanctions against Ukraine, the most significant being revoking the bilateral free trade agreement (FTA) on 1 January 2016 (in response to the entry into force of the EU-Ukraine FTA). To have a complete picture, one should also mention Ukraine's sanctions against Russia, such as banning direct passenger flights between Russia and Ukraine in October 2015 (Rainfords, 2015) and the energy and transport blockade of Crimea in November 2015 (Olearchyk & Farchy, 2015).

The Russian government also has extended restrictions on non-resident ownership in some sectors, for example, the media and industries that may be important for national defence and security. These restrictions came on top of those before 2014 and related to investment in natural resources and the financial sector, gas supply, and transportation via pipelines, medical equipment, and telecommunication, among others (European Commission, 2020). The government also tightened entry rules for incoming foreign investment (see Chapter 13) and several other regulations, such as public procurement (European Commission, 2020), international cooperation of non-government research institutions, and civil society organisations.

The reaction to Western sanctions and the increasing geopolitical confrontation with the West also led to a substantial reorientation of the entire economic policy. Earlier measures aimed at achieving competitiveness in global markets were replaced by initiatives to reduce dependence on foreign partners and international institutions, financed by the rents generated by traditional export markets. This strategy was implemented via an increasing interference of the government into business activity.

The postponement (or explicit refusal) of liberal economic reform became the most prominent feature of economic policy after 2014. No further liberalisation of regulated markets, no liberalisation of electricity prices, no reform of the financial and banking system, and no profound changes in the administrative regime or administrative control were undertaken.

Economic policy goals were shifted from diversification of economic structure, improvement of investment climate, and integration in the global economy to support for disintegration, the continuing promotion of traditional mineral export, and import substitution. It tried to support domestic producers in manufacturing and resource industries through tax incentives, government subsidies, investment support, export taxes and quotas (to decrease the domestic prices of many critical inputs), and preferences for domestic suppliers in public procurement, including purchases by state-owned and regulated companies (European Commission, 2020). An import-substitution policy and the associated economic, financial, and legal support to domestic producers contributed to building and strengthening various sectoral and industrial lobbies and helped them to capture government policies (Connolly & Hanson, 2016). Import-substitution programmes have also led to additional fiscal and quasi-fiscal costs and trade distortions, and often they have contradicted Russia's commitments to the World Trade Organization (WTO).

Several policy measures aimed to avoid, or at least reduce, the Russian economy's critical dependence on decisions taken abroad and potential new sanctions, increasing Russia's self-sufficiency.

One of the key actions to increase the country's 'economic security' focused on reforming the cashless payment system. In 2015, a national payment card system under the control of the Central Bank of the Russian Federation (CBRF) began to process all cashless transactions in Russia. The payment card 'MIR' (*peace* or *world* in the Russian language) was introduced and quickly expanded its scale of operations, among others, due to its use for payments from public funds. At the end of 2021, the share of the MIR payment system expanded to more than 25% of cashless payments in Russia, and its centralised national processing diminished the threats of the interruption of global payment systems.

The government has also tried to achieve digital independence by supporting Russian-born digital platforms in domestic markets. From 2014 to 2021, several remedies on Google were imposed to support Russian Yandex to promote digital services. From 2021, a rule on the compulsory pre-instalment of Russian applications to all devices sold in Russia is in force. In 2019, the Federal Assembly adopted a law to create a separate 'Russian Internet' (*Runet*).

Import-substitution policies and associated protectionist measures (usually having a non-tariff character) led to a response from Russia's trade partners. For example, the European Commission applied several anti-dumping procedures against Russian exporters of chemical and ferrous metal products (European Commission, 2020; see Chapter 12). As a result, non-tariff measures increased from both sides: Russia and its trade partners (European Commission, 2020).

Since 2014, Russia has refrained from re-establishing or promoting international trade with European countries, announcing a strategy to increase economic cooperation and exchange with Asia. However, the actual geography and structure of commodity exports and imports have changed very slowly, and the share of oil and natural gas in total exports further increased. In 2020, the EU remained the largest trade partner. The only destination with increasing Russian exports is China, but overall export volume in 2021 was still one-third lower than exports to Europe (USD 140 billion against USD 218 billion).

The Government of Russia also announced changes in the priorities for budget expenditures and the management of public programmes. Twelve government programmes along three priorities named 'Quality of Economic Environment', 'Economic Growth', and 'Human Capital Development', accounting for about 12% of annual budget expenditure, were initiated. Among these 12 priority programmes launched in 2019, nearly half of the expenses are allocated for infrastructure: roads, railroads, and energy. Substantial funds were spent on the social benefit programmes within the Human Capital Development programme. This spending increased during the COVID-19 pandemic in 2020–2021, exceeding the pre-2014 level.

14.4 Economic Impact of the First Two Rounds of Sanctions and Countersanctions

Assessing the impact on the Russian economy of the first two rounds (2014 and 2018) of sanctions and countersanctions is not an easy task because of the difficulty of disentangling their effects from other factors, such as the collapse of the oil price and other commodity prices in mid-2014 (Korhonen et al., 2018). Furthermore, most of the quantitative assessments were done during the early stage of sanctions implementation (2014–2016), and some of them were based on *ex-ante* forecasting rather than *ex-post* analysis.

Some early estimates (for example, Kholodilin & Netsunajev, 2016) found an annual negative impact ranging from 1 to 2% of gross domestic product (GDP). Gurvich and Prilepskiy (2015) estimated the cumulative loss of

Russian GDP from Western financial sanctions at 6% of GDP for 2014–2017. Bloomberg Economics obtained a similar result (cumulative 6%) for 2014–2018 (Doff, 2018).

The International Monetary Fund (IMF, 2015, p. 5) estimated the initial negative impact of sanctions between 1.0% and 1.5% of Russian GDP, with a long-term cumulative effect of up to 9% of GDP. However, in its later report (IMF, 2019, p. 58), it gave a much lower estimate: sanctions were to be responsible for 0.2 percentage points (pp) of GDP lower annual growth in comparison with the IMF 2013 World Economic Outlook (WEO) projection. This is in line with Pestova and Mamonov's (2019) estimates.

The World Bank (2016, p. 40) estimated that removing sanctions would increase forecasted GDP growth in 2017 by 0.9 pp (from 1.1 to 2%) because of the boost to investment and consumer confidence. However, the forecasted growth rate would remain unchanged in subsequent years because of other factors unrelated to sanctions, limiting Russia's growth potential.

Overall, the latest estimates based on actual data series gave lower estimates of growth losses (due to sanctions) than earlier estimates based on forecasting models.

Regarding the Russian countersanctions, Volchkova et al. (2018) estimated that they were responsible for an average annual loss of RUB 2,000 (about USD 30) per Russian consumer, or 0.00036% of Russian GDP per capita in 2014. Russian producers captured 63% of this amount, and non-sanctioned exporters, in particular from Belarus, took 26%. The remaining 10% constituted a deadweight loss.

None of the available studies measured the potential impact of the 2018 US CAATSA sanctions.

Overall, the sanctions and countersanctions aggravated the 2014–2016 currency crisis and recession (see Chapters 15 and 16). In 2014–2015, financial sanctions were particularly painful. By suddenly closing off the international financial market to large state-controlled companies such as Rosneft, Novatek, and Gazprom, the sanctions forced the Russian authorities, including the CBRF, to rescue them. This caused an additional diminution of the CBRF's international reserves and a depletion of National Wealth Fund (NWF) assets. Financial sanctions also triggered large-scale capital outflows from Russia in 2014–2015 (see Chapters 13 and 16). Therefore, they added to the market panic and the collapse of the rouble exchange rate in December 2014 and early 2015.

Beyond the effects of the sanctions, the Ukrainian conflict involved other direct and indirect costs for Russia, such as higher military spending, human losses, the social costs of refugee flows, and aid of various kinds to rebel-controlled territories, among others. Increased military expenditure crowds out expenditure on other public services, in particular education and health care, negatively contributing to potential economic growth, an argument frequently raised in Russian economic debates (Kudrin & Knobel, 2018; Kudrin & Sokolov, 2017).

The termination of the free trade regime with Ukraine and the various restrictions initiated by both sides of the conflict (see Sect. 14.2) hurt economic growth in both countries—more significant in Ukraine, more minor but still considerable in Russia (given the different sizes of both economies).

In addition, there have been substantial costs of integrating Crimea into the Russian economy. The costliest investment project was the construction of the Crimea Bridge over the Strait of Kerch, between the Kerch Peninsula (part of the Crimean Peninsula) and the Taman Peninsula in Krasnodarsky Krai (part of the Russian mainland), which was opened in May 2018. Its length is over 18 kms, and the total construction cost was in the region of USD 4 billion.

Aslund (2018) estimated the cost of integrating Crimea and providing support to occupied Donbas at USD 4 billion or 0.3% of Russia's GDP, not including the construction costs of the Crimea Bridge.

14.5 The 2022 Round of Western Sanctions

The military invasion of Ukraine launched on 24 February 2022 triggered an unprecedented wave of sanctions against Russia initiated by the US, EU, the UK, Canada, Japan, Australia, and several other countries. When writing this chapter, the war in Ukraine continues, and new sanctions are added to those introduced earlier. Below, we present a summary of the adopted and planned sanctions as of 15 May 2022.[4]

As in the case of the 2014 sanctions, they address various sectors and areas of relations with Russia and target different subjects (individuals, institutions of the Russian state, businesses, and banks, among others). However, they have much broader coverage and are more robust than those adopted eight years earlier.

14.5.1 Individual Sanctions

The US, EU, the UK, and other countries have sanctioned more than 1,000 Russian individuals and businesses, including top government officials and their families, members of the State Duma and National Security Council, military and security commanders involved in atrocities in Ukraine, key businesspeople close to the Kremlin (the 'oligarchs'), and others. For example, the sixth package of EU sanctions discussed in the first half of May 2022 includes a list of 58 individuals.

Individual sanctions involve visa bans and personal asset freezes in most cases.

---

[4] See https://www.bbc.com/news/world-europe-60125659, https://www.consilium.europa.eu/en/policies/sanctions/restrictive-measures-against-russia-over-ukraine/sanctions-against-russia-explained/, https://home.treasury.gov/policy-issues/financial-sanctions/sanctions-programs-and-country-information/ukraine-russia-related-sanctions.

14.5.2 Financial Sanctions

Financial sanctions involve a ban on transactions with the CBRF and the freezing of its assets (this affected approximately one-half of Russia's international reserves). They cut seven Russian banks off the Society for Worldwide Interbank Financial Telecommunication (SWIFT). They also banned the supply of euro-denominated banknotes to Russia and deposits to cryptowallets. They restrict the access of Russian banks, enterprises, and individuals to the capital and financial markets of the US, EU, and the UK. The US government also barred Russian entities from using their assets held in US banks to repay their debts.

The EU restricted financial and non-financial support to Russian publicly owned or controlled entities under the EU, Euratom, and Member States programmes.

In its sixth sanctions package, the EU plans to disconnect an additional three Russian banks from the SWIFT system.

14.5.3 Energy Sanctions

The US banned all oil and natural gas imports from Russia, and the UK will stop oil imports from Russia by the end of 2022. The EU is discussing the same measure. In August 2022, the EU will also stop coal imports from Russia. There is a broad debate within the EU about a substantial reduction of its natural gas imports from Russia.

Germany has finally suspended the opening of the Nord Stream 2 gas pipeline from Russia. This investment project raised a lot of political controversy within the EU and its relations with the US.

New sanctions also involve a ban on exports to Russia of goods and technologies in the oil refining sector and new investments in the Russian energy sector.

14.5.4 Trade Sanctions

Apart from sanctions related to energy trade (see Section 14.5.3), the EU imposed an embargo on importing iron, steel, wood, cement, rubber products, seafood, spirits, and liquor from Russia. The UK has imposed a 35% duty on some imports from Russia.

On the export side, the US, EU, and the UK have banned selling dual-use goods (which may serve both civilian and military purposes) to Russia. The respective list includes, among others, drones and software for drones, software for encryption devices, semiconductors, and advanced electronics. The EU and UK have also prohibited exporting some luxury goods to Russia.

The EU prohibited all Russian nationals and entities from participating in procurement contracts.

On 15 March 2022, the EU, in cooperation with other G7 partners, stopped treating Russia as a Most Favoured Nation according to WTO rules. In this way, Russia lost a substantial part of its membership rights and privileges in this organisation.

14.5.5 Transportation Sanctions

Transportation sanctions include the closure of EU, US, UK, and Canadian airspace to all Russian-owned, registered, or controlled aircraft. The airspace closure accompanies the ban on exports, sales, supply, or transfer of all aircraft, aircraft parts, and equipment to Russia and the provision of all related repair, maintenance, or financial services. Similar bans concern goods, technology, and services exports in the maritime and space sectors.

The countries mentioned above also closed their seaports to Russian vessels. The EU banned Russian road transport operators.

14.5.6 Media Sanctions

The first round of media sanctions included a ban on all forms of broadcasting of Russia Today and Sputnik. In its sixth sanctions package, the EU considers adding three main Russian television channels to this list.

14.5.7 Diplomatic Sanctions

Diplomatic sanctions included suspension of the EU-Russia visa facilitation agreement concerning Russian diplomats and other Russian officials and businesspeople and a reduction in the number of diplomatic staff in Russian embassies and consulates. Russia has also been suspended from the United Nations Human Rights Council and excluded from the Council of Europe.

14.5.8 Withdrawal from Russia and Spontaneous Boycott

Besides official sanctions, Russia as a country and Russian residents have become the subject of spontaneous international boycotts in various spheres, including sport, culture, scientific cooperation, and various forms of business activity. For example, by mid-May 2022, more than 1,000 international companies had either suspended or completely stopped their activities in Russia. This list includes, among others, 3 M, Acer, Adidas, Amazon, Apple, Asus, AXA, BMW, British Petroleum, Canon, Chevron, Daimler Truck, Decathlon, DHL, Deloitte, Deutsche Telekom, Dr. Oetker, Equinor, Exxon, Ernst & Young, FedEx, Fitch, Ford, Heineken, Henkel, Honda, Hyundai, Ikea, JYSK, KONE, KPMG, Maersk, McDonald's, McKinsey, Michelin, Mitsubishi, Moody's, Netflix, Nokia, OBI, Oracle, Panasonic, PwC,

Renault, Samsung, Schneider Electric, Shell, Siemens, Skoda, Spotify, Starbucks, TikTok, Uber, UPS, Volkswagen, and Volvo.[5]

Various considerations justified the decisions of individual companies: difficulties in continuing business in the environment of sanctions, countersanctions, partial inconvertibility of the rouble, the expected economic downturn in Russia, political arguments, and public relations motives, among others.

14.6 Russia's Response Measures to the 2022 Sanctions

Initiating a war in Ukraine, Russian authorities had to expect tough sanctions from the US and EU as Ukrainian allies. However, no one could perfectly predict what would be the exact content of the sanction measures and how tough, deep, and effective they would be. Consequently, most of the response measures (except those taken earlier to increase self-reliance in such areas as the payment system and digital sphere—see Sect. 14.3) were taken in reaction to the concrete sanction decisions presented in Sect. 14.5. These measures can be divided into four groups: (i) short-term stabilisation tools; (ii) support for aggregate demand and supply; (iii) retaliation (countersanctions) measures; and (iv) sectoral measures to compensate cuts in imports and the withdrawal of foreign direct investment.

14.6.1 Short-Term Stabilisation Measures

In the first month of the war, the Russian authorities' primary and most visible attempts were concentrated on preventing a banking and currency crisis. From the end of February, by mid-March, Russia introduced highly restrictive monetary policy instruments and restrictions on rouble convertibility. The CBRF increased its policy rate more than twice—from 9.5 to 20%. Exporters had to convert 80% of their export revenues into roubles (surrender requirements).

According to the new regulations, Russian residents were restricted from getting credit contracts with non-residents (special approval was necessary for new contracts). They also became obliged to register accounts in banks outside Russia. Russian debtors became obliged to repay debt obligations above RUB 10 million monthly (according to the current CBRF exchange rate) in roubles, irrespective of the currency of the contracts (exceptions could be allowed by the Ministry of Finance). In retail banking, withdrawals from individual currency deposits and transfers abroad were restricted to USD 10 thousand. In April and May 2022, some of the above restrictions (timing of conversion of export revenues and rules of buying currency in cash, among others) were partly relaxed, and the key CBRF policy rate was cut to 14%.

---

[5] https://som.yale.edu/story/2022/almost-1000-companies-have-curtailed-operations-russia-some-remain?company=Coca+Cola&country=.

These regulations are considered Russian retaliation to Western sanctions, but they hurt every foreign investor in Russia on a non-discriminatory basis, being an instrument of capital control. Until the end of 2022, Russian residents are prohibited from buying shares in any non-resident company or making payments to any non-resident under joint venture agreements unless they obtain a special permit from the CBRF. For specific contracts with non-residents, Russian residents are prohibited from making advance payments exceeding 30% of the sum of their obligations under the contract. Professional brokers in Russia are prohibited from selling securities on behalf of non-Russian companies or individuals. The issuance and trading outside of Russia of depositary receipts representing shares of Russian companies are not permitted (this means automatic de-listing from foreign stock exchanges). Russian corporations are obliged to terminate their respective agreements so that the depositary receipts are converted into underlying shares that can be traded only in Russia.

All these measures have mitigated capital flight from Russia. Capital outflow from Russia during the first quarter of 2022 amounted to USD 64 billion, which is slightly less than during the entire 2021 (USD 72 billion). When writing this chapter, annual capital outflows in 2022 are expected to be comparable with the outflows of 2008 and 2015.

14.6.2 Support for Aggregate Demand and Supply

The partial inconvertibility of the rouble will further deteriorate the business and investment climate (see Chapter 6) and, therefore, contribute to the deterioration of economic performance. Still, it provides more room for manoeuvring domestic fiscal and monetary policies in the short term. This allowed, among others, the weakening of the budgetary discipline rules (see Chapter 16). The fiscal rule on accumulating extra revenues from oil exports (above the threshold oil price) in the NWF was suspended. The government obtained the right to spend these additional revenues (if they occur) with high discretion. This allows the implementation of expansionary fiscal policies and applying demand-targeted and supply-targeted measures.

Demand-targeted measures include subsidising mortgages, applying negative effective interest rates to particular groups of domestic debtors, and the further extension of social expenditures.

Supply-targeted measures include easing administrative burdens and deferred tax payments. In monitoring and control, the government introduced a moratorium on regular inspections (except those related to health and safety), automatically renews most permissions, and simplifies and speeds up certification and compliance procedures.

The relaxation of the prudential regulation of Russian banks complemented the expansionary fiscal measures. This includes a moratorium on the capital adequacy requirements determined by the Basel-3 rules. The amount of credit provided to small and medium-sized enterprises without specific financial audits increased five times.

Among two groups of measures, demand-oriented ones prevail, desired to compensate for money outflow from Russian markets and to mitigate the expected decline in nominal GDP.

14.6.3 Retaliation (Countersanction) Measures

The reaction of the Russian government to Western sanctions adopted in February 2022 (see Sect. 14.5) was similar to that in 2014. It followed the tradition of symmetric response by adopting retaliatory measures against 'unfriendly' states, that is, countries that joined anti-Russian sanctions (despite their damaging impact on the Russian economy).

The most important and potentially influential countermeasure is the decision which obliges purchasers of Russian natural gas from 'unfriendly' countries to pay in roubles. The 'rouble payment rule' makes it mandatory for buyers to register a special account in Gazprombank and deposit the payment in the contract currency (euro or dollar) which would be converted into roubles by this bank. The proclaimed reason for this rule is the desire to evade sanctions technically. The purchase of roubles is expected to support the exchange rate and provide funds for the additional budget expenditure due to changes in fiscal rules (see Section 14.6.2). However, payments in roubles as a strategic instrument of Russian trade policies were discussed and designed long before 2022. One of the objectives was to discourage using US dollars in trade transactions. However, it was never achieved because residents and non-residents lacked interest in using the rouble as a transaction currency. Last but not the least, payments in roubles are expected to promote market segmentation for gas supply and potentially for other commodities.

Another retaliation instrument is the refusal to protect intellectual property rights (IPR) owned by residents of 'unfriendly' states. Inventions, utility models, or industrial designs are to be used for zero compensation without the consent of the rights holders.

The Government of the Russian Federation has also introduced an export ban on more than 200 products until the end of 2022, including telecoms; medical, vehicle, agricultural, and electrical equipment; and timber.[6]

It blocked interest payments to foreign investors who hold government bonds and banned Russian firms from paying dividends to foreign shareholders. It also prohibited foreign owners of Russian stocks and bonds from selling them.

Reciprocity measures were also adopted in the transportation sector. Russia closed its airspace and seaports to carriers and vessels from 'unfriendly' countries.

---

[6] See https://www.bbc.com/news/business-60689279.

The few Western and independent domestic media, including social networks and Internet outlets, that still operated in Russia at the beginning of 2022 were prohibited and cut off from broadcasting once the war started. Heavy criminal penalties were introduced for spreading supposedly false information—that is, information contradicting official government information and its interpretation of events.

Several drafts of legal documents that allow the direct confiscation of property of foreign owners are under consideration, including a draft bill on the 'external' administration of companies closing their business in Russia and the right to confiscate the property of 'unfriendly' countries and the persons associated with them. According to another draft bill, Russian banks are to be prohibited from providing information on clients and their transactions upon the request of any non-Russian authorities without the prior consent of Russian authorities. However, it remains unclear which of these drafts will be adopted, when, and in which form.

14.6.4 Sectoral Measures to Compensate for the Withdrawal of Imports and FDI

The exit of several foreign companies from Russia (see Section 14.5.8) will destroy technological ties and, therefore, put the functioning of the Russian economy under threat. Two types of measures were undertaken to mitigate the danger of technological unbundling. First, for particular import groups, import tariffs were reduced to zero. In addition, parallel imports (imports without the prior consent of the IPR-holder) were allowed for technological equipment for selected industries (including mining, energy, railroads and shipping, and agriculture), auto components and car engines, computers and smartphones, pharmaceuticals, and cosmetics. The intention is to evade sanctions for the producers of branded goods.

The second group of measures focuses on import substitution. The NWF is expected to be used for these purposes, for example, through subsidised credit programmes.

The policy to stop a brain drain from Russia is another form of policy response. In particular, a support programme was offered to companies and professionals in the information technologies (IT) sector. Until 2025, Russian IT companies are exempted from the profit tax and all forms of foreign exchange control, and they could obtain subsidised credits. There is a programme for IT professionals working in Russia, offering them mortgage credits with a near-zero interest rate (negative in real terms) and exempting them from mandatory military service.

There is a substantial overlap between the measures addressing different targets. Restrictions on capital outflows (i) hurt companies from 'unfriendly states' (iii) and every foreign investor in Russia. The 'gas for roubles' scheme was considered the most painful retaliatory measure (iii), but it also helped to stabilise the domestic financial market (i), which is necessary to stimulate aggregate demand (ii). By allowing parallel imports and removing the protection of IPR of 'unfriendly' state residents, the government tries to prevent shortages of critical goods and services in the domestic market (iv). However, it also penalises the companies which left Russia (iii).

14.7 Impact of Sanctions and Geopolitical Confrontation on Russia's Economic Development

When writing this chapter, it is impossible to forecast how extensive the economic damage would be to the Russian economy coming from the war in Ukraine, sanctions, countersanctions introduced in 2022, and other policy measures adopted by the Russian authorities in response to the new situation. In its April 2022 WEO, the IMF (2022) forecasts Russia's negative growth of real GDP at -8.5% in 2022 and -2.3% in 2023, inflation jumping to 24% at the end of 2022, and a deep contraction in imports and exports.

Going beyond quantitative forecasts, which are speculative and uncertain by their nature, qualitative changes in the Russian economic system and policies seem even more critical. Many of them will likely remain in force for a long time, even if the reasons for their introduction disappear. Below, we try to outline the most important of them:

- The disintegration of the Russian economy from the global economy. This may lead to the loss of a substantial part of the productivity gains obtained from trade, investment, and financial liberalisation since the 1990s (see Chapters 12, 13, and 15). The Russian economy will become partly closed to the external world, less competitive, less innovative, and more autarkic. Quality of life will suffer and the costs of production will increase. China, India, Turkey, South Africa, and some other developing economies that have not joined anti-Russian sanctions cannot substitute the US, EU, and other advanced economies as technology suppliers critical to continuing Russia's economic modernisation. Nor can Russia's domestic research and innovation sector fill the knowledge and technology gap.
- An increasing role of the government in managing the economy and a weakening of the role of the market mechanism. Sectoral import-substitution programmes with accompanying financial incentives and administrative support measures will inevitably lead to more structural, microeconomic, and social distortions.
- The increasing role of the government in economic management and Russia's decoupling from the global economy will further deteriorate the already poor business and investment climate (see Chapter 6). Geopolitical confrontation with the West and the atmosphere of war will also further increase the role of security and law enforcement agencies, reducing areas of economic and civil freedom.

- Although, until May 2022, the government refrained from the large-scale expropriation of foreign owners, the share of state-owned enterprises in the Russian economy (see Chapter 7) will inevitably increase due to the exit of foreign shareholders. The government may use the resources of the NWF for these purposes, including buying back the shares of foreign owners.
- The fragile macroeconomic stability (see Chapter 16) may deteriorate due to higher budget expenditures for supporting business activity and import substitution, military and security purposes, social programmes, and lower revenue (due to the recession and energy sector-related sanctions). Although a currency crisis in March 2022 (the depreciation of the domestic currency by more than 20% against the USD) was partly mitigated, thanks to capital controls and a dramatic hike in the CBRF policy rate (see Subsection 14.6.1), the rouble will remain vulnerable to new potential shocks. They may originate, for example, from lower international energy prices or new economic and financial sanctions.

Questions for students

1. What were the causes of the Western sanctions against Russia introduced in 2014, 2018, and 2022?
2. Please characterise the content of the sanction packages in 2014, 2018, and 2022.
3. How has Russia responded to the sanctions (in terms of retaliation measures against the countries which introduced sanctions and domestic policy adjustment)?
4. Please assess the negative impact of the 2014 sanctions on the Russian economy.
5. What will be the most likely economic consequences of the 2022 sanctions in the short, medium, and long terms?

References

Aslund, A. (2018). The Toll of Putin's Wars. Project Syndicate, 3 September. https://www.project-syndicate.org/commentary/cost-of-wars-for-russia-by-anders-aslund-2018-09

Connolly, R., & Hanson, P. (2016). *Import Substitution and Economic Sovereignty in Russia. Research Paper*. Russia and Eurasia Programme, Chatham House. https://www.chathamhouse.org/sites/default/files/publications/research/2016-06-09-import-substitution-russia-connolly-hanson.pdf

Dabrowski, M. (2019). Factors determining Russia's long-term growth rate. *Russian Journal of Economics*, 5(4), 328–353. https://rujec.org/article/49417/download/pdf/366392

Doff, N. (2018). Here's One Measure That Shows Sanctions on Russia are Working. Bloomberg, 16 November. https://www.bloomberg.com/news/articles/2018-11-16/here-s-one-measure-that-shows-sanctions-on-russia-are-working

European Commission. (2020). Commission Staff Working Document on significant distortions in the economy of the Russian Federation for the purposes of trade defence investigations. European Commission, Brussels. https://trade.ec.europa.eu/doclib/docs/2020/october/tradoc_158997.pdf

Gurvich. E., & Prilepskiy, I. (2015). The impact of financial sanctions on the Russian economy. *Russian Journal of Economics, 1*(4), 359–385. https://rujec.org/article/27956/

IMF. (2015). *Russian federation: Staff report for the 2015 Article IV Consultation. IMF Country Report 15/211.* International Monetary Fund, Washington DC. https://www.imf.org/~/media/Websites/IMF/imported-full-text-pdf/external/pubs/ft/scr/2015/_cr15211.ashx

IMF. (2019). *Russian Federation: 2019 Article IV Consultation-Press Release; Staff Report. IMF Country Report 19/260.* International Monetary Fund, Washington DC. https://www.imf.org/-/media/Files/Publications/CR/2019/1RUSEA2019001.ashx

IMF. (2022). *World Economic Outlook, April 2022: War Sets Back the Global Recovery.* International Monetary Fund, Washington DC. https://www.imf.org/-/media/Files/Publications/WEO/2022/April/English/text.ashx

Kholodilin, K.A., & Netsunajev, A. (2016). *Crimea and Punishment: The Impact of Sanctions on Russian and European Economies. DIW Berlin Discussion Papers 1569.* German Institute for Economic Research. http://www.diw.de/documents/publikationen/73/diw_01.c.530645.de/dp1569.pdf

Korhonen, I., Simola, H., & Solanko, L. (2018). Sanctions and countersanctions – Effects on economy, trade and finance. *Focus on European Economic Integration, Q3*, 68–76. Oesterreichische Nationalbank. https://www.oenb.at/dam/jcr:d45f7129-94eb-48f4-b4d7-e715d88c224a/06_Sanctions_and_countersanctions_feei_2018_q3.pdf

Kudrin, A., & Knobel, A. (2018). Russian budget structure efficiency: Empirical study. *Russian Journal of Economics, 4*(3), 197–214. https://rujec.org/article/30163/download/pdf/

Kudrin, A., & Sokolov, I. (2017). Fiscal maneuver and restructuring of the Russian economy. *Russian Journal of Economics, 3*(3), 221–239. https://rujec.org/article/27990/download/pdf/

Olearchyk ,R., & Farchy, J. (2015). Ukraine imposes economic blockade on a blacked-out Crimea. *Financial Times*, 23 November. https://www.ft.com/content/d5487eaa-9203-11e5-bd82-c1fb87bef7af

Pestova, A., & Mamonov, M. (2019). Should we care? The economic effects of financial sanctions on the Russian economy. BOFIT Discussion Papers 13/2019. https://doi.org/10.2139/ssrn.3428854

Rainfords, S. (2015). Ban due on direct flights between Russia and Ukraine. *BBC News*, 24 October. http://www.bbc.com/news/world-europe-34622665

Russell, M. (2016). Sanctions over Ukraine: Impact on Russia. Members' Research Service. European Parliamentary Research Service, PE 579.084. http://www.europarl.europa.eu/RegData/etudes/BRIE/2016/579084/EPRS_BRI(2016)579084_EN.pdf

Volchkova, N., Kuznetsova, P., & Turdyeva, N. (2018). Losers and Winners of Russian Countersanctions: A welfare analysis. Free Network Policy Brief Series, October. https://freepolicybriefs.org/2018/10/01/losers-and-winners-of-russian-countersanctions-a-welfare-analysis/

World Bank. (2016). Russia Economic Report: The Long Journey to Recovery, No. 35, April. The World Bank Group, Washington, DC. http://documents.worldbank.org/curated/en/657991467989516696/pdf/104825-NWP-P156290-PUBLIC-WB-RER-No-35-FINAL-ENG.pdf

PART VI

Economic and Social Policy Challenges

CHAPTER 15

Economic Growth

Ilya Voskoboynikov

Highlights

- Since 1990, economic growth in Russia has been volatile. The transformational recession, with a sharp output fall (−8.4% in 1990–1995), was followed by a post-transition recovery (6% growth in 2001–2005) and a long stagnation (1.7% in 2011–2019). These three periods differ in terms of the main sources of growth.
- The transformational recession of 1990–1998 was caused mostly by a fall in productivity, caused by initial disorganisation and mass disinvestments.
- Outstanding growth during the post-transition recovery was fuelled by the unique combination of favourable factors such as investment inflows not only from oil and gas export revenues but also from global integration. This included foreign direct investment (FDI) and technology catching up in manufacturing and financial services. Furthermore, new imported machinery and information and communication technologies enhanced growth.
- The stagnation of the 2010s was largely explained by the fall in productivity in oil and gas against the backdrop of the lost momentum for

I. Voskoboynikov (✉)
HSE University, Moscow, Russia
e-mail: ivoskoboynikov@hse.ru

© The Author(s), under exclusive license to Springer Nature Switzerland AG 2023
M. Dabrowski (ed.), *The Contemporary Russian Economy*,
https://doi.org/10.1007/978-3-031-17382-0_15

technology catching up in manufacturing. This was partially compensated by capital contributions from oil and gas and some small positive productivity contributions from manufacturing.
- Intensive structural change with the reallocation of economic activities from goods to market services was primarily growth-enhancing. However, the substantial share of oil and gas in the economy makes growth dependent on the volatile productivity of mining.
- In the future, sustainable growth depends on the success of diversification.

15.1 Introduction

Since 1990, Russian economic growth has been volatile. The transformational recession (1990–1998), with its sharp fall in output to a level of 59% in 1990, was followed by a fast recovery (1999–2007) with soaring growth of almost 7% per year, overperforming most economies in the world, and a decade of stagnation (2008–2019), with average growth rates below 1.5%. How can one understand this growth pattern and, possibly, outline growth prospects for the future? Many people think that Russian growth depends heavily on oil and gas exports. If so, why was there high growth during 1999–2007, when oil prices were just around USD 40 per barrel, while the stagnation of 2011–2019 corresponds to prices of USD 80?

The explanation, which the present chapter suggests, comes down to the interaction of three fundamental groups of factors—*geography*, *institutions* and *trade*. Geography includes rich natural resources, such as gas, oil, metals, land and other resources for agriculture, and its large territory, which makes Russia attractive as a bridge between the European market and South-East Asia, and dependent on transport infrastructure (see Chapter 1). Institutions include Russia's Soviet legacy (see Chapter 4), the intensive transformations of the 1990s, the business environment and corruption (see Chapters 6 and 8), and regional institutional diversity (see Chapter 11). Trade and openness are also important for growth. Since the early 1990s, Russia has been deeply integrated into the global economy (see Chapter 12). Openness has created new opportunities, such as FDI inflow (see Chapter 13), the enhancement of technology catching up, access to global investment resources, and opportunities for Russian firms to integrate into global value chains. The other side of the coin is that openness makes Russia much more sensitive to changes in terms of trade, shocks in global financial markets and global crises, such as the global financial crisis (GFC) of 2008–2009 and the ongoing consequences of the COVID-19 pandemic's shock to the global economy.

The conceptual framework for this chapter (see Fig. 15.2) follows the growth literature[1] and suggests two levels of analysis. First, it links the three

---

[1] See, for example, the textbook of Weil (2013). In a condensed form, it is also presented by Rodrik (2003).

fundamental groups of factors, geography, institutions, and trade, with factor endowments—labour, physical and human capital, and total factor productivity (TFP). Second, factor endowments form growth. The representation of aggregate real value growth rates as the sum of the contributions of labour, capital, and TFP refers to *growth accounting* (Sect. 15.4).

The chapter begins with two sections providing an overview of Russian growth (Sect. 15.2) and structural change (Sect. 15.3) over three decades (1990–2019) from a comparative perspective. These sections introduce three periods of Russian growth, put them in the context of global development, and discuss shifts in industrial structure and labour quality. The following three sections cover Russia's three stages of growth: the transformational recession (Sect. 15.4), the post-transition recovery (Sect. 15.5), and the stagnation (Sect. 15.6), focusing on the specificity of each period. The final Sect. 15.7, concludes, by comparing the three periods and summarising the main features of Russia's growth pattern.

15.2 The Global Economy and Russia During 1990–2019: An Overview

Russia is an important part of the global economy. Before its economic transition, the Soviet Union was involved in international trade and adapted advanced technologies from the West (Gregory & Stuart, 2001, Chapters 8 and 12). Since the early 1990s, along with trade and much more intensive technology transfer, Russia integrated into global financial markets, Russian enterprises gained access to international investment resources, and projects in Russia became interesting for FDI. This is why major global economic development trends are important in understanding Russia's growth pattern.

Three decades of global development include the end of the post-war convergence, including 'the golden age of economic growth' (1950–1973) and the following slowdown (1974–mid-1990s), the information and communication technology (ICT) revolution and 'the new economy' (1995–2004) (Crafts & Toniolo, 2010, p. 289), and the age of the global productivity slowdown (OECD, 2015, pp. 24–32). After the Second World War (WWII), the economies of Western Europe grew, being driven by catching up to the technology frontier provided by the United States. The economies of Eastern Europe, including the Soviet Union and Soviet Russia,[2] the largest Union republic, were also involved in this process, but the effects of convergence for them were less profound, and since the mid-1970s, have almost disappeared (Crafts & Toniolo, 2010). By 1995, Old Europe had approached the frontier. The next global growth engine was the ICT revolution. Personal computers and the Internet changed technologies in most industries, including retail and financial services. The growth-enhancing effects of the ICT revolution, however, disappeared by the mid-2000s. Since then, the global economy has

---

[2] The Russian Soviet Federative Socialist Republic or, in short, Soviet Russia.

Table 15.1 GDP yearly average growth rates in Russia and in the World 1990–2019, in comparable prices, %

Countries and regions	Real GDP			Labour productivity		
	1990–2000	2001–2010	2011–2019	1990–2000	2001–2010	2011–2019
Russia	−3.84	4.72	1.71	−2.05	4.56	1.86
World	2.63	3.50	2.85	1.24	2.25	1.83
Mature Economies	2.57	1.72	1.88	2.02	1.39	0.86
Emerging Markets and Developing Economies	2.73	5.67	3.75	1.13	4.11	2.73
Brazil	1.94	3.62	0.76	0.48	1.59	0.43
China (alternative)	5.79	8.50	4.32	3.93	7.41	4.79
Germany	1.46	0.85	1.71	2.26	1.01	0.96
India	5.63	7.09	6.60	3.82	5.39	5.81
Czechia	0.61	3.14	2.45	1.31	3.38	1.74

Notes See data description in Fig. 15.1
Source The Conference Board Total Economy Database™, August (2021).

entered a period of productivity slowdown (OECD, 2015, pp. 24–32). This slowdown has been observed in almost all major economies (Table 15.1), with the exception of the mature[3] economies, where growth has remained almost unchanged.

The Russian growth pattern differed, especially in the early transition. This is not a surprise, considering the low level of international integration of the Soviet economy and the specificity of transition for post-Socialist economies, such as Russia. In the early 1990s, Russia underwent a sharp transition from a planned economy with fixed prices to a market economy, accompanied by high inflation and a drastic fall in output. The recession lasted 8 years, and by 1998, gross domestic product (GDP) fell to 59% of the 1990 level (Fig. 15.1). The financial crisis of 1998 hit Russia and was caused mostly by domestic policy shortcomings, such as its chronic fiscal deficit combined with its exchange rate peg and the low level of international reserves of the central bank (see Chapter 16). Yearly average growth rates were negative: − 3.8%. Russia's growth demonstrated the opposite trend in comparison with the global economy, both mature and emerging markets.

---

[3] Mature economies include all current 27 members of the European Union, Australia, Canada, Hong Kong, Iceland, Israel, Japan, New Zealand, Norway, Singapore, South Korea, Switzerland, Taiwan, the United Kingdom, and the United States.

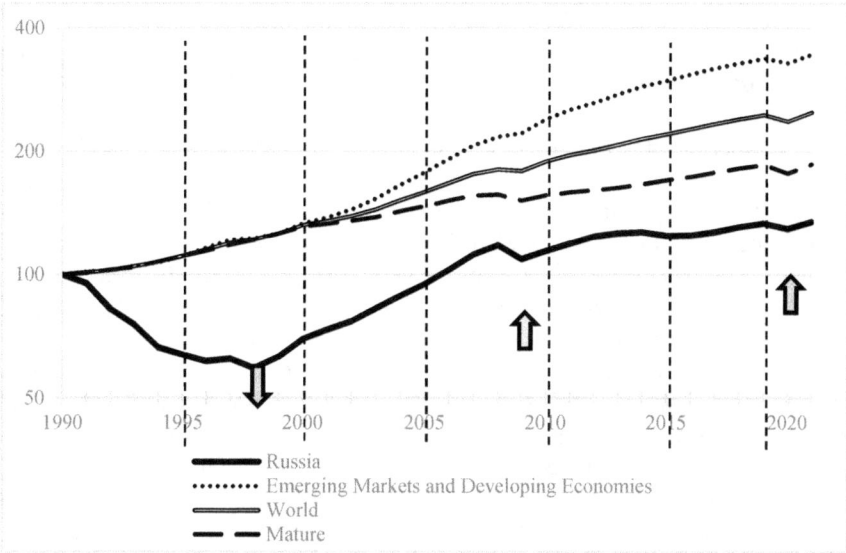

Fig. 15.1 Changes in real GDP in Russia in a comparative perspective, 1990 = 100, 1990–2021 (*Notes* The figure is represented in logarithmic or ratio scale. See more about ratio scale in [Weil, 2013, p. 31, Fig. 1.3]. For the country grouping—see Appendix 15.1. *Source* The Conference Board Total Economy Database™, August, 2021)

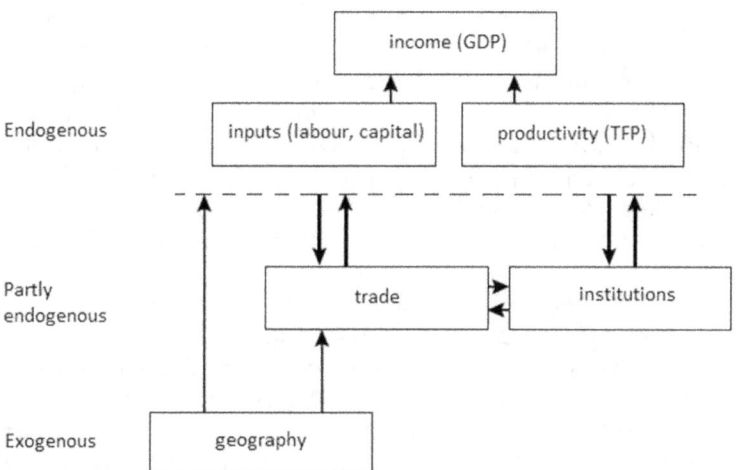

Fig. 15.2 Conceptual framework for understanding sources of economic growth (*Source* Rodrik, 2003, p. 5, and author's analysis)

Starting from the early 2000s, Russia has become much more dependent on global economic shocks and trends. However, in the 2000s, Russian growth was almost the highest in the world. As shown in Table 15.1, it gave way to China and India but exceeded mature economies. Finally, in the 2010s, it entered a period of slow growth and stagnation, after the GFC of 2008–2009.

An almost similar pattern can be observed if we shift from the output (Table 15.1, left panel) to labour productivity growth (Table 15.1, right panel). In post-industrialised economies with slow or negative population growth, GDP growth is largely driven by labour productivity. Its decline during Russia's transformational recession was not as strong as the decline of output (−2.05 and −3.84%, respectively), because the latter was partially compensated by the fall in employment. While the origins of the Russian crisis of 1998 were mostly[4] of a domestic nature, the GFC of 2008–2009 and the COVID-19 pandemic shock of 2020 hit both the world economy and Russia. Thus, since the early 1990s, the economy of Russia has been more globalised.

The above observations help us raise questions on the role of structural change and various intra-industry sources in each of the three analysed periods, which will be discussed in the following sections.

15.3 Structural Change, Labour Reallocation, and Productivity Growth

Structural change implies the reallocation of labour between activities with different levels of productivity. If a worker leaves a less productive job for a more productive one, aggregate productivity grows, and the other way around. This is why structural change impacts growth either positively or negatively. The economic structure of command economies before transition was distorted in favour of material production. This included agriculture and manufacturing, overinvested partially because of excessive militarisation. The intensive reallocation of economic activity to services is one of the stylised facts commonly observed in all transition economies, including Russia (Campos & Coricelli, 2002).

Table 15.2 provides an overview of the structural changes in five major sectors of the Russian economy, representing changes in shares of hours worked and value added and in relative labour productivity levels. As can be seen in Part A of Table 15.2, in 1995, almost one-half of the hours worked belonged to material production sectors—agriculture, manufacturing, and extended mining.[5] By 2015, this fell to 42%. Interestingly, in 1995, the

---

[4] Several analyses put the Russian crisis in the context of the late 1990s wave of emerging market financial crises. See, e.g., Chiodo and Owyang (2002).

[5] In the case of Russia, mining should be considered in a broader sense in comparison with the approach used in standard industry classifications. An extended oil and gas sector includes organisations which are involved in the process of the extraction, transportation, and wholesale trade of oil and gas. Some of these have establishments in different industries, such as mining, wholesale trade, fuel, and pipeline transport. Because of strong

share of agriculture exceeded one-quarter of the total working time, which was too high for a post-industrialised economy. However, in the case of Russia, this reflected not only employment in agricultural firms but also in households, which produced for own consumption (Kapelyushnikov et al., 2012). This household employment not only provided a substantial share of production for certain agricultural products but also absorbed negative labour market shocks during the transformational recession.

During the recovery, the share of agriculture diminished to one-fifth by 2016. It became a donor for more productive sectors. Another sector that lost labour was manufacturing. Its share diminished from almost 19% in 1995 to 14% in 2016. Market services, such as construction, retail, and telecom were the major recipients of labour. Their share expanded from 20% in 1995 to 28% in 2016. Finance and business services, extended mining, and non-market services also recorded an expansion.

Intensive structural change can also be observed if we look at the shares of value added, represented in Part B of Table 15.2. The shares of agriculture and manufacturing also fell, but in comparison with hours worked, it was relatively modest in agriculture (2.5 percentage points [pp]) and more sound in manufacturing (7 pp). Increasing government expenditures on public administration, education, and healthcare led to the expansion of non-market services by 5 pp. The expansion of the extended mining sector was relatively modest, just 2.5 pp, but during years of soaring oil prices (2010), its share reached one-quarter. This can reflect the comparative disadvantages of Russian manufacturing compared to its main trading partners. Finance and business services and retail, construction, and telecom expanded from 24[6] to 31%. Unlike other post-transition economies, Russia is a resource exporting country. The growth of global oil prices after 1999 led to the remarkable expansion of its mining and mining-related industries, combined in Table 15.2 into extended mining, from 20% in 1995 to almost one-quarter in 2015. Overall, the expanding shares of services and extended mining predetermine the leading contribution of these sectors to aggregate growth.

The ratio of value-added and employment shares represents the relative level of labour productivity (see Part C of Table 15.2). For example, in 1995, the labour productivity of extended mining was 5.7 times higher than the total economy average.[7] Correspondingly, the lowest relative labour productivity level, around 0.2, belonged to agriculture. Table 15.2 shows that cross-sector

---

vertical integration and transfer pricing, its share in total value added exceeds mining. This chapter assumes that this extended mining sector includes mining, wholesale trade, and fuel. See also Timmer and Voskoboynikov (2016) for further discussion.

[6] From Table 15.2 Part B, we have 24.1% = 19.1% + 5.0%.

[7] The productivity level of extended mining, which equals 5.7 of the average economy level, can be calculated with corresponding data from Table 15.2 Parts A and B. Denoting total economy nominal value added and hours worked with VA and H correspondingly, we have the labour productivity level of extended mining in 1995 (20.0% × VA)/(3.5% × H) = 5.7(VA/H).

Table 15.2 Structural changes in the Russian economy in 1995–2015

Sectors/industries	A. Shares of hours worked (%)					B. Shares of nominal value added (%)					C. Sectoral labour productivity				
	1995	2000	2005	2010	2015	1995	2000	2005	2010	2015	1995	2000	2005	2010	2015
TOTAL	100.0	100.0	100.0	100.0	100.0	100.0	100.0	100.0	100.0	100.0	1.00	1.00	1.00	1.00	1.00
Market economy	80.9	79.3	79.8	79.3	79.5	85.9	87.6	85.1	81.7	80.5	1.06	1.10	1.07	1.03	1.01
Agriculture	27.9	25.5	22.8	21.6	20.2	7.6	7.1	5.0	3.9	4.9	0.27	0.28	0.22	0.18	0.24
Extended Mining	3.5	4.2	4.5	4.9	4.7	20.0	25.7	26.7	25.0	23.2	5.74	6.08	5.95	5.11	4.90
Manufacturing	18.8	17.7	16.3	15.2	14.6	22.5	22.1	17.6	15.8	15.6	1.20	1.25	1.08	1.04	1.07
Construction, Retail, Telecom	19.7	22.2	25.6	26.5	28.0	19.1	18.4	18.6	18.9	17.9	0.97	0.83	0.73	0.71	0.64
Finance & Business Services	5.2	4.3	4.9	5.5	6.0	5.0	6.4	9.7	11.2	12.0	0.97	1.50	1.99	2.02	1.99
Transportation	5.7	5.4	5.7	5.7	6.0	11.7	7.8	7.7	7.0	6.9	2.03	1.44	1.35	1.23	1.16
Non-Market Services	19.1	20.7	20.2	20.7	20.5	14.1	12.4	14.9	18.3	19.5	0.74	0.60	0.74	0.89	0.95

Notes Non-market services include real estate, public administration, education, and health and social work. Transportation includes inland, water, and other transport, as well as transport services. Extended mining includes total mining, fuel, and wholesale trade. A detailed sectoral composition is available in (Voskoboynikov, 2017, Table A1)

Source Russia KLEMS (2019), author's calculations

differentiation in labour productivity was lower in 2016 than in 1995. It also demonstrates that market services in a modern economy differ in productivity. In 1995, the finance and business services sector was at the level of construction and retail. By 2015, the former grew to 2.1, while construction and retail fell below two-thirds of the economy's average. Finance attracts qualified people and engages ICT and intangible assets (software), while retail and construction absorb the unskilled labour force.

The contribution of labour reallocation to aggregate productivity growth includes positive and negative components. On the one hand, labour inflow to finance and business services and extended mining—sectors with above average productivity—contributes positively to labour productivity growth. Furthermore, a positive contribution is provided by labour outflow from low productive activities, such as agriculture and manufacturing.[8] On the other hand, labour inflow to low productive construction, retail, and telecom drags labour productivity growth down. Voskoboynikov (2020, Table 3) argues that the total reallocation effect was growth enhancing, being more intensive in 1995–2005 in comparison with the following years. This reflected a more efficient allocation of resources and the elimination of the distortions of the planned economy period.

Overall, the contribution of labour reallocation to aggregate growth rates in 1995–2005 does not exceed 0.23 pp—or almost one-quarter – of the total 5% annual labour productivity growth (Voskoboynikov, 2020, Table 3). Thus, in comparison with intra-industry sources, the impact of labour reallocation is of secondary importance. These sources will be discussed in the following three sections, starting from the early transition.

15.4 Transformational Recession (1990–1998)

In the late 1980s, the Soviet economy, including Soviet Russia as its largest part, as well as the socialist economies in Eastern Europe, entered a period of economic transformation from plan to market. This transition was accompanied by a sharp output fall, called by Kornai (1994), the *transformational recession*.

Transition economies varied by the duration of the transformational recession and the depth of the trough. Among the 20 transition economies, Poland was the luckiest. It started growing in 1991 from a level of 93% of GDP per capita relative to 1990. Compared with 20 Central and Eastern European economies, Russia had one of the longest periods of the transformational recession, which ended in 1998 with the deep fall of GDP per capita relative to 1990—57.4%. Only Moldova (1999, 34.1%) and Ukraine

---

[8] This is the average representation of these sectors. Manufacturing includes both high productive and low productive industries. Agriculture includes stagnant low productive households, which produce for own consumption, and capital-intensive modern agricultural firms (see Chapter 10).

(1999, 40.8%) performed worse (Voskoboynikov, 2021, p. 391).[9] In general, the economies of Central and Eastern Europe started to recover by 1994 (excluding Bulgaria), faster than the countries of the former Soviet Union (FSU) (Voskoboynikov, 2021, p. 391). Causes of the transformational recession are expected to have some similar features in all transition economies.[10]

The starting point for the explanation of the growth pattern of the transformational recession is a discussion on the changes in the fundamental exogenous factors of growth: *geography*, *trade*, and *institutions* (Fig. 15.2).[11]

The main changes in *geography*, common for all transition economies, are related to distance penalties, complemented by underdeveloped connective infrastructure, and trade policies and institutions, which often tended to increase the costs of cross-border trade (Kossev & Tompson, 2021, p. 437). Within the Soviet Union, the borders of Russia had a character of internal administrative lines. In 1990, the actual shares of inter-republic exports in the total exports of the 15 USSR republics varied from 68% (Russia) to 98% (Kyrgyzstan) (Kaminski et al., 1996, pp. 13–14, Table 2).

After the collapse of the Soviet Union, these administrative lines became state borders, creating barriers to the flow of goods and services. Russian enterprises lost free access to seaports in Ukraine (the Odesa seaport) and the Baltic countries (for example, Riga and Tallinn) and direct access to the pipeline system of Europe, critically important for Russian oil and gas exports. New state borders impacted existing production chains, transforming cooperation between enterprises within the Soviet economy into international trade relations. In many cases, the increasing costs of such operations stopped them. Enterprises had to find new partners or shut down.

Changes to state borders and production chains impacted international *trade reorientation* but were not the only factors of importance. Russia quickly found better markets for its major export products, hydrocarbons and metals, than FSU countries. The latter's share in Russia's exports declined from 64% in 1990 to 23% in 1996 (Kossev & Tompson, 2021, p. 444).

Before transition, foreign trade turnover was low relative to GDP and FDI did not exist or was negligible and state-controlled. Soviet institutions prevented managers from responding to changes in relative prices abroad. The state monopoly on foreign trade and controlled prices within the Soviet economy blocked all world price signals and prevented changes in domestic prices. For example, domestic prices on oil and gas remained unchanged even after the oil price shock in the mid-1970s. This is why after price and trade

---

[9] However, some other FSU countries faced a more severe transition. For example, the lowest GDP level in Georgia was 29% of 1990, Azerbaijan—55% (World Bank, 2002, p. 5).

[10] A comprehensive discussion of transformational recession is presented by Ickes (2018).

[11] There are various channels which link multiple primary sources of growth, exogenous and partially endogenous, with GDP growth. Some of the sources impact inputs. For example, infrastructure (geography) through capital and favourable business environment (institutions) through productivity. FDI inflow adds inputs, accelerating capital accumulation, and increases technology level, improving production methods (productivity).

liberalisation, Russian resource industries gained more than other industries (Kossev & Tompson, 2021, p. 435).

The last group of changes—and probably the most important one—is related to *institutions*. The Soviet economy had administratively controlled prices, rigid regulation of the labour market with no free wages and formally full employment, state-owned and -controlled enterprises, operating according to centrally set plans for production and investments, and a state monopoly on foreign trade.

The transition to a market economy in Russia meant an almost immediate discontinuation of all elements of a planned economy. In 1992, price controls for most goods and services were abandoned. Labour market regulations were also abandoned, which opened the door for unemployment. The state stopped financing investments for most enterprises. Producers were faced with the new challenge of looking for credit in private banks, which had not existed in the Soviet Union since the 1920s. The government abandoned the state monopoly on foreign trade. Russian firms gained access to international markets and could sell their products abroad for hard currency. However, Russian firms were faced with competition from imported goods, and many of them failed this competition, which was a small wonder. Most of them lacked international competition before the transition in many aspects, including in regard to their investment design, geographic location, and production profile. Some of them were initially adjusted for military production but were largely shut down by the early 1990s. Finally, the government launched mass privatisation and most Russian enterprises became private. This completely changed the landscape of the Russian economy in just a few years.

The transition to a market economy and free pricing in January 1992 generated both a macro- and microeconomic shock. Open high inflation (prices grew by 26 times in 1992, 9.4 times in 1993, 3.2 times in 1994—see Rosstat, 1999, Table 24.1), mass payments arrears, the increasing share of barter deals, a new taxation system, the inflow of imported goods, and the reduction of military procurement led to the closure of many enterprises. Economic instability was fuelled by political turmoil, for example, the confrontation of the populist majority in the Russian parliament, insistent on increasing budget expenditures, and the government, which aimed to bound inflation and achieve macroeconomic stabilisation.

As it follows from the conceptual framework, outlined in Fig. 15.2, an important step for the analysis is making the link between the growth rates of output Y, labour, capital, and *TFP*. In other words, it is central to know how much of Russia's income growth is accounted for by growth in *TFP* and by growth in the quantity of factors of production. These contributions can be expressed in the form of the growth accounting decomposition:

$$\hat{Y} = \overline{\alpha} \cdot \hat{K} + (1 - \overline{\alpha}) \cdot \hat{H} + (1 - \overline{\alpha}) \cdot \widehat{LC} + \widehat{TFP} \qquad (15.1)$$

which are labour, measured in hours worked (H), capital (K), labour composition (LC), and total factor productivity (TFP). Putting a hat $\left(\widehat{X}, \text{ where } X \equiv Y, K, H, LC \text{ or } TFP\right)$ on top of a variable indicates its growth rate. $\overline{\alpha}$ is the yearly average share of capital costs in nominal value added, which is equal to the elasticity of capital substitution in perfect market equilibrium. While conventional inputs, labour and capital, do not need additional comments, some clarification is needed for LC and TFP. The index of labour composition goes up if the share of more productive workers is expanded. In turn, TFP growth is positive when the real cost of production per output becomes lower. TFP growth is usually associated with technology improvements. However, many other factors could also accelerate it, such as economies of scale, better management practice, and unmeasured effects of human and social capital.

In summary, Eq. 15.1 states that output growth rates equal the sum of contributions of capital $\left(\overline{\alpha} \cdot \hat{K}\right)$, labour $\left((1-\overline{\alpha}) \cdot \hat{H}\right)$, labour composition $\left((1-\overline{\alpha}) \cdot \widehat{LC}\right)$, and TFP $\left(\hat{A}\right)$[12] (Table 15.3). Growth is called *extensive* if the contribution of inputs dominates. Alternatively, growth is *intensive* if it is fuelled by TFP or by diminishing the costs of production. Because of diminishing returns of capital ($\overline{\alpha} < 1$), extensive growth needs more inputs for backing the same growth rates in the future. This is why it is considered as unsustainable. In turn, intensive or TFP-based growth is sustainable.

Table 15.3 presents the results of growth accounting for Russia in 1990–2019 and, to some extent, clarifies the nature of the output fall in 1990–1995 by –8.4%. More than one-half of the fall, or –3.8 pp,[13] is due to the lower use of labour and capital. This is not surprising. Before the transition, a substantial share of production did not have market demand. Even excluding military production, Soviet factories produced an enormous amount of textiles, shoes, cars, and other goods that were internationally uncompetitive. These goods disappeared after the transition, being substituted by imports. In turn, many people in Russia found themselves out of work. They had to change activities, shift to part-time work, move to informal activities, or leave the labour market (see Chapter 17).

A similar explanation is applicable to capital. In a few years, a substantial share of fixed assets became deserted and idle. Under the conditions of an economic recession and combined with a lack of investment, the substitution of old and obsolete capital was not an easy task.

Next, there was one input which remained positive during the whole period in question. This is labour quality. In 1990–1995, it provided a substantial positive contribution by 0.4 pp of output growth. In the market

---

[12] See also Weil (2013, Chapter 7) for a further discussion of growth accounting and its interpretation. An advanced representation of growth accounting at the industry level can be found in Jorgenson et al. (2005).

[13] From the first column of Table 15.3, we have –3.8 = –1.3–2.53.

Table 15.3 Growth accounting of the Russian economy in 1990–2019

Indicator	1990–1995	1996–2000	2001–2005	2006–2010	2011–2015	2016–2019
Annual average growth rates, %						
1 Real value added (7 + 8 + 9 + 10)	−8.36	1.59	5.96	3.48	1.72	1.70
2 Labour	−2.91	−0.43	0.84	0.17	0.07	−0.43
3 Capital	−4.56	−3.31	0.29	2.20	2.36	1.89
4 Labour quality	0.86	0.89	0.49	0.53	0.66	0.54
Average share of value added, %						
5 Labour share (%)	44.5	45.6	43.4	47.1	45.9	47.2
6 Capital share (%)	55.5	54.4	56.6	52.9	54.1	52.8
Contributions (pp)						
7 Labour (2 × 5)/100	−1.30	−0.20	0.36	0.08	0.03	−0.20
8 Labour quality (4 × 5)/100	0.38	0.40	0.21	0.25	0.30	0.25
9 Capital (3 × 6)/100	−2.53	−1.80	0.16	1.17	1.28	0.99
10 Total Factor Productivity	−4.92	3.18	5.22	1.99	0.10	0.65

Note See also Sect. 15.4 and equation (Eq. 15.1) for methodology discussion
Source The Conference Board Total Economy Database™, August (2021); Own calculations

economy, more productive workers found better jobs, which enhanced aggregate growth. Interestingly, in the following years, this effect became smaller (around 0.2–0.3 pp of GDP) because the room for further improvements in labour structure was likely exhausted. The remarkable features of the whole analysed period are the increasing share of workers with a university degree and their ageing (see Chapter 2). Both factors contributed positively to labour quality. More educated people are usually more productive. Thus, the increasing share of skilled workers stimulates growth. Furthermore, aged workers, those who survived on the labour market, are usually experienced and more productive.

What is noticeable at first glance is the negative contribution of TFP. Indeed, one of the advances of the market economy in comparison with the planned economy is more efficient resource allocation. Therefore, we would expect a fall in production costs, rather than growth. However, TFP fall as the main source of the transformational recession was almost common in transition economies (Campos & Coricelli, 2002). This requires a theoretical explanation, which comes from the idea of institutional change.

A lack of rudimentary market institutions in transition economies to support long production chains, which is also referred to as disorganisation, as well as labour reallocation from state to private sectors are the core assumptions in the output fall model of Blanchard and Kremer (1997). It explains the output fall by inefficient bargaining and asymmetric information. According to the model, a large state-owned enterprise (SOE) critically depends on many inputs. If one of the inputs is not available, the SOE stops production.

Another explanation was suggested by Roland and Verdier (1999). They explained this fall as a consequence for a firm of increasing search frictions for a new business partner, either a client or a supplier. Indeed, after the transition almost all firms were faced with the need to find new long-term partners. High inflation made price signals less clear and increased search frictions. Hence, the search took longer and hit output growth because of disruptions to previous production links, a fall in investments, and capital depreciation. This explanation is similar to the previous one.

The influence of the major factors of the transformational recession largely disappeared in the second half of the 1990s. The Russian economy passed the most difficult and turbulent years of the transition and achieved some level of macroeconomic stabilisation. Inflation went down to 111% in 1997 (Rosstat, 1999, Table 24.1), which was still high but much lower in comparison with 2509% in 1992. In 1997, the Russian economy started growing for the first time since 1989—by 1.4% relative to 1996 (see Fig. 15.1). However, the financial crisis of 1998 (see Chapter 16) caused a GDP to decline by 5.5% this year. A deep rouble depreciation (see Chapter 16) accompanied by the initial growth of oil prices shifted the economy back to growth in 1999. However, the financial crisis was the bottom line of the transformational recession and the starting point for growth.

15.4.1 *The Post-Transition Recovery (1999–2008)*

The decade after the 1998 crisis was a period of outstanding growth for the Russian economy, which outperformed most countries in the world. Russia found itself a member of the BRIC countries—a club of four large emerging market economies, along with Brazil, China, and India. As it follows from Table 15.3, such performance came from two sources—*total factor productivity* (1996–2010) and *capital* (from 2006). An additional question concerns the origins of the productivity slowdown in the second half of the 2000s.

Initially, in 1999, the positive impact on growth and *productivity* came from the rouble devaluation, which made production in many industries competitive. Manufacturing industries started to grow, engaging idle capital capacity and hiring more workers. This was how output growth could be achieved with low additional costs. Considering the low level of capacity utilisation before 1998 and the availability of labour, the initial post-crisis growth did not require substantial investments.

Productivity could also be reinforced by an inflow of FDI, which increased sharply in 2004–2005 and was largely directed to the oil and gas sector (Kossev & Tompson, 2021, p. 451). FDI enabled technology improvements and stimulated technology catching up.

Manufacturing, banking, and retail also adapted better technologies. The long process of WTO accession, successfully completed in 2012, improved the institutional environment. WTO membership provided better access to global markets and the legal framework for the resolution of trade disputes. This was a remarkable step forward on a long path towards integration into the global economy, which started with the IMF and World Bank accessions in 1992. Finally, macroeconomic stabilisation after 1998 facilitated the growth of productivity. Improvements in the banking system made investments easier. As a result, complex production processes became more predictable.

Although the contribution of productivity was remarkable during these years, it was *capital* which made growth high and stable. The dependence of capital growth rates on yearly average global oil prices is shown in Fig. 15.3. Before 2003, capital growth was negative, which reflected the mass discarding of capital during the transition period (see Sect. 15.4).

The price of oil increased from its lowest point of USD 12.80 per barrel in 1998 to USD 17.90 in 1999 and USD 28.70 in 2000. By 2012, it reached its maximum level of USD 111.63, or almost 9 times as much as in 1998, reflecting increasing demand for natural resources, particularly in rapidly growing China and India. Export revenues were partly transformed into investments and increasing capital intensity and fuelled growth. Table 15.3 shows that the contribution of capital in 2006–2011 became remarkable.

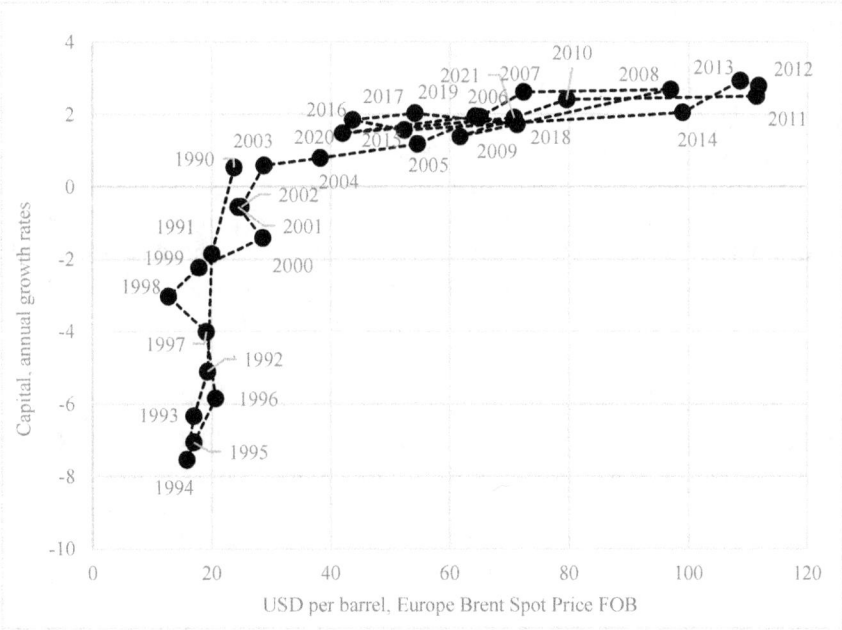

Fig. 15.3 Capital growth rates and oil prices in 1990–2021 (*Sources* The Conference Board Total Economy Database™, August [2021], Thomson Reuters, U.S. Energy Information Administration—for oil prices)

In the 2000s, Russian firms purchased new machinery. The share of machinery in total imports of machinery, equipment, and transport means in 2000–2007 expanded from 31.1% (2000) to 51.0% (2007) (Rosstat, 2008, Table 26.11); these years are referred to as the years of 'the second industrialisation'. Interestingly, from 2003 until the present, capital growth rates have demonstrated a strong correlation with the level of oil prices. Finally, Russia has also enjoyed the ICT revolution. Computers, ICT technologies, and online trade have penetrated everywhere.

Capital is the main driver of growth in extended mining and retail, construction, and telecom. These sectors enjoyed the inflow of capital in the 2000s. Extended mining transformed a share of oil and gas revenues into purchases of investment goods. The second sector, especially retail, passed through the technological revolution. In the early 1990s, with a few exceptions, the Soviet retail sector had only a few supermarkets. The retail sector in the Soviet Union lagged for a long time. In 1999, McKinsey (Unlocking economic growth in Russia, 1999, p. 5) reported that modern formats of retailing were rare, with less than 1% of market share. From the mid-1990s, Russia has experienced the expansion of modern retail centres, which in 2009 captured 35% of total retail sales (McKinsey Global Institute, 2009, p. 65).

Overall, the high growth of the 2000s was not only the outcome of oil and gas revenues transformed into investments but also resulted from the access of Russian firms to global financial markets, the inflow of FDI, and new technologies.

Starting from the mid-2000s, the productivity of the Russian economy began to slow down, while the contribution of capital continued to grow (Table 15.3). Due to the lower contribution of TFP, more capital was needed to support growth, which increased the dependence of economic growth on oil and gas export revenues. Although in the second half of the 2000s, the productivity slowdown was substituted with capital contributions, it made the economy more vulnerable to changes in oil and gas prices and other external shocks. This predetermined the stagnation of the 2010s.

15.5 The Decade of Stagnation (2009–2019)

In the late 2000s, particularly after the shock caused by the GFC, the Russian economy entered a long period of stagnation. Annual average growth rates of GDP slowed down to 1.71% in 2011–2019 and labour productivity growth—to 1.86% (Table 15.1). The origins of this stagnation are of both a global and a country-specific nature. We consider both, starting with the global origins.

The second half of the 2000s was the starting point for the global productivity slowdown. Almost all economies in the world experienced this phenomenon (Table 15.1). Inefficient investments in machinery, human capital, and organisational processes were contributing factors (OECD, 2015). This included skills mismatch and the lack of technology diffusion from advanced to laggard firms.

The GFC also contributed to global stagnation. In 2013, the average annual TFP growth in OECD economies was almost 2%. This is lower than the pre-crisis performance (OECD, 2015, p. 28). In terms of long-run consequences, three issues could impact post-crisis performance but are working in opposite directions. First, tangible investments were affected and recovered slower compared to the recoveries after the previous recession episodes in 1973, 1981, and 2000. An OECD report (OECD, 2015) links this with increased uncertainty. Investors were forced to delay investment decisions. Second, investments to knowledge-based capital (KBC) were more resilient. Before the crisis, long-term investments in research and development (R&D) and human capital assumed substantial opportunity costs, diverting resources from current production. After the crisis, however, opportunity costs became lower. Therefore, investments to human capital and R&D did not fall as much as tangibles. KBC investments also recovered faster. This global overview is helpful in understanding the productivity slowdown in Russia.

A growth accounting decomposition of the Russian economy unveils some similarities with OECD economies. First, TFP growth declined by 1.9 pp in 2011–2015. Second, similar to the United States, the TFP slowdown in Russia started before 2008—in the mid-2000s. In the 2010s, growth was supported by capital intensity and, to a lesser extent, labour quality. However, since the mid-2000s, the growth rates of ICT capital were lower than the non-ICT ones (Voskoboynikov, 2017, Table 2).

The fall of TFP was a major source of the post-GFC stagnation in Russia. Taking into account relatively small changes in the structure of the economy since 2010 (Table 15.2), major sources of stagnation are expected to be within individual industries. A detailed industry-level growth accounting decomposition (Voskoboynikov, 2017, Fig. 4) unveils such sectoral sources, which are extended mining and construction, retail, and telecom. Both grew in the 2000s and shifted into the negative zone in the 2010s (extended mining was the most important). Russia suffered from the sharp outflow of FDI in 2014 as a result of the Ukraine crisis (Kossev & Tompson, 2021). This factor, along with the economic sanctions against Russia (see Chapter 14), jeopardised technology transfer and affected TFP growth.

The nature of the TFP decline in extended mining is not clear and could be caused, for example, by increasing costs of extraction, inefficient tariffs for transportation, or the market power of natural monopolies. All these explanations could also be relevant in other economies. Negative productivity growth in mining is not unusual. For example, in 2011–2016, the TFP growth rates in the countries with the largest value-added share of mining in Europe were −9.3% in the Netherlands and −12.8% in Denmark. This was much higher than in Russia in the same year (−5.0%) (EU KLEMS, 2019). However, Russia's aggregate growth is much more sensitive to the performance of extended mining, because its value-added share is about one-fifth of the economy (Table 15.2), while, in the Netherlands and Denmark, it is below 3.5%.

Negative aggregate TFP growth was mitigated by two progressive sectors, agriculture and financial and business services. Agriculture performed very well since the early 2000s, but its tiny share in value added makes its contribution small. The potential of financial services in the 2000s to catch up was almost exhausted, but this sector quickly recovered after the GFC. The remaining source of growth was capital intensity. At the sectoral level, all industries demonstrated positive dynamics, with the leading contributions from extended mining and retail. Thus, it seems the major reasons for the slowdown of the 2010s are of a domestic nature. Global factors affected Russia in tradable sectors, such as manufacturing, and slowed down technology convergence.

15.6 Conclusions

Russian economic growth is volatile. Since the collapse of the Soviet Union and its transition to a market economy, Russia has passed through three main periods of growth: the transformational recession (1990–1998), the recovery (1999–2008), and the stagnation (2009–2019). The periodisation is connected with the transition from a planned to a market economy and the development of the global economy before and after the GFC of 2008–2009. Each period can be characterised by the different contributions of labour, capital, and TFP as well as by factors related to geography, trade, and institutions.

The three periods differ in terms of the main sources of growth. During the transformational recession, disorganisation (i.e., the inability of weak institutions to support long production chains) and macroeconomic instability caused a decline in productivity. This was accompanied by mass discarding of obsolete capital and a decline in the number of hours worked. Trade reorientation from the FSU to global markets as well as the unfavourable level of oil prices contributed to the fall of investments. By the second half of the 1990s, some of these negative factors were overcome. However, only the financial crisis of 1998 accompanied by the rouble devaluation and the growing demand for hydrocarbons and metals dragged the economy out of the transformational recession.

The post-crisis recovery was fuelled by a unique combination of favourable conditions. After the initial devaluation impulse, which made many Russian products competitive, TFP and labour and capital inputs started growing. The establishment of market economy institutions made business activities more stable and predictable. Many Russian manufacturing enterprises found ways to integrate globally. Since the mid-2000s, the inflow of FDI (mostly to extended mining) has facilitated the adaptation of better technologies. Technological catching up was remarkable not only in manufacturing and agriculture but also in services, especially in financial intermediation and retail.

Another important source of growth was the accelerating capital accumulation, mostly supported by growing revenues from exports of oil and gas, but also because of cheap investment resources abroad as well as FDI. In

1999–2008, many factors worked for growth. High oil prices reversed the negative investment trend. At the aggregate level, capital growth became positive from 2003, but in some industries, this happened earlier. Additionally, Russia enjoyed an ICT revolution, which contributed to capital and productivity growth all-around, especially in market services. Starting from the mid-2000s, capital contributions became remarkable, especially against the TFP slowdown.

The GFC of 2008–2009 was a notable shock for the Russian economy. However, it was not the main cause of the following stagnation. The poor performance of the Russian economy in the 2010s came from the slowdown of TFP growth in most sectors, especially in extended mining. Given the share of this sector in the aggregate value added (about 20%), it dragged the economy down. The causes of the TFP fall in extended mining need further research, but a clear takeaway is the weakness of an economy heavily dependent on such a volatile sector. This fall in productivity was attenuated by strong TFP performance in financial services and agriculture, but their contribution was not sufficient to reverse the negative TFP trend. The only remaining strong source of growth was the contribution of capital.

Growth enhancing structural changes supported growth through all three decades, being stronger during the transformational recession. Mass labour reallocation from manufacturing to agriculture had a controversial impact on the aggregate productivity growth. The expansion of finance and business services contributed positively, while the increasing share of retail and construction weighted the economy down. The same logic is applicable to the quality change of the labour force: it remained positive since the early 1990s. The shares of hours worked by more productive workers expanded, contributing 0.2–0.4 pp to aggregate output growth each year. On average, the positive contribution dominated, reflecting the healthy impact of the transition to market in terms of the efficiency of resource allocation.

The stagnation of the 2010s differs from the transformational recession. In contrast with the 1990s, the Russian economy of the 2010s did not suffer from a lack of capital or the intensive transformation of institutions, as in the 1990s.[14] Short-term macroeconomic policy also became more efficient. On the contrary, capital continued growing and the economy benefited from the infrastructure created in the previous two decades. The problem of the 2010s was primarily weak productivity performance. This was because of lagging technological adaptation, the weakness of rooted institutions, a poor business climate (Chapter 6), and geopolitical shocks (Chapter 14). One of the consequences was the sharp outflow of FDI since 2014. Last, but not least, is the lack of diversification. The substantial share of extended mining in the economy makes it vulnerable not only to oil and gas prices but also to the

---

[14] In the 2010s, the institutional environment changed. In many sectors, the government increased its share in the capital of large companies. This can impact *TFP* performance. However, these changes were minor in comparison with the 1990s.

productivity of this sector. Its low productivity drags the economy down even if the causes of this poor performance are objective, such as the age structure of mines or the conditions of mining extraction. At the same time, capital accumulation in extended mining remains an important backbone of Russian economic growth.

Future perspectives of Russian growth depend on its ability of structural diversification, improvements in the business environment, openness to technology adaptation, attention to knowledge-based capital, and *renewable* resources.

Questions for Students

1. What was the industrial structure of the Russian economy before the transition to market and what were the structural changes during transition and the impact of these changes on growth?
2. What explains the transformational recession in general, and why is Russia different?
3. Why did Russia recover faster than other post-transition economies?
4. What are the origins of the ensuing slowdown of the Russian economy in the 2010s?
5. What are the consequences of the large share of extended mining in Russian GDP?

Appendix 15.1: Country Grouping

Emerging Markets and Developing Economies: Other Developing Asia, Latin America, Middle East & North Africa, Sub-Saharan Africa, Russia, Central Asia and Southeast Europe, as well as India and China (Alternative).

China (Alternative): China is presented in the Total Economy Database (TED) in two series, China (Official) and China (Alternative). Over the years, scholars expressed concerns about the reliability and upward bias of the official series. The Conference Board (TCB) has reconstructed the Chinese GDP series bottom-up on a sector-by-sector basis, partly relying on official measures where those are found to be relatively unbiased and partly constructing new estimates where there are concerns about the methodology of the published estimates (de Vries & Erumban, 2017, pp. 8–9, Sect. 1.1.4). This chapter uses the alternative series. However, TCB includes also the official series for China. Thus, all estimations can be recalculated.

Other Developing Asia: Bangladesh, Cambodia, Indonesia, Malaysia, Myanmar, Pakistan, Philippines, Sri Lanka, Thailand, and Vietnam.

Latin America: Argentina, Bolivia, Brazil, Chile, Colombia, Costa Rica, Dominican Republic, Ecuador, Guatemala, Jamaica, Mexico, Paraguay, Peru, Trinidad & Tobago, Uruguay, and Venezuela.

Middle East & North Africa: Algeria, Bahrain, Egypt, Iran, Iraq, Jordan, Kuwait, Lebanon, Morocco, Oman, Qatar, Saudi Arabia, Sudan, Syria, Tunisia, United Arab Emirates, and Yemen.

Central Asia and Southeast Europe: Albania, Armenia, Azerbaijan, Belarus, Bosnia & Herzegovina, Georgia, Kazakhstan, the Kyrgyz Republic, Macedonia, Moldova, Russia, Serbia, Tajikistan, Turkey, Turkmenistan, Ukraine, and Uzbekistan.

Mature: all current 27 members of the European Union, Australia, Canada, Hong Kong, Iceland, Israel, Japan, New Zealand, Norway, Singapore, South Korea, Switzerland, Taiwan, the United Kingdom, and the United States.

Source: The Conference Board Total Economy Database™, August 2021.

References

Blanchard, O. J., & Kremer, M. (1997). Disorganization. *The Quarterly Journal of Economics, 112,* 1091–1126. https://doi.org/10.1162/003355300555439

Campos, N. F., & Coricelli, F. (2002). Growth in transition: What we know, what we don't, and what we should. *Journal of Economic Literature, 40,* 793–836. https://doi.org/10.1257/002205102760273797

Chiodo, A.J., Owyang, M.T. (2002). A case study of a currency crisis: The Russian default of 1998. *Federal Reserve Bank St. Louis Review, 84,* 7–18. https://doi.org/10.20955/r.84.7-18

Crafts, N., Toniolo, G. (2010). Aggregate growth, 1950–2005. In S. Broadberry & K. H. O'Rourke (Eds.), *The Cambridge Economic History of Modern Europe* (pp. 296–332). Cambridge University Press. https://doi.org/10.1017/CBO9780511794841.014

de Vries, K., & Erumban, A. A. (2017). *Total Economy Database. A detailed guide to its sources and methods.* The Conference Board. https://www.conference-board.org/data/economydatabase/total-economy-database-methodology. Accessed 15 December 2021.

EU KLEMS. (2019). The Vienna Institute for International Economic Studies, Vienna. https://euklems.eu/. Accessed 08 November 2021.

Gregory, P. R., & Stuart, R. C. (2001). *Russian and Soviet economic performance and structure* (7th ed.). Addison-Wesley.

Ickes, B. W. (2018). Output Fall—Transformational Recession. In Macmillan Publishers Ltd (Eds.), *The New Palgrave Dictionary of Economics.* Palgrave Macmillan. https://doi.org/10.1057/978-1-349-95189-5_2691

Jorgenson, D. W., Ho, M. S., & Stiroh, K. J. (2005). *Information Technology and the American Growth Resurgence.* The MIT Press.

Kaminski, B., Wang, Z. K., & Winters, A. L. (1996). Foreign trade in the transition. *The World Bank.* https://doi.org/10.1596/0-8213-3611-8

Kapelyushnikov, R. I., Kuznetsov, A., & Kuznetsova, O. (2012). The role of the informal sector, flexible working time and pay in the Russian labour market model. *Post-Communist Economies, 24,* 177–190. https://doi.org/10.1080/14631377.2012.675154

Kornai, J. (1994). Transformational Recession: The Main Causes. *Journal of Comparative Economics, 19*, 39–63. https://www.sciencedirect.com/science/article/pii/S0147596784710626

Kossev, K., & Tompson, W. (2021). Political and Economic Integration with the Western Economies. In M. Morys (Ed.), *The Economic History of Central, East and South-East Europe: 1800 to the Present* (pp. 434–467). Routledge.

McKinsey Global Institute. (1999). *Unlocking economic growth in Russia*. McKinsey Global Institute.

McKinsey Global Institute. (2009). Lean Russia: Sustaining economic growth through improved productivity. https://www.mckinsey.com/global-themes/employment-and-growth/lean-russia-sustaining-economic-growth

OECD. (2015). *The Future of Productivity*. OECD. http://www.oecd.org/economy/growth/OECD-2015-The-future-of-productivity-book.pdf

Rodrik, D. (2003). Introduction: What do we learn from country narratives? In D. Rodrik (Ed.), *In search of prosperity* (pp. 1–19). Princeton University Press, Princeton.

Roland, G., Verdier, T. (1999). Transition and the output fall. *Economics of Transition, 7*, 1–28. https://doi.org/10.1111/1468-0351.00002

Rosstat (1999) Russia in figures. (1999). *Concise statistical handbook*. State Statistical Committee of Russia.

Rosstat (2008) Russia in figures. (2008). *Statistical handbook*. Federal State Statistics Service (Rosstat).

Russia KLEMS. (2019). HSE University. https://www.hse.ru/mirror/pubs/share/322620037. Accessed 15 December 2021.

Timmer, M. P., & Voskoboynikov, I. B. (2016). Is Mining Fuelling Long-run Growth in Russia? Industry Productivity Growth Trends in 1995–2012. In D. W. Jorgenson, K. Fukao, & M. P. Timmer (Eds.), *Growth and Stagnation in the World Economy* (pp. 281–318). Cambridge University Press.

The Conference Board Total Economy Database™, August. (2021). *The Conference Board*. https://www.conference-board.org/data/economydatabase/total-economy-database-productivity. Accessed 03 September 2021.

Voskoboynikov, I. B. (2017). Sources of long run economic growth in Russia before and after the global financial crisis. *Russian Journal of Economics, 3*, 348–365. https://doi.org/10.1016/j.ruje.2017.12.003

Voskoboynikov, I. B. (2020). Structural change, expanding informality and labor productivity growth in Russia. *Review of Income and Wealth, 66*, 394–417. https://doi.org/10.1111/roiw.12417

Voskoboynikov, I. B. (2021). Economic growth and sectoral developments, 1990–2008. In M. Morys (Ed.), *The Economic History of Central, East and South-East Europe: 1800 to the Present* (pp. 387–415). Routledge.

Weil, D. N. (2013). *Economic Growth*, 3rd edn. Pearson, Addison Wesley.

World Bank. (2002). *Transition, the first ten years: Analysis and lessons for eastern Europe and the former Soviet Union*. World Bank, Washington. https://openknowledge.worldbank.org/handle/10986/14042. Accessed 15 April 2022.

Macroeconomic Vulnerability, Monetary, and Fiscal Policies

Marek Dabrowski

Highlights

- Since the collapse of the Soviet Union, Russia has suffered from six rounds of macroeconomic and financial instability. Some of them have been triggered by external shocks, but domestic economic and political factors have always played a role.
- Disinflation in Russia was a very gradual process with several reversals. Russia's inflation has consistently been above the level represented by most advanced and emerging market economies. In the 1990s, these were expansive monetary and fiscal policies responsible for a slow disinflation process. In the 2000s and 2010s, these were a mercantilist monetary policy bias and recurrent episodes of macroeconomic instability.
- After the period of chronic budget deficits in the 1990s, fiscal policy in the 2000s and 2010s became much more prudent, with frequent budget surpluses and the National Wealth Fund (NWF) playing the role of a

M. Dabrowski (✉)
Bruegel, Brussels, Belgium
e-mail: marek.dabrowski@bruegel.org

Higher School of Economics, Moscow, Russia

CASE—Center for Social and Economic Research, Warsaw, Poland

significant systemic buffer against the fluctuation of global oil and natural gas prices.
- Since 1992, Russia has built a market-based tax system similar to most other economies. However, the business community sees frequent changes to this system, numerous tax exemptions, and special tax regimes, and arbitrary tax enforcement practices contributing to a poor business and investment climate.

16.1 Introduction

Since the dissolution of the Soviet Union in 1991, Russia has suffered from at least six periods of macroeconomic and financial turbulences. Some were triggered by external shocks (the global financial crisis [GFC] of 2008–2009, the sharp decline of hydrocarbon prices in 2014–2015, and the COVID-19 crisis in 2020–2021). Others had primarily domestic roots. The Russian economy and financial system experienced limited resilience in dealing with adverse shocks in each case.

The recurrent episodes of macroeconomic and financial crises may be surprising in a country which records persistent current account surpluses and has one of the largest foreign currency reserves in the world, frequent fiscal surpluses, and relatively low public debt. To understand the root causes of this puzzle, one should consider both inconsistencies in macroeconomic management and vulnerabilities in microeconomic, structural, institutional, and political spheres.

This chapter[1] presents an overview of the subsequent episodes of macroeconomic and financial instability (Sect. 16.2), followed by an analysis of the root causes of balance-of-payments fragility (Sect. 16.3). Then we present the evolution of monetary policy and the history of disinflation efforts (Sect. 16.4), fiscal policy (Sect. 16.5), and the tax system (Sect. 16.6). The chapter is concluded with Sect. 16.7.

16.2 Episodes of Macroeconomic and Financial Instability

At the end of the 1980s, the Soviet economic system entered its gradual agony accompanied by deep monetary, fiscal, and balance-of-payments disequilibria (Gaidar, 2007). Since that time, there have been six episodes of macroeconomic and financial instability. These were: (i) the gradual collapse of the Soviet monetary system and the failure of macroeconomic stabilisation after the collapse of the Soviet Union (1989–1995); (ii) the financial crisis of 1998–1999 caused by sovereign default and numerous fragilities of the

---

[1] This chapter partly draws from Dabrowski (2016b, 2019).

banking system; (iii) fallout from the GFC of 2007–2009; (iv) the macroeconomic crisis of 2014–2016 caused by the decline of commodity prices and the Western sanctions against Russia following the annexation of Crimea and the war in Donbas; (v) the COVID-19 crisis (2020–2021); and (vi) the consequences of the Russian aggression against Ukraine in 2022. For the definition and typology of financial and currency crises—see Box 16.1.

Box 16.1 Typology of financial crises

A financial crisis is the broadest category and involves all kinds of instability related to monetary and financial systems (WEO, 1998, pp. 74–76). We define a financial crisis as a sudden decline in confidence regarding the ability of a government, central bank, and banking sector to respect their liabilities on committed terms.

There are four forms of a financial crisis (Dabrowski, 2003, p. 5). A banking crisis refers to actual or potential bank runs or failures that induce commercial banks to suspend the internal convertibility of their liabilities. A public debt crisis is when a government cannot service its foreign and domestic obligations. A balance-of-payments crisis is a structural misbalance between a deficit on the current account (absorption) and capital and financial accounts (sources of financing). A currency crisis is a sub-form of a balance-of-payments crisis. It is defined as a sudden decline in confidence in a given currency, usually leading to a speculative attack against it. Analytically, a currency crisis can be detected by either substantial depreciation of a given currency, the decline in a country's international reserves, or both. Finally, high inflation or hyperinflation means the failure of a central bank to deliver on a price stability mandate, that is, guaranteeing a stable nominal value of its liabilities (currency in circulation and deposits held by a central bank).

16.2.1 Collapse of the Soviet Rouble and Failure of Macroeconomic Stabilisation After the Collapse of the Soviet Union (1989–1995)

The former Soviet Union (FSU) never enjoyed macroeconomic stability even by standards of centrally planned economies (former Czechoslovakia or the German Democratic Republic [GDR] did perform better in this respect). However, due to extensive price and foreign exchange controls, the steadily increasing disequilibria did not lead to high open inflation or official exchange rate depreciation. Instead, they manifested themselves in a physical shortage of goods and services (a shortage economy according to Kornai, 1980) and a black-market exchange rate premium. This led to 'forced' saving (money holders could not spend their money balances to purchase the desired goods and services due to their physical absence) and monetary 'overhang' (Cottarelli & Blejer, 1991).

The situation got even worse in the second half of the 1980s (Gaidar, 2007) thanks to the triple shock: (i) a decline in oil prices (which led to a deterioration in the balance of payments and a decline in budget revenue); (ii) the anti-alcohol campaign (which caused further damage to budget revenue); and (iii) the gradual loss of control of the Union's authorities over state-owned enterprises (SOEs) and Soviet republics.

The third shock resulted from the reluctance to abandon a system of central planning in the situation where the political system entered the path of gradual liberalisation (Mau, 1996; Ofer, 1990). The administrative discipline and associated coercion tools could no longer work, but they were not replaced by market discipline. The partial economic reforms introduced in 1987–1988 (laws on SOEs, cooperatives, and leasing) did not offer a comprehensive market-based system. Instead, they only worsened macroeconomic discipline and the already existing disequilibria. They led to numerous distortions, including beginning oligarchic fortunes based on price and exchange rate arbitrage and stripping profits and assets outside SOEs (see Chapters 4 and 7).

The long and inconclusive debate on potential reforms in 1990–1991, especially on price liberalisation, led to an increase in inflationary expectations, flight from the rouble, and further worsened macroeconomic disequilibria.

One should also add the gradual political disintegration of the Soviet Union, which sped up after the first, partly democratic, elections to republican parliaments on 4 March 1990. The struggle for sovereignty of the Soviet republics included taking political control over republican central banks (before they were just branches of the State Bank of the USSR, popularly called the Gosbank), credit emission, SOEs, and stopping revenue transfers to the Union budget, among others (Dabrowski, 2016a). As a result, the Union's budget had to be financed mainly from money emissions, which led to very high inflation in both the open and hidden forms in 1991.

Despite the dissolution of the Soviet Union at the end of 1991, the Soviet rouble survived until the second half of 1993, complicating the process of macroeconomic stabilisation in the FSU successor states, including Russia.

The single currency was managed by 15 central banks of newly independent states, each subordinated to national parliaments and governments and, as a result, had their own economic policy priorities. The International Monetary Fund (IMF) attempts to help coordinate the monetary policy of post-Soviet central banks or the orderly dissolution of the rouble area (Odling-Smee & Pastor, 2001) brought no effects. Individual central banks learned and built capacities to conduct independent monetary policies in a market environment. On the other hand, the temptation for free riding, i.e., issuing excess money supply, which 'leaked' to neighbouring countries using the same currency, was too strong to resist.

The Central Bank of the Russian Federation (CBRF), which played a crucial role in the system (Russia was the only post-Soviet country that issued cash roubles), was slow in taking active steps towards the dissolution of the rouble area. Although on 1 July 1992, it introduced the requirement of the daily balancing of the correspondent accounts of other post-Soviet central banks at the CBRF, it softened this measure by providing them with generous 'technical credits' (this practice was continued until the spring of 1993). Only in July 1993 were the old Soviet cash roubles converted into new Russian roubles on the territory of Russia. Other countries that remained in the rouble area (Armenia, Azerbaijan, Belarus, Kazakhstan, Moldova, Turkmenistan, and Uzbekistan[2]) were forced to introduce their currencies in the second half of 1993 (Dabrowski, 2016a; Odling-Smee & Pastor, 2001).

The slow dissolution of the rouble area was not the only factor that delayed macroeconomic stabilisation in Russia and most other FSU countries. In January 1992, most consumer and producer prices in Russia were liberalised, leading to very high corrective inflation (see Sect. 16.4). Given the enormous initial disequilibria and monetary overhang accumulated in the Soviet era, this was, to some degree, unavoidable. However, the situation became worse than it could have been thanks to weak monetary and fiscal policies and the late dissolution of the rouble area.

Russia, which started radical but incomplete and inconsequent market reforms at the end of 1991 (the 'Gaidar programme'), continued to run high fiscal (see Sect. 16.5) and quasi-fiscal deficits financed by money emission. Among the quasi-fiscal operations carried out by the CBRF, one can mention the netting out of inter-enterprise payment arrears (*vzaimozachety*). Lax monetary and fiscal policies resulted in very high inflation and abrupt devaluations of the rouble. The 'Black Tuesday' of 11 October 1994, when the rouble depreciated by almost 40% against the USD in a single day, was the most spectacular symptom of continuous macroeconomic instability. It also served as the alarm bell for the federal government and CBRF, which tightened fiscal and monetary policies, leading to disinflation and relative rouble stabilisation in 1995–1997. The subsequent IMF-sponsored reform and macroeconomic adjustment programmes also helped in this process.

However, the prolonged period of macroeconomic instability negatively affected other areas of economic reforms, for example, privatisation and enterprise restructuring (see Chapter 7). It also made the transformation-related output decline longer and more profound (see Chapter 15) and increased its social costs (see Chapter 18). Furthermore, it undermined trust in the rouble and national macroeconomic policies leading to more abrupt market reactions to the subsequent economic and political shocks.

---

[2] Estonia, Latvia, Lithuania, Ukraine, Georgia, and Kyrgyzstan left the rouble area between June 1992 and May 1993. Tajikistan did so in May 1995 only.

16.2.2 The Crisis of 1998–1999

The relative stabilisation accomplished in 1996–1997 proved unsustainable. The money supply was taken under control, but the underlying fiscal disequilibria continued. They were partly reduced and financed by issuing Treasury securities to private investors rather than central bank lending.

However, domestic financial markets remained shallow and foreign purchasers required high-risk premia. Soon the slow pace of fiscal adjustment and structural reforms and continued output decline undermined the sustainability of such financing. The contagion effect coming from the Asian crises of 1997–1998, the strengthening of USD, and the collapse of oil prices (Fig. 16.1) added to market pressures.

As a result, on 17 August 1998, Russia defaulted on its public debt obligations. It abandoned the currency band to the USD, which led to rouble devaluation by three-quarters of its initial value against the USD between June 1998 and June 1999. Russia had to renegotiate its government debt obligations with creditors. Large government debt portfolios also caused a severe banking crisis in Russia. Commercial banks conducted imprudent lending (including connected lending to major shareholders) and had unbalanced assets and liabilities in foreign currencies.

The abrupt devaluation of the rouble led to a new wave of high inflation, fortunately, it was short-lived (see Sect. 16.4). On the other hand, it helped in post-transformation output recovery, especially in agriculture

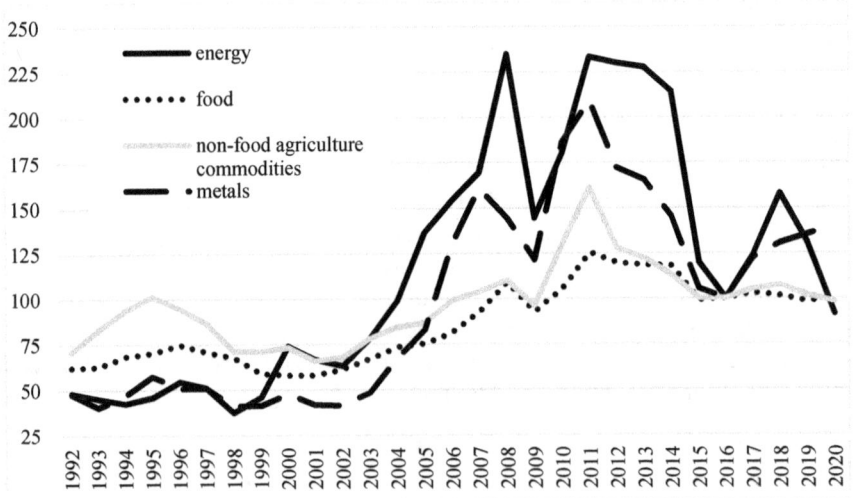

Fig. 16.1 Commodity price indices, 1992–2020, 2016 = 100 (*Source* IMF Primary Commodity Price System, http://www.imf.org/external/np/res/commod/External_Data.xls)

and manufacturing, by reducing the pressure of external competition (see Chapter 15).

16.2.3 Fallout from the Global Financial Crisis (2008–2009)

The 1998–1999 crisis was followed by almost a decade of high growth (see Chapter 15), much lower inflation, better fiscal performance, growing international reserves, higher demand for domestic money balances, and relative exchange rate stability. It resulted from favourable global conditions, i.e., abundant global liquidity, high oil and other commodity prices (Fig. 16.1), large-scale capital inflows, and grasping low-hanging fruits of the decade-long structural and institutional transformation.

However, the GFC triggered by the housing and financial crisis in the United States and part of Europe in 2007–2009 put most of those accomplishments under question. The global liquidity squeeze, especially after the bankruptcy of the Lehmann Brothers in September 2008, led to massive capital outflows from emerging markets. In the summer of 2008, the previous commodity bubble burst, with oil prices plummeting to one-third of this precrisis peak (Fig. 16.1). As a result, Russia experienced capital outflow, a decline in international reserves (Fig. 16.2), depreciation of the rouble by 23.8% between June 2008 and June 2009, a deterioration in fiscal accounts, a GDP fall of 7.8% in 2009, and again tensions in its banking system.

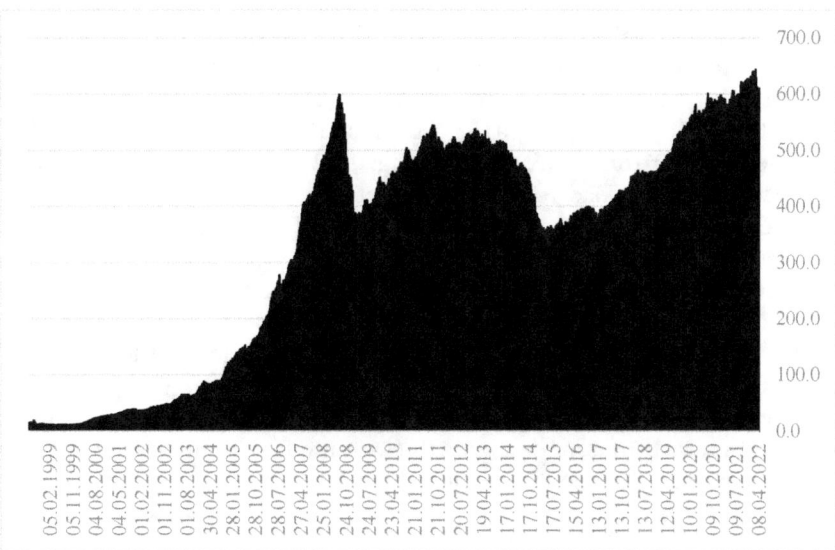

Fig. 16.2 Russia's international reserves in USD billion, 1998–2022 (*Source* http://www.cbr.ru/hd_base/mrrf/mrrf_7d/?UniDbQuery.Posted=True&UniDbQuery.From=05.1998&UniDbQuery.To=04.2022)

The global liquidity squeeze was overcome in the spring of 2009 by the aggressive monetary policy easing of major central banks. As a result, international trade, GDP, and commodity prices started to recover in the second half of 2009. However, Russia did not return to the previous high-growth rates (see Chapter 15). Other macroeconomic indicators also deteriorated as compared to the pre-2008 period.

16.2.4 The 2014–2016 Crisis

The next crisis episode started in Russia in early 2014 due to global, regional, and country-specific factors. Among the global factors, one can point to a gradual tightening of US monetary policy, some growth slowdown in China and India, and a far-reaching collapse of oil and other commodity prices (Fig. 16.1). Regionally, Russia's annexation of Crimea in March and its support for the separatist rebellion in Donbas in the following months led to a substantial deterioration in the business and investment climate in Ukraine, Russia, and other FSU countries (an increase in geopolitical risks), the wave of the Western sanctions against Russia, Russia's retaliation measures against the West, and Russia's sanctions against Ukraine (see Chapter 14). These global and regional factors overlapped with domestic economic stagnation and decreasing productivity in Russia (see Chapter 15) and the perception of reform stagnation or even their partial reversal, especially the increasing role of SOEs (see Chapters 7 and 19).

Overall, between December 2013 and December 2015, the rouble depreciated by 55.1% against the USD. Thus, the scale of currency depreciation was closer to the 1998–1999 crisis than to the GFC (2008–2009) and higher than in most other oil-exporting countries (Dabrowski, 2016b). Between November 2013 and April 2015, the international reserves of the CBRF decreased by approximately one-third (Fig. 16.2). The fiscal deficit increased, and the government had to partially deplete its sovereign wealth funds (see Sect. 16.5). Inflation returned to a two-digit level (see Sect. 16.4).

Russia was one of few oil exporters—apart from war-affected Iraq and Libya and Venezuela (which suffered from more than a decade of economic populism)—where GDP decreased in 2015 (by –2.0%). It was preceded by a meagre growth rate of 0.7% in 2014 and followed by an even lower growth rate of 0.2% in 2016.

Since 2016, following a partial recovery of oil prices (Fig. 16.1), the Russian economy returned to a modest growth (with the highest annual rate of 2.8% in 2018) and macroeconomic stability.

16.2.5 The COVID-19 Crisis (2020–2021)

Once again, the relative macroeconomic stability did not last long. In February and March 2020, the entire world economy was hit by the COVID-19 pandemic. Three factors negatively influenced the economic performance of Russia in 2020. The first factor was the lockdown measures. Compared to other countries, Russia represented a medium stringency of pandemic-related restrictions.[3] The second was a decline in oil prices in March–April 2020. However, in the second half of 2020, oil prices started to recover gradually, reaching a pre-crisis level in the last quarter of 2021. In addition, as a result of a global economic recovery, prices for natural gas, metals, and food products also started to grow rapidly. Third, the COVID-19 crisis also triggered a massive capital outflow from emerging markets, including Russia, in February and March 2020 (Lanau & Fortun, 2020). However, thanks to the ultra-lax monetary policy of the US Federal Reserve Board and other leading central banks, the liquidity crisis in the international financial market was overcome at the end of the second quarter of 2020. Capital flows to emerging markets resumed. Nevertheless, the rouble depreciated by approximately 20% against the USD between the end of January 2020 and the end of January 2022.

In 2020, Russia recorded a real GDP decline of 3%, less than many other advanced and emerging market economies. Its fiscal deficit increased modestly (to –4.0 of GDP). Although the pandemic is an unfinished story (at least at the time of writing this chapter, i.e., April 2022), its negative economic consequences for the Russian economy seemed to be overcome in 2021, with positive growth above 4% and an improvement of fiscal indicators.

16.2.6 Macroeconomic Consequences of the War with Ukraine (2022)

The invasion of Ukraine, which started on 24 February 2022, triggered another macroeconomic and financial crisis in the Russian economy, possibly the most serious one among those analysed in this section. An unprecedented large package of international economic and financial sanctions against Russia (see Chapter 14) is the main factor behind this adverse shock. Most importantly (for macroeconomic and financial stability), a substantial part of the CBRF international reserves was frozen. The largest Russian banks were cut off from the global financial markets and the SWIFT telecommunication network. The financial market immediately reacted to the war and sanctions. Russia experienced another wave of domestic financial panic and capital outflows, but they were stopped by heavy capital control measures and 80% foreign currency surrender requirements for exporters. When writing this chapter (April 2022), the rouble is no longer a convertible currency. However, it is too early to assess the potential impact of the war and sanctions on the Russian economy.

---

[3] https://ourworldindata.org/grapher/covid-stringency-index?tab=chart&country=~RUS.

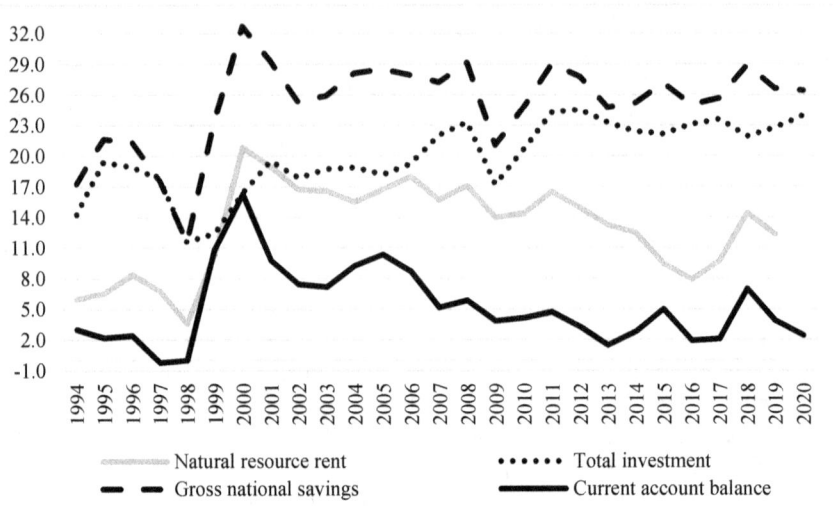

Fig. 16.3 Russia: savings, investment, current account balance, and natural resource rent, % of GDP, 1994–2020 (*Source* IMF World Economic Outlook database, October 2021; World Bank's World Development Indicators, last update 28 October 2021)

16.3 Sources of Balance-of-Payments and Currency Fragility

Russia is a country that runs a permanent current account surplus even in years of low oil prices[4] (Fig. 16.3). This originates from a relatively high gross national savings rate (in most years in the range of 25–30% of GDP) underpinned by high natural resource rents (mainly the oil rent). Since the early 2000s, the CBRF international reserves have increased rapidly (Fig. 16.2), achieving one of the highest levels in the world. Chronic fiscal deficits, responsible for the delayed stabilisation in the early 1990s and the 1998–1999 crisis, disappeared in the next two decades (see Sect. 16.5). Furthermore, since the mid-2000s, the federal government had built sovereign wealth funds out of fiscal surpluses when oil prices were high.

In the light of the above macroeconomic characteristics, identifying the causes of repeated balance-of-payments and rouble instability looks like a non-trivial task. Elementary balance-of-payments arithmetic suggests that developments on a capital account trigger the subsequent currency crises. Figure 16.4 confirms this suggestion. Russia has been a permanent net exporter of private capital (except for the short period of 2006–2007), which can be considered a common phenomenon in countries with a high savings rate and natural resource rent. However, Russia is characterised by a high volatility of capital flows.

---

[4] Only in 1997, Russia recorded a current account deficit of –0.2% of GDP.

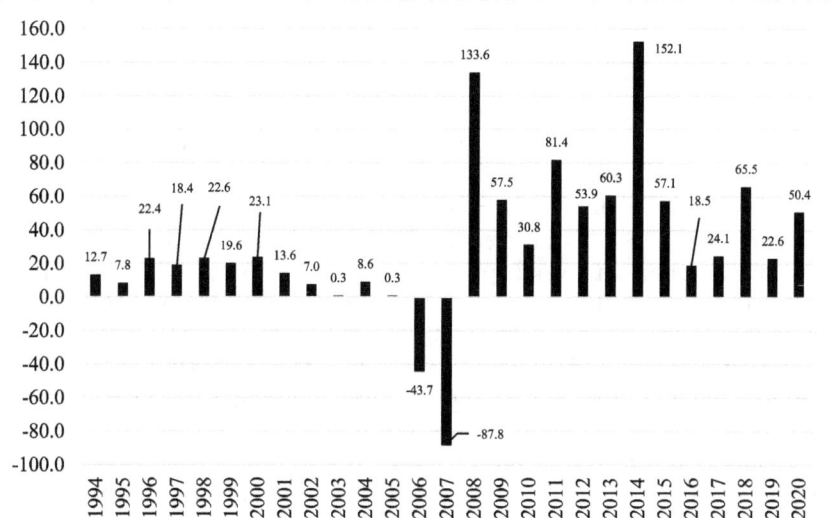

Fig. 16.4 Russia: net private capital flows, USD billion, 1994–2020 (*Note* Sign (−) means net capital inflows, sign (+)—net capital outflow. *Source* http://www.cbr.ru/statistics/credit_statistics/bop/outflow.xlsx)

As long as the macroeconomic and political environment was perceived stable (in particular, in the early and mid-2000s, before the GFC), economic agents were ready to invest in Russia and use the domestic currency (rouble). However, once the Russian economy was hit by an external economic shock (for example, in 2008–2009, 2014–2015, and 2020) or prospects of war and Western sanctions (2014–2015, 2022), they moved their financial assets outside the country on a massive scale. This concerned both residents and non-residents. Similar reactions have been observed in other emerging market economies hit by financial crises or political instability, such as in Latin America in the 1970s and 1980s.

The dominant business model has also facilitated the rapid capital outflow from Russia. Most large companies remain in close ownership relationships with their foreign subsidiaries or parent companies (owned by expatriates). They keep a substantial part of their assets abroad and finance their domestic operations through foreign borrowing (Rogov, 2014).

The entire post-2008 period has been marked by Russia's intensification of net capital outflows (Fig. 16.4). This can be explained by the continuous deterioration of Russia's business and investment climate. Widespread corruption, weak rule of law, unstable property rights (the danger of politically motivated expropriation), increasing red tape, and harassment by various law enforcement agencies are symptoms of such an unfavourable climate (see Chapters 5 and 6). Numerous restrictions have always characterised the policy towards foreign investors, but since 2014 it has become even more unfriendly (see Chapters 13 and 14).

While Russia's macroeconomic fragility is deeply rooted in its microeconomic and institutional imperfections, macroeconomic factors also play a role. Memories of the past crises have had a powerful impact on the behaviour of domestic economic agents. They have lost their savings several times due to high inflation in the 1990s, banking failures, and non-equivalent exchanges of money in 1991 and 1993 (and earlier, in the Soviet era—in 1947 and 1961). They have experienced several episodes of rouble devaluation (see Sect. 16.2). As a result, between the end of 1995 and 2020, the rouble lost 93.8% of its initial value against the USD.

Even after the end of the high inflation era of the 1990s, the continuous moderate inflation (two-digit or high low-digit—see Sect. 16.4) did not help build confidence in the domestic currency.

As a result, trust in the rouble and the domestic financial system remains limited. As long as there is no severe turbulence, this low level of trust might be sufficient to keep the currency stable and banks afloat. In an adverse shock, however, whether of economic or political origin, external or domestic source, domestic money-holders are the first to run from the rouble and banking deposits.

The widespread phenomenon of currency substitution (also known from other emerging market economies) illustrates the limited trust in the rouble. Even in the relatively stable periods such as the mid-2000s and the late 2010s, the share of foreign-exchange denominated liabilities in total liabilities of the Russian banking system was substantial, in the range of 20–25%. During the crisis periods, it increased, reaching, for example, 31.5% in 2009 and 39.9% in 2015. Apart from foreign-exchange denominated deposits, the Russian population and small- and medium-sized enterprises keep large amounts of USD and EUR cash. Still, there are no statistics that can provide concrete figures.

16.4 Inflation, Monetary Policy, Central Bank Independence

In the early 1990s, Russia experienced very high inflation, which decelerated only gradually and with periodic reversals associated with macroeconomic and financial instability episodes (see Sect. 16.2).

The initial outburst of very high inflation in 1992 was associated with a radical price liberalisation and the freeing of the 'monetary overhang' accumulated in the late Soviet era (see Subsection 16.2.1). However, the subsequent failures of tightening both monetary and fiscal policies in 1992–1994 extended the period of three-digit inflation until 1995 (Fig. 16.5). The macroeconomic stabilisation effort undertaken in 1994–1995 proved more successful than the previous ones. It resulted in the end-of-year inflation going down from 131.3% in 1995 to 21.8% in 1996 and 11.0% in 1997. However, the financial crisis of 1998-1999 reversed this trend. Inflation jumped to 84.4% at the end of 1998 and 36.6% in 1999. Then the slow disinflation process resumed. In 2006, inflation reached a one-digit level (9.0%) for the first time. After the return to a two-digit level in 2007–2008, it decreased below 10% again in 2009–2013 and since 2016. Only in 2017, it amounted to below 5%. The 2017 record (2.5%) was the best in the analysed period of 1992–2021. Overall, the cumulative inflation between the end of 1993 and the end of 2021 amounted to 215,370%. Between the end of 2000 and the end of 2021, it amounted to 767%. Between the end of 2010 and the end of 2021—248%.

Similar to chronic macroeconomic fragility (see Sect. 16.3), explaining the causes of the slow disinflation process (slower than in most other emerging markets and transition economies) is not easy. Chronic fiscal disequilibria and the resulting fiscal and quasi-fiscal pressures on monetary policy that could be rightly blamed for high inflation in the 1990s disappeared since the early 2000s (see Sect. 16.5). On the contrary, the creation of sovereign wealth funds helped sterilise a part of the rapidly increasing CBRF international reserves and, therefore, the CBRF monetary base. Thus, the reasons for slow disinflation should be searched within the monetary policy itself.

Between 1992 and 1995, the rouble exchange rate was freely floating, and the CBRF was expected to target monetary aggregates. However, it conducted various quasi-fiscal activities such as netting out inter-enterprise arrears and granting discounted credits to specific sectors and industries, and 'technical' credits to other post-Soviet countries remaining in the Soviet rouble area (see Subsection 16.2.1). All of them contradicted an anti-inflationary mandate. In the spring of 1995, the CBRF adopted an exchange rate targeting in the form

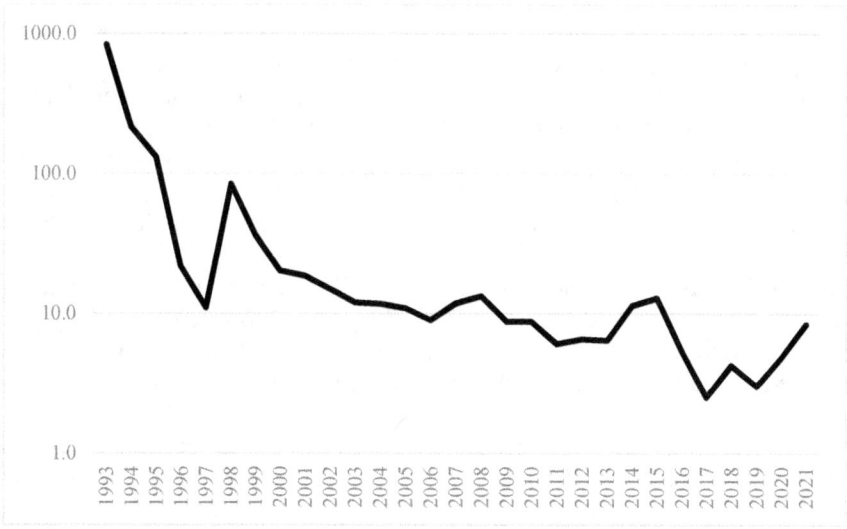

Fig. 16.5 Russia: Inflation, end of the period, annual % change, 1993–2021, logarithmic scale (*Source* IMF World Economic Outlook database, April 2022)

of a currency band against the USD. From time to time, this band was slightly depreciated. The new policy helped stabilise inflationary expectations and slow down inflation from 1996 to 1997. However, an exchange rate peg was fundamentally inconsistent with continuous large fiscal deficits and led to the rouble crash of 17 August 1998, a typical case of a 'first-generation currency crisis' (Flood & Garber, 1984; Krugman, 1979).

After the 1998–1999 financial crisis, the CBRF has never returned to explicit exchange rate targeting. Still, informally, it tried to follow a sort of exchange rate band against the basket of the USD and EUR (in changing proportions of both currencies). Formally, there was no explicitly stated nominal anchor (Dabrowski, 2013). Interestingly, the de facto exchange rate policy of the CBRF was asymmetric. During the subsequent crises (1998–1999, 2008–2009, 2014–2015), the CBRF allowed the rouble exchange rate to depreciate substantially (in the case of 1998–1999, it did not have other choices). However, it was reluctant to allow it to recover to the pre-crisis level when the macroeconomic situation improved. In the early 2000s, when Russia's terms of trade began to improve rapidly (as a result of rising oil prices), the CBRF continued the de facto crawling (depreciating) band.

In November 2014, at the peak of another crisis and after more than a decade of IMF agitation, the CBRF moved officially to an inflation targeting strategy under the floating exchange rate. It facilitated further disinflation progress in the second half of the 2010s. However, the CBRF international reserves (Fig. 16.2) demonstrate that net foreign exchange purchases were continued on a large scale, so the rouble exchange rate was not genuinely floating (note that free-floating is one of the conditions of effective inflation targeting).

For two reasons, a mercantilist policy does not help the disinflation process. First, a weak domestic currency paralyses the exchange rate channel of an anti-inflationary policy. Second, large international reserves mean large net foreign assets and a large monetary base of the CBRF, other things being equal.

A policy to keep the domestic currency weak is usually motivated by an export-oriented growth strategy (the example of several Asian economies at the end of the twentieth century) and pressures of the export lobbies. None of these motives seem to be present in Russia. Fuels and energy contribute over 70% of its merchandise exports (see Chapters 9 and 12). Manufacturing exports (the standard beneficiary of export support policies in emerging market economies) are less meaningful in Russia. Perhaps stimulation of import substitution in manufacturing and agriculture (see Chapter 14) plays some role.

However, two other arguments may be more critical. First, building up a large stock of international reserves (a traditional mercantilist motive) may be seen as a measure to increase macroeconomic resilience to adverse shocks, a policy adopted by several emerging market economies after the series of financial crises in the second half of the 1990s and early 2000s, and advocated by the IMF at that time. In the case of Russia, it could also be the desire to become independent of external financial aid (especially after the experience of the 1998–1999 crisis). Since 2014, there is also a question of resilience against potential Western sanctions (however, the 2022 financial sanctions hit the CBRF international reserves—see Chapter 14). Second, the rouble depreciation, resulting from lower oil and natural gas prices, compensates for budget revenue losses (export and natural resource taxes are denominated in foreign currency).

All this leads us to the question of CBRF independence. In the 1990s, the position of the CBRF governor and CBRF monetary policy were subjects of the continuous political struggle between President Boris Yeltsin's administration and the parliament dominated by an opposition led by the Communist Party of the Russian Federation. It was not easy to say about genuine central bank independence in such a political environment. In the next two decades, the situation stabilised with governors serving their full terms, increasing the level of CBRF professionalism and new legislation, which followed international experience. However, the Federal Law No. 86-FZ of 10 July 2002 'On the Central Bank of the Russian Federation (Bank of Russia)' with several further modifications[5] does not offer the CBRF comprehensive legal guarantees of its independence as most individual legislative acts in advanced economies do. For example, the list of reasons justifying the dismissal of the Governor and the members of the Board of Directors during their terms is relatively long (Articles 14 and 15).

The addition of the responsibility for regulation and supervision of the entire Russian financial sector in 2013 to the list of tasks of the CBRF (see Chapter 7) is also a mixed blessing for its monetary policy independence (sometimes, these tasks stay in conflict with a price stability goal).

The hyper-centralised system of executive power in Russia, with the dominant role of the President and his Administration and limited judicial independence (see Chapter 5), make the actual independence of the CBRF even more fragile and problematic. This could be observed in all crisis episodes when the CBRF participated in rescuing large banks and companies (European Commission, 2020).

16.5 Evolution of Fiscal Policy

In the 1990s, Russia experienced a chronic fiscal crisis caused by the transformation-related output decline (see Chapter 15), low international oil prices, and political inability to balance government expenditures with revenues. Since the early 2000s, the fiscal situation has improved due to economic recovery, high oil prices, and more conservative fiscal policies. Windfall gains from high oil prices allowed the creation of two sovereign wealth funds, which helped the federal government withstand the adverse budgetary

---

[5] https://www.cbr.ru/eng/about_br/bankstatus/.

effects of the macroeconomic and financial crises in 2008–2009, 2014–2015, and 2020–2021.

Figure 16.6 shows that in the early and mid-2000s, Russia produced substantial fiscal surpluses. This resulted in, among others, the rapid reduction of very high general government (GG) gross debt (Fig. 16.7). While in 1998, it amounted to 135% of GDP (there are no earlier IMF fiscal statistics on Russia), 8 years later (in 2006), it went down below 10% of GDP. Given the creation of sovereign wealth funds and the rapid increase in CBRF international reserves (see Sect. 16.3), the GG net debt was even lower, most probably—negative (there are no IMF WEO statistics on Russia's GG net debt).

The GFC and subsequent crises (2014–2015, 2020, and most probably 2022) caused a deterioration in fiscal indicators (Fig. 16.6). They improved between the crisis episodes but less spectacularly than before the GFC. The periods of positive GG balances were short (2011–2012, 2018–2019, and 2021) and surpluses were smaller than in the early and mid-2010s. GG gross debt fluctuated between 10 and 20% of GDP, which is still not a large number compared to other emerging market and advanced economies. However, in the era of comprehensive financial sanctions (the reality of early 2022), servicing even a small GG debt may meet serious market obstacles.

As mentioned earlier, Russia has had a sovereign wealth fund. Its beginning goes back to January 2004, when it was established as the Stabilisation Fund. In January 2008, the Stabilisation Fund was split into the Reserve Fund and the NWF. During the 2014–2015 crisis, the assets of the Reserve Fund were depleted. In 2017, the two funds were merged again under the name of the NWF. The NWF is formed from the federal budget's surplus of oil and natural

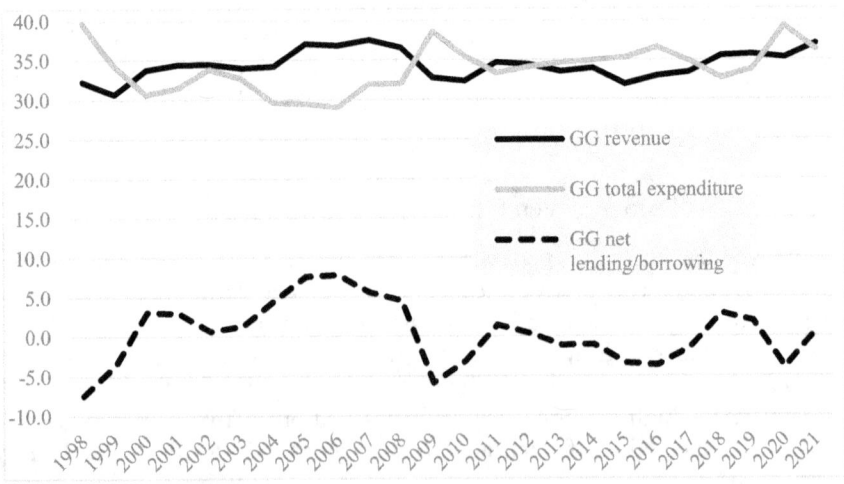

Fig. 16.6 Russia: fiscal indicators, in % of GDP, 1998–2021 (*Source* IMF World Economic Outlook database, April 2022)

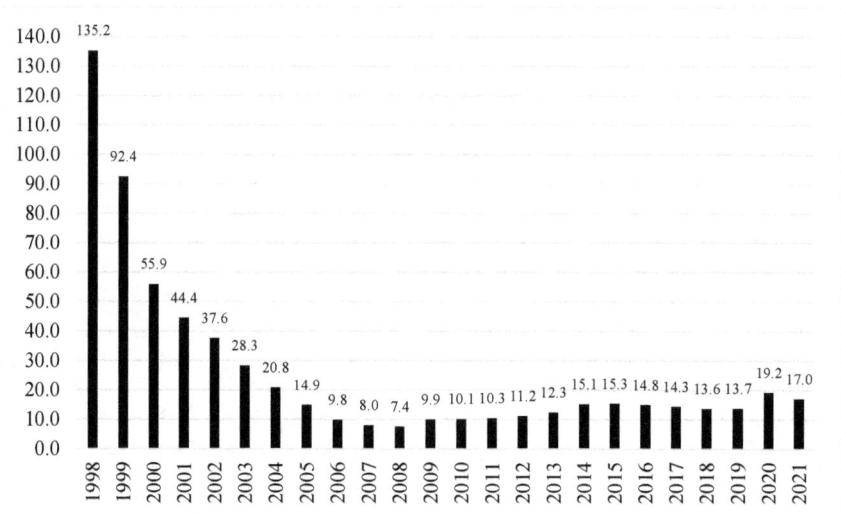

Fig. 16.7 Russia: General government gross debt, in % of GDP, 1998–2021 (*Source* IMF World Economic Outlook database, April 2022)

gas revenues, exceeding 3.7% of GDP forecasted for a given fiscal year. It is used for budgetary deficit financing when oil and natural gas prices are low. It also supports the pension system. Its size amounted to approximately 12% of GDP in November 2021.[6]

Figure 16.6 shows that the GG's total expenditure has fluctuated between 30 and 40% of GDP, with a somewhat increasing trend in the 2010s. By international comparison, Russia is a medium-size public spender, similar to many other emerging market economies from the upper middle-income group.

Table 16.1 presents a functional classification of GG expenditure and its evolution. Defence spending seems to be underestimated if one compares it with the World Bank's World Development Indicators statistics (based on analyses of the Stockholm International Peace Research Institute).[7] Between 2000 and 2020, expenditure on general public services and social protection (see Chapter 18) increased markedly. This may be explained by the low level of public sector salaries, pensions, and other social benefits in 2000 and, in the case of pensions, by population aging (see Chapter 2). Expenditure on economic affairs (mainly various subsidies) also moderately increased. On the other hand, spending on education and health stayed on a relatively modest level and represented a declining trend in the case of health.

Analysing the structure of GG revenue (Table 16.2), there is a substantial and increasing role of 'other revenue', which includes, among others, a mineral

---

[6] See https://minfin.gov.ru/en/key/nationalwealthfund/.
[7] See https://data.worldbank.org/indicator/MS.MIL.XPND.GD.ZS?locations=RU.

Table 16.1 Russia: structure of general government expenditure (functional classification), % of GDP, 2000–2020

Expenditure item	2000	2004	2008	2012	2016	2020
General public services	8.3	6.1	12.6	9.1	7.9	10.0
Defence	2.7	2.4	2.1	2.8	2.3	2.0
Public order & safety	1.5	2.5	2.3	2.6	2.3	2.3
Economic affairs	4.8	4.1	3.8	3.5	3.5	4.7
Environment protection	0.0	0.1	0.1	0.1	0.1	0.3
Housing & community amenities	2.7	1.6	1.9	1.2	1.0	1.3
Health	1.9	1.6	3.9	3.2	3.6	2.2
Recreation, culture, & religion	0.6	0.9	0.6	0.8	0.9	1.0
Education	2.7	3.2	3.8	3.6	3.6	3.7
Social protection	7.5	9.1	8.5	11.3	12.6	14.2

Source IMF Government Finance Statistics

extraction tax (MET) and other royalty-type payments for the exploitation of mineral resources and dividends from SOEs. Since the mid-2010s, the MET has replaced export taxes on oil and natural gas (see Chapters 9 and 12); shares of the latter in GG revenue have started to decline. Overall, oil-related revenue was estimated at 10.1% of GDP in 2018 and 8.2% in 2019 (IMF, 2021, p. 33). Among the 'standard' taxes, taxation of goods and services (VAT and excise taxes) and income, profit, and capital gains taxation bring similar portions of GDP.

16.6 Tax System

In 1992, Russia introduced a market-based tax system non-existent in the centrally planned economy. It consisted of the value-added tax (VAT), initially at a very high rate of 28% (which later came down to 20%), excise taxes, personal income tax (PIT), profit tax (the equivalent of a corporate income tax [CIT]), customs duties and export taxes (which had to be gradually decreased or removed as a result of the accession process to the World Trade Organization—see Chapter 12), the MET and other royalty-type payments and duties related to the extraction of mineral resources and the energy sector (see Chapter 9), and regional and local taxes. This reform also required a tax and customs administration compatible with a market system.

Implementation of the 1992 tax reform was neither easy nor straightforward. The initial tax legislation was not precise enough and contained numerous loopholes. Furthermore, newly introduced taxes were the subject of erosion due to the tax exemptions, holidays, and special tax regimes, among others, introduced under the pressure of various sectoral and regional lobbies. On the other hand, the resulting revenue losses were compensated by multiple ad hoc tax measures on the federal and regional levels. These measures (for

Table 16.2 Russia: Structure of general government revenue (selected items), % of GDP, 2000–2020

Revenue item	2000	2002	2004	2006	2008	2010	2012	2014	2016	2018	2020
Taxes on income, profits, and capital gains	7.5	7.3	8.3	9.6	9.4	7.7	7.3	6.6	6.3	7.8	8.0
Taxes on property		1.3	1.2	0.9	1.0	1.1	1.0	1.1	1.2	1.2	0.5
Taxes on goods and services		10.7	7.5	6.2	5.8	6.1	6.6	6.7	7.5	8.0	9.3
Taxes on international trade and transactions	3.0	2.8	4.7	8.0	8.0	6.4	7.4	6.8	3.1	3.6	1.8
Other taxes	1.1	0.1	0.1	0.0	0.0	0.0	0.0	0.0	0.0	0.0	0.0
Social contributions	6.6	11.0	6.9	5.2	5.0	5.1	5.9	6.6	8.0	7.2	7.8
Other revenue	6.0	13.2	8.5	7.7	16.2	11.7	12.7	11.5	10.3	10.8	11.6

Source IMF Government Finance Statistics

example, local sales taxes) were inconsistent with the essential components of the tax system, for example, VAT, and highly distortive.

Tax enforcement was ineffective (in terms of revenue collection) but arbitrary and rightly considered by many businesses as a mechanism of administrative harassment and rent extraction negatively influencing the business and investment climate (see Chapter 6). Worse, since the 2000s, it started to be used as an instrument of politically motivated expropriation and political repressions (the example of the crackdown on the Yukos company and its major shareholders in 2003–2005).

Gradually, during the 1990s and early 2000s, many pieces of the tax system, legislation, and administration were improved, for example, by the adoption of the comprehensive Tax Code in two parts (in 1998 and 2000, respectively). The introduction of the proportional personal income tax rate of 13% in 2001 (subject to changes in 2020–2021) was a flagship measure of a more liberal and pro-business tax policy of the early 2000s. Nevertheless, many shortcomings of the earlier period remained in place, for example, excessive tax exemptions (aimed at stimulating various industrial and regional policies—see Chapters 8 and 11) or the arbitrary functioning of the tax administration.

At the beginning of 2022, the main components of the federal tax system included (Fernandez, 2022):

- VAT with two rates: a basic rate of 20% and a lower rate of 10% (for food and some medical items, among others);
- Excise taxes;
- MET (see Chapter 9);
- PIT with two rates: 13% (up to an annual income of RUB 5 million) and 15% (above);
- CIT of 20%; 13% is paid for dividend profits;
- Unified social tax (contribution to the pension, medical insurance, and social insurance funds) of 30%.

16.7 Conclusions

In the first half of the 1990s, the subsequent attempts at macroeconomic stabilisation in Russia failed due to the late dissolution of the Soviet rouble area (in the second half of 1993) and expansive monetary and fiscal policies. A partial disinflation and stabilisation were achieved only in 1996–1997. However, the August 1998 financial crisis (due to insufficient fiscal adjustment) devastated these limited achievements.

Only in the early and mid-2000s, thanks to the post-transition economic recovery and global commodity boom, Russia radically strengthened its macroeconomic fundamentals. CBRF international reserves grew rapidly and fiscal surpluses allowed the formation of the sovereign wealth fund. However, despite these buffers and prudent monetary and fiscal policies, the Russian economy remained vulnerable to adverse shocks, which was visible, in particular, during the GFC and the 2014–2015 crisis. Apart from the memory of past crises, this vulnerability originates from a poor business and investment climate, numerous institutional deficiencies, excessive dependence on natural resource rents (especially on oil-related revenue), and, since 2014, assertive foreign and military policy. The war in Ukraine in 2022 and the associated package of international sanctions against Russia can damage Russia's macroeconomic stability and growth potential.

Questions for Students

1. Which have been the main episodes of macroeconomic and financial instability in Russia in the post-Soviet era?
2. What have been the reasons for continuous macroeconomic fragility despite current account surpluses and prudent fiscal policy (since the early 2000s)?
3. Please characterise the evolution of monetary and exchange rate policies since the early 1990s.
4. Please describe the macroeconomic role of the NWF, its institutional evolution, and the sources of its formation.
5. What are the strong and weak points of the Russian tax system?

References

Cottarelli, C., & Blejer, M. (1991, June). Forced Savings and Repressed Inflation in the Soviet Union: Some Empirical Results. IMF Working Paper WP/91/55. https://www.elibrary.imf.org/doc/IMF001/02566-9781451847550/02566-9781451847550/Other_formats/Source_PDF/02566-9781455298808.pdf

Dabrowski, M. (2003). Currency Crises in Emerging-Market Economies: An Overview. In M. Dabrowski (Ed.), *Currency Crises in Emerging Markets*. Kluwer Academic Publishers.

Dabrowski, M. (2013). Monetary policy regimes in CIS economies and their ability to provide price and financial stability. BOFIT Discussion Papers 8. Bank of Finland, Institute for Economies in Transition. http://www.suomenpankki.fi/bofit_en/tutkimus/tutkimusjulkaisut/dp/Documents/2013/dp0813.pdf

Dabrowski, M. (2016a). Post-Communist Transition and Monetary Disintegration. *CESifo Forum, 17*(4), 3–11. https://www.cesifo-group.de/DocDL/forum-2016a-4-dabrowski-ruble-zone-collapse-december.pdf

Dabrowski, M. (2016b). Currency crises in post-Soviet economies—a never ending story? *Russian Journal of Economics, 2*(3), 302–326. https://doi.org/10.1016/j.ruje.2016.08.002

Dabrowski, M. (2019). Factors determining Russia's long-term growth rate. *Russian Journal of Economics, 5*(4), 328–353. https://rujec.org/article/49417/download/pdf/366392

European Commission. (2020). Commission Staff Working Document on significant distortions in the economy of the Russian Federation for the purposes of trade defence investigations. European Commission, Brussels. https://trade.ec.europa.eu/doclib/docs/2020/october/tradoc_158997.pdf

Fernandez, K. (2022, February 7). Taxes in Russia: A guide to the Russian tax system. *Expatica*. https://www.expatica.com/ru/finance/taxes/taxes-in-russia-104125/#corporate

Flood, R. P., & Garber, P. M. (1984). Collapsing exchange rate regimes: Some linear examples. *Journal of International Economics, 17*, 1–13.

Gaidar, Y. (2007). *Collapse of an Empire: Lessons for Modern Russia*. Brookings Institution Press.

IMF. (2021). Russian Federation: 2020 Article IV Consultation-Press Release; Staff Report, IMF Country Report CR/2021/036. https://www.imf.org/-/media/Files/Publications/CR/2021/English/1RUSEA2021001.ashx

Kornai, J. (1980). *Economics of Shortage*. North-Holland.

Krugman, P. (1979). A model of balance of payments crises. *Journal of Money, Credit, and Banking, 11*, 311–325.

Lanau, S., & Fortun, J. (2020, March 17). The COVID-19 Shock to EM Flows. Economic Views. Institute for International Finance. https://www.iif.com/Portals/0/Files/content/EV_03172020.pdf

Mau, V. (1996). The Political History of Economic Reform in Russia, 1985–1994. Centre for Research into Communist Economies, London, U.K.

Odling-Smee, J., & Pastor, G. (2001, August). The IMF and the Ruble Area, 1991–1993. IMF Working Paper WP/01/101. http://www.imf.org/external/pubs/ft/wp/2001/wp01101.pdf

Ofer, G. (1990). Macroeconomic Issues of Soviet Reforms. *NBER Macroeconomics Annual, 5*, 297–334. https://www.journals.uchicago.edu/doi/pdf/10.1086/654147

Rogov, K. (2014, December 23). What will be the consequences of the Russian currency crisis? European Council of Foreign Relations, Commentary. http://www.ecfr.eu/article/commentary_what_will_be_the_consequences_of_the_russian_currency_crisis385

WEO. (1998, May). World Economic Outlook. International Monetary Fund, Washington DC. http://www.imf.org/external/pubs/ft/weo/weo0598/pdf/0598ch4.pdf

CHAPTER 17

Labour Market, Employment, and Migration

Vladimir Gimpelson

Highlights

- At the start of its transition, Russia was structurally and institutionally unfit for the requirements of the market economy. Substantial unemployment was expected given the scale of its GDP decline. However, during the 1990s, employment declined modestly and unemployment, though on the rise, increased only gradually. The 1998–1999 crisis brought about the lowest point of the transformational recession, with unemployment peaking at 14%.
- The post-crisis recovery brought strong GDP growth and stabilisation in the labour market. This successful period ended with a new crisis in 2008–2009. This next period was marked by a prolonged stagnation.
- For the Russian labour market, all boom and bust episodes were characterised by similar adjustment mechanisms. Adjustments always occurred through the wage (price) side while employment showed little change. Rigid employment and flexible wages allowed Russia to maintain low unemployment.

V. Gimpelson (✉)
Higher School of Economics, Moscow, Russia
e-mail: vladim.gimpelson@gmail.com

Institute of Labour Economics (IZA), Bonn, Germany

- This type of adjustment has specific institutional foundations: strict employment protection, low unemployment benefits and minimum wage levels, high wage flexibility, and substantial informality.
- Employment reallocated from agriculture and industry to the service sector, from large to small firms, and from the corporate to the non-corporate segment. The occupational composition also experienced a dramatic change, especially during the 1990s.
- The opposite side of this adjustment pattern is the high proportion of low-paid and low-quality jobs. In fact, higher unemployment was substituted by the higher vulnerability of labour income for those employed.
- The Russian labour force is highly educated. Over one-third of the employed hold a university degree, while only a small percentage are without a secondary education. Though this provides opportunities for the economy, it also creates structural problems (a mismatch between supply and demand). Demand for low-skilled labour is satisfied by the migrant labour force from Central Asia.

17.1 Introduction

This chapter discusses the labour market developments that have been taking place since the start of Russia's economic transition. There are many reasons why these developments are important and interesting. On the one side, the labour market contributes to shaping a healthy macroeconomic environment by ensuring a high level of employment and decent consumption without heating inflationary expectations; on the other, it is 'responsible' for translating economic performance into the well-being of households.

The Russian economy entered its transition period in the early 1990s, with the labour market having been both shaped and constrained by its Soviet legacy. This concerned a number of factors on the supply and demand sides as well as all labour market institutions. On the supply side, there was excessive employment and participation, outdated and over-specialised education, and low motivation among workers. The demand side was affected by the domination of heavy industries and the undeveloped production of consumer goods and services. On top of this, many firms were insolvent, and the fiscal system was in a deep crisis. Modern labour market institutions, including those providing social safety nets, did not exist or were critically underdeveloped. All of this made the labour market absolutely unfit to the needs and requirements of the market economy.

17.2 A Concise Story of Labour Market Adjustment

The story of the Russian labour market can be divided into three sub-periods which are separated from each other by major economic crises. The first sub-period lasted from early 1992—the beginning of Russia's transition

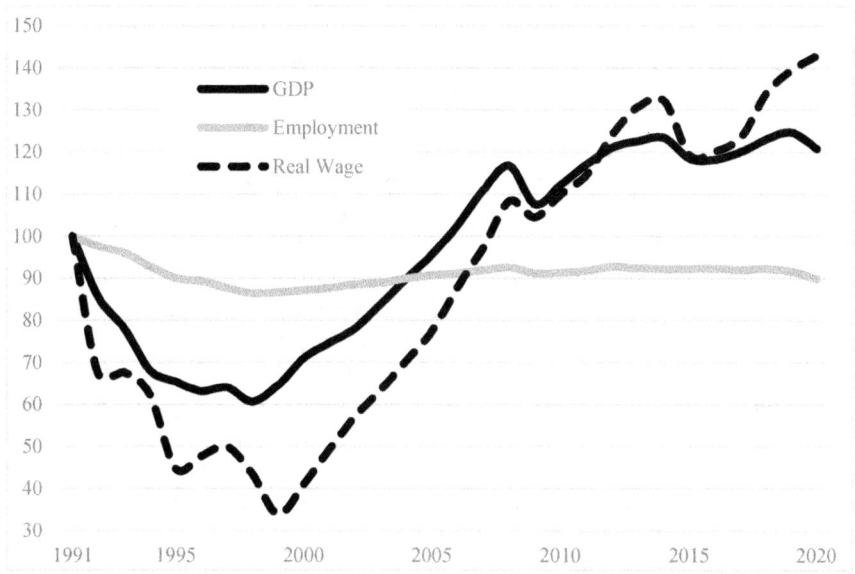

Fig. 17.1 GDP, employment, and real wage, 1991 = 100% (*Source* The Federal State Statistics Service [Rosstat])

reforms—until 1998 when the Asian financial crisis broke out, hitting Russia hard. The second began the following year (1999) and ended with the global financial crisis (GFC) in 2008. The third sub-period started in 2009 and continued through to the early 2020s.[1] This division is illustrated in Fig. 17.1, which shows the evolution of employment, the real wage, and gross domestic product (GDP) over the whole period.

17.2.1 The First Decade—From Plan to Turmoil

During the first sub-period, the Russian economy experienced a prolonged and very deep economic recession and was hit by a few strong macroeconomic shocks. By August 1998 (compared to 1991, which was the last year of the existence of the Soviet Union), the country's GDP lost about 40% of its 1991 value (see Chapter 15). This extraordinary 'performance' can be referred to as the Great Contraction. The shock of this scale was expected to cause a full collapse of the labour market. The loss of an equivalent number of jobs should have brought about skyrocketing unemployment. Most observers considered this outcome almost inevitable; however, to their surprise, this did not happen. Aggregate employment did lose a 'modest' 15% of all jobs, which was much less than the fall in GDP. Meanwhile, unemployment, while having somewhat

---

[1] An alternative dating is also possible. Another strong hit occurred in 2015; however, the turn towards stagnation came before.

increased, remained at moderate levels given the unprecedented depth of the transformation recession. Its rate reached an all-time peak level of 14% by early 1999. However, it only lasted for a short time and began to decrease quickly afterwards. How could this be if GDP had nosedived so steeply?

The explanation can be found on the side of wage adjustment. Though wages are usually downwardly rigid even in recessions (Bewley, 1998), in this case, the real value of the labour compensation that workers received decreased drastically and, by the end of the decade, lost about two-thirds of its pre-transition value. Persistently high inflation over the period coupled with various manipulations, such as delayed wage payments (wage arrears), administrative leaves, short-time work arrangements, and the expansion of informal employment helped to bring labour costs down in accordance with the fall in production (Earle & Sabirianova Peter, 2009; Lehmann & Wadsworth, 2007). All of this enabled the still high employment rates to be maintained. This type of adjustment—when unemployment for some workers is substituted with lower wages for all—would help Russia to weather future crises as well (Gimpelson, 2019; Gimpelson & Kapeliushnikov, 2013).

17.2.2   *Unexpected Boom and Surprising Recovery*

The rescue from the transformation recession of the 1990s arrived with the beginning of the second sub-period (which lasted from 1999 until 2008). Several factors were at work here. The first was the quick recovery in world commodity prices which began in the early 2000s. This enabled the repayment of debts and improved public finances. Second, the macro-management of the economy became more accurate and efficient (see Chapter 16). Third, the deep devaluation of the national currency as an outcome of the 1998 crisis made Russian producers more competitive against expensive imports. And fourth, by this period, the pro-market economic reforms of the 1990s, including privatisation, had begun to bear their first fruits. All of this ultimately helped the economy to return to a path of growth, though it was not an even one (see Chapter 15).

The key feature resulting from this sub-period was the impressive economic growth: the GDP value in 2008 was 85% higher than its initial 1999 value. Meanwhile, as shown in Fig. 17.1, the aggregate employment stock showed a subtle reaction to this performance and grew by a mere 9%. But what happened with the real wage? This time it behaved very flexibly upwards and gained 175% in 9 years!

17.2.3   *The New Crisis and Endless Stagnation*

The GFC that broke out in 2008 hit Russia one year later. Its cost to Russian GDP was around 8.5% and it put an end to the booming decade. What did it bring to the labour market? The massive dis-employment and skyrocketing unemployment that was naturally expected? Not at all. Due to active government measures supporting wages and non-employment benefits, the reaction was more mixed than before; however, real wages did fall again (Fig. 17.1).

Post-crisis development was characterised by a short, rapid recovery, which ended by 2013. Falling oil prices and the economic sanctions introduced after Russia's annexation of Crimea brought a new recession in subsequent years. Total GDP growth within this 8-year sub-period (2013–2020) was about 14%, or just under 2% per year. The real wage gained 17%, but employment gained less than 4%.

What is the common element among these episodes of booms and busts during the post-Soviet period? The common element is that the labour market reacted rapidly, adjusting the price of labour, but not the quantity. The real wage seemed to work as an equilibrating device to maintain stable employment. Its dynamics were always strongly procyclical. This behaviour is clearly different from that observed in developed countries in shock situations. In Sect. 17.5, we discuss how this can work.

17.3 A Miracle of Low Unemployment?

Unsurprisingly, the high and stable employment during all the above-mentioned episodes was coupled with relatively low and stable unemployment. Figure 17.2 shows the stylised unemployment story using two conventional measures—the total and the long-term unemployment rates (both are survey-based, according to the International Labour Organization [ILO] definition).

During the 1990s, both unemployment rates tended to rise until they reached their all-time peaks in 1999. This rise was gradual and much smaller than what could be expected given the actual GDP fall. Since the early 2000s, the unemployment rate has largely been on a decline, except for a few temporary hikes. The 2009 shock lifted it from 6 to 8%. This additional two percentage point (pp) rise was fairly mild given the depth of the recession. After 2012, the unemployment rate remained permanently under 6%; the long-term unemployment rate was on a gradual decline as well. In the aftermath of the crisis, about 40% of all unemployed were searching for a job for longer than one year; however, by the end of the sub-period, this amount was less than 30%.

'Registered' unemployment, as measured by the number of claimants to the Public Employment Service, was always much lower than the survey-based figure. The large disparity between the survey and claimant unemployment rates emerges as an outcome of two interacting factors. The first relates to the very limited support for jobseekers (low unemployment benefits and almost non-existent active labour market policies). The second includes the relatively large informal or semi-formal sector. If weak support does not allow a person to be without work for very long, the informal sector can easily absorb the extra labor supply.

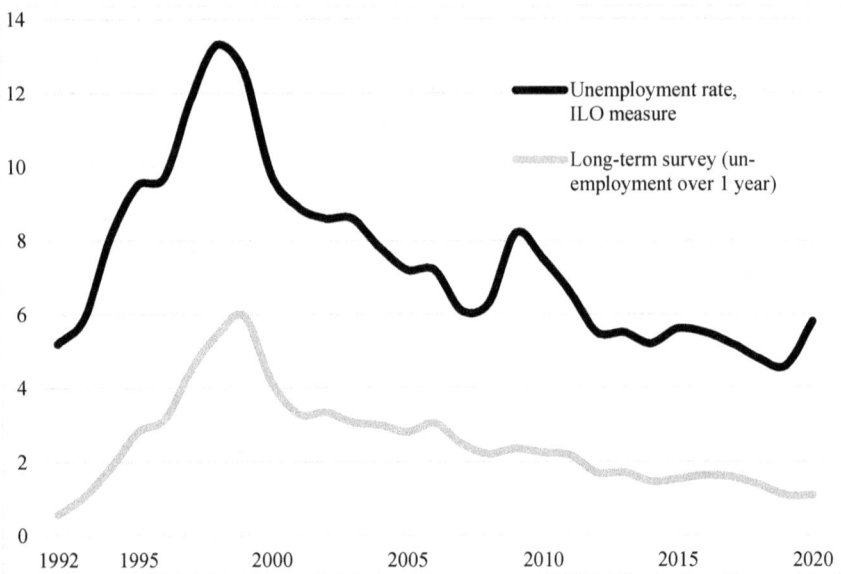

Fig. 17.2 Unemployment rates, %, 1992–2020 (*Source* Federal State Statistics Service [Rosstat])

According to the story painted by statistical data, unemployment has never emerged as a number one labour market or political issue. Of course, stable employment and low unemployment do not exclude the possibility that participation and employment rates could remain low. This would mean the significant underutilisation of labour potential with adverse implications for household well-being. In the Russian case, these rates remained persistently high most of the time. The employment rate, i.e., the employment to population ratio (e/p ratio) was on a downward slide until 1998, when it reached 58% (for the 15–64 age group). Since then, it has tended to climb gradually and monotonically, despite all crises, finally surpassing 70% in 2017. With such ratios, the Russian employment level is above the OECD average. Of course, men and women may differ in their employment. High total employment rates can hide gender disparities, though the female employment rate (about 65%) is among the highest in the world, behind only a few countries, including the Nordic ones. The gap in employment rates between men and women remained steady during the whole period at around 8–10 pp.

Do high employment/low unemployment rates mean that the Russian labour market functions perfectly and its agents do not experience any serious problems? Of course not. As a normal temperature of the human body is a positive indicator, it does not mean that excellent health is guaranteed. Here as well, there can be various other serious problems/illnesses that require careful analysis and painful treatment. These illnesses may have structural origins and often manifest themselves through wage distribution.

17.4 Puzzles of Adjustment: How Does It Work?

Two key indicators, one of which reflects the dynamics of employment, while the other follows the cost of labour, suggest that in all situations, when the labour market was not in a steady state, the wage side took the brunt of the adjustment. This combination may look unconventional and puzzling. It contradicts the standard expectation that wages are downwardly rigid, while employment has some room to adjust. Layard and Richter (1995), after observing in the 1990s the Russian wage rollercoasters, called this method of adjustment the 'Russian model'. However, this title is not entirely accurate as this method of adjusting to shocks is typical among many emerging market and developing economies, including those outside the former Soviet Union (FSU).

Khanna et al. (2011) reviewed evidence from 44 middle-income countries on how the 2008 GFC affected jobs and workers' income. They find that the crisis hit payrolls much more strongly than it hit the number of jobs. For a given drop in GDP, earnings declined more in countries with larger manufacturing sectors, smaller export sectors, and more stringent labour market regulations.

If employment remains constant in recessions, labour slack can be absorbed by various low-wage jobs. Workers who would lose their jobs in developed economies, in the Russian case retain employment. Either their wages are cut to adjust to falling demand or they move to various marginal and highly precarious positions—low-paid, informal, casual, part-time, or self-employed, among others. This erodes the conventional borderline between employment and unemployment as it is set by ILO guidelines.

The ILO (2008, p. 47) document questions the universal applicability of the standard approach to measuring unemployment: 'In developing countries, in particular, unemployment (as defined by the standard definition of unemployment adopted by the 13th ICLS[2] in 1982) tends to be low, and is often lower than in many industrialized countries'. When social protection is meagre or absent and vacancies are scarce, 'most people are ready to take any job that is available, or to create their own employment (mainly in the informal sector). Thus, in terms of a labor market model, the excess supply of labour gets absorbed through a decrease in earnings or productivity, rather than an increase in the number of unemployed persons. Most of the persons who cannot find work or create any job for themselves join the ranks of the economically inactive rather than of the unemployed'.

Economic crises make these adjustments even more salient.

Labour market institutions and the structural properties of the economy can affect the depth of the fall in earnings. If wages are not protected institutionally from deep falls, they can fall into crisis situations. If workers' bargaining power

---

[2] International Conference of Labour Statisticians—the ILO body responsible for the elaboration and dissemination of statistical standards.

and voices are weak, they find it hard to resist falls. If wages contain large variable and not ex ante contracted portions, they become more flexible. The Russian government has always considered low unemployment a top priority in domestic politics and has never tried to shift the institutional equilibrium. But what could motivate workers to accept wage cuts in order to keep jobs which are poorly rewarded? And what would make employers retain underutilised labour? Now, we turn to our discussion on the institutional peculiarities that beget this adjustment pattern.

17.5 THE ROLE OF LABOUR MARKET INSTITUTIONS

The choice of a particular wage–employment trade-off is largely a political economy problem and depends on the set of acting labour market institutions (Boeri & Terrell, 2002). Institutions, as we understand, are the rules and procedures that regulate the functioning of the labour market. Here, we address only those that play a major role in shaping the adjustment pattern. Employment protection legislation introduces firing costs which firms have to bear if they want to shed extra labour. Stricter rules protect workers and existing jobs but disincentivises new hiring. This slows down employment change in recessions as well as in booms. The flexibility of wages depends on basic wage-setting institutions, such as the rules for setting the minimum wage and unemployment benefits as well as collective bargaining. Minimum wage and unemployment benefits set the wage floor, below which the wage does not move. Bargaining rules affect wage differentiation and benefit policy. Though most countries have, in general, similar institutions, the latter may operate quite differently due to differences in specific settings and non-labour institutions and policies. What are the Russian specifics in the area of labour relations?

17.5.1 Employment Regulations

Stricter job protection makes employment adjustment costly and takes more time, causing longer periods of labour hoarding. This can put additional pressure on corporate finance, especially in recessions. In Russia, according to the estimates reported by the OECD, permanent contracts—which prevail in Russia—are excessively rigid. Job protection for this group of workers is scored at 3.06 compared to 2.11 for the OECD average.[3] Only Portugal, which is known for having the strictest job protection among all OECD member countries, has a higher score (3.14). Facing costly employment adjustment, firms may seek alternative instruments to keep labour costs under control.

Fixing the wage floor: minimum wage and unemployment benefits. In developed economies, employers cannot easily cut contracted wages even if

---

[3] The scale ranges from 0 to 6, where 6 relates to the highest possible level of strictness, https://stats.oecd.org/Index.aspx?DataSetCode=EPL_OV.

they are under financial stress. Even in recessions, wages do not fall. The minimum wage and unemployment benefits help fix the wage floor, which is usually high relative to the median wage. Performance-linked pay is more flexible, but its use is limited because monitoring individual outcomes can be difficult and expensive.

To be flexible, wages need a low floor and an easily movable ceiling. This provides room for wage movements. In the Russian case, the wage floor has always been low, while the ceiling moves easily. The minimum-to-average wage ratio (known as the Kaitz ratio) largely remained below 10% until 2007. In January 2009, as a result of the doubling of the minimum wage (from RUB 2300 to RUB 4330 in nominal terms), the ratio rose from 13 to 23%. Soon after, the Kaitz ratio dropped again, to 17%, and then rose to 20% by the end of 2017. During the entire period, this ratio was much lower than that in the countries of Central and Eastern Europe.

High inter-regional differentiation in wages also matters. Until 2006, the minimum wage was set at the national level regardless of specific regional situations. The average wage in better-performing regions was up to five times higher than in the worst-performing regions. The national minimum wage equalled a mere 15% of the average wage in the first group (such as Moscow city or the oil-rich Tyumen region) but might easily exceed 50% in the second group (the national republics of the North Caucasus, among others). In 2006, the Labour Code was amended, adding a clause allowing each region to set its own minimum wage at a level not lower than the national one. Some regions refrained from raising the regional minimum wage level, others raised it very modestly, and still others increased it but with significant caveats. One of the highest regional minimum wages was set in Moscow, but even here it amounted to only about one-quarter of the average wage.

Non-employment benefits can shape the actual wage floor as well. If these benefits are high, workers do not have incentives to work for low wages. This raises the reservation wage of workers and shifts a portion of low-wage employees into unemployment. The key non-employment benefit is unemployment benefits, which jobless individuals may receive if registered with an employment service. Were Russian unemployment benefits high? The data suggest that their level could hardly be binding. The replacement ratio (the ratio of the average unemployment benefit to the average wage) reached a peak level of 30% in 1998 but has since declined gradually. By the 2008 crisis, it fell below the 10% level and has remained at this level since. Clearly, this level of income does not appear as an attractive alternative to any paid employment. If a job is lost, a new one—of any quality—must be found as soon as possible. In this context, the unemployment benefit level has never been a binding wage floor either.

Labour market policies usually have two components. The first component—the passive policy—aims at income support, with unemployment benefit spending comprising a major component. The other—the active policy—aims at providing support to the unemployed for their job search, occupational orientation, and retraining, for example, to become an entrepreneur, among other things. Low unemployment benefits reflect the scarce spending on passive labour market programmes, while spending for active policy measures has also been negligible. Throughout the 1990s, the expenditures budgeted for active measures comprised less than 0.5% of GDP. In the 2000s, total annual spending on labour market programmes was less than 0.1% of GDP, only approaching 0.3% in 2009 due to additional anti-crisis spending (OECD 2011). For comparison, in the OECD countries, spending on passive programmes alone often surpasses 1% of GDP.[4]

But what could explain the Russian government's commitment to keeping the wage floor at such a low level? First, there are fiscal constraints, as generous social standards are expensive. Until 2000, a number of social benefits were tied to the minimum wage and an increase of the latter expanded social spending. Any rise in the minimum wage shifted the entire pay scale in the public sector upward, thus inflating total public spending. The government, being under fiscal stress in the 1990s, tried to maintain control of it. Second, the enormous heterogeneity of the Russian regions may also play a role. Any large increase in the national minimum wage or unemployment benefits could severely impact the most depressed regional labour markets, causing an uncontrolled rise in unemployment. Last, but not least, while the government considered high unemployment as a politically dangerous challenge, the low wage floor (in combination with other institutional features) helped to absorb low-skilled labour and replace unemployment with low-paid employment. Upward adjustments to the unemployment benefit and minimum wage levels were modest and implemented only when they were considered to be politically beneficial, which usually coincided with upcoming elections.

17.5.2 *Wage Setting and a Two-Tier Wage Structure*

If on the bottom side, the wage floor was not a binding constraint preventing it from falling too low, upward wage movement is also not constrained. Many Russian firms consider two components when setting individual wages. The first component is relatively rigid and fixed in labour contracts. The second is complementary and highly variable. On average, it comprises one-third of the total, being implicitly linked to the financial performance of firms. There can be even a third component—informal pay if it exists—which is the most flexible. The use of this type of wage-setting is widespread, with even public sector entities using the same two-tier scheme.

The variable component in the two-tier wage structure works as an automatic risk-sharing device. It expands when a firm performs well and it shrinks when things become worse or dangerously uncertain. In this way, it affects the wage distribution due to less equal allocation. This system reduces the room for trade unions to manoeuvre in wage bargaining.

---

[4] https://dx.doi.org/10.1787/empl_outlook-2016-table92-en.

17.5.3 Trade Unions and Wage Agreements

Though trade unions around the world have lost much of their power, they remain an important player in wage setting. National, industry-wide, and firm-level collective agreements provide a general framework within which individual wages are set. A high level of unionisation (membership in a trade union) is usually associated with lower wage differentiation. Russia inherited from the Soviet Union almost universal unionisation, but this has gradually been eroding. About 70% of workers in large- and medium-sized firms are still formally unionised; however, in wage setting, the role of the trade union is scarcely visible. Outside of large- and medium-sized establishments, they are largely non-existent, making the union density for the economy as a whole under 30%.

Another important feature of any wage setting system is the level of centralisation and coordination. If it is more centralised and coordinated, less scope is left for wage adjustment in case of shocks. Russia has a multi-layer bargaining structure, where the Tripartite Commission is on the top (adopting national level tripartite agreements), followed by industry-level tariff agreements between employer associations and sector-specific trade unions, with tripartite agreements at the regional level. Within this framework, firms might seem to be left with little room for any decentralised wage adjustments. However, the variable portion of the total wage is usually not rigidly determined and—being linked to performance and set by managerial discretion—introduces an element of the spot market. If trade unions were stronger and more influential, one would expect to see lower variation in wages, a smaller variable portion (if any) in the wage structure, lower quit rates, and a higher frequency of strikes across the economy compared to what has been documented during this period.

17.6 Structural Change and Informality

The Soviet economy had a one-sided specialisation. Its main investments went to heavy industry, including mining and military-oriented manufacturing. Various goods for everyday household consumption were largely imported, mostly from other socialist countries, sold for fixed prices, and were in short demand for ordinary consumers. The service sector was underdeveloped and its proportion in total employment was relatively small (see Chapters 8 and 15). The inherited economic structure—critically unfit to market needs—started eroding as soon as Russia began its transition. This process was associated with a fiscal crisis, the disruption of previous economic ties and the creation of new ones, the penetration of new technologies from the West, the opening up to global trade, the birth of the new private sector, and dramatic changes on the demand side. Unsurprisingly, this mix initiated a rapid and massive structural change (see Chapter 8).

There are a few figures that illustrate the scale of the industrial restructuring. In 1992, agricultural employment (together with fishery and forestry) comprised about 15% of the total; by 2000, it was under 9%, contracting further to 6.5% by 2020. In total, it shrank by 2.5 times. Over this period, industry and construction reduced their employment from 40% of the total to 27%, or by 1.5 times. Correspondingly, the service sector expanded from 44 to 67%. Retail and wholesale trade became major employers in terms of job quantity. This structural change moved the Russian economy from the group of industrial countries to the group of service sector economies. Though the proportion of service sector jobs in total employment is still smaller than that in the leading economies, this transformation has had a profound influence.

Another dimension of Russia's restructuring relates to firm size. Russian statistics highlight the activity of large- and medium-sized firms. This segment includes not only private companies but all public entities as well; they are all well monitored by the state, pay taxes, and are expected to protect workers according to the labour law. Aggregate employment in this segment, however, has been decreasing monotonically over time: from close to 100% in 1992 to less than one-half in 2019. The remaining segment of employment (if we subtract employment in large and medium firms from the total) comprises those working in small and micro businesses, individual entrepreneurs, and different types of self-employed.

These jobs are especially heterogeneous in terms of pay, working conditions, and social protection and include some element of informal relations at the very least. Though an exact identification of which job is informal or is not straightforward, many jobs in this segment have some informal components. Even if taxes are paid correctly, these jobs rarely provide the legally mandated social protection and are likely to be low-paid, short-term, or casual. Such jobs are extremely flexible and can be short-lived as they are easily created as well as easily destroyed. In total, they add flexibility to the labour market. All of this makes this segment an absorptive 'sponge' with free entry. Those who lose jobs in the corporate segment are absorbed by the sponge of the non-corporate segment. But many occupations in the 'corporate' segment are also highly absorptive. For example, the number of salesclerks and taxi drivers increased to close to 15% of all employed, and finding this type of job is not difficult, even in a recession.

The downsizing of industrial and agricultural employment and the shift from large to small firms triggered a massive occupational reallocation. Since the occupations and skills used in the contracting industries are often poorly transferable, job change leads workers to changing occupations and acquiring new skills. According to Sabirianova (2002), over 40% of all workers changed their occupation during 1991–1998. This was a process of a rapid depreciation of previously accumulated human capital and its replacement with a newly created one. The Great Human Capital Reallocation, as it was referred to by Sabirianova, was associated with the destruction of old jobs and occupations and the creation of new ones. Though the rate of reallocation tended to subside over time, it nevertheless remains high, as cumulative changes in the industrial structure may suggest.

The fact that such a tremendous scale of downsizing and reallocation brought relatively little unemployment hints at the high adjustment capacity of the labour market (see above). But where did all those workers who quit or were dismissed go? Some left the labour force, but the prevailing majority did not. Many of those who remained in (the labour force) found work in small or micro-businesses or became self-employed. This is the segment that functioned as the absorptive sponge we discussed earlier. Many of these jobs, even if not fully informal, have some features of informality.

Increasing labour market informality is a salient feature of most emerging market economies, and Russia does not stay here alone (Packard et al., 2012). Its expansion and persistence have various structural and institutional causes. The structural shift towards the small-scale service sector as well as a hostile business environment, including what might be called the 'grabbing hand' of the government (see Chapter 6), are among the factors feeding the search for a room in the shadows. Weak social protection also matters as jobless individuals cannot remain out of employment for long and therefore must accept any income-generating opportunity. Though scholars debate the definitions of informality and the approaches to measuring it, one common feature persists. This economic activity takes place in the shadow of the regulations, out of reach of state institutions, and is associated with unpaid taxes and/or the under-provision of social protection. This raises concerns about the quality of these jobs, the quality of state institutions, and the implications for the well-being of citizens.

Depending on the methodology of the measurement and the available data sets, estimates of informal employment in Russia vary from one-fifth to one-third. In the latter case, 'informal workers' are those who work outside of the 'legal entities' of the corporate sector. They include the self-employed as well as wage and salary workers hired by unincorporated micro-businesses or private individuals. Despite different approaches applying different measures, the trends they reveal are similar.

How do Russian estimates look from a cross-country perspective? According to a study conducted by the World Bank (Perry et al., 2007), Russian GDP per capita corresponds to an informality level of around 25–30%. Of course, any cross-country informality comparisons are approximate, allowing for a rough typology only. Ensuring the same definitions and measurements of informality across countries is difficult. One can safely say that the level of informality in Russia is comparable to that observed in other Eastern European countries as well as Southern Europe but is significantly higher than that in the most advanced market economies. It would also be fair to say that Russian labour market informality is more modest than that in most other emerging market economies of the FSU, except the Baltic countries.

In addition to tax avoidance and a lack of social protection, informal employment creates one more serious worry. It concerns the productivity of workers in these jobs. If they are less productive, and usually they are, than formal workers, then the reallocation of labour towards informal jobs affects economic growth and aggregate productivity negatively (see Chapter 15). This also means that an increasing proportion of the total labour force is being used less efficiently than it could be if these workers were in formal jobs in the same industries/occupations.

An important question relates to the composition of informal jobs. We have already mentioned that informal employment is highly heterogeneous and contains micro-entrepreneurs, the self-employed, and hired workers as well as casual workers involved in various irregular activities. Oftentimes, the lines dividing these groups are blurred.

Exposure to informality is not random and, for some groups, the chances to be informal are higher than for others. Informal salaried work and irregular activities are most prevalent among young men and women with low levels of formal schooling. Informal entrepreneurship and self-employment, in contrast, are more common among middle-aged men with technical or university degrees. Informal work is concentrated in service, agricultural, and low-skilled occupations. New labour market entrants may start their working career in the informal sector. Having gained work experience, they are able to find formal positions. Finally, many may move back into the informal sector after (or close to) retirement. This pattern can potentially apply to every cohort. We see these effects in the Russian data, but they are typical for most informality-ridden middle-income countries (Gimpelson & Kapeliushnikov, 2015).

17.7 WAGES, LOW PAY, AND INEQUALITY

17.7.1 Dynamics and Levels

The level of pay reflects the demand for labour services and the level of labour productivity. Wages comprise the largest part of household income and therefore play a key role in shaping the well-being of households. How have the wages of Russian workers evolved since the beginning of the market economy? Fig. 17.1 presents this story through the evolution of the monthly real wage (deflated by the consumer price index).

Although its trajectory is quite bumpy and the periods of monotonous wage growth are short, the accumulated growth is significant. If we take 1991— the last year of the Soviet Union—as the reference year, the real wage has demonstrated very impressive growth! But within selected sub-periods, the growth was very uneven. Much of this growth was achieved during the second decade of transition (2000s) when it increased by 290% as compared to its 2000 level. Since then, the growth in the real wage has become more modest and less stable. In nominal dollar terms, growth was more impressive though very unstable over time. Having started from about a miserable USD 10 in early 1992, the monthly wage rose to USD 80 in 1995, reaching USD 700 in

2008; it then lost over USD 100 in 2009, exceeded USD 900 by 2013, and finally ended up at about USD 700 in 2020. Major losses occurred during times of crises and were aggravated by deep devaluations of the rouble (see Chapter 16).

The main lesson for the Russian economy coming from Fig. 17.1 appears straightforward. Wage development in a resource-dependent economy is very much contingent on GDP growth: when the latter increases, the real wage follows the trend. However, any slowdown in GDP growth translates immediately into a negative wage change, bringing uncertainty to the prospects of workers' well-being.

17.7.2 Low Pay

High employment and low unemployment rates in the presence of low wage floors and almost unconstrained wage flexibility are supported by maintaining a vast array of low-paid jobs. These jobs substitute for more generous unemployment protection because if the wage floor were higher, low-productivity workers would be squeezed out of employment.

The absolute level of pay that can be considered 'low' differs greatly across countries. What is 'low' in Norway or Switzerland can be very 'high' in post-communist middle-income countries, for example, Russia, Bulgaria, or Romania, and even 'very high' in most developing countries. Therefore, the main conventional measure of 'low pay' is relative, equalling two-thirds of the median hourly wage. Those workers whose hourly earnings are below this line are considered low paid. Having defined it in this way, we can conduct comparisons over time and between countries.

The proportion of low-paid jobs has always been large, although it declines over time. A study using data for 2002–2016 shows that the size of this group was close to 30% in the beginning but decreased to 24% of total employment by the end of the period (Gimpelson et al., 2018). These rates are markedly higher than the average for European Union (EU) countries (17%) but are close to the rates observed in a number of the new EU Member States (e.g., Latvia, Lithuania, and Romania). Low levels of education and skills as well as residing outside of large cities significantly increase a worker's chances of being low paid. Low pay as a short-term phenomenon may not present a serious social issue as such jobs can work as stepping stones for better employment for labour market entrants or those with periods of non-employment. However, if persistent, low pay becomes more problematic. For Russian workers, being low paid is largely a long-term trap as two out of three low-paid workers are unable to exit from this state within a year. The trap effect appears stronger for women than for men. Though the stepping stone effect is also present, it is much weaker and relates to only one out of four low-paid workers.

17.7.3 Inequality

Since jobs (and workers) are highly heterogeneous among many dimensions, wage differentiation in modern labour markets is unavoidable. Russia is considered a country with a high degree of wage inequality. Many factors are at work here, stretching out the earnings distribution.

One factor is a highly concentrated economic structure, where the mining sector provides over one-fifth of GDP but employs only about 2% of the labour force. Much of Russia's mining is located in its north, where harsh weather conditions should be compensated for with much higher pay. Revenues generated by mining not only afford higher pay for workers but also higher rents for all related activities. On the opposite end of the scale is agriculture. In 2020, the average wage in mining was 2.75 times higher than in agriculture. But if we look at oil extraction alone, its average wage was 4.1 times higher than in agriculture. These inter-industry differences translate into inter-regional differences, as the spatial allocation of industries is far from even (see Chapter 11). As a result, the range of pay across regions is four times, which is much higher than in any other large country.

Another factor is the high incidence of low pay. As we have already discussed, the sizeable proportion of low-paid and free-entry jobs is the opposite side of low unemployment. But this also stretches out the earnings distribution, thus contributing to differentiation. Finally, the widespread use of performance-related wage setting can matter here as well, as performance pay is always distributed less equally.

What is the level of wage inequality in quantitative terms and how has it changed over time? Is this inequality driven by low pay or high pay? Various statistical measures can help in answering these questions. Among them are the Gini coefficient and two decile ratios, which grasp the upper (p90/p50[5]) and the lower parts (p50/p10) of the wage distribution. Figure 17.3, which uses data from the Russia Longitudinal Monitoring Survey of the Higher School of Economics (RLMS-HSE),[6] shows that inequality has been on a downward trend. If in 2000 the Gini coefficient was about 0.49—which was quite high— by 2020, it had slid down to 0.32, which corresponds to a medium level. Both decile ratios demonstrate a gradual decline in earnings inequality and suggest that this has been driven largely by stronger compression in the low pay segment. The Federal State Statistics Service (Rosstat) provides higher Gini values but documents the same declining trend: from 0.50 in 2000 to 0.41 in 2019. Its estimates are based on data from surveys of firms, which are likely to capture the segment comprised of those earning relatively higher wages better than the household budget surveys can. Of course, we need to

---

[5] The p90/p50 decile ratio is the ratio of the upper bound value of the ninth decile in the wage distribution to the median wage and, correspondingly, P50/P10 is the ratio of median wage to the upper bound of the first decile. The former reflects the inequality in the upper part of the earnings distribution and the latter—in the lower part.

[6] https://rlms-hse.cpc.unc.edu/.

remember here that all available data sources usually do a relatively poor job of capturing the wages of top earners. Therefore, any available statistical measures may underestimate the actual wage inequality and must be interpreted with caution.

What could be behind the observed compression in wage inequality? The literature does not suggest a conclusive answer. Interestingly, the fastest pace of inequality reduction was observed during the recovery period which began soon after the 1998 economic crisis. Two of the most obvious candidates for explanations include the commodity boom (which might 'lift all boats') and the rise in the minimum wage (which targets low earners). However, both should be rejected as they occurred later; thus, neither could be a factor here.

A tentative explanation is that low-wage earners benefited from the fast elimination of some of the cost-saving adjustment options which were widespread in the 1990s. Employers—state and private alike—used late payments, short-time work arrangements, and unpaid leave in order to adjust the wage bill and avoid mass dismissals. These non-standard adjustment practices affected low-paid workers relatively more frequently (Earle & Sabirianova Peter, 2009; Lehmann & Wadsworth, 2007). The recovery allowed firms to gradually repay wage arrears, though significantly devalued by high inflation, and diminish the underemployment of hired workers. An additional explanation hints at the structural changes in the economy which also accelerated at this moment. The lowest (agriculture and the public sector) and highest

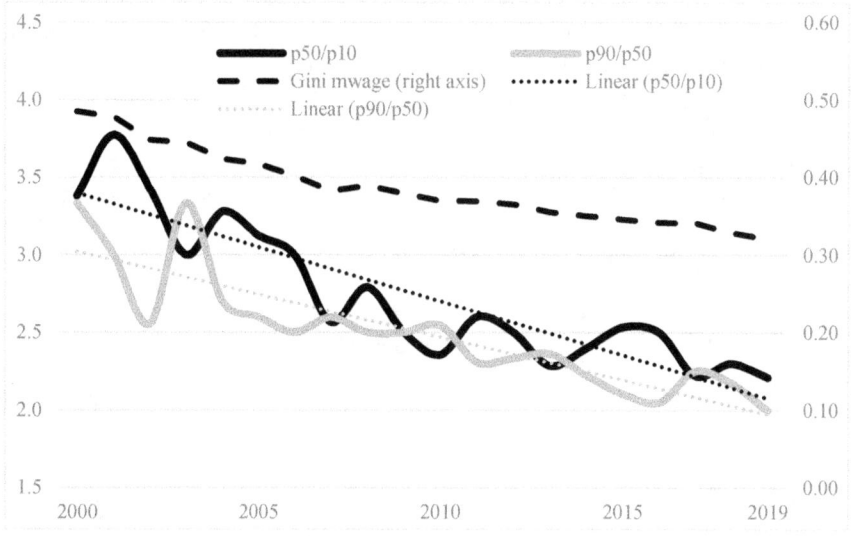

Fig. 17.3 Differentiation of earnings: Gini and decile ratios, p90/p50 and p50/p10 (*Source* Author's RLMS-HSE-based estimates)

(finance and mining) paying industries reduced their employment dramatically, thus contributing to the compression of inter-industry and inter-regional components in earnings inequality.

17.8 Human Capital, Educational Boom, and High Returns

There is consensus among economists that advanced human capital is a key ingredient for sustainable economic growth. In a nutshell, following the definition given by Nobel Prize economist Gary Becker, 'human capital' consists of the education and skills that individuals possess and use in their economic activity (Becker, 1964). Human capital increases labour productivity and, therefore, is well rewarded. In any modern economy, educated and skilled workers are in high demand; they are not only more productive and better paid but also are more adaptive to any turbulence. A considerable proportion of the labour force in high-income countries have a tertiary education, though the opposite is not always true. What can we say about Russian human capital and its utilisation?

The fast expansion of university level education and, simultaneously, the gradual disappearance of the low-educated workforce are among the salient features of the Russian labour market. If before the collapse of the Soviet Union, every sixth employed individual had a university-level education, in 2002, this increased to every fourth, and in 2015—more than every third (Table 17.1). Such a fast increase deserves to be called an educational boom! The abundance of tertiary education holders places Russia among the world leaders according to this indicator. Meanwhile, the uneducated labour force has almost disappeared. Workers who have not finished high school comprise under 4% of total employment, and they are mostly of pre-retirement or retirement age.

The generous supply of human capital opens up new economic opportunities but creates serious challenges as well. On the one hand, there is an increasing risk of overeducation if holders of college or university diplomas

Table 17.1 Educational composition of employment, of all employed, %

Level of education	1989	2002	2015
University (complete and incomplete)	15.9	26.3	37.4
College (2 years or short-cycled tertiary)	24.3	35.7	34.7
Vocational	17.8	15.3	9.8
General secondary	20.8	16.2	14.3
Basic (8–9 years) and lower	21.2	6.6	3.8
TOTAL	100	100	100

Source Population censuses of 1989 and 2002, Micro-census of 2015

take a job that does not require their level of skills. The human capital accumulated can be lost if it is not used efficiently.

On the other hand, the sizeable proportion of low-skilled jobs appears at odds with the supply of educated labour. The supply of workers willing to do simple and unskilled work in agriculture, construction, and services is insufficient. Either these jobs are taken by low-skilled migrants or are filled by overeducated Russians.

Both questions deserve to be answered. How was this fast increase in the educated labour supply absorbed and how was the existing demand for low-skilled labour met? In other words, how did 'the race between education and technology' (the famous expression of J. Tinbergen) proceed? The aggregate data suggest that, over the duration of the post-Soviet period, the demand for education did not lag far behind the supply.

Three major indicators may help us in understanding the trends in demand for education.

First, better-educated people face better employment prospects. The ratio of employed university graduates to all university graduates (e/p ratio) exceeded 80% over the whole period, and the ratios for college degree holders and vocational certificate holders remained high as well, though were somewhat lower. Meanwhile, workers with secondary and lower levels of education faced shrinking employment opportunities.

Another angle from which to view this problem is through an estimate of the 'return to education'. This measure (derived from the standard Mincerian equation[7]) shows how each additional year of schooling translates into wage growth. It was on a steady rise starting from 2–3% in the early 1990s to 8–9% by the mid-2000s. The estimates for years 2016–2019 reach 12–13% (Kapeliushnikov, 2021). This is a very decent return, especially given the booming supply of educated labour against the background of the stagnating economy.

Still another way to explore the utilisation of educated labour is to look at its allocation across major occupational groups. Do skilled occupations absorb the growing supply of college and university graduates? In the standard classification of occupations,[8] university graduates largely form the group of 'professionals' and college graduates belong to the group of 'associate professionals'. The group of 'managers' is also largely comprised of highly educated workers. Therefore, the larger supply of educated labour is expected to expand the aggregate size of these three groups correspondingly, especially the group of 'professionals'.

---

[7] The equation linking the wage an individual earns with their human capital measured as years of schooling and experience. This was first suggested by J. Mincer as a standard tool of labour economics (Mincer, 1974). The coefficient for schooling is often considered the rate of private return to investments in education.

[8] Here, we mean the ISCO—International Standard Classification of Occupations—suggested by the ILO and used by almost all countries, though some (like the United States or the United Kingdom) may have national versions.

So, how has the composition of employment changed over time? Fig. 17.4 may offer a clue. It compares the occupational structure of employment in 2000 and 2020, presenting its transformation (in pp).

The obvious beneficiary of this occupational reallocation is the group of professionals. It gained almost 11 pp relative to the 2000 level. In total, the most skilled occupations (managers, professionals, and associate professionals) gained over 10 pp, while the share of low-skilled occupations decreased. This is a crude test indicating that the increased supply of educated labour was largely absorbed by the growing demand. Of course, these groups are sufficiently heterogeneous and further research is needed. In addition, though skilled occupations are, on average, better paid than medium- or low-skilled occupations, there are many exceptions.

Training. Evaluating the stock of human capital, we often rely on variables which measure the level of education achieved or the length of schooling. These variables are usually easily available from national and international statistics and are very convenient for cross-country comparisons. However, there is a serious limitation: these variables measure human capital accumulated during formal schooling, which individuals usually complete by age 25. After this, the working life may continue for 40–45 years, during which the initial human capital does not remain intact. It can keep accumulating through on-the-job training and learning by doing. But it is also exposed to depreciation. This means that the actual productive skills which adult workers possess may

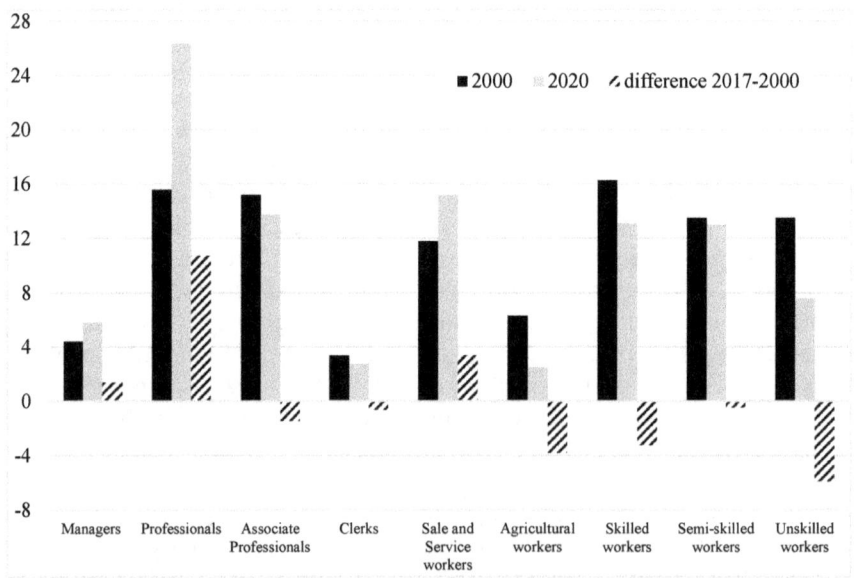

Fig. 17.4 Composition of employment by occupation, 2000 and 2020 (*Source* Rosstat, author's estimates)

differ significantly from what they received through formal education. Though measuring adult skills is a very difficult task, one can easily assume that life-long learning, including on-the-job training, should matter. Plotting the incidence of on-the-job training against per capita GDP measures across countries shows a positive linear relationship: countries with a higher incidence of on-the-job training are more productive and more wealthy. How does Russia look in this context? As we mentioned early, it is among the leaders on the higher education axis, but on the training incidence axis, the story is the opposite. Training incidence is low, which means that skills obtained during schooling are not maintained or further updated over the life cycle. Thus, this can contribute to potential explanations of why the leader in education remains a laggard in productivity.

Migration. The efficient utilisation of human capital assumes that its distribution over the working population is a rough match to the structure of labour demand. In other words, educated workers do more complex and skilled work, while the less educated and skilled take simpler jobs which do not require extensive schooling. Everyone has a job that roughly fits their skills. In Russia, as we see it, this match does not occur.

If all available native workers are well educated, who does the simple—manual and routine—work? Demand for this type of work is not going to disappear in the foreseeable future. Robots are thus far bad as nurses, fitness instructors, babysitters, cleaners, deliverers, and packers, among others. Partially, Russians select these jobs when they agree to slide down the occupational ladder and do not see better options. But the native labour supply for taking these jobs is limited, especially in the largest cities. Thus, migrants arrive to help in this situation, given the wage difference between Russia and some neighbouring FSU countries, where the level of pay is much lower.

Collecting high-quality data covering international migration is a daunting task, since migration regimes vary across time and across countries. Citizens of certain countries (members of the Eurasian Economic Union—see Chapter 12) do not need special permission to work in Russia; however, others may need work permits or licences. The trend of the increasing presence of migrants in the Russian labour market can be illustrated using data showing the number of foreigners registered for the first time at a place of temporary residence in Russia with the declared purpose 'work' (Fig. 17.5). This figure increased by 3.3 times between 2009 and 2019, reaching 5.5 million in 2019 (Brunarska & Denisenko, 2021). If compared to the officially measured labour force of 75 million, this amounts to over 7%. Over 60% of all migrants (Fig. 17.5) come from two Central Asian countries—Uzbekistan and Tajikistan. The actual number of labour migrants may be even larger, as not all migrants are captured by this statistic. Most migrants are employed in construction, transportation, and services. When the COVID-19-induced lockdown in 2020 prevented many migrants from travelling to Russia to work, the economy immediately felt the consequences—an acute shortage of workers in migrant-dependent industries.

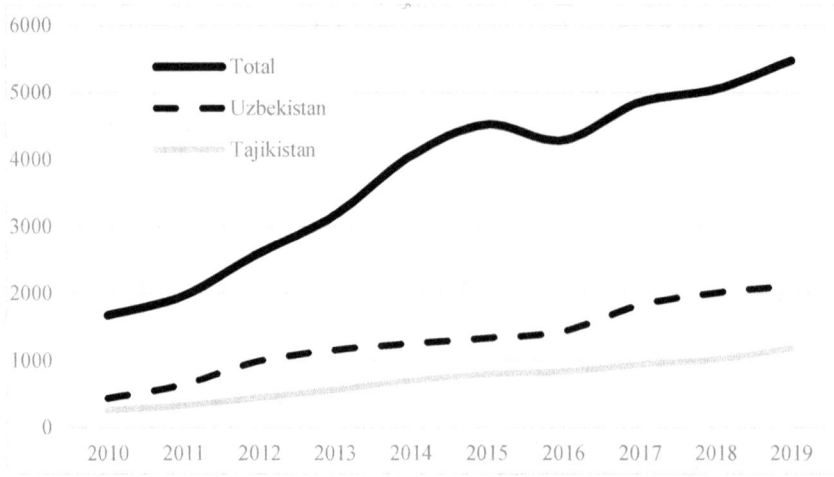

Fig. 17.5 Number of foreign workers,* 2010–2019, in thousands (*Note* * the number of foreigners registered for the first time at a place of temporary residence in Russia with the declared purpose 'work'. *Source* Brunarska & Denisenko, 2021, Table A6)

On the other side of the educational spectrum, the problem is the opposite and leads to out-migration to the United States and Western Europe. This is due primarily to economic reasons because the difference in work opportunities remains sufficiently large. The human capital drain, which began during the late Soviet era, has yet to stop. However, since 2014–2015, political reasons have begun to play a more significant role, as repressive pressure on the political opposition mounts. All this concerns the most educated Russians who seek academic, managerial, or IT-related jobs in the West and who want to live and work in a freer and more liberal environment.

17.9 Conclusions

In this chapter, we present a stylised story of labour market developments during the 30-year period from the early 1990s until 2020. During these years, the Russian labour market survived several deep crises and underwent substantial structural changes. Though the shocks that hit the economy were of different origins and intensities, the adjustments were surprisingly similar and almost always unconventional. If in a standard case, the adjustment is expected to be largely quantitative, where firms shed labour slack but keep wages intact, in Russia, they prefer to abstain from employee downsizing but instead eagerly manipulate using wage cuts. This kind of 'reverse flexibility' allows for cutting costs while aggregate employment and unemployment show little change. For this performance, workers must pay via volatile wages and a higher risk of low pay.

Was this type of adjustment a reflection of a particular culture, politics, or institutional foundations? We accept the latter explanation as the most convincing, though any economic or labour market institutions are usually endogenous to culture and politics in the long run. We consider a complex web of employment protection legislation, the unemployment benefit system, and the wage setting rules as creating a set of incentives and constraints that tended to shape the observed behaviour. A high level of informality and weak enforcement mechanisms add to the general labour market flexibility.

Can we evaluate the economic and social efficiency of the model? On the one hand, it has clear advantages if helps maintain employment at a high level and unemployment at a low one, even when GDP nosedives. On the other hand, it is not without costs. Some downward wage adjustments may concern everyone, thus depressing labour incomes. In-work poverty emerges as a grave consequence. Another feature of the model is low labour productivity. If a drop in output is not matched with a corresponding cut in employment, productivity suffers. If negative shocks are frequent, labour productivity is likely to stagnate. One can say the Russian model of labour market adjustment is helpful in absorbing strong shocks, but is not helpful in stimulating restructuring, modernisation, productivity growth, and a continuous increase in well-being.

Questions for students

1. What is the key systemic feature of the Russian labour market adjustment?
2. How can we explain this unconventional type of performance? Which institutions drive it and how they do it?
3. What are the pros and cons of this model?
4. What can we say about the main directions of structural change over this period?
5. Having a sizeable proportion of highly educated workers can be an advantage. However, structural problems and mismatches are also possible. What can we say about the Russian case?

References

Becker, G. (1964). *Human capital*. University of Chicago Press.
Bewley, T. (1998). Why not cut pay? *European Economic Review, 42*(3–5), 459–490.
Boeri, T., & Terrell, K. (2002). Institutional determinants of labor reallocation in transition. *Journal of Economic Perspectives, 16*(1), 51–76.
Brunarska, Z., & Denisenko, M. (2021). Russia: A 'Hidden' migration transition and a winding road towards a mature immigration country? *Central and Eastern European Migration Review, 10*(1), 143–172. https://doi.org/10.17467/ceemr.2021.08
Earle, J., & Sabirianova Peter, K. (2009). Complementarity and custom in wage contract violation. *Review of Economics and Statistics, 91*(4), 832–849.

Gimpelson, V., & Kapeliushnikov, R. (2013). Labor market adjustment: Is Russia different? In M. Alexeev & S. Weber (Eds.), *The Oxford Handbook of the Russian Economy* (pp. 693–724). Oxford University Press.

Gimpelson, V., Kapeliushnikov, R., & Sharunina, A. (2018). Nizkooplachivaemye rabochie mesta na rossiiskom rynke truda: est' li vykhod i kuda on vedet? [Low Paid Jobs in the Russian Labour Market: Does Exit Exist and Where Does It Lead to?]. *HSE Economic Journal, 22*(4), 489–530.

Gimpelson, V. (2019). The labor market in Russia, 2000–2017. *IZA World of Labor, 2019*(466) https://doi.org/10.15185/izawol.466

Gimpelson, V. E., & Kapeliushnikov, R. (2015). Between light and shadow: Informality in the Russian labour market. In O. Oxenstierna (Ed.), *The challenges for Russia's politicized economic system* (pp. 33–58). Routledge.

ILO. (2008). 18th International Conference of Labour Statisticians. General Report. ICLS/18/2008/IV/FINAL. https://www.ilo.org/wcmsp5/groups/public/---dgreports/---stat/documents/meetingdocument/wcms_101467.pdf

Kapeliushnikov, R. (2021). Otdacha ot obrazovaniya v Rossii: Nizhe nikuda? [Returns to education in Russia: Nowhere below?]. *Voprosy Ekonomiki, 2021*(8), 37–68. https://doi.org/10.32609/0042-8736-2021-8-37-68

Khanna, G., Newhouse, D., & Paci, P. (2011). Fewer Jobs or Smaller Paychecks? Aggregate Crisis Impacts in Selected Middle-Income Countries. IZA DP No.5956, September.

Layard, R., & Richter, A. (1995). How much unemployment is needed for restructuring. *Economics of Transition, 3*(1), 39–58.

Lehmann, H., & Wadsworth, J. (2007). Wage arrears and the distribution of earnings in Russia. *Research in Labor Economics, 26*, 125–155.

Mincer, J. (1974). *Schooling, experience, and earnings*. Columbia University Press for the National Bureau of Economic Research.

OECD. (2011). OECD *reviews of labour market and social policies*. Russian Federation. OECD, Paris.

Packard, T., Koettl, J., & Montenegro, C. (2012). In from the shadow: Integrating Europe's informal labor. *World Bank, Washington DC.* https://doi.org/10.1596/978-0-8213-9550-9

Perry, G., Maloney, W., Arias, O., Fajnzylber, P., Mason, A., & Saavedra-Chanduvi, J. (2007). *Informality: Exit and exclusion*. World Bank.

Sabirianova, K. (2002). The great human capital reallocation: A study of occupational mobility in transitional Russia. *Journal of Comparative Economics, 30*, 191–217. https://doi.org/10.1006/jcec.2001.1760

CHAPTER 18

Standard of Living and Social Policy

Irina Denisova and Marina Kartseva

Highlights

- Russia is an upper middle-income country as measured by GDP per capita and household disposable income. For sizeable groups of the population, however, the opportunities for high living standards are undermined by high income and wealth inequality.
- The prevalence of low-paid jobs in the formal and informal sectors is responsible for the high poverty risk of working adults. This risk is amplified if there are children in the families. Low intergenerational income mobility increases the risk of intergenerational poverty.
- Social protection in the Soviet era—provided largely by state-owned enterprises, collective farms, and other workplaces—has been replaced by a fully fledged social policy system with a sizeable public social insurance

I. Denisova (✉)
New Economic School, Moscow, Russia
e-mail: idenisova@nes.ru

Moscow State University, Moscow, Russia

M. Kartseva
Russian Academy of National Economy and Public Administration (RANEPA), Moscow, Russia
e-mail: kartseva-ma@ranepa.ru

© The Author(s), under exclusive license to Springer Nature Switzerland AG 2023
M. Dabrowski (ed.), *The Contemporary Russian Economy*,
https://doi.org/10.1007/978-3-031-17382-0_18

component. The system, however, is only moderately effective at insuring against the risks of income shortage due to job loss, health deterioration, and ageing. The informality of employment arrangements places large groups in the margins of this system.

- Social assistance is highly fragmented and poorly targeted to those in need. The shift of the financing burden from the federal to the regional level in the 2000s increased the risk of poverty in the least developed regions.

18.1 Introduction

In this chapter, we analyse the living standards of the Russian population according to income, wealth, and poverty indicators from an international perspective (Sect. 18.2). An overview of the evolution of income inequality in the 2000s is supplemented with a discussion of the factors behind inequality (Sect. 18.3). We also analyse poverty dynamics based on a number of different poverty measures and examine the poverty risks of different groups of the population (Sect. 18.4). In Sect. 18.5, we present the social safety net in Russia and examine the role of social assistance in mitigating poverty and inequality as well as in improving living standards. We devote particular attention to the changes in the public pension system in the 2000s. Section 18.6 presents our conclusions.

18.2 Living Standard, Income, and Wealth Inequality in Russia from an International Perspective

As discussed in Chapter 2, Russia ranks high as measured by gross national income (GNI) per capita—54 of 189 as of 2019.[1] This implies a high standard of living, provided that income inequality is not high.

Household per capita disposable income offers a more precise measure of population income than GNI per capita (Fig. 18.1).

The measure includes—in addition to estimates of monetary income from various sources net of taxes—social transfers in kind, such as health care and education provided for free or at reduced prices. The OECD's estimate of per capita disposable income for Russia in 2011 was USD 15.8 thousand and, in 2019, USD 20.8 thousand, both in purchasing power parity (PPP) terms. This is 63% of the European Union (EU) average, 50% of that of Germany, and 38% of that of the United States. At the same time, disposable per capita income in Russia is higher than in Chile or Mexico and slightly below that of Turkey and Latvia, both of which showed significant progress in the 2010s.

---

[1] http://hdr.undp.org/en/content/human-development-index-hdi.

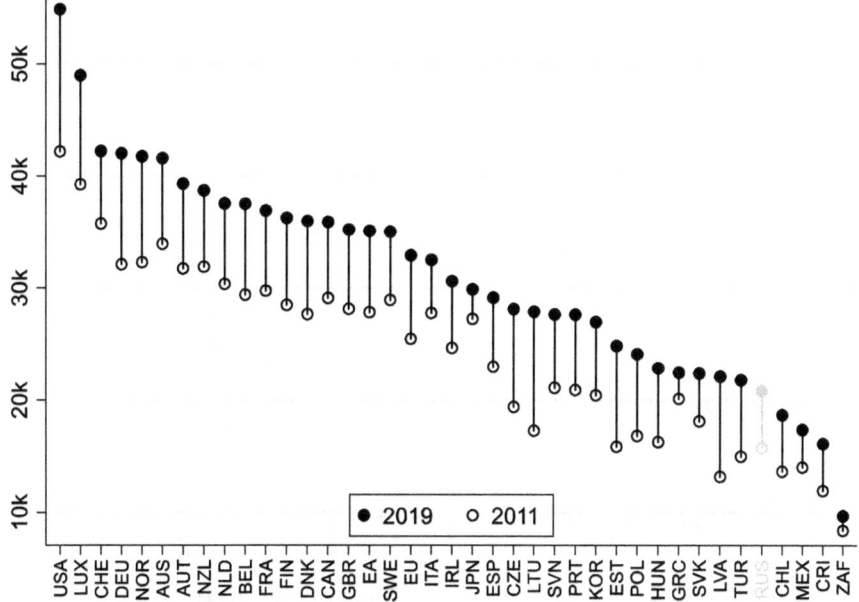

Fig. 18.1 Gross household disposable income, including social transfers in kind, PPP USD per capita, 2011–2019 (or nearest) (*Note* For Costa Rica [CRI], Japan [JPN], New Zealand [NZL], and Turkey [TUR]—2017 instead of 2019; for CRI—2012 instead of 2011. *Source* OECD statistics)

The ranking in terms of household per capita disposable income confirms Russia's position as an upper middle-income country, which would suggest a rather high standard of living. At the same time, the averaged across-population measure of income could be misleading if high inequality deprives large groups of the population of this high standard of living. Both income and wealth inequality are rather high in Russia.

Income inequality can be measured in many ways. Here, we use the Gini index and the S90/S10 decile share. The Gini index is a way to characterise how far the income distribution is from perfect equality. It takes values from 0 to 1, with a higher index value reflecting higher inequality. The S90/S10 decile share shows the ratio of the mean income of the richest 10% to the mean income of the poorest 10%.

In Russia, the Gini index of income inequality (as estimated by the World Bank) was 0.375 in 2018 (Fig. 18.2),[2] slightly below that of China and India, 37% higher than in Finland and Norway, 18% higher than in Germany, and

---

[2] The estimates by the World Bank are based on household survey data. These estimates differ from the estimate by the Federal State Statistics Service (Rosstat) due to differences in the data sources used and the methodology of income estimation (see Box 18.1).

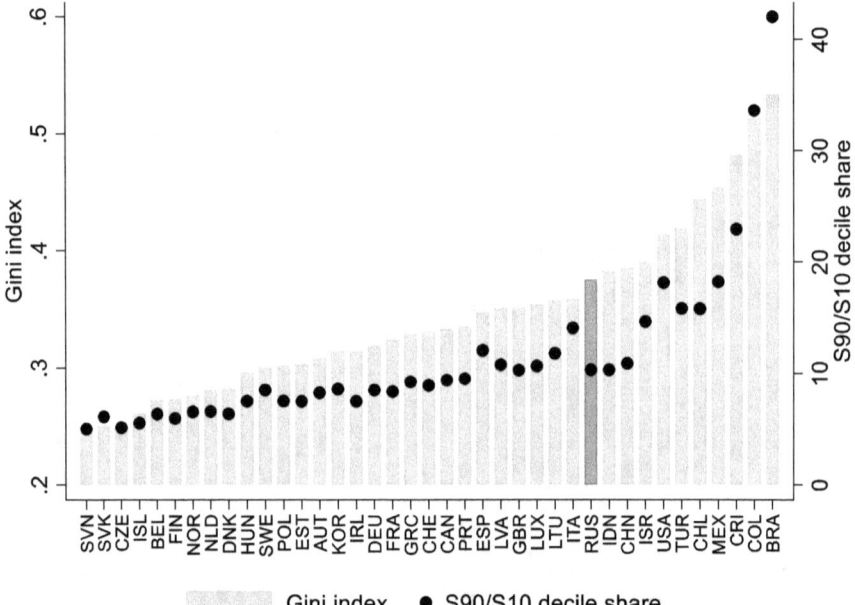

Fig. 18.2 Gini index and S90/S10 decile share, incomes, OECD member countries, candidate countries, and Russia, 2019 (or nearest) (*Source* World Bank's World Development Indicators)

8% higher than in the United Kingdom. However, it was lower than in the United States (0.414), Turkey (0.419), and Brazil (0.534).

If we use the S90/S10 decile share, inequality in Russia is at the same level as in China, India and the United Kingdom and only 10% higher than in Canada and 20% higher than in Sweden.

18.3 Income and Wealth Inequality: Measurement, Dynamics, and Determinants

18.3.1 Income Inequality

Income inequality in Russia increased throughout the 2000s before slightly declining in the 2010s (Fig. 18.3). Inequality as measured by the Gini index increased from 0.395 in 2000 to 0.422 in 2007, was rather stable until 2012, and then declined to 0.411 in 2019. The dynamic pattern of the S90/S10 decile ratio is the same: the ratio increased from 13.9 times in 2000 to 16.7 times in 2007, fluctuated around this level until 2012, and then gradually declined to 15.4 times in 2019.

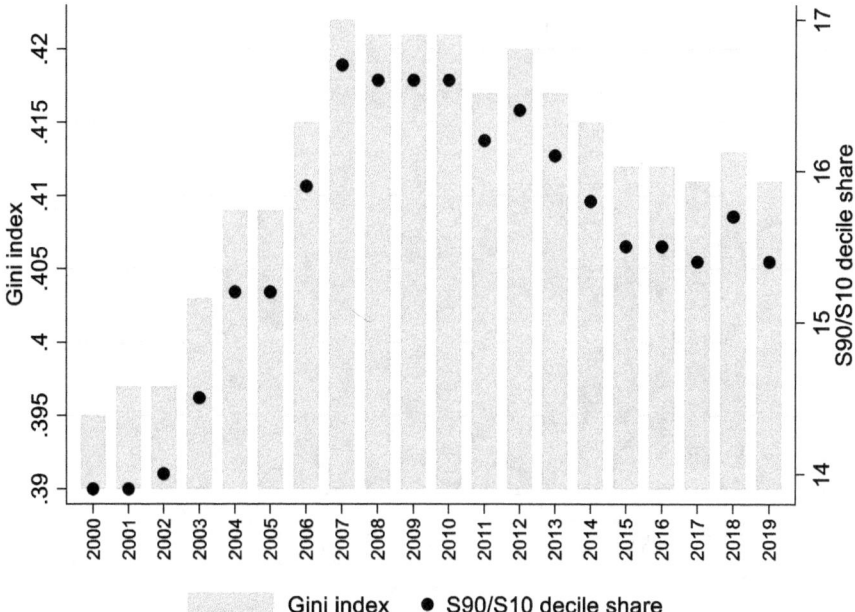

Fig. 18.3 Gini index and S90/S10 decile share, Russia, 2000–2019 (*Source* The Federal State Statistics Service [Rosstat])

Income distribution as measured by average monthly per capita household monetary income is depicted in Fig. 18.4, with the relevant shares by deciles in Fig. 18.5 (for more on the income measurement—see Box 18.1). The shape of the distribution suggests two things. First, income inequality in Russia is rather high. Indeed, 0.1% of the population reports an income higher than USD 2400, while the mean per capita monthly income is only USD 449 and the median income is even lower—USD 361.

Second, the inequality originates primarily from the gap between the top and bottom deciles, while the variation of income in the middle section of the distribution is rather low. The average income of the poorest decile is 73% lower than the average income of the next (second) decile. Similarly, the average income of the top (tenth) decile is 83% higher than the average income of the ninth decile. At the same time, the difference between the average incomes of the neighbouring deciles in the middle section of the income distribution is much lower—in the range of 21–33%.

18.3.2 *Regional Income Inequality*

The national income inequality level is the weighted average of the regional levels. Russia's regions are heterogeneous in terms of income inequality. The S90/S10 ratio varies from 18.6 in Yamal to 9.0 in Kalmykia and Ingushetia.

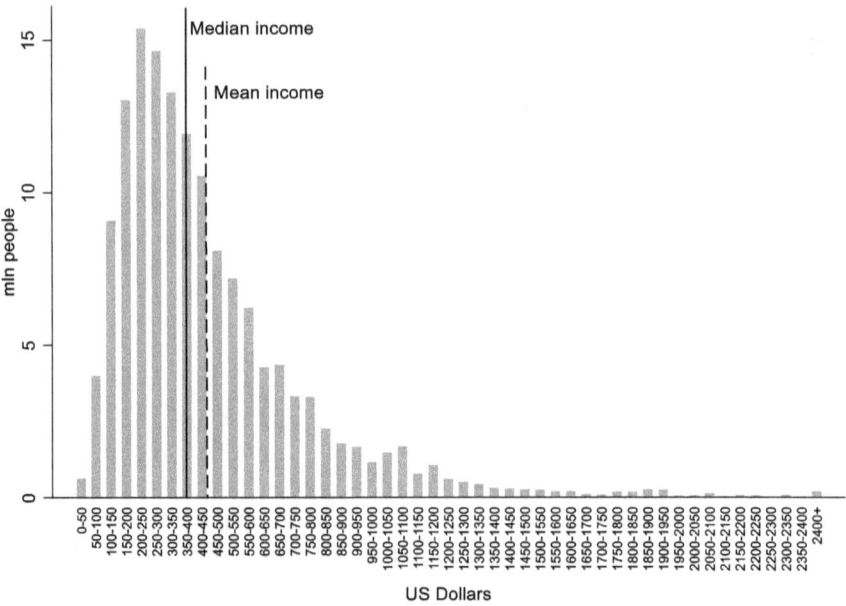

Fig. 18.4 Population distribution by average monthly household per capita monetary income (in USD) in Russia, 2018 (*Note* Annual average exchange rate in 2018 used for conversion into USD 2019. *Source* authors' calculations based on the Statistical Survey of Income and Participation in Social Programmes, Rosstat)

The Gini index is as high as 0.43 in Yamal and Tyumen while it amounts to only 0.33 in Kalmykia and Ingushetia. Hence, there are regions in Russia with income inequality at the level of France, and those with inequality at the level of Turkey, India, or China. Such regional variation complicates national-level policies to reduce inequality.

18.3.3 Determinants of Inequality: Inequality of Opportunities

Income inequality originates in the labour market, where the earnings of those working for wages in the formal and informal sectors or involved in entrepreneurship or self-employment vary substantially (see Chapter 17). On top of this, capital and business incomes are a significant component of the highest incomes. Income distribution is a result of the redistribution of earnings from high earners to relatively disadvantaged groups through formal channels of taxation, public transfers and subsidies, and informal inter-household transfers (see Sect. 18.5).

The sizeable variation in earnings is explained by the differences in productive capacity across people—that is, their human capital. Variation in human capital relates, on the one hand, to the volume of investment of time and effort into the accumulation of productive capacity, and on the other hand,

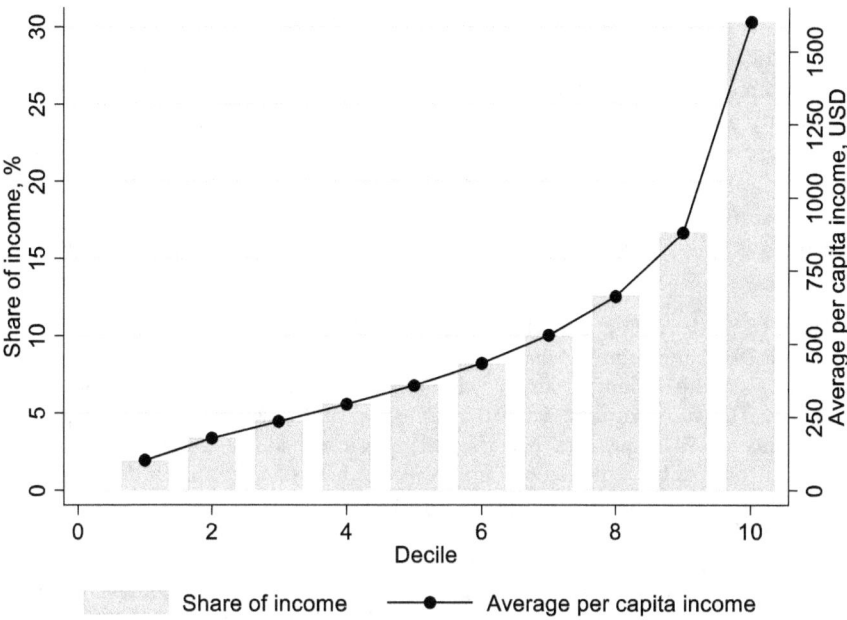

Fig. 18.5 Distribution of income and average per capita income in Russia in 2018, by decile (*Source* The Federal State Statistics Service [Rosstat])

to the human capital production technology, i.e., abilities. Differences in time preference rates, abilities, and opportunities shape individual choices of human capital formation (e.g., Rosen, 1986). Part of the resulting variation in productive capacity and earnings is perceived as fair because it reflects the differences in the efforts people make. At the same time, there are differences related to factors beyond the control of an individual, revealing that person's starting conditions or opportunities (gender, place of birth, education, occupation, and other characteristics of the parental family). This part of the earnings differential is viewed as unfair.

The share of unfair inequality amounts to 25% in earnings and 21% in incomes in Russia (Kartseva & Kuznetsova, 2020). This is similar to that of the United States, the United Kingdom, and China, less than in Latin America, and higher than in the majority of European countries (Checchi et al., 2015; Ferreira & Gignoux, 2008; Golley et al., 2019; Marrero & Rodríguez, 2012).

18.3.4 Wealth Inequality

Measuring the incomes of households is a complicated exercise, as discussed in Box 18.1. Measuring wealth or accumulated assets is an even bigger challenge as people are reluctant to report their savings in surveys; thus, administrative (tax office) and banking and finance industry data are widely used to fill the gap in information. The challenge is even higher in countries like Russia, where there is a large shadow economy, tax avoidance, and capital flight. This complicates estimates of wealth inequality. The best-known estimate of wealth inequality in Russia comes from Novokmet et al. (2018) who find it very high. The share of the top 10% in total wealth in 2015 amounted to 71%, which was at the level of the United States, 4 percentage points (pp) higher than in China, and 16 pp higher than in France. The share of the top 1% of the total wealth was as high as 42%, as compared to 30% in China and 23% in France.

Box 18.1 Measuring household income in Russia

Until 2012, the primary source of data on Russian households was the quarterly Household Budget Survey (HBS) by the Federal State Statistics Service (Rosstat), which provided detailed information on household expenditures, but not incomes. The raw data from the HBS was modified in a complicated way to adjust for possible sampling and non-response biases and to match the Balance of Monetary Incomes and Expenditures (BMIE) of certain statistical criteria. The BMIE of Russian households is based on all available sources of information (e.g., wage bills paid by employers and the purchase of currency at banks, among others) and is managed at the national and regional levels. The published household income statistics, which included poverty and inequality measures, were based on these complicated adjustments.

In 2012, Rosstat launched an annual Statistical Survey of Income and Participation in Social Programmes (SSIPSP)—the first official large household survey to collect information on household incomes. The survey is nationally and regionally representative. Since then, the HBS and BMIE have become additional sources used to adjust official income and poverty statistics from the SSIPSP. Russia's large shadow economy justifies these types of adjustments.

The State Tax Administration and Pension Fund are rich sources of data on all participants in the formal sector and can add to the estimates of income inequality. Importantly, the data are a unique source of information on top earners in both labour and capital income as the group is not reachable for household surveys. The data are not yet utilised on a regular basis thus leaving income inequality measures biased downward. The estimates by Novokmet et al. (2018), corrected for the missing incomes of top earners, increased the Gini index in 2015 for Russia from 0.41 to 0.52.

18.4 Poverty: Dynamics, Determinants, and Measurement Issues

18.4.1 Poverty Measures and Dynamics

The shape of the income distribution in Russia, with very flat lower and medium income segments of the distribution (Sect. 18.2), makes the poverty headcount rates especially sensitive to different definitions of poverty lines (Fig. 18.6) . The lowest poverty headcount ratios are seen when the poverty

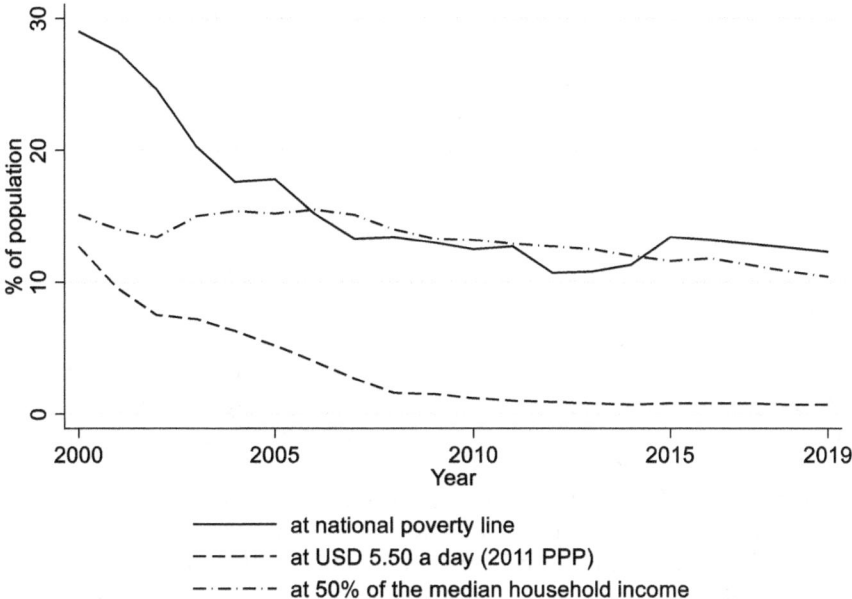

Fig. 18.6 Poverty headcount ratio, various poverty lines, Russia, 2000–2019 (*Sources* Federal State Statistics Service [Rosstat] https://www.fedstat.ru/indicator/33460; World Bank)

line is defined at USD 5.5 per day (in 2011 PPP)—the definition used by the World Bank for international comparisons. The rate was 12.7% in 2000, decreasing rapidly to 1% in 2011 and further to 0.7% in 2019. Hence, according to this definition, as of the 2010s, there is almost no poverty in Russia.

The official national poverty line used in Russia from 1992 to 2019 was based on the minimum subsistence level (see Box 18.2). It amounted to 29% in 2000, decreasing twofold by 2006 and further to 10.7% in 2012. There was then an increase to 13.4% in 2015 followed by a slight decline to 12.3% in 2019. The sizeable reduction in both absolute poverty measures in the 2000s is largely explained by rapid economic growth accompanied by an increase in pensions and transfers to families with children (see Sect. 18.5). The World Bank (2005) estimated that 60% of the poverty reduction during 1997–2002 was due to economic growth and 40% was due to decreased inequality. The reverse in the inequality trend in 2003 suggests partial losses in opportunities for poverty reduction provided by economic growth, while the decline in inequality after 2012 restored this potential.

The dynamics of the relative poverty measure—the share of those with an income below 50% of the median per capita household income—looks different. The share fluctuated around 14–15% in the 2000s and then slowly declined to 10.4% in 2019. The internationally moderate (see Subsect. 18.4.2) and rather stable relative poverty rate is a reflection of the rather flat low- and medium-income segments of the distribution.

18.4.2 International Perspective

To examine poverty rates in Russia from an international perspective, we use the OECD poverty rate, which is defined as the ratio of people (or a given age group) whose income falls below the poverty line. The poverty line is defined as half the median household income of the total population. Notice that this definition refers to half of the median income, i.e., a relative income threshold instead of an absolute income threshold. As a result, two countries with the same relative poverty rate may look different in terms of absolute poverty rates with the same absolute thresholds.

According to the poverty headcount ratio using half-median income, Russia, with 11.5%, was in the middle of the group of countries in 2019 (Fig. 18.7). For Costa Rica, this ratio amounted to 19.9%, and for the United States—17.8%. Iceland had the lowest relative poverty rate—4.9%, followed by Denmark (6.1%), Czechia (6.1%), and Finland (6.5%). Notice that the relative

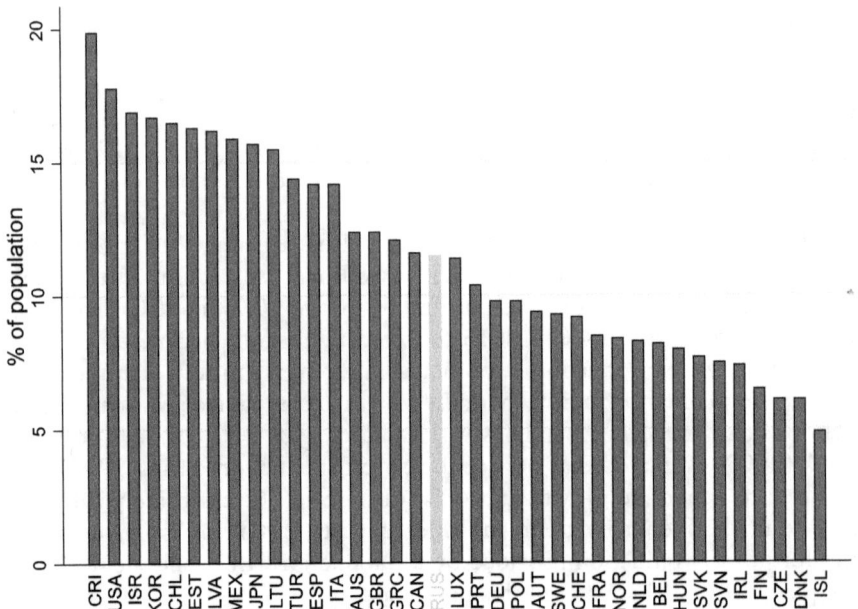

Fig. 18.7 Poverty headcount ratio at half of the median income, OECD member countries, candidate countries, and Russia, 2019 (or the nearest) (*Source* OECD statistics https://data.oecd.org/inequality/poverty-rate.htm)

poverty rate depends on the shape of the income distribution. The moderate level of relative poverty in Russia reflects the flat shape of the middle segment of the income distribution (Sect. 18.3).

The relative poverty measure is also available by broad age groups: child poverty (0–17 years old), working-age poverty (18–65 years old), and elderly poverty (66 years old or more). This enables an assessment of the relative risks of poverty across demographic groups. Interestingly, countries vary with respect to the age group with the highest risk of relative poverty and the size of the difference in risk across age groups. For instance, in 2019 in Russia, the relative poverty rate for children amounted to 17.9%, while for the elderly—12% and the working age population—9.5%. This suggests a high risk of poverty for families with children (see Subsect. 18.4.3). The relative poverty rate for children is also higher than the relative poverty rate of other age groups in Turkey, Chile, Slovakia, Italy, and Spain, making these countries' poverty profiles similar to that of Russia. In contrast, the relative poverty rate of the elderly group is much higher than the relative poverty rates of other age groups in Mexico, Latvia, Lithuania, Estonia, Australia, South Korea, and Japan. There are no visible differences in relative poverty rates across age groups in Sweden, Belgium, Ireland, Germany, Austria, and Canada.

18.4.3 Determinants of Poverty, Poverty Profiles, and Poverty Risk Factors

The age structure of poverty as measured by the absolute line at the minimum subsistence level (i.e., the official definition of poverty) confirms that poverty among the elderly is rather low in Russia. Only 7% of the poor in 2019 were of pension age, while 52% of the poor were of working age and 41% of the poor were younger than 15 years old (Rosstat, 2019). Importantly, in contrast to many other countries, the working-age poor in Russia are for the most part not the unemployed. Rather, it is employed people who form a large group of the poor in Russia. The explanation behind this phenomenon stems from the specificities of the Russian labour market, with its persistently large share of low-paid jobs in the formal sector, both public and private, and its large informal sector (see Chapter 17).

The vulnerable groups with high poverty risks are single parents and, more broadly, families with children, rural households, and families where the head of household is unemployed. Pensioners are relatively well buffered against poverty. A better education, especially a university degree, is also effective insurance against poverty, especially in urban areas (Denisova, 2012; Slobodenyuk & Mareeva, 2020).

In terms of persistency, poverty in Russia is largely transitory, with large flows into and out of poverty and a rather small proportion of chronic poor. Permanent poverty is estimated at a level of 1%, implying that there is almost no marginalised poverty (Mills & Mykerezi, 2009). This low share of chronic poverty is consistent with the observation that the poverty gap is small for the majority of families (Denisova, 2012). The large flows into and out of poverty are explained by the fact that many families 'fluctuate' around the poverty line, with negative shocks easily bringing them into poverty. This poverty pattern suggests there is significant potential for poverty escapes due to economic growth. It also points to the lack of insurance against macroeconomic shocks, making a sizeable proportion of Russian households vulnerable to poverty risks.

18.4.4 Regional Dimension of Poverty

Russia's average poverty rate conceals the substantial variation across regions (see Chapter 11). As of 2019, several regions in Russia had headcount poverty rates in the range of 10–17% (the average rate for Russia is 12.3%). At the same time, there were regions with much lower poverty rates (Moscow, St. Petersburg, and Tatarstan have poverty rates of less than 7%) and regions with poverty rates higher than 20% (Buryatia, Kalmykia, Mari El, and Kabardino-Balkaria) or 30% (Ingushetia and Tyva). Part of this difference in regional poverty rates is due to regional variations in rates of urbanisation, levels of education, employment opportunities, and family size; however, a sizeable share of this variation is left unexplained. As noted by the World Bank (2005), the chances of falling into poverty are three times higher for a person with the same characteristics in Dagestan or Tyva as compared to Tyumen or Moscow.

Variation in poverty rates across regions, reflecting differences in living standards, is a serious hazard for the country's integrity. A significant reduction in poverty is among the top national priorities (see Box 18.3).

Box 18.2 Official definition of the poverty rate in Russia

The official poverty rate in Russia is defined as the share of the population with an income below the subsistence level (1992–2020) or poverty line (since 2021). During 1992–2020, the official definition of poverty in Russia was based on the absolute income concept of poverty: a person was recognised as poor if their income (calculated as household per capita income) was less than the established minimum subsistence line—a cost estimate of the minimum set of goods and services necessary to maintain health and human activity. The minimum subsistence line was determined quarterly at both the national and regional levels for the population as a whole and for three separate age groups: the working age population, the population older than working age, and the population younger than working age. Starting from 2021, Russia shifted to the concept of relative poverty as a means to define poverty for anti-poverty policy purposes. Specifically, the subsistence level is now defined as 44.2% of the median per capita income in the country (or region) of the previous year. At the same time, for statistical purposes, the concept of absolute poverty is still

> used. Poverty line is now used instead of subsistence level for statistical calculations. The poverty line is set at the subsistence level at the end of 2020, indexed for inflation. The duality of the poverty definition—one for policy and another for statistics—complicates estimations of the resources needed for poverty reduction.

18.5 Social Security and Social Policy Instruments

In this section, we discuss the public policy instruments aimed at reducing income inequality and poverty. We begin with a description of the social security system in Russia.

18.5.1 Configuration of the Social Security System in Russia

Russia has a very comprehensive system of social security, covering support for the old-aged, families with children, medical treatments, parental and sick leave, and unemployment and disability benefits. There are three public social insurance funds in Russia: the Pension Fund, the Social Security Fund (to be integrated with the Pension Fund from 2023), and the Federal Fund for Mandatory Medical Insurance (FFMMI). Contribution to these funds via employer payroll taxes is obligatory for all employed persons in Russia (see Chapter 16). Contributions on behalf of the non-working population are paid from regional budgets and federal funds are used to balance the funds' budgets if necessary. Until 2001, there was a fourth fund—the Employment Fund; however, it has since been abolished and now unemployment insurance and assistance benefits are financed from general taxes.

Old-age, survivor, and disability pensions are paid from the Pension Fund. Additionally, the Pension Fund manages certain social protection programmes, maternity capital being the largest. The Pension Fund manages individual labour pension accounts, which are comprised of three parts: general, reflecting contributions to the insurance portion of the labour pension; special, reflecting contributions to the funded portion of the labour pension, including employer co-financing schemes and funds from maternity capital allocated to pensions; and professional, reflecting additional contributions for work conducted in difficult or dangerous conditions.

Sickness and maternity benefits, the one-time maternity benefit granted for those registered at medical centres at early periods of pregnancy, the one-time maternity benefit granted upon the birth of the child, and the monthly childcare allowance are paid from the Social Insurance Fund.

Medical expenses are paid from the FFMMI. Despite unequal access to high-quality services, major health risks are covered by the medical insurance system and all citizens of Russia have access to prepaid medical services. The important exclusion is medicine for outpatient care, which is not covered for non-vulnerable groups.

18.5.2 Social Protection Components

Social protection programmes in Russia consist of contributory and non-contributory social assistance programmes. Contributory social assistance programmes in Russia include old-age pensions and disability pensions for former employees and farmers, pensions for their dependents (survivorship), temporary disability benefits, maternity benefits, and unemployment benefits. Although with no explicit poverty alleviation mandate, these programmes have some components designed to reduce poverty, e.g., minimum pensions, social pensions, redistribution through the compression of pension benefits in comparison with contributions to the Pension Fund.

Non-contributory social assistance programmes in Russia consist of an extensive system of subsidies, transfers, benefits, and programmes. The level of fragmentation of social assistance in Russia is very high when compared internationally. An inventory conducted by a World Bank project in 2017 identified 756 federally mandated and—on average—150 regionally mandated programmes per region that are of a social assistance type (Yemtsov et al., 2019). For comparison, Turkey has about 40 programmes and Greece—about 200 (Yemtsov et al., 2019). Many programmes target privileged groups, with fewer programmes targeting the poor. The main privileged categories in Russia include vulnerable citizens (the disabled, war invalids, dependents of war victims, and those affected by radiation); citizens who provided exceptional service to the state and thus receive merit-based privileges; and occupational benefits holders and labour veterans who receive occupational privileges. Privileged groups are entitled to a wide list of services for free or only partly paid, for example, housing and utility discounted tariffs, transport, sanatorium and spa recreation, special arrangements for medical care, and the provision of medicine, among others.

Social assistance programmes targeted to the poor in Russia consist of three types: child benefits to low-income families; housing and utility subsidies to low-income households; and targeted social assistance programmes by regional or local governments. Additionally, social assistance is provided through institutionalised care to the elderly, orphans, and the disabled. Targeted social assistance to those in need is provided as monetary or in-kind payments on a monthly or one-time basis and is of a very limited scope. Poverty-targeted means-tested benefits were estimated at 0.44% of GDP in 2017 (Yemtsov et al., 2019).

Estimates by Zubarevich and Gorina (2015) show that total public expenditures on social protection in Russia amounted to 11.9% of GDP in 2014. Two-thirds of expenditures were for public social insurance programmes. According to World Bank data, social assistance per se was estimated at 1.61%

of GDP in 2018, with 1.13% of GDP for (unconditional) cash transfers and 0.48% of GDP for social pensions (ASPIRE, 2019). To compare, annual spending on social assistance in Chile was 3.78% of GDP (2018) and 3.11% of GDP in Estonia (2017). Russia's spending on social assistance is similar to that of Brazil, India, Armenia, and Slovakia and more than that of China, Turkey, Moldova, and Czechia.

18.5.3 *The Impact of Social Transfers on Poverty*

The impact of social assistance programmes on poverty in Russia is rather modest. Part of this explanation is that a large portion of the numerous programmes provided under the umbrella of social assistance do not prioritise the poor (Yemtsov et al., 2019). There is only a small subset of social assistance programmes which are means-tested, with child and poverty benefits being the largest. In 2017, the volume of federal programmes explicitly targeted to the poor was estimated at 0.04% of GDP, with regional programmes amounting to 0.4% of GDP (ASPIRE, 2019).

At the same time, the coverage of the poor in Russia by social assistance programmes is high and comparable to that of developed countries (Yemtsov et al., 2019). Rather, it is the limited ability to direct the allocated resources to the bottom segment of the income distribution (low benefit incidence) along with the limited size of the benefits (low adequacy of the benefit) that make their impact on poverty modest.

Indeed, Russia is among the leaders in terms of the coverage of the poor by social assistance programmes: 78.6% of the poorest quintile received some form of social assistance benefit in 2017. This was higher than in Poland (50% in 2015) and Turkey (40% in 2019). At the same time, there is room for improvement here as social assistance coverage amounted to 96% in Chile (2017), India (2011), and South Africa (2014).

Benefit incidence defined as percentage of social assistance benefits allocated to the poorest 20% of the population relative to the total benefits to the entire population was only 29.5% in Russia (2017), as compared to 56.4% in Poland (2015) and Brazil (2019), 40% in Mexico (2018), and 32% in India (2011). This implies that 70% of funds earmarked to help the poor are not allocated to the most vulnerable group either by design or misallocation (failure to identify or to deliver to the neediest groups).

The average volume of assistance provided to families in the poorest quintile in Russia was estimated at 19% of pre-transfer income in 2017. This was similar to that of Kazakhstan (2017) and Kyrgyzstan (2013), slightly higher than that of Turkey (2019), twice as high as that of India (10% in 2011), and 2.5 times higher than in China (7.5% in 2013). At the same time, it was twice as low as in Serbia (41% in 2015), Poland (35% in 2015), and Brazil (35% in 2019). Even though the poverty gap in Russia, on average, is not large, the size of social assistance transfers is, in many instances, insufficient to bring families out of poverty.

The analysis suggests that to further fight poverty, more resources must be channelled to programmes targeting the poor. Some argue that better targeting would allow for a sizeable decrease in poverty without the need for additional funds to be allocated to social assistance (Yemtsov et al., 2019).

18.5.4 Social Policy Instruments: Maternity and Child Benefits

Maternity and child benefits consist of both contributory and non-contributory items, with financing originating from the Social Insurance Fund for the former and the federal and regional budgets for the latter. The benefits paid under the umbrella of mandatory social insurance from the Social Insurance Fund include maternity benefits, one-time maternity benefits granted for those registered at medical centres at early periods of pregnancy, one-time maternity benefits granted upon the birth of a child, and a monthly childcare allowance.

The maternity benefit is paid cumulatively for the period of maternity leave defined as 70 (84 if siblings) calendar days before child delivery and 70(86 if complications during delivery and 110 if siblings) calendar days after delivery. The size of the maternity benefit is defined as 100% of the average (within 12 months) monthly wage. Those with less than 6 months of labour experience receive the federally defined minimum wage. Benefits are paid from the Social Insurance Fund for the non-military and those not in full-time education and from the federal budget otherwise. Regions may add additional benefits.

In addition to maternity benefits and the child allowance, which is paid until the child is 1.5 years old, families with children are eligible for monthly child benefits. Until 1999, monthly child benefits were universal and financed from the federal budget. In 1999, benefits became means-tested, with eligibility based on a per capita household income less than the regional subsistence level. As of 2005, monthly child benefits are determined by regional authorities and paid from regional budgets. The size of the benefit varies across regions, with richer regions paying much higher amounts. Detailed information on financial support to families with children as of 2021 is presented in Box 18.4.

Since January 2006, a maternity certificate system was introduced. The system aims to provide additional incentives for the public healthcare system to deliver better quality medical care to pregnant women during labour and to children during the first year of life. Certificates are financed from the federal budget.

18.5.5 Social Policy Instruments: Labour Pension

The labour pension is defined as a monthly monetary payment to compensate the insured for loss of wages, salaries, and other labour reimbursement payments due to the loss of the own ability to work (either due to old age or disability) or the loss of income by dependents of the insured due to the death of the insured. The labour pension in Russia consists of three types of pensions: the old-age pension, the disability pension, and the survivor pension.

As of 2015, the old-age labour pension is comprised of three parts: the insurance pension, the funded pension, and the fixed pension payment. There are three conditions for labour insurance pension eligibility: reaching the retirement age, meeting the minimum contribution experience (15 years contributing to the Pension Fund from 2025), and accumulating minimum pension rights equivalent to 30 individual 'pension points'. The retirement age had long been set at 55 for females and 60 for males; however, in 2019, it was changed during the retirement age reform to gradually reach 60 for women and 65 for men by 2028 (see Box 2.3 in Chapter 2).

The pension reform of 2015 aimed to stimulate employment in the formal sector, longer employment life, and later retirement. The minimum contribution period necessary to be eligible for the labour pension was gradually extended from 5 to 15 years, and those not meeting the criteria are eligible for the social (basic) pension, with the eligibility age for social pensioners being 5 years higher than for labour pensioners.

The key innovation of the reform was the introduction of individual 'pension points' or coefficients. Since then, the insurance pension benefit is the product of the total accumulated pension points and the monetary value of one pension point (defined by the government each year). The number of individual pension points attributed to a year of employment (and contribution to the Pension Fund) depends on the annual contribution to the Pension Fund. It is calculated as the ratio of the sum of the annual individual insurance contribution to the normative (maximum possible) insurance contribution to the Pension Fund. There is an upper limit of the points attributed to a year of employment.

Late retirement is stimulated via the premium pension coefficients for employment beyond retirement age and the augmented fixed portion of the labour pension. Low trust in general and in government in particular, however, leads to people claiming public pension benefits at the earliest possible point. The numerous changes in the rules governing the provision of pensions during the last 25 years have also added to public scepticism about the value of the benefits promised in the long run.

As a result, the magnitude of the insurance pension benefit depends on (official) wages during working life, the length of the contribution to the Pension Fund, and the age at retirement. It is estimated that to earn 30 pension points (the eligibility minimum), it is sufficient to have 15 years of contribution to the Pension Fund paid from a wage not less than twice the minimum wage, or 30 years of contribution from a wage equal to the minimum wage (Denisova, 2014).

The pension points formula and the limits to the taxable wage bill result in the strong compression of the pension benefits distribution as compared to the wage distribution. The estimates of the gross pension replacement rate (the level of pension benefits in retirement from mandatory public and private pension schemes relative to earnings when working) in 2020 varied from 57% for low earners to 47% for average earners and 42% for high earners (OECD, 2021). The minimum pension is set higher than the minimum subsistence level, reducing the (absolute) poverty risk of the group.

There is also a second tier to Russia's old-age pension—the funded defined contribution benefit. The funded component was introduced during the pension reform of 2002, with its rules further updated in 2014. As of 2014, those entering the labour market may choose whether or not they want the funded component (if not all contributions are made to the insurance portion). The funded portion of the old-age pension is accumulated in the special part of individual pension accounts at the Pension Fund or in private funds. From 2014, the Pension Fund introduced a moratorium (as of early 2022, until the end of 2023) on the formation of the funded portion of the old-age pension, with all contributions temporarily paid into the insurance portion.

Box 18.3 Evolution of the social protection system

By 1995, much of Russia's legislation on social protection had already been put in place. However, even until the mid-2000s, Russia's social protection system lacked clarity, as certain benefits and privileges inherited from the Soviet era were neither fully abolished nor fully granted, but rather provided based on discretion. As of 2004, Russia had more than 100 types of in-kind social benefits and subsidies which amounted to 5% of GDP (World Bank, 2005). Meanwhile, new benefits were introduced during the transition period (i.e., unemployment benefits, housing and utility subsidies, and poverty assistance programmes). In 1999, benefits targeted to low-income families were introduced and child benefits—which also existed during Soviet times—became means-tested; only families with per capita incomes below the subsistence level were eligible for the benefits.

The division of financial responsibilities for state obligations between the federal and regional budgets was not clearly defined until 2004 when the system was restructured. In particular, an option to monetise basic in-kind benefits was introduced. Responsibilities between regional and federal budgets were divided clearly and federal and regional groups of the population eligible for social support were defined. A uniform system for housing subsidies was introduced. The shift of part of the burden to the regional level resulted in a reduction in the provision of the regional component in some regions due to the lack of funds in their budgets.

In 2006, the priorities in social policy were changed in favour of families with children. Various maternity-related insurance benefits and allowances were increased significantly. Additionally, maternity capital was introduced for the second and higher order child (see Chapter 2). The policy received additional support in 2018 under the umbrella of national projects (see Box 18.4).

In the early 2020s, the government continued to pay several monetary benefits and allowances and provided subsidies and selected in-kind services. In particular, the government was responsible for the provision of labour pensions, social pensions, including disability pensions, unemployment benefits, child benefits, and family and maternity allowances. Additionally, it provided subsidies for maintenance and utility services and food subsidies for children in full-time education and children in kindergarten. The largest in-kind services were provided in transport and sanatorium and spa recreation.

Box 18.4 Poverty reduction as a national policy priority: families with children

In 2018, Russian President Vladimir Putin declared the aim to halve poverty—from 13.2% as of 2017 to 6.6% by 2024—as the top national development goal. In 2020, the target date was reset to 2030. With the main responsibility for poverty reduction falling on regional authorities, the federal government has allocated additional resources to families with children, a group highly vulnerable to poverty risk. The efficiency of the support is monitored under the umbrella of the Demography National Project.

The key measures supporting families with children as of 2021 include:

- Maternity capital, which as of 2022 increased to RUB 524.5 thousand for the first child and RUB 693.1 thousand for the second (under the condition that the family did not receive maternity capital for the first child, or RUB 168.6 thousand if they did). Constraints on the use of the money were further relaxed to enable funding for the current needs of the family. Eligibility does not depend on household income.
- Monthly payment for children from birth to 3 years old (for the first and second child). Eligibility is means-based.
- Monthly payment for children aged 3–7 (introduced by Presidential Decree in 2020). Eligibility is means-based.
- Monthly payment for children aged 8–17. Only incomplete families are eligible, subject to means test (amendment to the Federal Law in 2021).
- Preferential mortgage rates for families with children (with two or more children as of 2018, expanded to families with one child in 2021). Eligibility does not depend on family income.

Source Ministry of Labour and Social Protection of the Russian Federation.

18.6 Conclusions

Russia is an upper middle-income country as measured by both GDP per capita and per capita household disposable income. Its high level of development provides opportunities for high standards of living for the population. However, high income and—especially—wealth inequality challenges the bright prospects for large groups of the population. The prevalence of low-paid jobs in the formal and informal sectors of the labour market is responsible for the high risk of poverty of working adults. The risks amplify if there are children in the families.

There is a fully fledged social protection system in Russia, with a sizeable public social insurance component. This social insurance is nevertheless only moderately effective in insuring against the risks of income shortage due to job loss, health deterioration, and ageing. Moreover, informality and the absence of working contracts place large groups of the population at the boundaries of the public social insurance system, as they are eligible for minimum (social) pensions and unemployment benefits.

The social assistance system is highly fragmented and poorly targeted to those in need. The reforms of the 2000s shifted the burden of financing the social assistance system from the federal to the regional level. Given Russia's vast regional heterogeneity, this increased the risks of poverty in the least developed regions. To further fight poverty, more resources must be channelled to the poor; the size of the benefits targeted to the poor must also be increased.

There are concerns about the relatively high earnings differential in Russia due to the inequality of opportunities and low intergenerational income mobility. These increase the risks of intergenerational poverty.

Questions for students

1. Russia ranks high in terms of GDP per capita. Does this imply high living standards for the population? What are the major challenges you see?
2. Characterise the income distribution in Russia using different measures of income inequality. What are the sources of unequal incomes in Russia?
3. What are the most vulnerable groups in Russia in terms of poverty risks? Do you see anything unusual in Russia's poverty profile? Compare with the situation in your native country.
4. What are the main challenges for the social assistance system in Russia? Hint: consider the coverage, incidence, and adequacy of social assistance benefits.

References

ASPIRE. (2019). *The Atlas of social protection indicators of resilience and equity*. The World Bank. https://www.worldbank.org/en/data/datatopics/aspire

Checchi, D., Peragine, V., & Serlenga, L. (2015). *Income inequality and opportunity inequality in Europe: Recent trends and explaining factors*. Paper presented at the 5th ECINEQ meeting, University of Luxembourg, July 2015.

Denisova, I. (2012). *Income distribution and poverty in Russia* (OECD Social, Employment and Migration Working Papers No. 132). OECD Publishing. https://doi.org/10.1787/5k9csf9zcz7c-en

Denisova, I. (2014). *Social protection system and social policy in Russia*—background paper prepared for the World Bank.

Ferreira, F., & Gignoux, J. (2008). The measurement of inequality of opportunity: Theory and an application to Latin America. *Review of Income and Wealth, 57*(4), 622–657. https://doi.org/10.1111/j.1475-4991.2011.00467.x

Golley, J., Zhou, Y., & Wang, M. (2019). Inequality of opportunity in China's labour earnings: The gender dimension. *China & World Economy, 27*(1), 28–50. https://doi.org/10.1111/cwe.12266

Kartseva, M., & Kuznetsova, P. (2020). Is income inequality fair in Russia? Inequality of opportunity and income inequality. *Applied Econometrics, 58*(2), 5–31 (In Russ.). https://doi.org/10.22394/1993-7601-2020-58-5-31

Marrero, G. A., & Rodríguez, J. G. (2012). Inequality of opportunity in Europe. *Review of Income and Wealth, 58*(4), 597–621. https://doi.org/10.1111/j.1475-4991.2012.00496.x

Mills, B. F., & Mykerezi, E. (2009). Chronic and transient poverty in the Russian Federation. *Post-Communist Economies, 21*(3), 283–306. https://doi.org/10.1080/14631370903090590

Novokmet, F., Piketty, T., & Zucman, G. (2018). From Soviets to oligarchs: Inequality and property in Russia 1905–2016. *The Journal of Economic Inequality, 16*(2), 189–223. https://doi.org/10.1007/s10888-018-9383-0

OECD. (2021). Pensions at a glance 2021: OECD and G20 indicators. *OECD Publishing*. https://doi.org/10.1787/ca401ebd-en

Rosen, S. (1986). The theory of equalizing differences. In O. Ashenfelter, P. R. G. Layard (Eds.), *Handbook of Labor Economics* (Vol. 1). Elsevier.

Rosstat. (2019). *The demographic yearbook of Russia 2019*. The Federal State Statistics Service (Rosstat). https://gks.ru/bgd/regl/B19_16/Main.htm. Accessed 25 Jan 2022.

Slobodenyuk, E. D., & Mareeva, S. V. (2020). Relative poverty in Russia: Evidence from different thresholds. *Social Indicators Research, 151*, 135–153. https://doi.org/10.1007/s11205-020-02364-1

World Bank. (2005). *Russian Federation. Reducing Poverty through Growth and Social Policy Reform* (Report No. 28923-RU). World Bank. https://documents1.worldbank.org/curated/en/391591564381077495/pdf/Strengthening-Social-Protection-Towards-more-effective-social-assistance-in-Russia-An-update-of-the-system-performance-considering-new-national-target-of-halving-poverty-by-2024.pdf

Yemtsov, R., Posarac, A., Nagernyak, M., & Albegova, I. (2019). *Towards more effective social assistance in Russia: An update of the system performance considering new national target of halving poverty by 2024*. World Bank. https://openknowledge.worldbank.org/handle/10986/32255

Zubarevich, N., & Gorina, E. (2015). *Social'nye raskhody v Rossii: Federal'nyi i regional'nye byudzhety (Social expenditures in Russia: Federal and regional budgets).* Higher School of Economics. https://www.hse.ru/data/2015/05/19/1097215048/2015_3q_SocialSpendings_fin_z.pdf

PART VII

Summary

CHAPTER 19

Russia's Two Transitions (1992–2003 and 2003–2022)

Marek Dabrowski

Highlights

- After the dissolution of the Soviet Union in 1991, Russia experienced two political and economic transitions, going in opposite directions.
- In the 1990s and early 2000s, the centrally planned economy based on the almost monopoly of state ownership and largely closed to the external world was transformed to a more open market system based predominantly on private ownership. Parallelly, the political system became freer and more democratic, a continuation of reforms started in the perestroika era.
- However, in 2003, the economic system started moving towards more state ownership, government interference in economic life, and inward-oriented economic policies. The global financial crisis (GFC) of 2008–2009, the annexation of Crimea and the war in Donbas (2014–2015), the invasion of Ukraine in February 2022, and the associated sanctions

M. Dabrowski (✉)
Bruegel, Brussels, Belgium
e-mail: marek.dabrowski@bruegel.org

Higher School of Economics, Moscow, Russia

CASE—Center for Social and Economic Research, Warsaw, Poland

© The Author(s), under exclusive license to Springer Nature Switzerland AG 2023
M. Dabrowski (ed.), *The Contemporary Russian Economy*,
https://doi.org/10.1007/978-3-031-17382-0_19

and countersanctions accelerated this process. It was associated with a gradual but systematic autocratic drift in the political sphere.
- The experience of two Russian transitions confirms an interrelation between economic and political changes, with the latter determining the prospects of the former.

19.1 Introduction

Since the collapse of the communist regime and the dissolution of the Soviet Union in 1991, Russia has experienced two political and economic transitions.

In the first decade, the Russian economy was transformed from the command system of a central planning based on the almost monopoly of state ownership and largely closed to the external world to a more open market system based predominantly on private ownership. However, in 2003, the economic system started moving towards more state ownership, government interference in economic life, and inward-oriented economic policies. The global financial crisis (GFC) of 2008–2009, the annexation of Crimea and the war in Donbas (2014–2015), the invasion of Ukraine in February 2022, and the associated sanctions and countersanctions (see Chapter 14) accelerated this process.

In parallel to economic transitions, political transitions also took place, and, as we argue in this chapter, political changes determined the economic ones. In the early 1990s, the Russian political system became freer and more democratic (compared to the Soviet era), although still far from the standards of mature liberal democracies. The Freedom House's Freedom in the World (FHFIW) survey rated Russia as a partly free country then.[1] However, since the early 2000s, under Vladimir Putin's presidency, the political system has become more autocratic and centralised, with decreasing room for civil liberties and political rights. In the early 2020s, the process of consolidating a 'power vertical', as popularly called in the Russian political debate (around the institution of the president[2]), and eliminating systemic checks and balances was completed.

The purpose of this chapter is to present a synthetic picture of these two political and economic transitions, first from communist dictatorship to democracy and from the command system to a market-based system, and then back—from democracy to a new autocratic regime and from the dominant role of the market to more government dirigisme in an economic sphere. In doing so, we will refer to the findings of other chapters of this volume.

---

[1] See https://freedomhouse.org/sites/default/files/2022-03/Country_and_Territory_Ratings_and_Statuses_FIW_1973-2022%20.xlsx.

[2] Amendments to the Constitution of the Russian Federation adopted in 2020 (see Chapter 5) further increased the prerogatives of the president and practically eliminated the time limit (two consecutive 6-year terms) for holding this office.

Section 19.2 begins with the transition from a communist regime to democracy and from plan to market in the 1990s. Then, in Sect. 19.3, we concentrate on the early 2000s, when several critical economic reforms initiated in the 1990s were completed and Russia returned to economic growth after a decade of output decline. However, the same period started the autocratic drift observed in the next two decades. Section 19.4 deals with the period between 2003 and 2014 when the autocratic tendencies in the political sphere intensified. Simultaneously, the share of state ownership in the economy increased from its lowest level in the early 2000s. Section 19.5 is devoted to the period since 2014 when the annexation of Crimea and engagement in the war in Donbas led to Western sanctions against Russia and Russian retaliatory measures against Western partners. Apart from the further increase of autocratic tendencies in the political sphere and the government's interference in economic life, this period set off the inward-oriented economic policies. The invasion of Ukraine generated the next and much stronger shock of the same type in February 2022. In Sect. 19.6, we summarise how the Russian economy, economic system, and economic policy operate in the early 2020s, including the expected impact of the war in Ukraine and associated sanctions, and analyse the future challenges.

19.2 FROM PLAN TO MARKET: THE HEROIC DECADE OF THE 1990S

Russia's economic transition towards a market-oriented system in the 1990s was long and painful because of the complicated legacy of the Soviet system (structural distortions, including excessive militarisation, macroeconomic imbalances, and the absence of market institutions) and insufficient political support for market-oriented reforms. Both resulted in their slow and inconsequent implementation (Dabrowski, 2001; Dabrowski et al., 2004).

Political changes in 1990–1991 facilitated the economic transition. They included, among others, partially democratic elections of the Congress of People's Deputies and Supreme Council of the Russian Federation in March 1990, the declaration of the state sovereignty of Russia on 12 June 1990, the democratic election of Boris Yeltsin as the first president of the Russian Federation a year later, democratic amendments to the Constitution of the Russian Federation (still within the Soviet Union) in 1990–1991, the failure of the anti-reform *coup d'état* in August 1991, followed by the dissolution of the Communist Party of the Soviet Union just after the coup and the Soviet Union in December 1991. These changes unblocked the market-oriented economic reforms stalled in the final years of the *perestroika* period (see Chapter 4).

Nevertheless, the window of political opportunity opened by these changes proved too short and narrow[3] to guarantee the adoption of the upfront package of comprehensive and radical market reforms as happened in the Central European and Baltic countries. The limited pro-reform consensus within the political elite came to an end already in the spring of 1992. The following political windows of opportunity were created by Yeltsin's victory in the April 1993 referendum,[4] the dissolution of the pro-communist Supreme Council in September 1993, cracking down on the communist unrest in Moscow at the beginning of October 1993, and Yeltsin's re-election in June 1996. However, they appeared to also be narrow and short-lived and were largely missed opportunities for economic reforms.

The anti-reform opposition, represented by the newly (re)created Communist Party of the Russian Federation (CPRF) and other populist political parties, remained strong until the end of the 1990s and dominated the State Duma for the first two terms (1993–1995 and 1995–1999). They represented the anti-reform lobbies, particularly managers of state-owned and collective farms and state-owned industrial enterprises (the so-called red directors). Representatives of these lobbies were also present in the subsequent governments. The legislative branch of government was in permanent political confrontation with the executive branch (president and government).

This unfavourable political environment forced subsequent governments and key economic policymakers to make various bad compromises with the anti-reform forces and search for the second-and-third-best solutions to increase their room for manoeuvre and move reforms forward.

There were many examples of such bad compromises, suboptimal policy choices, and reform 'gaps' caused by a political inability to adopt fundamental reform components wholly and promptly.

When reforms started in the fall of 1991, monetary policy could not become a part of the macroeconomic stabilisation package. There were two reasons: the anti-reform camp controlled the Central Bank of the Russian Federation (CBRF) and the Soviet rouble zone with fifteen independent central banks continued to operate until the second half of 1993 (see Chapter 16). As a result, a price liberalisation in January 1992 had to be carried out with a substantial monetary overhang accumulated during the Soviet era and without the possibility of controlling the current money supply. In addition, the subsequent governments could not reduce the fiscal deficit because they did not have majority support in the parliament. As a result, disinflation took several years. Russia experienced several currency crises (the most spectacular in October 1994 and August 1998) that undermined trust

---

[3] The discussion of why this window of political opportunity was narrow and short-lived as compared with Central European and Baltic countries goes beyond the agenda of this chapter and this textbook.

[4] One of the questions concerned support for the socio-economic policy conducted by the president and the government.

in the national currency and domestic financial systems for many years (see Chapter 16).

The delay also concerned external liberalisation and the liberalisation of domestic energy and oil prices. The exchange rate was unified only in September 1992, and the elimination of centralised export, import subsidies, export quotas, and licences lasted until the end of 1994. Domestic energy and oil prices were never adjusted to the international level (see Chapter 9). The distortions created by the delayed macroeconomic stabilisation and liberalisation led to the beginnings of many oligarchs' fortunes.

Political compromises also concerned the privatisation process (see Chapter 7). First, privatisation was carried out in a volatile macroeconomic environment (high inflation, frequent devaluations of the rouble), which negatively influenced the quality and social perception of this process. Second, the resistance of various sectoral lobbies and 'red' directors did not allow the mass de-concentration and de-monopolisation prior to privatisation, as done in Central European and Baltic countries. It complicated enterprise restructuring, made the domestic market less competitive, and contributed to the emergence of large financial-industrial groups. Third, the political circumstances also determined the choice of privatisation strategy and methods.

At the end of 1992, the choice was made in favour of mass voucher privatisation, following the experience of Czechia. With the benefit of hindsight, this decision seemed to be correct. First, other privatisation methods could not bring fast ownership changes in large enterprises for technical reasons (lack of a well-functioning stock exchange and financial market, the limited interest of foreign investors, and difficulties with the valuation of privatised assets, among others). Second, this was the only politically acceptable method at that time. Third, it allowed stopping the spontaneous and non-transparent privatisation based on so-called leasing (*arenda*), the law on cooperatives, and other ownership experiments of the perestroika era.

For the same political reasons, the government gave a significant stake of shares to insiders – employees and managers (see Chapter 7). The privileges to insiders slowed down the process of enterprise restructuring. However, they allowed both gaining parliamentary approval and creating a strong interest in ownership changes on the enterprise level. Other transition countries that limited incentives to insiders had to deal with resistance from this important social constituency.

An even more controversial decision was taken in 1995 after the mass voucher privatisation ended and the follow-up cash privatisation had problems taking off for political and administrative reasons. The biggest Russian private banks invented the loans-for-shares scheme (*zalogovye aukciony*), and the government accepted this idea (see Chapter 7). The rationale of this project was purely political, as owners of private banks wanted to receive a reward for the promised support of Boris Yeltsin in the 1996 presidential election.

The loans-for-shares scheme led to the beginning of the very non-transparent phase of the Russian privatisation, which had several negative consequences. First, the federal budget lost potential proceeds from privatisation because the most attractive assets were sold much below their market price. Second, this scheme helped build strong financial-industrial groups to control Russia's economic and political life in the next few years. Third, the social legitimisation of privatisation became seriously damaged. As a result, it was easier to question its results and renationalise some crucial sectors in the 2000s and 2010s (see Sect. 19.4).

Another essential political compromise worth mentioning in this historical overview related to the limits on the entry of foreign banks into Russia. They were adopted as a presidential decree before the December 1993 parliamentary elections, on demand of the Association of Russian Banks. In a modified legal form, they are still in force. This decision helped to create large financial-industrial groups owned by oligarchs. It also limited competition in the banking sector and the inflow of modern know-how as well as facilitated imprudent banking practices such as connected lending. Eventually, it led to the banking crises in 1998 and 2008–2009.

As a result of a slow reform process and the associated political compromises, macroeconomic stabilisation and building the foundations of an open market economy took longer, and they were more painful compared to Central European and Baltic countries.[5] The transformation-related output decline lasted ten years and amounted to more than 40% on a cumulative basis (see Chapter 15). Real wages and real population incomes[6] also significantly dropped (see Chapters 17 and 18). All this led to the perception of the 'lost decade' (which was not true, given the scale of systemic transformation) and 'the poor 1990s', the arguments actively used by the advocates of the autocratic drift and greater government interventionism in the next two decades.

The post-Soviet structural and institutional legacies also played a role in determining the scale of transition-related hardships (see Chapters 8 and 15). They were more complicated in the FSU than in the rest of the former communist bloc, especially in the countries which were experimenting earlier with 'socialist-market' reforms, such as the former Yugoslavia, Hungary, and Poland. A shorter period of the communist regime in the latter, their greater openness to the West, greater enterprise autonomy, and some enclaves of the private sector also did matter. On the other hand, socialist industrialisation in the former Soviet Union (FSU) lasted much longer, was more intensive, and

---

[5] To be fair, in the 1990s, Russia's economic reform progress looked better as compared with many other FSU and South-East European countries—see e.g., World Bank (1996, 2002); EBRD (1999).

[6] What was the real wage and income level in the early 1990s, in the presence of a widespread physical shortage of goods (a form of hidden inflation) and black market, is another question. Taking this factor into account, perhaps the actual decline in living standard in the 1990s was less dramatic than that statistically recorded.

subordinated to military needs, creating greater structural distortions (Chapters 4 and 8). However, the experience of the Baltic countries, which also had to deal with the Soviet structural and institutional legacy and recorded a substantial output decline but overcame it much earlier (in the mid-1990s), suggests that speed, comprehensiveness, and quality of reforms played an important role (WEO, 2000, Chapter 3).

Insufficient support for democratic and liberal reforms also negatively influenced changes in the political and institutional system. Although the new constitution adopted in December 1993 broke radically with the Soviet past and set the foundation for a market economy, human rights, civil and political freedoms, and democratic governance (see Chapter 5), it suffered from a fundamental institutional imbalance in favour of executive power, especially the president. Such a solution resulted from the Russian historical tradition of a strong executive power (see Chapters 3 and 4) and the political landscape of 1992–1993, when the reform-oriented president was permanently challenged by the anti-reform opposition in the Congress of Peoples' Deputies and the Supreme Council.

Furthermore, the political circumstances that led to the constitutional referendum and parliamentary elections in December 1993, namely, the forceful dissolution of the parliament in September 1993, which was controversial on the grounds of the previous constitution, could be considered as another 'original sin' (Gel'man, 2015). It undermined the legitimacy of the new political and institutional order.

Following the adoption of the 1993 Constitution, several other pieces of legislation, which were to set institutional foundations for a market economic order and liberal democracy, were approved. Some of them, especially those related to the economic sphere, draw from the experience of matured market economies. However, the anti-reform opposition in the first and second Duma compromised the quality and consistency of many new laws (see Chapter 5) and delayed their implementation.

Looking back, four crucial areas (the judiciary, law enforcement and security agencies, the army, and the public administration) were not sufficiently reformed in the 1990s, which negatively influenced the course of political developments and the business and investment climate (see Chapter 6) in the next two decades.

19.3 The Turning Point of the Russian Transition (the Early 2000s)

Despite all hardships, market reforms started to bear fruit at the beginning of the new millennium. In 1999, the Russian economy entered a phase of post-transformation growth recovery, which accelerated in the early and mid-2000s on the back of the global economic boom and increasing oil prices (see Chapter 15).

Furthermore, the first years of Vladimir Putin's presidency (2000–2003) brought the completion of many overdue reforms. They included land reform, simplification of the tax system (the flat 13% personal income tax rate), judicial reform, continued privatisation, broader opening to foreign investors (see Chapter 13), deregulation, and the adoption of several pieces of market-oriented legislation. Fiscal imbalances were eliminated, disinflation continued (although at a slow pace), and the international reserves of the CBRF increased substantially. These positive changes were possible thanks to changes in the political composition of the State Duma after parliamentary elections in December 1999. They resulted in a weaker position of the CPRF and its political allies and the forming of a sort of pro-reform coalition. Vladimir Putin, who became Acting President after the resignation of Boris Yeltsin on 31 December 1999 and whose mandate was confirmed by the presidential election in March 2000, also actively supported the continuation of the market transformation of the Russian economy (Treisman, 2011).

As a result of reforms conducted in the 1990s and early 2000s, Russia completed its primary transition to a market economy based on private ownership, which seemed to be an unrealistic dream at the end of the 1980s. In the early 2000s, according to an EBRD estimate,[7] the private sector contributed about 70% of the Russian gross domestic product (GDP), an imposing figure compared to other post-communist economies. The temptation to return to a command economy did not look like a real political danger anymore.

However, some enclaves of the old economic system (only slightly reformed) remained. These were, among others, municipal and housing services, a significant part of the energy sector, social services, the social safety net, and the pension system. The natural monopolies suffered from non-transparent regulations, excessive political interference, incomplete privatisation, and administratively imposed low tariffs. These sectors continued to be the object of intensive rent-seeking by the competing oligarchic groups.

The opening up of the Russian economy to external trade and the painful restructuring in the 1990s (see Chapter 8) removed a substantial part of the uncompetitive industries created in the Soviet era and revealed the genuine comparative advantages of the Russian economy. These were a large part of the energy sector, mining other than oil and natural gas, metallurgy, and the chemical industry which already contributed to exports in the Soviet era. However, there was also a revival of the agriculture sector, especially grain production (see Chapter 10), and the rapid development of market-oriented services.

Despite the successes in reforming the economy and advancing the economic recovery, the first presidential term of Vladimir Putin planted the seeds of the future autocratic reversal. Although the deterioration of Russia's FHFIW score started in 1998, and 'the voice and accountability' component of the World Bank's World Development Indicators—even earlier (see

---

[7] See http://www.ebrd.com/downloads/research/economics/macrodata/sci.xls.

Chapter 6), in the early 2000s, the autocratic drift took a more systematic character. Looking back, one can say it looked like an intentional political plan to consolidate, step by step, political power around the institution of the president.

The consolidation of executive power started during the second Chechen war in 1999–2000, called a counterterrorist operation and conducted with violations of fundamental human rights. Another step was taking over the independent TV station NTV, owned by Vladimir Gusinskii, by Gazprom in the spring of 2001. This operation was carried out using various coercive tools such as criminal investigation against the company owner and management, presenting tax claims (for supposed tax avoidance), commercial litigation, intimidation, or corrupting company officials and journalists. Its implementation involved politically dependent prosecutors, judges, tax inspectors and bailiffs, security agencies, and police. Such a scheme was later repeated in other cases of media takeovers and the politically motivated expropriation of other business assets. For the Russian and international public, it was presented as the result of a commercial dispute, on the one hand, and the government struggle with omnipotent oligarchs, on the other.

Following the NTV takeover, other leading media companies were also taken under the control of the Presidential Administration using various instruments. In most cases, these were sales of controlling packages by private owners under political pressure.

On another front, in May 2000, the presidential decree established seven federal districts (their number increased to eight in 2010) to facilitate the stricter control of regional authorities by federal ones. In subsequent years, this additional administrative level (which did not have constitutional foundations) was used to limit the autonomy of federal entities (regions) and recentralise the Russian state.

In the economic sphere, the turning point came in 2003 with the politically motivated crackdown on the most prominent Russian private oil company, Yukos. Its assets were subsequently taken over by the state-owned company Rosneft. Its founder and significant shareholder, Mikhail Khodorkovskii, had to spend more than ten years in prison after being sentenced in the two subsequent politically motivated criminal trials on numerous charges that included supposed tax avoidance, fraud, embezzlement, and money laundering.

19.4 The Autocratic and Dirigiste Drift (2003–2014)

The takeover of Yukos initiated Russia's gradual departure from market-oriented reforms towards building a sort of hybrid system heavily controlled and dominated by the state bureaucracy and the ruling elite.

A tighter political and administrative grip on the economy was accompanied and determined by progress in building an autocratic regime in the political sphere. It included a further clamp-down on free media, political control of the judicial system, the increasingly oppressive behaviour of various law enforcement and security agencies, the systematically decreasing autonomy of federal entities (regions) and local self-government, the gradual departure from free and competitive elections and a pluralist party system, and the elimination of other institutional checks and balances.

One can mention a few critical milestones in tightening the autocratic regime. First, the parliamentary elections in 2003 and the presidential elections in 2004 were less free, fair, and competitive than the previous ones (Treisman, 2011). Second, in the 2003 parliamentary election, the pro-presidential United Russia (Edinaya Rossiya) party gained a two-thirds constitutional majority in the State Duma. Such a result was repeated in each subsequent election. It eliminated the remaining constraints on presidential power from the side of the legislature. Third, in 2004, the direct elections of regional governors were cancelled and replaced by the president nominating candidates for governors and approving them by regional legislative assemblies. The direct elections of governors returned in 2012 but in a more restricted and controlled (by the federal centre) form.

The presidential term of Dmitrii Medvedev (2008–2012), during which Vladimir Putin occupied the position of the Prime Minister (with a broadened range of prerogatives), slowed down the autocratic drift but did not stop it completely. After returning Vladimir Putin to the Office of President in 2012, this drift intensified again with the adoption of several pieces of repressive legislation. Among them, the infamous law on foreign agents of 2012 (with several subsequent changes) targeted independent civil society organisations and media.

In this context, the increasing government interference in business activity was part of a broader process of building the 'power vertical'—a mechanism of hierarchical control extending down from federal authorities to regions, municipalities, enterprises, media, and civil society organisations.

The most noticeable tendency was increasing the share of state ownership in the economy (see Chapter 7). Due to the nationalisation of Yukos, between 2004 and 2005, the private sector share of GDP decreased from 70 to 65% (EBRD estimates). In the following years, this policy continued, especially in the oil and gas industry. For example, in 2005, Gazprom acquired the private oil company Sibneft, which was transformed into Gazprom's daughter company Gazprom Neft.

The activities of foreign oil and gas firms were marginalised. The best-known case, in 2006, was the downsizing of the shares held by Shell, Mitsubishi, and Mitsui in the Sakhalin-2 project in favour of Gazprom by using administrative pressure on foreign companies (Sprenger, 2010 and Chapter 6). In 2013, Rosneft acquired the third-largest oil company, TNK-BP. In 2014, another oil company, Bashneft, was renationalised forcefully, and two years later, it became part of Rosneft.

State-owned holdings were also created in other sectors and industries. It concerned the defence industry (Rostekhnologii, Rosoboronexport), nuclear energy (Rosatom), the production of alcohol (Rosspirtprom), nanotechnologies (Rosnano), the banking sector, heavy industry, energy, transport, communication, and other sectors considered to be 'strategically important' (see Chapter 7).

The adverse effects of renationalisation became evident in 2008–2009 when the GFC hit the Russian economy heavily (see Chapters 15 and 16). Several large enterprises and banks, both private and state-owned, overborrowed before the crisis and could not roll over their debts. Various factors caused overborrowing. Among them, mergers and acquisitions (M&As) conducted before the GFC, including those related to the renationalisation of the formerly privately-owned companies, played a prominent role. Overborrowing also resulted from investing outside Russia both by state-owned and private companies.

As part of its anti-crisis package, the Russian government offered bailouts to troubled companies via either their direct nationalisation or takeovers by state-owned firms and banks. As a result, the share of state ownership in the Russian economy further increased (see Chapters 5 and 7), especially in the financial sector. At the end of 2013, more than 80% of the shares in the ten largest Russian firms belonged to the state, and the three largest state-owned banks accounted for almost 60% of total banking assets (IMF 2014, pp. 30–33).

The state-owned enterprises were less efficient, less dynamic, non-transparent, overly politicised, and favoured by the government in its regulatory and procurement activities. The natural gas monopolist Gazprom might be the best example of the negative consequences of government control. Its gas production in physical volume has stagnated since its formation in the early 1990s. At the same time, its business model has remained highly opaque and often served Russia's foreign policy goals rather than a purely business strategy aiming to maximise profit (Aslund, 2012).

Although privatisation policies were not abandoned entirely, the subsequent privatisation plans were less and less ambitious and usually not implemented or only partly implemented (Chapter 7).

However, changes in economic policy and the economic system did not go only in a statist direction. The actual policy landscape was more complex and nuanced. Several essential reforms were continued or launched. They included, for example, a pension system, social and family policies (see Chapter 18), education and healthcare (see Chapter 2), and the energy sector (see Chapter 9). In the latter, the most critical step involved a comprehensive electricity sector reform. Between 2002 and 2008, the former natural monopolist, the Russian Joint-Stock Company 'United Energy Systems' (the Russian language abbreviation RAO EES), was split into several independent power generation and distribution companies (most of them privatised), and the Federal Grid Company (FGC). A wholesale electricity market was also created (see Chapter 9).

In 2012, Russia became a member of the World Trade Organization (WTO). WTO accession required a substantial liberalisation of Russian trade and investment regulations, including a significant lowering of tariff- and non-tariff barriers to trade (see Chapter 12) and a broader opening to foreign direct and portfolio investment (see Chapter 13). Russia also had to harmonise its technical standards, sanitary and phytosanitary measures, customs procedures, intellectual property rights protection, public procurement, state aid, financial support to the agriculture sector, and other legislation to WTO standards.

Russia's partnership with the Organisation for Economic Co-operation and Development (OECD) had a similar positive, although less significant, impact. Russia's accession negotiations to this organisation were opened in 2007, but they were suspended in 2014 after the annexation of Crimea. A period of active cooperation with the OECD helped increase Russia's financial openness, adopting some transparency standards related to public administration, corporate governance, the anti-bribery convention, and others.

The implementation of the Partnership and Cooperation Agreement (PCA) between the European Union (EU) and Russia (which entered into force in 1997), the signing of a joint declaration on the roadmaps for four common spaces with the EU (economic; freedom, security, and justice; external security; and research, education, and culture) in 2005, and the beginning of negotiations in 2008 on a new agreement which would succeed the PCA (Dabrowski, 2014) also facilitated trade and investment liberalisation via the adoption of part of the WTO rules in bilateral relations before Russia acceded to this organisation and the harmonisation of various pieces of Russian legislation with the EU standards. Negotiations on the common spaces and new agreements were suspended in 2014 after the annexation of Crimea.

Finally, in the first two decades of the twenty-first century, macroeconomic policy, especially fiscal policy, became more prudent than it was in the 1990s. Apart from a few crisis years, a budget deficit was replaced with a budget surplus. The Soviet-era foreign debt was repaid. Furthermore, in 2004, the first sovereign wealth fund was created (see Chapter 16). It cumulated part of the natural resource rent in years of high oil prices to be spent in crisis years (2008–2009, 2014–2015, 2020).

19.5 Towards the War Economy (2014–2022)

The annexation of Crimea and active engagement in the separatist rebellion in Donbas in 2014 marked another turning point in contemporary Russian political and economic history.

The costs of the conflict itself and the following Western sanctions and Russian countersanctions were substantial but not catastrophic for the Russian economy (see Chapter 14). Since 2016, it began to recover after the 2014–2015 macroeconomic crisis caused by the collapse of oil prices and sanctions (see Chapters 15 and 16), but the pace of recovery was meagre.

However, the Ukrainian crisis signalled new worrying tendencies in Russian politics, which had significant long-term consequences for the Russian economy and economic policy.

First, it meant prioritising geopolitical ambitions over the goals of economic and social development and modernisation. Russia's more assertive foreign and security policy against some of its neighbours, the EU, the United States, and their allies was not an entirely new phenomenon. It started in the second half of the 2000s and included such episodes as the military intervention in Georgia in 2008. However, since 2014, it has become a dominant strategic goal of Russian foreign policy.

Second, Western sanctions, although not so heavy in respect to Russia's trade and investment relations with the EU and United States (most of them concentrated on personal, diplomatic, and financial measures), suspended various tracks of Russia's cooperation with their Western partners, for example, the OECD accession process, or its membership in the G8. It eliminated external incentives to continue many institutional reforms (see Sect. 19.4).

Third and most important, the Ukrainian crisis and associated sanctions triggered a broad spectrum of inward-oriented policies aimed at making Russia less dependent on global markets and potential new sanctions (see Chapter 14). They involved a wide range of protectionist and import-substitution measures and programmes, creating a new domestic payment system, increasing Russia's digital 'independence' from the outside world (and its ability to control internal information flows), and others. With the benefit of hindsight, they can be interpreted as either the result of pressure from various lobbies, for example, the agriculture lobby, or purposeful preparation for the next round of geopolitical confrontation with the United States and the EU, or perhaps both.

An even more prudent fiscal policy after 2014 (compared to previous periods) can also be considered a measure aimed at increasing Russia's independence from global financial markets. The same can be said about various monetary and financial policy measures of the CBRF: adopting inflation targeting, diversification of the CBRF international reserves out of the USD denominated assets (in favour of gold and the Chinese Yuan), and tighter macroprudential policy, among others. Most of these measures deserve a positive assessment from the macroeconomic policy point of view but might also be motivated by non-economic considerations.

The invasion of Ukraine in February 2022 caused a new wave of Western sanctions (see Chapter 14). This time they hit almost all spheres of Russia's external economic relations: most of its trade, investment, financial system, transportation and transit, technology transfer, and many others. Assessing their consequences on Russia's economic and social development is not possible yet (at the time of writing this chapter). The war itself must be more costly than the conflict of 2014–2015.

The war also further increased the degree of the repressiveness of the Russian political system by banning the remaining independent media, introducing heavy criminal penalties for spreading 'fake' news, challenging the government information and propaganda monopoly, and cracking down on all symptoms of anti-war protests, among others.

19.6 THE RUSSIAN ECONOMY IN THE EARLY 2020S

Despite the two transitions analysed in the chapter, with the second one reversing a part of the gains of the first one, the Russian economy has not returned to its starting point, that is, to where it was in the late 1980s and early 1990s. Rebuilding the command system of central planning with an almost monopoly of state ownership and far-reaching isolation from the external world does not look like a feasible and rational option, even in war and extensive sanctions.

Before the invasion of Ukraine, but taking into account damages caused by the earlier (2014–2015) stage of this conflict, the long-lasting autocratic and dirigiste drift, and the consequences of the COVID-19 pandemic, the Russian economy could be characterised as predominantly market-oriented and open to the external world. However, it suffered from various institutional and structural distortions, a poor business and investment climate, and poor governance (Chapters 5 and 6). These deficiencies have been determined by the autocratic trend which started in the early 2000s and continues until now. The Russian experience confirms that there are no market-friendly autocracies (or they are sporadic phenomena) and that the autocratic tendencies in the political sphere negatively influence economic freedom and transparency and cause more corruption and institutional and structural distortions, among others (Dabrowski, 2021). In the case of Russia, they also involve the risk of wasting its relatively high level of human capital (see Chapters 2 and 17).

Depending on its length and outcome, the war will worsen things. It will mean less personal and economic freedom, a further tightening of political control over society, and more repression. Therefore, the Russian political system may return to the Soviet era, even if the dominant state ideology (nationalism instead of communism) has changed.

In the economic sphere, there will be attempts to replace trade, investment, and financial relations with the EU, the United States, and other advanced economies with other partners who did not join sanctions or joined them only partly (China, India, Brazil, South Africa, Turkey, Indonesia, and other emerging market and developing economies) and by more import-substitution and other inward-oriented policies. However, they cannot fully substitute the role of advanced economies as Russia's export markets, source of investment and consumer imports, and source of new technologies, among others. Besides, trade reorientation requires time and investments, especially in the energy sphere.

Russia will likely face years of negative or stagnant growth, which may challenge its status as an upper-middle-income economy, and deteriorating living standards (see Chapter 18).

The war and sanctions-related crisis may also overshadow other critical long-term challenges, such as the consequences of the green transition, which will decrease the global demand for hydrocarbons in the medium and long run (see Chapters 1 and 9), and its demographic crisis, which will further reduce the number of the working-age population and increase the costs of population ageing (see Chapters 2, 17, and 18).

Questions for students

1. Please characterise the major stages of Russia's economic and political transition after the dissolution of the Soviet Union in 1991.
2. How did the political compromises at the early stage of transition (the early and mid-1990s) influence its quality and the socio-political conditions of economic policy in the 2000s and 2010s?
3. How can changes in the political system impact the economic system and vice versa?
4. How can the war Ukraine change the external conditions in which the Russian economy functions and Russia's economic policy and economic system?
5. What are the future challenges for the Russian economy, apart from the consequences of the war in Ukraine?

REFERENCES

Aslund, A. (2012). Why Gazprom Resembles a Crime Syndicate. *The Moscow Times*, 28 February, http://www.themoscowtimes.com/opinion/article/why-gazprom-resembles-a-crime-syndicate/453762.html

Dabrowski, M. (2001). Some Thoughts on the Russian Transition, 1990–2000. 30 March. https://www.researchgate.net/publication/281289143_Some_Thoughts_on_the_Russian_Transition_1990-2000

Dabrowski, M. (2014). EU cooperation with non-member neighboring countries: the principle of variable geometry. *CASE Network Reports* 114. http://www.case-research.eu/files/?id_plik=5073

Dabrowski, M. (2021). The Antidemocratic Drift in the Early 21st Century: Some Thoughts on its Roots, Dynamics and Prospects. *Central European Business Review* 10(2):63–83. https://cebr.vse.cz/pdfs/cbr/2021/02/04.pdf

Dabrowski, M., Mau, V., Yanovskiy, K., Sinitsina, I., Antczak, R., Zhavoronkov, S., & Shapovalov, A. (2004). Russia: Political and Institutional Determinants of Economic Reforms. *CASE Reports* 56. http://www.case-research.eu/sites/default/files/publications/2437193_RC%2056_0.pdf

EBRD. (1999). *Transition Report 1999: Ten years of transition*. European Bank for Reconstruction and Development, London. https://www.ebrd.com/publications/transition-report-1999-english.pdf

Gel'man, V. (2015). *Authoritarian Russia: Analyzing Post-Soviet Regime Changes*. University of Pittsburgh Press

IMF. (2014). Russian Federation: 2014 Article IV Consultation-Staff Report; Informational Annex; Press Release. *IMF Country Report* 14/175. International Monetary Fund, Washington DC, http://www.imf.org/external/pubs/ft/scr/2014/cr14175.pdf

Sprenger, C. (2010). State ownership in the Russian economy: Its magnitude, structure and governance problems. *The Journal of the Institute of Public Enterprise* 33(1–2), http://papers.ssrn.com/sol3/Delivery.cfm/SSRN_ID1657905_code438253.pdf?abstractid=1311223&mirid=1

Treisman, D. (2011). *The Return: Russia's Journey from Gorbachev to Medvedev*. Free Press, New York, NY, London, Toronto & Sydney

WEO. (2000). *World Economic Outlook: Focus on Transition Economies*. September. International Monetary Fund, Washington, DC

World Bank. (1996). *World Development Report: From Plan to Market*. Oxford University Press.

World Bank. (2002). *Transition – The First Ten Years: Analysis and Lessons for Eastern Europe and Former Soviet Union*. The World Bank, Washington, DC. http://documents.worldbank.org/curated/en/319481468770972868/pdf/multi0page.pdf

Index

A
aging, 31
agrarian reform, 54, 75
agrarian transformation, 189, 191
agribusiness, 190, 200
agricultural lands, 8
agricultural production, 152, 188, 191, 193, 195, 198–200
agricultural sector, 53, 64, 71, 152, 187, 193, 197, 200
agriculture, 8, 9, 32, 46, 53, 55, 56, 62–68, 70–72, 74, 146, 162, 187–191, 193, 195, 197–201, 210, 233, 241, 274, 284, 292, 296, 297, 299, 308, 309, 318, 326, 336, 350, 351, 353, 390, 394, 395
airports, 18
alcohol, 35, 55, 56, 75, 316, 393
aluminium, 240, 242, 243
Amur River, 7
anti-dumping, 234, 276
anti-inflationary policy, 326
aquatic resources, 5
Archangelsk, 13
Arctic Ocean, 4, 6
Asia, 4, 11, 18, 158, 171, 174, 176, 228, 240, 276, 292, 310, 311, 336
autarky, 66
autocratic drift, 99

B
Baikal, 4, 6, 220
balance-of-payments, 315
Baltic Sea, 4, 6
banking system, 63, 122, 134, 135, 275, 305, 315, 319, 324
Bank of Russia, 127, 128, 130, 131, 135, 327
Bashkortostan, 10, 211, 212, 222
birth rate, 24, 25
Black Sea, 6, 16
boards of directors, 125, 126, 128, 129, 137
Bologna process, 37
Brezhnev, Leonid, 73, 74
brownfield companies, 150, 153
brownfield industries, 145
budget, 18, 52, 55, 66, 86, 94, 105, 119, 124, 134, 146, 163, 167, 189, 191, 195, 219, 220, 267, 276, 283, 286, 301, 313, 316, 327, 328, 350, 374, 388, 394
Buryatia, 12, 14, 210, 211, 370
business activity, 99, 101, 108, 111, 156, 275, 280, 286, 392
business and investment climate, 100, 111
business cycle, 101
business registration, 111
business services, 297, 299

© The Editor(s) (if applicable) and The Author(s), under exclusive license to Springer Nature Switzerland AG 2023
M. Dabrowski (ed.), *The Contemporary Russian Economy*,
https://doi.org/10.1007/978-3-031-17382-0

C

capital outflows, 100, 112, 277, 282, 284, 319, 321, 323
carbon, 5–7, 179, 183, 198, 228, 243, 268
Carbon Border Adjustment Mechanism CBAM, 243
carbon capture, 183
cardiovascular diseases, 26, 33, 34
cardiovascular revolution, 21, 26, 33, 36, 39
car producers, 156, 157
Caspian Sea, 4, 6, 205
Caucasus, 4, 7, 72, 205, 210, 216, 223, 343
Central Bank of the Russian Federation CBRF, 13, 256, 263, 275, 277, 279, 281, 282, 286, 316, 317, 320–322, 325–328, 332, 386, 390, 395
centralisation, 72, 91, 99, 219, 220, 222, 345
centralised planning, 68, 70, 72
Chechnya, 25, 26, 205
checks and balances, 99, 109, 110, 137, 384, 392
chemicals, 163
Chernobyl disaster, 74
child benefits, 28, 372, 374, 376, 377
China, 7, 8, 10–14, 22, 26, 31, 37, 38, 148, 168, 171, 174, 176, 177, 227–229, 232, 234, 237–240, 242, 244, 258, 259, 261, 268, 276, 285, 294, 296, 304, 305, 310, 320, 361, 362, 364–366, 373, 396
Chuvash Republic, 213, 215
Civil Code, 81–83, 85, 87, 90, 92, 96, 126, 137, 190
civil liberties, 107, 108, 110, 384
civil rights, 63, 87, 108
civil society, 52, 91, 96, 102, 107, 109, 257, 258, 274, 392
climate, 4, 5, 8, 14, 17, 19, 86, 99–102, 108, 110–112, 134, 155, 162, 164, 179, 181, 182, 184, 187, 198, 242, 243, 248, 268, 272, 275, 282, 285, 309, 314, 320, 323, 332, 333, 389, 396
climate change, 182, 241

CO_2, 162, 164, 180, 181, 187, 243
CO_2 emission, 162
coal, 4, 8, 9, 11, 15, 47, 54, 63, 68, 146, 151, 162, 164, 167, 168, 176–179, 183, 243, 279
collective farms, 68, 70, 359, 386
collectivisation, 62, 67, 68, 70, 71, 74, 188, 189
COMECON, 228, 229, 237, 241
command economy, 67, 70, 71, 147, 390
Communist Party, 72, 76, 85, 327, 385, 386
Communist Party of the Soviet Union CPSU, 72, 73, 76
competition, 84, 86, 102, 105, 111, 122, 124, 129, 134, 136, 138, 145, 147, 150, 151, 153, 157, 158, 166, 173, 222, 232, 235, 243, 244, 265, 301, 319, 388
competitive advantage, 154, 264
Congress of People's Deputies, 75
Constitution, 81–92, 94, 96, 384, 385, 389
Constitutional changes, 88, 91
Constitutional Court, 84, 94
construction, 7, 11, 12, 15, 45–47, 53, 70, 72, 75, 82, 102, 103, 110, 147, 157, 158, 173, 220, 278, 297, 299, 306, 307, 309, 346, 353, 355
consumer goods, 64, 66, 68, 71, 74, 147, 150, 151, 153, 258, 336
continental shelf, 4, 6, 8, 10, 11
copper, 4, 8, 9, 12
coronavirus, 220
corporate governance, 102, 116, 124–129, 137
Corporate Governance Code, 124, 127, 128, 130, 137
corporate inversion, 247, 256, 265
corruption, 63, 75, 95, 100, 104–107, 109, 110, 158, 195, 292, 323, 396
countersanctions, 104, 146, 157, 241, 242, 257, 272, 276, 277, 281, 285, 384, 394
COVID-19, 25, 129, 167, 239, 248, 249, 252, 267–269, 276, 292, 296, 314, 315, 320, 355, 396

INDEX   401

Crimea, 50, 89, 92, 94, 195, 271–274, 278, 315, 320, 339, 383–385, 394
Crimean War, 47, 48
Criminal Code, 109
crops, 68, 154, 187, 188, 193, 194, 199
cross-subsidisation, 174
currency crisis, 277, 281, 286, 315, 326
currency depreciation, 320

D

Dagestan, 7, 25, 26, 205, 210, 211, 213, 214, 217, 370
death rate, 24, 25, 33, 34
debt, 47, 54, 55, 66, 116, 119, 124, 125, 135, 137, 281, 314, 315, 318, 328, 329, 394
deindustrialisation, 148, 149, 158, 239, 240
democracy, 107, 108, 384, 385, 389
democracy score, 107
democratisation, 99, 106
demographic burden, 31, 205
demographic structure, 205
deregulation, 100, 110, 166, 170, 178, 390
devaluation, 152, 193, 213, 304, 308, 318, 324, 338
diabetes, 34, 35
diamonds, 4, 8, 9, 13
direct investment, 152, 221, 227, 247, 249–251, 262, 269, 281, 291
disinflation, 313, 314, 317, 325, 326, 332, 386, 390
disposable income, 359–361, 377
dividend, 123, 332
Doing Business, 102
domestic market, 17, 147, 151, 153, 154, 275
domestic money, 319, 324
Donbas, 92, 271–273, 278, 315, 320, 383–385, 394
downstream industries, 151, 172
Duma, 47, 48, 51–53, 59, 83, 85, 86, 88, 90, 167, 278, 386, 389, 390, 392

E

EAEU, 228, 234, 236–238, 240, 241, 244. *See also* Eurasian Economic Union
EBRD, 101, 102, 122, 127, 232, 388, 390, 392. *See also* European Bank of Reconstruction and Development
economic freedom, 110, 396
economic growth, 21, 22, 46, 48, 74, 76, 115, 154, 171, 180, 219, 222, 241, 277, 278, 291–293, 295, 306, 308, 310, 338, 348, 352, 367, 370, 385
economic liberalisation, 64, 100
economic performance, 46, 69, 74, 94, 107, 166, 207, 272, 282, 321, 336
economic system, 62, 70, 74, 82, 147, 188, 285, 383–385, 390, 393, 397
economic transformation, 86, 107, 299
education, 21, 23, 29, 36–40, 46, 48–51, 55, 57, 58, 73, 110, 156, 200, 201, 263, 277, 297, 298, 329, 336, 349, 352–354, 360, 365, 369, 370, 374, 377, 393, 394
electoral process, 107, 108
emancipation of the serfs, 45
embargo, 274, 279
emerging market economies, 100, 110, 112, 304, 313, 321, 323, 324, 326, 329, 347
employee ownership, 117
employment, 16, 50, 65, 71, 73, 92, 101, 122, 137, 145, 146, 148, 149, 163, 296, 297, 301, 335–349, 352–354, 356, 357, 360, 364, 370, 375
energy prices, 74, 161, 163, 166, 167, 286
energy sector, 92, 112, 158, 161–163, 165–167, 169, 180, 182, 184, 279, 286, 330, 390, 393
environmental conditions, 4, 14
environmental sustainability, 187, 197, 199
ethnic, 21, 25, 75
EU, 37, 123, 137, 195, 198, 234, 236–243, 259, 271–274, 276, 278–281, 285, 307, 349, 360, 394–396. *See also* European Union

Eurasian Economic Union, 228, 355. *See also* EAEU
Europe, 4–6, 10, 11, 15, 18, 46, 50, 53, 56–58, 69, 75, 107, 157, 164, 171, 172, 174, 176, 227, 228, 237–239, 241, 242, 253, 254, 273, 276, 280, 293, 299, 300, 307, 310, 311, 319, 343, 347, 356
European Bank of Reconstruction and Development, 101. *See also* EBRD
European Union, 37, 123, 148, 195, 228, 259, 271, 294, 311, 349, 360, 394. *See also* EU
exchange rate, 67, 132, 146, 149, 152, 155, 174, 231, 249, 277, 281, 283, 294, 315, 316, 319, 325, 326, 333, 364, 387
exchange rate peg, 294, 326
executive branch, 83, 109, 386
executive power, 87, 89, 92, 93, 96, 133, 327, 389, 391
expenditures, 53, 55, 92, 94, 175, 219, 220, 276, 282, 286, 297, 301, 327, 344, 366, 372
export, 4, 8, 11, 15, 18, 47, 53, 66, 67, 149, 151, 154, 163, 166, 167, 171–174, 178, 179, 195, 216, 223, 228, 240–242, 264, 275, 276, 279, 281, 283, 291, 300, 306, 326, 327, 330, 341, 387, 396
extreme weather conditions, 5

F
family farms, 68, 187, 190
famine, 49, 64, 71, 195
Far East, 7, 13, 15, 170, 204, 205, 220, 222, 223, 235, 240
farmer, 64
FDI, 152–154, 227, 235, 247, 249, 251–265, 267, 268, 284, 291–293, 300, 304, 306–309
February Revolution, 46, 59
Federal Agency for State Property Management, 120, 135
Federal Antimonopoly Service FAS, 122, 166, 179
Federal District, 10, 11, 210, 220

Federal Fund for Mandatory Medical Insurance, 371
federal government, 82, 220, 317, 322, 327, 377
Federal Grid Company, 134, 178, 393
Federal Security Service, 90
Federal State Statistics Service, 6, 7, 154, 163, 165, 192–197, 204, 206, 207, 209–212, 215–218, 337, 340, 350, 361, 363, 365–367
federal transfers, 220
Federation Council, 89, 90
ferrous metallurgy, 151
fertiliser, 6
fertility, 24, 27, 28, 30, 31, 39, 40, 199
financial crises, 110, 112, 130, 296, 314, 315, 323, 326, 328
financial crisis of 1998, 88, 193, 294, 304, 308, 314, 324
financial instability, 100, 313, 314, 324, 333
financial regulation, 116, 138
financial sector, 99, 100, 135, 274, 327, 393
financial turbulences, 314
fiscal decentralisation, 220
fiscal federalism, 220
fiscal policies, 110, 112, 282, 313, 317, 324, 327, 332
fiscal stability, 54, 107
fishing, 6
five-year plan, 61, 66, 68, 70
fixed assets, 119, 121, 132, 136, 213, 302
flexible wages, 335
food, 46, 59, 63, 64, 66–70, 151–154, 187–189, 191–196, 198–201, 239, 241, 274, 321, 332, 377
Food and Agriculture Organization, 6, 8, 234
Foreign Agent Law, 109
foreign currency, 67, 88, 228, 314, 321, 327
foreign investment, 45, 47, 56, 101, 131, 133, 135, 153, 247–249, 251, 253, 254, 256, 258, 259, 261, 262, 264, 265, 267–269, 274
forest, 8
Forest lands, 8

fossil fuel, 163
free trade agreement
  FTA, 237, 241, 274
FSU countries, 133, 171, 174, 190, 236, 239, 300, 317, 320, 355
fuel, 6, 7, 12, 17, 122, 124, 149, 151, 161, 163, 167, 169, 174, 178, 195, 230, 237–239, 243, 296, 298

G

Gaidar, 76, 116, 314, 316, 317
gas pipelines, 11, 157, 170
Gazprom, 110, 134, 146, 157, 158, 166, 170–175, 178, 266, 267, 277, 391–393
General Agreement on Tariffs and Trade (GATT), 232, 241, 242
GFC, 119, 126, 131, 135, 138, 153, 157, 193, 207, 212, 213, 231, 239, 249, 252, 292, 296, 306–309, 314, 315, 319, 320, 323, 328, 333, 337, 338, 341, 383, 384, 393. *See also* global financial crisis
Gini index, 361–364, 366
glasnost, 74
Global Competitiveness Report, 102
global economy, 17, 180, 183, 275, 285, 292–294, 305, 308
global financial crisis, 92, 119, 153, 193, 207, 231, 249, 292, 314, 319, 337, 383, 384. *See also* GFC
globalisation, 124
global trade, 17, 238
global value chains, 17, 292
global warming, 4, 5, 198
gold, 4, 8, 9, 13, 45, 47, 54–56, 67, 74, 210, 395
Gorbachev, Mikhail, 62, 74–76
Gosbank, 67, 316
Gosplan, 65, 75
governance, 37, 49–51, 65, 70, 99–102, 106–108, 110–112, 115, 116, 124–130, 137, 138, 389, 396
governors, 91, 327, 392
Great Patriotic War, 69
green economy, 180, 182
greenfield investment, 155, 247, 251

greenhouse gas emissions, 180, 182, 183, 198, 199
gross domestic product
  GDP, 47, 55, 69, 71, 73, 86, 92, 93, 95, 115, 120–123, 130–132, 134–138, 148, 149, 152, 153, 155, 162–164, 182, 193, 197, 213, 229, 230, 259, 261, 276–278, 283, 285, 294–296, 299, 300, 303, 304, 306, 310, 319–322, 328–331, 335, 337–339, 341, 344, 347, 349, 350, 355, 357, 359, 372, 373, 376–378, 390, 392
Gross Regional Product, 207. *See also* GRP
GRP, 207, 210–216, 223. *See also* Gross Regional Product

H

HDI, 22, 23, 40. *See also* Human Development Index
health care infrastructure, 207
health policy, 36
household plots, 187, 190, 197
human capital, 17, 22, 23, 71, 100, 111, 293, 306, 307, 346, 352–356, 364, 396
human development, 22, 23, 37, 40
Human Development Index, 22, 23. *See also* HDI
human resources, 22, 39, 110
Human settlement patterns, 14
hydrocarbons, 10, 210, 221, 300, 308, 396
hydropower, 7, 168, 180

I

IMF, 92, 122, 131, 132, 136, 163, 164, 168, 230–232, 249, 250, 259–261, 277, 285, 305, 316–318, 322, 325, 326, 328–331, 393. *See also* International Monetary Fund
import, 9, 12, 67, 149, 152, 156–158, 187, 193, 195, 232, 235, 242, 275, 284–286, 326, 387, 395, 396
income distribution, 361, 363, 366, 369, 373, 378

independent directors, 125, 126, 128, 129
industrial enterprises, 15, 17, 386
industrialisation, 15, 45–47, 54, 58, 61, 62, 64, 65, 67, 70, 148, 161, 163, 232, 235, 240, 306, 388
industrialisation policies, 71
industrial policies, 145, 155, 156
inequality, 204, 218–220, 222, 348, 350–352, 359–367, 371, 377, 378
inflation, 29, 59, 63, 89, 134, 149, 172, 192, 195, 207, 285, 294, 301, 304, 313, 315–319, 324–326, 338, 351, 371, 387, 388, 395
inflationary expectations, 316, 326, 336
information and telecommunication technologies
  ICT, 104, 105, 111, 112, 293, 299, 306, 307, 309
Ingushetia, 25, 26, 205, 213, 214, 217, 218, 363, 370
initial public offering, 126. *See also* IPO
innovation, 39, 62, 71, 73, 104, 126, 155, 158, 180, 184, 187, 197, 205, 220, 221, 285, 375
institutional transformation, 45, 51, 52, 319
inter-enterprise credit, 75
intergovernmental transfers, 219
internal market, 100, 173, 236
international division of labour, 155
International Labour Organization
  ILO, 339, 341
International Monetary Fund, 92, 136, 230, 249, 277, 316. *See also* IMF
international reserves, 277, 279, 294, 315, 319–322, 325, 326, 328, 332, 390, 395
investment goods, 68, 306
IPO, 126, 134, 138. *See also* initial public offering
Irkutsk, 14, 213, 214
iron ore, 8, 12, 151, 210

J

job, 118, 221, 249, 263, 296, 339, 341–343, 346, 351, 353–355, 360, 378

joint stock companies, 117, 121, 124, 125, 128, 130, 132, 133, 137, 138
joint stock company law, 88
judicial reform, 46, 49, 390
judicial system, 49, 52, 89, 95, 392
judiciary, 83, 85, 90, 94, 96, 99, 109, 111, 389

K

Kabardino-Balkarian Republic, 205, 213, 215, 217
Kaliningrad Oblast, 4, 211, 220
Kalmykia, 205, 210, 211, 213, 215, 218, 363, 370
Kamchatka, 4, 13, 205, 210, 211
Karelia, 211
Khodorkovskii, Mikhail, 391
Khrushchev, Nikita, 72–74
kolkhozes, 188, 189
Komi, 14, 205, 210, 211, 213, 214, 217
Kosygin, Alexei, 73, 76
Krasnoyarsk, 12, 13, 211–214, 217, 218
kulaks, 66, 68
Kursk Magnetic Anomaly, 12
Kuzbass, 11, 176

L

labour, 15, 16, 32, 46, 47, 50, 53, 58, 62, 64–68, 70, 72, 73, 104, 105, 118, 119, 129, 134, 146–148, 153, 155, 188, 195, 197, 198, 200, 204, 205, 236, 263, 293, 296–299, 301–304, 306–309, 335–342, 344, 346–350, 352–357, 364, 366, 369, 371, 372, 374–378
labour market, 104, 297, 301–303, 335–342, 344, 346–349, 352, 355–357, 364, 369, 376, 378
labour migrants, 355
labour productivity, 32, 118, 119, 188, 195, 296–299, 306, 348, 352, 357
land, 8
Land Code, 87, 88, 90
law enforcement agencies, 100, 109, 111, 285, 323
legislation, 47, 51, 52, 82, 83, 85, 87–90, 109, 110, 117, 118, 124,

126, 127, 129, 134, 137, 236, 327, 330, 332, 342, 357, 376, 389, 390, 392, 394
Lenin, Vladimir, 58, 63, 65
life expectancy, 23, 26, 30, 31, 33–36, 40, 75, 207
liquified natural gas
  LNG, 11, 18, 167, 170, 171
living standard, 388
loans-for-shares, 133, 387, 388
low pay, 348–350, 356
Lukoil, 133, 134, 146, 170, 175, 266

M

M&As, 119, 124, 126, 247, 251–253, 393
macroeconomic policy, 100, 309, 394, 395
macroeconomic stabilisation, 86, 301, 304, 305, 314–317, 324, 332, 386–388
macroeconomic stability, 53, 95, 100, 104, 105, 154, 286, 315, 320, 333
Magadan, 13, 205, 211, 213, 214, 217
manufacturing, 64, 112, 145, 146, 148, 149, 152, 157, 158, 210, 223, 230, 238–240, 244, 257, 264, 275, 291, 292, 296, 297, 299, 308, 309, 319, 326, 341, 345
Mari El, 213, 215, 370
market economy, 62, 81–86, 93, 96, 110, 145, 147, 149, 150, 153, 155, 158, 193, 248, 261, 264, 294, 301, 303, 308, 335, 336, 348, 388–390
market failure, 147
mass privatisation, 117, 118, 121
maternity benefits, 371, 372, 374
maternity capital, 29, 377
Medvedev, Dimitry, 92, 232, 392
metallurgical industry, 54
metallurgy, 153, 154, 163, 177, 190, 253, 390
migration, 14, 25, 32, 200, 201, 203–205, 217, 236, 355, 356
military aggression, 164, 183
mineral extraction tax
  MET, 167, 330
mineral resources, 8–10, 18

minimum wage, 89, 336, 342–344, 351, 374, 375
modernisation, 17, 27, 32, 39, 40, 46, 47, 56, 58, 60, 68, 75, 157, 167, 187, 285, 357, 395
monetary overhang, 317, 324, 386
monetary policy, 146, 207, 281, 313, 314, 316, 320, 321, 324, 325, 327, 386
monetary privatisation, 119
monetary system, 314
Mordovia, 25
mortality, 21, 24–27, 30, 31, 33–35, 39, 56, 57, 71, 207, 208
Moscow, 15, 16, 25, 57, 63, 65, 72, 76, 91, 128, 131, 135, 136, 204, 205, 210–214, 216–218, 343, 370, 386
Most Favoured Nation, 233, 280
motherhood, 28, 39
motorways, 18
multi-national enterprises
  MNEs, 248, 253
municipal authorities, 84
Murmansk, 13, 14, 205, 211, 213, 214

N

national champions, 93, 120
natural disaster, 5
natural gas, 4, 8–11, 149, 151, 154, 157, 161, 162, 164, 166–173, 178–180, 241, 243, 276, 279, 283, 314, 321, 327, 329, 330, 390, 393
natural population growth rate, 24, 25
natural resources, 3, 5, 14
neoplasms, 34, 36
NEP, 61, 64, 65–68, 76. *See also* New Economic Policy
New Economic Policy, 61, 64. *See also* NEP
NGOs, 102. *See also* non-governmental organisations
nickel, 4, 8, 9, 12, 146
non-governmental organisations, 102. *See also* NGOs
Nord Stream, 11, 241, 279
Northern Sea Route, 5, 18
Novatek, 170, 171, 175, 277
Novgorod, 15, 25, 26

nuclear energy, 158, 164, 168, 177, 183, 243, 393

O
oil, 4, 8–10, 15, 18, 55, 67, 74, 92, 110, 119, 131, 132, 134, 135, 146, 149, 151, 152, 154, 157, 162, 164, 166–168, 173–180, 183, 189, 194, 205, 230–232, 241, 243, 253, 265, 273, 276, 279, 282, 291, 292, 296, 297, 300, 304–306, 308, 309, 314, 316, 318–322, 326–328, 330, 333, 339, 343, 350, 387, 389–392, 394
oil pipeline, 157
oligarchs, 87
open economy, 149, 229
open joint stock company, 121
Organisation for Economic Co-operation and Development
    OECD, 22, 32–34, 36–39, 124, 127, 128, 137, 167, 191, 235, 293, 306, 307, 340, 342, 344, 360–362, 368, 376, 394, 395
Organization of the Petroleum Exporting Countries
    OPEC, 174
outmigration, 16
output recovery, 318
ownership structure, 117, 121, 126, 128, 138

P
Pacific Ocean, 4, 7, 15
palladium, 8, 146
payments arrears, 301
Pension Fund, 366, 371, 372, 375, 376
pension system, 135, 329, 360, 390, 393
per capita investment, 216
perestroika, 74–76, 232, 383, 385, 387
Perm, 10, 14
Permafrost, 5
personal asset freezes, 278
plan indicators, 74
planned economy, 15, 62, 73, 150, 158, 192, 232, 294, 299, 301, 303, 330, 383, 384

Polar Circle, 4
political economy, 161, 163, 342
political system, 16, 47, 72, 83, 89, 100, 102, 106, 107, 109, 316, 383, 384, 395–397
population, 15–17, 21, 22, 24, 25, 30–33, 35, 36, 39, 46, 52, 53, 56, 62, 67–69, 71, 75, 111, 132, 136, 191, 192, 197, 198, 200, 201, 203–206, 208, 212, 219, 223, 265, 296, 324, 329, 340, 355, 359–361, 363, 368–371, 373, 376–378, 388, 397
population aging, 21, 31, 205, 329, 397
population growth, 21, 22, 24, 25, 39, 71, 204, 205, 296
portfolio investment, 134, 136, 138, 249, 250, 394
post-communist countries, 107, 117
post-communist transformation, 116
post-privatisation, 117
post-Soviet Russia, 93, 96, 154, 188
poverty, 46, 57, 101, 155, 357, 359, 360, 366–374, 376–378
poverty reduction, 367, 371, 377
PPP, 23, 213, 360, 361, 367. *See also* purchasing power parity
price controls, 65, 191, 301
price distortions, 174
primary energy, 146, 162–164, 168, 180
priority social and economic development areas, 221
private capital, 112, 322, 323
private sector, 62, 69, 75, 84, 86, 91, 92, 95, 102, 200, 345, 388, 390, 392
privatisation, 8, 86, 100, 109, 116–120, 124, 130, 131, 133, 134, 136–138, 150, 151, 178, 189, 201, 251, 301, 317, 338, 387, 388, 390, 393
privatisation method, 121
property rights, 48, 51, 52, 62, 63, 71, 86, 87, 90, 99–101, 103, 105, 108, 111, 112, 117, 129, 283, 323, 394
Prosecutor General, 90, 135
Pskov, 25, 211, 217, 218
public administration, 109, 297, 298, 389, 394
public finances, 21, 219, 338

public goods, 108, 109, 219
public sector, 115–118, 120–122, 137, 138, 329, 344, 351
purchasing power parity, 23, 136, 163, 164, 213, 360. *See also* PPP
Putin, Vladimir, 83, 87–89, 91, 92, 94, 96, 232, 377, 384, 390, 392

Q
quasi-fiscal, 275, 317, 325

R
railway, 18, 71, 177
raw materials, 9, 16, 134, 146, 147, 151–154, 190, 268
real wage, 337–339, 348, 349, 388
recession, 73, 272, 277, 286, 291–294, 296, 297, 299, 300, 302–304, 307–310, 335, 337–339, 346
regional development, 204, 218–221
regulatory environment, 99–102, 112
religion, 25, 330
renationalisation, 111, 393
renewable, 7, 118, 167, 168, 177, 179, 180, 184, 310
renewable energy, 7, 167, 168, 177, 179, 180, 184
rent-seeking, 87, 109, 155, 158, 390
research and development
R&D, 39, 155, 156, 158, 200, 307
restructuring, 86, 119, 134, 145, 149–152, 154, 157, 167, 189, 191, 205, 317, 346, 357, 387, 390
retaliatory measures, 111, 146, 271, 283, 385
retirement age, 32, 33, 352, 375
return on equity, 124. *See also* ROE
Revealed Comparative Advantage, 147
revenues, 4, 53–55, 59, 63, 92, 118, 119, 122, 163, 167, 197, 219, 220, 231, 281, 282, 291, 305, 306, 308, 327, 329
ROE, 124, 125. *See also* return on equity
Rosatom, 12, 135, 158, 178, 393
Rosneft, 134, 135, 146, 170, 171, 175, 266, 267, 277, 391, 392

rouble, 67, 146, 149, 152, 155, 193, 213, 228, 231, 277, 281–283, 286, 304, 308, 315–327, 332, 349, 386, 387
round-tripping, 247, 256, 257
rule of law, 85, 88, 93, 95, 99, 101, 104, 106, 107, 323
rural areas, 39, 49, 197, 200, 201, 205
rural development, 187, 197, 200, 201
rural infrastructure, 201
Russian economy, 4, 56, 62, 82, 88, 91–94, 96, 102, 111, 122, 138, 145–150, 152, 153, 155, 158, 163, 165, 184, 195, 221, 261, 262, 267, 268, 271, 272, 275, 276, 278, 283–286, 296, 298, 301, 303, 304, 306, 307, 309, 310, 314, 320, 321, 323, 333, 336, 337, 346, 349, 384, 385, 389, 390, 393, 394, 396, 397
Russian Empire, 15, 55, 154
Russian Federation, 6, 7, 9–14, 17, 18, 76, 82–85, 89, 90, 93, 95, 121, 126, 127, 129, 132, 135, 172, 175–177, 181, 182, 204, 207–210, 218, 219, 256, 264, 274, 275, 283, 316, 327, 377, 384–386
Russian government, 17, 34, 50, 54, 59, 82, 83, 86, 90–92, 94, 95, 134, 146, 153, 155, 156, 248, 262, 267–269, 274, 283, 342, 344, 393
Russian monarchy, 46, 62
Russian Soviet Federative Socialist Republic
RSFSR, 83, 84

S
Saint-Petersburg International Mercantile Exchange
SPIMEX, 173
Sakhalin, 4, 11, 110, 171, 210, 211, 213, 214, 217, 218, 392
sanctions, 11, 92, 94, 104, 111, 128, 135, 138, 146, 153, 157, 183, 195, 236, 241, 242, 257, 271–286, 307, 315, 320, 321, 323, 327, 328, 333, 339, 383–385, 394–396
seaport, 18, 300
secondary school, 36, 37, 50

self-government, 47, 50, 392
services, 17–19, 57, 64, 68, 72, 74, 75, 84, 101, 105, 112, 122, 145, 146, 156, 162, 166, 179, 192, 219, 227, 230, 232, 235, 236, 258, 264, 268, 273–275, 277, 280, 285, 291–293, 296–301, 308, 309, 315, 329–331, 336, 348, 353, 355, 370–372, 377, 390
Sevastopol, 89
shareholder, 102, 117, 175, 391
Siberia, 4–7, 11–15, 52, 53, 72, 168, 170, 176, 179, 198, 204, 205, 216
single-industry towns, 16, 221
skills, 104, 249, 263, 264, 306, 346, 349, 352–355
smoking, 35, 36
Smolensk, 25, 26
social assistance, 360, 372–374, 378
social networks, 152, 284
social policy, 22, 40, 359, 371, 376
social security, 371
sovereign default, 314
sovereign wealth funds, 320, 322, 325, 327, 328
Soviet agriculture, 189
Soviet Constitution, 83, 84
Soviet economic system, 70, 72, 314
Soviet economy, 66, 73, 117, 146, 149, 189, 193, 294, 299–301, 345
Soviet era, 21, 73, 153, 187, 192–194, 317, 324, 333, 356, 359, 376, 384, 386, 390, 396
Soviet legacy, 16, 292, 336
Soviet period, 8, 21, 86, 91, 150, 154, 192, 193, 217, 228, 339, 353
Soviet Union, 6, 15, 16, 32, 62, 69–76, 82–87, 90, 107, 118, 150, 154, 158, 164, 165, 189, 193, 204, 227–229, 232, 237, 248, 293, 300, 301, 306, 308, 313–316, 337, 341, 345, 348, 352, 383–385, 388, 397
sovkhozes, 188, 189
special administrative regions, 221
special economic zones, 221
spontaneous privatisation, 118
Stalin, Iosif, 61, 62, 65, 66, 68, 70–72
starting a business, 103, 105
state budget, 75

state capitalism, 120
state capture, 100, 110
state intervention, 81, 91, 93, 165
state monopoly, 67, 300, 301
state-owned enterprises
  SOEs, 86, 111, 117–126, 128, 130, 132, 133, 135–138, 175, 304, 316, 320, 330
state ownership, 62, 116–119, 135, 137, 155, 267, 272, 383–385, 392, 393, 396
state procurements, 191
stock exchange, 55, 127, 134, 166, 387
stock market, 116, 119, 121, 123, 129–136, 138
Stolypin, Petr, 48, 51, 52
St. Petersburg, 15, 16, 18, 25, 51, 57, 204, 205, 210–212, 217, 218, 235, 240, 370
structural diversification, 100, 221, 310
subsidies, 86, 165, 167, 168, 189, 191, 193–195, 234, 242, 275, 329, 364, 372, 376, 377, 387
subsistence level, 201, 205–207, 367, 369, 370, 374, 376
supervisory board, 129
Supreme Council, 63, 83, 121, 385, 386, 389
Supreme Council of the National Economy, 63
Supreme Court, 89, 90
Sustainable Development Goals
  SDGs, 198

T
Tambov Revolt, 64
Tatarstan, 10, 25, 175, 211–214, 218, 222, 370
technical infrastructure, 100, 110, 200
technological revolution, 306
tertiary education, 37, 39, 352
tobacco, 35, 36, 53, 55
total factor productivity
  TFP, 73, 195, 293, 302, 304
total fertility rate, 27
trade, 4, 6, 11, 15–17, 19, 47, 50, 51, 53, 63, 64, 66–68, 70, 74, 75, 103, 105, 111, 119, 146, 148–150, 162,

171, 173, 174, 191, 192, 194, 196, 200, 227–244, 248, 253, 258, 262, 268, 272–276, 278, 279, 283, 285, 292, 293, 296, 298, 300, 301, 305, 306, 308, 320, 326, 331, 342, 344–346, 390, 393–396
trade unions, 50, 344, 345
transaction costs, 100, 112, 192
transfers in kind, 360, 361
transhipping, 247, 256
transition, 28, 31, 82, 85–87, 116, 118, 126, 146–150, 153, 155, 159, 162, 167, 179–184, 188, 193, 197, 227–229, 233, 237, 240–243, 247, 248, 254, 259, 261, 262, 265, 268, 291, 293, 294, 296, 297, 299–305, 308–310, 325, 332, 335, 336, 338, 345, 348, 376, 385, 387–390, 396, 397
Transparency International Corruption Perception Index, 102
transport, 16, 18, 19
transportation routes, 14, 16, 17
transportation tariffs, 170, 177
transport infrastructure, 16, 17, 292
transport system, 17
tuberculosis, 34, 35
Tula, 14, 25
Turkish Stream, 11
Tver, 25, 26
twentieth century, 6, 15, 18, 21, 27, 46, 48, 74, 326
twenty-first century, 7, 18, 33, 110, 152, 157, 201, 223, 394
two-tier wage structure, 344
Tyumen, 10, 198, 205, 211–214, 217, 218, 343, 364, 370
Tyva, 25, 26, 205, 214, 218, 370

U

Ukraine, 12, 63, 90, 92, 104, 111, 119, 162, 164, 171, 183, 184, 228, 229, 236, 237, 240–242, 247, 248, 268, 271–274, 278, 281, 285, 299, 300, 307, 311, 315, 317, 320, 321, 333, 383–385, 395–397
unemployment benefits, 336, 339, 342–344, 372, 376–378

unemployment rate, 201, 339
Unified Gas Supply System
    UGGS, 166
Unified State Examination, 39
Union of the Soviet Socialist Republics
    USSR, 67, 69, 84, 93, 228, 248, 316
United Energy System, 134, 178
United Nations
    UN, 8, 22, 101, 182, 198, 280
United Nations Conference on Trade and Development
    UNCTAD, 148, 233, 250–255, 257–261, 265, 267
United States, 7, 8, 10, 11, 25–28, 31, 32, 35, 37, 53, 56, 63, 69, 74, 90, 126, 168, 174, 176, 177, 195, 213, 229, 234, 238, 240, 242, 254, 259, 271, 272, 293, 294, 307, 311, 319, 353, 356, 360, 362, 365, 366, 368, 395, 396
university, 37, 39, 50, 303, 336, 348, 352, 353, 369
urbanisation, 15, 56, 198, 205, 370
urban system, 15

V

value added, 122, 146–149, 155, 157, 167, 193, 197, 199, 207, 296–298, 302, 303, 308, 309
value added tax
    VAT, 167, 221, 330, 332
visa bans, 273, 278
Vladivostok, 18, 204
Vnesheconombank
    VEB, 158
voice and accountability, 106, 390
Volgograd, 14

W

wage bargaining, 344
wage setting, 345, 350, 357
War Communism, 61–65
wealth inequality, 361, 366
West Siberian Plain, 4, 205
WGI, 101. *See also* World Governance Indicators
White Sea, 6, 15

wholesale markets, 179, 192
working-age population, 21, 31, 32, 40, 205, 397
working capital, 151, 188
World Bank, 24, 27, 86, 93, 95, 101, 102, 106, 131, 132, 136, 229, 230, 232, 277, 300, 305, 322, 329, 347, 361, 362, 367, 370, 372, 376, 388, 390
World Bank Doing Business WBDB, 102, 103, 111
world commodity markets, 207
World Development Indicators, 93, 95, 131, 132, 136, 148, 229, 230, 322, 329, 362, 390
World Governance Indicators, 101, 106. *See also* WGI
world market, 194
World Trade Organization, 228, 275, 393. *See also* WTO
World War I, 46, 59, 60, 62. *See also* WWI
World War II, 16, 31, 62, 69. *See also* WWII
WTO, 174, 227, 228, 232–236, 240–243, 275, 280, 304, 393, 394. *See also* World Trade Organization
WTO membership, 232–235, 243, 305
WWI, 46, 47, 48, 54–56, 59, 62, 63, 66, 69. *See also* World War I
WWII, 16, 69, 71, 72, 293. *See also* World War II

Y

Yakutia, 12, 13, 176, 205, 214, 217
Yamal Peninsula, 11, 18
Yeltsin, Boris, 76, 83–85, 88, 232, 327, 385–387, 390
Yukos, 134, 267, 332, 391, 392

Z

zemstvo, 48, 59
zinc, 8, 9

GPSR Compliance

The European Union's (EU) General Product Safety Regulation (GPSR) is a set of rules that requires consumer products to be safe and our obligations to ensure this.

If you have any concerns about our products, you can contact us on

ProductSafety@springernature.com

In case Publisher is established outside the EU, the EU authorized representative is:

Springer Nature Customer Service Center GmbH
Europaplatz 3
69115 Heidelberg, Germany